Vertically Inclined Rock Gym
Income Statement
For Month Ended March 31, 2014

Revenues:		
Teaching revenue	$ 3,800	
Equipment rental revenue	300	
Total revenues		$ 4,100
Operating expenses:		
Rent expense	$ 1,000	
Salaries expense	700	
Total operating expenses		1,700
Net income		$ 2,400

Vertically Inclined Rock Gym
Statement of Changes in Equity
For Month Ended March 31, 2014

Virgil Klimb, capital, March 1		$ -0-
Add: Investments by owner	$ 10,000	
Net income	2,400	12,400
Total		$ 12,400
Less: Withdrawals by owner		600
Virgil Klimb, capital, March 31		$ 11,800

Vertically Inclined Rock Gym
Balance Sheet
March 31, 2014

Assets		Liabilities	
Cash	$ 8,400	Accounts payable	$ 200
Supplies	3,600	Notes payable	6,000
Equipment	6,000	Total liabilities	$ 6,200
		Equity	
		Virgil Klimb, capital	11,800
Total assets	$18,000	Total liabilities and equity	$ 18,000

Vertically Inclined Rock Gym
Statement of Cash Flows
For Month Ended March 31, 2014

Cash flows from operating activities		
Cash received from clients	$ 4,100	
Cash paid for supplies	(3,400)	
Cash paid for rent	(1,000)	
Cash paid to employee	(700)	
Net cash used by operating activities		$ (1,000)
Cash flows from investing activities		-0-
Cash flows from financing activities		
Investment by owner	$10,000	
Withdrawal by owner	(600)	
Net cash provided by financing activities		9,400
Net increase in cash		$ 8,400
Cash balance, March 1		-0-
Cash balance, March 31		$ 8,400

DIFFERENTIATING THE FINANCIAL STATEMENTS

Fundamental Accounting Principles uses a colour scheme to help students differentiate among the four key financial statements.

The arrows are imaginary but they emphasize the link between statements.

FUNDAMENTAL
ACCOUNTING PRINCIPLES

FOURTEENTH CANADIAN EDITION | VOLUME 1

Kermit D. Larson
University of Texas—Austin

Tilly Jensen
Athabasca University—Alberta

McGraw-Hill
Ryerson
Connect. Learn. Succeed.

McGraw-Hill
Ryerson
Connect. Learn. Succeed.

Fundamental Accounting Principles
Volume 1
Fourteenth Canadian Edition

The Internet addresses listed in the text were accurate at the time of publication. The inclusion of a website does not indicate an endorsement by the authors or McGraw-Hill Ryerson, and McGraw-Hill Ryerson does not guarantee the accuracy of the information presented at these sites.

ISBN-13: 978-0-07-105150-7
ISBN-10: 0-07-105150-3

3 4 5 6 7 8 9 10 TCP 1 9 8 7 6 5 4

Printed and bound in Canada.

Care has been taken to trace ownership of copyright material contained in this text; however, the publisher will welcome any information that enables them to rectify any reference or credit for subsequent editions.

Director of Product Management: Rhondda McNabb
Product Manager: Keara Emmett
Executive Marketing Manager: Joy Armitage Taylor
Developmental Editors: Suzanne Simpson Millar & Sarah Fulton
Senior Product Team Associate: Christine Lomas
Supervising Editor: Jessica Barnoski
Photo/Permissions Researcher: Tracy Leonard
Copy Editor: Laurel Sparrow
Production Coordinator: Tammy Mavroudi
Cover Design: Greg Devitt
Cover Image: Classroom: Muntz/Getty Images; Drawing: Pinkfish
Interior Design: Greg Devitt
Page Layout: Aptara®, Inc.
Printer: Transcontinental Printing Group

Library and Archives Canada Cataloguing in Publication

Larson, Kermit D.
    Fundamental accounting principles / Kermit D. Larson, Tilly Jensen.—14th Canadian ed.

Includes bibliographical references and index.
Contents: v. 1. chapters 1-9.
ISBN 978-0-07-105150-7 (v. 1).

    1. Accounting—Textbooks.   I. Jensen, Tilly   II. Title.

HF5636.L343 2012   657   C2012-906304-5

Kermit D. Larson, University of Texas – Austin

Kermit D. Larson is the Arthur Andersen & Co. Alumni Professor of Accounting Emeritus at the University of Texas at Austin. He served as chair of the University of Texas, Department of Accounting, and was visiting associate professor at Tulane University. His scholarly articles have been published in a variety of journals, including *The Accounting Review, Journal of Accountancy,* and *Abacus.* He is the author of several books, including *Financial Accounting* and *Fundamentals of Financial* and *Managerial Accounting,* both published by Irwin/McGraw-Hill.

Professor Larson is a member of the American Accounting Association, the Texas Society of CPAs, and the American Institute of CPAs. His positions with the AAA have included vice president, southwest regional service president, and chair of several committees, including the Committee of Concepts and Standards. He was a member of the committee that planned the first AAA doctoral consortium and served as its director.

Tilly Jensen, Athabasca University – Alberta

Tilly Jensen graduated from the University of Alberta with a Bachelor of Commerce and later attained the designation of Certified Management Accountant. She worked in private industry for a number of years before making teaching her full-time career. Tilly was an accounting instructor at the Northern Alberta Institute of Technology (NAIT) in Edmonton, Alberta, for a number of years and is now an Assistant Professor of Accounting at Athabasca University, Canada's open, online university. She obtained her M.Ed. at the University of Sheffield in Britain while travelling abroad and completed her doctoral studies at the University of Calgary focusing on how educational technologies might be used to enhance critical thinking. Tilly spent four years in the Middle East teaching at Dubai Men's College of the Higher Colleges of Technology in the United Arab Emirates. While overseas, she also taught financial accounting to students enrolled in the Chartered Institute of Management Accountants (CIMA) program, a British professional accounting designation. During a sabbatical, Tilly also taught accounting in China to ESL students at Shenyang Ligong University. She authored LIFA—Lyryx Interactive Financial Accounting—a dynamic, leading-edge, Web-based teaching and learning tool produced by Lyryx. Tilly has also authored material for CGA-Canada. In addition to her professional interests, Tilly places a priority on time spent with her family and friends.

Brief Contents

Midterm
6, 8, 9, 10, 11
↓
Question 10.6
Ex→ 10.9
Ex→ 10.12
Ex→ 10.16

Contents

CHAPTER 6
Merchandise Inventory and Cost of Sales 331

CHAPTER 7
Accounting Information Systems 385

CHAPTER 8
Internal Control and Cash 432

CHAPTER 9
Receivables 490

APPENDIX I
Payroll Liabilities A-1

APPENDIX II
Financial Statement Information A-34

APPENDIX III
Chart of Accounts A-76

connect™

The integrated solutions for Larson, *Fundamental Accounting Principles*, *Volume 1*, have been proven to help you achieve your course goals of improving student readiness, enhancing student engagement, and increasing student comprehension of content. Known for its engaging style, the Larson solution employs the use of current companies, LearnSmart, and instant feedback on practice problems to help students engage with course materials, understand the content, and achieve higher outcomes in the course.

McGraw-Hill's adaptive learning component, **LearnSmart**, provides assignable modules that help students master core concepts and come to class more prepared.

Finally, our new **Intelligent Response Technology**-based content offers students an intelligent homework experience that helps them stay focused on learning instead of navigating the technology.

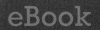

PROVEN EFFECTIVE

FEATURES

eBook

Connect includes a media-rich eBook that allows you to share your notes with your students. Your students can insert and review their own notes, highlight the text, search for specific information, and interact with media resources. Using an eBook with Connect gives your students a complete digital solution that allows them to access their materials from any computer.

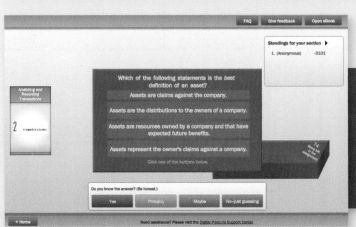

LearnSmart™

McGraw-Hill LearnSmart™ is an adaptive learning program that identifies what an individual student knows and doesn't know. LearnSmart's adaptive learning path helps students learn faster, study more efficiently, and retain more knowledge.

Get Connected. Get Engaged.

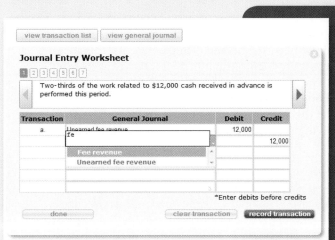

Intelligent Response Technology

Intelligent Response Technology (IRT) is Connect Accounting's new student interface for end-of-chapter assessment content. Intelligent Response Technology provides a general journal application that looks and feels more like what you would find in a general ledger software package, improves answer acceptance to reduce student frustration with formatting issues (such as rounding), and, for select questions, provides an expanded table that guides students through the process of solving the problem.

Help Me Solve It

New *Help Me Solve It* tutorials are available on **Connect** for Larson's *Fundamental Accounting Principles*. The tutorials guide students through two of the more challenging end-of-chapter problems per chapter, providing them with an engaging visual and audio walkthrough of the problem. The *Help Me Solve It* tutorials allow for the power of technology to bring the content to life for students, help to reinforce concepts, and appeal to all learning styles.

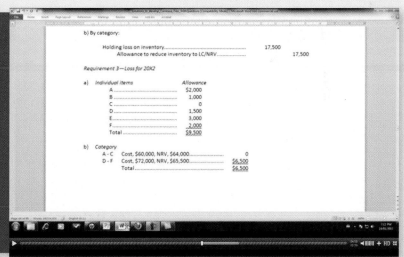

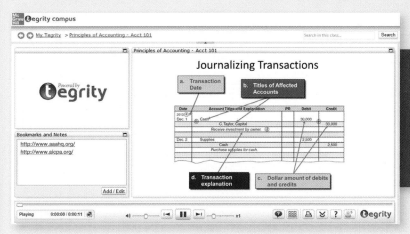

Lecture Capture

Make your classes available anytime, anywhere. With simple, one-click recording, students can search for a word or phrase and be taken to the exact place in your lecture that they need to review.

Preface

INSIDE THE CHAPTERS

As educators, instructors strive to create an environment that fosters learning and provides students with the tools they need to succeed. The Fourteenth Canadian Edition continues to meet and surpass the high standards the market expects from *Fundamental Accounting Principles*. We continue to put learning first, with student-centred pedagogy and critical thinking lessons throughout the text.

All the pedagogical tools are carefully designed for ease of use and understanding, helping the instructor teach and giving the students what they need to succeed.

Pedagogy

Student Success Cycle

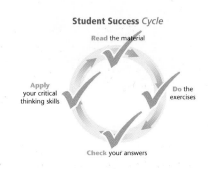

Student Success *Cycle*

Read the material
Do the exercises
Check your answers
Apply your critical thinking skills

Student success at the post-secondary level is not measured by how much knowledge a student has acquired, but rather by how well a student can *use* knowledge. The Student Success Cycle, illustrated by a circular icon (shown at left), reinforces decision-making skills by highlighting key steps toward understanding and critically evaluating the information the student has just read. **Read–Do–Check–Apply** reinforces active learning rather than passive learning. This tool is integrated throughout the text, including the chapter opening page, Checkpoint questions, Demonstration Problems, and end-of-chapter material.

Critical Thinking Challenge

An essential element of critical thinking is the ability to ask questions while reading (or listening or speaking). These exercises are designed to help students develop the skills related to questioning. Suggested answers are posted on **Connect**.

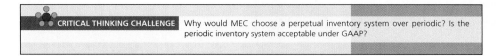

CRITICAL THINKING CHALLENGE Why would MEC choose a perpetual inventory system over periodic? Is the periodic inventory system acceptable under GAAP?

IFRS and ASPE—The Differences

This box appears at the end of every chapter to highlight any differences or important points about reporting and terminology as they relate to the financial accounting course. The chapter content is IFRS 2012 compliant throughout both volumes; references are provided where appropriate.

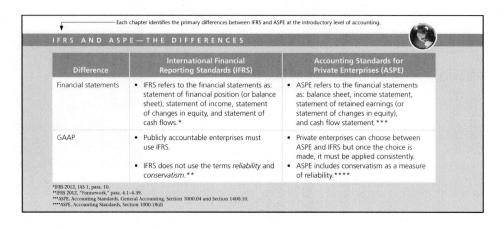

Each chapter identifies the primary differences between IFRS and ASPE at the introductory level of accounting.

IFRS AND ASPE—THE DIFFERENCES

Difference	International Financial Reporting Standards (IFRS)	Accounting Standards for Private Enterprises (ASPE)
Financial statements	• IFRS refers to the financial statements as: statement of financial position (or balance sheet), statement of income, statement of changes in equity, and statement of cash flows.*	• ASPE refers to the financial statements as: balance sheet, income statement, statement of retained earnings (or statement of changes in equity), and cash flow statement.***
GAAP	• Publicly accountable enterprises must use IFRS. • IFRS does not use the terms *reliability* and *conservatism*.**	• Private enterprises can choose between ASPE and IFRS but once the choice is made, it must be applied consistently. • ASPE includes conservatism as a measure of reliability.****

*IFRS 2012, IAS 1, para. 10.
**IFRS 2012, "Framework," para. 4.1–4.39.
***ASPE, Accounting Standards, General Accounting, Section 1000.04 and Section 1400.10.
****ASPE, Accounting Standards, Section 1000.18(d)

Real-World Focus

The Fourteenth Canadian Edition has increased the use of real business examples to reflect the most current information available. This continues the text's strong ties to the real world of accounting, be it through detailed interviews with businesspeople for the chapter-opening vignettes, examples of ethical standards and treatments, or annual reports for end-of-chapter material. When an actual business is used, its name is highlighted and bold for emphasis. This integration with real-world companies helps engage students while they read.

> Prepaids are common in business. For example, **Cameco** reported $182,037,000 of prepaid expenses at December 31, 2011, $24,688,000 of prepaids appear on **Maple Leaf Foods'** December 31, 2011, balance sheet, and **Canadian Tire** showed

Learning Objectives

Learning Objectives have long been a standard in the Larson textbook. By giving students a head start on what the following material encompasses, the text readies them for the work ahead.

Checkpoint

This series of questions within the chapter reinforces the material presented immediately before it. These questions allow the students to "Do" problem material by referencing what they have just learned. Answers at the end of each chapter will then allow them to "Check" their work, further supporting the Student Success Cycle. Under each set of Checkpoints is a reference to the Quick Study questions (single-topic exercises) available at the end of each chapter. Students can go ahead and try them at this point. Checkpoint solutions are at the end of the chapter. Quick Study solutions are available on **Connect**.

CHECKPOINT

1. Explain the accounting cycle.
2. Classify the following accounts as either assets, liabilities, or equity: (1) Prepaid Rent, (2) Rent Expense, (3) Unearned Rent, (4) Rent Revenue, (5) Buildings, (6) Owner Capital, (7) Wages Payable, (8) Wages Expense, (9) Office Supplies, and (10) Owner Withdrawals.
3. What is the difference between the accounts Rent Earned, Rent Revenue, and Earned Rent?

Do Quick Study question: QS 2-1

Decision Insight

Social responsibility continues to be important for students to learn early in their accounting courses. Through the Decision Insight feature, accounting's role in ethics and social responsibility is described by both reporting and assessing its impact. Relating theory to a real-life situation piques interest and reinforces active learning.

DECISION INSIGHT

In September 2011, the federal Competition Bureau, after conducting a joint investigation with the RCMP, charged four Montreal-based telemarketing companies with fraud: Mega Byte Information Inc., Express Transaction Services Inc., International Business Logistics Inc., and Comexco Management Inc. It is alleged that after falsely claiming to be regular suppliers, the telemarketers tricked customers into believing that a purchase order had already been pre-authorized. As a result, more than $172 million worth of supplies changed hands between 2001 and 2007 at prices inflated up to 10 times the market value. This situation occurred because of inadequate internal controls.

SOURCE: *The Globe and Mail*, 2011.

Decision Maker

This feature requires students to make accounting and business decisions by using role-playing to show the interaction of judgement, awareness, and the impact of decisions made. Guidance answers are available at the end of each chapter.

> **DECISION MAKER**   Answer—End of chapter
>
> **Accounting Clerk**
> You recently got a job as a part-time accounting clerk to earn extra cash while you attend college. Today, your employer, the owner of the business, made some purchases and instructed you to debit Office Supplies and credit Accounts Payable for the entire amount. He tells you that the invoice is for a few office supplies but mainly for some items that he needed for personal use at home. Explain which GAAP is being violated, and the impact of this error on the financial statements of the business.

Extend Your Knowledge (EYK)

EYK
1-1

Supplementary material has been developed to explore some topics in more detail than the textbook can allow. When available, the EYK icon is displayed in the margin, alerting students to visit **Connect** if they choose to delve deeper into the material.

Financial Statements

Features and assignments that highlight companies such as WestJet (a company that provides services) and Danier (a merchandiser) show accounting in a modern and global context. Because students go directly to the financial statements of real companies, they remain engaged in the active learning process. The audited annual financial statement section of these annual reports are reproduced at the end of Volume 1. In Volume 2, the annual audited financial statements, **excluding** notes to the financial statements, for WestJet, Danier, High Liner Foods, and Shoppers Drug Mart are included.

END-OF-CHAPTER MATERIAL

Fundamental Accounting Principles sets the standard for quantity and quality of end-of-chapter material.

SUMMARY

LO¹ Explain the accounting cycle. The accounting cycle includes the steps in preparing financial statements for users that are repeated each reporting period.

LO² Describe an account, its use, and its relationship to the ledger. An account is a detailed record of increases and decreases in a specific asset, liability, or equity item. Information is taken from accounts, analyzed, summarized, and presented in useful reports and financial statements for users.

LO³ Define debits and credits and explain their role in double-entry accounting. Debit refers to left, and credit refers to right. The following table summarizes debit and credit effects by account type:

| | Assets = Liabilities + | | Equity | | | |
			Owner's Capital	Owner's Withdrawals	Revenues	Expenses
Increases	Debits	Credits	Credits	Debits	Credits	Debits
Decreases	Credits	Debits	Debits	Credits	Debits	Credits

LO⁴ Describe a chart of accounts and its relationship to the ledger. A ledger is a record that contains all accounts used by a company. This is what is referred to as *the books*. The chart of accounts is a listing of all accounts and usually includes an identification number that is assigned to each account.

LO⁵ Analyze the impact of transactions on accounts. We analyze transactions using the concepts of double-entry accounting. This analysis is performed by determining a transaction's effects on accounts. These effects are recorded in journals and posted to accounts in the ledger.

LO⁶ Record transactions in a journal and post entries to a ledger. We record transactions in a journal to give a record of their effects. Each entry in a journal is posted to the accounts in the ledger. This provides information in accounts that is used to produce financial statements. Balance column ledger accounts are widely used and include columns for debits, credits, and the account balance after each entry.

Summary

Each chapter includes a Summary of the chapter by Learning Objective, to reinforce what students have just learned.

GUIDANCE ANSWER TO DECISION MAKER

Accounting Clerk
The business entity principle is being violated because it requires that the owner's personal expenses be recorded separately from those of his business. By debiting the entire amount to Office Supplies, assets will be overstated on the balance sheet. By crediting Accounts Payable for the whole amount, liabilities will also be overstated. At the end of the accounting period when the amount of supplies used is recorded, Office Supplies Expense will be overstated on the income statement, causing net income to be understated. When net income is too low, equity is also understated.

Guidance Answers to Decision Maker

These discuss the Decision Maker boxes presented earlier in the chapter, and reinforce the need for decision making and critical thinking skills. This feature fits into the Student Success Cycle by reinforcing the "Apply" step.

GUIDANCE ANSWERS TO CHECKPOINT

1. The accounting cycle represents the steps followed each reporting period for the purpose of preparing financial statements.
2. Assets   Liabilities   Equity
   1, 5, 9   3, 7   2, 4, 6, 8, 10
3. The difference between the three accounts is in the name only; they are variations of a revenue account for rent.
4. An account is a record in the ledger where increases and decreases in a specific asset, liability, or equity item are recorded and stored. A ledger is a collection of all accounts used by a business. A chart of accounts is a numerical list of the accounts in the ledger. The numbers represent whether the account is an asset, liability, or type of equity.
5. A company's size and diversity affect the number of accounts needed in its ledger. The types of accounts used by a business depend on information that the business needs both to operative effectively and to report its activities in financial statements.

Guidance Answers to Checkpoint

The Checkpoint material throughout the chapter allows students to pause and check their progress. This feature reinforces the "Do," "Check," and "Apply" steps of the Student Success Cycle.

GLOSSARY

Account A place or location within an accounting system in which the increases and decreases in a specific asset, liability, or equity are recorded and stored.

Account balance The difference between the increases (including the beginning balance) and decreases recorded in an account.

Accounting cycle The steps repeated each reporting period for the purpose of preparing financial statements for users.

Accounts payable Obligations that arise when a promise to pay later is made in connection with purchases of merchandise, supplies, or equipment.

Journal A record where transactions are recorded before they are recorded in accounts; amounts are posted from the journal to the ledger; also called the *book of original entry*.

Journalizing Recording transactions in a journal.

Ledger A record containing all accounts used by a business.

Normal balance The debit or credit side on which an account increases. For example, assets increase with debits, therefore the normal balance for an asset is a debit. Revenues increase with credits, therefore a credit is the normal balance for a revenue account.

Glossary

All terms highlighted in the chapter are included.

Problem Material

Demonstration Problems

These problems reinforce the chapter material and further bolster the Student Success Cycle.

DEMONSTRATION PROBLEM

After several months of planning, Joane Cardinal started a haircutting business called The Cutlery. The following business activities occurred during its first month, August 2014:

a. On August 1, Cardinal put $16,000 cash into a chequing account in the name of The Cutlery. She also invested $10,000 of equipment that she already owned.
b. On August 2, she paid $2,000 cash for furniture for the shop.
c. On August 3, she paid $3,200 cash to rent space in a strip mall for August.
d. On August 4, she equipped the shop by installing the old equipment and some new equipment that she bought on credit for $21,000. This amount is to be repaid in three equal payments at the end of August, September, and October.

Analysis Component

An analysis component is included in each Mid- and End-of-Chapter Demonstration Problem, as well as several Exercises, Problems, and Focus on Financial Statements questions. These promote critical thinking and give students opportunities to practise these skills.

Analysis Component:
a. Identify how much of the assets held by The Cutlery are owned by the owner, Joane Cardinal.

Concept Review Questions

These short-answer questions reinforce the chapter content by Learning Objective.

CONCEPT REVIEW QUESTIONS

1. Describe the fundamental steps in the accounting process.
2. What is the difference between a note receivable and an account receivable?
3. Reread the chapter's opening scenario describing Black Feather Wilderness Adventure Company. Assume that Black Feather's expenses are about 75% of total revenues. Suggest appropriate account titles for 15 possible expense accounts.
6. Review the WestJet balance sheet for fiscal year-end December 31, 2011, in Appendix II. Identify three accounts on the balance sheet that would carry debit balances and three accounts on the balance sheet that would carry credit balances.
7. What kinds of transactions can be recorded in a General Journal?

Quick Study

These single-topic exercises give the students a quick test of each key element in the chapter and are referenced to Learning Objectives. Answers to these items are available on **Connect**.

QUICK STUDY

QS 2-1 Identifying accounts LO²

Identify the account as an asset, liability, or equity by entering the letter of the account type beside the account name. If the item is an equity account, indicate the type of equity account.

A = Asset   OE = Owner's Capital (Equity)   R = Revenues (Equity)
L = Liability   W = Owner's Withdrawals (Equity)   E = Expenses (Equity)

____ 1. Buildings   ____ 11. Advertising Fees Earned   ____ 21. Unearned Rent Revenue
____ 2. Building Repair Expense   ____ 12. Interest Earned   ____ 22. Prepaid Rent
____ 3. Wages Expense   ____ 13. Interest Expense   ____ 23. Rent Payable

Exercises

Exercises provide students with an additional opportunity to reinforce basic chapter concepts by Learning Objective. Note: Selected end-of-chapter exercises and problems are marked with this icon: e**X**cel. These have Excel templates located on **Connect**.

EXERCISES   ▣ connect

CHECK FIGURE:
Total cash = $17,975

Help Me
SOLVE IT

e**X**cel

Exercise 2-1 Recording the effects of transactions directly in T-accounts LO³,⁵

Set up the following T-accounts: Cash; Accounts Receivable; Office Supplies; Office Equipment; Accounts Payable; Sandra Moses, Capital; Sandra Moses, Withdrawals; Fees Earned; and Rent Expense. Next, record these transactions of the Northern Lights Company by recording the debit and credit entries directly in the T-accounts. Use the letters beside the transactions to identify the entries. Finally, determine the balance of each account.

a. Sandra Moses invested $32,600 cash in the business.
b. Purchased $925 of office supplies for cash.
c. Purchased $13,600 of office equipment on credit.
d. Received $3,000 cash as fees for services provided to a customer.

PROBLEMS

CHECK FIGURE:
2. Cash balance, Nov. 30,
2014 = $12,600

Problem 2-1A Recording transactions in T-accounts LO3,5

Following are business activities completed by Joel Douglas during the month of November 2014:

a. Invested $100,000 cash and office equipment with a $9,000 fair value in a new sole proprietorship named Douglas Tax Consulting.

b. Purchased land and a small office building. The land was worth $115,000, and the building was worth $85,000. The purchase price was paid with $80,000 cash and a long-term note payable for the balance.

Required

1. Set up the following T-accounts: Cash; Accounts Receivable; Office Supplies; Automobiles; Office Equipment; Building; Land; Accounts Payable; Long-Term Notes Payable; Joel Douglas, Capital; Joel Douglas, Withdrawals; Fees Earned; Wages Expense; and Utilities Expense.

Problems

Problems typically incorporate two or more concepts. As well, there are two groups of Problems: A Problems and Alternate or B Problems. B Problems mirror the A Problems to help improve understanding through repetition.

ETHICS CHALLENGE

EC 2-1

You are a cashier at a retail convenience store. When you were hired, the owner explained to you the policy of immediately ringing up each sale. Recently, lunch hour traffic has increased dramatically and the manager asks you to take customers' cash and make change without ringing up sales to avoid delays. The manager says she will add up cash and ring up sales equal to the cash amount after lunch. She says that in this way the register will always be accurate when the owner arrives at 3:00 p.m.

Required

1. Identify the advantages and disadvantages of the manager's suggestion.
2. Identify the ethical dilemma and evaluate at least two courses of action you might consider and why.

Ethics Challenge

Each chapter includes at least one Ethics Challenge to reinforce critical thinking skills for the students and open up discussion about various ethical topics.

FOCUS ON FINANCIAL STATEMENTS

FFS 4-1

CHECK FIGURES:
1. Net income =
$70,575; Total assets =
$95,850
3. Post-closing trial
balance = $121,350

Sarda Electrical Servicing began operations two years ago. Its adjusted account balances at December 31, 2014, are listed alphabetically below. The owner, Nymeth Sarda, made a $20,000 investment early in the year just ended December 31, 2014.

Required

1. Prepare an income statement, statement of changes in equity, and classified balance sheet based on the information provided.

2. Prepare the closing entries.   3. Prepare the post-closing trial balance.

Focus on Financial Statements

Each chapter includes a technical and analytical question that incorporates into the financial statements all major topics covered up to that point. Additional questions are available online on **Connect**.

CRITICAL THINKING MINI CASE

Prairie Insurance sells life insurance, disability insurance, vehicle insurance, crop insurance, and homeowners' insurance. You are employed by Prairie Insurance and have been promoted to sales division manager for the Western Canadian division. You will be supervising approximately 25 salespeople, along with five administrative assistants at various locations. The salespeople travel extensively and submit expense reports along with sales information monthly. A sample expense report for September shows:

Prairie Insurance—Western Canadian Division Sales Report: John Bishop Month Ended September 30, 2014	
Sales revenue*	$56,000
Expenses**	34,000

*Sales invoices attached
**Receipts attached

Critical Thinking Mini Cases

These cases give students the opportunity to apply critical thinking skills to concepts learned in the chapter, thus further reinforcing the "Apply" step of the Student Success Cycle.

Help Me Solve It

New *Help Me Solve It* tutorials are available on **Connect** for Larson's *Fundamental Accounting Principles*. The tutorials guide students through two of the more challenging end-of-chapter problems per chapter, providing them with an engaging visual and audio walkthrough of the problem. The *Help Me Solve It* tutorials allow for the power of technology to bring the content to life for students, help to reinforce concepts, and appeal to all learning styles.

THE ACCOUNTING STANDARD

We listened! In addition to obtaining numerous individual reviewer comments, we have held focus groups in cities throughout Canada to hear the issues and concerns instructors like you have about the materials you use to teach introductory financial accounting. We were the first textbook to go to these lengths for market research. Based on this sort of research and our extensive review process, you will find a list of new changes to specific chapters that our author has made to ensure the content of Larson's FAP remains current and fresh. Whether you are new to using FAP or new to this edition, you can see that McGraw-Hill Ryerson and Larson/Jensen are setting the accounting standard in *Fundamental Accounting Principles*. We think you'll like what you see.

General Updates

- Appendix II for Volume 1 includes the complete annual audited financial statements, including notes to the financial statements, for WestJet and Danier Leather, while Appendix II for Volume 2 includes the annual audited financial statements, excluding notes to the financial statements, for WestJet, Danier Leather, High Liner Foods, and Shoppers Drug Mart.
- Throughout Volumes 1 and 2, the exercises and problems have been refreshed in terms of numbers and/or business name/owner.
- Various end-of-chapter exercises/problems have been adjusted to incorporate reviewer suggestions.
- The chapter content is IFRS 2012 compliant throughout both volumes; IFRS 2012 references are included where appropriate.
- Actual businesses used as examples throughout Volumes 1 and 2 are bolded and highlighted to emphasize integration of accounting concepts with actual business practice.
- IFRS and ASPE differences are identified at the end of each chapter.
- Judgement Call feature has been replaced by Decision Maker.
- Did You Know? feature has been replaced by Decision Insight.
- Exhibits have been updated as appropriate with current information.
- Actual business examples reflect most current information available.
- Number of actual business examples increased based on review requests; these have been bolded and highlighted in magenta for emphasis.

Chapter-by-Chapter Updates

Chapter 1 (former Chapters 1 and 2)

- Combined and condensed the former Chapters 1 and 2
- GAAP updated to comply with IFRS 2012 (prudence/conservatism deleted and replaced by emphasis on faithful representation)
- New Extend Your Knowledge supplements added

Chapter 2 (former Chapter 3)

- New chapter opening story
- New Extend Your Knowledge supplement added
- New Mid-Chapter Demonstration Problem
- Accounting cycle exhibit changed to clockwise from counter clockwise direction

Chapter 3 (former Chapter 4)

- New chapter opening story
- Accounting cycle exhibit changed to clockwise from counter clockwise direction

Chapter 4 (former Chapter 5)

- New chapter opening story
- Accounting cycle exhibit changed to clockwise from counter clockwise direction
- Updated worksheet to Excel spreadsheet representation
- Exhibit 4.14 footnote converted to symbol to enhance pedagogy

Chapter 5 (former Chapter 6)

- New chapter opening story
- Replaced fictitious demonstration company used throughout this chapter (formerly Z-Mart) with actual business: Mountain Equipment Co-op
- Demonstration problems in appendix removed based on reviewer requests

Chapter 6 (former Chapter 7)

- Replaced fictitious demonstration company used throughout this chapter (formerly Z-Mart) with actual business: Mountain Equipment Co-op
- Replaced prudence with faithful representation
- PST rates updated to information available at time of printing

Chapter 7 (former Chapter 8)

– New chapter opening story

Chapter 8 (former Chapter 9)

– New chapter opening story
– New Extend Your Knowledge added to supplement information regarding need for internal controls, entitled "Profile of a Canadian Fraudster"
– New section under Technology and Internal Control, titled Increased E-Commerce

Chapter 9 (former Chapter 10)

– Updated chapter opening story

Appendix I (former Chapter 11)

– Appendix I is the former Payroll chapter
– All rates (i.e., EI, CPP, Provincial Tax, Federal Tax) updated to 2012

Appendix II (former Appendix I)

– Volume 1 includes annual audited financial statements (including notes to the financial statements) for WestJet and Danier Leather
– Volume 2 includes annual audited financial statements (excluding notes to the financial statements) for WestJet, Danier Leather, High Liner Foods, and Shoppers Drug Mart

Appendix III (former Appendix II)

– Sample chart of accounts updated to reflect textbook content

INNOVATIVE TECHNOLOGY SUPPORTING STUDENT SUCCESS

Fundamental Accounting Principles offers a wealth of resources unmatched in educational publishing.

CONNECT

McGraw-Hill Connect™ is a web-based assignment and assessment platform that gives students the means to better connect with their coursework, with their instructors, and with the important concepts that they will need to know for success now and in the future.

With Connect, instructors can deliver assignments, quizzes, and tests online. Nearly all the questions from the text are presented in an auto-gradeable format and tied to the textbook's learning objectives. Instructors can edit existing questions and author entirely new problems. Track individual student performance—by question, by assignment, or in relation to the class overall—with detailed grade reports. Integrate grade reports easily with learning management systems such as WebCT and Blackboard. And much more.

By choosing Connect, instructors are providing their students with a powerful tool for improving academic performance and truly mastering course material. Connect allows students to practise important skills at their own pace and on their own schedule. Importantly, students' assessment results and instructors' feedback are all saved online—so students can continually review their progress and plot their course to success.

Connect also provides 24/7 online access to an eBook—an online edition of the textbook—to aid students in successfully completing their work, wherever and whenever they choose.

Key Features

Simple Assignment Management

With Connect, creating assignments is easier than ever, so you can spend more time teaching and less time managing.

- Create and deliver assignments easily with selectable end-of-chapter questions and test bank material to assign online

- Streamline lesson planning, student progress reporting, and assignment grading to make classroom management more efficient than ever
- Go paperless with the eBook and online submission and grading of student assignments

Smart Grading

When it comes to studying, time is precious. Connect helps students learn more efficiently by providing feedback and practice material when they need it, where they need it.

- Automatically score assignments, giving students immediate feedback on their work and side-by-side comparisons with correct answers
- Access and review each response; manually change grades; or leave comments for students to review
- Reinforce classroom concepts with practice tests and instant quizzes

Instructor Library

The Connect Instructor Library is your course creation hub. It provides all the critical resources you'll need to build your course, just how you want to teach it.

- Assign eBook readings and draw from a rich collection of textbook-specific assignments
- Access instructor resources, including ready-made PowerPoint presentations and media to use in your lectures
- View assignments and resources created for past sections
- Post your own resources for students to use

eBook

Connect reinvents the textbook learning experience for the modern student. Every Connect subject area is seamlessly integrated with Connect eBooks, which are designed to keep students focused on the concepts key to their success.

- Provide students with a Connect eBook, allowing for anytime, anywhere access to the textbook
- Merge media, animation, and assessments with the text's narrative to engage students and improve learning and retention
- Pinpoint and connect key concepts in a snap using the powerful eBook search engine
- Manage notes, highlights, and bookmarks in one place for simple, comprehensive review

No two students are alike. McGraw-Hill LearnSmart™ is an intelligent learning system that uses a series of adaptive questions to pinpoint each student's knowledge gaps. LearnSmart then provides an optimal learning path for each student, so that they spend less time in areas they already know and more time in areas they don't. The result is LearnSmart's adaptive learning path helps students retain more knowledge, learn faster, and study more efficiently.

LYRYX INTERACTIVE FINANCIAL ACCOUNTING

Lyryx Interactive Financial Accounting (LIFA) contains algorithmic problems based upon the Larson text End-of-Chapter problem material, unlimited opportunity for students to practice, and automatic grading with detailed feedback for students and instructors. *LIFA* contains Lessons, Explorations, and Labs. The Labs may be attempted by students as many times as they wish, with only the best grade being recorded. Optional *Lyryx LIFA* is available to package with the Larson 14th Canadian edition text at an additional cost.

INSTRUCTOR RESOURCES

Instructor supplements are available within **Connect**.

Solutions Manual

Fundamental Accounting Principles continues to set the standard for accuracy of its problem material. The Solutions Manual has been revised by Tilly Jensen, Athabasca University; Wendy Popowich, Northern Alberta Institute of Technology; Susan Hurley, Northern Alberta Institute of Technology; and Ruby So Koumarelas, Northern Alberta Institute of Technology. Additional accuracy checking was provided by Ross Meacher, CA; Betty Young, Red River College; and ANSR Source. Available in both Microsoft Word and PDF format, solutions for all problem material are included.

Computerized Test Bank

The test bank has been revised and technically checked for accuracy to reflect the changes in the Fourteenth Canadian Edition. Sarah Magdalinski, Northern Alberta Institute of Technology, revised the test bank for this edition, and Elizabeth Hicks, Douglas College, provided additional technical checking. Grouped according to Learning Objective, difficulty level, and by level of Bloom's Taxonomy, the questions in the computerized test bank include true/false, multiple choice, matching, short essay, and problem material.

PowerPoint® Presentations

These presentation slides, revised by Joe Pidutti, Durham College, and checked by Betty Young, Red River College, are fully integrated with the text to visually present chapter concepts.

Instructor's Manual

The Instructor's Manual, revised by Jeanine Wall, Red River College, cross-references assignment materials by Learning Objective and also provides a convenient chapter outline.

Focus on Financial Statements

These include technical and analytical questions which incorporate major topics covered. These, and accompanying solutions in the Solutions Manual, have been revised by Stephanie Ibach, MacEwan University.

Extend Your Knowledge

This supplemental material has been developed to delve into more detail for specific topics. These have been revised by Stephanie Ibach, MacEwan University.

Excel Template Solutions

Solutions to the problems using Excel templates are available for instructors. These have been revised by Ian Feltmate, Acadia University.

Image Bank

All exhibits and tables displayed in the text are available for your use, whether for creating transparencies or handouts, or customizing your own PowerPoint presentations.

OTHER SUPPLEMENTS FOR STUDENTS

Working Papers

Available for purchase by students, printed Working Papers for Volumes 1 and 2 match the end-of-chapter material. They include papers that can be used to solve all of the Quick Study questions, Exercises, and A and B Problem sets. The Working Papers for the Fourteenth Canadian Edition have been revised by Wendy Popowich, NAIT; Susan Hurley, NAIT; and Ruby So Koumarelas, NAIT. Additional technical checking was completed by Joan Baines, Red River College.

SUPERIOR LEARNING SOLUTIONS AND SUPPORT

The McGraw-Hill Ryerson team is ready to help you assess and integrate any of our products, technology, and services into your course for optimal teaching and learning performance. Whether it's helping your students improve their grades, or putting your entire course online, the McGraw-Hill Ryerson team is here to help you do it. Contact your iLearning Sales Specialist today to learn how to maximize all of McGraw-Hill Ryerson's resources!

For more information on the latest technology and Learning Solutions offered by McGraw-Hill Ryerson and its partners, please visit us online: www.mcgrawhill.ca/he/solutions.

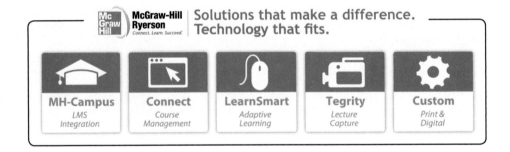

DEVELOPING A MARKET-DRIVEN TEXT

The success of this text is the result of an exhaustive process, which has gone beyond the scope of a single edition. Hundreds of instructors and educators across the country have been involved in giving their feedback to help develop the most successful accounting fundamentals text in the country. We owe thanks to all of those who took the time to evaluate this textbook and its supplemental products.

Fourteenth Canadian Edition reviewers

Joan Baines	*Red River College*	Lorrene Laursen	*Olds College*
Cam Beck	*Holland College*	Doug Leatherdale	*Georgian College*
Maria Belanger	*Algonquin College*	Kayla Levesque	*Cambrian College*
Neil Bishop	*Fanshawe College*	Richard MacKay	*Everest College*
Martha Brant	*Algoma University*	Bruce MacLean	*Dalhousie University*
Ruby Brar	*SAIT Polytechnic*	Geoff Milne	*Assiniboine Community College*
Robert Briggs	*New Brunswick Community College*	Richard Murphy	*Eastern College*
Kim Calder	*Nova Scotia Community College*	Michelle Nicholson	*Okanagan College*
Barbara Chapple	*St. Clair College*	Norma Pelletier	*North Island College*
Shelly Chlan	*Red River College*	Joe Pidutti	*Durham College*
Carole Clyne	*Centennial College*	Bill Pierias	*Humber College*
Derek Cook	*Okanagan College*	Traven Reed	*Canadore College*
Meredith Delaney	*Seneca College*	Doug Ringrose	*Grant MacEwan University*
Alison Dubois	*Algonquin College*	Don Smith	*Georgian College*
Andrew Dykstra	*Georgian College*	Tiffany Snauwaert	*Selkirk College*
John Harris	*Centennial College*	Glen Stanger	*Douglas College*
Michael Hockenstein	*Vanier College*	Clayton Stone	*George Brown*
Paul Hurley	*Durham College*	Barrie Tober	*Niagara College*
Jane Kaake	*Durham College*	Joe Toste	*Centennial College*
Michael Konkin	*Selkirk College*	Helen Vallee	*Kwantlen Polytechnic University*
Helene Labelle	*Canadore College*	Brad Witt	*Humber College*
Steve Landry	*John Abbott College*	Gerald Woudstra	*Concordia University College*

Fundamental Accounting Principles continues to set the bar in terms of its quality, accuracy, and depth and breadth of supplemental resources. This has been possible only because of the outstanding efforts and contributions of a dedicated group of individuals. I owe many thanks to their expertise and commitment that was extensively drawn upon during the process of writing this textbook. Particular thanks go out to: Joan Baines, Ian Feltmate, Liz Hicks, Michael Hockenstein, Susan Hurley, Stephanie Ibach, Ruby So Koumarelas, Sarah Magdalinski, Ross Meacher, Joe Pidutti, Wendy Popowich, Don Smith, Vijayshree Vethantham (and team), Jeanine Wall, and Betty Young. Thanks goes out to Reilly Dow (www.pinkfish.ca), as well, for the unique drawing and video she created for the cover of the textbook.

I am also appreciative to my colleagues from across Canada who suggested enhancements for this edition. Their knowledge and experience in the classroom are invaluable in directing and improving this book.

With sincere appreciation,
Tilly Jensen

Accounting in Business

YIELDING VERTICAL RESULTS

Vertically Inclined Rock Gym is an indoor climbing facility with more than 7,500 square feet of sculpted cliff walls, ledges, and boulders, a "leap of faith," and more than 4,000 handholds that can challenge the most accomplished climber or provide a unique fitness experience to the novice. Jake Kreutzer, the gym's founder and owner, was a struggling artist and waiter in Vancouver before moving to Victoria where he earned an economics degree. This was followed by short stints at an advertising agency and a sports and fitness magazine as a photographer. After receiving his MBA from the University of Calgary, Jake and his soon-to-be wife, Nancy, moved to Edmonton in 1994. The couple took up rock climbing in the Rockies but because indoor facilities were scarce, they found that climbing wasn't easy to learn or practise. Jake thought that more people would welcome the challenge and excitement of climbing, as he had done, if it was more accessible. From that realization, combined with Jake's desire to own his own business, Vertically Inclined was born … or at least the concept was. Rock climbing gyms were a novel and unproven industry, and the banks were not interested in lending money to a risky startup. So Jake put everything he had into the business and raised the rest of the cash privately. Jake's passion fuelled the persistence needed to navigate around what seemed like endless roadblocks. While establishing the business and creating brand recognition, he was working more than 90 hours per week … on top of helping his wife care for their newly born twin daughters!

Jake's life is more settled now. He is the sole owner and has a strong management team and reliable staff giving him more time to spend with his family. "Getting to the top of a difficult climb is a lot like succeeding in business. It takes tenacity, perseverance, and an ability to tolerate risk. My accounting and business knowledge helped me understand and learn from the mistakes I inevitably made." Jake chuckles and recounts the story of the licensed lounge and cappuccino bar he opened on the second floor. "The climbers loved it … but it didn't take long for the numbers to show me that selling 5 beer, 20 cappuccinos, and a few chocolate bars a day didn't cover the additional staffing and product costs … and it took up most of my time! So, we converted the space to a bouldering wall that increased the number of climbers we could accommodate and added to the variety of types of climbing available in the facility.

"My focus is marketing but I have learned that accounting is invaluable … it's the language that allows me to talk to and understand my accountant, bookkeeper, banker, lawyer, contractors, and customers … accounting gives you an advantage."

LEARNING OBJECTIVES

LO¹ Describe the purpose and importance of accounting.

LO² Describe forms of business organization.

LO³ Identify users and uses of, and opportunities in, accounting.

LO⁴ Identify and explain why ethics and social responsibility are crucial to accounting.

LO⁵ Identify, explain, and apply accounting principles.

LO⁶ Identify and explain the content and reporting aims of financial statements.

LO⁷ Analyze business transactions by applying the accounting equation.

LO⁸ Prepare financial statements reflecting business transactions.

www.verticallyinclined.com

An essential element of critical thinking is the ability to ask questions while reading (or listening or speaking). This exercise is designed to help students develop the skills related to questioning. Suggested answers are available on Connect.

CRITICAL THINKING CHALLENGE What questions might Jake need the answers to in order to get a loan from a bank? Who else might require accounting information from Jake's business?

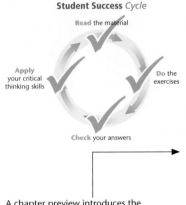

Student Success *Cycle*

Read the material

Apply
your critical
thinking skills

Do the
exercises

Check your answers

A chapter preview introduces the importance and relevance of the material, and also links these materials to the opening article to motivate you, the reader.

CHAPTER PREVIEW

Accounting is at the heart of business: accounting information pulsates throughout an organization, feeding decision makers with details needed to give them an edge over competitors. Decision makers like Jake in the chapter opening story cannot rely on hunches and guesses. Decision makers depend on their knowledge of accounting principles and practices to help them identify and take advantage of opportunities discovered from reviewing large volumes of information. Through your study of this book, you will learn about many of the accounting concepts, procedures, and analyses common to both small and large businesses. This knowledge will provide you with the basics necessary to make better business decisions.

This first chapter accomplishes three goals. First, it introduces the subject of accounting, providing a foundation for those students who have little or no understanding of business or the role of accounting in business.

Second, it focuses on how accounting information is created and communicated in the form of *financial statements*, which report on the financial performance and condition of an organization. This chapter will illustrate how transactions are reflected in financial statements, by using fictitious examples related to the first month of operations for Vertically Inclined Rock Gym, the business featured in the opening story. Vertically Inclined was assumed to have been opened on March 1, 2014, by owner Virgil Klimb. (Virgil Klimb is a pseudonym for the actual business owner. **Vir***gil* was derived from the name of the business: **V**ertically **I**nclined **R**ock **G**ym.)

Third, it introduces you to each of the learning features found in most chapters. For example, immediately to the left of the first paragraph above is an explanation of purpose regarding the chapter preview, and three additional features are described in the lower left margin. Some of the features refer to Connect, located on the web. Take the time in this chapter to explore and learn the value of these additional resources.

WHAT IS ACCOUNTING?

LO¹ Describe the purpose and importance of accounting.

Each chapter is separated into chunks of information called learning objectives (LO). Each LO tells you what needs to be mastered in that section of reading.

Accounting knowledge is a powerful tool; it is your key to success, according to Jake in the chapter opening story. How does accounting knowledge give you power? What exactly is the focus of accounting? This section answers these fundamental questions.

Power of Accounting

Boldfaced words or phrases represent new terminology that is explained here and defined in the glossary at the end of the chapter.

Accounting is an information system that identifies, measures, records, and communicates *relevant* information that *faithfully represents* an organization's economic activities,[1,2] as shown in Exhibit 1.1. Its objective is to help people make better decisions. It also helps people better assess opportunities, products, investments, and social and community responsibilities. In addition to reporting on the performance of a business, what the business owns, and what it owes, accounting opens our eyes to new and exciting possibilities. Put more simply, accounting involves collecting information, recording it, and then reporting it to various decision makers. In the chapter opening story, for example, **Vertically Inclined Rock Gym** collected and recorded accounting information so that it could be

Real company names are printed in bold magenta.

---

1 IFRS 2012, "Framework," para. QC5.
2 When information makes a difference in the decisions made by users, it is *relevant*. For information to possess the quality of *faithful representation*, it must be complete, neutral, and free from error. These primary qualitative characteristics of useful accounting information will be discussed in more detail later in this chapter.

EXHIBIT 1.1

Accounting Activities

Exhibits aid in visual learning of key accounting and business topics.

reported to Jake, the business's owner, to help him make important decisions such as those involved in setting selling prices for various services.

Focus of Accounting

Accounting affects many parts of life. Some examples of common contacts with accounting are through credit approvals, bank accounts, student loan forms, and payroll. These experiences are limited and tend to focus on the *recordkeeping* (or *bookkeeping*) parts of accounting. **Recordkeeping**, or **bookkeeping**, is the recording of financial transactions, either manually or electronically, for the purpose of creating a bank of data that is complete, neutral, and free from error. Accounting *involves* the recordkeeping process but *is* much more.

Accounting also involves designing information systems to provide useful reports that will be of aid in monitoring and controlling an organization's activities. In order to use the reports effectively, decision makers must be able to interpret the information. The skills needed to understand and interpret accounting information come from an insight into each aspect of accounting, including recordkeeping. The use of technology in recordkeeping reduces the time, effort, and cost of accounting while improving clerical accuracy. As technology has changed the way we store, process, and summarize masses of data, accounting has been freed to expand. Consulting, planning, and other financial services are now closely linked to accounting. These services require sorting through data, interpreting their meaning, identifying key factors, and analyzing their implications. Because accounting is part of so much that we do in business and our everyday lives, you can enjoy greater opportunities if you understand and are able to use accounting information effectively.

A series of Checkpoint questions in the chapter reinforces the immediately preceding materials. It gives you feedback on your comprehension before you go on to new topics. Answers to these Checkpoint questions are available for you at the end of each chapter.

CHECKPOINT

1. What is the major objective of accounting?
2. Distinguish between accounting and recordkeeping.

Do Quick Study questions: QS 1-1, QS 1-2

Answers to the Quick Study (QS) questions are available on Connect.

FORMS OF ORGANIZATION

A **business** is one or more individuals selling products or services for profit. Products like athletic apparel (**CCM, Bauer, NIKE, Reebok**), computers (**Dell, Hewlett-Packard, Apple**), and clothing (**Tilley, Levi's, GAP**) are part of our daily lives. Services like information communication (**Sympatico, AOL Canada, CompuServe, Microsoft**), dining (**Tim Hortons, Harvey's, McDonald's, Burger King**), and car rental (**Tilden, Hertz, Budget**) make our lives easier. A business can be as small as an in-home childcare service or as large as **Canadian Tire**. Nearly 100,000 new businesses are started in Canada each year, with most of

 LO² Describe forms of business organization.

them being founded by people who want freedom from ordinary jobs, a new challenge in life, or the advantage of earning extra money.

Most organizations engage in economic activities, such as the business activities of purchasing materials and labour, and selling products and services. They can also involve activities for non-business organizations, more commonly referred to as not-for-profit organizations, such as government, schools, and churches. Non-business organizations do not plan and operate for profit, but rather for other goals such as health, education, religious services, and cultural and social activities. A common feature in all organizations, both business and non-business, is the power and use of accounting.

Business Organizations

Businesses take one of three forms: sole proprietorship, partnership, or corporation.

Sole Proprietorship

A **sole proprietorship**, or **single proprietorship**, is a business owned by one person. No special legal requirements must be met in order to start this form of business, other than to file for a business licence and register the business name. While it is a separate entity[3] for accounting purposes, it is *not* a separate legal entity from its owner. This means, for example, that a court can order an owner to sell personal belongings to pay a proprietorship's debt. An owner is even responsible for debts that are greater than the resources of the proprietorship; this is known as **unlimited liability**, and is an obvious disadvantage of a sole proprietorship. Because tax authorities do not separate a proprietorship from its owner, the profits of the business are reported and taxed on the owner's personal income tax return. Small retail stores and service businesses often are organized as proprietorships.

Partnership

A **partnership**[4] is owned by two or more persons called *partners*. As for a proprietorship, no special legal requirements must be met in order to start a partnership, other than to register the business name and obtain a business licence. To run the business together, the partners need an oral or written agreement that usually indicates how profits and losses are to be shared. A partnership, like a proprietorship, is not legally separate from its owners, therefore each partner's share of profits is reported and taxed on that partner's tax return. Partners are usually subject to *unlimited liability*.

Corporation

A **corporation**[5] is a business that is a separate legal entity chartered (or *incorporated*) under provincial or federal laws. A corporation is responsible for its own acts and its own debts. It can enter into its own contracts, and it can buy, own, and sell property. It can also sue and be sued. Not only does separate legal status give a corporation an unlimited life, but it also entitles the corporation to conduct business with the rights, duties, and responsibilities of a person. As a result, a corporation files a tax return and pays tax on its profits. A corporation acts through its managers, who are its legal agents. Separate legal status also means that the shareholders are not personally liable for corporate acts and debts. Shareholders are legally distinct from the business and their loss is limited to what they invested. This **limited liability** is a key to why corporations can raise resources from shareholders who are not active in managing

---

3 The *business entity principle* is one of a group of accounting rules, the *generally accepted accounting principles (GAAP)*, which are discussed later in this chapter. This principle states that each economic entity or business of the owner must keep accounting records and reports separate from the owner and any other economic entity of the owner.

4 Partnerships are discussed in greater detail in Chapter 12 in Volume 2 of the textbook.

5 Corporations are discussed in greater detail in Chapter 13 in Volume 2 of the textbook.

the business. Ownership, or equity, of all corporations is divided into units called **shares**. Owners of shares are called **shareholders** (the American term for shares is *stock* and for shareholders, *stockholders*). A shareholder can sell or transfer shares to another person without affecting the operations of a corporation. When a corporation issues (or sells) only one class of shares, we call them **common shares**. A corporation that sells its shares to the public is called a **publicly accountable enterprise (PAE)**. The **public sale of shares** refers to the trading of shares in an organized stock market such as the Montreal or Toronto stock exchanges. A **private enterprise (PE)** is a corporation that does not offer its shares for public sale. **Agrium Inc.** is an example of a publicly accountable enterprise. Its shares are available on the Toronto Stock Exchange, and as of December 31, 2011, Agrium Inc. had issued a total of 158 million common shares to the public. This means that Agrium Inc.'s ownership is divided into 158 million units. A shareholder who owns 1,580,000 shares of Agrium Inc. owns 1%. **McCain Foods Limited** is a Canadian corporation that is a private enterprise. McCain's shares are held by a small group of individuals and are not for sale to the public. Exhibit 1.2 lists some of the characteristics of each business form:

	Sole Proprietorship	Partnership	Corporation
Business entity	yes	yes	yes
Legal entity	no	no	yes
Limited liability	no	no	yes
Unlimited life	no	no	yes
Business income is taxed	no	no	yes
One owner allowed	yes	no	yes

EXHIBIT 1.2

Characteristics of Business Organizations

CHECKPOINT

3. Identify examples of non-business organizations.
4. What are the three common forms of business organization?

Do Quick Study question: QS 1-3

USERS OF ACCOUNTING INFORMATION

Accounting is a service activity that serves the decision-making needs of *external* and *internal* users, as shown in Exhibit 1.3.

LO³ Identify users and uses of, and opportunities in, accounting.

External users

- Lenders
- Shareholders
- Governments
- Consumer groups
- External auditors
- Customers

Internal users

- Officers
- Managers
- Internal auditors
- Sales staff
- Budget officers
- Controllers

EXHIBIT 1.3

Users of Accounting Information

Infographics reinforce key concepts through visual learning.

External Information Users

External users of accounting information are *not* directly involved in running the organization. They include shareholders, lenders, directors, customers, suppliers, regulators, lawyers, brokers, and the press. Each external user has special information needs that depend on the kind of decision to be made. To make a decision, key questions need to be answered; this is often done using information available in accounting reports. Extend Your Knowledge 1-1 (EYK 1–1) identifies several external users and decisions that require accounting information.

External Reporting

Financial accounting is the area of accounting aimed at serving external users. Its primary objective is to provide external reports called *financial statements* to help users analyze an organization's activities. Because external users have limited access to an organization's information, their own success depends on getting external reports that communicate relevant information that is faithfully represented. Some governmental and regulatory agencies have the power to get reports in specific forms, but most external users must rely on *general-purpose financial statements*. The term *general-purpose* refers to the broad range of purposes for which external users rely on these statements. *Generally accepted accounting principles (GAAP)* are important in increasing the usefulness of financial statements to users. GAAP are the underlying concepts that make up acceptable accounting practices. GAAP in Canada follow International Financial Reporting Standards (IFRS). IFRS are the "accounting laws" that must be applied by accountants to public companies in Canada, when recording and reporting accounting information. We discuss GAAP and IFRS along with the financial statements in more detail later.

Internal Information Users

Internal users of accounting information are those individuals directly involved in managing and operating an organization. The internal role of accounting is to provide information to help internal users improve the efficiency and effectiveness of an organization in delivering products or services.

Internal Reporting

Managerial accounting is the area of accounting aimed at serving the decision-making needs of internal users. Managerial accounting provides special-purpose reports customized to meet the information needs of internal users. An example of such a report is a listing of credit customers who are late in paying their accounts to Vertically Inclined Rock Gym (refer to the chapter opening story). Another example would be a report showing suppliers owed money by Jake for credit purchases. Internal reports aim to answer such questions as:

- What are the manufacturing expenses per unit of product?
- What is the most profitable mix of goods and/or services?
- What level of revenues is necessary to show net income?
- Which service activities are most profitable?
- Which expenses change with a change in revenues?

This book will help you to learn the skills needed to use accounting information effectively to answer questions like these and others.

Internal Operating Functions

The responsibilities and duties of internal users extend to every function of an organization such as purchasing, production, human resources, distribution, marketing, and research and development. Accounting is essential to the smooth operation of each. Extend Your Knowledge 1-2 identifies several internal operating functions that require accounting information.

EYK
1-1

This Extend Your Knowledge icon appears when more information about a topic can be found on the Connect website accompanying this text. Go to Connect to find out more. A complete list of Extend Your Knowledge items is located on the back inside cover of the textbook.

EYK
1-2

To monitor operating functions, managers rely on **internal controls**—procedures set up to protect assets (like cash, equipment, and buildings), ensure that accounting reports are free from error, neutral, and complete, promote efficiency, and ensure that company policies are followed. For example, certain actions require verification, such as a manager's approval before materials enter production. Internal controls are crucial if accounting reports are to provide relevant and trustworthy information.

DECISION INSIGHT

In September 2011, the federal Competition Bureau, after conducting a joint investigation with the RCMP, charged four Montreal-based telemarketing companies with fraud: Mega Byte Information Inc., Express Transaction Services Inc., International Business Logistics Inc., and Comexco Management Inc. It is alleged that after falsely claiming to be regular suppliers, the telemarketers tricked customers into believing that a purchase order had already been pre-authorized. As a result, more than $172 million worth of supplies changed hands between 2001 and 2007 at prices inflated up to 10 times the market value. This situation occurred because of inadequate internal controls.

SOURCE: *The Globe and Mail*, 2011.

ACCOUNTING OPPORTUNITIES

Exhibit 1.4 identifies some of the countless job opportunities in accounting by classifying accountants according to the kind of work that they perform. In general, accountants work in four broad fields:

- Financial
- Managerial
- Taxation
- Accounting-related

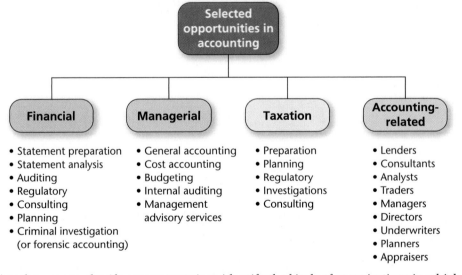

EXHIBIT 1.4

Opportunities in Practice

Another way to classify accountants is to identify the kinds of organizations in which they work. Most accountants are **private accountants** and work for a single employer, which is often a business. The services of **public accountants** are available to the public, which means that services are provided to many different clients. **Government accountants** work for local, provincial, and federal government agencies. Exhibit 1.5 shows the average annual salaries for various accounting groups.

Financial Accounting

Financial accounting serves the needs of external users by providing financial statements. Many organizations, both business and non-business, issue their financial statements only after an audit. An **audit** is an independent review and test of an

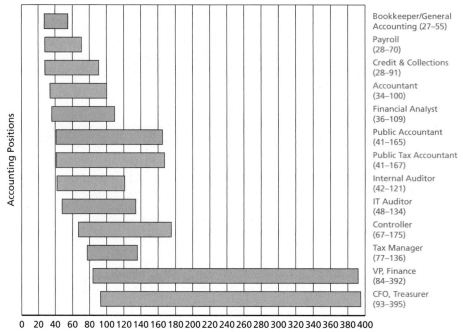

Accounting Positions

Bookkeeper/General
Accounting (27–55)
Payroll
(28–70)
Credit & Collections
(28–91)
Accountant
(34–100)
Financial Analyst
(36–109)
Public Accountant
(41–165)
Public Tax Accountant
(41–167)
Internal Auditor
(42–121)
IT Auditor
(48–134)
Controller
(67–175)
Tax Manager
(77–136)
VP, Finance
(84–392)
CFO, Treasurer
(93–395)

0 20 40 60 80 100 120 140 160 180 200 220 240 260 280 300 320 340 360 380 400

Salary Ranges for 2011 ($000s)

*These values do not include benefits/bonuses.
SOURCE: *2012 Salary Guide* from Robert Half.

organization's accounting systems and records; it is performed to add credibility to the financial statements.[6] **External auditors** perform the audit function at the request of the board of directors to protect shareholder interests.

Managerial Accounting

Managerial accounting serves the needs of internal users by providing special-purpose reports. These special-purpose reports are the result of general accounting, cost accounting, budgeting, internal auditing, and management consulting.

General accounting	The task of recording transactions, processing the recorded data, and preparing reports for members of the management team such as the **controller** (the chief accounting officer of an organization).
Cost accounting	The process of accumulating the information that managers need about the various **costs** within the organization.
Budgeting	The process of developing formal plans for an organization's future activities.
Internal auditing	Function performed by auditors employed within the organization for the purpose of evaluating the efficiency and effectiveness of procedures.
Management consulting	Service provided by external accountants who suggest improvements to a company's procedures; suggestions may concern new accounting and internal control systems, new computer systems, budgeting, and employee benefit plans.

Taxation

Income tax raised by federal and provincial governments is based on the income earned by taxpayers. These taxpayers include both individuals and corporate businesses. Sole proprietorships and partnerships are not subject to income tax, but owners of these two non-corporate business forms must pay tax on income earned

---

6   To achieve this result, audits are performed by independent professionals who are public accountants. Little or no credibility would be added to statements if they were audited by a company's own employees.

from these business forms. The amount of tax is based on what the laws define to be income. In the field of **taxation**, tax accountants help taxpayers comply with these laws by preparing their tax returns and providing assistance with tax planning for the future. The government (specifically, the **Canada Revenue Agency (CRA)**) employs tax accountants for collection and enforcement.

Professional Certification

Many accountants (financial, managerial, tax, and other) have professional accounting status. Accounting is a profession, like law and medicine, because accountants have special abilities and responsibilities. The professional status of an accountant is often indicated by one or more professional certifications. In Canada, several accounting organizations currently provide the education and training required in order to obtain professional certification. These include the Certified General Accountants' Association (for the designation of Certified General Accountant **(CGA)**), the Society of Management Accountants (for the Certified Management Accountant **(CMA)** designation), and the Institute of Chartered Accountants (for the designation of Chartered Accountant **(CA)**). At the time of writing, the CGA, CMA, and CA organizations were working together to unite the Canadian accounting profession under the new Canadian Chartered Professional Accountant **(CPA)** designation. The CPA certification program will be ready for delivery in parts of Canada by the autumn of 2013, and in the fall of 2015, the first CPA exams will be available.

The preceding discussions show how important accounting is for organizations. Regardless of your career goals, you will use accounting information because it is the language of business. The discussion also emphasizes the broad scope and growing number of opportunities available in accounting. This book will help you to take advantage of those opportunities.

Relevant links are included as a source of additional information.

For detailed information regarding professional accounting education programs and journals, refer to the following websites: www.cpacanada.ca, www.cga-canada.org, www.cma-canada.org, and www.cica.ca.

CHECKPOINT

5. What is the difference between private and public accountants?
6. What are the four broad fields of accounting?
7. What is the purpose of an audit?
8. Distinguish between managerial and financial accounting.
9. What is the difference between external and internal users of accounting information?
10. Why are internal controls important?

Do Quick Study questions: QS 1-4, QS 1-5

ETHICS AND SOCIAL RESPONSIBILITY

LO⁴ Identify and explain why ethics and social responsibility are crucial to accounting.

Ethics and ethical behaviour are important to the accounting profession and to those who use accounting information. We are reminded of this when we find stories in the media of cheating, or when we witness wrongful actions by individuals in business. A lack of ethics makes it harder for people to trust one another. If trust is missing, our lives are more difficult, inefficient, and unpleasant. An important goal of accounting is to provide useful information for decision making. For information to be useful, it must be trusted; this demands ethics in accounting. Closely related to ethics is social responsibility. Both are discussed in this section.

Understanding Ethics

Ethics are beliefs that differentiate right from wrong. Ethics and laws often coincide, with the result that many unethical actions (such as theft and physical violence) are also illegal. Yet other actions are not against the law but are considered unethical, such as not helping people with certain needs or deliberately withholding critical information from the user.

Identifying the ethical path is sometimes difficult. The preferred ethical path is to take a course of action that avoids casting doubt on one's decision. For example, as a member of the board for a not-for-profit organization, you are involved in a decision through which your brother's company could win a profitable contract to do work for the organization … do you participate in the decision or do you remove yourself from the discussion? The ethical answer would be to avoid this conflict of interest by not participating. Accountants have ethical obligations in at least four general areas: they are expected to maintain a high level of professional competence, treat sensitive information as confidential, exercise personal integrity, and be objective in matters of financial disclosure. Extend Your Knowledge 1-3 lets you apply the Rotary 4-Way Test, shown next.

EYK
1-3

DECISION INSIGHT

Ethics Are Timeless
The Rotary 4-Way Test, created by Herbert J. Taylor in 1932, is an internationally renowned guideline for making ethical business choices:
"Of the things we think, say or do:
1. Is it the Truth?
2. Is it Fair to all concerned?
3. Will it build goodwill and better friendships?
4. Will it be beneficial to all concerned?"

SOURCE: www.rotary.org, ® Rotary International. Used with permission.

Organizational Ethics

Organizational ethics are likely learned through management example and leadership. Companies like **Shell Canada**, **The Body Shop**, and **Royal Bank of Canada** work hard to convey the importance of ethics to employees. For example, Shell Canada states:

"We set high standards of performance and ethical behavior that we apply internationally. The Shell General Business Principles, Code of Conduct and Code of Ethics help everyone at Shell act according to our core values of honesty, integrity and respect for people to comply with relevant legislation and regulations."
SOURCE: http://shell.ca. Information accessed September, 2011

Ethical practices build trust, which promotes loyalty and long-term relationships with customers, suppliers, employees, and investors. Good ethics add to an organization's reputation and its success.

DECISION INSIGHT

Corporate Governance Promotes Corporate Good
Ethical companies are said to have excellent **corporate governance**, the mechanism by which individuals in a company, in particular the board of directors, are motivated to align their behaviours with the overall corporate good. Since the demise of corporations like Enron and WorldCom, caused by fraudulent accounting activities, corporate governance is in the spotlight. Royal Bank of Canada, with its head office in Montreal, has detailed corporate governance guidelines, an excerpt of which follows:

"RBC and its Board of Directors are committed to maintaining high standards of governance which comply with all regulatory standards and incorporate best practices appropriate to the organization."

In Extend Your Knowledge 1-4, you will find an example of corporate governance.

EYK
1-4

SOURCE: http://www.rbc.com (accessed September 2011).

Accounting Ethics

Ethics are crucial in accounting. As they prepare financial reports, providers of accounting information often face ethical choices that can affect both the use and the receipt of money, including taxes owed and money shared with owners. Accounting information can affect the price that a buyer pays and the wages paid to workers. It can even affect the success of products, services, and divisions. Misleading information can lead to a wrongful closing of a division, causing workers, customers, and suppliers to be seriously harmed.

Because of the importance of accounting ethics, codes of ethics for accountants are set up and enforced by the Provincial Certified General Accountants' Associations, the Provincial Societies of Management Accountants, and the Provincial Institutes of Chartered Accountants. The codes of all three professional accounting bodies state that accountants have a responsibility to society, they must act in the interest of their client or employer, they must exercise due care and professional judgment and continually upgrade their skills, and they must not be associated with deceptive information. Samples from these codes are presented in Extend Your Knowledge 1-5 on Connect. These codes can be of help when one confronts ethical dilemmas.

EYK
1-5

Ethics codes are also useful when one is dealing with confidential information. For example, auditors have access to confidential salaries and an organization's strategies. Organizations can be harmed if auditors pass this information to others. To prevent this, auditors' ethics codes require them to keep information confidential. Internal accountants are also not to use confidential information for personal gain.

DECISION INSIGHT

Silvercorp Metals Inc. — Wrongly Accused of Unethical Accounting?
An anonymous group has accused Silvercorp, a Vancouver-based company, of inflating its earnings. Although these statements of wrongdoing are being investigated, the company is working with police and securities regulators to determine the source of the allegations because it may be that the "whistle blowers" are the criminals. Why? The accusations caused a decrease in Silvercorp's share price ... if the accusers were short sellers*, they would have made a lot of money at Silvercorp's expense. Time will tell whether Silvercorp or the accusers are the unethical party.

SOURCE: www.theglobeandmail.com; September 2011.
* Short sellers are investors who sell shares that they do not have. The goal of a short seller is to make a profit from selling the shares for an amount greater than what they will have to pay when they buy them. A short seller will lose money if they have to pay more for the shares than the amount they sold them for.

Ethical Challenge

In our lives, we encounter many situations requiring ethical decisions. We need to remember that accounting must be practised ethically if it is to be useful, and must always ensure that our actions and decisions are ethical.

Social Responsibility

Social responsibility is a concern for the impact of our actions on society as a whole. It requires that an organization identify issues, analyze options, and make socially responsible decisions.

Socially conscious employees, customers, investors, and others see to it that organizations follow claims of social awareness with action, by placing significant pressure on organizations to contribute positively to society. Organizations such as

Appendix II at the end of the text includes two sets of real-life financial statements to provide you with a frame of reference.

DANIER

WestJet and **Danier Leather** take social responsibility seriously. WestJet invests in the community through WestJet Cares, a program that supports ten national charities such as the Boys and Girls Clubs of Canada, Big Brothers Big Sisters Canada, CNIB, Kids Help Phone Canada, KidSport Canada, and Make-A-Wish Canada. Danier Leather sponsors not only Because I Am a Girl, a campaign to fight global gender inequality, but also the construction of the Barlonyo Trade and Vocational Institute in Uganda, and supports more than 150 children through Plan Canada.

CHECKPOINT

11. What are the guidelines to use in making ethical and socially responsible decisions?
12. Why are ethics and social responsibility valuable to organizations?
13. Why are ethics crucial to accounting?

Do Quick Study question: QS 1-6

GENERALLY ACCEPTED ACCOUNTING PRINCIPLES (GAAP)

LO⁵ Identify, explain, and apply accounting principles.

As has already been stated, the goal of accounting is to provide useful information for decision making. For information to be useful, it must be trusted and relevant. This demands not only ethics in accounting but also generally accepted underlying concepts. The underlying concepts that make up acceptable accounting practices are referred to as **generally accepted accounting principles (GAAP)**.

GAAP for Public vs. Private Enterprises

The responsibility for setting accounting principles in Canada changed recently because of Canada's adoption of **International Financial Reporting Standards (IFRS)**. IFRS have replaced Canadian accounting standards for publicly accountable enterprises (PAEs). The **Accounting Standards Board (AcSB)**, the body that originally governed accounting standards in Canada, has developed a set of "made in Canada" **Accounting Standards for Private Enterprises (ASPE)**.

	Publicly Accountable Enterprises (PAEs)	Private Enterprises (PEs)
GAAP to be used	IFRS	ASPE or IFRS

Why IFRS? Although professional accountants around the world all follow GAAP, how GAAP are interpreted and applied in the recording and reporting of accounting information differs from country to country. These differences can prevent investors, creditors, and other users of global accounting information from making the most informed decisions possible. To improve the comparability of accounting information, the **International Accounting Standards Board (IASB)** was established to try to achieve global agreement on the use of a common set of accounting standards, namely, IFRS. The long-term goal of the IASB is to have all countries use IFRS, and current IFRS adopters include the European Union, Australia, China, South Africa, Russia, Hong Kong, Malaysia, Canada, and others. With the signing of the Norwalk Agreement, the United States may soon adopt IFRS.

Why ASPE? Private enterprises are privately owned so have some different reporting needs than public enterprises. For example, a small sole proprietorship with *employee future benefits*[7] might incur significant costs if it had to comply with the

---

7   The accounting for employee future benefits is well beyond the scope of an introductory financial accounting course but the issue is raised to provide an example of an area of difference between IFRS and ASPE.

complexities of the related IFRS. The AcSB developed ASPE to meet the need for simplification in areas where the adoption of IFRS might have caused significant cost/benefit concerns for private enterprises. Private enterprises can choose whether to follow ASPE or IFRS.

Accounting Standards for Private Enterprises have significant parallels to IFRS but there are differences between the two. The differences, within the scope of an introductory financial accounting textbook, are identified and briefly discussed in the 'IFRS and ASPE—The Differences' section at the end of each chapter. This textbook focuses on GAAP as they relate to IFRS and we begin emphasizing these in the early chapters of this book.

Purpose of GAAP

The primary purpose of GAAP is to ensure the usefulness of financial information. For financial information to be useful, it must possess the primary qualitative characteristics of *relevance* and *faithful representation*.[8] Information that has **relevance** is capable of making a difference in the decisions made by users.[9] When information is a **faithful representation** of what it claims to represent, it is complete, neutral, and free from error.[10] Usefulness is enhanced if the financial information is *comparable, verifiable, timely,* and *understandable*. If companies use similar practices, users are able to compare companies and the information possesses **comparability**.[11] **Verifiability** means that different knowledgeable users could agree that financial information was faithfully represented.[12] Information has **timeliness** if it is available to decision makers in time to influence their decisions.[13] Presenting information clearly and concisely gives it **understandability**.[14]

GAAP impose limits on the range of accounting practices that companies can use. We describe in the next section some of the important accounting principles.

Fundamental Building Blocks of Accounting

GAAP, as illustrated in Exhibit 1.6, are the building blocks of accounting. The GAAP described in this chapter include: business entity, cost, going concern, monetary unit, and revenue recognition. General principles described in later chapters (with their relevant chapter in parentheses) include: timeliness (3), matching (3), full disclosure (5), materiality (6), and consistency (6).

EXHIBIT 1.6

Building Blocks of GAAP*

For ease of reference, these principles are also summarized on the inside cover of both Volumes 1 and 2 of the textbook.

*A complete discussion of the complexities encompassing the IFRS conceptual framework is beyond the scope of a fundamentals textbook and is left for a more advanced course.

---

8   IFRS 2012, "Framework," para. QC4.
9   IFRS 2012, "Framework," para. QC6.
10 IFRS 2012, "Framework," para. QC12.
11 IFRS 2012, "Framework," para. QC20.
12 IFRS 2012, "Framework," para. QC26.
13 IFRS 2012, "Framework," para. QC29.
14 IFRS 2012, "Framework," para. QC30.

Business Entity Principle

The **business entity principle** requires that each economic entity or business of the owner must keep accounting records separate from those of the owner and any other economic entity of the owner. Users want information about the performance of a specific entity. If information is mixed between two or more entities, its usefulness decreases.

> *Example:* Looking at Vertically Inclined, Virgil Klimb must not include personal expenses, such as personal clothing and the cost of going to the movies, as expenses of his business.

Cost Principle

The **cost principle** requires that all transactions be recorded based on the actual cash amount received or paid. In the absence of cash, the cash equivalent amount of the exchange is recorded.[15]

> *Example:* If Vertically Inclined purchased used equipment for $5,000 cash, it is recorded in the accounting records at $5,000. It makes no difference if Virgil Klimb thinks that the value of the equipment is $7,000.

Going Concern Principle

According to the **going concern principle**, financial statement users can safely assume that the statements reflect a business that is going to continue its operations instead of being closed or sold. Therefore, assets are maintained in the accounting records at cost and not reduced to a liquidation value as if the business were being bought or sold. If a company is to be bought or sold, buyers and sellers are advised to obtain additional information, such as estimated market values, from other sources.[16]

> *Example:* It is assumed from a review of Vertically Inclined's financial statements that the business is continuing its operations, because information to the contrary is not included.

Monetary Unit Principle

The **monetary unit principle** requires that transactions be expressed using units of money as the common denominator. It is assumed that the monetary unit is stable; therefore, a transaction is left as originally recorded and is not later adjusted for changes in currency value or inflation. The greater the changes in currency value and inflation, the more difficult it is to use and interpret financial statements across time.

> *Example:* Assume that in August 2014 Vertically Inclined purchased equipment from a supplier in the United States at a total cost of $1,000 (U.S.), or $950 (Cdn) ($1,000/1.0526 exchange rate). If the exchange rate changes several months later to 1.0256, Vertically Inclined does not restate the value of the equipment to $975 ($1,000/1.0256 current exchange rate). The equipment remains in the accounting records at $950 (Cdn). This is also consistent with the *cost principle*.

Revenue Recognition Principle

The **revenue recognition principle** requires that revenue be recorded at the time that it is earned regardless of whether cash or another asset has been exchanged.[17] The amount of revenue to be recorded is measured by the cash plus the cash equivalent value (market value) of any other assets received.

---

15 IFRS 2012, IAS 16, para. 23.
16 IFRS 2012, IAS 1, para. 25.
17 IFRS 2012, IAS 18, para. 9–34; "Framework," para. 4.37–4.39.

Example: Assume that on April 3, Vertically Inclined performed work for a client in the amount of $600. The client did not pay the $600 until May 15. Revenue is recorded when actually earned on April 3 in the amount of $600, the value of the noncash asset received by Vertically Inclined. Alternatively, if Vertically Inclined received $1,000 on April 15 for work to be done next month, revenue is *not* recorded until the work is actually done in May.

Extend Your Knowledge 1-6 provides a supplement on the generally accepted accounting principles.

EYK
1-6

CHECKPOINT

14. Why is the business entity principle important?
15. Describe the cost principle and explain why it might be considered verifiable.
16. A customer pays cash today for a product that is to be delivered to her next month. When should revenue be recognized?

Do Quick Study questions: QS 1-7, QS 1-8, QS 1-9

COMMUNICATING THROUGH FINANCIAL STATEMENTS

Financial statements are an organization's primary means of financial communication and are the end result of a process, or cycle, that begins with a business transaction like a sale. These transactions are recorded, classified, sorted, and summarized in order to produce the statements.

LO⁶ Identify and explain the content and reporting aims of financial statements.

Previewing Financial Statements

We will begin our study of the four major financial statements—the income statement, balance sheet, statement of changes in equity, and statement of cash flows—with a brief description of each. How these statements are linked is shown in Exhibit 1.7. Examples of financial statements are illustrated in the following pages using Vertically Inclined Rock Gym.

NOTE: Flexibility is permitted in the naming of financial statements. For example, the *statement of financial position* is another name for the *balance sheet*. In Appendix II at the end of the textbook, notice that WestJet uses the term *statement of financial position*, while Danier Leather uses *balance sheet*. The *statement of profit and loss (P&L)*, *statement of earnings*, and other names are used instead of *income statement*. For consistency, the financial statements will be named throughout this textbook as introduced in Exhibit 1.7.

DANIER

EXHIBIT 1.7

Links Between Financial Statements

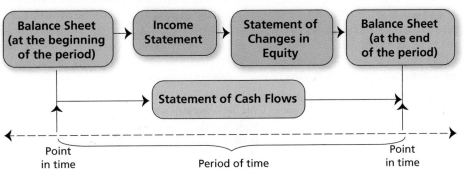

Transactions occur over a period of time, or during the accounting period, and are reported on the income statement, statement of changes in equity, and statement of cash flows. These transactions result in a new balance sheet at the end of the period.

A balance sheet reports on an organization's financial position at a *point in time*. The income statement, statement of changes in equity, and statement of cash flows report on performance over a *period of time*.

Selection of a reporting period is up to preparers and users (including regulatory agencies). A one-year, or annual, reporting period is common, as are semi-annual, quarterly, and monthly periods. The one-year reporting period is also known as the accounting or **fiscal year**. Businesses whose reporting period follows the **calendar year** begin on January 1 and end on December 31. Many companies choose a fiscal year based on their **natural business year** that ends when sales and inventories are low. For example, **Reitman's (Canada) Limited's** fiscal year-end is January 31, after the holiday season.

Income Statement

Revenues − Expenses = Net income
or
Net loss
For example:
$100   − $75   = $25
Revenues   Expenses   Net income
OR
$300   − $360   = $60
Revenues   Expenses   Net loss

An **income statement** reports *revenues* earned less *expenses* incurred by a business over a period of time.

Revenues are the value of assets exchanged for products and services provided to customers as part of a business's main operations. Assets are economic resources held by a business and include cash, equipment, buildings, and land. Later in the chapter, we will define assets more precisely. The income statement for Vertically Inclined's first month of operations is shown in Exhibit 1.8. It shows that Vertically Inclined earned total revenues of $4,100 during March: $3,800 from teaching revenue plus $300 from equipment rental revenue.

Expenses are costs incurred or the using up of assets from generating revenue. The income statement in Exhibit 1.8 shows that Vertically Inclined used up some of its assets in paying for rented space. The $1,000 expense for rental space is reported in the income statement as rent expense. Vertically Inclined also paid for an employee's salary at a cost of $700. This is reported on the income statement as salaries expense. The income statement heading in Exhibit 1.8 identifies the business, the type of statement, and the time period covered. Knowledge of the time period is important for us in judging whether the $2,400 net income earned in March is satisfactory.

A **net income**, or **profit**, means that revenues are more than expenses. A **net loss** means that expenses are more than revenues.

An income statement lists the types and amounts of both revenues and expenses to help users understand and predict company performance. This detailed information is more useful for making decisions than a simple profit or loss number would be.

Statement of Changes in Equity

Equity is equal to total assets minus total liabilities; it represents how much of the assets *belong* to the owner. Equity increases with *owner investments* and net income and decreases with *owner withdrawals* and net loss. **Owner investments** occur when the owner transfers personal assets, such as cash, into the business. Since owner investments do not result from the sale of a product or service, they are **not** a revenue and are therefore not reported on the income statement. **Owner withdrawals**, or **withdrawals**, occur when the owner takes cash or other assets from the business. Withdrawals represent a distribution of net income to the owner. Since withdrawals do not help to create revenue, they are **not** expenses and therefore are not reported on the income statement.

The **statement of changes in equity** reports on changes in equity over the reporting period. This statement starts with beginning equity and adjusts it for transactions that (1) increase it (investments by the owner and net income), and (2) decrease it (owner withdrawals and net loss).

The statement of changes in equity for Vertically Inclined's first month of operations is shown in Exhibit 1.9. This statement describes transactions that changed

Vertically Inclined Rock Gym
Income Statement
For Month Ended March 31, 2014

Revenues:		
Teaching revenue	$ 3,800	
Equipment rental revenue	300	
Total revenues		$ 4,100
Operating expenses:		
Rent expense	$ 1,000	
Salaries expense	700	
Total operating expenses		1,700
Net income		$ 2,400

EXHIBIT 1.8

Income Statement for Vertically Inclined Rock Gym

Vertically Inclined Rock Gym
Statement of Changes in Equity
For Month Ended March 31, 2014

Virgil Klimb, capital, March 1	$ -0-	
Add: Investments by owner	$ 10,000	
Net income	2,400	12,400
Total		$ 12,400
Less: Withdrawals by owner		600
Virgil Klimb, capital, March 31		$ 11,800

EXHIBIT 1.9

Statement of Changes in Equity for Vertically Inclined Rock Gym

Vertically Inclined Rock Gym
Balance Sheet
March 31, 2014

Assets		Liabilities		
Cash	$ 8,400	Accounts payable	$ 200	
Supplies	3,600	Notes payable	6,000	
Equipment	6,000	Total liabilities		$ 6,200
		Equity		
		Virgil Klimb, capital		11,800
Total assets	$18,000	Total liabilities and equity . . .		$ 18,000

EXHIBIT 1.10

Balance Sheet for Vertically Inclined Rock Gym

Vertically Inclined Rock Gym
Statement of Cash Flows
For Month Ended March 31, 2014

Cash flows from operating activities		
Cash received from clients	$ 4,100	
Cash paid for supplies	(3,400)	
Cash paid for rent	(1,000)	
Cash paid to employee	(700)	
Net cash used by operating activities		$ (1,000)
Cash flows from investing activities		-0-
Cash flows from financing activities		
Investment by owner	$10,000	
Withdrawal by owner	(600)	
Net cash provided by financing activities		9,400
Net increase in cash		$ 8,400
Cash balance, March 1		-0-
Cash balance, March 31		$ 8,400

EXHIBIT 1.11

Statement of Cash Flows for Vertically Inclined Rock Gym

> The arrows are imaginary but they emphasize the link between statements.

equity during the month. It shows $10,000 of equity created by Virgil Klimb's initial investment. It also shows $2,400 of net income earned during the month. The statement also reports the owner's $600 withdrawal. Vertically Inclined's equity balance at the end of the month is $11,800.

Balance Sheet

The **balance sheet**, or **statement of financial position**, reports the financial position of a business at a point in time, usually at the end of a month or year. It describes financial position by listing the types and dollar amounts of *assets, liabilities,* and *equity*. **Assets** are the properties or economic resources held by a business. A common characteristic of assets is their ability to provide future benefits to the company.[18] A familiar asset is *cash*. Another is **accounts receivable**, an asset created by selling products or services on credit. It reflects amounts owed to a business by its credit customers. These customers, and other individuals and organizations who owe amounts to a business, are called its **debtors**. Other common assets include merchandise held for sale, supplies, equipment, buildings, and land. Discussed in Chapter 4 are other assets having intangible rights, such as those granted by a patent or copyright.

Liabilities are debts or obligations of a business. They are claims of others against the assets of the business. A common characteristic of liabilities is their capacity to reduce future assets or to require future services or products.[19] Typical liabilities include *accounts payable* and *notes payable*. An **account payable** is a liability created by buying products or services on credit. It reflects amounts owed to others. A **note payable** is a liability expressed by a written promise to make a future payment at a specific time. Other common liabilities are salaries and wages owed to employees, and interest payable.

Individuals and organizations who own the right to receive payments from a business are called its **creditors**. One entity's payable is another entity's receivable. If a business fails to pay its obligations, the law gives creditors a right to force sale of its assets to obtain the money to meet their claims. When assets are sold under these conditions, creditors are paid first but only up to the amount of their claims. Any remaining money goes to the owner of the business. Creditors often compare the amounts of liabilities and assets on a balance sheet to help them decide whether to lend money to a business. A loan is less risky if liabilities are small in comparison to assets, because there are more resources than claims on resources. A loan is more risky if liabilities are large compared to assets.

Equity is the owner's claim on the assets of a business. It represents the assets that remain after deducting liabilities,[20] called **net assets**. We explained that net income is the difference between revenues and expenses of a business over a period of time. Net income is also equal to the change in equity due to operating activities over a period of time. In this way, an income statement links balance sheets from the beginning and the end of a reporting period. The causes of changes in equity are highlighted in Exhibit 1.12. Changes in equity are reported in the statement of changes in equity, and give us the ending balance of equity that is reported in the balance sheet.

Exhibit 1.10 shows the balance sheet for Vertically Inclined as of March 31, 2014. The balance sheet heading lists the business name, the statement, and the specific date on which assets and liabilities are identified and measured. The amounts in the balance sheet are measured as of the close of business on that specific date.

The balance sheet for Vertically Inclined shows that it has three different assets at the close of business on March 31, 2014. The assets are cash, supplies, and equipment,

---

EXHIBIT 1.12

The Causes of Changes in Equity

Increases in equity are caused by:
- owner investments
- revenues

Decreases in equity are caused by:
- owner withdrawals
- expenses

EYK

1-7

---

18 IFRS 2012, IAS 1, para. 15; "Framework," para. 4.8.
19 IFRS 2012, IAS 1, para. 15; "Framework," para. 4.15.
20 IFRS 2012, IAS 1, para. 15; "Framework," para. 4.20.

for a total dollar amount of $18,000. The balance sheet also shows total liabilities of $6,200. Equity is $11,800. Equity is the difference between assets and liabilities. The statement is named a *balance sheet* because: (1) the total amounts on both sides of the statement are equal; and (2) the reporting of assets, liabilities, and equity is in *balance*.

Statement of Cash Flows

The **statement of cash flows** describes the sources and uses of cash for a reporting period. It also reports the amount of cash at both the beginning and the end of a period. The statement of cash flows is organized by a company's major activities: operating, investing, and financing. Since a company must carefully manage cash if it is to survive and prosper, cash flow information is important.

As an example, the statement of cash flows for Vertically Inclined is shown in Exhibit 1.11 (notice that Vertically Inclined shows both operating and financing activities but it had no investing activities during March). To fully appreciate this financial statement, a solid understanding of some basic accounting concepts is required. Therefore, a detailed discussion has been left to Chapter 17.

Financial Statements and Forms of Organization

Earlier in the chapter, three different forms of business organization were described: sole proprietorships, partnerships, and corporations. Exhibit 1.13 summarizes key differences among these three forms of business ownership. While many differences exist, financial statements for these three types of organizations are very similar.

Difference	Type of Business Organization		
	Sole Proprietorship	Partnership	Corporation
Equity on the balance sheet belongs to:	Sole owner	Partners	Shareholders
Distributions to owners are called:	Withdrawals	Withdrawals	Dividends
When managers are also owners, their salaries are:	Not an expense	Not an expense	Expense

EXHIBIT 1.13

Financial Statement Differences Based on Type of Business Organization

The emphasis in the early chapters of this book is on sole proprietorships. This allows us to focus on important measurement and reporting issues in accounting without getting caught up in the complexities of additional forms of organization. We do discuss other forms of organization, however, and provide examples when appropriate. Chapters 12, 13, and 14 return to this topic and provide additional detail about the financial statements of partnerships and corporations.

EYK
1-8

CHECKPOINT

17. What are the four major financial statements?
18. Describe revenues and expenses.
19. Explain assets, liablities, and equity.
20. What are three differences in financial statements for different forms of organization?

Do Quick Study question: QS 1-10

THE ACCOUNTING EQUATION

LO7 Analyze business transactions by applying the accounting equation.

Notice in Exhibit 1.10 that there are two main sections of the balance sheet: assets on one side and liabilities and equity on the other side. Observe that the total assets of $18,000 equal the total liabilities and equity of $18,000. This equality is known as the *accounting equation*. This equation is based on relationships fundamental to accounting.

When an organization invests in assets, it is the result of an equal amount of financing. This relationship is expressed in the following equation:

$$Investing = Financing$$

Since invested amounts are referred to as *assets*, and financing is made up of owner and non-owner financing, we can also express this equality as:

$$Assets = Non\text{-}Owner\ Financing + Owner\ Financing$$

Non-owners are creditors. Creditors and owners hold claims or rights in the assets. Creditors' claims are called *liabilities* and the owner's claim is called *equity*. The equation can be rewritten as shown in Exhibit 1.14.

EXHIBIT 1.14

The Accounting Equation

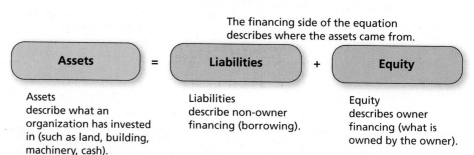

The financing side of the equation describes where the assets came from.

| Assets | = | Liabilities | + | Equity |

Assets describe what an organization has invested in (such as land, building, machinery, cash).

Liabilities describe non-owner financing (borrowing).

Equity describes owner financing (what is owned by the owner).

It is called the **accounting equation** or **balance sheet equation** because of its link to the balance sheet. It describes the relationship between a company's assets, liabilities, and equity. To demonstrate, assume you want to buy a car that costs $25,000. The bank lends you $15,000 and you pay $10,000 out of your personal savings account.

| Assets | = | Liabilities | + | Equity |

$25,000 = **$15,000** + **$10,000**

You have invested in a car that costs $25,000.

Borrowing $15,000 from the bank has financed part of your investment.

You, the owner, have financed part of the investment in the car; you own $10,000 of the car; in other words, your equity in the car is $10,000.

The accounting equation can be changed by moving liabilities to the left side of the equation:

$$\underline{Assets - Liabilities} = Equity$$

Net assets

Assets less liabilities equals *net assets*, another name for equity.

Transaction Analysis

Business activities can be described in terms of **transactions** and **events**. A **business transaction** is an exchange of *economic consideration* between two parties

CAUTION: The illustration of transaction analysis on the following pages is a learning tool to demonstrate the effects of transactions on the accounting equation. How transactions are recorded in the real world is the topic of Chapter 2.

that causes a change in assets, liabilities, or equity. An **economic consideration** is something of value, and examples include products, services, money, and rights to collect money. These transactions cause changes in the accounting equation. **Source documents** identify and describe transactions entering the accounting process. They are the *source* of accounting information, and can be in either paper or electronic form. Source documents, especially if obtained from outside the organization, provide objective evidence about transactions and their amounts, making information more reliable and useful. Examples of source documents are sales invoices, cheques, purchase orders, charges to customers, bills from suppliers, employee earnings records, and bank statements.

Not all business activities are transactions. **Business events** are activities that do not involve an exchange of economic consideration between two parties and therefore do not affect the accounting equation. Examples include placing an order for supplies, interviewing job applicants, signing a contract, and making a hotel reservation for an out-of-town business trip.

Every transaction leaves the equation in balance. Assets *always* equal the sum of liabilities and equity. We show how this equality is maintained by looking at the assumed activities of Vertically Inclined Rock Gym in its first month of operations.

EYK

1-9 AND **1-10**

1. Investment by Owner. On March 1, 2014, Virgil Klimb formed his indoor rock climbing business and set it up as a sole proprietorship. Klimb is the owner and manager of the business. The marketing plan for the business is to focus primarily on providing a safe, high quality, indoor rock climbing facility that offers programs for novice, recreational, and expert climbers. Klimb invests $10,000 cash in the new company, which he deposits in a bank account opened under the name of Vertically Inclined Rock Gym. An exchange has taken place, so this is a transaction. Transactions affect the accounting equation. As shown, this transaction affects both Vertically Inclined's cash (an asset) and equity (called *Virgil Klimb, Capital*), each for $10,000.

	Assets	=	Liabilities	+	Equity	Explanation of Equity Transaction
	Cash	=			Virgil Klimb, Capital	
(1)	+$10,000	=			+$10,000	Investment by Owner

The source of increase in equity is identified as an investment to distinguish it from subsequent transactions affecting equity.

2. Purchase Supplies for Cash. Vertically Inclined uses $2,500 of its cash to purchase supplies. This is a transaction because it involves an exchange of cash, an asset, for another kind of asset, supplies. The transaction produces no expense because no value is lost. The decrease in cash is exactly equal to the increase in supplies. The equation remains in balance.

	Assets			=	Liabilities	+	Equity	Explanation of Equity Transaction
	Cash	+	Supplies	=			Virgil Klimb, Capital	
Old Bal.	$10,000			=			$10,000	
(2)	−$ 2,500		+$2,500					
New Bal.	$ 7,500	+	$2,500	=			$10,000	
		$10,000		=		$10,000		

3. Purchase Equipment and Supplies on Credit. The owner decides that the business needs equipment and more supplies; these purchases total $7,100. As we see from the accounting equation in (2) above, however, Vertically Inclined has only $7,500 in cash. Concerned that these purchases would use nearly all of Vertically Inclined's cash, Klimb arranges to purchase the items on credit from CanTech Supply Company. This is a transaction because an exchange has occurred: Vertically Inclined has acquired items in exchange for a promise to pay for them later. Supplies cost $1,100, and the equipment costs $6,000. The total liability to CanTech Supply is $7,100. Vertically Inclined will pay for the supplies in 30 days, but has arranged to pay for the equipment by signing a note. The effects of this transaction on the accounting equation are:

	Assets			=	Liabilities		+	Equity	Explanation of Equity Transaction
	Cash	+ Supplies	+ Equipment	=	Accounts Payable	+ Notes Payable	+	Virgil Klimb, Capital	
Old Bal.	$7,500	$2,500		=				$10,000	
(3)		+$1,100	+$6,000		+$1,100	+$6,000			
New Bal.	$7,500 +	$3,600 +	$6,000	=	$1,100 +	$6,000	+	$10,000	
		$17,100				$17,100			

This purchase increases assets by $7,100, while liabilities (called *accounts payable* and *notes payable*) increase by the same amount. Both of these payables are promises by Vertically Inclined to repay its debt, where the note payable reflects a more formal written agreement. We will discuss these liabilities in detail in later chapters.

4. Services Rendered for Cash. A primary objective of a business is to increase its owner's wealth. This goal is met when a business produces a profit, also called *net income*. Net income is reflected in the accounting equation as an increase in equity. Vertically Inclined earns revenues by teaching climbing in the specially constructed indoor gym, and renting equipment. On March 10, Vertically Inclined provides teaching services to a group of school children in exchange for $2,200 cash. This is a transaction since an exchange has taken place. When revenue is earned in exchange for cash, it affects the accounting equation by increasing cash and equity. Here, cash increases by $2,200 and equity also increases by $2,200, identified in the far right column as a revenue. These explanations are useful in preparing and understanding a statement of changes in equity and an income statement.

	Assets			=	Liabilities		+	Equity	Explanation of Equity Transaction
	Cash	+ Supplies	+ Equipment	=	Accounts Payable	+ Notes Payable	+	Virgil Klimb, Capital	
Old Bal.	$7,500	$3,600 +	$6,000	=	$1,100 +	$6,000	+	$10,000	
(4)	+$2,200							+$ 2,200	Teaching Revenue
New Bal.	$9,700 +	$3,600 +	$6,000	=	$1,100 +	$6,000	+	$12,200	
		$19,300				$19,300			

5. and 6. Payment of Expenses in Cash. On March 10, Vertically Inclined pays its building landlord $1,000 to cover March's rent for space. Since an exchange has taken place, this is a transaction and affects the accounting equation as shown below in line (5). On March 14, Vertically Inclined pays the $700 salary of the business's only employee. This is also a transaction because an exchange has occurred, and it is therefore reflected in the accounting equation in line (6).

	Assets			=	Liabilities		+	Equity	Explanation of Equity Transaction
	Cash	+ Supplies	+ Equipment	=	Accounts Payable	+ Notes Payable	+	Virgil Klimb, Capital	
Old Bal.	$9,700	+ $3,600	+ $6,000	=	$1,100	+ $6,000	+	$12,200	
(5)	−$1,000							−$ 1,000	Rent Expense
Bal.	$8,700	+ $3,600	+ $6,000	=	$1,100	+ $6,000	+	$11,200	
(6)	−$ 700							−$ 700	Salaries Expense
New Bal.	$8,000	+ $3,600	+ $6,000	=	$1,100	+ $6,000	+	$10,500	
		$17,600				$17,600			

Both (5) and (6) produce expenses for Vertically Inclined as noted in the far right column. They use up cash for the purpose of providing services to clients. Unlike the asset purchase in (2), the cash payments in (5) and (6) acquire services. The benefits of these services do *not* last beyond the end of this month. The accounting equation remains in balance, and shows that both transactions reduce cash and Klimb's equity.

7. Service Contract Signed for April. On March 11, a customer and Virgil Klimb sign a $2,700 contract that requires Vertically Inclined to teach rock climbing to a group of executives as a team building exercise. Vertically Inclined is expected to perform the services during April.

	Assets			=	Liabilities		+	Equity	Explanation of Equity Transaction
	Cash	+ Supplies	+ Equipment	=	Accounts Payable	+ Notes Payable	+	Virgil Klimb, Capital	
Old Bal.	$8,000	+ $3,600	+ $6,000	=	$1,100	+ $6,000		$10,500	
(7)									
New Bal.	$8,000	+ $3,600	+ $6,000	=	$1,100	+ $6,000	+	$10,500	
		$17,600				$17,600			

This is a business event and *not* a business transaction because there was no economic exchange (nothing has yet been received by Vertically Inclined *and* nothing has been provided to the customer as of March 11). Therefore, this has no effect on the accounting equation.

8. Services and Rental Revenues Rendered for Credit. On March 17, Vertically Inclined provided teaching services of $1,600 and rented climbing equipment for $300 to a group of friends; the group's coordinator is billed for $1,900. This is a transaction because an exchange has occurred: Vertically Inclined provided services to a customer and in exchange received an asset, an account receivable, from the customer. The $1,900 increase in assets produces an equal increase in equity. Notice that the increase in equity is identified as two revenue components in the far right column of the accounting equation:

	Assets				=	Liabilities		+	Equity	Explanation of Equity Transaction
	Cash	+ Accounts Receivable	+ Supplies	+ Equipment	=	Accounts Payable	+ Notes Payable	+	Virgil Klimb, Capital	
Old Bal.	$8,000		+ $3,600	+ $6,000	=	$1,100	+ $6,000	+	$10,500	
(8)		+$1,900							+$ 1,600	Teaching Revenue
									+$ 300	Equipment Rental Revenue
New Bal.	$8,000	+ $1,900	+ $3,600	+ $6,000	=	$1,100	+ $6,000	+	$12,400	
		$19,500					$19,500			

9. Receipt of Cash on Account. The amount of $1,900 is received from the client on March 27, ten days after the billing for services in (8). This exchange between Vertically Inclined and the customer represents a transaction and therefore affects the accounting equation. This transaction does not change the total amount of assets and does not affect liabilities or equity. It converts the receivable to cash and *does not* create new revenue. Revenue was recognized when Vertically Inclined provided the services on March 17. Therefore, revenue is *not* recorded on March 27 when the cash is collected. The new balances are:

	Assets				=	Liabilities		+	Equity	Explanation of Equity Transaction
	Cash	+ Accounts Receivable	+ Supplies	+ Equipment	=	Accounts Payable	+ Notes Payable	+	Virgil Klimb, Capital	
Old Bal.	$8,000	+ $1,900	+ $3,600	+ $6,000	=	$1,100	+ $6,000	+	$12,400	
(9)	+$1,900	−$1,900								
New Bal.	$9,900	+ $ -0-	+ $3,600	+ $6,000	=	$1,100	+ $6,000	+	$12,400	
			$19,500				$19,500			

10. Payment of Accounts Payable. Vertically Inclined pays $900 to CanTech Supply on March 27. This is a transaction since an exchange has occurred between Vertically Inclined and CanTech Supply. It therefore affects the accounting equation. The $900 payment is for the earlier $1,100 purchase of supplies from CanTech, leaving $200 unpaid. The $6,000 amount due to CanTech for equipment remains unpaid. The accounting equation shows that this transaction decreases Vertically Inclined's cash by $900 and decreases its liability to CanTech Supply by the same amount. As a result, equity does not change. This transaction does not create an expense, even though cash flows out of Vertically Inclined.

	Assets				=	Liabilities		+	Equity	Explanation of Equity Transaction
	Cash	+ Accounts Receivable	+ Supplies	+ Equipment	=	Accounts Payable	+ Notes Payable	+	Virgil Klimb, Capital	
Old Bal.	$9,900	+ $ -0-	+ $3,600	+ $6,000	=	$1,100	+ $6,000	+	$12,400	
(10)	−$ 900					−$ 900				
New Bal.	$9,000	+ $ -0-	+ $3,600	+ $6,000	=	$ 200	+ $6,000	+	$12,400	
			$18,600				$18,600			

11. Withdrawal of Cash by Owner. Klimb withdraws $600 in cash from Vertically Inclined for personal living expenses. An exchange has taken place between the owner and the business, so this is a transaction and affects the accounting equation. Withdrawals are not expenses because they are not part of the company's earnings process. Therefore, withdrawals are not used in calculating net income.

	Assets				=	Liabilities		+	Equity	Explanation of Equity Transaction
	Cash	+ Accounts Receivable	+ Supplies	+ Equipment	=	Accounts Payable	+ Notes Payable	+	Virgil Klimb, Capital	
Old Bal.	$9,000	+ $ -0-	+ $3,600	+ $6,000	=	$ 200	+ $6,000	+	$12,400	
(11)	−$ 600								−$ 600	Withdrawal by Owner
New Bal.	$8,400	+ $ -0-	+ $3,600	+ $6,000	=	$ 200	+ $6,000	+	$11,800	
			$18,000				$18,000			

Summary of Transactions

Summarized in Exhibit 1.15 are the effects of all of Vertically Inclined's March transactions using the accounting equation. Five points should be noted.

1. The accounting equation remains in balance after every transaction.

2. Transactions can be analyzed by their effects on components of the accounting equation. For example, total assets and equity increase by equal amounts in (1), (4), and (8). In (2) and (9), one asset increases while another decreases by an equal amount. For (3), we see equal increases in assets and liabilities. Both assets and equity decrease by equal amounts in (5), (6), and (11). In (10), we see equal decreases in an asset and a liability.

3. Transactions cause assets, liabilities, or equity to change. Notice in Exhibit 1.15 that (1)–(6) and (8)–(11) caused changes to the accounting equation because each transaction involved an exchange; (7) did not involve an exchange and so did not affect the accounting equation.

4. The format of the preceding analysis was used to demonstrate the effects of transactions on the components of the accounting equation; transactions in the real world are not recorded in this manner.

5. The equality of effects in the accounting equation is fundamental to the *double-entry accounting system* that is discussed in the next chapter.

It is important to recognize that the accounting equation is a representation of the balance sheet. Therefore, we can take the information in Exhibit 1.15 and prepare financial statements for Vertically Inclined. This will be done in the next section.

EXHIBIT 1.15

Summary Analysis of Vertically Inclined's Transactions Using the Accounting Equation

		Assets			=	Liabilities		+	Equity	Explanation of Equity Transaction
	Cash	+ Accounts + Receivable	Supplies	+ Equipment	=	Accounts Payable	+ Notes Payable	+	Virgil Klimb, Capital	
(1)	$10,000								$10,000	Investment by Owner
(2)	− 2,500		+$ 2,500							
Bal.	$ 7,500		$ 2,500						$10,000	
(3)			+1,100	+6,000		+$1,100	+$6,000			
Bal.	$ 7,500		$ 3,600	$6,000		$1,100	$6,000		$10,000	
(4)	+ 2,200								+ 2,200	Teaching Revenue
Bal.	$ 9,700		$ 3,600	$6,000		$1,100	$6,000		$12,200	
(5)	− 1,000								− 1,000	Rent Expense
Bal.	$ 8,700		$ 3,600	$6,000		$1,100	$6,000		$11,200	
(6)	− 700								− 700	Salaries Expense
Bal.	$ 8,000		$ 3,600	$6,000		$1,100	$6,000		$10,500	
(7)	No entry*									
(8)		+$ 1,900							+ 1,600	Teaching Revenue
									+ 300	Equipment Rental Revenue
Bal.	$ 8,000	$ 1,900	$ 3,600	$6,000		$1,100	$6,000		$12,400	
(9)	+ 1,900	−1,900								
Bal.	$ 9,900	$ -0-	$ 3,600	$6,000		$1,100	$6,000		$12,400	
(10)	− 900					− 900				
Bal.	$ 9,000	$ -0-	$ 3,600	$6,000		$ 200	$6,000		$12,400	
(11)	− 600								− 600	Withdrawal by Owner
Bal.	$ 8,400 +	$ -0- +	$ 3,600 +	$6,000	=	$ 200 +	$6,000 +		$11,800	
		$18,000					$18,000			

*Note: (7) did not involve an economic transaction between two parties, so it is an event and does not affect the accounting equation.

CHECKPOINT

21. How can a transaction *not* affect liability and equity accounts?
22. Describe a transaction that increases equity and one that decreases it.
23. Identify a transaction that decreases both assets and liabilities.
24. When is the accounting equation in balance, and what does it mean?
25. Explain the difference between a transaction and an event.
26. Identify examples of accounting source documents.
27. Explain the importance of source documents.

Do Quick Study questions: QS 1-11, QS 1-12, QS 1-13, QS 1-14, QS 1-15, QS 1-16

MID-CHAPTER DEMONSTRATION PROBLEM

Part A

All chapters have a Mid-Chapter and End-of-Chapter Demonstration Problem to illustrate and reinforce important topics.

Bob Delgado founded a new moving firm as a proprietorship on May 1. The accounting equation showed the following *balances* after each of the company's first five transactions. Analyze the equations and describe each of the five transactions with their amounts.

	Assets					=	Liabilities	+	Equity
Transaction	Cash +	Accounts Receivable +	Office Supplies +	Truck +	Office Furniture =		Accounts Payable +		Bob Delgado, Capital
1	$10,000	$ -0-	$ -0-	$45,000	$ -0-		$ -0-		$55,000
2	9,000	-0-	-0-	45,000	1,000		-0-		55,000
3	9,000	-0-	-0-	45,000	6,000		5,000		55,000
4	9,000	3,000	-0-	45,000	6,000		5,000		58,000
5	11,000	1,000	-0-	45,000	6,000		5,000		58,000

Part B

During June, Bob Delgado's second month of operations, transactions occurred, resulting in a $68,000 balance in the column 'Bob Delgado, Capital.' Calculate the net income or loss for June under each of the following independent situations:

1. Bob made no investments or withdrawals during June.
2. Bob invested $15,000 during June and made no withdrawals.
3. Bob withdrew a total of $5,000 during June and made no additional investments.
4. Bob invested $5,000 during June and made withdrawals of $3,000.

Analysis Component:

Several activities cause equity to change. Of those activities, which one will help build equity over the long term?

SOLUTION

Part A

1. Started the business by investing $10,000 cash and a $45,000 truck.
2. Purchased $1,000 of office furniture by paying cash.
3. Purchased $5,000 of office furniture on account.
4. Billed a customer $3,000 for services performed.
5. Collected $2,000 from a credit customer.

Part B

1.

Assets	=	Liabilities	+	Equity	
$63,000		$5,000		$58,000	Beginning assets, liabilities, and capital on June 1
				+ 0	Plus owner investments during June
				− 0	Less owner withdrawals during June
				+ 10,000	**Plus net income (less net loss) realized during June**
				=$68,000	Equals ending capital on June 30

Calculations: $68,000 − $58,000 = $10,000 net income.

2.

Assets	=	Liabilities	+	Equity	
$63,000		$5,000		$58,000	Beginning assets, liabilities, and capital on June 1
				+ 15,000	Plus owner investments during June
				− 0	Less owner withdrawals during June
				− 5,000	**Plus net income (less net loss) realized during June**
				=$68,000	Equals ending capital on June 30

Calculations: $68,000 − $15,000 − $58,000 = $5,000 net loss.

3.

Assets	=	Liabilities	+	Equity	
$63,000		$5,000		$58,000	Beginning assets, liabilities, and capital on June 1
				+ 0	Plus owner investments during June
				− 5,000	Less owner withdrawals during June
				+ 15,000	**Plus net income (less net loss) realized during June**
				=$68,000	Equals ending capital on June 30

Calculations: $68,000 + $5,000 − $58,000 = $15,000 net income.

4.

Assets	=	Liabilities	+	Equity	
$63,000		$5,000		$58,000	Beginning assets, liabilities, and capital on June 1
				+ 5,000	Plus owner investments during June
				− 3,000	Less owner withdrawals during June
				+ 8,000	**Plus net income (less net loss) realized during June**
				=$68,000	Equals ending capital on June 30

Calculations: $68,000 + $3,000 − $5,000 − $58,000 = $8,000 net income.

Analysis Component:

Equity increases because of owner investments and net income (when revenues are greater than expenses) and decreases because of owner withdrawals and net losses (when expenses are greater than revenues). Recurring net income will help build (or grow) equity over the long term.

FINANCIAL STATEMENTS

LO8 Prepare financial statements reflecting business transactions.

We illustrated financial statements earlier in this chapter. These statements are required under GAAP. In this section, we describe how the financial statements shown in Exhibits 1.8 to 1.10 were prepared from the business transactions summarized in Exhibit 1.15. The statement of cash flows, Exhibit 1.11, is left to Chapter 17.

Income Statement

Vertically Inclined's income statement is shown on the right side of Exhibit 1.16. It was prepared using revenue and expense information taken from the equity column in Exhibit 1.15, copied in Exhibit 1.16 on the left side.

EXHIBIT 1.16

Vertically Inclined's Financial Statements

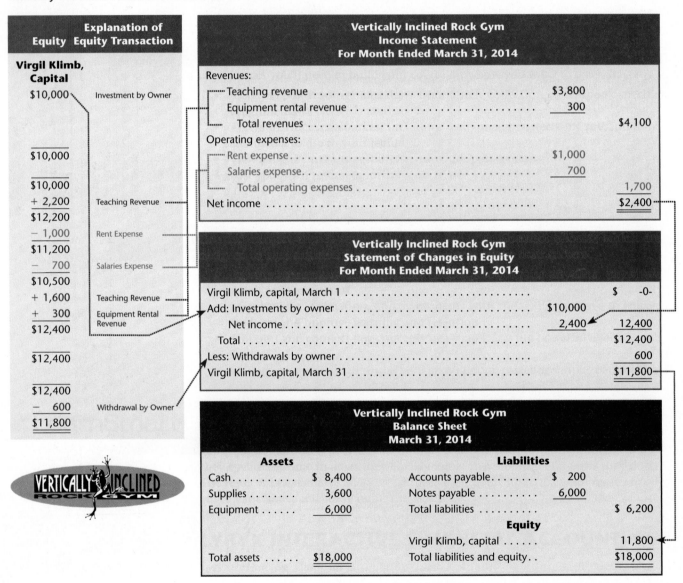

Revenues of $4,100 are reported first and include teaching revenues of $3,800 ($2,200 + $1,600) plus equipment rental revenue of $300. Expenses follow revenues, and can be listed in different ways. For convenience in this chapter, we list larger amounts first. Rent of $1,000 and salaries expenses of $700 result in total operating expenses of $1,700. Net income is reported at the bottom and is the amount earned during March. Owner's investments and withdrawals are *not* part of measuring income; they are shown on the statement of changes in equity.

Statement of Changes in Equity

The second report in Exhibit 1.16 is the statement of changes in equity for Vertically Inclined. Its heading lists the month as March 2014 because this statement describes transactions that happened during that month. The beginning balance of equity is measured as of the start of business on March 1. It is zero because Vertically Inclined did not exist before then. An existing business reports the beginning balance as of the end of the prior reporting period. Vertically Inclined's statement shows that $10,000 of equity is created by Virgil Klimb's initial investment. It also shows the $2,400 of net income earned during the month. This item links the income statement to the statement of changes in equity as shown in Exhibit 1.16. The statement also reports the owner's $600 withdrawal and Vertically Inclined's $11,800 equity balance at the end of the month.

Balance Sheet

The balance sheet in Exhibit 1.16 is the same statement that we described in Exhibit 1.10. Its heading tells us that the statement refers to Vertically Inclined's financial position at the close of business on March 31, 2014. ***Notice that the amounts appearing on the balance sheet came from the column totals summarized in Exhibit 1.15.***

The left side of the balance sheet lists Vertically Inclined's assets: cash, supplies, and equipment. The right side of the balance sheet shows that Vertically Inclined owes $6,200 to creditors, an amount made up of $200 for accounts payable and $6,000 for notes payable. The equity section shows an ending balance of $11,800. Note the link between the ending balance from the statement of changes in equity and the equity balance of the capital account. Also, note that the balance sheet equation, Assets = Liabilities + Equity, is still true ($18,000 = $6,200 + $11,800).

The financial statements for Vertically Inclined can be useful to both internal and external users for making decisions.

DECISION MAKER   Answer—End of chapter

Extending Credit
You open a wholesale business selling entertainment equipment to retail outlets such as **Future Shop**, **Leon's**, and **Best Buy Canada**. You find that most of your customers demand to buy on credit. How can you use the balance sheets of these customers to help you decide which ones are worthy of credit?

CHECKPOINT

28. Explain the link between an income statement and the statement of changes in equity.
29. Describe the link between a balance sheet and the statement of changes in equity.

Do Quick Study questions: QS 1-17, QS 1-18, QS 1-19, QS 1-20

After studying the content of each chapter, students are encouraged to return to the Critical Thinking Challenge questions for reflection.

CRITICAL THINKING CHALLENGE   Refer to the Critical Thinking Challenge questions at the beginning of the chapter. Compare your answers to those suggested on Connect.

Each chapter identifies the primary differences between IFRS and ASPE at the introductory level of accounting.

IFRS AND ASPE—THE DIFFERENCES

Difference	International Financial Reporting Standards (IFRS)	Accounting Standards for Private Enterprises (ASPE)
Financial statements	• IFRS refers to the financial statements as: statement of financial position (or balance sheet), statement of income, statement of changes in equity, and statement of cash flows.*	• ASPE refers to the financial statements as: balance sheet, income statement, statement of retained earnings (or statement of changes in equity), and cash flow statement.***
GAAP	• Publicly accountable enterprises must use IFRS. • IFRS does not use the terms *reliability* and *conservatism*.**	• Private enterprises can choose between ASPE and IFRS but once the choice is made, it must be applied consistently. • ASPE includes conservatism as a measure of reliability.****

*IFRS 2012, IAS 1, para. 10.
**IFRS 2012, "Framework," para. 4.1–4.39.
***ASPE, Accounting Standards, General Accounting, Section 1000.04 and Section 1400.10.
****ASPE, Accounting Standards, Section 1000.18(d)

Each chapter includes a summary of the chapter by learning objective.

SUMMARY

LO¹ Describe the purpose and importance of accounting. Accounting is an information and measurement system that aims to identify, measure, record, and communicate relevant information that faithfully represents an organization's economic activities. It helps us better assess opportunities, products, investments, and social and community responsibilities. The power of accounting is in opening our eyes to new and exciting opportunities. The greatest benefits of understanding accounting often come to those outside of accounting, because an improved understanding of accounting helps us to compete better in today's globally focused and technologically challenging world.

LO² Describe forms of business organization. Organizations can be classified either as businesses or as non-businesses. Businesses are organized for profit, while non-businesses serve us in ways not always measured by profit. Businesses take one of three forms: sole proprietorship, partnership, or corporation. These forms of organization have characteristics that hold important implications for legal liability, taxation, continuity, number of owners, and legal status.

LO³ Identify users and uses of, and opportunities in, accounting. There are both internal and external users of accounting. Some users and uses of accounting include: (a) management for control, monitoring, and planning; (b) lenders for making decisions regarding loan applications;

(c) shareholders for making investment decisions; (d) directors for overseeing management; and (e) employees for judging employment opportunities. Opportunities in accounting encompass traditional financial and managerial accounting, and taxation, but also include accounting-related fields such as lending, consulting, managing, and planning.

LO⁴ Identify and explain why ethics and social responsibility are crucial to accounting. The goal of accounting is to provide useful information for decision making. For information to be useful, it must be trusted. This demands ethics and socially responsible behaviour in accounting. Without these, accounting information loses its reliability.

LO⁵ Identify, explain, and apply accounting principles. Accounting principles aid in producing relevant information that faithfully represents an organization's economic activities. The general principles described in this chapter include: business entity, cost, going concern, monetary unit, and revenue recognition. We will discuss others in later chapters. The business entity principle requires that a business be accounted for separately from its owners. The cost principle requires that financial statements be based on actual costs incurred in business transactions. The going concern principle requires that financial statements reflect an assumption that the business continues to operate. The monetary unit principle assumes that transactions can be captured in money terms and that the monetary unit is stable over time. The revenue recognition principle assumes that revenue is recognized when earned, assets received from selling products and services do not have to be in cash, and revenue recognized is measured by cash received plus the cash equivalent (market) value of other assets received.

LO⁶   Identify and explain the content and reporting aims of financial statements. The major financial statements are: income statement (shows a company's profitability determined as revenues less expenses equals net income or loss), statement of changes in equity (explains how equity changes from the beginning to the end of a period), balance sheet (reports on a company's financial position, including assets, liabilities, and equity), and statement of cash flows (identifying all cash inflows and outflows for the period). The differences in financial statements across forms of business organization are: (1) The equity on the balance sheet belongs to: the sole owner in a sole proprietorship, to the partners in a partnership, and to the shareholders in a corporation; (2) Distributions of assets to the owner(s) are called withdrawals for both a sole proprietorship and a partnership, and dividends for a corporation; (3) When the owner of a proprietorship or partnership is its manager, no salary expense is reported, while in a corporation, salaries

paid to managers who are also shareholders are reported as expenses.

LO⁷   Analyze business transactions by applying the accounting equation. Investing activities are funded by an organization's financing activities. An organization's assets (investments) must equal its financing (from liabilities and from equity). This basic relation gives us the accounting equation: Assets = Liabilities + Equity. A transaction is an exchange of economic consideration between two parties and affects the accounting equation. The equation is always in balance when business transactions are properly recorded. An economic consideration is something of value; examples include products, services, money, and rights to collect money. Source documents are the source of accounting information. An event does not involve an economic exchange; it has no effect on the accounting equation.

LO⁸   Prepare financial statements reflecting business transactions. Using the accounting equation, business transactions can be summarized and organized so that we can readily prepare the financial statements. The balance sheet uses the ending balances in the accounting equation at a point in time. The statement of changes in equity and the income statement use data from the equity account for the period.

GUIDANCE ANSWER TO **DECISION MAKER**

Extending Credit
You can use the accounting equation (Assets = Liabilities + Equity) to help identify risky customers to whom you would likely not want to extend credit. A balance sheet provides

amounts for each of these key components. The lower a customer's equity is relative to liabilities, the less likely you would be to extend credit. A low equity means the business has little value that does not already have creditor claims to it.

GUIDANCE ANSWERS TO **CHECKPOINT**

1. Accounting is an information and measurement system that identifies, measures, records, and communicates relevant and faithfully representative information to people that helps them in making better decisions. It helps people in business to identify and react to investment opportunities, and better assess opportunities, products, investments, and social and community responsibilities.

2. Recordkeeping is the recording of financial transactions and events, either manually or electronically. While recordkeeping is essential to ensuring data is complete, free from error, and neutral, accounting is this and much more. Accounting includes identifying, measuring, recording, reporting, and analyzing economic events and transactions. It involves interpreting information, and designing information systems to

provide useful reports that monitor and control an organization's activities.

3. Non-business organizations may include public airports, libraries, museums, religious institutions, municipal governments, law enforcement organizations, postal services, colleges, universities, highways, shelters, parks, hospitals, and schools.

4. The three common forms of business organization are sole proprietorships, partnerships, and corporations.

5. Private accountants work for a single employer, which is often a business. A public accountant is available to the public, which means that services are provided to many different clients.

6. The four broad fields of accounting are: financial, managerial, taxation, and accounting-related.

7. The purpose of an audit is to add credibility to the financial statements.

8. Managerial accounting is for internal users, while financial accounting is for external users.

9. External users of accounting information are not directly involved in running the organization. Internal users of accounting information are those individuals directly involved in managing and operating an organization.

10. Internal controls are procedures set up to protect assets; ensure that accounting reports are complete, free from error, and neutral; promote efficiency; and encourage adherence to company policies. Internal controls are crucial if accounting reports are to provide relevant and trustworthy information.

11. The guidelines for ethical and socially responsible decisions are threefold: (1) identify the ethical and/or social issue; (2) analyze options, considering both good and bad consequences for all individuals affected; and (3) make an ethical/socially responsible decision, choosing the best option after weighing all consequences.

12. Ethics and social responsibility are important for people because, without them, existence is more difficult, inefficient, and unpleasant. They are equally important to organizations, for this same reason. In addition, they often translate into higher profits and a better working environment.

13. Accounting aims to provide useful information for decision making. For information to be useful, it must be trusted. Trustworthiness of information demands ethics in accounting.

14. The business entity principle is important to the usefulness of accounting. Users desire information about the performance of a *specific* entity. If information is mixed between two or more entities, its usefulness decreases. It is imperative that the business entity principle be followed.

15. The cost principle determines that financial statements are based on actual costs incurred in business transactions. Information prepared using the cost principle is considered verifiable because it can be confirmed and is not subject to arbitrary manipulation.

16. Revenue should be recognized next month when the product is delivered, according to the revenue recognition principle. This principle states that revenue is recognized when the product has been provided and not necessarily when cash has been received. In this case, the business has received the cash from the customer without providing the product. Therefore, the business has not realized a revenue but instead has incurred a liability; it owes the customer the product.

17. The four major financial statements are: income statement, statement of changes in equity, balance sheet, and statement of cash flows.

18. Revenues are the value of assets received in exchange for products or services provided to customers as part of a business's main operations. Expenses are costs incurred or the using up of assets that results from providing products or services to customers. Expenses also can arise from increases in liabilities.

19. Assets are the properties or economic resources owned by a business. Liabilities are the obligations of a business, representing the claims of others against the assets of a business. Equity is the owner's claim on the assets of the business. It is the assets of a business that remain after deducting liabilities.

20. Three differences in financial statements for different forms of organization are: (1) A proprietorship's equity belongs to one owner. A partnership's equity belongs to the partners. A corporation's equity belongs to the shareholders. (2) Distributions of cash or other assets to owners of a proprietorship or partnership are called withdrawals. Distributions of cash or other assets to owners of a corporation are called dividends. (3) When the owner of a sole proprietorship is also its manager, no salary expense is reported on the income statement. The same is true for a partnership. In a corporation, however, salaries paid to all employees, including managers who are shareholders, are reported as expenses.

21. A transaction, such as (2) that involves changing the form of one asset for another asset would *not* affect any liability and equity accounts.

22. Performing services for a customer, such as in (4) increases the equity (and assets). Incurring expenses while servicing clients, such as in (5) and (6) decreases the equity (and assets). Other examples include owner investments, such as (1) that increase equity, and owner withdrawals, such as (11) that decrease equity.

23. Payment of a liability with an asset reduces both asset and liability totals. An example is (10) where an account payable is settled by paying cash.

24. The accounting equation is: Assets = Liabilities + Equity. It is in balance when the sum of the assets is equal to the sum of the liabilities and equity accounts. This equation is always in balance, both before and after every transaction. Balance refers to the equality in this equation, which is always maintained.

25. Business transactions are exchanges between two parties and affect the accounting equation. Events do not involve an exchange and therefore do not affect the accounting equation.

26. Examples of source documents are sales invoices, cheques, purchase orders, charges to customers, bills from suppliers, employee earnings records, and bank statements.

27. Source documents serve many purposes, including recordkeeping and internal control. Source documents,

especially if obtained from outside the organization, provide evidence about transactions and their amounts for recording. Evidence is important because it makes information more reliable and useful.

28. An income statement describes a company's revenues and expenses along with the resulting net income or loss. A statement of changes in equity describes changes in equity that *include* net income or loss. Also, both statements report transactions occurring over a period of time.

29. A balance sheet describes a company's financial position (assets, liabilities, and equity) at a point in time. The equity account in the balance sheet is obtained from the statement of changes in equity.

DEMONSTRATION PROBLEM

After several months of planning, Joane Cardinal started a haircutting business called The Cutlery. The following business activities occurred during its first month, August 2014:

a. On August 1, Cardinal put $16,000 cash into a chequing account in the name of The Cutlery. She also invested $10,000 of equipment that she already owned.

b. On August 2, she paid $2,000 cash for furniture for the shop.

c. On August 3, she paid $3,200 cash to rent space in a strip mall for August.

d. On August 4, she equipped the shop by installing the old equipment and some new equipment that she bought on credit for $21,000. This amount is to be repaid in three equal payments at the end of August, September, and October.

e. On August 5, The Cutlery opened for business. Receipts from services provided for cash in the first week and a half of business (ended August 15) were $1,100.

f. On August 15, Cardinal provided haircutting services on account for $750.

g. On August 17, Cardinal received a $750 cheque in the mail for services previously rendered on account.

h. On August 17, Cardinal paid wages of $250 to an assistant for working during the grand opening.

i. On August 18, Cardinal interviewed a job applicant. The applicant was successful in getting the position and will receive $750 per week for part-time work starting in September.

j. Cash receipts from services provided during the second half of August were $1,950.

k. On August 31, Cardinal paid an installment on the account payable created in (d).

l. On August 31, the August hydro bill for $450 was received. It will be paid on September 14.

m. On August 31, Cardinal withdrew $500 cash for her personal use.

Required

1. Arrange the following asset, liability, and equity titles in a table similar to the one in Exhibit 1.15: Cash; Accounts Receivable; Furniture; Store Equipment; Accounts Payable; and Joane Cardinal, Capital. Show the effects of each transaction on the equation. Explain each of the changes in equity.

2. Prepare an income statement for August.

3. Prepare a statement of changes in equity for August.

4. Prepare a balance sheet as of August 31.

Analysis Component:

a. Identify how much of the assets held by The Cutlery are owned by the owner, Joane Cardinal.

b. How much of the total assets are financed by equity? by debt? Explain what it means to 'finance assets by equity' and to 'finance assets by debt.'

Planning the Solution

- Set up a table with the appropriate columns, including a final column for describing the transactions that affect equity.
- Identify and analyze each transaction and show its effects as increases or decreases in the appropriate columns. Be sure that the accounting equation remains in balance after each transaction.
- To prepare the income statement, find the revenues and expenses in the Explanation of Equity Transaction column. List those items on the statement, calculate the difference, and label the result as *net income* or *net loss*.
- Use the information in the Explanation of Equity Transaction column to prepare the statement of changes in equity.
- Use the information in the last row of the table to prepare the balance sheet.
- Prepare an answer to each part of the **analysis component** question.

SOLUTION

1.

	Cash +	Accounts Receivable +	Furniture +	Store Equipment =	Accounts Payable +	Joane Cardinal, Capital	Explanation of Equity Transaction
				Assets			
a.	$16,000			$10,000		$26,000	Investment by Owner
b.	− 2,000		+$2,000				
Bal.	$14,000		$2,000	$10,000		$26,000	
c.	− 3,200					− 3,200	Rent Expense
Bal.	$10,800		$2,000	$10,000		$22,800	
d.				+21,000	+$21,000		
Bal.	$10,800		$2,000	$31,000	$21,000	$22,800	
e.	+ 1,100					+ 1,100	Haircutting Services Revenue
Bal.	$11,900		$2,000	$31,000	$21,000	$23,900	
f.		+$750				+ 750	Haircutting Services Revenue
Bal.	$11,900	$750	$2,000	$31,000	$21,000	$24,650	
g.	+ 750	− 750					
Bal.	$12,650	$ -0-	$2,000	$31,000	$21,000	$24,650	
h.	− 250					− 250	Wages Expense
Bal.	$12,400		$2,000	$31,000	$21,000	$24,400	
i.	No entry*						
j.	+ 1,950					+ 1,950	Haircutting Services Revenue
Bal.	$14,350		$2,000	$31,000	$21,000	$26,350	
k.	− 7,000				− 7,000		
Bal.	$ 7,350		$2,000	$31,000	$14,000	$26,350	
l.					+ 450	− 450	Hydro Expense
Bal.	$ 7,350		$2,000	$31,000	$14,450	$25,900	
m.	− 500					− 500	Withdrawal by Owner
Bal.	$ 6,850 +	$ -0- +	$2,000 +	$31,000 =	$14,450 +	$25,400	

= $39,850   = $39,850

*Note: (i) does not involve an economic exchange between two parties; therefore it does not affect the accounting equation.

2.

The Cutlery
Income Statement
For Month Ended August 31, 2014

Revenues:		
Haircutting services revenue		$ 3,800
Operating expenses:		
Rent expense.	$3,200	
Hydro expense	450	
Wages expense	250	
Total operating expenses		3,900
Net loss		$ 100

3.

The Cutlery
Statement of Changes in Equity
For Month Ended August 31, 2014

Joane Cardinal, capital, August 1		$ –0–
Add: Investments by owner		26,000
Total		$26,000
Less: Withdrawals by owner	$500	
Net loss	100	600
Joane Cardinal, capital, August 31		$25,400

> The arrows are imaginary but they emphasize the link between statements.

4.

The Cutlery
Balance Sheet
August 31, 2014

Assets		Liabilities	
Cash.	$ 6,850	Accounts payable	$14,450
Furniture.	2,000		
Store equipment.	31,000	**Equity**	
		Joane Cardinal, capital	25,400
Total assets	$39,850	Total liabilities and equity	$39,850

Analysis Component:

a. $25,400 or 64% ($25,400/$39,850 × 100% = 63.74% or 64%) of the total assets are owned by the owner, Joane Cardinal.

b. $25,400 or 64% ($25,400/$39,850 × 100% = 63.74% or 64%) of the total assets are financed by equity. $14,450 or 36% ($14,450/$39,850 × 100% = 36.26% or 36%) of the total assets are financed by debt.

To *finance assets by equity* means that the equity transactions of owner investment, plus net income (or less net loss), and less owner withdrawals resulted in a portion of the assets. In the case of The Cutlery, 64% of the assets at August 31, 2014, resulted from these equity transactions.

To *finance assets by debt* (or liabilities) means that a portion of the assets resulted from borrowings. In the case of The Cutlery, 36% of the assets at August 31, 2014, resulted from, specifically, accounts payable.

The glossary includes terms and phrases explained in the chapter.

GLOSSARY

Accounting An information system that identifies, measures, records, and communicates relevant information that faithfully represents an organization's economic activities.

Accounting equation A description of the relationship between a company's assets, liabilities, and equity; expressed as Assets = Liabilities + Equity; also called the *balance sheet equation*.

Accounting Standards Board (AcSB) Prior to Canada's adoption of IFRS, the AcSB was the authoritative body that set accounting standards for Canada. With IFRS being set by the IASB, the AcSB's new role is evolving.

Accounting Standards for Private Enterprises (ASPE) Rules created by the Accounting Standards Board to govern accounting for Canadian private enterprises.

Account payable A liability created by buying goods or services on credit.

Accounts receivable Assets created by selling products or services on credit.

AcSB See *Accounting Standards Board*.

ASPE See *Accounting Standards for Private Enterprises*.

Assets Properties or economic resources owned by the business; more precisely, resources with an ability to provide future benefits to the business.

Audit A check of an organization's accounting systems and records.

Balance sheet A financial statement that reports the financial position of a business at a point in time; lists the types and dollar amounts of assets, liabilities, and equity as of a specific date; also called the *statement of financial position*.

Balance sheet equation Another name for the *accounting equation*.

Bookkeeping The part of accounting that involves recording economic transactions, either electronically or manually; also called *recordkeeping*.

Budgeting The process of developing formal plans for future activities, which often serve as a basis for evaluating actual performance.

Business One or more individuals selling products or services for profit.

Business activities All of the transactions and events experienced by a business.

Business entity principle The principle that requires every business to be accounted for separately from its owner or owners; based on the goal of providing relevant information about each business to users.

Business events Activities that do not involve an exchange of economic consideration between two parties and therefore do not affect the accounting equation.

Business transaction An exchange of economic consideration between two parties that causes a change in assets, liabilities, or equity. Examples of economic considerations include products, services, money, and rights to collect money.

CA Chartered Accountant; an accountant who has met the examination, education, and experience requirements of the Institute of Chartered Accountants for an individual professionally competent in accounting.

Calendar year An accounting year that begins on January 1 and ends on December 31.

Canada Revenue Agency (CRA) The federal government agency responsible for the collection of tax and enforcement of tax laws.

CGA Certified General Accountant; an accountant who has met the examination, education, and experience requirements of the Certified General Accountants' Association for an individual professionally competent in accounting.

CMA Certified Management Accountant; an accountant who has met the examination, education, and experience requirements of the Society of Management Accountants for an individual professionally competent in accounting.

Common shares The name for a corporation's shares when only one class of share capital is issued.

Comparability Similarity; ability to be compared with other information.

Controller The chief accounting officer of an organization.

Corporate governance The mechanism by which individuals in a company, in particular the board of directors, are motivated to align their behaviours with the overall corporate good.

Corporation A business that is a separate legal entity under provincial or federal laws with owners who are called shareholders.

Cost accounting A managerial accounting activity designed to help managers identify, measure, and control operating costs.

Cost principle The accounting principle that requires financial statement information to be based on actual costs incurred in business transactions; it requires assets and services to be recorded initially at the cash or cash equivalent amount given in exchange.

Costs The expenses incurred to earn revenues (or sales).

CPA Chartered Professional Accountant.

Creditors Individuals or organizations entitled to receive payments from a company.

Debtors Individuals or organizations that owe amounts to a business.

Economic consideration Something of value (e.g., products, services, money, and rights to collect money).

Equity The owner's claim on the assets of a business; more precisely, the assets of an entity that remain after deducting its liabilities. Increases with owner investments and net income and decreases with owner withdrawals and net loss, also called *net assets*.

Ethics Beliefs that differentiate right from wrong.

Events See *business events*.

Expenses Costs incurred or the using up of assets as a result of the major or central operations of a business.

External auditors Accountants outside the company who examine and provide assurance that financial statements are prepared according to generally accepted accounting principles (GAAP).

External users Persons using accounting information who are not directly involved in the running of the organization; examples include shareholders, customers, regulators, and suppliers.

Faithful representation A quality of information that is complete, neutral, and free from error.

Financial accounting The area of accounting that report on the financial performance and condition of an organization. They aimed at serving external users.

Financial statements The products of accounting that report on the financial performance and condition of an organization. They include the income statement, statement of changes in equity, balance sheet, and statement of cash flows.

Fiscal year A one-year reporting period.

GAAP See *generally accepted accounting principles*.

General accounting The task of recording transactions, processing data, and preparing reports for managers; includes preparing financial statements for disclosure to external users.

Generally accepted accounting principles (GAAP) The underlying concepts adopted by the accounting profession that make up acceptable accounting practices for the preparation of financial statements.

Going concern principle The rule that requires financial statements to reflect the assumption that the business will continue operating instead of being closed or sold, unless evidence shows that it will not continue.

Government accountants Accountants who work for local, provincial, and federal government agencies.

IASB See *International Accounting Standards Board*.

IFRS See *International Financial Reporting Standards*.

Income statement The financial statement that shows, by subtracting expenses from revenues, whether the business earned a profit; it lists the types and amounts of revenues earned and expenses incurred by a business over a period of time.

Internal auditing Function performed by employees within organizations who assess whether managers are following established operating procedures and evaluate the efficiency of operating procedures.

Internal controls Procedures set up to protect assets, ensure reliable accounting reports, promote efficiency, and encourage adherence to company policies.

Internal users Persons using accounting information who are directly involved in managing and operating an organization; examples include managers and officers.

International Accounting Standards Board (IASB) The body responsible for setting IFRS.

International Financial Reporting Standards (IFRS) The standards for financial reporting that came into effect January 2011 in Canada for publicly accountable entities.

Liabilities The debts or obligations of a business; claims by others that will reduce the future assets of a business or require future services or products.

Limited liability The owner's liability is limited to the amount of investment in the business.

Management consulting Activity in which suggestions are offered for improving a company's procedures; the suggestions may concern new accounting and internal control systems, new computer systems, budgeting, and employee benefit plans.

Managerial accounting The area of accounting aimed at serving the decision-making needs of internal users.

Monetary unit principle The expression of transactions in money units; examples include units such as the Canadian dollar, American dollar, peso, and pound sterling.

Natural business year A 12-month period that ends when a company's sales activities are at their lowest point.

Net assets Assets minus liabilities; another name for *equity*.

Net income The excess of revenues over expenses for a period; also called *profit*.

Net loss The excess of expenses over revenues for a period.

Note payable A liability expressed by a written promise to make a future payment at a specific time.

Owner investments The transfer of an owner's personal assets to the business.

Owner withdrawals See *withdrawals*.

Partnership A business owned by two or more people that is not organized as a corporation.

Private accountants Accountants who work for a single employer other than the government or a public accounting firm.

Private enterprise (PE) A corporation that does not offer its shares for public sale.

Profit Another name for *net income*.

Public accountants Accountants who provide their services to many different clients.

Publicly accountable enterprise (PAE) A corporation that sells its shares to the public.

Public sale of shares The trading of shares in an organized stock market.

Recordkeeping The recording of financial transactions, either manually or electronically; also called *bookkeeping*.

Relevance Information must make a difference in the decision-making process.

Revenue recognition principle Provides guidance on when revenue should be reflected on the income statement; the rule states that revenue is recorded at the time it is earned regardless of whether cash or another asset has been exchanged.

Revenues The value of assets exchanged for goods or services provided to customers as part of a business's main operations; may occur as inflows of assets or decreases in liabilities.

Shareholders The owners of a corporation; also known as stockholders.

Shares Units of ownership in a corporation; also known as stocks.

Single proprietorship A business owned by one individual that is not organized as a corporation; also called a *sole proprietorship*.

Social responsibility A commitment to considering the impact and being accountable for the effects that actions might have on society.

Sole proprietorship A business owned by one person that is not organized as a corporation; also called a *single proprietorship*.

Source documents Documents that identify and describe transactions entering the accounting process; the source of accounting information, whether in paper or electronic form.

Statement of cash flows A financial statement that describes the sources and uses of cash for a reporting period, i.e., where a company's cash came from (receipts) and where it went during the period (payments); the cash flows are arranged by an organization's major activities: operating, investing, and financing activities.

Statement of changes in equity A financial statement that reports the changes in equity over the reporting period; beginning equity is adjusted for increases such as owner investment or net income and for decreases such as owner withdrawals or a net loss.

Statement of financial position See *balance sheet*.

Taxation The field of accounting that includes preparing tax returns and planning future transactions to minimize the amount of tax paid; involves private, public, and government accountants.

Timeliness A quality of information that is available to decision makers in time to influence their decisions.

Transaction See *business transaction*.

Understandability A quality of information that is useful to users with reasonable knowledge of accounting and business and economic activities.

Unlimited liability When the debts of a sole proprietorship or partnership are greater than its resources, the owner(s) is (are) financially responsible.

Verifiability A quality of information that different knowledgeable users could agree was faithfully represented.

Withdrawals The distributions of cash or other assets from a proprietorship or partnership to its owner or owners.

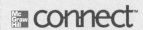 Visit **Connect** for additional study tools, practice quizzes, to search an interactive eBook, and much more.

——— Short-answer questions reinforce key chapter concepts in order of learning objectives.

CONCEPT REVIEW QUESTIONS

1. In the chapter's opening article, what does Jake identify as the key to success in business?

2. Name three real product-based businesses and specify the product that each provides. Name three real service-based businesses and specify the service that each provides.

3. Describe three forms of business organization and their characteristics.

4. Review Vertically Inclined's financial statements presented in the chapter for the month ended March 31, 2014. Review the balance sheet and determine the business form Virgil Klimb has chosen to organize his business.

5. Identify the two organizations for which accounting information is available in Appendix II at the end of the book.

6. Identify three types of organizations that can be formed as either profit-oriented businesses, government units, or not-for-profit establishments.

7. What type of accounting information might be useful to those who carry out the marketing activities of a business?

8. Identify four external and internal users and their uses of accounting information.

9. Describe the internal role of accounting for organizations.

10. Identify four managerial accounting tasks performed by both private and government accountants.

11. Identify two management-consulting services offered by public accounting professionals.

12. What work do tax accounting professionals perform in addition to preparing tax returns?

13. Identify the auditing firm that audited the financial statements of Danier Leather in Appendix II.

14. What is the purpose of accounting in society?

15. What ethical issues might accounting professionals face in dealing with confidential information?

16. Why does the user of an income statement need to know the time period that it covers?

17. Why is the revenue recognition principle needed? What does it require?

18. Identify four financial statements that a proprietorship presents to its owner and other users.

19. What information is presented in an income statement?

20. What do accountants mean by the term *revenue*?

21. What transactions change equity?

22. What information is presented in a balance sheet?

23. Define (a) assets, (b) liabilities, (c) equity, and (d) net assets.

Quick Study questions are single-topic exercises that give the reader a brief test of each key element in the chapter. Answers to the Quick Study (QS) questions are available on Connect.

QUICK STUDY

Each Quick Study, Exercise, and Problem is referenced to a learning objective in the chapter.

QS 1-1 Uses of accounting LO¹

You have just graduated from the finance program at a local post-secondary institution. An opportunity to become the marketing manager for a medium-sized florist chain is available to you. You are concerned because you know that accounting plays a major role in the successful execution of this role and accounting was not your best subject. Identify at least two questions or issues for which the marketing manager would require accounting information.

QS 1-2 Accounting vs. recordkeeping LO¹

Identify whether each of the following functions would be classified as accounting or recordkeeping.

a. Meeting with the mechanical staff to determine new machine requirements for next year.

b. Data entry of sales orders received via the telephone.

c. Analyzing a sales report to determine if the discount policy is effective in getting customers to buy in multiple quantities.

d. Listing cheques received in the mail.

QS 1-3 Business vs. non-business organizations LO²

Identify whether each of the following represents a business or non-business organization.
Hint: Enhance your research skills and check the Internet to confirm your answers.

a. Highlands United Church   d. CDI College

b. Royal Alexandra Hospital   e. Loblaw

c. Royal Bank of Canada   f. World Vision

QS 1-4 Accounting and accounting-related opportunities LO³

Identify at least three main areas of accounting for accounting professionals. For each accounting area, identify at least three accounting-related opportunities in practice.

QS 1-5 Identifying uses of accounting information LO³

Identify two possible uses of accounting information.

QS 1-6 Ethics in accounting—applying the Rotary 4-Way Test LO⁴

You are a salesperson. At the end of each month, you submit an expense report for reimbursement of personal funds you spent performing business duties such as client luncheons and travel. Last month, you included in your expense report two personal dinners with your spouse. By applying the Rotary 4-Way Test to this situation as identified earlier in the chapter, determine whether the behaviour is ethical or not.

QS 1-7 Identifying accounting principles LO⁵

Identify which GAAP most directly describes each of the following correct practices:

_____ a. Tracy Regis owns two businesses, Second Time Around Clothing and Antique Accents, both of which are sole proprietorships. In having financial statements prepared for the antique store, Regis should be sure that the revenue and expense transactions of Second Time Around are excluded from the statements of Antique Accents.

_____ b. In December 2013, Classic Coverings received a customer's order to install carpet and tile in a new house that would not be ready for completion until March 2014. Classic Coverings should record the revenue for the order in March 2014, not in December 2013.

_____ c. If $30,000 cash is paid to buy land, the land should be reported on the purchaser's balance sheet at $30,000 although the purchaser was offered $35,000 the following week.

QS 1-8 Identifying accounting principles LO⁵

For each of the following, identify which GAAP, if any, has been violated.

_____ **1.** A customer called and made arrangements for Jay's Plumbing to provide $6,000 of services _next month_. Jay, the owner, recorded revenue of $6,000 _this month_. No cash was exchanged.

_____ **2.** Land was purchased for $50,000. The bank appraised it for loan purposes at $68,000. Therefore, the owner of the land recorded it on the balance sheet at $68,000.

_____ **3.** The owner of Dallas Pizza and Don's Deli combines all transactions by keeping only one set of accounting records for both businesses.

_____ **4.** The owner of Pella's Junk Removal has become ill suddenly and is unable to continue the business. Pella's spouse, in need of cash to finance growing personal expenses, took the business's most recent financial statements to the bank and was granted a loan. She did not inform the bank of her husband's inability to work.

_____ **5.** Dale's Consulting Services completed a contract with an organization located overseas. Dale included the revenue on the income statement without converting the foreign currency to Canadian dollars.

QS 1-9 Identifying accounting principles LO⁵

For each of the following, identify which GAAP was violated by Delco Consulting. In cases where more than one GAAP applies, name the primary GAAP that was not followed.

_____ **a.** Delco performed work for a client located in China and collected 8,450,000 RMB (renminbi, the Chinese currency), the equivalent of about $1,320,000 Canadian. Delco recorded it as 8,450,000.

_____ **b.** Delco collected $180,000 from a customer on December 20, 2014, for work to be done in February 2015. The $180,000 was recorded as revenue during 2014. Delco's year-end is December 31.

_____ **c.** Delco's December 31, 2014, balance sheet showed total assets of $840,000 and liabilities of $1,120,000. The income statements for the past six years have shown a trend of increasing losses.

_____ **d.** Included in Delco's assets was land and a building purchased for $310,000 and reported on the balance sheet at $470,000.

_____ **e.** Delco's owner, Tom Del, consistently buys personal supplies and charges them to the company.

QS 1-10 Financial statements and forms of organization LO²,⁶

    SP – Sole proprietorship
    P – Partnership
    C – Corporation

Identify the type of business organization based on the following independent financial statement findings:

_____ **1.** The equity section of the balance sheet has one capital account.

_____ **2.** The owners receive dividends, a distribution of earnings, in the form of cash.

_____ **3.** There are two capital accounts: Tara Davis, Capital, and Sheila Kelton, Capital.

_____ **4.** The one owner receives distributions of earnings in the form of withdrawals.

_____ **5.** A manager, also the owner of the business, is paid a salary that is recorded as an expense.

_____ **6.** The equity on the balance sheet is held by shareholders.

_____ **7.** The five owners receive distributions of earnings in the form of withdrawals.

QS 1-11 Applying the accounting equation LO⁷

Determine the missing amount for each of the following equations:

	Assets	=	Liabilities	+	Equity
a.	$ 75,000		$ 40,500		?
b.	$300,000		?		$85,500
c.	?		$187,500		$95,400

QS 1-12 Applying the accounting equation LO⁷

Use the accounting equation to determine:

a. The equity in a business that has $374,700 of assets and $252,450 of liabilities.

b. The liabilities of a business having $150,900 of assets and $126,000 of equity.

c. The assets of a business having $37,650 of liabilities and $112,500 of equity.

QS 1-13 Applying the accounting equation LO⁷

The balance sheet is a more detailed presentation of the accounting equation. The income statement and statement of changes in equity are linked to the balance sheet (by the accounting equation). Calculate the missing amounts below.

a.

Allin Servicing
Income Statement
For Month Ended April 30, 2014

Revenues	$300
Expenses......................................	?
Net income (loss)	?

Allin Servicing
Statement of Changes in Equity
For Month Ended April 30, 2014

Tim Allin, capital, April 1		$ 50
Add: Investments by owner	$ 30	
Net income..............................	?	?
Total		$255
Less: Withdrawals by owner		?
Tim Allin, capital, April 30............		?

Allin Servicing
Balance Sheet
April 30, 2014

Assets		Liabilities	
Cash	$ 60	Accounts payable	$ 25
Equipment...	?	**Equity**	
		Tim Allin, capital	?
		Total liabilities	
Total assets ..	$265	and equity	?

b.

Allin Servicing
Income Statement
For Month Ended May 31, 2014

Revenues	?
Expenses......................................	$ 85
Net income (loss)	?

Allin Servicing
Statement of Changes in Equity
For Month Ended May 31, 2014

Tim Allin, capital, May 1		?
Add: Investments by owner	$ 60	
Net income..............................	?	$110
Total		?
Less: Withdrawals by owner		75
Tim Allin, capital, May 31		?

Allin Servicing
Balance Sheet
May 31, 2014

Assets		Liabilities	
Cash	$120	Accounts payable	$ 45
Equipment...	?	**Equity**	
		Tim Allin, capital	?
		Total liabilities	
Total assets ..	?	and equity	?

QS 1-14 Applying the accounting equation LO⁷

Using the accounting equation provided, calculate:

1. Beginning capital on January 1, 2014, and
2. Ending capital at December 31, 2014.

Assets	=	Liabilities	+	Equity	
$20,000		$15,000		?	Beginning capital on January 1, 2014
				+3,000	Plus owner investments during the year
				+8,000	Plus net income earned during the year
				−4,000	Less owner withdrawals during the year
				?	Equals ending capital on December 31, 2014

Hint: Review Part B of the Mid-Chapter Demonstration Problem before trying this question.

QS 1-15 Identifying source documents LO⁷

Select the items from the following list that are likely to serve as source documents:

a. Income statement

b. Statement of cash flows

c. Telephone bill

d. Invoice from supplier

e. Owner's withdrawals account

f. Balance sheet

g. Bank statement

h. Sales invoice

QS 1-16 Transaction analysis LO⁷

For each transaction described, identify which component of the accounting equation increases and/or decreases. The first one is done as an example.

Example: Services were performed for a client on credit.

a. A credit customer paid his account.

b. Supplies were purchased on credit.

c. The balance owing regarding the supplies purchased in part (b) was paid.

d. Last month's telephone bill was received today. It will be paid on the due date, which is 10 days from now.

e. Paid the employees their weekly wage.

Assets	=	Liabilities	+	Equity
Example: Increase				*Increases*
a.				
b.				
c.				
d.				
e.				

QS 1-17 Identifying financial statement items LO⁵,⁸

Tim Roadster began Roadster Servicing on April 1, 2014, and showed the following items after the first month of operations. Match each of these items with the financial statement or statements on which it should be presented. Indicate your answer by writing the letter or letters for the correct statement(s) in the blank space next to each item.

a. Income statement   b. Statement of changes in equity   c. Balance sheet

_____	1. Supplies	$10	_____	8. Utilities expense	$10
_____	2. Supplies expense	22	_____	9. Furniture	20
_____	3. Accounts receivable	25	_____	10. Fees earned	70
_____	4. Accounts payable	12	_____	11. Rent revenue	35
_____	5. Equipment	40	_____	12. Salaries expense	45
_____	6. Tim Roadster's withdrawals in April	35	_____	13. Tim Roadster's investments in April	60
_____	7. Notes payable	30	_____	14. Net income	?

QS 1-18 Calculating financial statement elements LO⁵,⁸

Using the information provided in QS 1-17, calculate each of the following financial statement elements.

1. Total revenues
2. Total operating expenses
3. Net income
4. Total assets

5. Total liabilities
6. Tim Roadster, capital (April 30, 2014)
7. Total liabilities and equity

QS 1-19 Balance sheet LO⁵,⁸

Joan Bennish began Bennish Consulting on May 1, 2014, and reported the items below at May 31, 2014. Match each numbered item with the part of the balance sheet on which it should be presented. If the item does not appear on the balance sheet, choose (d) and identify on which financial statement(s) the item would appear.

a. Asset
b. Liability

c. Equity
d. Does not appear on the balance sheet

_____	1. Net loss	$?	_____	8. Repair supplies	$ 5
_____	2. Rent expense	22	_____	9. Notes payable	25
_____	3. Rent payable	6	_____	10. Joan Bennish's withdrawals in May	5
_____	4. Accounts receivable	14			
_____	5. Joan Bennish's investments in May	30	_____	11. Truck	15
			_____	12. Consulting fees earned	18
_____	6. Interest revenue	2	_____	13. Joan Bennish, capital, May 31, 2014	?
_____	7. Joan Bennish, capital, May 1, 2014	0	_____	14. Cash	20

QS 1-20 Calculating financial statement elements LO⁵,⁸

Using the information in QS 1-19, prepare an income statement and statement of changes in equity for the month ended May 31, 2014, and a balance sheet at May 31, 2014.

This icon indicates that the questions in this section are available on Connect.

EXERCISES

Exercises provide you with an additional opportunity to reinforce basic chapter concepts.

Exercise 1-1 Distinguishing business organizations LO²

Presented below are descriptions of several different business organizations. Determine whether the situation described refers to a sole proprietorship, partnership, or corporation.

a. Ownership of Cola Corp. is divided into 1,000 shares.

b. Text Tech is owned by Kimberly Fisher, who is personally liable for the debts of the business.

c. Jerry Forrentes and Susan Montgomery own Financial Services, a financial and personal services provider. Neither Forrentes nor Montgomery has personal responsibility for the debts of Financial Services.

d. Nancy Kerr and Frank Levens own Runners, a courier service. Both Kerr and Levens are personally liable for the debts of the business.

e. MRS Consulting Services does not have a separate legal existence apart from the one person who owns it.

f. Biotech Company has one owner and does not pay income taxes.

g. Torby Technologies has two owners and pays its own income taxes.

Exercise 1-2 Users of accounting information LO³

Identify the users of TLC Daycare's accounting information as internal (I) or external (E).

	I or E		I or E
Bank manager		Parent	
Owner		Canada Revenue Agency	
Toy supplier		Cleaner contracted by TLC Daycare	

Exercise 1-3 Describing accounting responsibilities LO³

Many accounting professionals work in one of the following three areas:

a. Financial accounting

b. Managerial accounting

c. Taxation accounting

For each of the following responsibilities, identify the area of accounting that most likely involves that responsibility:

_____ **1.** Auditing financial statements.

_____ **2.** Planning transactions to minimize taxes paid.

_____ **3.** Cost accounting.

_____ **4.** Preparing financial statements.

_____ **5.** Reviewing financial reports for compliance with provincial securities commissions requirements.

_____ **6.** Budgeting.

_____ **7.** Internal auditing.

_____ **8.** Investigating violations of tax laws.

Exercise 1-4 Applying the Rotary 4-Way Test LO⁴

Required For each situation described below, apply the Rotary 4-Way Test as identified earlier in the chapter to determine whether the behaviour is ethical or not.

a. In performing your job, you and a colleague often need to use your company phones to make long distance calls to suppliers. On a number of occasions, you have observed your colleague secretly using his company phone to make personal long distance calls.

b. You and a friend go to the movie theatre and purchase tickets. As you and your friend approach the ticket-taker, you both notice that the three people ahead of you have no tickets. The group and the ticket-taker, who appear to know each other, have a brief conversation and the group is admitted without having purchased tickets.

c. To use the facilities at the local fitness centre, clients can pay a $5 drop-in fee each visit or they can purchase an annual pass for unlimited access. The cashier collects the $5 from drop-in clients and provides them with a cash register receipt only if they ask.

Exercise 1-5 Accounting principles LO⁵

Match each of these numbered descriptions with the term it best describes. Indicate your answer by writing the letter for the correct principle in the blank space next to each description.

a. Cost principle

b. Business entity principle

c. Revenue recognition principle

d. Going concern principle

_____ **1.** Requires every business to be accounted for separately from its owner or owners.

_____ **2.** Requires financial statement information to be based on costs incurred in transactions.

_____ **3.** Requires financial statements to reflect the assumption that the business will continue operating instead of being closed or sold.

_____ **4.** Requires revenue to be recorded only when the earnings process is complete.

Exercise 1-6 Determining net income LO⁶

Net income (net loss), owner withdrawals, and owner investment cause equity to change. We also know that revenues less expenses equals net income (loss). Using the following information, calculate net income (loss) for each independent situation.

a. The business earned revenues of $516,000 and had expenses of $492,000.

b. The business showed expenses of $240,000 and revenues of $165,000.

c. The equity at the beginning of the month was $32,000. During the month, the owner made no investments or withdrawals. At the end of the month, equity totalled $86,000.

d. The equity at the beginning of the month was $48,000. During the month, the owner made an investment of $40,000 but made no withdrawals. Equity at the end of the month totalled $52,000.

Exercise 1-7 Missing information LO⁶

Referring to Exhibit 1.9, calculate the amount of the missing item in each of the following independent cases:

	a	b	c	d	e
Equity, January 1	$ -0-	$ -0-	$ -0-	$ -0-	$?
Owner's investments during the year	60,000	?	31,500	37,500	140,000
Net income (loss) for the year	15,750	30,500	(4,500)	?	(8,000)
Owner's withdrawals during the year	?	(27,000)	(20,000)	(15,750)	(63,000)
Equity, December 31	56,000	49,500	?	32,000	171,000

Exercise 1-8 Income statement LO⁶

On November 1, 2014, Jean Higgins organized a new consulting firm called The Higgins Group. On November 30, 2014, the company's records showed the following items. Use this information to prepare a November income statement for the business, similar to Exhibit 1.8.

Cash	$16,000	Owner's withdrawals	$ 3,360
Accounts receivable	17,000	Consulting fees earned	22,000
Office supplies	5,000	Rent expense	2,550
Automobiles	36,000	Salaries expense	6,000
Office equipment	25,250	Telephone expense	1,680
Accounts payable	7,500	Utilities expenses	660
Owner's investments	84,000		

Exercise 1-9 Statement of changes in equity LO⁶

Use the facts in Exercise 1-8 to prepare a November statement of changes in equity for The Higgins Group, similar to Exhibit 1.9.

Analysis Component: What activities caused equity to increase during the month of November 2014?

Exercise 1-10 Balance sheet LO⁶

Use the facts in Exercise 1-8 to prepare a November 30 balance sheet for The Higgins Group, similar to Exhibit 1.10.

Analysis Component: Identify how much of the assets held by The Higgins Group are financed by the owner, Jean Higgins.

Exercise 1-11 Income statement LO⁶

On July 1, 2014, Windsor Learning Services entered its second month of operations. On July 31, 2014, Milton Windsor, the owner, finalized the company's records that showed the following items. Use this information to prepare a July income statement similar to Exhibit 1.8.

Accounts payable	$1,500	Owner's investments during	
Accounts receivable	2,000	July 2014	$1,200
Cash	1,600	Owner's withdrawals	1,000
Computer equipment	2,200	Supplies	1,280
Furniture	1,800	Textbook rental revenue	300
Milton Windsor, capital,		Tutoring fees earned	4,200
June 30, 2014*	7,400	Tutors' wages expense	1,540
Office rent expense	2,500	Utilities expense	680

Hint: The ending capital balance for one period is the beginning capital balance for the next period.

Exercise 1-12 Statement of changes in equity LO[6]

Use the facts in Exercise 1-11 to prepare a July statement of changes in equity for Windsor Learning Services, similar to Exhibit 1.9.

Analysis Component: Identify those activities that caused equity to decrease during July 2014.

Exercise 1-13 Balance sheet LO[6]

Use the facts in Exercise 1-11 to prepare a July 31 balance sheet for Windsor Learning Services, similar to Exhibit 1.10.

Analysis Component: Identify how much of the assets held by Windsor Learning Services are financed by debt.

Exercise 1-14 Determining net income LO[6,7]

A business had the following amounts of assets and liabilities at the beginning and end of a recent year:

	Assets	Liabilities
Beginning of the year	$ 75,000	$30,000
End of the year	120,000	46,000

Determine the net income earned or net loss incurred by the business during the year under each of the following unrelated assumptions:

a. The owner made no additional investments in the business and withdrew no assets during the year.

b. The owner made no additional investments in the business during the year but withdrew $4,750 **per month** to pay personal living expenses.

c. The owner withdrew no assets during the year but invested an additional $80,000 cash.

d. The owner withdrew $3,500 **per month** to pay personal living expenses and invested an additional $75,000 cash in the business.

Hint: Review the Mid-Chapter Demonstration Problem before trying this question.

Exercise 1-15 Accounting equation LO[7]

In the following table, the accounting equation is applied to Business A:

	Assets	=	Liabilities	+	Equity
At August 1, 2014	?		$10,000		?
At August 31, 2014	$25,000		?		?

Calculate the missing amounts assuming that:

a. Assets decreased by $15,000 during August, and

b. Liabilities increased by $9,000 during August.

Exercise 1-16 Effects of transactions on the accounting equation LO[5,7]

Wesson Servicing provides support to customers in the area of ecommerce. Using the format provided, show the effects of the activities listed in (a) through (f).

	Assets					=	Liabilities	+	Equity
	Cash	+	Accounts Receivable	+	Office Supplies	=	Accounts Payable	+	Marnie Wesson, Capital

a. Marnie Wesson, the owner, invested cash of $25,000 into the business.

b. The owner purchased office supplies on credit; $600.

c. Wesson Servicing did work for a client and received $7,000 cash.

d. Completed an application form for a $10,000 government grant.

e. The owner paid her assistant's salary; $4,500 cash.

f. Completed work for a customer on credit; $1,250.

Exercise 1-17 Effects of transactions on the accounting equation LO[6,7]

DigiCom repairs computers. Using the format provided below, show the effects of the activities listed in (a) through (i).

	Assets				=	Liabilities	+	Equity
Cash	+	Accounts Receivable	+	Parts Supplies	+	Equipment	=	Accounts Payable	+	Stacey Crowe, Capital

a. Stacey Crowe, owner of DigiCom, invested cash of $14,000 into her business.

b. DigiCom paid $2,500 to cover rent for the current month.

c. DigiCom purchased supplies on credit; $800.

d. DigiCom completed work for a client on credit; $3,400.

e. DigiCom purchased a new piece of equipment by paying cash of $1,950.

f. DigiCom hired a technician, to start next month, who will get paid $5,000 per month.

g. DigiCom paid for the supplies purchased in (c).

h. DigiCom performed work for a client and received cash of $3,400.

i. DigiCom paid the assistant's salary of $2,700.

Exercise 1-18 Analyzing the accounting equation LO[6,7]

Paula Caine began a new consulting firm on January 3. The accounting equation showed the following transactions. Analyze the equation and describe each of the transactions with their amounts. Transaction (a) has been done as an example for you.

		Assets						=	Liabilities	+	Equity
Transaction	Cash	+	Accounts Receivable	+	Office Supplies	+	Office Furniture	=	Accounts Payable	+	Paula Caine, Capital
Beginning Balances	-0-		-0-		-0-		-0-		-0-		-0-
a.	+15,000										+15,000
b.	− 500				+500						
c.	− 8,000						+8,000				
d.			+1,000								+ 1,000
e.					+400				+400		
f.	− 250								−250		
g.	+ 750		− 750								
Totals	7,000		250		900		8,000		150		16,000

Description of transaction (a):

a. *The owner invested $15,000 cash into the business.*

Exercise 1-19 Effects of transactions on the accounting equation LO[6,7]

Mailin Moon is a freelance writer who submits articles to various magazines and newspapers. She operates out of a small office where she employs one administrative assistant. The following activities occurred during March 2014, her first month of business:

a. Mailin invested $2,500 worth of equipment into her business along with $3,000 cash.

b. Submitted a series of articles to *The Globe and Mail* and received $6,500 cash.

c. Purchased supplies on credit; $600.

d. Paid the part-time administrative assistant's salary of $1,450.

e. Mailin ordered $3,000 of office equipment from the IKEA catalogue. It is scheduled to arrive in April or May.

f. Paid the rent for the first month; $1,400.

g. Submitted an article to *Report on Business*; will receive $4,500 next month.

Using the format provided below, show the effects of the activities listed in (a) through (g). For each transaction that affects equity, include a brief description beside it (owner investment, owner withdrawal, revenue, expense).

Assets				=	Liabilities	+	Equity	
Cash	+ Accounts Receivable	+ Supplies	+ Equipment	=	Accounts Payable	+	Mailin Moon, Capital	Explanation of Equity Transaction

Exercise 1-20 Financial statements LO[8]

Using your answer from Exercise 1-19, prepare an income statement, a statement of changes in equity, and a balance sheet using the formats provided.

Mailin Moon—Freelance Writing
Income Statement
For Month Ended March 31, 2014

Revenues:. . . . .
   Freelance writing revenue . . . .
Operating expenses:. . . . .
   Salaries expense . . . .
   Rent expense. . . . . _____
      Total operating expenses . . . .
Net income . . . .

Mailin Moon—Freelance Writing
Statement of Changes in Equity
For Month Ended March 31, 2014

Mailin Moon, capital, March 1 . . . .
Add: Investments by owner . . . .
   Net income. . . . . _____
Mailin Moon, capital, March 31 . . . .

Mailin Moon—Freelance Writing
Balance Sheet
March 31, 2014

Assets	**Liabilities**
Cash.	Accounts payable . . . .
Accounts receivable	
Supplies	**Equity**
Equipment	Mailin Moon, capital . . . .
Total assets . . . . _____	Total liabilities and equity . . . . . . _____

Analysis Component: Identify which assets were financed by:

a. Liabilities   **b.** Owner investment   **c.** Net income

Also identify the amount(s) for each.

CHECK FIGURE:
Accounts payable,
March 31,
2014 = $2,350

Exercise 1-21 Effects of transactions on the accounting equation LO[6,7]

Pete Kequahtooway opened a yard care business, Pete's Yard Care, on March 1, 2014. The following activities occurred during his first month of operations:

a. Pete Kequahtooway invested $4,300 cash and $15,000 of equipment into his business.

b. Purchased various supplies on account; $1,600.

c. Bought supplies on credit; $950.

d. Pete signed a $4,000 contract to do yard work beginning in May.

e. Did work for a client on account; $550.

f. Performed services for a customer on credit; $600.

g. Paid $200 for the supplies purchased in (c).

h. Paid $250 for advertising in the local newspaper.

i. Collected the amount owed from the customer in (f).

Using the format provided below, show the effects of the activities listed in (a) through (i). For each transaction that affects equity, include a brief description beside it (owner investment, owner withdrawal, revenue, expense).

Assets				=	Liabilities	+	Equity	
Cash +	Accounts Receivable +	Supplies +	Equipment =		Accounts Payable +		Pete Kequahtooway, Capital	Explanation of Equity Transaction

CHECK FIGURE:
Pete Kequahtooway,
Capital, March 31,
2014 = $20,200

Exercise 1-22 Financial statements LO[8]

Using your answer from Exercise 1-21, prepare an income statement, statement of changes in equity, and balance sheet for March 2014.

Analysis Component: Review Pete's income statement. Does the net income of $900 represent $900 of cash? Explain.

CHECK FIGURE:
Otto Ingles, Capital,
July 31, 2014 = $11,550

Exercise 1-23 Effects of transactions on the accounting equation LO[6,7]

The June transactions for Otto's Wrecking Service resulted in totals at June 30, 2014, as shown in the following accounting equation format:

Assets				=	Liabilities	+	Equity	
Cash +	Receivable Accounts +	Supplies +	Equipment =		Accounts Payable +		Otto Ingles, Capital	Explanation of Equity Transaction
$6,000 +	$1,200 +	$1,900 +	$6,500 =		$4,000 +		$11,600	

During July, the following occurred:

a. Collected $800 from a credit customer.

b. Paid $2,500 for equipment purchased on account in June.

c. Did work for a client and collected cash; $1,100.

d. Paid the part-time worker's wages; $950.

e. Paid the July rent; $1,200.

f. Paid the July utilities; $600.

g. Performed services for a customer on credit; $1,600.

h. Called a repair person to fix the equipment in August; it will cost $350.

Using the format provided above, show the effects of the activities listed in (a) through (h). For each transaction that affects equity, include a brief description beside it (owner investment, owner withdrawal, revenue, expense).

Exercise 1-24 Financial statements LO⁸

Using your answer from Exercise 1-23, prepare an income statement, a statement of changes in equity, and a balance sheet for July 2014.

Analysis Component: Review Otto's balance sheet. How much of the assets are financed by Otto Ingles? How much of the assets are financed by debt?

Problems typically incorporate two or more concepts. There are two groups of problems: A problems and Alternate or B problems. B problems mirror the A problems to help you improve your understanding through repetition.

PROBLEMS

Problem 1-1A Identifying type of business organization LO²

Complete the chart below by placing a checkmark in the appropriate column.

Characteristic	Type of Business Organization		
	Sole Proprietorship	**Partnership**	**Corporation**
Limited liability			
Unlimited liability			
Owners are shareholders			
Owners are partners			
Taxed as a separate legal entity			

Problem 1-2A Financial statements: analysis of statement of changes in equity LO⁶

BT Pool Cleaners began operations on January 1, 2013. The owner invested $10,000 during the first year and was able to withdraw cash of $42,000 after a successful first year.

During 2014, the second year of operations, the business reported net income of $175,000, owner withdrawals of $78,000, and no owner investments.

In 2015, the third year, BT Pool Cleaners incurred a loss of $5,000. The owner made no withdrawals and no owner investments during this period. At the end of 2015, owner's capital was $120,000.

Required Calculate the net income or loss for 2013.

Problem 1-3A Financial statements LO⁶

On August 1, 2013, Bee Clean entered its second year of operations, providing housekeeping services to the elderly and disabled as well as doing small household repairs. On July 31, 2014, Bee Cummins, the owner, finalized the company's records, which showed the following items.

Accounts payable	$ 9,400		Office equipment	$ 19,200
Accounts receivable	42,000		Prepaid rent	4,000
Bee Cummins, capital,			Rent expense	14,000
July 31, 2013*	79,300		Repair revenue	2,500
Bee Cummins, withdrawals	46,000		Service revenue	131,000
Cash	5,600		Supplies	2,400
Furniture	13,200		Supplies expense	15,900
Interest expense	2,100		Utilities expense	9,800
Notes payable	20,000		Wages expense	68,000

Hint: The ending capital balance for one period is the beginning capital balance for the next period. There were no owner investments during the year ended July 31, 2014.

Required Prepare an income statement and statement of changes in equity for the year ended July 31, 2014, and balance sheet at July 31, 2014, similar to Exhibits 1.8, 1.9, and 1.10.

Analysis Component: Analyze the balance sheet and calculate what percentage of the assets at July 31, 2014, were financed by (a) debt and (b) equity.

Problem 1-4A Calculating and interpreting net income and preparing a balance sheet LO6,7,8

The accounting records of LeClaire Delivery Services show the following assets and liabilities as of the end of 2014 and 2013:

	December 31	
	2014	2013
Cash	$ 9,375	$26,250
Accounts receivable	11,175	14,250
Office supplies	1,650	2,250
Trucks	27,000	27,000
Office equipment	73,500	69,000
Land	22,500	
Building	90,000	
Accounts payable	18,750	3,750
Notes payable	52,500	

During December 2014, the owner, Jess LeClaire, purchased a small office building and moved the business from rented quarters to the new building. The building and the land it occupies cost $112,500. The business paid $60,000 in cash and a note payable was signed for the balance. LeClaire had to invest $17,500 cash in the business to enable it to pay the $60,000. The business earned a net income during 2014, which enabled LeClaire to withdraw $1,500 per month from the business for personal expenses.

Required

1. Prepare balance sheets for the business as of the end of 2013 and the end of 2014.

2. Prepare a calculation to show how much net income was earned by the business during 2014.

Analysis Component: Assets increased from $138,750 at December 31, 2013, to $235,200 at December 31, 2014. Using numbers wherever possible, explain how these assets were financed.

Problem 1-5A Missing information LO7

The following financial statement information is known about five unrelated companies:

	Company A	Company B	Company C	Company D	Company E
December 31, 2013:					
Assets	$90,000	$105,000	$58,000	$160,000	$246,000
Liabilities	38,000	45,000	28,000	76,000	?
December 31, 2014:					
Assets	96,000	82,000	?	250,000	225,000
Liabilities	?	55,000	38,000	128,000	150,000
During 2014:					
Owner investments	10,000	19,000	15,500	?	9,000
Net income (loss)	(16,000)	?	18,000	24,000	36,000
Owner withdrawals	5,000	6,000	7,750	-0-	18,000

Required

1. Answer the following questions about Company A:
   a. What was the equity on December 31, 2013?
   b. What was the equity on December 31, 2014?
   c. What was the amount of liabilities owed on December 31, 2014?

2. Answer the following questions about Company B:
   a. What was the equity on December 31, 2013?
   b. What was the equity on December 31, 2014?
   c. What was the net income (loss) for 2014?

3. Calculate the amount of assets owned by Company C on December 31, 2014.

4. Calculate the amount of owner investments in Company D made during 2014.

5. Calculate the amount of liabilities owed by Company E on December 31, 2013.

Problem 1-6A Analyzing transactions and preparing financial statements LO^{6,7,8}

George Littlechild started a new kitchen and bath design business called Littlechild Enterprises. The following activities occurred during its first month of operations, March 2014:

a. Littlechild invested $160,000 cash and office equipment valued at $20,000 in the business.

b. Purchased a small building for $600,000 to be used as an office. Paid $100,000 in cash and signed a note payable promising to pay the balance over several years.

c. Purchased $3,000 of office supplies for cash.

d. Purchased $72,000 of office equipment on credit.

e. George Littlechild made reservations at a hotel hosting a kitchen and bath design conference in August 2014. He will send a $1,000 deposit on July 1, 2014.

f. Completed a project on credit and billed the client $5,200 for the work.

g. Paid a local newspaper $3,500 for an announcement that the office had opened.

h. Completed a project for a client and collected $4,000 cash.

i. Made a $4,000 payment on the equipment purchased in (d).

j. Received $2,500 from the client described in (f).

k. Paid $7,000 cash for the office secretary's wages.

l. Littlechild withdrew $3,600 cash from the company bank account to pay personal living expenses.

Littlechild Enterprises
Income Statement
For Month Ended March 31, 2014

Revenues:
  Service revenue . . . .
Operating expenses:
  Wages expense . . . .
  Advertising expense . . . . _____
    Total operating expenses . . . .
Net loss . . . .

Littlechild Enterprises
Statement of Changes in Equity
For Month Ended March 31, 2014

George Littlechild, capital, March 1 . . . .
Add: Investments by owner . . . .
    Total . . . . _____
Less: Withdrawals by owner
        Net loss . . . . _____
George Littlechild, capital, March 31 . . . .

Littlechild Enterprises
Balance Sheet
March 31, 2014

Assets		**Liabilities**	
Cash		Accounts payable	
Accounts receivable		Notes payable	_____
Office supplies		Total liabilities	
Office equipment			
Building		**Equity**	
		George Littlechild, capital	
Total assets	_____	Total liabilities and equity	_____

Required

1. Create a table like the one in Exhibit 1.15, using the following headings for the columns: Cash; Accounts Receivable; Office Supplies; Office Equipment; Building; Accounts Payable; Notes Payable; and George Littlechild, Capital. Leave space for an Explanation of Equity Transaction column to the right of the Capital column. Identify revenues and expenses by name in the Explanation of Equity Transaction column.

2. Use additions and subtractions to show the transactions' effects on the elements of the equation. **Do not determine new totals for the items of the equation after each transaction.** Next to each change in equity, state whether the change was caused by an investment, a revenue, an expense, or a withdrawal. Determine the final total for each item and verify that the equation is in balance.

3. Prepare an income statement, a statement of changes in equity, and a balance sheet using the formats provided.

Analysis Component: Littlechild Enterprises' assets are financed 76% by debt. What does this mean? As part of your answer, include an explanation of how the 76% was calculated.

CHECK FIGURE:
Accounts payable
balance, November 30,
2014 = $27,000

Larry Power, Capital
balance, November 30,
2014 = $69,100

Problem 1-7A Analyzing transactions LO[5,7]

Larry Power started a new business in the name of Power Electrical on October 1, 2014. During October, a number of activities occurred and the following totals resulted at October 31, 2014 (shown in accounting equation format):

		Assets					=	Liabilities	+	Equity
Cash	+	Accounts Receivable	+	Office Supplies	+	Office Equip.	+	Electrical Equip.	=	Accounts Payable	+	Larry Power, Capital
$30,000	+	$7,000	+	$1,900	+	$28,000	+	$14,000	=	$18,000	+	$62,900

During November, the following occurred:

Nov.	1	Rented office space and paid cash for the month's rent of $7,200.
	3	Purchased electrical equipment for $18,000 from an electrician who was going out of business, by using $10,000 in personal funds and agreeing to pay the balance in 30 days.
	5	Purchased office supplies by paying $1,800 cash.
Nov.	6	Completed electrical work and immediately collected $2,000 for doing the work.
	8	Purchased $5,200 of office equipment on credit.
	15	Completed electrical work on credit in the amount of $6,000.
	16	Interviewed and hired a part-time electrician who will be paid $5,300 each month. He will begin work in three weeks.
	18	Purchased $1,000 of office supplies on credit.
	20	Paid for the office equipment purchased on November 8.
	24	Billed a client $4,800 for electrical work; the balance is due in 30 days.
	28	Received $6,000 for the work completed on November 15.
	30	Paid the office assistant's salary of $4,400.
	30	Paid the monthly utility bills of $3,600.
	30	Power withdrew $1,400 from the business for personal use.

Required Use additions and subtractions to show the effects of each November activity on the items in the equation. **Do not determine new totals for the items of the equation after each transaction.** Next to each change in equity, state whether the change was caused by an investment, a revenue, an expense, or a withdrawal. Determine the final total for each item and verify that the equation is in balance.

Analysis Component: Revenue is not recorded on November 28. Explain, using your understanding of GAAP.

Problem 1-8A Preparing financial statements LO⁸

Required Using your answer to Problem 1-7A, prepare an income statement, a statement of changes in equity, and a balance sheet.

Analysis Component: Assets are financed by debt and equity. Net income is a component of equity. Therefore, net income helps to finance assets. Explain how/if net income helped to finance assets for Power Electrical for the month ended November 30, 2014.

Problem 1-9A Identifying the effects of transactions on the financial statements LO⁷,⁸

Identify how each of the following transactions affects the company's financial statements. For the balance sheet, identify how each transaction affects total assets, total liabilities, and equity. For the income statement, identify how each transaction affects net income. If there is an increase, place a "+" in the column or columns. If there is a decrease, place a "−" in the column or columns. If there is both an increase and a decrease, place a "+/−" in the column or columns. The line for the first transaction is completed as an example.

		Balance Sheet			Income Statement
	Transaction	**Total Assets**	**Total Liabilities**	**Equity**	**Net Income**
1	Owner invests cash	+		+	
2	Sell services for cash				
3	Acquire services on credit				
4	Pay wages with cash				
5	Owner withdraws cash				
6	Borrow cash with note payable				
7	Sell services on credit				
8	Buy office equipment for cash				
9	Collect receivable from (7)				
10	Buy asset with note payable				

ALTERNATE PROBLEMS

Problem 1-1B Identifying type of business organization LO²

a.   Refer to Appendix II at the end of the book. Determine if WestJet Airlines is a sole proprietorship, partnership, or corporation.

b.   Refer to Appendix II at the end of the book. Determine if Danier Leather is a sole proprietorship, partnership, or corporation.

Problem 1-2B Financial statements: analysis of statement of changes in equity LO⁶

Dublin Window Cleaners began operations on January 1, 2013. The owner invested $400,000 during the first year and made no withdrawals.

During 2014, the business reported net income of $192,000, owner withdrawals of $104,000, and zero owner investments.

In 2015, Dublin Window Cleaners earned net income of $366,000. The owner withdrew $218,000 during 2015 and made no investments. Owner's capital at December 31, 2015, was $605,000.

Required Calculate the net income or loss for the year 2013.

Problem 1-3B Financial statements LO⁶

On January 1, 2014, Fireworks Fantasia entered its third year of operations. On December 31, 2014, Wes Gandalf, the owner, finalized the company's records that showed the following items.

Accounts payable................................	$ 58,000	Office equipment......................................	$ 14,000
Accounts receivable	14,000	Office supplies..	3,000
Advertising expense............................	9,000	Office supplies expense............................	3,600
Building...	81,000	Rent revenue..	66,000
Cash..	8,000	Tools..	18,000
Fees earned	140,000	Utilities expense	25,100
Fireworks supplies..............................	49,000	Wages expense	92,000
Fireworks supplies expense	77,500	Wes Gandalf, capital,	
Land..	63,000	December 31, 2013	175,200
		Wes Gandalf, withdrawals	12,000

Hint: The ending capital balance for one period is the beginning capital balance for the next period. The owner made investments of $30,000 during the year ended December 31, 2014.

Required Prepare an income statement and statement of changes in equity for the year ended December 31, 2014, and a December 31, 2014, balance sheet, similar to Exhibits 1.8, 1.9, and 1.10.

Analysis Component: Analyze the balance sheet and calculate what percentage of the assets at December 31, 2014, were financed by (a) debt and (b) equity.

Problem 1-4B Calculating and interpreting net income and preparing a balance sheet LO⁶,⁷,⁸

The accounting records of Carmen Creek Gourmet Meats show the following assets and liabilities as of the end of 2014 and 2013:

	December 31	
	2014	**2013**
Cash...	$ 20,000	$ 28,000
Accounts receivable	60,000	50,000
Office supplies	25,000	20,000
Office equipment...	120,000	120,000
Machinery	61,000	61,000
Land..	130,000	
Building..	520,000	
Accounts payable...	30,000	10,000
Notes payable...	520,000	

During 2014, Carmen Munch, the owner, purchased a small office building and moved the business from rented quarters to the new building. The building and the land it occupies cost $650,000. The business paid $130,000 in cash and a note payable was signed for the balance. Munch had to invest an additional $50,000 to enable it to pay the $130,000. The business earned a net income during 2014, which enabled Munch to withdraw $2,000 per month from the business for personal use.

Required

1. Prepare balance sheets for the business as of the end of 2013 and the end of 2014.

2. Prepare a calculation to show how much net income was earned by the business during 2014.

Analysis Component: Assets increased from $279,000 at December 31, 2013, to $936,000 at December 31, 2014. Using numbers wherever possible, explain how these assets were financed.

Problem 1-5B Missing information LO⁷

The following financial statement information is known about five unrelated companies:

	Company V	Company W	Company X	Company Y	Company Z
December 31, 2013:					
Assets....................................	$165,000	$70,000	$121,500	$82,500	$124,000
Liabilities	30,000	50,000	58,500	50,000	?
December 31, 2014:					
Assets....................................	192,000	90,000	136,500	?	160,000
Liabilities	26,000	?	55,500	72,000	52,000
During 2014:					
Owner investments	60,000	10,000	?	38,100	40,000
Net income (loss)...................	?	30,000	16,500	(46,000)	32,000
Owner withdrawals................	4,500	2,000	-0-	18,000	6,000

Required

1. Answer the following questions about Company V:
   a. What was the equity on December 31, 2013?
   b. What was the equity on December 31, 2014?
   c. What was the net income (loss) for 2014?
2. Answer the following questions about Company W:
   a. What was the equity on December 31, 2013?
   b. What was the equity on December 31, 2014?
   c. What was the amount of liabilities owed on December 31, 2014?
3. Calculate the amount of owner investments in Company X made during 2014.
4. Calculate the amount of assets owned by Company Y on December 31, 2014.
5. Calculate the amount of liabilities owed by Company Z on December 31, 2013.

CHECK FIGURES:
2. Cash balance,
December 31,
2014 = $43,800
3. Net income = $5,700;
Total assets = $324,200

Problem 1-6B Analyzing transactions and preparing financial statements LO⁶,⁷,⁸

Lily Coe started a new business on January 1, 2014, called Coe Consulting. She develops financial invest-ment plans for young adults. During the business's first year of operations, the following activities occurred:

a. Coe invested $120,000 cash and office equipment valued at $10,000 in the business.
b. Purchased a small building for $240,000 to be used as an office. Paid $50,000 in cash and signed a note payable promising to pay the balance over several years.
c. Purchased $18,000 of office equipment for cash.
d. Purchased $4,000 of office supplies and $6,400 of office equipment on credit.
e. Paid a local newspaper $4,500 for an announcement that the office had opened.
f. Completed a financial plan on credit and billed the client $6,000 for the service.
g. Designed a financial plan for another client and collected an $8,000 cash fee.
h. Coe withdrew $5,500 cash from the company bank account to pay personal expenses.
i. Coe signed a $20,000 contract for the office to be painted in February 2015. A deposit of $6,000 will be paid on January 15, 2015.
j. Received $4,000 from the client described in (f).
k. Paid for the equipment purchased in (d).
l. Paid $3,800 cash for the office secretary's wages.

Required

1. Create a table like the one presented in Exhibit 1.15, using the following headings for the columns: Cash; Accounts Receivable; Office Supplies; Office Equipment; Building; Accounts Payable; Notes Payable; and Lily Coe, Capital. Leave space for an Explanation of Equity Transaction column to the right of the Capital column. Identify revenues and expenses by name in the Explanation column.

2. Use additions and subtractions to show the effects of the above transactions on the elements of the equation. **Do not determine new totals for the items of the equation after each transaction.** Next to each change in equity, state whether the change was caused by an investment, a revenue, an expense, or a withdrawal. Determine the final total for each item and verify that the equation is in balance.

3. Prepare an income statement, a statement of changes in equity, and a balance sheet for 2014 using the formats provided.

Coe Consulting
Income Statement
For Year Ended December 31, 2014

Revenues:
  Consulting services revenue ....
Operating expenses:
  Wages expense ....
  Advertising expense ....
    Total operating expenses ....
Net income ....

Coe Consulting
Statement of Changes in Equity
For Year Ended December 31, 2014

Lily Coe, capital, January 1..
Add: Investments by owner ....
    Net income ....
  Total..
Less: Withdrawals by owner..
Lily Coe, capital, December 31 ....

Coe Consulting
Balance Sheet
December 31, 2014

Assets	Liabilities
Cash	Accounts payable.....................
Accounts receivable	Notes payable..........................
Office supplies	Total liabilities ....
Office equipment......................	
Building.....................................	**Equity**
	Lily Coe, capital........................
Total assets	Total liabilities and equity.........

Analysis Component: Coe's assets are financed 60% by debt. What does this mean? As part of your answer, include an explanation of how the 60% was calculated.

Problem 1-7B Analyzing transactions LO^{5,7}

Cantu Excavating digs basements for building contractors. It is owned by Robert Cantu and began operations June 1, 2014. The June activities resulted in totals at June 30, 2014, as follows (illustrated in accounting equation format):

									Assets						=	Liabilities	+	Equity
	Cash	+	Accounts Receivable	+	Office Supplies	+	Office Equip.	+	Excavating Equip.	=	Accounts Payable	+	Robert Cantu, Capital
	$12,000	+	$4,600	+	$1,560	+	$9,600	+	$24,000	=	$6,200	+	$45,560

During July, the following occurred:

July	1	Cantu invested $20,000 cash in the business.
	1	Rented office space and paid the month's rent of $1,000.
	1	Purchased excavating equipment for $8,000 by paying $3,000 in cash and agreeing to pay the balance in 30 days.
	6	Purchased office supplies by paying $1,000 cash.
	8	Completed work for a customer and immediately collected $4,400 for doing the work.
	10	Purchased $7,600 of office equipment on credit.
	15	Completed work for a customer on credit in the amount of $4,800.
	17	Purchased $3,840 of office supplies on credit.
	23	Paid for the office equipment purchased on July 10.
	25	Billed a customer $10,000 for completed work; the balance is due in 30 days.
	28	Received $4,800 for the work completed on July 15.
	31	Paid an assistant's salary of $4,500.
	31	Paid the monthly utility bills of $1,700.
	31	Cantu withdrew $2,400 cash from the business to pay personal expenses.

Required Use additions and subtractions to show the effects of each July transaction on the items in the equation. **Do not determine new totals for the items of the equation after each transaction.** Next to each change in equity, state whether the change was caused by an investment, a revenue, an expense, or a withdrawal. Determine the final total for each item and verify that the equation is in balance.

Analysis Component: Identify which GAAP guides your treatment of the July 15 transaction. Explain your answer.

Problem 1-8B Preparing financial statements LO^8

Required Using your answer to Problem 1-7B, prepare an income statement, a statement of changes in equity, and a balance sheet.

Analysis Component: Assets are financed by debt and equity. Owner investment is a component of equity. Therefore, owner investment helps to finance assets. Explain how/if owner investment helped to finance assets for Cantu Excavating for the month ended July 31, 2014.

Problem 1-9B Identifying the effects of transactions on the financial statements LO[7,8]

You are to identify how each of the following transactions affects the company's financial statements. For the balance sheet, you are to identify how each transaction affects total assets, total liabilities, and equity. For the income statement, you are to identify how each transaction affects net income. If there is an increase, place a "+" in the column or columns. If there is a decrease, place a "−" in the column or columns. If there is both an increase and a decrease, place "+/−" in the column or columns. The line for the first transaction is completed as an example.

	Transaction	Balance Sheet Total Assets	Total Liabilities	Equity	Income Statement Net Income
1	Owner invests cash	+		+	
2	Pay wages with cash				
3	Acquire services on credit				
4	Buy store equipment for cash				
5	Borrow cash with note payable				
6	Sell services for cash				
7	Sell services on credit				
8	Pay rent with cash				
9	Owner withdraws cash				
10	Collect receivable from (7)				

ANALYTICAL AND REVIEW PROBLEMS

CHECK FIGURE:
Total assets = $89,775

A & R Problem 1-1

Jack Tasker opened his Auto Repair Shop in November 2014. The balance sheet at November 30, 2014, prepared by an inexperienced part-time bookkeeper, is shown below.

Required Prepare a correct balance sheet.

Tasker Auto Repair Shop
Balance Sheet
November 30, 2014

Assets		Liabilities and Equity	
Cash	$ 6,300	Parts and supplies	$14,175
Accounts payable	34,650	Accounts receivable	47,250
Equipment	22,050	Mortgage payable	28,350
Jack Tasker, capital	26,775		
Total income	$89,775	Total equities	$89,775

A & R Problem 1-2

Susan Huang began the practice of law October 1, 2014, with an initial investment of $10,500 in cash. She made no withdrawals during the month. After completing the first month of practice, the financial statements were prepared by Ryan Player, the secretary/bookkeeper Ms. Huang had hired. Ms. Huang almost burst out laughing when she saw them. She had completed a course in legal accounting in law school and knew the statements prepared by Mr. Player left much to be desired. Consequently, she asked you to revise the statements. The Player version is presented as follows:

Susan Huang, Lawyer
Balance Sheet
October 31, 2014

Assets		Liabilities and Equity	
Cash......................	$ 3,780	Susan Huang, capital........	$10,500
Furniture..................	2,100		
Supplies expense	420		
Accounts payable	1,050		
Rent expense	2,100		
Supplies	1,050		
	$10,500		$10,500

Susan Huang, Lawyer
Income Statement
For Month Ended October 31, 2014

Revenues:		
Legal fees	$11,550	
Accounts receivable....................................	2,100	$13,650
Expenses:		
Salaries expense	$ 2,940	
Telephone expense	210	
Law library	8,400	11,550
Profit		$ 2,100

Required Prepare the corrected financial statements for Susan Huang.

A & R Problem 1-3

For each of the following activities, identify the effect on each component of the income statement and balance sheet. The first one has been done as an example for you.

1. $14,000 of services were provided to clients on credit today.

	Income Statement		Balance Sheet		
	Revenues	Expenses	Assets	Liabilities	Equity
1.	⬆ $14,000		⬆ $14,000		⬆ $14,000

2. $5,000 cash was collected for services performed on credit last month.

3. $25,000 cash was borrowed from the bank.

4. $500 of advertising was done in the local newspaper today on account.

5. $500 was paid regarding the advertising in (4) above.

6. The owner invested an additional $10,000 cash into the business.

7. The owner withdrew $5,000 of cash from the business.

8. The owner took $200 worth of office supplies home for personal use.

9. A new computer was purchased for $2,000 cash.

10. A one-year insurance policy costing $12,000 was purchased today.

11. Purchased $45 of fuel for the van; paid cash.

12. Collected $900 from a client for work performed today.

ETHICS CHALLENGE

EC 1-1

Sue Ryskiak is a new entry-level accountant for a mail order company that specializes in supplying skateboards and accessories for the sport. At the end of the fiscal period, Sue is advised by a supervisor to include as revenue for the period any orders that have been charged by phone but not yet completed by shipping the product. Sue is also advised to include as revenue any orders received by mail with cheques enclosed that are also pending fulfillment.

Required

1. Identify relevant accounting principles that Sue should be aware of in view of the supervisor's instructions.

2. What are the ethical factors in this situation?

3. Would you recommend that Sue follow the supervisor's directives?

4. What alternatives might be available to Sue if she decides not to follow the supervisor's directions?

FOCUS ON FINANCIAL STATEMENTS

FFS 1-1

Glenrose Servicing began operations on June 1, 2014. The transactions for the first two months follow:

CHECK FIGURES:
3. Cash, June 30,
2014 = $15,000;
Total assets, June 30,
2014 = $23,000;
Cash, July 31,
2014 = $12,500;
Total assets, July 31,
2014 = $23,800

2014		
June	1	The owner, Diane Towbell, invested $20,000 cash and office equipment with a value of $6,000.
	5	Glenrose Servicing performed $3,000 of services for a client on account.
	7	Paid rent for June in the amount of $1,500.
	9	Collected $1,000 from the customer of June 5.
	15	Paid $5,000 of mid-month wages to part-time employees.
	17	Provided $2,000 of services to a client and collected the cash immediately.
	29	Received the $300 June utilities bill. It will be paid in July.
	30	Paid $1,500 in wages to part-time employees.
July	5	Did work for a customer on account; $3,500.
	8	Collected $2,000 from credit customers.
	9	Paid $1,500 rent for July.
	12	Purchased $1,800 of additional office equipment on account.
	14	Paid $1,000 of the amount owing regarding July 12.
	15	Paid mid-month wages to part-time staff; $2,500.
	17	Performed services for a customer and immediately collected $4,800.
	25	Paid $300 in utilities for the month of July plus the balance owing from June.
	31	Paid $1,700 in wages to part-time employees.
	31	The owner withdrew cash of $2,000 for personal use.

Required

1. Create two tables like the one in Exhibit 1.15 for each of June and July using the following headings for the columns: Cash; Accounts Receivable; Office Equipment; Accounts Payable; Diane Towbell, Capital; and Explanation of Equity Transaction.

2. Use additions and subtractions to show the effects of the above transactions on the elements of the equation for each of June and July.

3. Prepare an income statement and statement of changes in equity for each of the months ended June 30, and July 31, 2014. Also prepare a balance sheet at June 30, 2014, and July 31, 2014.

Analysis Component: Answer each of the following questions:

1. Assets increased by $800 from June 30, 2014, to July 31, 2014. How was this increase financed?

2. Which financial statement reports on a company's

   a. performance?

   b. financial position?

   Explain what is meant by each of these terms.

3. Explain how Glenrose Servicing's July income statement, statement of changes in equity, and balance sheet are linked.

FFS 1-2

Part A:

1. Refer to Appendix II at the end of the textbook for the December 31, 2011, balance sheet for WestJet Airlines Ltd., a Canadian airline based in Calgary, Alberta. What types of assets does WestJet have?

2. To what level of significance are the dollar amounts rounded on the financial statements?

3. Prove the accounting equation for WestJet at December 31, 2011.

4. Assume that the personal home of one of the owners of WestJet (a shareholder) is valued at over $2,000,000. Should it be included as an asset on the balance sheet for WestJet? Why or why not?

5. Identify a potential internal user who would be interested in WestJet's statements and explain their interest.

DANIER **Part B:**

6. Refer to Appendix II at the end of the textbook for the June 25, 2011, balance sheet for Danier Leather Inc., a Canadian specialty clothing designer, manufacturer, and retailer based in Toronto, Ontario. Identify the following for Danier at June 25, 2011:

   a. Total assets

   b. Total net assets

   c. Prove the accounting equation for Danier at June 25, 2011.

7. Notice that the balance sheet provides data for two years. Why do you think information has been presented for both June 25, 2011, and June 26, 2010?

8. Identify a potential external user that would be interested in Danier's statements and explain their interest.

CRITICAL THINKING MINI CASE

You have worked with XYZ Contractors as the marketing manager for a number of years. Each of your salespeople must submit a monthly report detailing money they spent while conducting business on behalf of XYZ Contractors. Each item on the monthly report must be coded as to the effect on assets, liabilities, and equity. As marketing manager, one of your duties is to review the monthly reports. One salesperson's report for September shows the following:

Date	Description of Transaction	Amount of Transaction	Effect on Assets	Effect on Liabilities	Effect on Equity
Aug. 28	Sold 80 units of product to a customer for cash	$150,000	Increased cash	No effect	Increased revenue
Sept. 10	Purchased new desk for office to be paid in October	$1,500	No effect	Increased accounts payable	Increased office expense
Sept. 2–30	Took clients for lunch and paid cash	$680	Decreased cash		Increased owner investments
Oct. 5	Paid for September cell phone usage	$130	Decreased cash		Increased expenses

Required Using the elements of critical thinking described on the inside front cover, respond.

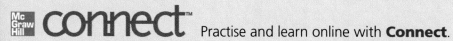

Practise and learn online with **Connect**.

Analyzing and Recording Transactions

LIVING THE DREAM

Many of us dream of creating a business based on a passion … for Wendy Grater, director/owner of Black Feather Wilderness Adventure Company, the fulfillment of a lifelong ambition began in 1984 when she joined the former Black Feather and Trailhead Outdoor Stores as part-owner. Having graduated from the University of Toronto in physical and health education and having taken a small business management course at Georgian Community College, Wendy had the foundational knowledge to take over managing the day-to-day logistics of Black Feather. In 1998 she became the company's sole owner.

From its inception in 1972, Black Feather has grown from a small operation offering a few canoe trips in Ontario and Quebec each summer, to an extensive ecotourism business hosting canoeing, hiking, and sea kayaking trips across Canada, in Greenland, and in Baja, Mexico.

Wendy says that, as a travel company, Black Feather's biggest challenge is anticipating increasing prices from suppliers during the season. "We publish our trip prices up to a year in advance … we can't change these at the last minute or after the fact because a costly emergency client evacuation is required or because of a change in air charter costs." Wendy has no doubt that "Accounting information is essential … it allows me to have an accurate picture of the financial health of the company as a whole and also for each trip. I use the information in planning the pricing, marketing, staffing, and operational logistics for each excursion. It would be foolhardy to have little or no knowledge of accounting while trying to run a small business." Her advice to aspiring entrepreneurs is, "Embrace it . . . an understanding of basic accounting is critical to ensuring a business's long-term health and viability."

www.blackfeather.com

Black Feather
the wilderness adventure company

LEARNING OBJECTIVES

LO¹ Explain the accounting cycle.

LO² Describe an account, its use, and its relationship to the ledger.

LO³ Define debits and credits and explain their role in double-entry accounting.

LO⁴ Describe a chart of accounts and its relationship to the ledger.

LO⁵ Analyze the impact of transactions on accounts.

LO⁶ Record transactions in a journal and post entries to a ledger.

LO⁷ Prepare and explain the use of a trial balance.

CRITICAL THINKING CHALLENGE | What does Wendy mean when she refers to the "financial health" of a company?

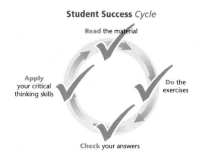

CHAPTER PREVIEW

We explained in Chapter 1 how the accounting equation helps us understand and analyze transactions and events. Analyzing financial transactions is the first step in the *accounting cycle*. Chapters 2 through 4 continue to explain and demonstrate each of the steps in the accounting cycle. All accounting systems use steps similar to those described here. These procedures are important because they lead to financial statements. Financial statement information is what Wendy Grater in the opening article uses to help her assess the health of her business.

We begin by providing an overview of the accounting cycle. We describe *accounts* and explain their purpose. *Debits* and *credits* are introduced, which enables us to describe the process of recording transactions in a *journal* and *posting* them to a *ledger*. We return to transactions of Vertically Inclined, first introduced in Chapter 1, to illustrate many of these procedures.

THE ACCOUNTING CYCLE

LO¹ Explain the accounting cycle.

The **accounting cycle** refers to the steps in preparing financial statements for users. It is called a cycle because the steps are repeated each reporting period. Exhibit 2.1 illustrates the accounting cycle. Chapter 1 introduced transaction analysis, the first step in the accounting cycle. Chapter 2 will focus on the next three steps of the accounting cycle. Step 7, the preparation of financial statements, was introduced in Chapter 1 but is reinforced in Chapters 2 and 3 and is expanded upon in Chapter 4.

EXHIBIT 2.1

Accounting Cycle

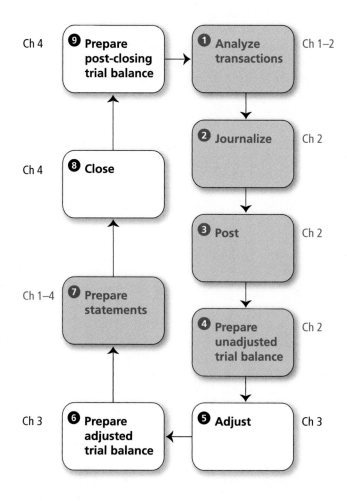

ACCOUNTS

This section explains the importance of an account to accounting and business. We also describe several crucial elements of an accounting system, including ledgers, T-accounts, debits and credits, double-entry accounting, and the chart of accounts.

 Describe an account, its use, and its relationship to the ledger.

The Account

An **account** is a detailed record of increases and decreases in a specific asset, liability, or equity item. Information is taken from accounts, analyzed, summarized, and presented in useful reports and financial statements for users. Separate accounts[1] are kept for each type of asset, liability, and equity item. Exhibit 2.2 shows examples of the different types of accounts used by Vertically Inclined.

Cash
Notes Receivable
Supplies
Furniture

Accounts Payable
Notes Payable

Virgil Klimb, Capital
Virgil Klimb, Withdrawals
Service Revenue
Rental Revenue
Salaries Expense
Advertising Expense

EXHIBIT 2.2

Types of Accounts for Vertically Inclined

A **ledger** is a record containing all accounts used by a business. A ledger is typically in electronic form and is sometimes referred to as the **books**. The term *books* originated when accounting records were maintained manually by recording accounts on separate pages in a special booklet. Books include both the ledger and the *journal*. Each company will have its own unique set of accounts to suit its type of operation. The remainder of this section introduces accounts that are important to most organizations.

Asset Accounts

Assets are resources controlled by an organization that have future benefits.[2] They have value and are used in the operations of the business to create revenue. For example, Equipment is an asset held by Vertically Inclined for the purpose of creating rental revenue in current and future periods. A separate account is maintained for each asset.

Cash increases and decreases are recorded in a Cash account. Examples are coins, currency, cheques, money orders, and chequing account balances.

Receivables are amounts that the business is expecting to receive in the future. Types of receivables include:

- **Accounts receivable**, which occur when services are performed for or goods are sold to customers in return for promises to pay in the future. These transactions are said to be on credit or *on account*. Accounts receivable are *increased* by services performed or goods sold on credit and *decreased* by customer payments.

- **Notes receivable** (or **promissory notes**), which are unconditional written promises to pay a definite sum of money on demand or on a defined future date(s).

Prepaid Expenses is an account containing payments made for assets that are to be used in the near future. As these assets are used up, the costs of the used assets become expenses. Examples include Office Supplies, Store Supplies, Prepaid Rent, and

---

1 As an example of an account, Exhibit 2.5 shows the Cash account as one of several asset accounts used by Vertically Inclined.
2 IFRS 2012, "Framework," para. 4.44.

Prepaid Insurance. A prepaid cost can be initially recorded as an expense *if* it is used up before the end of the period.

Equipment includes assets such as computers, printers, desks, chairs, counters, showcases, and cash registers. These assets are used in the operations of a business for more than one accounting period.

Buildings are assets owned by an organization that can provide space for a store, an office, a warehouse, or a factory. Buildings are assets because they provide benefits.

Land owned by a business is shown as an asset. The cost of land is separated from the cost of buildings located on the land to provide more useful information in financial statements.

Liability Accounts

Liabilities are obligations to transfer assets or provide services to other entities.[3] An organization often has several different liabilities, each of which is represented by a separate account that shows amounts owed to each creditor. The more common liability accounts are described here.

Payables are promises by a business to pay later for an asset or service already received. Types of payables include:

- **Accounts payable**, which occur with the purchase of merchandise, supplies, equipment, or services made by a promise to pay later.
- **Notes payable**, which occur when an organization formally recognizes a promise to pay by signing a promissory note.

Unearned revenues result when customers pay in advance for products or services. Because cash from these transactions is received before revenues are earned, the seller considers them unearned revenues in accordance with the revenue recognition principle. Unearned revenue is a liability because a service or product is *owed* to a customer. It will be earned when the service or product is delivered in the future. Examples of unearned revenue include magazine subscriptions collected in advance by a publisher, sales of gift certificates by stores, airline tickets sold in advance, and rent collected in advance by a landlord.

> WestJet Airlines Ltd. reported *advance ticket sales* of $432,186,000 on December 31, 2011.
>
> See Appendix II.

Other Liabilities include wages payable, taxes payable, and interest payable. Each of these is often recorded in a separate liability account. If they are not large in amount, two or more of them may be added and reported as a single amount on the balance sheet.

> The liabilities section of WestJet Airlines Ltd.'s balance sheet at December 31, 2011, included accounts payable and accrued liabilities of $307,279,000.
>
> See Appendix II.

Equity Accounts

We described in the previous chapter four types of transactions that affect equity: (1) investments by the owner, (2) withdrawals by the owner, (3) revenues, and (4) expenses. In Chapter 1, we entered all equity transactions in a single column under the owner's name as copied in Exhibit 2.3. When we later prepared the income

EXHIBIT 2.3

Equity Transactions as Analyzed in Chapter 1

Equity	Explanation of Equity Transaction
Virgil Klimb, Capital	
$10,000	Investment by Owner
$10,000	
$10,000	
+ 2,200	Teaching Revenue
$12,200	
− 1,000	Rent Expense
$11,200	
− 700	Salaries Expense
$10,500	
+ 1,600	Teaching Revenue
+ 300	Equipment Rental Revenue
$12,400	
$12,400	
$12,400	
− 600	Withdrawal by Owner
$11,800	

---

3 IFRS 2012, "Framework," para. 4.46.

statement and the statement of changes in equity, we had to review the items in that column to classify them properly in financial statements.

A preferred approach is to use separate accounts, as illustrated under the Equity heading in Exhibit 2.2.

Owner Capital records owner investments. The capital account is identified by including the owner's name. The owner's capital account includes transactions in addition to owner investments, as discussed in the following two paragraphs.

Owner withdrawals are recorded in an account with the name of the owner and the word *Withdrawals*. This account is also sometimes called the owner's *Personal* account or *Drawing* account.

Revenues and expenses incurred for a period must be known to decision makers. Businesses use a variety of accounts to report revenues earned and expenses incurred on income statements. Examples of revenue accounts are Sales, Commissions Earned, Professional Fees Earned, Rent Revenue, Earned Subscription Fees, and Interest Earned. Examples of expense accounts are Advertising Expense, Store Supplies Expense, Office Salaries Expense, Office Supplies Expense, Rent Expense, Utilities Expense, and Insurance Expense.

We can get an idea of the variety of revenues by looking at the chart of accounts in Appendix III. It lists accounts needed to solve some of the exercises and problems in this book.[4]

CHECKPOINT

1. Explain the accounting cycle.
2. Classify the following accounts as either assets, liabilities, or equity: (1) Prepaid Rent, (2) Rent Expense, (3) Unearned Rent, (4) Rent Revenue, (5) Buildings, (6) Owner Capital, (7) Wages Payable, (8) Wages Expense, (9) Office Supplies, and (10) Owner Withdrawals.
3. What is the difference between the accounts Rent Earned, Rent Revenue, and Earned Rent?

Do Quick Study question: QS 2-1

T-Account

A **T-account** is a helpful learning tool that represents an account in the ledger. It shows the effects of individual transactions on specific accounts. The T-account is so named because it looks like the letter T. It is shown in Exhibit 2.4.

The format of a T-account includes: (1) the account title on top, (2) a left or debit side, and (3) a right or credit side. Debits and credits are explained in the next section. A T-account provides one side for recording increases in the item and the other side for decreases. As an example, the T-account for Vertically Inclined's Cash account after recording the transactions in Chapter 1 is in Exhibit 2.5.

T-accounts are used throughout this text to help illustrate debits and credits and to solve accounting problems. *This form of account is a learning tool and is typically not used in actual accounting systems. However, many professional accountants often find T-accounts useful for analytical purposes.*

EXHIBIT 2.4

The T-Account

Account Title	
(Left side)	(Right side)
Debit	*Credit*

---

4   Different companies can use account titles different from those listed in Appendix III. For example, a company might use *Interest Revenue* instead of *Interest Earned*, or *Subscription Fees Revenue* or *Subscription Fees Earned* instead of *Earned Subscription Fees*, or *Rental Expense* instead of *Rent Expense*. It is only important that an account title describes the item it represents. We must use our good judgement when reading financial statements since titles can differ even within the same industry.

Balance of an Account

An **account balance** is the difference between the increases and decreases recorded in an account. To determine the balance, we:

1. Calculate the total increases shown on one side (including the beginning balance)
2. Calculate the total decreases shown on the other side
3. Subtract the sum of the decreases from the sum of the increases, and
4. Calculate the account balance.

The total increases in Vertically Inclined's Cash account are $14,100, the total decreases are $5,700, and the account balance is $8,400. The T-account in Exhibit 2.5 shows how we calculate the $8,400 balance:

EXHIBIT 2.5

Calculating the Balance of a T-Account

Cash			
Investment by owner	10,000	2,500	Purchase of supplies
Received from providing		1,000	Payment of rent
consulting services	2,200	700	Payment of salary
Collection of account		900	Payment of account payable
receivable	1,900	600	Withdrawal by owner
Total increases	14,100	5,700	Total decreases
Less decreases	−5,700		
Balance	8,400		

Debits and Credits

LO³ Define debits and credits and explain their role in double-entry accounting.

The left side of a T-account is always called the **debit** side, often abbreviated Dr. The right side is always called the **credit** side, abbreviated Cr.[5] To enter amounts on the left side of an account is to *debit* the account. To enter amounts on the right side is to *credit* the account. The difference between total debits and total credits for an account is the account balance. When the sum of debits exceeds the sum of credits, the account has a *debit balance*.[6] It has a *credit balance* when the sum of credits exceeds the sum of debits.[7] When the sum of debits equals the sum of credits, the account has a zero balance.

This dual method of recording transactions as debits and credits is an essential feature of *double-entry accounting*, and is the topic of the next section.

---

5   These abbreviations are remnants of 18th-century English recordkeeping practices in which the terms *Debitor* and *Creditor* were used instead of *debit* and *credit*. The abbreviations use the first and last letters of these terms where **Dr** resulted from **D**ebito**r**, and **Cr** from **C**reditor, just as we still do for *Saint* (St.) and *Doctor* (Dr.).

6

Office Supplies	
100	60
300	200
Balance 140	

100 + 300 = 400 total debits; 60 + 200 = 260 total credits; debits are greater than credits, so the 140 balance is a debit (400 − 260).

7

Accounts Payable	
350	400
500	600
	150 Balance

350 + 500 = 850 total debits; 400 + 600 = 1,000 total credits; credits are greater than debits, so the 150 balance is a credit (1,000 − 850).

Double-Entry Accounting

Double-entry accounting means every transaction affects and is recorded in at least two accounts. *The total amount debited must equal the total amount credited* for each transaction. Therefore, the sum of the debits for all entries must equal the sum of the credits for all entries. As well, the sum of debit account balances in the ledger must equal the sum of credit account balances. The only reason that the sum of debit balances would not equal the sum of credit balances is if an error had occurred. Double-entry accounting helps to prevent errors by ensuring that debits and credits for each transaction are equal.

The system for recording debits and credits follows from the accounting equation in Exhibit 2.6.

EXHIBIT 2.6

Accounting Equation

Assets are on the left side of this equation. Liabilities and equity are on the right side. Like any mathematical equation, increases or decreases on one side have equal effects on the other side. For example, the net increase in assets must be accompanied by an identical net increase in the liabilities and equity side. Some transactions affect only one side of the equation. This means that two or more accounts on one side are affected, but their net effect on this one side is zero.

The debit and credit effects for asset, liability, and equity accounts are captured in Exhibit 2.7.

EXHIBIT 2.7

Debit and Credit Effects for Accounts

Three important rules for recording transactions in a double-entry accounting system follow from Exhibit 2.7:

1. Increases in assets are debited to asset accounts. Decreases in assets are credited to asset accounts.
2. Increases in liabilities are credited to liability accounts. Decreases in liabilities are debited to liability accounts.
3. Increases in equity are credited to equity accounts. Decreases in equity are debited to equity accounts.

CAUTION: We must guard against the error of thinking that the terms debit and credit mean increase or decrease. In an account where a *debit is an increase*, such as an asset, a credit is a decrease. *But* notice that in an account where a debit is a decrease, such as a liability, a *credit is an increase*.

We explained in Chapter 1 how equity increases with owner investments and revenues and decreases with expenses and owner withdrawals. We can therefore expand the accounting equation and debit and credit effects as shown in Exhibit 2.8.

EXHIBIT 2.8

**Debit and Credit Effects
for Accounts**

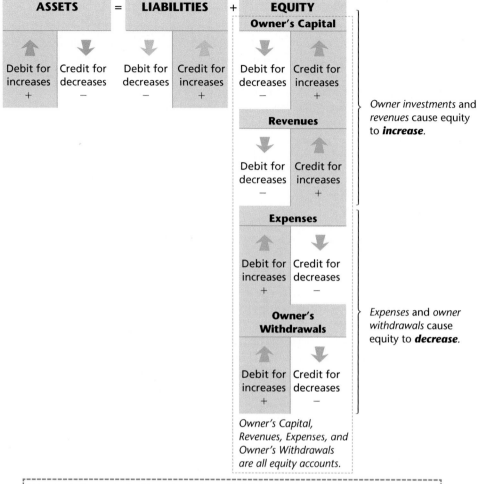

The shaded areas in the T-accounts above highlight the *normal balance* of each type of account. The **normal balance** refers to the debit or credit side where *increases* are recorded. For example, the normal balance for an asset account would be a debit because debits cause assets to increase. The normal balance for a revenue account would be a credit because revenues are increased by credits.

Increases in owner's capital or revenues *increase* equity. Increases in owner's withdrawals or expenses *decrease* equity. These important relations are reflected in the following four additional rules:

4. Investments by the owner are credited to owner's capital because they increase equity.
5. Revenues are credited to revenue accounts because they increase equity.
6. Expenses are debited to expense accounts because they decrease equity.
7. Withdrawals made by the owner are debited to owner's withdrawals because they decrease equity.

Our understanding of these diagrams and rules is crucial to analyzing and recording transactions. This also helps us to prepare and analyze financial statements.[8]

Chart of Accounts

LO⁴ Describe a chart of accounts and its relationship to the ledger.

Recall that the collection of all accounts for an information system is called a *ledger*. The number of accounts needed in the ledger is affected by a company's size and

---

8 We can use good judgement to our advantage in applying double-entry accounting. For example, revenues and expenses normally (but not always) accumulate in business. This means they increase and rarely decrease during an accounting period. Accordingly, we should be alert to decreases in these accounts (debit revenues or credit expenses) to be certain that this is our intent.

diversity of operations. A small company may have as few as 20 accounts, while a large company may need several thousand.

The **chart of accounts** is a list of all accounts used in the ledger by a company. The chart includes an identification number assigned to each account. The chart of accounts in Appendix III of the text uses the following numbering system for its accounts:

101–199	Asset accounts
201–299	Liability accounts
301–399	Owner capital and withdrawals accounts
401–499	Revenue accounts
501–599[9]	Cost of sales expense accounts
601–699	Operating expense accounts

The numbers provide a three-digit code that is useful in recordkeeping. In this case, the first digit assigned to asset accounts is 1, while the first digit assigned to liability accounts is 2, and so on. The first digit of an account's number also shows whether the account appears on the balance sheet or the income statement. The second and subsequent digits may also relate to the accounts' categories. The numerical basis of a chart of accounts is a fundamental component of a computerized accounting system. A partial chart of accounts for Vertically Inclined follows.

Account Number	Account Name	Account Number	Account Name
101	Cash	301	Virgil Klimb, Capital
106	Accounts Receivable	302	Virgil Klimb, Withdrawals
125	Supplies	403	Teaching Revenue
128	Prepaid Insurance	406	Equipment Rental Revenue
167	Equipment	622	Salaries Expense
201	Accounts Payable	641	Rent Expense
236	Unearned Teaching Revenue	690	Utilities Expense
240	Notes Payable		

CHECKPOINT

4. What is the relationship of an account to the ledger and chart of accounts?
5. What determines the quantity and types of accounts used in the ledger by a company?

Do Quick Study questions: QS 2-2, QS 2-3, QS 2-4, QS 2-5, QS 2-6

DECISION INSIGHT

ClubLink Enterprises Limited is engaged in golf club and resort operations, and is Canada's largest owner and operator of golf clubs. Its income statement for the year ended December 31, 2011, showed total revenues of $216,254,000. On the December 31, 2011, balance sheet, there were total assets of $662,132,000, total liabilities of $472,590,000, and total equity of $189,542,000. Although the details of ClubLink's chart of accounts can't be seen on its financial statements, it likely has hundreds of accounts to track its wide range of transactions.

www.clublinkenterprises.com

---

9   Vertically Inclined does not use accounts 501–599. These accounts are used by merchandisers (such as Danier Leather in Appendix II), a topic discussed in Chapter 5.

ANALYZING TRANSACTIONS

LO⁵ Analyze the impact of transactions on accounts.

EYK 2-1

EYK 2-2

We return to the activities of Vertically Inclined to show how debit and credit rules and double-entry accounting are useful in analyzing and processing transactions. We analyze Vertically Inclined's transactions in two steps.

- *Step One* analyzes a transaction and its source document(s).
- *Step Two* applies double-entry accounting to identify the effect of a transaction on account balances.

We should study each transaction thoroughly before proceeding to the next transaction. The first 11 activities are familiar to us from Chapter 1. We expand our analysis of these items and consider four new transactions (numbered 12 through 15) of Vertically Inclined.

1. Investment by owner.

Cash		101
(1)	10,000	

Virgil Klimb, Capital		301
	10,000	(1)

Transaction. Virgil Klimb invested $10,000 in Vertically Inclined on March 1, 2014.
Analysis. Assets increase. Equity increases.
Double-entry. Debit the Cash asset account for $10,000. Credit the Virgil Klimb, Capital account in equity for $10,000.

$A = L + E^{10}$
$\uparrow \qquad \uparrow$

2. Purchase supplies for cash.

Supplies		125
(2)	2,500	

Cash		101
(1)	10,000	2,500	(2)

Transaction. Vertically Inclined purchases supplies by paying $2,500 cash.
Analysis. Assets increase. Assets decrease. This changes the composition of assets, but does not change the total amount of assets.
Double-entry. Debit the Supplies asset account for $2,500. Credit the Cash asset account for $2,500.

$A = L + E$
$\uparrow\downarrow$

3. Purchase equipment and supplies on credit.

Supplies		125
(2)	2,500	
(3)	1,100	

Equipment		167
(3)	6,000	

Accounts Payable		201
	1,100	(3)

Notes Payable		240
	6,000	(3)

Transaction. Vertically Inclined purchases $1,100 of supplies and $6,000 of equipment on credit. Vertically Inclined signs a promissory note for the $6,000 of equipment.
Analysis. Assets increase. Liabilities increase.
Double-entry. Debit two asset accounts: Supplies for $1,100 and Equipment for $6,000. Credit two liability accounts: Accounts Payable for $1,100 and Notes Payable for $6,000.

$A = L + E$
$\uparrow \quad \uparrow$

4. Services rendered for cash.

Cash		101
(1)	10,000	2,500	(2)
(4)	2,200	

Teaching Revenue		403
	2,200	(4)

Transaction. Vertically Inclined provided teaching services to a group of school children and immediately collected $2,200 cash.
Analysis. Assets increase. Equity increases from Revenue.
Double-entry. Debit the Cash asset account for $2,200. Credit the Teaching Revenue account for $2,200 (this increases equity).

$A = L + E$
$\uparrow \qquad \uparrow$

---

10 The effect of each transaction on the accounting equation is repeated here from Chapter 1 to help you transition to debits and credits.

5. Payment of expense in cash.

Rent Expense		641
(5)	1,000	

Cash		101
(1)	10,000	2,500	(2)
(4)	2,200	1,000	(5)

Transaction. Vertically Inclined pays $1,000 cash for March rent.

Analysis. Assets decrease. Equity decreases from Expense.

Double-entry. Debit the Rent Expense account for $1,000 (this decreases equity). Credit the Cash asset account for $1,000.

A = L + E
↓   ↓

6. Payment of expense in cash.

Salaries Expense		622
(6)	700	

Cash		101
(1)	10,000	2,500	(2)
(4)	2,200	1,000	(5)
		700	(6)

Transaction. Vertically Inclined pays $700 cash for employee's salary for the pay period ending on March 14.

Analysis. Assets decrease. Equity decreases from Expense.

Double-entry. Debit the Salaries Expense account for $700 (this decreases equity). Credit the Cash asset account for $700.

A = L + E
↓   ↓

7. Service contract signed for April.

Event. Vertically Inclined signed a contract to teach rock climbing to a group of executives for $2,700 during April.

Analysis. There has been no economic exchange between two parties (the services have not been provided and Vertically Inclined did not receive any assets), therefore this has no effect on the accounting equation.

8. Services and rental revenues rendered on credit.

Accounts Receivable		106
(8)	1,900	

Teaching Revenue		403
	2,200	(4)
	1,600	(8)

Equipment Rental Revenue		406
	300	(8)

Transaction. Vertically Inclined provided teaching services of $1,600 and rented climbing equipment for $300 to a customer. The customer is billed $1,900 for the services and Vertically Inclined expects to collect this money in the near future.

Analysis. Assets increase. Equity increases from Revenue.

Double-entry. Debit the Accounts Receivable asset account for $1,900. Credit two revenue accounts: Teaching Revenue for $1,600 (this increases equity) and Equipment Rental Revenue for $300 (this increases equity).

A = L + E
↑   ↑

9. Receipt of cash on account.

Cash		101
(1)	10,000	2,500	(2)
(4)	2,200	1,000	(5)
(9)	1,900	700	(6)

Accounts Receivable		106
(8)	1,900	1,900	(9)

Transaction. On March 27, an amount of $1,900 is received from the client in Transaction 8.

Analysis. Assets increase. Assets decrease. This changes the composition of assets, but does not change the total amount of assets.

Double-entry. Debit the Cash asset account for $1,900. Credit the Accounts Receivable asset account for $1,900.

A = L + E
↑↓

10. Partial payment of accounts payable.

Accounts Payable			201
(10)	900	1,100	(3)

Cash			101
(1)	10,000	2,500	(2)
(4)	2,200	1,000	(5)
(9)	1,900	700	(6)
		900	(10)

Transaction. Vertically Inclined pays CanTech Supply $900 cash toward the account payable of $1,100 owed from the purchase of supplies in Transaction 4.
Analysis. Assets decrease. Liabilities decrease.
Double-entry. Debit the Accounts Payable liability account for $900. Credit the Cash asset account for $900.

$A = L + E$
$\downarrow \quad \downarrow$

11. Withdrawal of cash by owner.

Virgil Klimb, Withdrawals			302
(11)	600		

Cash			101
(1)	10,000	2,500	(2)
(4)	2,200	1,000	(5)
(9)	1,900	700	(6)
		900	(10)
		600	(11)

Transaction. Virgil Klimb withdraws $600 from Vertically Inclined for personal living expenses.
Analysis. Assets decrease. Equity decreases.
Double-entry. Debit the Virgil Klimb, Withdrawals account in equity for $600. Credit the Cash asset account for $600.

$A = L + E$
$\downarrow \qquad \downarrow$

12. Receipt of cash for future services.

Cash			101
(1)	10,000	2,500	(2)
(4)	2,200	1,000	(5)
(9)	1,900	700	(6)
(12)	3,000	900	(10)
		600	(11)

Unearned Teaching Revenue			236
		3,000	(12)

Transaction. Vertically Inclined enters into (signs) a contract with a customer to provide future indoor rock climbing lessons. Vertically Inclined receives $3,000 cash in advance of providing these teaching services.
Analysis. Assets increase. Liabilities increase. Accepting the $3,000 cash obligates Vertically Inclined to perform future services, and is a liability. No revenue is earned until services are provided.
Double-entry. Debit the Cash asset account for $3,000. Credit the Unearned Teaching Revenue liability account for $3,000.

$A = L + E$
$\uparrow \quad \uparrow$

13. Payment of cash for future insurance coverage.

Prepaid Insurance			128
(13)	2,400		

Cash			101
(1)	10,000	2,500	(2)
(4)	2,200	1,000	(5)
(9)	1,900	700	(6)
(12)	3,000	900	(10)
		600	(11)
		2,400	(13)

Transaction. Vertically Inclined pays $2,400 cash (premium) for a two-year insurance policy. Coverage begins on March 1.
Analysis. Assets increase. Assets decrease. This changes the composition of assets from cash to a "right" of insurance coverage. This does not change the total amount of assets. Expense will be incurred as insurance coverage is provided.
Double-entry. Debit the Prepaid Insurance asset account for $2,400. Credit the Cash asset account for $2,400.

$A = L + E$
$\uparrow\downarrow$

14. Payment of expense in cash.

Utilities Expense		690
(14)	230	

	Cash		101
(1)	10,000	2,500	(2)
(4)	2,200	1,000	(5)
(9)	1,900	700	(6)
(12)	3,000	900	(10)
		600	(11)
		2,400	(13)
		230	(14)

Transaction. Vertically Inclined pays $230 cash for March utilities.
Analysis. Assets decrease. Equity decreases from Expense.
Double-entry. Debit the Utilities Expense account for $230 (this decreases equity). Credit the Cash asset account for $230.

$A = L + E$
$\downarrow \qquad \downarrow$

15. Payment of expense in cash.

Salaries Expense		622
(6)	700	
(15)	700	

	Cash		101
(1)	10,000	2,500	(2)
(4)	2,200	1,000	(5)
(9)	1,900	700	(6)
(12)	3,000	900	(10)
		600	(11)
		2,400	(13)
		230	(14)
		700	(15)

Transaction. Vertically Inclined pays $700 cash for employee's salary for the two-week pay period ending on March 28.
Analysis. Assets decrease. Equity decreases from Expense.
Double-entry. Debit the Salaries Expense account for $700 (this decreases equity). Credit the Cash asset account for $700.

$A = L + E$
$\downarrow \qquad \downarrow$

ACCOUNTING EQUATION ANALYSIS

Exhibit 2.9 shows Vertically Inclined's accounts in the ledger after all March transactions are recorded and the balances calculated. For emphasis, the accounts are grouped into three major columns representing the terms in the accounting equation: assets, liabilities, and equity.

DECISION MAKER Answer—End of chapter

Accounting Clerk
You recently got a job as a part-time accounting clerk to earn extra cash while you attend college. Today, your employer, the owner of the business, made some purchases and instructed you to debit Office Supplies and credit Accounts Payable for the entire amount. He tells you that the invoice is for a few office supplies but mainly for some items that he needed for personal use at home. Explain which GAAP is being violated, and the impact of this error on the financial statements of the business.

EXHIBIT 2.9

Ledger for Vertically Inclined at March 31, 2014

Assets				=	Liabilities			+	Equity		

Cash   101

(1)	10,000	2,500	(2)
(4)	2,200	1,000	(5)
(9)	1,900	700	(6)
(12)	3,000	900	(10)
		600	(11)
		2,400	(13)
		230	(14)
		700	(15)
Balance	8,070		

Accounts Receivable   106

(8)	1,900	1,900	(9)
Balance	0		

Supplies   125

(2)	2,500	
(3)	1,100	
Balance	3,600	

Prepaid Insurance   128

(13)	2,400	
Balance	2,400	

Equipment   167

(3)	6,000	
Balance	6,000	

Accounts Payable   201

(10)	900	1,100	(3)
		200	Balance

Unearned Teaching Revenue   236

	3,000	(12)
	3,000	Balance

Notes Payable   240

	6,000	(3)
	6,000	Balance

Virgil Klimb, Capital   301

	10,000	(1)
	10,000	Balance

Virgil Klimb, Withdrawals   302

(11)	600		
Balance	600		

Teaching Revenue   403

	2,200	(4)
	1,600	(8)
	3,800	Balance

Equipment Rental Revenue   406

	300	(8)
	300	Balance

Salaries Expense   622

(6)	700	
(15)	700	
Balance	1,400	

Rent Expense   641

(5)	1,000	
Balance	1,000	

> Accounts in the white area reflect increases and decreases in equity. Their balances are reported on the income statement or the statement of changes in equity.

Utilities Expense   690

(14)	230	
Balance	230	

TOTALS:	**$20,070[1]**	=	**$9,200[2]**	+	**$10,870[3]**

[1] $8,070 + $0 + $3,600 + $2,400 + $6,000 = $20,070
[2] $200 + $3,000 + $6,000 = $9,200
[3] $10,000 − $600 + $3,800 + $300 − $1,400 − $1,000 − $230 = $10,870

Exhibit 2.9 highlights three important points.

1. The totals for the three columns show that the accounting equation is in balance:

Assets $20,070	=	Liabilities $9,200	+	Equity $10,870

2. The owner's investment is recorded in the capital account and the withdrawals, revenue, and expense accounts reflect the transactions that change equity. Their ending balances make up the statement of changes in equity.

3. The revenue and expense account balances are summarized and reported in the income statement.

EYK
2-3

CHECKPOINT

6. Does debit always mean increase and credit always mean decrease?
7. What kinds of transactions increase equity? What kinds decrease equity?
8. Why are most accounting systems called *double-entry*?
9. Double-entry accounting requires that (select the best answer):
   a. All transactions that create debits to asset accounts must create credits to liability or equity accounts.
   b. A transaction that requires a debit to a liability account also requires a credit to an asset account.
   c. Every transaction must be recorded with total debits equal to total credits.

Do Quick Study questions: QS 2-7, QS 2-8

MID-CHAPTER DEMONSTRATION PROBLEM

Kara Morris founded her dream business, called Kara's Kiteboarding Adventures. The following transactions occurred during June 2014, her first month of operations.

a. Kara invested $15,000 cash into the business on June 1.

b. Kara's Kiteboarding purchased $12,000 worth of kiteboarding equipment on credit.

c. The business rented additional kiteboarding equipment for $1,500 on account.

d. Kara's Kiteboarding paid $400 to cover insurance for the month of June.

e. The business provided lessons to a group of clients for $3,500 on account.

f. The business collected $2,000 from its credit customers.

g. The kiteboarding equipment purchased on credit was paid for today.

Required

1. Open the following T-accounts: Cash; Accounts Receivable; Equipment; Accounts Payable; Kara Morris, Capital; Teaching Revenue; Insurance Expense; Equipment Rental Expense.
2. Post the June entries directly into the T-accounts.

Analysis Component:
Using your answer in Part 2, prove that the accounting equation balances at the end of June.

SOLUTION

1 and 2.

Cash			
(a)	15,000	400	(d)
(f)	2,000	12,000	(g)
(Bal.)	4,600		

Accounts Receivable			
(e)	3,500	2,000	(f)
(Bal.)	1,500		

Equipment			
(b)	12,000		

Accounts Payable			
(g)	12,000	12,000	(b)
		1,500	(c)
		1,500	(Bal.)

Kara Morris, Capital		
	15,000	(a)

Teaching Revenue		
	3,500	(e)

Insurance Expense		
(d)	400	

Equipment Rental Expense		
(c)	1,500	

Analysis Component:

Total assets   = Cash 4,600 + Accounts Receivable 1,500 + Equipment 12,000 = 18,100
Total liabilities   = Accounts Payable 1,500
Total equity   = Kara Morris, Capital 15,000 + Teaching Revenue 3,500 − Insurance Expense 400 − Equipment Rental Expense 1,500 = 16,600

Assets 18,100   = Liabilities 1,500 + Equity 16,600
18,100   = 18,100

RECORDING AND POSTING TRANSACTIONS

LO⁶ Record transactions in a journal and post entries to a ledger.

In the previous section, we analyzed transactions, *Step One* of the accounting cycle, and recorded their effects directly in T-accounts to help you understand the double-entry accounting system. Yet accounting systems rarely record transactions directly in accounts. Instead, *Step Two* of the accounting cycle requires that we record transactions in a record called a **journal** before recording them in accounts. This is to avoid the potential for error and the difficulty in tracking mistakes. A journal gives us a complete record of each transaction in one place. It also directly links the debits and credits for each transaction. The process of recording transactions in a journal is called **journalizing**.

Step Three of the accounting cycle is to **post**, or transfer, entries from the journal to the ledger. ***Posting occurs after debits and credits for each transaction are entered into a journal***. This process leaves a helpful trail that can be followed in checking for accuracy. This section describes both journalizing and posting of transactions. *Step Four* of the accounting cycle, preparing a *trial balance*, is explained in the next section. Each of these steps in processing transactions is shown in Exhibit 2.10.

EXHIBIT 2.10

First Four Steps of the Accounting Cycle

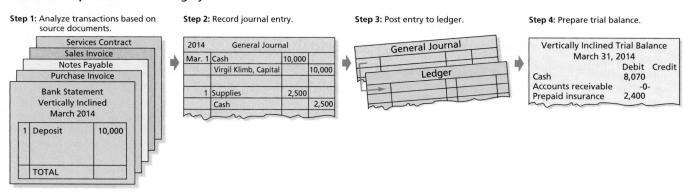

The Journal Entry

The **General Journal** is flexible in that it can be used to record any economic transaction. A General Journal entry includes the following information about each transaction:

1. Date of transaction
2. Titles of affected accounts
3. Dollar amount of each debit and credit
4. Explanation of transaction

Exhibit 2.11 shows how the first three transactions of Vertically Inclined are recorded in a General Journal. A journal is often referred to as the *book of original entry*. Although businesses use computerized systems, this textbook will demonstrate the accounting processes of journalizing and posting using a manual system. Computerized journals and ledgers all operate on the same bases and processes as manual systems.

The third entry in Exhibit 2.11 uses four accounts. There are debits to the two assets purchased, Supplies and Equipment. There are also credits to the two sources of payment, Accounts Payable and Notes Payable. A transaction affecting three or more accounts is called a **compound journal entry**.

EXHIBIT 2.11

Partial General Journal for Vertically Inclined

General Journal				Page 1
Date	Account Titles and Explanation	PR	Debit	Credit
2014				
Mar. 1	Cash		10,000	
	Virgil Klimb, Capital			10,000
	Investment by owner.			
1	Supplies		2,500	
	Cash			2,500
	Purchased store supplies for cash.			
1	Supplies		1,100	
	Equipment		6,000	
	Accounts Payable			1,100
	Notes Payable			6,000
	Purchased supplies and equipment			
	on credit.			

Journalizing Transactions

We can identify nine steps in journalizing entries in a General Journal. Review the entries in Exhibit 2.11 when studying these steps.

1. Enter the year on the first line at the top of the first column.

2. Enter the month in Column One on the first line of the journal entry. Later entries for the same month and year on the same page of the journal do not require re-entering the same month and year.

3. Enter the day of the transaction in Column Two on the first line of each entry. Transactions are journalized in date order.

4. Enter the titles of accounts debited. Account titles are taken from the chart of accounts and are aligned with the left margin of the Account Titles and Explanation column.

5. Enter the debit amounts in the Debit column on the same line as the accounts to be debited.

6. Enter the titles of accounts credited. Account titles are taken from the chart of accounts and are indented from the left margin of the Account Titles and Explanation column to distinguish them from debited accounts (an indent of 1 cm is common).

7. Enter the credit amounts in the Credit column on the same line as the accounts to be credited.

8. Enter a brief explanation of the transaction on the line below the entry. This explanation is indented about half as far as the credited account titles to avoid confusing an explanation with accounts. For illustrative purposes, the textbook italicizes explanations so they stand out. This is not normally done.

9. Skip a line after each journal entry for clarity.

A complete journal entry gives us a useful description of the transaction and its effects on the organization.

The **posting reference (PR) column** is left blank when a transaction is initially recorded. Individual account numbers are later entered into the PR column when entries are posted to the ledger.

Computerized systems include error-checking routines that ensure that debits equal credits for each entry. Shortcuts often allow recordkeepers to enter account numbers instead of names, and to enter account names and numbers with pull-down menus.

Balance Column Ledger

T-accounts are a simple and direct learning tool to show how the accounting process works. They allow us to omit less relevant details and concentrate on main ideas. Accounting systems in practice need more structure and use **balance column ledger accounts**. Exhibit 2.12 is an example.

EXHIBIT 2.12

Cash Account in Balance Column Ledger

Cash						Account No. 101
Date		Explanation	PR	Debit	Credit	Balance
2014						
Mar.	1		G1	10,000		10,000
	1		G1		2,500	7,500
	10		G1	2,200		9,700

The T-account was derived from the balance column ledger account format and it too has a column for debits and a column for credits. Look at the imaginary T-account superimposed over Exhibit 2.12. The balance column ledger account is different from a T-account because it includes a transaction's date and explanation and has a third column with the balance of the account after each entry is posted. This means that the amount on the last line in this column is the account's current balance. For example, Vertically Inclined's Cash account in Exhibit 2.12 is debited on March 1 for the $10,000 investment by Virgil Klimb. The account then shows a $10,000 debit balance. The account is also credited on March 1 for $2,500, and its new $7,500 balance is shown in the third column. The Cash account is debited for $2,200 on March 10, and its balance increases to a $9,700 debit.

When a balance column ledger is used, the heading of the Balance column does not show whether it is a debit or credit balance. This omission is no problem because every account has a normal balance, as previously highlighted in Exhibit 2.8.

Abnormal Balance

Unusual transactions can sometimes give an abnormal balance to an account. An *abnormal balance* refers to a balance on the side where decreases are recorded. For example, a customer might mistakenly overpay a bill. This gives that customer's account receivable an abnormal credit balance.[11]

Zero Balance

A zero balance for an account is usually shown by writing zeros or a dash in the Balance column. This practice avoids confusion between a zero balance and one omitted in error.

---

11 Assume a customer overpaid an account, causing an abnormal balance. To highlight this, brackets can be used as illustrated below or the value could be shown in red.

Accounts Receivable						Account No. 106
Date		Explanation	PR	Debit	Credit	Balance
2014						
May	1		G1	100		100
	15		G6		125	(25)

Posting Journal Entries

To ensure that the ledger is up to date, entries are posted as soon as possible. This might be daily, weekly, or monthly. All entries must be posted to the ledger by the end of a reporting period. This is so that account balances are current when financial statements are prepared. Because the ledger is the final destination for individual transactions, it is referred to as the *book of final entry*.

When posting entries to the ledger, the debits in journal entries are copied into ledger accounts as debits, and credits are copied into the ledger as credits. To demonstrate the posting process, Exhibit 2.13 lists six steps to post each debit and credit from a journal entry.

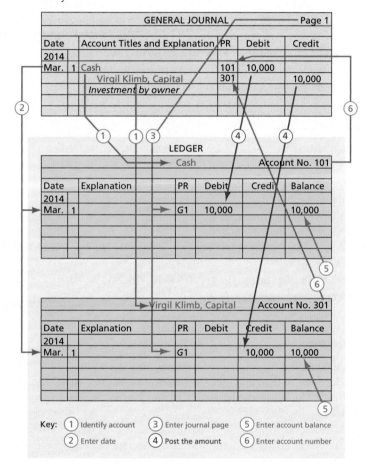

EXHIBIT 2.13

Posting an Entry to the Ledger

EYK

2-4

For each journal entry, the usual process is to post debit(s) and then credit(s). The steps in posting are:

(1) Identify the ledger account that was debited in the journal entry.

(2) Enter the date of the journal entry in this ledger account.

(3) Enter the source of the debit in the PR column, both the journal and page. The letter G shows it came from the General Journal.[12]

(4) Enter the amount debited from the journal entry into the Debit column of the ledger account.

(5) Calculate and enter the account's new balance in the Balance column.

(6) Enter the ledger account number in the PR column of the journal entry.

---

12 Other journals are identified by their own letters. We discuss other journals later in the book.

Repeat the six steps for credit amounts and Credit columns. Notice that posting does not create new information; posting simply transfers (or copies) information from the General Journal to the appropriate account in the ledger.

Step Six in the posting process for both debit and credit amounts of an entry inserts the account number in the journal's PR column. This creates a cross-reference between the ledger and the journal entry for tracing an amount from one record to another.

Posting in Computerized Systems

Computerized systems require no added effort to post journal entries to the ledger. These systems automatically transfer debit and credit entries from the journal to the ledger database. Journal entries are posted directly to ledger accounts. Many systems have programs that test the reasonableness of a journal entry and the account balance when recorded. For example, a payroll program might alert a preparer to hourly wage rates that are greater than $100.

CHECKPOINT

10. Assume Maria Sanchez, the owner of a new business called RecordLink, invested $15,000 cash and equipment with a market value of $23,000. Assume that RecordLink also took responsibility for an $18,000 note payable issued to finance the purchase of equipment. Prepare the journal entry to record Sanchez's investment.

11. Explain what a compound journal entry is.

12. Why are posting reference numbers entered in the journal when entries are posted to accounts?

Do Quick Study questions: QS 2-9, QS 2-10, QS 2-11

Trial Balance

LO7 Prepare and explain the use of a trial balance.

Double-entry accounting records every transaction with equal debits and credits. An error exists if the sum of debit entries in the ledger does not equal the sum of credit entries. The sum of debit account balances must always equal the sum of credit account balances.

Step Four of the accounting cycle shown in Exhibit 2.1 requires the preparation of a trial balance to check whether debit and credit account balances are equal. A **trial balance** is a list of accounts and their balances at a point in time. Account balances are reported in the debit or credit column of the trial balance. Exhibit 2.14 shows the trial balance for Vertically Inclined after the entries described earlier in the chapter are posted to the ledger.

Another use of the trial balance is as an internal report for preparing financial statements. Preparing statements is easier when we can take account balances from a trial balance instead of searching the ledger. The preparation of financial statements using a trial balance is illustrated in the End-of-Chapter Demonstration Problem. We expand on this process in Chapter 3.

Vertically Inclined Rock Gym Trial Balance March 31, 2014			
Acct. No.	Account	Debit	Credit
101	Cash	$ 8,070	
106	Accounts receivable	-0-	
125	Supplies	3,600	
128	Prepaid insurance	2,400	
167	Equipment	6,000	
201	Accounts payable		$ 200
236	Unearned teaching revenue		3,000
240	Notes payable		6,000
301	Virgil Klimb, capital		10,000
302	Virgil Klimb, withdrawals	600	
403	Teaching revenue		3,800
406	Equipment rental revenue		300
622	Salaries expense	1,400	
641	Rent expense	1,000	
690	Utilities expense	230	
	Totals	$23,300	$23,300

EXHIBIT 2.14

Trial Balance

Preparing a Trial Balance

Preparing a trial balance involves five steps:

1. Identify each account balance from the ledger.
2. List each account and its balance (in the same order as the Chart of Accounts). Debit balances are entered in the Debit column and credit balances in the Credit column.[13]
3. Calculate the total of debit balances.
4. Calculate the total of credit balances.
5. Verify that total debit balances equal total credit balances.

EYK
2-5

Notice that the total debit balance equals the total credit balance for the trial balance in Exhibit 2.14. If these two totals were not equal, we would know that one or more errors exist. Equality of these two totals does ***not*** guarantee the absence of errors.

Using a Trial Balance

We know that one or more errors exist when a trial balance does not *balance* (when its columns are not equal). When one or more errors exist, they often arise from one of the following steps in the accounting process:

1. Preparing journal entries
2. Posting entries to the ledger
3. Calculating account balances
4. Copying account balances to the trial balance
5. Totalling the trial balance columns

---

13 If an account has a zero balance, it can be listed in the trial balance with a zero in the column for its
   normal balance.

When a trial balance does balance, the accounts are likely free of the kinds of errors that create unequal debits and credits. Yet errors can still exist. One example is when a debit or credit of a correct amount is made to a wrong account. This can occur when either journalizing or posting. The error would produce incorrect balances in two accounts but the trial balance would balance. Another error is to record equal debits and credits of an incorrect amount. This error produces incorrect balances in two accounts but again the debits and credits are equal. We give these examples to show that when a trial balance does balance, it does not prove that all journal entries are recorded and posted correctly.

In a computerized accounting system, the trial balance would **always** balance. Accounting software is such that unbalanced entries would not be accepted by the system. However, errors as described in the last paragraph can still exist in a computerized system.

Searching for Errors

When performing accounting manually, if the trial balance does not balance, the error (or errors) must be found and corrected before financial statements are prepared. To search for the error, we check the journalizing, posting, and trial balance preparation process in *reverse order*. Otherwise we would need to look at every transaction until the error was found. The steps involved are:

1. Verify that the trial balance columns are correctly added. If this fails to show the error, then
2. Verify that account balances are accurately copied from the ledger.
3. Determine if a debit or credit balance is mistakenly listed in the trial balance as a credit or debit. Look for this when the difference between total debits and total credits in the trial balance equals twice the amount of the incorrect account balance.
4. Recalculate each account balance. If the error remains, then
5. Verify that each journal entry is properly posted to ledger accounts.
6. Verify that the original journal entry has equal debits and credits.

One frequent error is called a **transposition error**, in which two digits are switched or transposed within a number (e.g., 619 instead of 691). Another type of error, a **slide**,[14] occurs when adding or deleting a zero (or zeros) in a value (e.g., 32 instead of 320). If transposition or a slide is the only error, then the difference between the totals of the trial balance columns will be *evenly divisible by 9*. For example, to find a transposition error:

1. Subtract total debits in the trial balance from total credits.
   Based on the transposition given above, the difference between total debits and credits is $72 ($691 − $619).
2. Divide the difference by 9.
   $72 ÷ 9 = 8
3. The quotient equals the difference between the two transposed numbers.
   8 is the difference between '9' and '1' in both '91' of '691' and '19' of '619.'
4. The number of digits in the quotient tells us the location of the transposition.
   The quotient of 8 is only one digit, so the transposition can be found by checking the first digit from the right in each number.[15]

---

14 To find a slide error, follow steps 1 and 2 for a transposition error. The quotient resulting from step 2 identifies the correct value (the incorrect value +/− the correct zeros).

15 Consider another example where a transposition error involves posting $961 instead of the correct $691. The difference in these numbers is $270, and its quotient is $30 ($270/9). Because the quotient has two digits, it tells us to check the second digits from the right for a transposition of two numbers that have a difference of 3.

Formatting Conventions

Dollar signs are *not* used in journals and ledgers. They *do* appear in financial statements and other reports, including trial balances, to identify the kind of currency being used. This book follows the usual practice of putting a dollar sign beside the first amount in each column of numbers and the first amount appearing after a ruled line that indicates that an addition or subtraction has been performed. The financial statements in Exhibit 1.15 demonstrate how dollar signs are used in this book. Different companies use various conventions for dollar signs.

When amounts are entered manually in a formal journal, ledger, or trial balance, commas are not needed to indicate thousands, millions, and so forth. Also, decimal points are not needed to separate dollars and cents. If an amount consists of even dollars without cents, a convenient shortcut uses a dash in the cents column instead of two zeros. However, commas and decimal points are used in financial statements and other reports. An exception is when this detail is not important to users.

It is common for companies to round amounts to the nearest dollar, and to an even higher level for certain accounts. **WestJet** is typical of many companies in that it rounds its financial statement amounts to the nearest thousand dollars.

CHECKPOINT

13. If a $4,000 debit to Equipment in a journal entry is incorrectly posted as a $4,000 credit to the Equipment account in the ledger, what is the effect of this error on the trial balance column totals, assuming no other errors?

14. When are dollar signs typically used in accounting reports?

Do Quick Study questions: QS 2-12, QS 2-13, QS 2-14, QS 2-15

CRITICAL THINKING CHALLENGE Refer to the Critical Thinking Challenge questions at the beginning of the chapter. Compare your answers to those suggested on Connect.

IFRS AND ASPE—THE DIFFERENCES

Difference	International Financial Reporting Standards (IFRS)	Accounting Standards for Private Enterprises (ASPE)
Financial statement elements	• The level of account detail for expenses must allow the income statement to show the nature and/or function of expenses incurred for the purpose of providing relevant information to financial statement users.* The nature vs. function of an expense is discussed in greater detail in Chapter 5.	• No minimum level of account detail is prescribed for expenses under ASPE.

*IFRS 2012, IAS 1, para. 99–105.

SUMMARY

LO¹ Explain the accounting cycle. The accounting cycle includes the steps in preparing financial statements for users that are repeated each reporting period.

LO² Describe an account, its use, and its relationship to the ledger. An account is a detailed record of increases and decreases in a specific asset, liability, or equity item. Information is taken from accounts, analyzed, summarized, and presented in useful reports and financial statements for users.

LO³ Define debits and credits and explain their role in double-entry accounting. Debit refers to left, and credit refers to right. The following table summarizes debit and credit effects by account type:

	Assets	= Liabilities +		Equity		
			Owner's Capital	Owner's Withdrawals	Revenues	Expenses
Increases	Debits	Credits	Credits	Debits	Credits	Debits
Decreases	Credits	Debits	Debits	Credits	Debits	Credits

Double-entry accounting means that every transaction affects at least two accounts. The total amount debited must equal the total amount credited for each transaction. The system for recording debits and credits follows from the accounting equation. The debit side is the normal balance for assets, owner's withdrawals, and expenses, and the credit side is the normal balance for liabilities, owner's capital, and revenues.

LO⁴ Describe a chart of accounts and its relationship to the ledger. A ledger is a record that contains all accounts used by a company. This is what is referred to as *the books*. The chart of accounts is a listing of all accounts and usually includes an identification number that is assigned to each account.

LO⁵ Analyze the impact of transactions on accounts. We analyze transactions using the concepts of double-entry accounting. This analysis is performed by determining a transaction's effects on accounts. These effects are recorded in journals and posted to accounts in the ledger.

LO⁶ Record transactions in a journal and post entries to a ledger. We record transactions in a journal to give a record of their effects. Each entry in a journal is posted to the accounts in the ledger. This provides information in accounts that is used to produce financial statements. Balance column ledger accounts are widely used and include columns for debits, credits, and the account balance after each entry.

LO⁷ Prepare and explain the use of a trial balance. A trial balance is a list of accounts in the ledger showing their debit and credit balances in separate columns. The trial balance is a convenient summary of the ledger's contents and is useful in preparing financial statements. It reveals errors of the kind that produce unequal debit and credit account balances.

GUIDANCE ANSWER TO **DECISION MAKER**

Accounting Clerk
The business entity principle is being violated because it requires that the owner's personal expenses be recorded separately from those of his business. By debiting the entire amount to Office Supplies, assets will be overstated on the balance sheet. By crediting Accounts Payable for the whole amount, liabilities will also be overstated. At the end of the accounting period when the amount of supplies used is recorded, Office Supplies Expense will be overstated on the income statement, causing net income to be understated. When net income is too low, equity is also understated.

GUIDANCE ANSWERS TO **CHECKPOINT**

1. The accounting cycle represents the steps followed each reporting period for the purpose of preparing financial statements.

2.
Assets	Liabilities	Equity
1, 5, 9	3, 7	2, 4, 6, 8, 10

3. The difference between the three accounts is in the name only; they are variations of a revenue account for rent.

4. An account is a record in the ledger where increases and decreases in a specific asset, liability, or equity item are recorded and stored. A ledger is a collection of all accounts used by a business. A chart of accounts is a numerical list of the accounts in the ledger. The numbers represent whether the account is an asset, liability, or type of equity.

5. A company's size and diversity affect the number of accounts needed in its ledger. The types of accounts used by a business depend on information that the business needs both to operative effectively and to report its activities in financial statements.

6. No. Debit and credit both can mean increase or decrease. The particular meaning depends on the type of account.

7. Equity is increased by revenues and owner's investments in the company. Equity is decreased by expenses and owner's withdrawals.

8. The name *double-entry* is used because all transactions affect and are recorded in at least two accounts. There must be at least one debit in one account and at least one credit in another.

9. c

10. The entry is:

Cash	15,000	
Equipment	23,000	
Notes Payable		18,000
Maria Sanchez, Capital		20,000

11. A compound journal entry is one that affects three or more accounts.

12. Posting reference numbers are entered in the journal when posting to the ledger as a control over the posting process. They provide a cross-reference that allows the bookkeeper or auditor to trace debits and credits from journals to ledgers and vice versa.

13. This error, if uncorrected, will cause the trial balance's debit column total to be understated by $8,000.

14. Dollar signs are used in financial statements and other reports to identify the kind of currency being used in the reports. At a minimum, they are placed beside the first and last numbers in each column. Some companies place dollar signs beside any amount that appears after a ruled line to indicate that an addition or subtraction has taken place.

DEMONSTRATION PROBLEM

This Demonstration Problem is based on the same facts as the Demonstration Problem at the end of Chapter 1 except for two additional items: (b) August 1 and (k) August 18. The following activities occurred during the first month of Joane Cardinal's new haircutting business called The Cutlery:

a. On August 1, Cardinal put $16,000 cash into a chequing account in the name of The Cutlery. She also invested $10,000 of equipment that she already owned.

b. On August 1, Cardinal paid $2,400 for six months of insurance effective immediately.

c. On August 2, she paid $2,000 cash for furniture for the shop.

d. On August 3, she paid $3,200 cash to rent space in a strip mall for August.

e. On August 4, she furnished the shop by installing the old equipment and some new equipment that she bought on credit for $21,000. This amount is to be repaid in three equal payments at the end of August, September, and October.

f. On August 5, The Cutlery opened for business. Cash receipts from haircutting services provided in the first week and a half of business (ended August 15) were $1,100.

g. On August 15, Cardinal provided haircutting services on account for $750.

h. On August 17, Cardinal received a $750 cheque in the mail for services previously rendered on account.

i. On August 17, Cardinal paid $250 to an assistant for working during the grand opening.

j. On August 18, Cardinal interviewed a job applicant. The applicant was successful in getting the position and will receive $750 per week for part-time work starting in September.

k. On August 18, a regular customer paid $500 for services to be provided over the next three months.

l. Cash receipts from haircutting services provided during the second half of August were $1,950.

m. On August 31, Cardinal paid an installment on the account payable created in (e) above.

n. On August 31, the August hydro bill for $450 was received. It will be paid on September 14.

o. On August 31, she withdrew $500 cash for her personal use.

Required

1. Prepare General Journal entries for the preceding transactions.
2. Open the following accounts: Cash, 101; Accounts Receivable, 106; Prepaid Insurance, 128; Furniture, 161; Store Equipment, 165; Accounts Payable, 201; Unearned Haircutting Services Revenue, 236; Joane Cardinal, Capital, 301; Joane Cardinal, Withdrawals, 302; Haircutting Services Revenue, 403; Wages Expense, 623; Rent Expense, 640; and Hydro Expense, 690.
3. Post the journal entries to the ledger accounts.
4. Prepare a trial balance as of August 31, 2014.
5. Prepare an income statement and a statement of changes in equity for the month ended August 31, 2014, and a balance sheet at August 31, 2014.

Analysis Component:

Refer to The Cutlery's August 31, 2014, financial statements. What do each of *equity* and *liabilities* represent?

Planning the Solution

*   Analyze each activity to determine if it is a transaction.
*   For each transaction, identify the accounts affected and the amount of each effect.
*   Use the debit and credit rules to prepare a journal entry for each transaction.
*   Post each debit and each credit in the journal entries to the appropriate ledger accounts and cross-reference each amount in the Posting Reference columns in the journal and account.
*   Calculate each account balance and list the accounts with their balances on a trial balance.
*   Verify that the total debits in the trial balance equal total credits.
*   Prepare an income statement, statement of changes in equity, and balance sheet using the information in the trial balance.
*   Prepare an answer to each part of the *analysis component* question.

SOLUTION

1. General Journal entries:

Date	General Journal Account Titles and Explanations	PR	Debit	Page G1 Credit
2014 Aug. 1	Cash	101	16,000	
	Store Equipment....................................	165	10,000	
	Joane Cardinal, Capital	301		26,000
	Owner's initial investment.			
1	Prepaid Insurance..................................	128	2,400	
	Cash...	101		2,400
	Purchased six months of insurance.			
2	Furniture	161	2,000	
	Cash...	101		2,000
	Purchased furniture for cash.			
3	Rent Expense..	640	3,200	
	Cash...	101		3,200
	Paid rent for August.			
4	Store Equipment....................................	165	21,000	
	Accounts Payable...........................	201		21,000
	Purchased additional equipment on credit.			
15	Cash	101	1,100	
	Haircutting Services Revenue	403		1,100
	Cash receipts from 10 days of operations.			
15	Accounts Receivable	106	750	
	Haircutting Services Revenue	403		750
	To record revenue for services provided on account.			
17	Cash	101	750	
	Accounts Receivable	106		750
	To record cash received as payment on account.			
17	Wages Expense....................................	623	250	
	Cash...	101		250
	Paid wages to assistant.			
18	No entry required since there has been no economic exchange.			
18	Cash	101	500	
	Unearned Haircutting Services Revenue	236		500
	To record payment in advance.			
31	Cash	101	1,950	
	Haircutting Services Revenue	403		1,950
	Cash receipts from second half of August.			
31	Accounts Payable...................................	201	7,000	
	Cash...	101		7,000
	Paid an installment on accounts payable.			
31	Hydro Expense	690	450	
	Accounts Payable...........................	201		450
	August hydro to be paid by Sept. 14.			
31	Joane Cardinal, Withdrawals.................................	302	500	
	Cash...	101		500
	Owner withdrew cash from the business.			

2. & 3. Accounts in the ledger:

Cash						Account No. 101
Date		Explanation	PR	Debit	Credit	Balance
2014						
Aug.	1		G1	16,000		16,000
	1		G1		2,400	13,600
	2		G1		2,000	11,600
	3		G1		3,200	8,400
	15		G1	1,100		9,500
	17		G1	750		10,250
	17		G1		250	10,000
	18		G1	500		10,500
	31		G1	1,950		12,450
	31		G1		7,000	5,450
	31		G1		500	4,950

Accounts Receivable						Account No. 106
Date		Explanation	PR	Debit	Credit	Balance
2014						
Aug.	15		G1	750		750
	17		G1		750	-0-

Prepaid Insurance						Account No. 128
Date		Explanation	PR	Debit	Credit	Balance
2014						
Aug.	1		G1	2,400		2,400

Furniture						Account No. 161
Date		Explanation	PR	Debit	Credit	Balance
2014						
Aug.	2		G1	2,000		2,000

Store Equipment						Account No. 165
Date		Explanation	PR	Debit	Credit	Balance
2014						
Aug.	1		G1	10,000		10,000
	4		G1	21,000		31,000

Accounts Payable						Account No. 201
Date		Explanation	PR	Debit	Credit	Balance
2014						
Aug.	4		G1		21,000	21,000
	31		G1	7,000		14,000
	31		G1		450	14,450

Note: The T-account has been superimposed on each balance column ledger account for illustrative purposes only. It emphasizes that using T-accounts will produce identical balances to the balance column ledger account but in a shortened form. This shortened form is what makes the T-account a convenient tool.

2. & 3.

Unearned Haircutting Services Revenue — Account No. 236

Date		Explanation	PR	Debit	Credit	Balance
2014 Aug.	18		G1		500	500

Joane Cardinal, Capital — Account No. 301

Date		Explanation	PR	Debit	Credit	Balance
2014 Aug.	1		G1		26,000	26,000

Joane Cardinal, Withdrawals — Account No. 302

Date		Explanation	PR	Debit	Credit	Balance
2014 Aug.	31		G1	500		500

Haircutting Services Revenue — Account No. 403

Date		Explanation	PR	Debit	Credit	Balance
2014 Aug.	15		G1		1,100	1,100
	15		G1		750	1,850
	31		G1		1,950	3,800

Wages Expense — Account No. 623

Date		Explanation	PR	Debit	Credit	Balance
2014 Aug.	17		G1	250		250

Rent Expense — Account No. 640

Date		Explanation	PR	Debit	Credit	Balance
2014 Aug.	3		G1	3,200		3,200

Hydro Expense — Account No. 690

Date		Explanation	PR	Debit	Credit	Balance
2014 Aug.	31		G1	450		450

4.

The Cutlery
Trial Balance
August 31, 2014

Acct. No.	Account	Debit	Credit
101	Cash	$ 4,950	
106	Accounts receivable	-0-	
128	Prepaid insurance	2,400	
161	Furniture	2,000	
165	Store equipment	31,000	
201	Accounts payable		$14,450
236	Unearned haircutting services revenue		500
301	Joane Cardinal, capital		26,000
302	Joane Cardinal, withdrawals	500	
403	Haircutting services revenue		3,800
623	Wages expenses	250	
640	Rent expense	3,200	
690	Hydro expense	450	
	Totals	$44,750	$44,750

> The arrows are imaginary but they emphasize:
> 1. How the statements are prepared from the trial balance and
> 2. The link between statements.

5.

The Cutlery
Income Statement
For Month Ended August 31, 2014

Revenues:		
Haircutting services revenue		$3,800
Operating expenses:		
Rent expense	$3,200	
Hydro expense	450	
Wages expense	250	
Total operating expenses		3,900
Net loss		$ 100

The Cutlery
Statement of Changes in Equity
For Month Ended August 31, 2014

Joane Cardinal, capital, August 1		$ -0-
Add: Investments by owner		26,000
Total		$26,000
Less: Withdrawals by owner	$500	
Net loss	100	600
Joane Cardinal, capital, August 31		$25,400

The Cutlery
Balance Sheet
August 31, 2014

Assets

Cash	$ 4,950
Prepaid insurance	2,400
Furniture	2,000
Store equipment	31,000
Total assets	$40,350

Liabilities

Accounts payable	$14,450	
Unearned haircutting services revenue	500	
Total liabilities		$14,950

Equity

Joane Cardinal, capital	25,400
Total liabilities and equity	$40,350

Analysis Component:

Equity represents how much of the total assets are owned (or financed) by the owner of the business. In the case of The Cutlery, the owner, Joane Cardinal, owns $25,400 of the total $40,350 in assets or 63% ($25,400/$40,350 × 100% = 62.949% or 63%). Most of her equity in the business is a result of her $26,000 investment at start-up. The original $26,000 investment was decreased during the month by a $100 net loss and a $500 withdrawal by the owner.

Liabilities represent how much of the total assets have been financed by debt. In the case of The Cutlery, $14,950 or 37% of the total assets are financed by liabilities ($14,950/$40,350 × 100% = 37.051% or 37%).

GLOSSARY

Account A place or location within an accounting system in which the increases and decreases in a specific asset, liability, or equity are recorded and stored.

Account balance The difference between the increases (including the beginning balance) and decreases recorded in an account.

Accounting cycle The steps repeated each reporting period for the purpose of preparing financial statements for users.

Accounts payable Obligations that arise when a promise to pay later is made in connection with purchases of merchandise, supplies, or equipment.

Accounts receivable When services are performed for or goods are sold to customers in return for promises to pay in the future, an *account receivable* is recorded. These transactions are said to be *on credit* or *on account*. Accounts receivable are *increased* by services performed or goods sold on credit and *decreased* by customer payments.

Balance column ledger accounts Accounts with debit and credit columns for recording entries and a third column showing the balance of the account after each entry is posted.

Books So named when accounting records were maintained manually by recording accounts on separate pages in a special booklet; the books include both the ledger and the journal.

Chart of accounts A list of all accounts used by a company; includes the identification number assigned to each account.

Compound journal entry A journal entry that affects at least three accounts.

Credit An entry that decreases asset, expense, and owner's withdrawals accounts or increases liability, owner's capital, and revenue accounts; recorded on the right side of a T-account.

Debit An entry that increases asset, expense, and owner's withdrawals accounts or decreases liability, owner's capital, and revenue accounts; recorded on the left side of a T-account.

Double-entry accounting An accounting system where every transaction affects and is recorded in at least two accounts; the sum of the debits for all entries must equal the sum of the credits for all entries.

General Journal The most flexible type of journal; can be used to record any kind of transaction.

Journal A record where transactions are recorded before they are recorded in accounts; amounts are posted from the journal to the ledger; also called the *book of original entry*.

Journalizing Recording transactions in a journal.

Ledger A record containing all accounts used by a business.

Normal balance The debit or credit side on which an account increases. For example, assets increase with debits, therefore the normal balance for an asset is a debit. Revenues increase with credits, therefore a credit is the normal balance for a revenue account.

Notes payable Obligations that arise when an organization formally recognizes a promise to pay by signing a promissory note.

Notes receivable Unconditional written promises to pay a definite sum of money on demand or on a defined future date(s); also called *promissory notes*.

Post(ing) Transfer(ring) journal entry information to ledger accounts.

Posting reference (PR) column A column in *journals* where individual account numbers are entered when entries are posted to the ledger. A column in *ledgers* where journal page numbers are entered when entries are posted.

Prepaid Expenses An asset account containing payments made for assets that are not to be used until later.

Promissory notes Unconditional written promises to pay a definite sum of money on demand or on a defined future date(s); also called *notes receivable*.

Slide An error that results from adding or deleting a zero (or zeros) in a value.

T-account A simple characterization of an account form used as a helpful tool in showing the effects of transactions on specific accounts.

Transposition error Error due to two digits being switched or transposed within a number.

Trial balance A list of accounts and their balances at a point in time; the total debit balances should equal the total credit balances.

Unearned revenues Liabilities created when customers pay in advance for products or services; created when cash is received before revenues are earned; satisfied by delivering the products or services in the future.

 Visit **Connect** for additional study tools, practice quizzes, to search an interactive eBook, and much more.

CONCEPT REVIEW QUESTIONS

1. Describe the fundamental steps in the accounting process.

2. What is the difference between a note receivable and an account receivable?

3. Reread the chapter's opening scenario describing Black Feather Wilderness Adventure Company. Assume that Black Feather's expenses are about 75% of total revenues. Suggest appropriate account titles for 15 possible expense accounts.

4. Review the Danier Leather balance **DANIER** sheet for fiscal year-end June 25, 2011, in Appendix II. Identify four different asset accounts and three different liability accounts.

5. If assets are valuable resources and asset accounts have debit balances, why do expense accounts have debit balances?

6. Review the WestJet balance sheet for fiscal year-end December 31, 2011, in Appendix II. Identify three accounts on the balance sheet that would carry debit balances and three accounts on the balance sheet that would carry credit balances.

7. What kinds of transactions can be recorded in a General Journal?

8. Are debits or credits listed first in General Journal entries? Are the debits or the credits indented?

9. Should a transaction be recorded first in a journal or the ledger? Why?

10. Why does the bookkeeper prepare a trial balance?

QUICK STUDY

QS 2-1 Identifying accounts LO^2

Identify the account as an asset, liability, or equity by entering the letter of the account type beside the account name. If the item is an equity account, indicate the type of equity account.

A = Asset   OE = Owner's Capital (Equity)   R = Revenues (Equity)
L = Liability   W = Owner's Withdrawals (Equity)   E = Expenses (Equity)

_____ 1. Buildings	_____ 11. Advertising Fees Earned	_____ 21. Unearned Rent Revenue
_____ 2. Building Repair Expense	_____ 12. Interest Earned	_____ 22. Prepaid Rent
_____ 3. Wages Expense	_____ 13. Interest Expense	_____ 23. Rent Payable
_____ 4. Wages Payable	_____ 14. Interest Payable	_____ 24. Service Fees Earned
_____ 5. Notes Receivable	_____ 15. Earned Subscription Fees	_____ 25. Jan Sted, Withdrawals
_____ 6. Notes Payable	_____ 16. Unearned Subscription Fees	_____ 26. Jan Sted, Capital
_____ 7. Prepaid Advertising	_____ 17. Prepaid Subscription Fees	_____ 27. Salaries Expense
_____ 8. Advertising Expense	_____ 18. Supplies	_____ 28. Salaries Payable
_____ 9. Advertising Payable	_____ 19. Supplies Expense	_____ 29. Furniture
_____ 10. Unearned Advertising	_____ 20. Rent Revenue	_____ 30. Equipment

QS 2-2 Calculating account balances LO^2

Calculate the account balance for each of the following:

Accounts Receivable		Accounts Payable		Service Revenue	
1,000	650	250	250		13,000
400	920	900	1,800		2,500
920	1,500	650	1,400		810
3,000			650		3,500

Utilities Expense		Cash		Notes Payable	
610		3,900	2,400	4,000	50,000
520		17,800	3,900	8,000	
390		14,500	21,800		
275		340			

QS 2-3 Identifying normal balance as a debit or credit LO^3

Indicate whether the normal balance of each of the following accounts is a debit or a credit:

a. Equipment	**f.** Prepaid Rent	**k.** Al Tait, Capital
b. Land	**g.** Accounts Receivable	**l.** Rent Earned
c. Al Tait, Withdrawals	**h.** Office Supplies	**m.** Rent Payable
d. Rent Expense	**i.** Notes Receivable	**n.** Interest Expense
e. Interest Revenue	**j.** Notes Payable	**o.** Interest Payable

QS 2-4 Analyzing debit or credit by account LO^3

Identify whether a debit or credit entry would be made to record the indicated change in each of the following accounts:

a. To increase Notes Payable	**i.** To increase Store Equipment
b. To decrease Accounts Receivable	**j.** To increase Owner, Withdrawals
c. To increase Owner, Capital	**k.** To decrease Rent Payable
d. To decrease Unearned Fees	**l.** To decrease Prepaid Rent
e. To decrease Prepaid Insurance	**m.** To increase Supplies
f. To decrease Cash	**n.** To increase Supplies Expense
g. To increase Utilities Expense	**o.** To decrease Accounts Payable
h. To increase Fees Earned	

QS 2-5 Linking credit or debit with normal balance LO^3

Indicate whether a debit or credit is necessary to *decrease* the normal balance of each of the following accounts:

a. Buildings	**f.** Interest Payable	**k.** Interest Expense
b. Interest Revenue	**g.** Accounts Receivable	**l.** Unearned Revenue
c. Bob Norton, Withdrawals	**h.** Salaries Expense	**m.** Salaries Payable
d. Bob Norton, Capital	**i.** Office Supplies	**n.** Furniture
e. Prepaid Insurance	**j.** Repair Services Revenue	**o.** Interest Receivable

QS 2-6 Developing a chart of accounts LO^4

Using the chart of accounts numbering system, develop a chart of accounts that assigns an account number to each of the following accounts:

a. Buildings	**f.** Interest Payable	**k.** Interest Expense
b. Interest Revenue	**g.** Accounts Receivable	**l.** Unearned Revenue
c. Bob Norton, Withdrawals	**h.** Salaries Expense	**m.** Salaries Payable
d. Bob Norton, Capital	**i.** Office Supplies	**n.** Furniture
e. Prepaid Insurance	**j.** Repair Services Revenue	**o.** Interest Receivable

QS 2-7 Recording directly into T-accounts LO^5

1. Record the following transactions directly in the T-accounts provided:

    a. Del Martin invested $15,000 cash into his new business.

    b. Purchased $2,000 of furniture on account.

    c. Purchased $500 of furniture, paying cash.

    d. Did $1,000 of work for a customer; collected cash.

    e. Did $700 of work for a customer on account.

    f. Paid $500 regarding (b).

    g. Collected $300 regarding (e).

    h. Did $400 of work for a client on credit.

2. Calculate the balance in each T-account and prove the accounting equation.

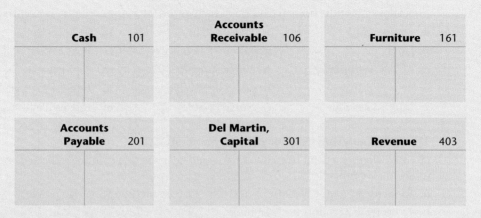

QS 2-8 Recording directly into T-accounts LO5

Bell Company's records showed the following April 30, 2014, account balances:

Cash			Accounts Receivable			Car			Accounts Payable		
Apr 30 15,000			Apr 30 3,200							6,000 Apr 30

Unearned Revenue			Dee Bell, Capital			Revenue			Wages Expense		
	1,800 Apr 30			8,900 Apr 30			3,000 Apr 30		Apr 30 1,500	

1. Using the chart of accounts numbering system, assign an account number to each account.
2. Record the May 2014 transactions directly in the T-accounts provided:

May	2	Dee Bell transferred her personal car valued at $8,000 into the business.
	10	Did $4,000 of work for a customer on account.
	12	Collected $10,000 from a customer for work to be done in July 2014.
	15	Paid wages of $6,000.
	16	Collected $4,000 from the customer of May 10.
	22	Paid half of the outstanding accounts payable.

3. Calculate the May 31, 2014, balance in each T-account and prove the accounting equation.

QS 2-9 Preparing journal entries LO3,5,6

Prepare journal entries for the following transactions that occurred during 2014:

May	1	Purchased equipment on account; $500.
	2	Paid for the equipment purchased on May 1.
	3	Purchased supplies for cash; $100.
	4	Paid wages to employees; $2,000.
	5	Performed services for a client and collected cash; $750.
	6	Did work for a customer on credit; $2,500.
	7	Collected the amount owing from the customer of May 6.

QS 2-10 Preparing journal entries LO[3,5,6]

Prepare journal entries for the following transactions that occurred during January 2014:

January	3	Stan Adams opened a landscaping business by investing $60,000 cash and equipment having a $40,000 fair value.
	4	Purchased office supplies on credit for $340.
	6	Received $5,200 for providing landscaping services to a customer.
	15	Paid $200 regarding the office supplies purchase of January 4.
	16	Purchased $700 of office supplies on account.
	30	Paid the balance owing regarding the office supplies purchase of January 4.

QS 2-11 Recording in T-accounts LO[5,6]

a. Set up the following accounts (use the balance column format as illustrated in Exhibit 2.12: Cash (101), Office Supplies (124), Equipment (163), Accounts Payable (201), Stan Adams, Capital (301), and Landscaping Services Revenue (403).

b. Post the journal entries from QS 2-10 to the accounts and enter the balance after each posting.

QS 2-12 Preparing a trial balance LO[7]

Using the account information shown below, prepare a trial balance at January 31, 2014.

Vahn Landscaping
General Ledger

Cash	101
5,000	6,000
2,000	4,000
3,000	1,000
8,000	

Equipment	163
9,000	

Unearned Fees	233
	2,000

Brea Vahn, Capital	301
	14,000

Brea Vahn, Withdrawals	302
1,000	

Fees Earned	401
	3,000
	8,000

Rent Expense	640
6,000	

Utilities Expense	690
4,000	

QS 2-13 Identifying a posting error LO[3,5,6,7]

A trial balance has total debits of $21,000 and total credits of $25,500. Which one of the following errors would create this imbalance? Explain.

a. A $4,500 debit to Salaries Expense in a journal entry was incorrectly posted to the ledger as a $4,500 credit, leaving the Salaries Expense account with a $750 debit balance.

b. A $2,250 credit to Teaching Fees Earned in a journal entry was incorrectly posted to the ledger as a $2,250 debit, leaving the Teaching Fees Earned account with a $6,300 credit balance.

c. A $2,250 debit to Rent Expense in a journal entry was incorrectly posted to the ledger as a $2,250 credit, leaving the Rent Expense account with a $3,000 debit balance.

QS 2-14 Identifying a transposition error LO7

Identify the transposition error in the following trial balance, assuming this is the only error.

	SunFlowers Trial Balance September 30, 2014		
Acct. No.	**Account**	**Debit**	**Credit**
101	Cash	$ 9,800	
165	Equipment...	10,350	
201	Accounts payable...		$ 750
301	Tracy Rumanko, Capital		3,800
403	Consulting revenue......................................		17,000
640	Rent expense	4,100	
	Totals..	$24,250	$21,550

QS 2-15 Identifying a slide error LO7

Identify the slide error in the following trial balance, assuming this is the only error.

Delwin's Fitness Training Trial Balance April 30, 2014		
Cash	$330	
Supplies	38	
Notes payable...		$ 25
Jane Delwin, capital..		100
Fees earned..		378
Wages expense	360	
Totals	$728	$503

EXERCISES

CHECK FIGURE:
Total cash = $17,975

Exercise 2-1 Recording the effects of transactions directly in T-accounts LO3,5

Set up the following T-accounts: Cash; Accounts Receivable; Office Supplies; Office Equipment; Accounts Payable; Sandra Moses, Capital; Sandra Moses, Withdrawals; Fees Earned; and Rent Expense. Next, record these transactions of the Northern Lights Company by recording the debit and credit entries directly in the T-accounts. Use the letters beside the transactions to identify the entries. Finally, determine the balance of each account.

a. Sandra Moses invested $32,600 cash in the business.

b. Purchased $925 of office supplies for cash.

c. Purchased $13,600 of office equipment on credit.

d. Received $3,000 cash as fees for services provided to a customer.

e. Paid for the office equipment purchased in transaction (c).

f. Billed a customer $5,400 as fees for services.

g. Paid the monthly rent with $3,500 cash.

h. Collected the account receivable created in transaction (f).

i. Moses withdrew $5,000 cash from the business for personal use.

CHECK FIGURE:
Total cash = $9,665

Exercise 2-2 Recording the effects of transactions directly in T-accounts LO3,5

Poundmaker Accounting Services began operations on January 1, 2014. Set up the following T-accounts, which show balances at January 31: Cash $890; Accounts Receivable $1,200; Prepaid Insurance $0; Computer Equipment $480; Accounts Payable $250; Notes Payable $0; Neil Poundmaker, Capital $800; Neil Poundmaker, Withdrawals $0; Service Revenue $2,600; Wages Expense $1,080. The activities below occurred during February. Identify the transactions and record them directly in the T-accounts. Use the dates beside the transactions to identify the entries. Also, determine the balance of each account.

Feb.	2	Neil Poundmaker provided services to a customer and collected cash of $3,100.
	10	Purchased $7,600 of new computer equipment for the business by signing a note.
	12	Performed $15,000 of accounting services for a client on account.
	14	Paid the $4,000 annual insurance premium covering the next 12 months.
	18	Billed a client $1,900 for work performed today.
	20	Collected $2,400 from a credit customer.
	21	Poundmaker ordered $1,600 in new accounting software from a local vendor; it will be paid for when it arrives in about two weeks.
	22	Collected $10,000 from the customer of February 12.
	23	Paid half of the outstanding accounts payable.
	25	Poundmaker withdrew $1,000 cash for personal use.
	26	Paid part-time employee wages of $1,600.

Analysis Component: Regarding February 12, which GAAP must be considered in determining the appropriate accounting treatment for this item?

CHECK FIGURE:
Total cash = $3,250

Exercise 2-3 Recording the effects of transactions directly in T-accounts LO^{3,5}

On March 1, 2014, Nels Sigurdsen opened an automotive repair shop called Nels Car Repairs. Set up the following T-accounts that show balances at March 31, 2014: Cash $1,800; Accounts Receivable $4,800; Repair Supplies $1,400; Equipment $7,400; Accounts Payable $500; Nels Sigurdsen, Capital $2,350; Nels Sigurdsen, Withdrawals $500; Repair Revenue $14,000; Rent Expense $950. The activities below occurred during April. Identify the transactions and record them directly in the T-accounts. Use the dates beside the transactions to identify the entries. Also, determine the balance of each account.

Apr.	2	Nels Sigurdsen did some repairs on a car today and immediately collected $2,100.
	5	Sigurdsen hired a tune-up specialist who will start next month and get paid $4,500 per month.
	9	Repair supplies were purchased on credit; $1,500.
	10	Paid $1,000 regarding the supplies purchased on April 9.
	15	Bought a small piece of equipment, paying cash of $950.
	18	Did work for a customer on account; $1,200.
	19	Collected $2,800 regarding a customer's account.
	25	Rented some specialized equipment from Ace Rentals; $820 on account.
	29	Sigurdsen withdrew $1,500 cash for personal use.

CHECK FIGURES:
4. Total debits = $19,000
5. Total assets = $15,250

Exercise 2-4 Journalizing, posting, preparing a trial balance, and financial statements LO^{3,5,6,7}

MiraCom incurred the following transactions during July 2014, its first month of operations:

July	1	The owner, Mira Delco, invested $5,000 cash.
	10	Purchased $2,500 worth of equipment on credit.
	12	Performed services for a client and received $10,000 cash.
	14	Paid for expenses; $3,500.
	15	Completed services for a client and sent a bill for $1,500.
	31	The owner withdrew $250 cash for personal use.

Required

1. Create a General Ledger by setting up the following accounts: Cash, 101; Accounts Receivable, 106; Equipment, 150; Accounts Payable, 201; Mira Delco, Capital, 301; Mira Delco, Withdrawals, 302; Revenue, 401; Expenses, 501.

2. Journalize the July transactions in the General Journal.

3. Post the July transactions from your General Journal into your General Ledger accounts.

4. Prepare a trial balance based on the balances in your General Ledger accounts.

5. Prepare an income statement, statement of changes in equity, and balance sheet based on your trial balance.

Analysis Component: Assets are financed by debt and equity transactions, a concept reinforced by the accounting equation: A = L + E. Since accounts receivable are an asset, are they financed by debt and/or equity? Explain.

Exercise 2-5 Chart of accounts LO⁴

You have been given the following guide regarding the chart of accounts for Paquette Advisors:

100–199	Assets	400–499	Revenues
200–299	Liabilities	500–599	Expenses
300–399	Equity		

Using the account information from Exercise 2-6, develop a chart of accounts for Paquette Advisors.

CHECK FIGURES:
4. Net income = $21,700
6. Total assets = $35,400

Exercise 2-6 Journalizing, posting, preparing a trial balance, and financial statements LO³,⁵,⁶,⁷

After its first month of operations, Paquette Advisors showed the following account balances in its General Ledger accounts as at January 31, 2014.

Cash		Accounts Receivable		Office Equipment	
15,000		3,800		22,500	

Accounts Payable		Unearned Revenue		Aaron Paquette, Capital	
	8,000		2,600		9,500

Aaron Paquette, Withdrawals		Consulting Revenues		Salaries Expense	
2,000			41,700	10,000	

Rent Expense		Utilities Expense	
7,500		1,000	

During February, the following transactions occurred:

Feb.	1	Performed work for a client and received cash of $8,500.
	5	Paid $5,000 regarding outstanding accounts payable.
	10	Received cash of $3,600 for work to be done in March.
	12	Called FasCo Rentals to book the use of some equipment next month. The $400 rental fee will be paid in full when the equipment is returned.
	17	The owner withdrew cash of $3,000 for personal use.
	28	Paid salaries of $10,000.

Required

1. Journalize the February transactions in the General Journal.

2. Post the transactions from your General Journal to the General Ledger (T-accounts above).

3. Prepare a trial balance based on the balances in your General Ledger.

4. Prepare an income statement for the two months ended February 28, 2014.

5. Prepare a statement of changes in equity for the two months ended February 28, 2014.

6. Prepare the balance sheet as at February 28, 2014.

Analysis Component: Paquette Advisors shows Unearned Revenue on its February 28, 2014, balance sheet. Explain what Unearned Revenue is. As part of your answer, be sure to address why Unearned Revenue is reported as a liability.

Exercise 2-7 Analyzing transactions from T-accounts LO^{3,5}

Prepare General Journal entries for each of the seven transactions posted to the following T-accounts. Provide a short description of each transaction. The first description is done as an example.

(a) *The owner invested cash, an automobile, and equipment in the business.*

Cash			
(a)	7,000	3,600	(b)
(e)	2,500	600	(c)
		2,400	(f)
		700	(g)

Office Supplies		
(c)	600	
(d)	200	

Prepaid Insurance		
(b)	3,600	

Equipment		
(a)	5,600	
(d)	9,400	

Automobiles		
(a)	11,000	

Accounts Payable			
(f)	2,400	9,600	(d)

Jerry Steiner, Capital		
	23,600	(a)

Delivery Services Revenue		
	2,500	(e)

Gas and Oil Expense		
(g)	700	

Exercise 2-8 General Journal entries LO^{3,5,6}

TLC Laser Eye Centres showed the following selected activities during the month of April 2014. Journalize the transactions in your General Journal.

April	5	Performed surgery on a customer today and collected $4,600 cash.
	8	Purchased surgical supplies on credit; $19,000.
	15	Paid salaries; $41,000.
	20	Paid for the surgical supplies purchased on April 8.
	21	Contacted a client's lawyer today regarding a complaint about the surgery. The client is planning to sue for $100,000.
	22	Performed six surgeries today, all on credit; $3,800 each.
	29	Collected from four of the credit customers of April 22.
	30	Paid the April utilities bill today; $1,800.

Exercise 2-9 Analyzing and journalizing revenue transactions LO^{3,5,6}

Examine the following transactions and identify those that created revenues for TI Servicing, a sole proprietorship owned by Todd Iver. Prepare General Journal entries to record those transactions and explain why the other transactions did not create revenues.

a. Todd Iver invested $76,500 cash in the business.

b. Provided $2,700 of services on credit.

c. Received $3,150 cash for services provided to a client.

d. Received $18,300 from a client in payment for services to be provided next year.

e. Received $9,000 from a client in partial payment of an account receivable.

f. Borrowed $300,000 from the bank by signing a promissory note.

Exercise 2-10 Analyzing and journalizing expense transactions LO^{3,5,6}

Examine the following transactions and identify those that created expenses for EK Servicing. Prepare General Journal entries to record those transactions and explain why the other transactions did not create expenses.

a. Paid $14,100 cash for office supplies purchased 30 days previously.

b. Paid the $1,125 salary of the receptionist.

c. Paid $45,000 cash for equipment.

d. Paid utility bill with $930 cash.

e. Elijah Kunnuk withdrew $5,000 from the business account for personal use.

Exercise 2-11 Posting from the General Journal to the ledger LO⁴,⁶

Walker's Inspection Services is in its second month of operations. You have been given the following journal entries regarding its January 2014 transactions.

Required

a. Set up the following accounts (use the balance column format) entering the opening balances brought forward from the end of last month, December 31, 2013: Cash (101) $850; Accounts Receivable (106) $300; Equipment (167) $1,500; Accounts Payable (201) $325; Jay Walker, Capital (301) $2,325; Jay Walker, Withdrawals (302) $300; Fees Earned (401) $1,800; and Salaries Expense (622) $1,500.

b. Post the journal entries to the accounts and enter the balance after each posting.

	General Journal			Page 1
Date	**Account Titles and Explanation**	**PR**	**Debit**	**Credit**
2014				
Jan. 1	Cash...		3,500	
	Jay Walker, Capital			3,500
	Additional owner investment.			
12	Accounts Receivable..		9,000	
	Fees Earned..			9,000
	Performed work for a customer on account.			
20	Equipment		12,000	
	Accounts Payable			10,000
	Cash			2,000
	Purchased equipment by paying cash and the balance on credit.			
31	Cash...		5,000	
	Accounts Receivable.............................			5,000
	Collected cash from credit customer.			
31	Salaries Expense		3,000	
	Cash			3,000
	Paid month-end salaries.			
31	Jay Walker, Withdrawals		750	
	Cash			750
	Jay Walker withdrew cash for personal use.			

Analysis Component: The accounting cycle requires that transactions be journalized in the General Journal and then posted in the General Ledger. This seems to indicate that we are recording the same information in two different places. Why can't we eliminate journalizing or posting?

Exercise 2-12 General Journal entries LO³,⁵,⁶

Prepare General Journal entries to record the following August 2014 transactions of a new business called The Pixel Shop.

Aug.   1   Joseph Eetok, the owner, invested $20,000 cash and photography equipment with a fair value of $42,000.
          1   Rented a studio, paying $12,000 for the next three months in advance.
          5   Purchased office supplies for $1,800 cash.
          20   Received $9,200 in photography fees.
          31   Paid $1,400 for August utilities.

Exercise 2-13 Ledger accounts and the trial balance LO³,⁵,⁶,⁷

Set up the following accounts (use the balance column format): Cash (101); Office Supplies (124); Prepaid Rent (131); Photography Equipment (167); Joseph Eetok, Capital (301); Photography Fees Earned (401); and Utilities Expense (690). Then, using your General Journal entries from Exercise 2-12, post to the ledger. Finally, prepare the August 31, 2014, trial balance.

Analysis Component: Joseph Eetok wanted to buy a building for his business and took the August 31, 2014, trial balance to his bank manager. Is the trial balance used for external reporting? Explain.

Exercise 2-14 T-accounts and the trial balance LO3,5,6,7

Follow the instructions in Exercise 2-13, but instead of using a balance column format for the accounts, use T-accounts.

Exercise 2-15 Preparing financial statements from a trial balance LO7

Hogan's Consulting showed the following trial balances for its first year just ended December 31, 2014:

Account Title	Debit	Credit
Cash..	$ 18,000	
Accounts receivable	5,200	
Prepaid rent	13,000	
Machinery	57,100	
Accounts payable		$ 17,300
Notes payable..		47,000
Lisa Hogan, capital		50,000
Lisa Hogan, withdrawals	2,000	
Consulting fees earned		18,000
Wages expense...	29,000	
Rent expense	8,000	
Totals	$132,300	$132,300

Required Use the information provided to complete an income statement, statement of changes in equity, and balance sheet.

Analysis Component: If Hogan's Consulting continues to experience losses, what alternatives are available to prevent assets from decreasing?

Exercise 2-16 Preparing financial statements from a trial balance LO7

JenCo showed the following trial balance information (in alphabetical order) for its first month just ended March 31, 2014:

Account	Debit	Credit
Accounts payable...		$ 500
Accounts receivable	$ 1,950	
Cash..	500	
Equipment...	700	
Interest expense	10	
Marie Jensen, capital....................................		2,050
Marie Jensen, withdrawals	1,500	
Notes payable..		1,100
Prepaid insurance	300	
Salaries expense...	800	
Service revenue		1,650
Unearned service revenue............................		460
Totals...	$ 5,760	$5,760

Required Use the information provided to complete an income statement, statement of changes in equity, and balance sheet.

Exercise 2-17 Preparing financial statements from a trial balance LO[7]

Nanimahoo Marketing Services has been operating for several years. It showed the following trial balance information (in alphabetical order) for the month just ended March 31, 2014:

Account	Debit	Credit
Accounts payable..		$ 46,000
Accounts receivable	$ 3,000	
Building..	80,000	
Cash	17,000	
Fees earned		126,000
Dee Nanimahoo, capital*..............................		122,000
Dee Nanimahoo, withdrawals.......................	18,000	
Land..	84,000	
Machinery	50,000	
Notes payable...		114,000
Office supplies	3,000	
Office supplies expense................................	7,000	
Wages expense..	146,000	
Totals...	$408,000	$408,000

*The $122,000 balance includes $35,000 invested by the owner during March.

Required Using the information provided, prepare an income statement and a statement of changes in equity for the month ended March 31, 2014, and a balance sheet at March 31, 2014.

Exercise 2-18 Effects of posting errors on the trial balance LO[3,5,6,7]

Complete the following table by filling in the blanks. For each of the listed posting errors:

1. Enter in column (1) the amount of the difference that the error would create between the two trial balance columns (show a zero if the columns would balance).

2. Identify if there would be a difference between the two columns, and identify in column (2) the trial balance column that would be larger.

3. Identify the account(s) affected in column (3).

4. Identify the amount by which the account(s) is (are) under- or overstated in column (4). The answer for the first error is provided as an example.

	Description	(1) Difference Between Debit and Credit Columns	(2) Column With the Larger Total	(3) Identify Account(s) Incorrectly Stated	(4) Amount That Account(s) Is (Are) Over- or Understated
a.	A $2,400 debit to Rent Expense was posted as a $1,590 debit.	$810	Credit	Rent Expense	Rent Expense is understated by $810
b.	A $42,000 debit to Machinery was posted as a debit to Accounts Payable.				
c.	A $4,950 credit to Services Revenue was posted as a $495 credit.				
d.	A $1,440 debit to Store Supplies was not posted at all.				
e.	A $2,250 debit to Prepaid Insurance was posted as a debit to Insurance Expense.				
f.	A $4,050 credit to Cash was posted twice as two credits to the Cash account.				
g.	A $9,900 debit to the owner's withdrawals account was debited to the owner's capital account.				

Exercise 2-19 Analyzing the trial balance LO^{3,5,6,7}

During March, Bonnie Doan, the owner of Doan Cleaning Services, had trouble keeping her debits and credits equal. The following errors were noted:

a. Bonnie did not post the entry to record $3,500 of services performed on account.

b. In posting a $300 payment on account, Bonnie debited Cash and credited Accounts Payable.

c. In posting a cash payment, Bonnie correctly debited Accounts Payable for $425 but incorrectly credited Cash for $245.

d. In posting a cash receipt of $750, Bonnie debited Cash but forgot to post the credit to Accounts Receivable.

e. In posting the purchase of $1,000 of equipment on credit, Bonnie debited Accounts Payable and credited Equipment.

Required For each of the errors described, indicate:

1. Whether debits equal credits on the trial balance, and

2. Which account(s) have incorrect balances.

Exercise 2-20 Transposition and slide errors on the trial balance LO^7

Required Identify the single transposition or slide error in each of the following independent trial balances.

	Case A		Case B		Case C	
Cash	$ 120		$ 3,900		$ 59	
Accounts receivable	260		1,900		46	
Equipment	3,170		12,900		791	
Accounts payable.................		$ 190		$ 2,350		$ 72
Capital		1,100		16,150		229
Withdrawals.........................	850		7,000		-0-	
Revenue...............................		3,000		9,600		641
Wages expense	610		8,700		10	
Totals....................................	$5,010	$4,290	$34,400	$28,100	$906	$942

PROBLEMS

CHECK FIGURE:
2. Cash balance, Nov. 30,
2014 = $12,600

Problem 2-1A Recording transactions in T-accounts LO^{3,5}

Following are business activities completed by Joel Douglas during the month of November 2014:

a. Invested $100,000 cash and office equipment with a $9,000 fair value in a new sole proprietorship named Douglas Tax Consulting.

b. Purchased land and a small office building. The land was worth $115,000, and the building was worth $85,000. The purchase price was paid with $80,000 cash and a long-term note payable for the balance.

c. Purchased $4,600 of office supplies on credit.

d. Joel Douglas transferred title of his personal automobile to the business. The automobile had a value of $9,000 and was to be used exclusively in the business.

e. Purchased $3,000 of additional office equipment on credit.

f. Paid $3,200 wages to an assistant.

g. Provided services to a client and collected $16,000 cash.

h. Paid $1,800 for the month's utilities.

i. Signed an equipment rental agreement to commence in January. A deposit of $250 must be paid by December 15.

j. Paid the account payable created in transaction (c).

k. Purchased $10,000 of new office equipment by paying $9,300 cash and trading in old equipment with a recorded cost of $700.

l. Completed $5,100 of services for a client. This amount is to be paid within 30 days.

m. Paid $3,200 wages to an assistant.

n. Received $1,900 payment on the receivable created in transaction (l).

o. Withdrew $3,200 cash from the business for personal use.

Required

1. Set up the following T-accounts: Cash; Accounts Receivable; Office Supplies; Automobiles; Office Equipment; Building; Land; Accounts Payable; Long-Term Notes Payable; Joel Douglas, Capital; Joel Douglas, Withdrawals; Fees Earned; Wages Expense; and Utilities Expense.

2. Record the effects of the transactions by entering debits and credits directly in the T-accounts. Use the transaction letters to identify each debit and credit entry.

Problem 2-2A Preparing General Journal entries LO^{3,5,6}

Bruce Ibach owns Biotech Fitness Centre, which showed the following selected transactions for the month ended May 31, 2014:

May	1	Purchased new equipment, paying cash of $14,000 and signing a 90-day note payable for the balance of $32,000.
	2	Purchased 12 months of insurance to begin May 2; paid $24,000.
	3	Completed a fitness contract for a group of clients today and received $6,000.
	4	Purchased office supplies on account; $3,750.
	6	Returned to the supplier $750 of defective office supplies purchased on May 4.
	10	Provided services to a client today on account; $11,500.
	15	Paid for the May 4 purchase less the return of May 6.
	20	Received payment from the client of May 10.
	25	Received cash of $2,500 from a client for work to be done in June.
	31	Paid month-end salaries of $47,000.
	31	Paid the May telephone bill today; $2,250.
	31	Received the May electrical bill today; $3,100. It will be paid on June 15.

Required Prepare General Journal entries for each of the above transactions.

Problem 2-3A Preparing General Journal entries LO^{3,5,6}

Abe Factor opened a new accounting practice called X-Factor Accounting and completed these activities during March 2014:

Mar.	1	Invested $50,000 in cash and office equipment that had a fair value of $12,000.
	1	Prepaid $9,000 cash for three months' rent for an office.
	3	Made credit purchases of used office equipment for $6,000 and office supplies for $1,200.
	5	Completed work for a client and immediately received $6,200 cash.
	9	Completed a $4,000 project for a client, who will pay within 30 days.
	11	Paid the account payable created on March 3.
	15	Paid $3,000 cash for the annual premium on an insurance policy.
	20	Received $1,500 as partial payment for the work completed on March 9.
	22	Placed an order with a supplier for $4,800 of supplies to be delivered April 7. They must be paid for within 15 days of being received.
	23	Completed work for another client for $2,850 on credit.
	27	Abe Factor withdrew $3,600 cash from the business to pay some personal expenses.
	30	Purchased $650 of additional office supplies on credit.
	31	Paid $860 for the month's utility bill.

Required Prepare General Journal entries to record the transactions.

CHECK FIGURE:
3. Total Dr = $75,700

Problem 2-4A Posting, preparing a trial balance LO[4,6,7]

Required Using the General Journal entries prepared in Problem 2-3A, complete the following:

1. Set up the following accounts (use the balance column format or T-accounts): Cash (101); Accounts Receivable (106); Office Supplies (124); Prepaid Insurance (128); Prepaid Rent (131); Office Equipment (163); Accounts Payable (201); Abe Factor, Capital (301); Abe Factor, Withdrawals (302); Accounting Fees Earned (401); and Utilities Expense (690).

2. Post the entries to the accounts and enter the balance after each posting.

3. Prepare a trial balance as of the end of the month.

CHECK FIGURES:
Net income = $12,190;
Total assets = $71,240

Problem 2-5A Preparing financial statements from a trial balance LO[7]

Using the trial balance prepared for X-Factor Accounting in Part 3 of Problem 2-4A, prepare an income statement and statement of changes in equity for the month ended March 31, 2014, and a balance sheet at March 31, 2014.

CHECK FIGURE:
4. Total Dr = $168,280

Problem 2-6A Preparing and posting General Journal entries; preparing a trial balance LO[3,4,5,6,7]

Jill Wahpoosywan opened a computer consulting business called Techno Wizards and completed the following transactions during May 2014:

May	1	Jill Wahpoosywan invested $75,000 in cash and office equipment that had a fair value of $48,000 in the business.
	1	Prepaid $14,400 cash for three months' rent for an office.
	2	Made credit purchases of office equipment for $24,000 and office supplies for $4,800.
	6	Completed services for a client and immediately received $8,000 cash.
	9	Completed a $16,000 project for a client, who will pay within 30 days.
	10	Paid half of the account payable created on May 2.
	19	Paid $7,500 cash for the annual premium on an insurance policy.
	22	Received $12,800 as partial payment for the work completed on May 9.
	25	Completed work for another client for $5,280 on credit.
	25	Paid wages for May totalling $34,000.
	31	Wahpoosywan withdrew $5,000 cash from the business for personal use.
	31	Purchased $1,600 of additional office supplies on credit.
	31	Paid $1,400 for the month's utility bill.

Required

1. Prepare General Journal entries to record the transactions. Use page 1 for the journal.

2. Set up the following accounts (use the balance column format or T-accounts): Cash (101); Accounts Receivable (106); Office Supplies (124); Prepaid Insurance (128); Prepaid Rent (131); Office Equipment (163); Accounts Payable (201); Jill Wahpoosywan, Capital (301); Jill Wahpoosywan, Withdrawals (302); Services Revenue (403); Wages Expense (623); and Utilities Expense (690).

3. Post the entries to the accounts and enter the balance after each posting.

4. Prepare a trial balance at May 31, 2014.

Analysis Component: Utilities Expense, Services Revenue, and Jill Wahpoosywan, Withdrawals are equity accounts. Explain why.

Problem 2-7A Preparing financial statements from a trial balance LO[7]

Using the trial balance prepared for Techno Wizards in Part 4 of Problem 2-6A, prepare an income statement and statement of changes in equity for the month ended May 31, 2014, and a balance sheet at May 31, 2014.

Problem 2-8A Preparing financial statements from a trial balance LO[7]

Wildcat Opticians Trial Balance May 31, 2014			
Acct. No.	**Account Title**	**Debit**	**Credit**
101	Cash	$18,500	
106	Accounts receivable	8,480	
124	Office supplies	6,400	
128	Prepaid insurance	9,820	
163	Office equipment	25,600	
201	Accounts payable		$ 1,600
230	Unearned service revenue		7,800
301	Bo Wildcat, capital		56,300
302	Bo Wildcat, withdrawals	1,480	
403	Services revenue		25,280
623	Wages expense	15,000	
640	Rent expense	4,300	
690	Utilities expense	1,400	
	Totals	$90,980	$90,980

Required Using the trial balance provided above, prepare an income statement and statement of changes in equity for the first month ended May 31, 2014, and a balance sheet at May 31, 2014.

Analysis Component: Prepare two different journal entries, including explanations, that might have created the May 31, 2014, balance in Utilities Expense of $1,400. Use May 31, 2014, as the date for your entries.

Problem 2-9A Journalizing, posting, preparing a trial balance LO[3,4,5,6,7]

Binbutti Engineering, a sole proprietorship, completed the following transactions during July 2014, the third month of operations:

July	1	Bishr Binbutti, the owner, invested $300,000 cash, office equipment with a value of $12,000, and $90,000 of drafting equipment in the business.
	2	Purchased land for an office. The land was worth $108,000, which was paid with $10,800 cash and a long-term note payable for $97,200.
	3	Purchased a portable building with $150,000 cash and moved it onto the land.
	5	Paid $12,000 cash for the premiums on two one-year insurance policies.
	7	Completed and delivered a set of plans for a client and collected $1,400 cash.
	9	Purchased additional drafting equipment for $45,000. Paid $21,000 cash and signed a long-term note payable for the $24,000 balance.
	10	Completed $4,000 of engineering services for a client. This amount is to be paid within 30 days.
	12	Purchased $4,500 of additional office equipment on credit.
	15	Completed engineering services for $7,000 on credit.
	16	Received a bill for rent on equipment that was used on a completed job. The $13,800 rent must be paid within 30 days.
	17	Collected $400 from the client of July 10.
	19	Paid $12,000 wages to the drafting assistants.
	22	Paid the account payable created on July 12.
	25	Paid $1,350 cash for some repairs to an item of drafting equipment.
	26	Binbutti withdrew $800 cash from the business for personal use.
	30	Paid $12,000 wages to the drafting assistants.
	31	Paid $6,000 cash for advertising in the local newspaper during July.

Required

1. Prepare General Journal entries to record the transactions. Use page 1 for the journal.

2. Set up the following accounts (use the balance column format or T-accounts), entering the balances brought forward from June 30, 2014: Cash (101) $26,000; Accounts Receivable (106) $3,000; Prepaid Insurance (128) $500; Office Equipment (163) $1,700; Drafting Equipment (167) $1,200; Building (173) $42,000; Land (183) $28,000; Accounts Payable (201) $1,740; Long-Term Notes Payable (251) $24,000; Bishr Binbutti, Capital (301) $54,000; Bishr Binbutti, Withdrawals (302) $1,000; Engineering Fees Earned (401) $29,600; Wages Expense (623) $4,000; Equipment Rental Expense (645) $1,000; Advertising Expense (655) $640; and Repairs Expense (684) $300.

3. Post the entries to the accounts and enter the balance after each posting.

4. Prepare a trial balance at July 31, 2014.

CHECK FIGURES:
Net loss = $9,090;
Total assets = $605,850

Problem 2-10A Preparing financial statements from a trial balance LO[7]

Using the trial balance prepared for Binbutti Engineering in Part 4 of Problem 2-9A, prepare an income statement and statement of changes in equity for the three months ended July 31, 2014, and a balance sheet at July 31, 2014.

CHECK FIGURES:
4. Dr = $66,200
5. Net income = $11,350;
Total assets = $16,050

Problem 2-11A Journalizing, posting, preparing a trial balance and financial statements LO[1,3,4,5,6,7]

Ted Ng began Ng's English School on May 1, 2014. The following activities occurred during July, the third month of operations:

July	1	Purchased supplies on account; $100.
	2	Collected $4,000 for August teaching fees.
	3	Collected $2,000 for July teaching fees.
	4	Paid July rent of $3,000.
	5	Paid $500 for supplies purchased on account last month.
	15	Ted Ng withdrew cash of $500 for personal use.
	20	Paid wages of $1,300.
	31	Purchased a new chair on account; $300.

Required

1. Prepare General Journal entries to record the July transactions.

2. Set up the following T-accounts, entering the balances brought forward from June 30, 2014: Cash (101) $6,000; Supplies (126) $950; Furniture (161) $8,000; Accounts Payable (201) $1,500; Unearned Teaching Revenue (233) $9,800; Ted Ng, Capital (301) $3,000; Ted Ng, Withdrawals (302) $13,000; Teaching Revenue (401) $46,000; Wages Expense (623) $26,350; and Rent Expense (640) $6,000.

3. Post the entries to the accounts; calculate the ending balance in each account.

4. Prepare a trial balance at July 31, 2014.

5. Use the trial balance to prepare an income statement and statement of changes in equity for the three months ended July 31, 2014, as well as a balance sheet at July 31, 2014.

Problem 2-12A Preparing financial statements from a trial balance LO[7]

	Feline Pet Care Trial Balance July 31, 2014			
Acct. No.	**Account Title**		**Debit**	**Credit**
101	Cash		$ 23,000	
106	Accounts receivable		11,600	
128	Prepaid insurance		12,500	
163	Equipment		18,200	
173	Building		192,000	
183	Land		136,000	
201	Accounts payable			$ 15,540
230	Unearned fees			92,000
301	Betty Lark, capital			292,760
302	Betty Lark, withdrawals		5,000	
401	Fees earned			117,000
623	Wages expense		58,000	
645	Equipment rental expense		34,000	
655	Advertising expense		9,200	
684	Pet food expense		17,800	
	Totals		$517,300	$517,300

Required Using the trial balance provided above, prepare an income statement and statement of changes in equity for the first year ended July 31, 2014, and a balance sheet at July 31, 2014.

Analysis Component: Prepare two different journal entries, including explanations, that might have created the July 31, 2014, balance in Fees Earned of $117,000. Use July 31, 2014, as the date for your entries.

Problem 2-13A Analyzing trial balance errors LO[3,5,6,7]

Wilm Schmidt, the owner of Wilm's Window Washing Services, had difficulty getting the debits to equal credits on the January 31, 2014, trial balance.

Wilm's Window Washing Services Trial Balance January 31, 2014		
	Debit	**Credit**
Cash	$ 11,600	
Accounts receivable	9,240	
Prepaid insurance	2,400	
Equipment	24,000	
Accounts payable		$ 5,400
Wilm Schmidt, capital		45,000
Wilm Schmidt, withdrawals	8,960	
Service revenues		60,400
Salaries expense	32,000	
Insurance expense	5,200	
Maintenance expense	13,000	
Utilities expense	5,200	
Totals	$111,600	$110,800

The following errors were discovered:

a. Wilm did not post a $4,000 purchase of equipment on credit.

b. In posting a $1,400 collection from a credit customer, Wilm debited Accounts Receivable and credited Cash.

c. In posting a cash receipt, Wilm correctly debited Cash for $2,660 but incorrectly credited Accounts Receivable for $6,260.

d. In posting a $4,400 payment on account, Wilm debited Accounts Payable but forgot to post the credit to Cash.

e. In posting the entry for services of $3,600 performed for a customer on credit, Wilm debited Accounts Receivable but credited Maintenance Expense.

Required Prepare a corrected trial balance.

ALTERNATE PROBLEMS

Problem 2-1B Recording transactions in T-accounts LO^{3,5}

Peeters Consulting completed these transactions during June 2014:

a. Trevor Peeters, the sole proprietor, invested $46,000 cash and office equipment with a $24,000 fair value in the business.

b. Purchased land and a small office building. The land was worth $268,000 and the building was worth $66,000. The purchase price was paid with $30,000 cash and a long-term note payable for $304,000.

c. Purchased $600 of office supplies on credit.

d. Trevor Peeters transferred title of his personal automobile to the business. The automobile had a value of $7,000 and was to be used exclusively in the business.

e. Purchased $4,600 of additional office equipment on credit.

f. Paid $1,800 salary to an assistant.

g. Provided services to a client and collected $2,700 cash.

h. Paid $1,430 for the month's utilities.

i. Paid the account payable created in transaction (c).

j. Purchased $4,000 of new office equipment by paying $2,400 cash and trading in old equipment with a recorded cost of $1,600.

k. Completed $2,400 of services for a client. This amount is to be paid within 30 days.

l. Paid $1,800 salary to an assistant.

m. Received $1,000 payment on the receivable created in transaction (k).

n. Trevor Peeters withdrew $1,050 cash from the business for personal use.

Required

1. Set up the following T-accounts: Cash; Accounts Receivable; Office Supplies; Automobiles; Office Equipment; Building; Land; Accounts Payable; Long-Term Notes Payable; Trevor Peeters, Capital; Trevor Peeters, Withdrawals; Fees Earned; Salaries Expense; and Utilities Expense.

2. Record the effects of the listed transactions by entering debits and credits directly in the T-accounts. Use the transaction letters to identify each debit and credit entry.

Problem 2-2B Preparing General Journal entries LO^{3,5,6}

Airdrie Advertising showed the following selected transactions for the month ended March 31, 2014:

Mar.		
	1	Purchased a new portable building, paying cash of $75,000 and signing a five-year note payable for the balance of $300,000.
	1	Purchased six months of insurance to begin March 1; paid $5,700.
	2	Made a hotel reservation by phone regarding a business meeting to be held on March 28. The full payment of $240 will be required upon arrival at the hotel.
	4	Purchased cleaning supplies on account; $450.
	15	Paid for the March 4 purchase.
	19	Performed advertising work for a client today on account; $35,000.
	20	Collected cash of $8,000 from a customer. The advertising work will be done in April.
	28	Registered at the hotel booked on March 2 and paid the bill. Attended the out-of-town business meeting and returned to the office the next day.
	29	Provided advertising services to the local botanical garden society; collected $5,000.
	30	Paid month-end salaries of $25,600.
	30	Received the March telephone bill today; $1,300. It will be paid April 14.
	30	Collected half of the amount owed by the customer of March 19.

Required Prepare General Journal entries for each of the above transactions.

Problem 2-3B Preparing General Journal entries LO[3,5,6]

Susan Hurley, Public Accountant, completed these activities during September 2014, the first month of operations:

Sept.	1	Began a public accounting practice by investing $20,000 in cash and office equipment having a $9,200 fair value.
	1	Prepaid two months' rent in advance on suitable office space, $5,600.
	2	Purchased on credit used office equipment, $3,800, and office supplies, $1,380.
	4	Completed accounting work for a client and immediately received payment of $2,900 cash.
	8	Completed accounting work on credit for Frontier Bank, $5,080.
	10	Paid for the items purchased on credit on September 2.
	14	Paid the annual $3,300 premium on an insurance policy.
	15	Paid $1,250 to attend an all-day seminar on September 20 regarding ethical accounting practices.
	18	Received payment in full from Frontier Bank for the work completed on September 8.
	20	Attended the seminar paid for on September 15.
	24	Completed accounting work on credit for Travis Realty, $5,000.
	28	Hurley withdrew $2,500 cash from the practice to pay personal expenses.
	29	Purchased additional office supplies on credit, $450.
	30	Paid the September utility bills, $1,750.

Required Prepare General Journal entries to record the transactions.

CHECK FIGURE:
3. Total Dr = $42,630

Problem 2-4B Posting, preparing a trial balance LO[4,6,7]

Required Using the General Journal entries prepared in Problem 2-3B, complete the following:

1. Set up the following accounts (use the balance column format or T-accounts): Cash (101); Accounts Receivable (106); Office Supplies (124); Prepaid Insurance (128); Prepaid Rent (131); Office Equipment (163); Accounts Payable (201); Susan Hurley, Capital (301); Susan Hurley, Withdrawals (302); Accounting Fees Earned (401); Professional Development Expense (680); and Utilities Expense (690).

2. Post the entries to the accounts and enter the balance after each posting.

3. Prepare a trial balance as of September 30, 2014.

CHECK FIGURES:
Net income = $9,980;
Total assets = $37,130

Problem 2-5B Preparing financial statements from a trial balance LO[7]

Using the trial balance prepared in Part 3 of Problem 2-4B, prepare an income statement and statement of changes in equity for the month ended September 30, 2014, and a balance sheet at September 30, 2014.

CHECK FIGURE:
4. Total Dr = $96,300

Problem 2-6B Preparing and posting General Journal entries; preparing a trial balance LO[3,4,5,6,7]

WiCom Servicing completed these transactions during November 2014, its first month of operations:

Nov.	1	Tait Unger, the owner, invested $62,000 cash and office equipment that had a fair value of $19,000 in the business.
	2	Prepaid $21,000 cash for three months' rent for an office.
	4	Made credit purchases of used office equipment for $9,000 and office supplies for $1,650.
	8	Completed work for a client and immediately received $5,200 cash.
	12	Completed a $4,800 project for a client, who will pay within 30 days.
	13	Paid the account payable created on November 4.
	19	Paid $3,750 cash as the annual premium on an insurance policy.
	22	Received $2,000 as partial payment for the work completed on November 12.
	24	Completed work for another client for $3,600 on credit.
	28	Unger withdrew $5,300 from the business for personal use.
	29	Purchased $1,700 of additional office supplies on credit.
	30	Paid $19,000 in wages.
	30	Paid $1,650 for the month's utility bill.

Required

1. Prepare General Journal entries to record the transactions. Use General Journal page 1.

2. Set up the following accounts (use the balance column format or T-accounts): Cash (101); Accounts Receivable (106); Office Supplies (124); Prepaid Insurance (128); Prepaid Rent (131); Office Equipment (163); Accounts Payable (201); Tait Unger, Capital (301); Tait Unger, Withdrawals (302); Service Fees Earned (401); Wages Expense (680); and Utilities Expense (690).

3. Post the entries to the accounts, and enter the balance after each posting.

4. Prepare a trial balance at November 30, 2014.

Analysis Component: Is the November 29 purchase of office supplies recorded as a debit to an asset or an expense account? Explain.

CHECK FIGURES:
Net loss = $7,050;
Total assets = $70,350

Problem 2-7B Preparing financial statements from a trial balance LO⁷

Using the trial balance prepared in Part 4 of Problem 2-6B, prepare an income statement and statement of changes in equity for the month ended November 30, 2014, and a balance sheet at November 30, 2014.

CHECK FIGURES:
Net loss = $3,120;
Total assets = $135,680

Problem 2-8B Preparing financial statements from a trial balance LO⁷

	Rush Innovations Trial Balance November 30, 2014		
Acct. No.	**Account Title**	**Debit**	**Credit**
101	Cash	$ 23,480	
106	Accounts receivable	7,000	
124	Office supplies	5,800	
128	Prepaid insurance	10,400	
131	Prepaid rent	21,000	
163	Office equipment	68,000	
201	Accounts payable		$ 3,400
301	Jay Rush, capital		146,000
302	Jay Rush, withdrawals	10,600	
401	Service fees earned		15,800
680	Wages expense	16,000	
690	Utilities expense	2,920	
	Totals	$165,200	$165,200

Required Use the trial balance provided above to prepare an income statement and statement of changes in equity for the first month ended November 30, 2014, and a balance sheet at November 30, 2014.

Analysis Component: Prepare two journal entries, including explanations: one that would have caused Accounts Receivable to increase, and one that would have caused it to decrease. Use November 30, 2014, as the date for your entries.

Problem 2-9B Journalizing, posting, preparing a trial balance LO[3,4,5,6,7]

At the beginning of June 2014, Brett Wilson created a moving company called Frog Box Company. The company had the following transactions during July, its second month of operations:

July	1	Purchased office equipment for $9,000 and a truck for $56,000 by signing a long-term note payable.
	2	Purchased land for an office. The land was worth $124,000, which was paid with $40,800 cash and a long-term note payable for the balance.
	3	Purchased a used portable building with $21,000 cash and moved it onto the land.
	5	Paid $9,600 cash for the premiums on two one-year insurance policies.
	9	Provided services to a client and collected $3,200 cash.
	12	Purchased additional office equipment for $6,500. Paid $700 cash and signed a long-term note payable for the balance.
	15	Completed $3,750 of services for a client. This amount is due within 30 days.
	20	Completed another hauling job for $9,200 on credit.
	21	Received a bill for rent on a specialized hauling truck that was used to complete the job done on July 20. The $1,300 rent must be paid within 30 days.
	22	Collected $5,000 from the client described in the transaction on July 20.
	23	Paid $1,600 wages to an assistant.
	24	Paid the account payable created in the transaction of July 21.
	25	Paid $1,425 cash for some repairs to the truck.
	26	Wilson withdrew $3,875 in cash from the business for personal use.
	27	Paid $1,600 wages to an assistant.
	28	Paid $800 cash for advertising in the local newspaper during July.
	29	Received $1,400 from a client for services to be performed in August.

Required

1. Prepare General Journal entries to record the transactions. Use page 1 for the journal.

2. Set up the following accounts (use the balance column format or T-accounts), entering the balances brought forward from June 30, 2014: Cash (101) $75,000; Accounts Receivable (106) $950; Prepaid Insurance (128) $275; Trucks (153) $20,800; Office Equipment (163) $1,200; Building (173) $-0-; Land (183) $-0-; Accounts Payable (201) $725; Unearned Fees (233) $-0-; Long-Term Notes Payable (251) $7,000; Brett Wilson, Capital (301) $83,825; Brett Wilson, Withdrawals (302) $600; Fees Earned (401) $8,400; Wages Expense (623) $780; Truck Rental Expense (645) $230; Advertising Expense (655) $75; and Repairs Expense (684) $40.

3. Post the entries to the accounts and enter the balance after each posting.

4. Prepare a trial balance as of the end of the month.

Problem 2-10B Preparing financial statements from a trial balance LO[7]

Using the trial balance prepared in Part 4 of Problem 2-9B, prepare an income statement and statement of changes in equity for the two months ended July 31, 2014, and a balance sheet at July 31, 2014.

Problem 2-11B Journalizing, posting, preparing a trial balance and financial statements LO[1,3,4,5,6,7]

Ike Petrov started a tour company, Tour-Along, on October 1, 2014. The following activities occurred during November, the second month of operations:

Nov.	1	Paid $10,000 regarding purchases made on account during October.
	2	Purchased a $34,000 photocopier, paying $6,000 cash and signing a note payable for the balance.
	3	Purchased office supplies for cash; $800.
	4	Signed a $200,000 contract with RBC to arrange travel for its employees beginning January 1, 2015.
	14	Paid wages of $6,000.
	20	Collected $14,000 for clients travelling in November.
	25	Ike Petrov withdrew $2,000 cash for personal use.
	30	Paid interest on the notes payable; $150.

Required

1. Prepare General Journal entries to record the November transactions.

2. Set up the following T-accounts, entering the balances brought forward from October 31, 2014: Cash (101) $26,000; Office Supplies (124) $900; Office Equipment (163) $36,000; Accounts Payable (201) $43,000; Notes Payable (205) $20,000; Ike Petrov, Capital (301) $8,000; Ike Petrov, Withdrawals (302) $4,000; Travel Revenue (401) $34,000; Wages Expense (623) $38,000; and Interest Expense (633) $100.

3. Post the entries to the accounts; calculate the ending balance in each account.

4. Prepare a trial balance at November 30, 2014.

5. Use the trial balance to prepare an income statement and statement of changes in equity for the two months ended November 30, 2014, as well as a balance sheet at November 30, 2014.

Analysis Component: Part 2 of the *Required* states that the account Ike Petrov, Capital had a balance of $8,000 at October 31, 2014. Explain what this balance represents.

CHECK FIGURES:
Net loss = $33,680;
Total assets = $120,670

Problem 2-12B Preparing financial statements from a trial balance LO⁷

Lincoln Landscaping Trial Balance July 31, 2014		
Acct. No. **Account Title**	**Debit**	**Credit**
101 Cash	$ 23,720	
106 Accounts receivable	18,600	
128 Prepaid insurance	13,750	
167 Equipment	64,600	
201 Accounts payable		$ 37,500
233 Unearned fees		2,800
251 Long-term notes payable		58,000
301 Brielle Lincoln, capital		65,000
302 Brielle Lincoln, withdrawals	8,950	
401 Fees earned		29,100
623 Wages expense	59,000	
645 Rental expense	1,100	
655 Advertising expense	1,750	
684 Repairs expense	930	
Totals	$192,400	$192,400

Required Using the trial balance provided above, prepare an income statement and a statement of changes in equity for the first three months ended July 31, 2014, and a balance sheet at July 31, 2014.

Analysis Component: Analyze the balance sheet and calculate what percentage of the assets is financed by (a) debt and (b) equity.

CHECK FIGURE:
Total Dr = $49,860

Problem 2-13B Analyzing trial balance errors LO[3,5,6,7]

On January 1, 2014, Bev Horricks started a new business called Dance-A-Lot. Near the end of the year, she hired a new bookkeeper without making a careful reference check. As a result, a number of mistakes have been made in preparing the following trial balance:

Dance-A-Lot Trial Balance December 31, 2014		
	Debit	**Credit**
Cash	$ 5,500	
Accounts receivable		$ 7,900
Office supplies............................	2,650	
Office equipment.......................	20,500	
Accounts payable.......................		9,465
Bev Horricks, capital..................	16,745	
Services revenue.........................		22,350
Wages expense		6,000
Rent expense		4,800
Advertising expense..................		1,250
Totals..	$45,395	$52,340

Bev's analysis of the situation has uncovered these errors:

a. The sum of the debits in the Cash account is $37,175 and the sum of the credits is $30,540.

b. A $275 payment from a credit customer was posted to Cash but was not posted to Accounts Receivable.

c. A credit purchase of office supplies for $400 was not posted at all.

d. A transposition error occurred in copying the balance of the Services Revenue account to the trial balance. The correct amount was $23,250.

Other errors were made in placing account balances in the wrong trial balance columns and in taking the totals of the columns.

Required Prepare a corrected trial balance.

ANALYTICAL AND REVIEW PROBLEMS

A & R Problem 2-1

Carlos Young started an engineering firm called Young Engineering. He began operations in March 2014 and completed seven transactions, including his initial investment of $17,000 cash. After these transactions, the ledger included the following accounts with their normal balances:

Cash	$26,660
Office Supplies	660
Prepaid Insurance...	3,200
Office Equipment..	16,500
Accounts Payable	16,500
Carlos Young, Capital....................................	17,000
Carlos Young, Withdrawals	3,740
Engineering Fees Earned	24,000
Rent Expense	6,740

Required
Preparation Component: Prepare a trial balance for the business.

Analysis Component: Analyze the accounts and balances and prepare narratives that describe each of the seven most likely transactions and their amounts.

A & R Problem 2-2

Nice-n-Fresh Drycleaning showed the following information for its first and second months just ended, March and April of 2014:

Account Title	April 30, 2014	March 31, 2014
Cash	7,000	3,000
Cleaning supplies......................	3,500	900
Prepaid rent	12,000	16,000
Equipment	76,000	30,000
Accounts payable......................	700	500
Notes payable...........................	40,000	15,000
Ed Fresh, capital*	?	?

*Ed Fresh made a $10,000 investment during March and had withdrawals of $1,000 in March and $25,100 in April.

Required Use the information provided to complete a statement of changes in equity and a balance sheet for each of March and April 2014. *NOTE: Prepare the statements on a comparative*[16] *basis similar to the statements for* **Danier Leather** *and* **WestJet** *in Appendix II at the end of the textbook.*

Analysis Component:

a. Liabilities increased by $25,200 from March 31, 2014, to April 30, 2014. Review the balance sheet and identify why liabilities increased.

b. Equity increased by $34,400 during March and by $23,400 during April, yet net income was much higher in April. Explain.

ETHICS CHALLENGE

EC 2-1

You are a cashier at a retail convenience store. When you were hired, the owner explained to you the policy of immediately ringing up each sale. Recently, lunch hour traffic has increased dramatically and the manager asks you to take customers' cash and make change without ringing up sales to avoid delays. The manager says she will add up cash and ring up sales equal to the cash amount after lunch. She says that in this way the register will always be accurate when the owner arrives at 3:00 p.m.

Required

1. Identify the advantages and disadvantages of the manager's suggestion.
2. Identify the ethical dilemma and evaluate at least two courses of action you might consider and why.

---

16 Preparing statements on a *comparative basis* means to have numbers for at least two periods side by side. This kind of presentation provides decision makers with something meaningful against which the current period can be compared.

FOCUS ON FINANCIAL STATEMENTS

FFS 2-1

Travis McAllister operates a surveying company. For the first few months of the company's life (through April), the accounting records were maintained by an outside bookkeeping service. According to those records, McAllister's equity balance was $75,000 as of April 30. To save on expenses, McAllister decided to keep the records himself. He managed to record May's transactions properly, but was a bit rusty when the time came to prepare the financial statements. His first versions of the balance sheet and income statement follow. McAllister is bothered that the company apparently operated at a loss during the month, even though he was very busy.

McAllister Surveying
Income Statement
For Month Ended May 31, 2014

Revenue:		
Investments by owner		$ 3,000
Unearned surveying fees..........		6,000
Total revenues......................		$ 9,000
Operating expenses:		
Rent expense	$3,100	
Telephone expense..................	600	
Surveying equipment	5,400	
Advertising expense................	3,200	
Utilities expense......................	300	
Insurance expense	900	
Withdrawals by owner.............	6,000	
Total operating expenses		19,500
Net income (loss)........................		$(10,500)

McAllister Surveying
Balance Sheet
May 31, 2014

Assets			**Liabilities**		
Cash	$ 3,900		Accounts payable	$ 2,400	
Accounts receivable	2,700		Surveying fees earned.............	18,000	
Prepaid insurance..................	1,800		Short-term notes payable	48,000	
Prepaid rent	4,200		Total liabilities	$ 68,400	
Office supplies........................	300				
Buildings................................	81,000		**Equity**		
Land	36,000		Travis McAllister, capital..........	64,500	
Salaries expense	3,000				
Total assets.............................	$132,900		Total liabilities and equity	$132,900	

Required Using the information contained in the original financial statements, prepare revised statements, including a statement of changes in equity, for the month of May.

Analysis Component: The owner, Travis McAllister, made a withdrawal during May. Withdrawals cause equity to decrease. Why would the owner intentionally cause equity to decrease by making a withdrawal?

FFS 2-2

1. Refer to **WestJet's** income statement in Appendix II at the end of the textbook.
    a. Total *Guest revenues* for 2011 were $2,790,299 (thousand).
       (i)   Prepare two possible journal entries that might have been recorded to create this result.
       (ii) What effect do revenues have on the balance sheet?
       (iii) What assurances do we have that the revenues appearing on the income statement are for the year 2011? *Hint:* Which GAAP?
    b. Total *Finance costs* for 2011 were $60,911 (thousand).
       (i)   Prepare a possible journal entry that might have recorded the interest expense.
       (ii) Do expenses affect the balance sheet? Explain.
2. Refer to **WestJet's** balance sheet in Appendix II at the end of the textbook. Find the line showing *Advance ticket sales* of $432,186 (thousand).
    a. Explain what you think the account *Advance ticket sales* represents.
    b. Prepare the journal entry that might have recorded this account balance.

CRITICAL THINKING MINI CASE

Prairie Insurance sells life insurance, disability insurance, vehicle insurance, crop insurance, and home-owners' insurance. You are employed by Prairie Insurance and have been promoted to sales division manager for the Western Canadian division. You will be supervising approximately 25 salespeople, along with five administrative assistants at various locations. The salespeople travel extensively and submit expense reports along with sales information monthly. A sample expense report for September shows:

Prairie Insurance—Western Canadian Division **Sales Report: John Bishop** **Month Ended September 30, 2014**	
Sales revenue*...	$56,000
Expenses**	34,000
*Sales invoices attached **Receipts attached	

The former manager was dismissed because division results have been deteriorating. The consolidated sales report for the past three months shows the following:

Prairie Insurance—Western Canadian Division **Sales Report** **Month Ended**			
	September 30, 2014	**August 31, 2014**	**July 31, 2014**
Sales revenue	$680,000	$510,000	$440,000
Expenses...............................	544,000	382,500	321,200
Net income...........................	$136,000	$127,500	$118,800

You learn that the company has one revenue account called Sales Revenue and one expense account called Expenses. You proceed to prepare a brief memo to the company's accountant requesting information that is needed to help you analyze the situation.

Required

Using the elements of critical thinking described on the inside front cover, respond.

SERIAL PROBLEM

Echo Systems

(This comprehensive problem starts in this chapter and continues in Chapters 3, 4, and 5. Because of its length, this problem is most easily solved if you use the Working Papers[17] that accompany this text.)

On October 1, 2014, Mary Graham organized a computer service company called Echo Systems. Echo is organized as a sole proprietorship and will provide consulting services, computer system installations, and custom program development. Graham has adopted the calendar year for reporting, and expects to prepare the company's first set of financial statements as of December 31, 2014. The initial chart of accounts for the accounting system includes these items:

Account Number	Account Name	Account Number	Account Name
101	Cash	301	Mary Graham, Capital
106	Accounts Receivable	302	Mary Graham, Withdrawals
126	Computer Supplies	403	Computer Services Revenue
128	Prepaid Insurance	623	Wages Expense
131	Prepaid Rent	655	Advertising Expense
163	Office Equipment	676	Mileage Expense
167	Computer Equipment	684	Repairs Expense, Computer
201	Accounts Payable	699	Charitable Donations Expense

---

17 If students have not purchased the Working Paper package, the Working Papers for the Serial Problem are available on Connect.

Part A

Required

1. Set up balance column accounts based on the chart of accounts provided.

2. Prepare journal entries to record each of the following October transactions.

3. Post the October entries.

4. Prepare a trial balance at October 31, 2014.

5. Prepare an income statement and a statement of changes in equity for the month ended October 31, 2014, as well as a balance sheet at October 31, 2014.

Oct.	1	Mary Graham invested $90,000 cash, a $36,000 computer system, and $18,000 of office equipment in the business.
	2	Paid rent in advance of $9,000.
	3	Purchased computer supplies on credit for $2,640 from Abbott Office Products.
	5	Paid $4,320 cash for one year's premium on a property and liability insurance policy.
	6	Billed Capital Leasing $6,600 for installing a new computer.
	8	Paid for the computer supplies purchased from Abbott Office Products.
	10	Hired Carly Smith as a part-time assistant for $200 per day, as needed.
	12	Billed Capital Leasing another $2,400 for computer services rendered.
	15	Received $6,600 from Capital Leasing on its account.
	17	Paid $1,410 to repair computer equipment damaged when moving into the new office.
	20	Paid $3,720 for an advertisement in the local newspaper.
	22	Received $2,400 from Capital Leasing on its account.
	28	Billed Decker Company $6,450 for services.
	31	Paid Carly Smith for seven days' work.
	31	Mary Graham withdrew $7,200 cash from the business for personal use.

Part B

Required

6. Prepare journal entries to record each of the following November transactions.

7. Post the November entries.

8. Prepare a trial balance at November 30, 2014.

9. Prepare an income statement and a statement of changes in equity for the two months ended November 30, 2014, as well as a balance sheet at November 30, 2014.

Nov.	1	Reimbursed Mary Graham's business automobile expense for 1,000 kilometres at $1.00 per kilometre.
	2	Received $9,300 cash from Elite Corporation for computer services rendered.
	5	Purchased $1,920 of computer supplies for cash from Abbott Office Products.
	8	Billed Fostek Co. $8,700 for computer services rendered.
	13	Notified by Alamo Engineering Co. that Echo's bid of $7,500 for an upcoming project was accepted.
	18	Received $3,750 from Decker Company against the bill dated October 28.
	22	Donated $1,500 to the United Way in the company's name.
	24	Completed work for Alamo Engineering Co. and sent a bill for $7,500.
	25	Sent another bill to Decker Company for the past due amount of $2,700.
	28	Reimbursed Mary Graham's business automobile expense for 1,200 kilometres at $1.00 per kilometre.
	30	Paid Carly Smith for 14 days' work.
	30	Mary Graham withdrew $3,600 cash from the business for personal use.

Adjusting Accounts for Financial Statements

LEAPING AHEAD

Doug Burgoyne founded Vancouver-based Frogbox Inc. in 2008 to pursue his goal of filling a niche in the $5 billion residential moving market by creating an eco-friendly alternative to cardboard moving boxes. The business plan? To drop off green, reusable boxes to your current home or office and pick them up empty at your new place. It's convenient and affordable as well as appealing to the go-green mindset. Cardboard boxes can be used twice, on average, while a plastic Frogbox can be cleaned and reused about 400 times before needing to be recycled. Frogbox doesn't stop there ... in addition to providing recycled packing paper and other eco-friendly moving supplies, its delivery trucks are equipped with software that maps routes and schedules to efficiently schedule deliveries and pick-ups to reduce mileage thereby reducing greenhouse gas emissions.

Doug says that "As an entrepreneur it's critical to have proper accounting data to drive strategic decisions in the business. Without proper accounting it's not possible to fully understand the impact of the decisions a business makes." Frogbox seems to have all its bases covered ... in addition to managing the business from an accounting perspective, it has also consciously taken steps to be socially responsible—Frogbox donates 1 percent of its gross revenues to frog-habitat restoration projects, including the Vancouver Aquarium's Oregon Spotted Frog Recovery and BC Frogwatch programs.

After only three years in operation, the business has 19 locations and plans to expand into numerous U.S. cities within the next two years. The exposure from their appearance on the popular CBC television show *Dragons' Den* attracted significant attention from prospective North American franchisees. As a result, Frogbox is set to grow in leaps and bounds!

www.frogbox.com

LEARNING OBJECTIVES

LO¹ Describe the purpose of adjusting accounts at the end of a period.

LO² Explain how the timeliness, matching, and revenue recognition principles affect the adjusting process.

LO³ Explain accrual accounting and cash basis accounting and how accrual accounting adds to the usefulness of financial statements.

LO⁴ Prepare and explain adjusting entries for prepaid expenses, depreciation, unearned revenues, accrued expenses, and accrued revenues.

LO⁵ Explain how accounting adjustments link to financial statements.

LO⁶ Explain and prepare an adjusted trial balance.

LO⁷ Prepare financial statements from an adjusted trial balance.

*Appendix 3A

LO⁸ Explain and prepare correcting entries.

*Appendix 3B

LO⁹ Identify and explain an alternative in recording prepaids and unearned revenues.

An asterisk (*) identifies appendix material.

CRITICAL THINKING CHALLENGE Assuming you were an executive in Frogbox Inc., how might you intentionally inflate earnings to create a better image with potential investors? Explain how GAAP would be violated by this strategy.

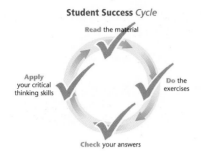

Student Success *Cycle*

Read the material

Apply your critical thinking skills

Do the exercises

Check your answers

CHAPTER PREVIEW

Financial statements reflect revenues when earned and expenses when incurred. This is known as *accrual basis accounting*. Accrual basis accounting is achieved by following the steps of the accounting cycle. We described the first four of these steps in Chapter 2.

An important part of the accounting cycle is the adjustment of account balances. The adjusted account balances are what is reported in financial statements that are prepared according to generally accepted accounting principles. Adjustment of accounts is necessary so that financial statements at the end of a reporting period reflect the effects of all transactions. This chapter emphasizes Steps Five and Six of the accounting cycle as highlighted in Exhibit 3.1. Preparation of financial statements, Step Seven of the accounting cycle, is reinforced in this chapter, with an emphasis on how *adjusting entries* impact the financial statements. **Frogbox Inc.**, in the chapter opener, likely used adjusting entries to play an important role in producing accurate financial statements. To illustrate the adjusting process, we continue with the example of Vertically Inclined used in previous chapters.

PURPOSE OF ADJUSTING

LO¹ Describe the purpose of adjusting accounts at the end of a period.

The usual process during an accounting period is to record *external transactions*. **External transactions** are exchanges between two parties; these were the focus of Chapters 1 and 2. After external transactions are recorded, several accounts in the ledger need adjustment for their balances to appear in financial statements. This need arises because *internal transactions* remain unrecorded. **Internal transactions** represent exchanges within an organization that affect the accounting equation and are the focus of this chapter.

EXHIBIT 3.1

Steps in the Accounting Cycle Introduced in Chapter 3

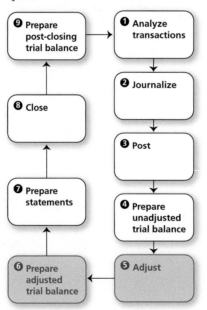

An example is the cost of certain assets that expire or are used up as time passes. The Prepaid Insurance account of Vertically Inclined is one of these. Vertically Inclined's trial balance (Exhibit 3.2) shows Prepaid Insurance with a balance of $2,400. This amount is the premium for two years of insurance protection beginning on March 1, 2014. By March 31, 2014, because one month's coverage is used up, the $2,400 is no longer the correct account balance for Prepaid Insurance. The Prepaid Insurance account balance must be reduced by one month's cost, or $100 ($2,400/24 months). The income statement must report this $100 cost as insurance expense for March.

Another example is the $3,600 balance in Supplies. Part of this balance includes the cost of supplies that were used in March. The cost of the supplies used must be reported as an expense in March. The balances of both the Prepaid Insurance and Supplies accounts must be *adjusted* before they are reported on the March 31 balance sheet.

Another adjustment necessary for Vertically Inclined relates to one month's usage of equipment. The balances of the Unearned Teaching Revenue, Teaching Revenue, and Salaries Expense accounts often also need adjusting before they appear on the statements. We explain *why* this adjusting process is carried out in the next section.

Vertically Inclined Rock Gym Trial Balance March 31, 2014		
	Debit	**Credit**
Cash..	$ 8,070	
Accounts receivable...	-0-	
Prepaid insurance	2,400	
Supplies..	3,600	
Equipment...	6,000	
Accounts payable..		$ 200
Unearned teaching revenue......................................		3,000
Notes payable..		6,000
Virgil Klimb, capital..		10,000
Virgil Klimb, withdrawals	600	
Teaching revenue		3,800
Equipment rental revenue..		300
Rent expense	1,000	
Salaries expense...	1,400	
Utilities expense...	230	
Totals...	$23,300	$23,300

GAAP AND THE ADJUSTING PROCESS

The adjusting process is based on three generally accepted accounting principles: the timeliness principle, the revenue recognition principle, and the matching principle. In this section, we explain how GAAP add to the usefulness of financial statements.

LO² Explain how the timeliness, matching, and revenue recognition principles affect the adjusting process.

The Accounting Period

The adjusting process is often linked to timeliness of information. Information must reach decision makers frequently and promptly, therefore accounting systems need to prepare periodic reports at regular intervals. This results in an accounting process impacted by the *timeliness principle*.[1] The **timeliness principle** assumes that an organization's activities can be divided into specific time periods such as a month, a three-month quarter, or a year, as illustrated in Exhibit 3.3. It requires that statements be presented at least annually.

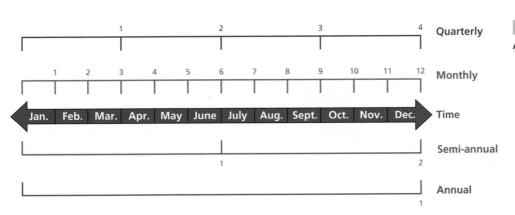

---

1   IFRS 2012, IAS 1, para. 36; "Framework," para. QC29.

Time periods covered by statements are called **accounting periods** (or **reporting periods**). Reports covering a one-year period are known as *annual financial statements*. Recall that a company can adopt a *fiscal year* based on the *calendar year* or its *natural business year*.

Many organizations also prepare **interim financial reports** covering one, three (quarterly), or six (semi-annual) months of activity.

Recognizing Revenues and Expenses

Because of the need for regular reporting of information, activities are often reported on or before their completion so as not to mislead decision makers. These activities are recorded through the adjusting process. Two main generally accepted accounting principles are used in the adjusting process: the *matching principle* and the *revenue recognition principle*. The **matching principle** aims to report or *match* expenses in the same accounting period as the revenues they helped to earn.[2] For example, assume that as part of a $500 teaching services contract Vertically Inclined is to supply a detailed written plan to one of its customers in May. In the process of earning this $500 in revenue, Vertically Inclined will use $150 of office supplies purchased and paid for in April. The $150 of office supplies used in *May* is an expense that will be reported on the *May* income statement even though the supplies were purchased and paid for in April. The $150 of office supplies used in May must be ***matched*** against the $500 of May revenues in accordance with the matching principle. Financial statements will reflect accurate information about the income actually earned during the period only if expenses are properly matched against the revenues they helped to create.

To illustrate *revenue recognition*, we will look at two situations. First, assume that in May, Vertically Inclined provides $500 of teaching services to a client and collects the cash immediately. The $500 of revenue is earned in May and is reported on the May income statement in accordance with the revenue recognition principle. Second, assume that Vertically Inclined collected $1,000 cash in May for work to be done in June. The $1,000 of revenue will be earned in June and will therefore be reported on the June income statement; the $1,000 will *not* be reported as revenue in May because it has not yet been earned. A major goal of the adjusting process is to have revenue *recognized* (reported) in the time period when it is *earned* regardless of when the cash is actually received. This concept is the foundation on which the *accrual basis of accounting* was developed.

Accrual Basis Compared to Cash Basis

Accrual basis accounting is founded on the revenue recognition principle, where revenues and expenses are *recognized* or recorded when earned or incurred regardless of when cash is received or paid. The word *accrual* and its root word *accrue* mean *to accumulate* or *to add*. So accrual basis accounting means that revenues and expenses must be *added* or *matched* to the *time period* in which they actually happened; when cash was received or paid is irrelevant to the recording of revenues and expenses. Accrual basis accounting, then, is based on the three GAAP of *revenue recognition*, *matching*, and *timeliness*.

In contrast, **cash basis accounting** recognizes revenues and expenses when *cash* is received or paid. Cash basis accounting for the income statement, balance sheet, and statement of changes in equity is *not* consistent with generally accepted accounting principles. It is commonly held that accrual basis accounting provides a better indication of business performance than information about current cash receipts and payments. Accrual basis accounting also increases the comparability of financial statements from one period to another. Yet information about cash flows is also useful. This is why companies also include a cash flow statement, discussed in Chapter 17.

LO³ Explain accrual accounting and cash basis accounting and how accrual accounting adds to the usefulness of financial statements.

Accrual Basis Accounting
Revenues (= when earned)
− Expenses (= when incurred)
Net Income

Cash Basis Accounting
Revenues (= cash receipts)
− Expenses (= cash payments)
Net Income

---

2   IFRS 2012, IAS 18, para. 19; "Framework," para. 4.50.

DECISION INSIGHT

Matching False Revenues Against Real Expenses?
British Columbia–based Chronico Music Group purchases talent and organizes concerts. Based on a poolside conversation at the MTV Music Awards hosted at the Hollywood Roosevelt Hotel, Chronico paid a deposit to an individual in exchange for scheduling a concert at the Pacific Coliseum in Vancouver on November 10, 2011, featuring the hip hop and R&B star Chris Brown. The questionable individual set up a fake bank account and Chronico, which did not appropriately verify the booking, has no revenues to match against the expense related to the booking fee that was paid.

SOURCE: *The Globe and Mail*, September 2011.

CHECKPOINT

1. Describe a company's annual reporting period.
2. Why do companies prepare interim financial statements?
3. What accounting principles most directly lead to the adjusting process?
4. Is cash basis accounting consistent with generally accepted accounting principles?

Do Quick Study questions: QS 3-1, QS 3-2

ADJUSTING ACCOUNTS

The process of adjusting accounts is similar to our process of analyzing and recording transactions in Chapter 2. We must analyze each account balance and the transactions that affect it to determine any needed adjustments. An **adjusting entry** is recorded at the **end** of the accounting period to bring an asset or liability account balance to its proper amount. This entry also updates the related expense or revenue account and is necessary to prepare the financial statements. Adjustments are journalized in the General Journal and then posted to accounts in the ledger like any other entry. This next section shows the mechanics of adjusting entries and their links to financial statements.

Framework for Adjustments

It is helpful to group adjustments by their timing of cash receipt or payment in comparison to when they are recognized as revenues or expenses. Exhibit 3.4 identifies the five main adjustments, each of which is detailed in the following sections.

LO⁴ Prepare and explain adjusting entries for prepaid expenses, depreciation, unearned revenues, accrued expenses, and accrued revenues.

EXHIBIT 3.4
Framework For Adjustments

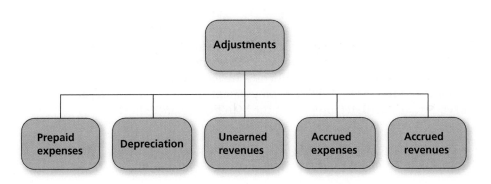

EYK
3-1

Adjusting Prepaid Expenses

Prepaid expenses[3] refer to items *paid for* in advance of receiving their benefits. Prepaid expenses are assets. As these assets are used, their costs become expenses. Prepaids are common in business. For example, **Cameco** reported $182,037,000 of prepaid expenses at December 31, 2011, $24,688,000 of prepaids appear on **Maple Leaf Foods'** December 31, 2011, balance sheet, and **Canadian Tire** showed $44,300,000 of prepaid expenses on its December 31, 2011, financial statements. Adjusting entries for prepaids involve increasing (debiting) expenses and decreasing (crediting) assets as shown in Exhibit 3.5.

EXHIBIT 3.5

Adjusting for Prepaid Expenses

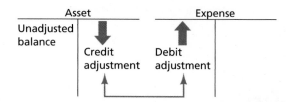

The three common prepaid expenses are insurance, supplies, and depreciation.

Prepaid Insurance

We illustrate prepaid insurance using Vertically Inclined's payment of $2,400 for two years of insurance protection beginning on March 1, 2014. The following entry records the purchase of the insurance:

Mar.	1	Prepaid Insurance	2,400	
		Cash		2,400
		To record purchase of insurance for 24 months.		

By March 31, one month's insurance coverage is used, causing a portion of the asset Prepaid Insurance to become an expense. This expense is $100 ($2,400 × 1/24). Our adjusting entry to record this expense and reduce the asset is:

Adjustment (a)

$$A = L + E^*$$
$$\downarrow \qquad \downarrow$$

* Recall that expenses cause equity to decrease.

Mar.	31	Insurance Expense...	100	
		Prepaid Insurance		100
		To record expired insurance.		

Posting this adjusting entry affects the accounts shown in Exhibit 3.6:

EXHIBIT 3.6

Insurance Accounts After Adjusting for Prepaids

Prepaid Insurance				Insurance Expense		
Mar. 1	2,400	100	Mar. 31	Mar. 31	100	
Balance	2,300					

After posting, the $100 balance in Insurance Expense and the $2,300 balance in Prepaid Insurance are ready for reporting in the financial statements. If the adjustment is *not* made at March 31, then (a) expenses are *understated* by $100 and net income is *overstated* by $100 for the March income statement, and (b) both Prepaid Insurance and equity are overstated by $100 in the March 31 balance sheet.

---

3 Prepaids are also called *deferrals* because the recognition of the expense or revenue on the income statement is *deferred* to a future accounting period.

An **understated account** is too low. For example, if Revenue has a balance of $100 and it is understated by $20, the correct balance is $120. An **overstated account** is too high. For example, if Equipment has a balance of $450 and it is overstated by $40, the correct balance is $410.

Supplies

Vertically Inclined purchased $3,600 of supplies in March and used some of them during this month. Daily usage of supplies was not recorded in Vertically Inclined's accounts because this information was not needed. When we report account balances in financial statements only at the end of a month, recordkeeping costs can be reduced by making only one adjusting entry at that time. This entry needs to record the total cost of all supplies used in the month.

The cost of supplies used during March must be recognized as an expense. Vertically Inclined calculates ("takes inventory of") the remaining unused supplies. The cost of the remaining supplies is then deducted from the cost of the purchased supplies to calculate the amount used. Vertically Inclined has $2,550 of supplies remaining out of the $3,600 ($2,500 + $1,100) purchased in March. The $1,050 difference between these two amounts is the cost of the supplies used. This amount is March's Supplies Expense. Our adjusting entry to record this expense and reduce the Supplies asset account is:

Adjustment (b)

Mar. 31	Supplies Expense...	1,050		$A = L + E$
	Supplies...		1,050	↓ ↓
	To record supplies used.			

Posting this adjusting entry affects the accounts shown in Exhibit 3.7:

Supplies			
Mar. 1	2,500	1,050	Mar. 31
1	1,100		
Balance	2,550		

Supplies Expense		
Mar. 31	1,050	

EXHIBIT 3.7

Supplies Accounts After Adjusting for Prepaids

The balance of the Supplies account is $2,550 after posting and equals the cost of remaining unused supplies. If the adjustment is *not* made at March 31, then (a) expenses are understated by $1,050 and net income overstated by $1,050 for the March income statement, and (b) both Supplies and equity are overstated by $1,050 in the March 31 balance sheet.

Other Prepaid Expenses

There are other prepaid expenses (including Prepaid Rent), which are accounted for in exactly the same manner as Insurance and Supplies above. We should also note that some prepaid expenses are both paid for and fully used up within a single accounting period. One example is when a company pays monthly rent on the first day of each month. The payment creates a prepaid expense on the first day of each month that fully expires by the end of the month. In these special cases, we can record the cash paid with a debit to the expense account instead of an asset account.

Investor

A small publishing company signed a well known athlete to write a book. The company paid the athlete $500,000 today plus will pay future book royalties. A note to the company's financial statements says that "prepaid expenses include $500,000 in author signing fees to be matched against future expected sales." Is this accounting for the signing bonus acceptable? How might it affect your analysis as an investor in the publishing company?

CHECKPOINT

5. If the entry to adjust Prepaid Insurance was not recorded, what effect would this have on each component of the accounting equation?

Do Quick Study question: QS 3-3

Adjusting for Depreciation[4]

Property, plant and equipment (PPE) assets are used to produce and sell products and services, and **intangible assets** (such as patents) convey the right to use a product or process. Both of these asset groups are expected to provide benefits for more than one accounting period. Examples of property, plant and equipment assets are land, buildings, machines, vehicles, and fixtures. Because these assets (except for land) wear out or decline in usefulness as they are used, an expense must be recorded to match the cost of the asset over the time the asset helped earn revenues. **Depreciation** is the process of calculating expense from matching (or allocating) the cost of plant and equipment assets over their expected useful lives. Businesses that have significant dollars invested in plant and equipment can have large amounts of depreciation appearing on the income statement. For example, **Bombardier Inc.** reported buildings and equipment that cost $4,010 million with $178 million of corresponding depreciation in its December 31, 2011, financial statements. On its December 31, 2011, statements, **Suncor** reported depreciation of $1.8 billion related to plant and equipment that cost $45 billion.

Vertically Inclined uses equipment in earning revenue. This equipment's cost must be depreciated to match the cost of the equipment over the time that the equipment helps earn revenue. Recall that Vertically Inclined purchased equipment for $6,000 on March 1. Virgil Klimb expects the equipment to have a useful life (benefit period) of two years. Virgil expects to sell the equipment for about $1,200 at the end of two years. This means that the *net cost* expected to expire over the estimated useful life is $4,800 (=$6,000 − $1,200).

Straight-Line Depreciation

Calculated as:

$$= \frac{\text{Cost of asset} - \text{Estimated value at end of estimated useful life}}{\text{Estimated useful life}}$$

$$= \frac{\$6,000 - \$1,200}{24 \text{ months}}$$

$$= \$200 \text{ per month}$$

---

4 Prior to 2011, the term **amortization** was used instead of *depreciation*. In 2011, IFRS were adopted in Canada and the term *depreciation* is to be used for plant and equipment (IFRS 2012, IAS 16, para. 43). *Amortization* will continue to be used for intangible assets (IFRS 2012, IAS 38, para. 97). *Intangible assets* are introduced in Chapter 4. *Amortization* for intangible assets is discussed in more detail in Chapter 10.

There are several methods that we can use to allocate this $4,800 net cost to expense. Vertically Inclined uses *straight-line depreciation.*[5] The **straight-line depreciation method** allocates equal amounts of an asset's net cost over its estimated useful life. When the $4,800 net cost is divided by the asset's useful life of 24 months (2 years × 12 months per year), we get an average monthly cost of $200 ($4,800/24). Our adjusting entry to record monthly depreciation expense is:

Adjustment (c)

Mar. 31	Depreciation Expense, Equipment.................	200		$A = L + E$
	Accumulated Depreciation, Equipment		200	$\downarrow$ $\quad$ $\downarrow$
	To record monthly depreciation on equipment			

Posting this adjusting entry affects the accounts shown in Exhibit 3.8:

Equipment	
Mar. 1	6,000
Bal.	6,000

Accumulated Depreciation, Equipment	
	200 Mar. 31

Depreciation Expense, Equipment	
Mar. 31 200	

EXHIBIT 3.8

Accounts After Depreciation Adjustments

Accumulated depreciation is recorded in a *contra asset account.* A **contra account** is an account that is linked with another account and has an opposite normal balance to its counterpart. It is reported as a subtraction from the other account's balance. On Vertically Inclined's balance sheet, the balance in the contra asset account, *Accumulated Depreciation, Equipment,* will be subtracted from the Equipment account balance as shown in Exhibit 3.10. The cost of an asset less its accumulated depreciation is the **book value of an asset**. The **market value of an asset** is the amount it can be sold for. Market value is not tied to the book value of an asset.

After posting the adjustment, the *Equipment* account less its *Accumulated Depreciation, Equipment* account equals the March 31 balance sheet amount for this asset. The balance in the Depreciation Expense, Equipment account is the expense reported in the March income statement. If the adjustment is *not* made at March 31, then (a) expenses are understated by $200 and net income is overstated by $200 for the March income statement, and (b) both assets and equity are overstated by $200 in the March 31 balance sheet.

The use of the contra asset account Accumulated Depreciation allows balance sheet readers to know both the cost of assets and the total amount of depreciation charged to expense to date. Notice that the title of the contra account is *Accumulated* Depreciation. This means that the account includes *total* depreciation expense for all prior periods when the assets were being used. Vertically Inclined's Equipment and Accumulated Depreciation, Equipment accounts would appear on

---

5 We explain the details of *depreciation* methods in Chapter 10 (Volume 2). We briefly describe the straight-line method here to help you understand the adjusting process.

May 31, 2011, as shown in Exhibit 3.10, after the three monthly adjusting entries detailed in Exhibit 3.9.

EXHIBIT 3.9

Accounts After Three Months of Depreciation Adjustments

Equipment		
Mar. 1	6,000	
Total	6,000	

Accumulated Depreciation, Equipment	
200	Mar. 31
200	Apr. 30
200	May 31
600	Total

EXHIBIT 3.10

Accumulated Depreciation Contra Account in the Balance Sheet

Assets		
Cash		$
Equipment	$6,000	
Less: Accumulated depreciation	600	5,400
Total assets		$

CHECKPOINT

6. If the year-end adjusting entry to record depreciation expense was not recorded, what effect would this have on each component of the accounting equation?
7. Explain what a contra account is.

Do Quick Study question: QS 3-4

DECISION MAKER   Answer—End of chapter

Small Business Owner
You are preparing to make an offer to purchase a small family-run restaurant. The manager gives you a copy of her depreciation schedule for the restaurant's building and equipment. It shows costs of $75,000 and accumulated depreciation of $55,000. This leaves a net total for building and equipment of $20,000. Is this information valuable in deciding on a purchase offer for the restaurant?

Adjusting Unearned Revenues

Unearned revenues refer to cash received in advance of providing products and services. Unearned revenues, also known as *deferred revenues*, are a *liability*. When cash is accepted, an obligation to provide products and services is also accepted. As products and services are provided, the amount of unearned revenues becomes *earned* revenues. Adjusting entries for unearned revenues involve increasing (crediting) revenues and decreasing (debiting) unearned revenues as shown in Exhibit 3.11. These adjustments reflect economic events (including passage of time) that impact unearned revenues.

We see an example of unearned revenues in **Rogers Communications'** 2011 annual report. Rogers reports unearned revenue of $335 million on its balance sheet

EXHIBIT 3.11

Adjusting for Unearned Revenues

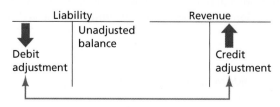

that includes subscriber deposits and amounts received related to services to be provided in the future. Another example is **WestJet**, which reports advance (unearned) ticket sales at December 31, 2011, of $432 million.

Vertically Inclined also has unearned revenues. On March 26, Vertically Inclined agreed to provide teaching services to a client for a fixed fee of $1,500 per month. On that same day, this client paid the first two months' fees in advance, covering the period from March 27 to May 27. The entry to record the cash received in advance is:

Mar. 26	Cash	3,000	
	Unearned Teaching Revenue................		3,000
	Received advance payment for services over the next two months.		

This advance payment increases cash and creates an obligation to provide teaching services over the next two months. As time passes, Vertically Inclined will earn this payment. No external transactions are linked with this earnings process. By March 31, Vertically Inclined provides five days of teaching that amounts to revenue of $250 (=$1,500 × 5/30). The revenue recognition principle requires that $250 of unearned revenue is reported as revenue on the March income statement. The adjusting entry to reduce the liability account and recognize earned revenue is:

Adjustment (d)

Mar. 31	Unearned Teaching Revenue..........................	250	
	Teaching Revenue...............................		250
	To record the earned portion of revenue received in advance calculated as $1,500 × 5/30.		

$A = L + E*$
$\quad\quad\downarrow\quad\uparrow$

* Recall that revenues cause equity to increase.

The accounts look as shown in Exhibit 3.12 after posting the adjusting entry.

Unearned Teaching Revenue			
Mar. 31	250	3,000	Mar. 26
		2,750	Balance

Teaching Revenue			
		2,200	Mar. 10
		1,600	15
		250	31
		4,050	Total

EXHIBIT 3.12

Unearned Revenue and Revenue Accounts After Adjustments

The adjusting entry transfers $250 out of Unearned Teaching Revenue (a liability account) to a revenue account. If the adjustment is *not* made, then (a) revenue and net income are understated by $250 in the March income statement, and (b) Unearned Teaching Revenue is overstated and equity understated by $250 on the March 31 balance sheet.

CHECKPOINT

8. AltaCo credited Unearned Revenue for $20,000 received on November 3, 2011, for work to be done just prior to Christmas. The work was completed as scheduled. If Unearned Revenue is not adjusted at year-end to reflect the completion of the work, which GAAP will be violated and why?

9. Describe how an unearned revenue arises. Give an example.

Do Quick Study question: QS 3-5

Adjusting Accrued Expenses

Accrued expenses refer to costs incurred in a period that are both unpaid and unrecorded. For example, **Loblaw Companies Limited** reported $3,677 million of accounts payable and accrued liabilities on its December 31, 2011, balance sheet. Accrued expenses are part of expenses and reported on the income statement. Adjusting entries for recording accrued expenses involve increasing (debiting) expenses and increasing (crediting) liabilities as shown in Exhibit 3.13.

EXHIBIT 3.13

Adjusting for Accrued Expenses

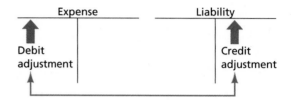

Common examples of accrued expenses are interest, salaries, rent, and taxes. We use interest and salaries to show how to adjust accounts for accrued expenses.

Accrued Interest Expense

It is common for companies to have accrued interest expense on notes payable and certain accounts payable at the end of a period. Interest expense is incurred with the passage of time. Unless interest is paid on the last day of an accounting period, we need to adjust accounts for interest expense incurred but not yet paid.

Interest of $35 has accrued on Vertically Inclined's $6,000, 7%, six-month note payable for the month of March.[6] The journal entry is:

Adjustment (e)

$$A = L + E$$
$$\uparrow \quad \downarrow$$

Mar.	31	Interest Expense..	35	
		Interest Payable		35
		To record accrued interest.		

After the adjusting entry is posted, the expense and liability accounts appear as shown in Exhibit 3.14.

EXHIBIT 3.14

Notes Payable and Interest Accounts After Accrual Adjustments

Notes Payable	
	6,000 Mar. 1

Interest Expense	
Mar. 31 35	

Interest Payable	
	35 Mar. 31

This means that $35 of interest expense is reported on the income statement and that $35 interest payable is reported on the balance sheet. Notice that the Notes Payable account is *not* affected by recording interest. If the interest adjustment is not made, then (a) Interest Expense is understated and net income overstated by $35 in

---

6   Interest on the $6,000, 7%, six-month note payable was calculated using the formula

Interest = Principal of the note × Annual interest rate × Time expressed in years OR $i = Prt$.

Therefore $6,000 × 7% × ¹⁄₁₂ = $35.
Where the term of the note is in days, Interest = Principal × Rate × $\dfrac{\text{Exact days}}{365}$.
Interest is discussed in greater detail in Chapter 9.

the March income statement, and (b) Interest Payable is understated and equity overstated by $35 on the March 31 balance sheet.

The $6,000 principal and total interest of $210 ($6,000 $\times$ 7% $\times$ 6/12 = $210) will be paid six months from March 1, the date the note was issued.[7]

Accrued Salaries Expense

Vertically Inclined's only employee earns $70 per day or $350 for a five-day work-week beginning on Monday and ending on Friday. This employee gets paid every two weeks on Friday. On the 14th and the 28th of March, the wages are paid, recorded in the journal, and posted to the ledger. The *unadjusted* Salaries Expense and Cash paid for salaries appear as shown in Exhibit 3.15.

Cash			
	700	Mar. 14	
	700	28	

Salaries Expense			
Mar. 14	700		
28	700		

EXHIBIT 3.15

Salary and Cash Accounts Before Adjusting

The calendar in Exhibit 3.16 shows one working day after the March 28 payday (March 31). This means that the employee earns one day's salary by the close of business on Monday, March 31. While this salary expense is incurred, it is not yet paid or recorded by the company. The period-end adjusting entry to account for accrued salaries is:

Adjustment (f)

Mar.	31	Salaries Expense...	70	
		Salaries Payable.....................................		70
		To record one day's accrued salary;		
		1 × $70.		

$A = L + E$
    $\uparrow$ $\downarrow$

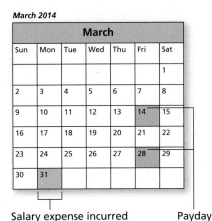

March 2014

March						
Sun	Mon	Tue	Wed	Thu	Fri	Sat
						1
2	3	4	5	6	7	8
9	10	11	12	13	14	15
16	17	18	19	20	21	22
23	24	25	26	27	28	29
30	31					

Salary expense incurred   Payday

April 2014

April						
Sun	Mon	Tue	Wed	Thu	Fri	Sat
		1	2	3	4	5
6	7	8	9	10	11	12
13	14	15	16	17	18	19
20	21	22	23	24	25	26
27	28					

Payday

EXHIBIT 3.16

Salary Accrual Period and Paydays

---

7   When the note payable and accrued interest are paid on September 1, six months after the date of issue on March 1, the entry would be (assuming interest expense of $35 per month has accrued):

Sept.	1	Notes Payable...	6,000	
		Interest Payable...	210	
		Cash...		6,210
		To record payment of note payable and		
		accrued interest.		

After the adjusting entry is posted, the expense and liability accounts appear as shown in Exhibit 3.17.

EXHIBIT 3.17

Salary Accounts After Accrual Adjustments

Salaries Expense		
Mar. 14	700	
28	700	
31	70	
Total	1,470	

Salaries Payable	
70	Mar. 31

EYK
3-2

This means that $1,470 of salaries expense is reported on the income statement and that $70 in salaries payable (liability) is reported in the balance sheet. If the adjustment is *not* made, then (a) Salaries Expense is understated and net income overstated by $70 in the March income statement, and (b) Salaries Payable is understated and equity overstated by $70 on the March 31 balance sheet.

The accrued salaries are paid on the first payday of the next bi-weekly period, which occurs on Friday, April 11. The entry includes the added salaries expense for the nine days worked in April:

Apr.	11	Salaries Payable...	70	
		Salaries Expense	630	
		Cash		700
		Paid two weeks' salary including one day accrued in March (1 day at $70; 9 days at $70 = $630).		

CHECKPOINT

10. In error, the May utility bill for $6,900 was not included in the May 31 adjusting entries. What effect would this error have on the components of the accounting equation?
11. What is an accrued expense? Give an example.
12. Music-Mart records $1,000 of accrued salaries on December 31. Five days later on January 5 (the next payday), salaries of $7,000 are paid. What is the January 5 entry?

Do Quick Study question: QS 3-6

DECISION MAKER   Answer—End of chapter

Financial Officer
At year-end, the president instructs you, the financial officer, not to record accrued expenses until next year because they will not be paid until then. The president also directs you to record in current-year sales a recent purchase order from a customer that requires merchandise to be delivered two weeks after the year-end. Your company would report a net income instead of a net loss if you carried out these instructions. What do you do?

Adjusting Accrued Revenues

When products and services are delivered, we expect to receive payment for them. **Accrued revenues** refer to revenues earned in a period that are both unrecorded and not yet received in cash (or other assets). Accrued revenues are part of revenues and must be reported on the income statement. The adjusting entries increase (debit) assets and increase (credit) revenues as shown in Exhibit 3.18.

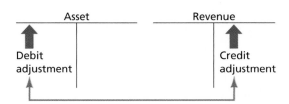

EXHIBIT 3.18

Adjusting for Accrued Revenues

Common examples of accrued revenues are fees for services and products, interest revenue, and rent revenue. We use service fees and interest revenue to show how to adjust accounts for accrued revenues.

Accrued Services Revenue

Accrued revenues are earned but unrecorded because either the customer has not paid for them or the seller has not yet billed the customer. Vertically Inclined provides us with an example of an accrued revenue. In the second week of March, Vertically Inclined agrees to provide teaching services to a client for a fixed fee of $2,700 per month from March 11 to April 10, or 30 days of service. The client agrees to pay $2,700 cash to Vertically Inclined on April 10, 2014, when the service period is complete.

At March 31, 2014, 20 days of services are already provided to the client. Since the contracted services are not yet entirely provided, the client is not yet billed nor has Vertically Inclined recorded the services already provided. Vertically Inclined has earned $1,800 (=$2,700 × 20/30). The *revenue recognition principle* requires that we report the $1,800 on the March income statement because it is earned in March. The balance sheet also must report that this client owes Vertically Inclined $1,800. The adjusting entry to account for accrued teaching services revenue is:

Adjustment (g)

Mar.	31	Accounts Receivable....................................	1,800	
		Teaching Revenue................................		1,800
		To record 20 days' accrued revenue.		

$A = L + E$
$\uparrow \qquad \uparrow$

After the adjusting entry is posted, the affected accounts look as shown in Exhibit 3.19.

Accounts Receivable			
Mar. 15	1,900	1,900	Mar. 25
31	1,800		
Balance	1,800		

Teaching Revenue		
	2,200	Mar. 10
	1,600	15
	250	31
	1,800	31
	5,850	Total

EXHIBIT 3.19

Receivable and Revenue Accounts After Accrual Adjustments

Accounts receivable are reported on the balance sheet at $1,800, and $5,850 of revenues are reported on the income statement. If the adjustment is *not* made, then (a) both Teaching Revenue and net income are understated by $1,800 in the March income statement, and (b) both Accounts Receivable and equity are understated by $1,800 on the March 31 balance sheet.

When the first month's fee is received on April 10, Vertically Inclined makes the following entry to remove the accrued asset (accounts receivable) and recognize the added 10 days of revenue earned in April:

Apr.	10	Cash	2,700	
		Accounts Receivable		1,800
		Teaching Revenue.................................		900
		Received cash for accrued asset and earned teaching revenue; $900 = $2,700 \times 10/30$.		

Accrued Interest Revenue

In addition to the accrued interest expense we described earlier, interest can yield an accrued revenue when a company is owed money (or other assets) by a debtor. If a company is holding notes or accounts receivable that produce interest revenue, we must adjust the accounts to record any earned and yet uncollected interest revenue. The adjusting entry is recorded as a debit to Interest Receivable (asset) and a credit to Interest Revenue (equity).

 CHECKPOINT

13. An adjusting entry to record $6,000 of accrued interest revenue was omitted due to an oversight. What effect would this error have on the components of the accounting equation?

Do Quick Study questions: QS 3-7, QS 3-8

ADJUSTMENTS AND FINANCIAL STATEMENTS

 Explain how accounting adjustments link to financial statements.

Exhibit 3.20 lists the five major types of transactions requiring adjustment. Adjusting entries are necessary for each. Understanding this exhibit is important to understanding the adjusting process and its link to financial statements. Remember that each adjusting entry affects both income statement accounts and balance sheet accounts.

EXHIBIT 3.20

Summary of Adjustments and Financial Statement Links

Type	Before Adjusting Balance Sheet Account	Income Statement Account	Adjusting Entry	
Prepaid Expense	Asset & equity overstated	Expense understated	Dr Expense .... XX Cr Asset XX	where XX = how much of the prepaid was used during the period
Depreciation	Asset & equity overstated	Expense understated	Dr Expense .... XX Cr Contra Asset.... XX	where XX = how much of the asset's cost was matched as an expense to the period
Unearned Revenues	Liability overstated; equity understated	Revenue understated	Dr Liability................ XX Cr Revenue XX	where XX = how much of the liability was earned during the period
Accrued Expenses	Liability understated; equity overstated	Expense understated	Dr Expense .... XX Cr Liability............ XX	where XX = the amount of the unpaid and unrecorded expense for the period
Accrued Revenues	Asset & equity understated	Revenue understated	Dr Asset................... XX Cr Revenue XX	where XX = the amount of the uncollected and unrecorded revenue for the period

Note that adjusting entries related to the framework in Exhibit 3.20 never affect cash.[8] A common error made by students learning to prepare adjusting entries is either to debit or to credit cash. In the case of prepaids and unearned revenues, cash has already been correctly recorded; it is the prepaids and unearned revenues account balances that need to be *fixed* or adjusted. In the case of accrued revenues and expenses, cash will be received or paid in the future and is not to be accounted for until that time; it is the revenue or expense account balance that needs to be fixed or adjusted. Depreciation is a non-cash transaction and therefore does not affect cash.

Exhibit 3.21 summarizes the adjusting entries of Vertically Inclined on March 31. The posting of adjusting entries to individual ledger accounts was shown when we described the transactions above and is not repeated here. Adjusting entries are often set apart from other journal entries with the caption *Adjusting Entries*, as shown in Exhibit 3.21.

GENERAL JOURNAL				Page 2
Date	Account Titles and Explanations	PR	Debit	Credit
2014	**Adjusting Entries**			
Mar. 31	Insurance Expense..		100	
	Prepaid Insurance...			100
	To record expired insurance; $2,400/24.			
31	Supplies Expense...		1,050	
	Supplies			1,050
	To record supplies used; $3,600 − $2,550.			
31	Depreciation Expense, Equipment......................		200	
	Accumulated Depreciation, Equipment			200
	To record monthly depreciation on equipment; $6,000 − $1,200 = $4,800/24.			
31	Unearned Teaching Revenue..............................		250	
	Teaching Revenue.......................................			250
	To record earned revenue received in advance; $1,500 × 5/30.			
31	Interest Expense..		35	
	Interest Payable...			35
	To record one month of accrued interest.			
31	Salaries Expense		70	
	Salaries Payable...			70
	To record one day's accrued salary; 1 × $70.			
31	Accounts Receivable..		1,800	
	Teaching Revenue.......................................			1,800
	To record 20 days of accrued revenue; $2,700 × 20/30.			

EXHIBIT 3.21

Journalizing Adjusting Entries of Vertically Inclined

CHECKPOINT

14. Explain how adjusting entries are linked to the components of the accounting equation.

Do Quick Study questions: QS 3-9, QS 3-10

---

8   Adjusting entries related to bank reconciliations affect cash but these adjustments are excluded from the framework in Exhibit 3.20 and will be discussed in Chapter 8.

MID-CHAPTER DEMONSTRATION PROBLEM

The owner of a lawn service company prepares **annual** financial statements.

Part A

Prepare the appropriate adjusting entries for July 31, 2014, based on the following information available at the end of July.

a. The annual insurance amounting to $1,200 went into effect on May 1, 2014. The Prepaid Insurance account was debited and Cash credited on the same date.

b. The lawn service company's lawn tractor was purchased for $3,200 in 2012. The value of the lawn tractor at the end of its estimated four-year useful life was determined to be $800. This information was made available to record depreciation for the year ended July 31, 2014.

c. On April 1, 2014, a customer paid for a six-month lawn service plan to begin June 1, 2014. The journal entry credited the Unearned Service Fees account when the $3,000 payment was received. The monthly fee is $500.

d. The last weekly salary of $1,400 was paid to employees on Friday, July 25. Employees are paid based on a five-day workweek. Salaries for July 28, 29, 30, and 31 have accrued.

e. Service fees of $1,800 were earned by July 31 but not recorded.

Part B

Refer to (d) above. Prepare the entry to pay the salaries on Friday, August 1.

Analysis Component:
Assume a business understated its earnings. Omitting which of the adjustments in Part A would accomplish this?

SOLUTION

Part A

a. July 31	Insurance Expense..	300	
	Prepaid Insurance		300
	To record insurance for May, June, and July; calculated as: $1,200/12 = $100 × 3 = $300.		

b. 31	Depreciation Expense, Lawn Tractor	600	
	Accumulated Depreciation, Lawn Tractor		600
	Annual depreciation, calculated as $3,200 − $800 = $2,400/4 years = $600/year.		

c. 31	Unearned Service Fees	1,000	
	Service Fees Earned...............................		1,000
	To record service fees earned for June and July; calculated as $500 × 2 = $1,000.		

d. 31	Salaries Expense	1,120	
	Salaries Payable......................................		1,120
	To record salaries for the last two days of July, calculated as $1,400/5 = $280/day × 4 days = $1,120.		

e. 31	Accounts Receivable..	1,800	
	Service Fees Earned...............................		1,800
	To record accrued service revenue for July.		

Part B

Aug. 1	Salaries Payable...	1,120	
	Salaries Expense..	280	
	Cash		1,400
	To record payment of weekly salaries; where salaries expense is calculated as $1,400/5 = $280/day \times 1$ day = $280.		

Analysis Component:

Omitting adjustments (c) and (e) would cause revenues to be understated; hence, earnings or net income would also be understated.

ADJUSTED TRIAL BALANCE

An **unadjusted trial balance** is a listing of accounts and balances prepared *before* adjustments are recorded. An **adjusted trial balance** is a list of accounts and balances prepared *after* adjusting entries are recorded and posted to the ledger. Exhibit 3.22 shows the unadjusted and adjusted trial balances for Vertically

LO6 Explain and prepare an adjusted trial balance.

EXHIBIT 3.22

Unadjusted and Adjusted Trial Balance for Vertically Inclined

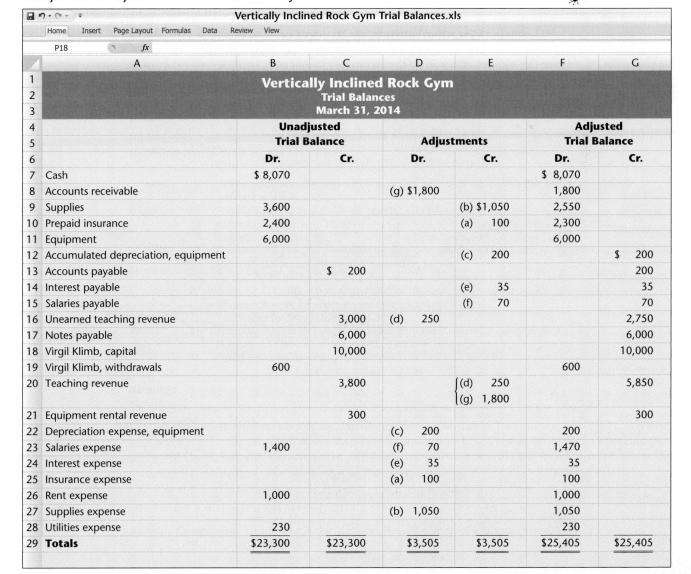

	A	B	C	D	E	F	G
		Vertically Inclined Rock Gym					
		Trial Balances					
		March 31, 2014					
		Unadjusted Trial Balance		Adjustments		Adjusted Trial Balance	
		Dr.	Cr.	Dr.	Cr.	Dr.	Cr.
7	Cash	$ 8,070				$ 8,070	
8	Accounts receivable			(g) $1,800		1,800	
9	Supplies	3,600			(b) $1,050	2,550	
10	Prepaid insurance	2,400			(a) 100	2,300	
11	Equipment	6,000				6,000	
12	Accumulated depreciation, equipment				(c) 200		$ 200
13	Accounts payable		$ 200				200
14	Interest payable				(e) 35		35
15	Salaries payable				(f) 70		70
16	Unearned teaching revenue		3,000	(d) 250			2,750
17	Notes payable		6,000				6,000
18	Virgil Klimb, capital		10,000				10,000
19	Virgil Klimb, withdrawals	600				600	
20	Teaching revenue		3,800		(d) 250 (g) 1,800		5,850
21	Equipment rental revenue		300				300
22	Depreciation expense, equipment			(c) 200		200	
23	Salaries expense	1,400		(f) 70		1,470	
24	Interest expense			(e) 35		35	
25	Insurance expense			(a) 100		100	
26	Rent expense	1,000				1,000	
27	Supplies expense			(b) 1,050		1,050	
28	Utilities expense	230				230	
29	**Totals**	$23,300	$23,300	$3,505	$3,505	$25,405	$25,405

Inclined at March 31, 2014, using an electronic spreadsheet. Electronic spreadsheet software such as Excel allows us to compile and manipulate numbers easily.

In Exhibit 3.22, notice several new accounts arising from the adjusting entries. The listing of accounts is also slightly changed to match the order listed in the Chart of Accounts in Appendix III at the end of the book.

PREPARING FINANCIAL STATEMENTS

LO⁷ Prepare financial statements from an adjusted trial balance.

We prepare financial statements directly from information in the *adjusted* trial balance. An adjusted trial balance includes all balances appearing in financial statements. We know that a trial balance summarizes information in the ledger by listing accounts and their balances. This summary is easier to work from than the entire ledger when preparing financial statements.

Exhibit 3.23 shows how Vertically Inclined's revenue and expense balances are transferred from the adjusted trial balance to (1) the income statement, and (2) the statement of changes in equity. Note how we use the net income and withdrawals account to prepare the statement of changes in equity.

Exhibit 3.23 also shows how Vertically Inclined's asset and liability balances on the adjusted trial balance are transferred to the balance sheet. The ending equity is determined on the statement of changes in equity and transferred to the balance sheet. There are different formats for the balance sheet. The **account form balance sheet**, used in previous chapters, lists assets on the left and liabilities and equity on the right side of the balance sheet. Its name comes from its link to the accounting equation, *Assets = Liabilities + Equity*. The balance sheet in Exhibit 1.15 is in account form. The **report form balance sheet** lists items vertically, as shown in Exhibit 3.23. Both forms are widely used and are considered equally helpful to users. For consistency, we will use the report form in the preparation of financial statements from this point forward.

We usually prepare financial statements in the order shown: income statement, statement of changes in equity, and balance sheet. This order makes sense since the balance sheet uses information from the statement of changes in equity, which in turn uses information from the income statement.

CHECKPOINT

15. Jordan Air Company has the following information in its unadjusted and adjusted trial balances:

	Unadjusted		Adjusted	
	Debit	Credit	Debit	Credit
Prepaid insurance............................	$6,200		$5,900	
Salaries payable................................		$ -0-		$1,400

What are the adjusting entries that Jordan Air likely recorded?

16. What types of accounts are taken from the adjusted trial balance to prepare an income statement?

17. In preparing financial statements from an adjusted trial balance, what statement is usually prepared first? second? third? Explain why.

Do Quick Study question: QS 3-11

EXHIBIT 3.23

Preparing the Income Statement, Statement of Changes in Equity, and Balance Sheet From the Adjusted Trial Balance

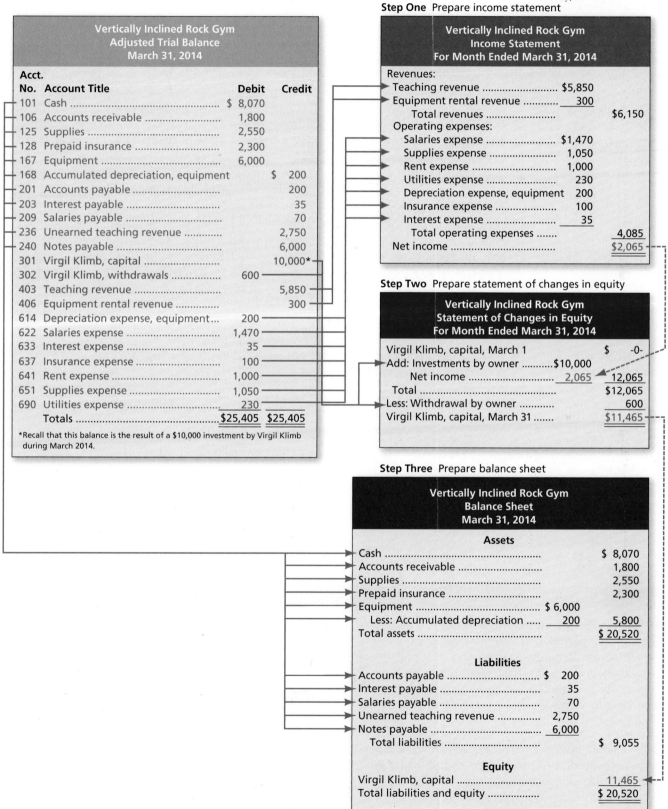

Step One Prepare income statement

Vertically Inclined Rock Gym
Adjusted Trial Balance
March 31, 2014

Acct. No.	Account Title	Debit	Credit
101	Cash	$ 8,070	
106	Accounts receivable	1,800	
125	Supplies	2,550	
128	Prepaid insurance	2,300	
167	Equipment	6,000	
168	Accumulated depreciation, equipment		$ 200
201	Accounts payable		200
203	Interest payable		35
209	Salaries payable		70
236	Unearned teaching revenue		2,750
240	Notes payable		6,000
301	Virgil Klimb, capital		10,000*
302	Virgil Klimb, withdrawals	600	
403	Teaching revenue		5,850
406	Equipment rental revenue		300
614	Depreciation expense, equipment	200	
622	Salaries expense	1,470	
633	Interest expense	35	
637	Insurance expense	100	
641	Rent expense	1,000	
651	Supplies expense	1,050	
690	Utilities expense	230	
	Totals	$25,405	$25,405

*Recall that this balance is the result of a $10,000 investment by Virgil Klimb during March 2014.

Vertically Inclined Rock Gym
Income Statement
For Month Ended March 31, 2014

Revenues:		
Teaching revenue	$5,850	
Equipment rental revenue	300	
Total revenues		$6,150
Operating expenses:		
Salaries expense	$1,470	
Supplies expense	1,050	
Rent expense	1,000	
Utilities expense	230	
Depreciation expense, equipment	200	
Insurance expense	100	
Interest expense	35	
Total operating expenses		4,085
Net income		$2,065

Step Two Prepare statement of changes in equity

Vertically Inclined Rock Gym
Statement of Changes in Equity
For Month Ended March 31, 2014

Virgil Klimb, capital, March 1		$ -0-
Add: Investments by owner	$10,000	
Net income	2,065	12,065
Total		$12,065
Less: Withdrawal by owner		600
Virgil Klimb, capital, March 31		$11,465

Step Three Prepare balance sheet

Vertically Inclined Rock Gym
Balance Sheet
March 31, 2014

Assets

Cash		$ 8,070
Accounts receivable		1,800
Supplies		2,550
Prepaid insurance		2,300
Equipment	$ 6,000	
Less: Accumulated depreciation	200	5,800
Total assets		$ 20,520

Liabilities

Accounts payable	$ 200	
Interest payable	35	
Salaries payable	70	
Unearned teaching revenue	2,750	
Notes payable	6,000	
Total liabilities		$ 9,055

Equity

Virgil Klimb, capital		11,465
Total liabilities and equity		$ 20,520

CRITICAL THINKING CHALLENGE   Refer to the Critical Thinking Challenge questions at the beginning of the chapter. Compare your answers to those suggested on Connect.

IFRS AND ASPE—THE DIFFERENCES

Difference	International Financial Reporting Standards (IFRS)	Accounting Standards for Private Enterprises (ASPE)
Recording adjusting entries	• IFRS require that financial statements be presented at least annually,* therefore adjustments would be prepared at least annually. However, Securities Commissions' Law typically requires public companies to present quarterly financial statements which, in turn, would require that adjusting entries be prepared at least quarterly.	• Unlike IFRS, ASPE does not explicitly require that financial statements be presented at least annually although it is implied given that financial statements must be presented in a timely manner** and items must be presented consistently from period to period.*** In actuality, adjustments are prepared at least annually for tax purposes and, for example, to meet any banking requirements.
	• Both public and private enterprises may prepare adjusting entries more frequently, such as monthly, to enhance the accuracy of information required for decision making.	
Depreciation vs. amortization	• IFRS uses the term *depreciation***** (although it uses *amortization* for intangible assets).*****	• ASPE uses the term *amortization*.******

* IFRS 2012, IAS 1 para. 36.
** ASPE, Accounting Standards, Section 1000.17(b).
*** ASPE, Accounting Standards, Section 1000.19-20.
**** IFRS 2012, IAS 16 para. 6.
*****IFRS 2012, IAS 38 para. 8.
****** ASPE, Accounting Standards, Section 3061.16.

SUMMARY

LO¹ Describe the purpose of adjusting accounts at the end of a period. After external transactions are recorded, several accounts need adjusting for their balances to be correct because internal transactions remain unrecorded. The purpose of adjusting accounts at the end of a period is to recognize unrecorded revenues and expenses.

LO² Explain how the timeliness, matching, and revenue recognition principles affect the adjusting process. The value of information is often linked to its timeliness, so accounting systems prepare periodic reports at regular intervals such as a month, a three-month quarter, or

at minimum, once a year. Adjustments are made so that revenues and expenses are recognized as they occur and matched to the proper period.

LO³ Explain accrual accounting and cash basis accounting and how accrual accounting adds to the usefulness of financial statements. Accrual accounting recognizes revenue when earned and expenses when incurred, not necessarily when cash inflows and outflows occur. Cash basis accounting recognizes revenues when cash is received and expenses when cash is paid; it is not in accordance with GAAP.

LO⁴   Prepare and explain adjusting entries for prepaid expenses, depreciation, unearned revenues, accrued expenses, and accrued revenues. Prepaid expenses, an asset, refer to items paid for in advance of receiving their benefits. As this asset is used, its cost becomes an expense.

Dr. Expense xx
    Cr. Prepaid.. xx
    To adjust prepaid for amount used.

Depreciation is the expense created by spreading the cost of plant and equipment assets over the periods these assets are used. Accumulated Depreciation, a contra asset account, is credited to track the total amount of the plant and equipment asset used.

Dr. Depreciation Expense.................................... xx
    Cr. Accumulated Depreciation xx
    To adjust for depreciation.

Unearned revenues, a liability, refer to cash received in advance of providing products and services. As products and services are provided, the amount of unearned revenues becomes earned revenues.

Dr. Unearned Revenue.. xx
    Cr. Revenue xx
    To adjust for unearned revenue that is earned.

Accrued expenses are costs incurred in a period that are unpaid and unrecorded.

Dr. Expense xx
    Cr. Liability xx
    To adjust for unrecorded and unpaid expenses.

Accrued revenues are revenues earned in a period that are unrecorded and not yet collected.

Dr. Receivable... xx
    Cr. Revenue xx
    To adjust for unrecorded revenues not yet collected.

LO⁵   Explain how accounting adjustments link to financial statements. Accounting adjustments bring an asset or liability account balance to its correct amount and update related expense or revenue accounts. Every adjusting entry affects one or more income statement *and* balance sheet accounts. An adjusting entry never affects cash. Adjustments are necessary for transactions that extend over more than one period. Exhibit 3.20 summarizes financial statement links by type of adjustment.

LO⁶   Explain and prepare an adjusted trial balance. An adjusted trial balance is a list of accounts and balances prepared after adjusting entries are recorded and posted to the ledger. Financial statements are often prepared from the adjusted trial balance.

LO⁷   Prepare financial statements from an adjusted trial balance. We can prepare financial statements directly from the adjusted trial balance that includes all account balances. Revenue and expense balances are transferred to the income statement and statement of changes in equity. Asset, liability, and equity balances are transferred to the balance sheet. We usually prepare statements in the following order: income statement, statement of changes in equity, and balance sheet.

GUIDANCE ANSWERS TO **DECISION MAKER**

Investor
Prepaid expenses are items paid for in advance of receiving their benefits. They are assets and are expensed as they are used up. The publishing company's treatment of the signing bonus is acceptable provided future book sales can at least match the $500,000 expense. As an investor, you are concerned about the risk of future book sales. The more uncertain future book sales are, the more likely your analysis is to treat the $500,000, or a portion of it, as an expense in the current accounting period, not a prepaid expense (an asset on the balance sheet).

Small Business Owner
We know that depreciation is a process of cost allocation, not asset valuation. Knowing the depreciation schedule of the restaurant is not especially useful in your estimation of what the restaurant's building and equipment are currently worth. Your assessment of the age, quality, and usefulness of the building and equipment is much more important. Also, you would use the current market values of similar assets in estimating the value of this restaurant's building and equipment.

Financial Officer
Omitting accrued expenses and recognizing revenue early can mislead financial statement users. One action is to request a second meeting with the president so you can explain that accruing expenses when incurred and recognizing revenue when earned are required practices. If the president persists, you might discuss the situation with legal counsel and any auditors involved. Your ethical action might cost you this job, but the potential pitfalls for falsification of statements, reputation and personal integrity loss, and other costs are too great.

GUIDANCE ANSWERS TO CHECKPOINT

1. An annual reporting (or accounting) period covers one year and refers to the preparation of annual financial statements. The annual reporting period can follow the calendar year or a fiscal year. The fiscal year can follow the business's natural business year.

2. Interim (less than one year) financial statements are prepared to provide decision makers with information frequently and promptly.

3. The revenue recognition principle, the timeliness principle, and the matching principle lead most directly to the adjusting process.

4. No. Cash basis accounting is not consistent with generally accepted accounting principles.

5. If Prepaid Insurance is not adjusted, assets and equity will be overstated.

6. If the adjusting entry to record depreciation was not recorded, assets and equity would be overstated.

7. A contra account is an account that is subtracted from the balance of a related account. Use of a contra account often provides more complete information than simply reporting a net amount.

8. The revenue recognition principle will be violated because revenues earned have not been recognized. The matching principle will also be violated because revenues earned will not be assigned to the correct accounting period— the period in which the expenses related to the revenues were incurred.

9. An unearned revenue arises when cash is (or other assets are) received from a customer before the services and products are delivered to the customer. Magazine subscription receipts in advance are one example.

10. The omission of the $6,900 interest expense accrual will cause liabilities to be understated by $6,900 and equity to be overstated by $6,900.

11. An accrued expense refers to costs incurred in a period that are both unpaid and unrecorded prior to adjusting entries. One example is salaries earned by employees but not yet paid at the end of a period.

12. The January 5 entry to settle the accrued salaries and pay for added salaries is:

Jan. 5	Salaries Payable............................	1,000	
	Salaries Expense	6,000	
	Cash		7,000

Paid salary including accrual from December.

13. The omission of an adjusting entry to record $6,000 of accrued interest would cause assets and equity to be understated by $6,000 each.

14. The various adjusting entries are linked to the accounting equation as follows: (a) adjustment of prepaids and the recording of depreciation cause assets and equity to decrease; (b) adjustment of unearned amounts causes liabilities to decrease and equity to increase; (c) accrual of revenues causes assets and equity to increase; and (d) accrual of expenses causes liabilities to increase and equity to decrease.

15. The probable adjusting entries of Jordan Air are:

Insurance Expense......................................	300	
Prepaid Insurance		300

To record insurance expired.

Salaries Expense	1,400	
Salaries Payable...............................		1,400

To record accrued salaries.

16. Revenue accounts and expense accounts.

17. The income statement is usually prepared first, followed by the statement of changes in equity because net income (loss) from the income statement flows into the statement of changes in equity. The balance sheet is then prepared since the ending capital balance from the statement of changes in equity flows into the equity section of the balance sheet.

DEMONSTRATION PROBLEM

The following information continues with The Cutlery, featured in the Chapter 1 and 2 Demonstration Problems. After the first month of business, The Cutlery's August 31, 2014, unadjusted trial balance appeared as follows:

The Cutlery Trial Balance August 31, 2014		
Account	**Debit**	**Credit**
Cash..................................	$ 4,950	
Accounts receivable......................	-0-	
Prepaid insurance..........................	2,400	
Furniture	2,000	
Store equipment	31,000	
Accounts payable		$14,450
Unearned haircutting services revenue.........................		500
Joane Cardinal, capital...................		26,000
Joane Cardinal, withdrawals	500	
Haircutting services revenue..........		3,800
Wages expense	250	
Rent expense................................	3,200	
Hydro expense	450	
Totals	$44,750	$44,750

The following additional information is available for the *month* just ended:

a. Depreciation of $100 per month will be taken on the furniture.
b. It is estimated that the store equipment will have a $1,000 value at the end of its estimated five-year (or 60-month) useful life. Joane Cardinal will record a full month of depreciation for August.
c. It was determined that the balance in unearned haircutting services revenue at August 31 should be $420.
d. The prepaid insurance represents six months of insurance beginning August 1.
e. On August 31, The Cutlery provided $130 of services to a client who will pay in September.
f. On August 31, Joane Cardinal received the business's August cell phone bill totalling $50. It will be paid in September.

Required
1. Prepare the adjusting entries needed on August 31, 2014, to record the previously unrecorded items.
2. Prepare T-accounts for accounts affected by the adjusting entries. Post the adjusting entries to the T-accounts.
3. Prepare an adjusted trial balance.
4. Prepare an income statement, a statement of changes in equity, and a balance sheet.

Analysis Component:
Calculate the net effect of the adjusting entries on the balance sheet. Is net income positively or negatively affected by these adjusting entries overall? Could the opposite effect be achieved? If so, how?

Planning the Solution

- Analyze the information for each situation to determine which accounts need to be updated with an adjustment.
- Calculate the dollar amount of each adjustment and prepare the necessary journal entries.
- Show the amount entered by each adjustment in the designated accounts and determine the adjusted balance.
- Determine each entry's effect on net income for the year and on total assets, total liabilities, and equity at the end of the year.
- Using the adjusted balances, prepare an adjusted trial balance.
- Using the adjusted trial balance, prepare the income statement, statement of changes in equity, and balance sheet.
- Analyze the adjusting entries and calculate the effect on each component of the accounting equation.

SOLUTION

1. Adjusting journal entries.

a.	Aug. 31	Depreciation Expense, Furniture.....................	100	
		Accumulated Depreciation, Furniture....		100
		To record depreciation expense for the month of August for the furniture.		

b.	31	Depreciation Expense, Store Equipment.........	500	
		Accumulated Depreciation, Store Equipment....................................		500
		To record depreciation expense for the month; ($31,000 − $1,000)/60 months = $500/month.		

c.	31	Unearned Haircutting Services Revenue	80	
		Haircutting Services Revenue		80
		To recognize haircutting services revenue earned; $500 − $420 = $80.		

d.	31	Insurance Expense..	400	
		Prepaid Insurance		400
		To adjust for the expired portion of prepaid insurance; $2,400/6 months = $400/month.		

e.	31	Accounts Receivable.......................................	130	
		Haircutting Services Revenue		130
		To record revenue earned.		

f.	31	Phone Expense..	50	
		Accounts Payable.....................................		50
		To record August cell phone bill.		

2.

Accounts Receivable		
(e)	130	

Prepaid Insurance			
Balance	2,400	400	(d)
Balance	2,000		

Accumulated Depreciation, Furniture		
	100	(a)

Accumulated Depreciation, Store Equipment		
	500	(b)

Accounts Payable			
	14,450	Balance	
	50	(f)	
	14,500	Balance	

Unearned Haircutting Services Revenue			
(c)	80	500	Balance
		420	Balance

Haircutting Services Revenue		
	3,800	Balance
	80	(c)
	130	(e)
	4,010	Balance

Depreciation Expense, Furniture		
(a)	100	

Depreciation Expense, Store Equipment		
(b)	500	

Insurance Expense		
(d)	400	

Phone Expense		
(f)	50	

3.

The Cutlery
Adjusted Trial Balance
August 31, 2014

Account	Debit	Credit
Cash	$ 4,950	
Accounts receivable	130	
Prepaid insurance	2,000	
Furniture	2,000	
Accumulated depreciation, furniture		$ 100
Store equipment	31,000	
Accumulated depreciation, store equipment		500
Accounts payable		14,500
Unearned haircutting services revenue		420
Joane Cardinal, capital		26,000
Joane Cardinal, withdrawals	500	
Haircutting services revenue		4,010
Depreciation expense, furniture	100	
Depreciation expense, store equipment	500	
Wages expense	250	
Insurance expense	400	
Rent expense	3,200	
Hydro expense	450	
Phone expense	50	
Totals	$45,530	$45,530

4.

The Cutlery
Income Statement
For Month Ended August 31, 2014

Revenues:		
Haircutting services revenue		$4,010
Operating expenses:		
Rent expense	$3,200	
Depreciation expense, store equipment.......	500	
Hydro expense...	450	
Insurance expense	400	
Wages expense..	250	
Depreciation expense, furniture..................	100	
Phone expense	50	
Total operating expenses.........................		4,950
Net loss...		$ 940

The Cutlery
Statement of Changes in Equity
For Month Ended August 31, 2014

Joane Cardinal, capital, August 1 ...		$ -0-
Add: Investments by owner...........		26,000
Total		$26,000
Less: Withdrawals by owner	$500	
Net loss.................................	940	1,440
Joane Cardinal, capital, August 31 ..		$24,560

The Cutlery
Balance Sheet
August 31, 2014

Assets

Cash...		$ 4,950
Accounts receivable..		130
Prepaid insurance...		2,000
Furniture	$ 2,000	
Less: Accumulated depreciation...............	100	1,900
Store equipment	$ 31,000	
Less: Accumulated depreciation...............	500	30,500
Total assets..		$39,480

Liabilities

Accounts payable...	$14,500	
Unearned haircutting services revenue	420	
Total liabilities...		$14,920

Equity

Joane Cardinal, capital.......................................		24,560
Total liabilities and equity		$ 39,480

> Reminder: The net loss on the income statement flows into the statement of changes in equity. The August 31 balance in capital on the statement of changes in equity is reported on the balance sheet.

Analysis Component:

The net effect of the adjustments on assets, liabilities, and equity is detailed below.

Entry	a.	b.	c.	d.	e.	f.	Net effect
Assets	$100 ↓	$500 ↓	No effect	$400 ↓	$130 ↑	No effect	$870 ↓
Liabilities	No effect	No effect	$80 ↓	No effect	No effect	$50 ↑	$30 ↓
Equity	$100 ↓	$500 ↓	$80 ↑	$400 ↓	$130 ↑	$50 ↓	$840 ↓

Equity decreased by $840 as a result of the adjusting entries. All of the adjustments that affected equity were income statement items (revenues or expenses), therefore net income was negatively affected by the adjusting entries (a net decrease in income of $840).

The opposite effect could have been achieved if accrued revenues (Dr Receivables and Cr Revenues) plus the adjustment of unearned amounts (Dr Unearned Revenues and Cr Revenues) were greater than the adjustment of prepaids (Dr Expense and Cr Prepaid) plus depreciation (Dr Depreciation Expense and Cr Accumulated Depreciation) and accrued expenses (Dr Expense and Cr Payable).

APPENDIX 3A

Correcting Errors

Correcting entries, as the term implies, account for the correction of errors, and are not to be confused with adjusting entries.

LO8 Explain and prepare correcting entries.

If an error in a journal entry is discovered before the error is posted, it can be corrected in a manual system by drawing a line through the incorrect information. The correct information is written above it to create a record of change for the auditor. Many computerized systems allow the operator to replace the incorrect information directly.

When an error in a journal entry is *not* discovered until after it is posted, the usual practice is to correct the error by creating *another* journal entry.[9] This *correcting entry* removes the amount from the wrong account and records it to the correct account. For example, suppose we recorded a purchase of office supplies with an incorrect debit to Office Equipment as follows:

Oct. 14	Office Equipment..	1,600	
	Cash		1,600
	To record the purchase of office supplies.		

Once posted, the Office Supplies account balance is understated by $1,600 and the Office Equipment account balance is overstated by the same amount. When we discover the error three days later, a correcting entry is made using either one or two entries as shown below:

17	Office Supplies...............................	1,600	
	Office Equipment		1,600
	To correct the entry of October 14 that incorrectly debited Office Equipment instead of Office Supplies.		

OR

17	Cash	1,600	
	Office Equipment		1,600
	To reverse the incorrect entry.		
17	Office Supplies...............................	1,600	
	Cash		1,600
	To journalize the purchase of office supplies correctly.		

In the approach to the left, the credit removes the error and the debit correctly records supplies. Alternatively, the two entries on the right could be used: the first entry reverses the incorrect entry *entirely*, and the second entry records the transaction as it should have been. Both methods achieve the same final results.

Computerized systems often use similar correcting entries. The exact procedure depends on the system used and management policy. Yet nearly all systems include controls to show when and where a correction is made.

CHECKPOINT

18. On March 14, Accounts Receivable was debited for $4,100 and Service Revenue was credited for $4,100. At the end of the month, it was discovered that the March 14 entry should have been credited to Rent Revenue. What correcting entry is required?

Do Quick Study questions: *QS 3-12, *QS 3-13

---

9 For tracking purposes, correcting entries must be referenced to the incorrect entry and any calculations are to be documented.

APPENDIX 3B

An Alternative in Recording Prepaids and Unearned Revenues

LO⁹ Identify and explain an alternative in recording prepaids and unearned revenues.

This section explains an alternative in recording prepaid expenses and unearned revenues.

RECORDING PREPAID EXPENSES IN EXPENSE ACCOUNTS

We explained that prepaid expenses are assets when they are purchased and are recorded with debits to asset accounts. Adjusting entries transfer the used amounts to expense accounts at the end of an accounting period.

There is an acceptable alternative practice of recording *all* prepaid expenses with debits to expense accounts. If any prepaids remain unused at the end of an accounting period, then adjusting entries transfer the unused portions from expense accounts to asset accounts. The financial statements are identical under either procedure, but the adjusting entries are different.

To illustrate, let's look at Vertically Inclined's cash payment for 24 months of insurance coverage beginning on March 1. Vertically Inclined recorded that payment with a debit to an asset account, but alternatively it could have been recorded as a debit to an expense account. Exhibit 3B.1 shows the two approaches.

EXHIBIT 3B.1

Initial Entry for Prepaid Expenses for Two Approaches

		Payment Recorded as Asset		Payment Recorded as Expense	
Mar. 1	Prepaid Insurance	2,400			
	Cash		2,400		
1	Insurance Expense			2,400	
	Cash				2,400

On March 31, insurance protection for one month is used up. This means $100 ($2,400/24) is the expense for March. Exhibit 3B.2 shows that the adjusting entry depends on how the original payment is recorded:

EXHIBIT 3B.2

Adjusting Entry for Prepaid Expenses for Two Approaches

		Payment Recorded as Asset		Payment Recorded as Expense	
Mar. 31	Insurance Expense	100			
	Prepaid Insurance		100		
31	Prepaid Insurance			2,300	
	Insurance Expense				2,300

When these entries are posted, we can see in Exhibit 3B.3 that these two approaches give identical adjusted account balances at March 31.

Payment Recorded as Asset				Payment Recorded as Expense			
Prepaid Insurance				**Prepaid Insurance**			
Mar. 1	2,400	100	Mar. 31	Mar. 31	2,300		
Balance	2,300						
Insurance Expense				**Insurance Expense**			
				Mar. 1	2,400	2,300	Mar. 31
Mar. 31	100			Balance	100		

EXHIBIT 3B.3

Account Balances Under Two Approaches for Recording Prepaid Expenses

Recording Unearned Revenues in Revenue Accounts

Unearned revenues are liabilities requiring delivery of products and services and are recorded as credits to liability accounts when cash and other assets are received. Adjusting entries at the end of an accounting period transfer to revenue accounts the earned portion of unearned revenues.

An acceptable alternative is to record *all* unearned revenues with credits to revenue accounts. If any revenues are unearned at the end of an accounting period, then adjusting entries transfer the unearned portions from revenue accounts to unearned revenue accounts. While the adjusting entries are different for these two approaches, the financial statements are identical.

To illustrate, let's look at Vertically Inclined's March 26 receipt of $3,000 for teaching services covering the period March 27 to April 27. Vertically Inclined recorded this transaction with a credit to a liability account. The alternative, shown in Exhibit 3B.4, is to record it with a credit to a revenue account as follows:

		Receipt Recorded as Liability		Receipt Recorded as Revenue	
Mar. 26	Cash	3,000			
	Unearned Teaching Revenue		3,000		
26	Cash			3,000	
	Teaching Revenue........................				3,000

EXHIBIT 3B.4

Initial Entry for Unearned Revenues for Two Approaches

By the end of the accounting period (March 31), Vertically Inclined earns $250 of this revenue. This means that $250 of the liability is satisfied. Depending on how the initial receipt is recorded, Exhibit 3B.5 shows the adjusting entry:

		Receipt Recorded as Liability		Receipt Recorded as Revenue	
Mar. 31	Unearned Teaching Revenue............	250			
	Teaching Revenue........................		250		
31	Teaching Revenue............................			2,750	
	Unearned Teaching Revenue				2,750

EXHIBIT 3B.5

Adjusting Entry for Unearned Revenues for Two Approaches

After adjusting entries are posted, the two approaches give identical adjusted account balances at March 31 as shown in Exhibit 3B.6.

EXHIBIT 3B.6

Account Balances Under Two Approaches for Recording Unearned Revenues

Receipt Recorded as Liability			
Unearned Teaching Revenue			
Mar. 31	250	3,000	Mar. 26
		2,750	Balance

Teaching Revenue		
	250	Mar. 31

Receipt Recorded as Revenue		
Unearned Teaching Revenue		
	2,750	Mar. 31

Teaching Revenue			
Mar. 31	2,750	3,000	Mar. 26
		250	Balance

CHECKPOINT

19. Miller Company records cash receipts of unearned revenues and cash payments of prepaid expenses in balance sheet accounts. Bud Company records these items in income statement accounts. Explain any difference in the financial statements of these two companies from their different ways of recording prepaids.

Do Quick Study question: *QS 3-14

SUMMARY OF APPENDIX 3A AND APPENDIX 3B

LO8 Explain and prepare correcting entries. A correcting entry is required when an error in a journal entry is not discovered until after it has been posted. The correcting entry can be done in one of two ways: the incorrect portion of the entry can be corrected, or the entire incorrect entry can be reversed and the correct entry recorded; both methods accomplish the same result.

LO9 Identify and explain an alternative in recording prepaids and unearned revenues. It is acceptable to charge all prepaid expenses to expense accounts when they are purchased. When this is done, adjusting entries must transfer any unexpired amounts from expense accounts to asset accounts. It is also acceptable to credit all unearned revenues to revenue accounts when cash is received. In this case the adjusting entries must transfer any unearned amounts from revenue accounts to unearned revenue accounts.

GUIDANCE ANSWERS TO CHECKPOINT

18. The correcting entry can be done in one of two ways:

31	Service Revenue	4,100	
	Rent Revenue		4,100
	To correct the March 14 entry.		

OR

31	Service Revenue............................	4,100	
	Accounts Receivable		4,100
	To reverse the incorrect		
	March 14 entry.		
31	Accounts Receivable	4,100	
	Rent Revenue		4,100
	To enter the correct entry for		
	March 14.		

19. When adjusting entries are correctly prepared, the financial statements of these companies will be identical under both approaches.

GLOSSARY

Account form balance sheet A balance sheet that lists assets on the left and liabilities and equity on the right side of the balance sheet.

Accounting periods Time frames covered by financial statements and other reports; also called *reporting periods*.

Accrual basis accounting The approach to preparing financial statements that uses the adjusting process to recognize revenues when earned and expenses when incurred, not when cash is paid or received; the basis for generally accepted accounting principles.

Accrued expenses Costs incurred in a period that are both unpaid and unrecorded; adjusting entries for recording accrued expenses involve increasing (debiting) expenses and increasing (crediting) liabilities.

Accrued revenues Revenues earned in a period that are both unrecorded and not yet received in cash (or other assets); adjusting entries for recording accrued revenues involve increasing (debiting) assets and increasing (crediting) revenues.

Adjusted trial balance A listing of accounts and balances prepared after adjustments are recorded and posted to the ledger.

Adjusting entry A journal entry at the end of an accounting period to bring an asset or liability account balance to its proper amount while also updating the related expense or revenue account.

Amortization The expense created by allocating the cost of intangible assets to the periods in which they are used; represents the expense of using these assets.

Book value of an asset The cost of the asset less its accumulated depreciation.

Cash basis accounting Revenues are recognized when cash is received, and expenses are recorded when cash is paid.

Contra account An account linked with another account and having an opposite normal balance; reported as a subtraction from the other account's balance so that more complete information than simply the net amount is provided.

Correcting entries Accounting entries made in order to correct errors.

Depreciation The expense created by allocating the cost of plant and equipment to the periods in which they are used; represents the expense of using the assets.

External transactions Exchanges between the entity and some other person or organization.

Intangible assets Long-lived assets that have no physical substance but convey a right to use a product or process.

Interim financial reports Financial reports covering less than one year; usually based on one-, three- or six-month periods.

Internal transactions Exchanges within an organization that can also affect the accounting equation.

Market value of an asset Amount an asset can be sold for. Market value is not tied to the book value of an asset.

Matching principle The broad principle that requires expenses to be reported in the same period as the revenues that were earned as a result of the expenses.

Overstated account An account that is too high.

Prepaid expenses Items that are paid for in advance of receiving their benefits. These are assets.

Property, plant and equipment (PPE) Tangible long-lived assets used to produce goods or services.

Report form balance sheet A balance sheet that lists items vertically with assets above the liabilities and equity.

Reporting periods See *accounting periods*.

Straight-line depreciation method Allocates equal amounts of an asset's cost to depreciation expense during its useful life.

Timeliness principle A broad principle that assumes that an organization's activities can be divided into specific time periods such as months, quarters, or years.

Unadjusted trial balance A listing of accounts and balances prepared before adjustments are recorded and posted to the ledger.

Understated account An account that is too low.

Unearned revenues Liabilities created when customers pay in advance for products or services; created when cash is received before revenues are earned; satisfied by delivering the products or services in the future.

 Visit **Connect** for additional study tools, practice quizzes, to search an interactive eBook, and much more.

CONCEPT REVIEW QUESTIONS

1. What type of business is most likely to select a fiscal year that corresponds to the natural business year instead of the calendar year?

2. What is the difference between the cash basis and accrual basis of accounting?

3. Why is the accrual basis of accounting preferred over the cash basis?

4. Where is a prepaid expense reported in the financial statements?

5. What kinds of assets require adjusting entries to record depreciation?

6. What contra account is used when recording and reporting the effects of depreciation? Why is it used?

7. Where is an unearned revenue reported in the financial statements?

8. What is an accrued revenue? Give an example.

9. Review the consolidated balance sheet of **Danier Leather** in Appendix II. DANIER Identify an asset account that requires adjustment before annual financial statements

can be prepared. What would be the effect on the income statement if this asset account were not adjusted?

10. Review the income statement of **WestJet** in Appendix II. How much depreciation was recorded in the adjusting entry for depreciation at the end of 2011?

*11. If a company initially records prepaid expenses with debits to expense accounts, what type of account is debited in the adjusting entries for prepaid expenses?

QUICK STUDY

QS 3-1 GAAP and adjusting entries LO²

For each of the following, identify the primary GAAP that has been violated and explain why.

1. Delta Company prepared its first set of financial statements for the three years ended July 31, 2014.

2. Warren Consulting purchased $9,800 of supplies on September 30, 2014, and debited Office Supplies Expense. Warren's year-end is September 30.

3. On May 3, 2014, Mindy Car Wash collected $3,000 in advance from a new limousine company to begin operating June 1, 2014. Mindy credited a revenue account for the $3,000.

4. On November 15, 2014, TelsCo rented equipment for $1,500. TelsCo is not recording the transaction until it pays (payment is required 15 days from the rental date).

QS 3-2 Accrual and cash accounting LO³

In its first year of operations, Harris Co. earned $39,000 in revenues and received $33,000 cash from customers. The company incurred expenses of $22,500, but had not paid for $2,250 of them at year-end. In addition, Harris prepaid $3,750 for expenses that would be incurred the next year. Calculate the first year's net income under the cash basis and calculate the first year's net income under the accrual basis.

QS 3-3 Preparing adjusting entries—prepaid expense LO⁴

Fargo's Detective Agency purchased a two-year insurance policy on April 1, 2014, paying cash of $7,680. Its year-end is December 31.

a. Record the journal entry on April 1, 2014.

b. Record the adjusting entry on December 31, 2014.

c. Record the adjusting entry on December 31, 2015.

d. How much of the insurance policy purchased on April 1, 2014, was actually used during the year 2016?

QS 3-4 Preparing adjusting entries—depreciation expense LO⁴

Softrock Minerals purchased a vehicle on March 1, 2014, for cash of $32,000. It will be used by the president for business purposes for four years and then sold for about $8,000. Softrock's year-end is December 31. Record the entry on March 1, 2014, and the adjusting entry required at the year-ends of 2014 and 2015.

QS 3-5 Preparing adjusting entries—unearned revenue LO⁴

On November 1, 2014, Fastfoot Industries collected $12,000 from a customer for services to be provided in the future. On December 31, 2014, Fastfoot's year-end, it was determined that $3,000 of this amount remained unearned. Prepare the entries for November 1 and December 31.

QS 3-6 Preparing adjusting entries—accrued expenses LO⁴

On December 31, 2014, Allied Consulting received the telephone bill for December usage of $1,840. It must be paid by January 14, 2015. Record the adjusting entry on December 31, 2014, and the entry to record the payment on January 14, 2015.

QS 3-7 Preparing adjusting entries—accrued revenues LO⁴

TigrSoft recorded unbilled and uncollected revenues of $17,000 on March 31, 2014. On April 16, $12,000 of these were collected. Prepare the entries for March 31 and April 16.

QS 3-8 Preparing adjusting entries LO⁴

Stark Company records prepayments of expenses in asset accounts and receipts of unearned revenues in liability accounts. Using the list of accounts provided, identify the debit and credit entry required for each of the annual adjustments described in (a) through (e). The first one is done as an example.

1. Cash
2. Prepaid Advertising
3. Advertising Payable
4. Advertising Expense
5. Accounts Receivable
6. Equipment Expense

7. Depreciation Expense
8. Accumulated Depreciation—Equipment
9. Equipment
10. Services Revenue Earned
11. Unearned Services Revenue

	Debits	Credits
Example: Accrual of uncollected and unrecorded services earned.	5	10
a. Accrual of unpaid and unrecorded advertising that was used by Stark Company.	_____	_____
b. Adjustment of Unearned Services Revenue to recognize earned revenue.	_____	_____
c. Recorded revenue for work completed this accounting period; the cash will be received in the next period.	_____	_____
d. The cost of Equipment was matched to the time periods benefited.	_____	_____
e. Adjustment of Prepaid Advertising to recognize the portion used.	_____	_____

QS 3-9 Recording and analyzing adjusting entries LO⁴,⁵

Adjusting entries affect one balance sheet account and one income statement account. For the entries listed below, identify the account to be debited and the account to be credited. Indicate which of the two accounts is the income statement account and which is the balance sheet account.

a. Entry to record annual depreciation expense.
b. Entry to show wages earned by employees but not yet paid.
c. Entry to show revenue earned that was previously received as cash in advance.
d. Entry to show expiration of prepaid insurance.
e. Entry to show revenue earned but not yet billed.

QS 3-10 Linking adjustments to financial statements LO⁵

For each type of adjustment in (a) through (e), indicate the effect on net income (overstated or understated) if the adjustment is not recorded.

	If adjustment is not recorded:			
Type of Adjustment	**Net income will be overstated, understated, or no effect**	**Assets will be overstated, understated, or no effect**	**Liabilities will be overstated, understated, or no effect**	**Equity will be overstated, understated, or no effect**
a. Prepaid Expenses				
b. Depreciation				
c. Unearned Revenues				
d. Accrued Expenses				
e. Accrued Revenues				

QS 3-11 Interpreting adjusting entries LO[4,6]

The following information has been taken from Shank Company's unadjusted and adjusted trial balances at October 31, 2014.

	Unadjusted		Adjusted	
	Debit	Credit	Debit	Credit
Prepaid insurance..	$3,100		$2,350	
Interest payable..		$ -0-		$ 750
Insurance expense..	-0-		750	
Interest expense...	-0-		750	

Given this trial balance information, prepare the adjusting journal entries.

*QS 3-12 Correcting entries LO[8]

The following entry was recorded on November 14.

Nov. 14	Salaries Expense..	14,800	
	Cash		14,800
	To record supplies expense.		

At month-end, it was discovered that *Supplies Expense* should have been debited on November 14 instead of *Salaries Expense*. Prepare the correcting entry required on November 30.

*QS 3-13 Correcting entries LO[8]

The following entry was recorded on January 10.

Jan. 10	Office Furniture..	25,000	
	Accounts Payable...................................		25,000
	To record purchase of computer equipment by borrowing from the bank.		

At month-end, it was discovered that on January 10, computer equipment was purchased for $25,000 by borrowing from the bank. Prepare the correcting entry required on January 31.

*QS 3-14 Recording prepaids and unearned amounts as expenses and revenues LO[9]

Foster Company initially records prepaid and unearned items in income statement accounts. Given Foster Company's practices, what is the appropriate adjusting entry for each of the following at November 30, 2014, the end of the company's first accounting period?

a. There are unpaid salaries of $3,000.

b. Unused office supplies of $800 were counted at year-end.
There was no beginning balance in office supplies.

c. Earned but unbilled consulting fees of $2,300 were discovered.

d. It was determined that there were unearned fees of $4,200.

EXERCISES

MGraw Hill **connect**

Exercise 3-1 Identifying adjusting entries LO[4]

For each entry (1) to (12) below, enter the letter of the explanation that describes it in the blank space to the left. You can use some letters more than once.

a. To record depreciation expense.

b. To record an accrued expense.

c. To record the use of a prepaid expense.

d. To record accrued revenue.

e. To record the earning of previously unearned revenue.

f. Not an adjusting entry.

An asterisk (*) identifies assignment material based on Appendix 3A or Appendix 3B.

____ 1.	Depreciation Expense.................	3,000		____ 7.	Insurance Expense......................	6,000	
	Accumulated Depreciation ..		3,000		Prepaid Insurance................		6,000
____ 2.	Unearned Professional Fees	2,000		____ 8.	Salaries Payable...........................	1,500	
	Professional Fees Earned......		2,000		Cash.....................................		1,500
____ 3.	Rent Expense	1,000		____ 9.	Cash	6,500	
	Prepaid Rent.......................		1,000		Unearned Professional Fees ..		6,500
____ 4.	Interest Expense.........................	4,000		____10.	Cash	9,000	
	Interest Payable..................		4,000		Interest Receivable...............		9,000
____ 5.	Prepaid Rent	3,500		____11.	Interest Receivable	7,000	
	Cash...................................		3,500		Interest Earned		7,000
____ 6.	Salaries Expense	5,000		____12.	Cash	8,000	
	Salaries Payable..................		5,000		Accounts Receivable............		8,000

Exercise 3-2 Adjusting entries LO⁴

Prepare adjusting journal entries for the year ended December 31, 2014, for each of the independent situations in (a) to (f). Assume that prepaid expenses are initially recorded in asset accounts. Assume that fees collected in advance of work are initially recorded as liabilities.

a. Depreciation on the company's machinery for 2014 was estimated to be $43,000.

b. The Prepaid Insurance account had a $26,000 debit balance at December 31, 2014, before adjusting for the costs of any expired coverage. An analysis of the company's insurance policies showed $19,200 of unexpired insurance remaining.

c. The Office Supplies account had a $600 debit balance on January 1, 2014; $3,100 of office supplies were purchased during the year; and the December 31, 2014, count showed that $240 of supplies are on hand.

d. Two-thirds of the work for a $45,000 fee received in advance has now been performed.

e. The Prepaid Insurance account had an $11,200 debit balance at December 31, 2014, before adjusting for the costs of any expired coverage. An analysis of the company's insurance policies showed that $8,600 of coverage had expired.

f. Wages of $46,000 have been earned by workers but not paid as of December 31, 2014.

g. Record the January 6, 2015, payment of $91,000 in wages, inclusive of the $46,000 December 31, 2014, accrual in (f) above.

Exercise 3-3 Adjusting entries LO⁴

Enviro Waste's year-end is December 31. The information in (a) to (e) is available at year-end for the preparation of adjusting entries:

a. Of the $18,500 balance in Unearned Revenue, $3,050 remains unearned.

b. The annual building depreciation is $14,600.

c. The Spare Parts Inventory account shows an unadjusted balance of $1,200. A physical count reveals a balance on hand of $980.

d. Unbilled and uncollected services provided to customers totalled $14,600.

e. The utility bill for the month of December was received but is unpaid; $2,100.

Required Prepare the required adjusting entries at December 31, 2014, for (a) to (e) and the subsequent cash entries required for (f) and (g).

f. The accrued revenues of $14,600 recorded in (d) were collected on January 4, 2015.

g. The $2,100 utility bill accrued in (e) was paid on January 14, 2015.

Exercise 3-4 Adjusting entries LO⁴

Monague Company prepares monthly financial statements. The information in (a) to (e) is available for the preparation of adjusting entries for the month ended September 30, 2014:

a. Of the $18,000 balance in Unearned Revenue, $11,800 has been earned.

b. Furniture costing $14,800 was purchased last year. It will be used for four years and donated to charity after that time.

c. The Office Supplies account shows an unadjusted balance of $7,200. A physical count reveals that $6,100 has been used.

d. Services provided to customers today (month-end) but unbilled total $14,350.

e. Rent of $12,400 for the month of September is unpaid and unrecorded.

Required Prepare the required adjusting entries at September 30, 2014, for (a) to (e) and the subsequent entries required for (f) and (g).

f. The $14,350 of service revenue accrued in (d) was collected on October 3, 2014.

g. The $12,400 of rent accrued in (e) was paid on October 4, 2014.

Exercise 3-5 Unearned and accrued revenues LO⁴

Landmark Properties owns and operates an apartment building and prepares annual financial statements based on a March 31 fiscal year-end.

Required Journalize the adjusting entry for each of (a) and (b) and the subsequent entry required in (c).

a. The tenants of one of the apartments paid five months' rent in advance on November 1, 2013. The monthly rental is $2,200 per month. The journal entry credited the Unearned Rent account when the payment was received. No other entry had been recorded prior to March 31, 2014. Give the adjusting journal entry that should be recorded on March 31, 2014.

b. On January 1, 2014, the tenants of another apartment moved in and paid the first month's rent. The $2,650 payment was recorded with a credit to the Rent Earned account. However, the tenants have not paid the rent for February or March. They have agreed to pay it as soon as possible. Give the adjusting journal entry that should be recorded on March 31, 2014.

c. On April 22, 2014, the tenants described in (b) paid $7,950 rent for February, March, and April. Give the journal entry to record the cash collection.

Exercise 3-6 Identifying adjusting entries LO⁴

Selected information in T-account format is presented below. Journalize the most likely adjustments that caused the balances to change.

a. Accounts Receivable	
Unadjusted Bal. 8,000 Dec. 31/14	
Adjusted Bal. 9,800 Dec. 31/14	

b. Prepaid Rent	
Unadjusted Bal. 32,000 Dec. 31/14	
Adjusted Bal. 26,400 Dec. 31/14	

c. Accumulated Depreciation, Machinery	
	9,200 Unadjusted Bal. Dec. 31/14
	12,600 Adjusted Bal. Dec. 31/14

d. Unearned Fees	
	6,100 Unadjusted Bal. Dec. 31/14
	1,500 Adjusted Bal. Dec. 31/14

e. Salaries Expense	
Unadjusted Bal. 62,000 Dec. 31/14	
Adjusted Bal. 65,000 Dec. 31/14	

Exercise 3-7 Missing data in supplies expense calculations LO⁴,⁵

Determine the missing amounts in each of these four independent situations:

	a	b	c	d
Supplies on hand, January 1	$ 300	$ 900	$ 2,600	?
Supplies purchased during the year	2,900	3,100	?	$78,800
Supplies on hand, December 31	1,000	?	3,300	9,100
Supplies expense for the year	?	850	26,000	86,000

Exercise 3-8 Adjusting and subsequent cash entries for accrued expenses LO⁴

Delcor Management has five part-time employees, each of whom earns $280 per day. They are normally paid on Fridays for work completed on Monday through Friday of the same week. They were all paid in full on Friday, December 26, 2014. The next week, all five of the employees worked only four days because New Year's Day was an unpaid holiday. Show the adjusting entry that would be recorded on Wednesday, December 31, 2014, Delcor's year-end, and the journal entry that would be made to record paying the employees' wages on Friday, January 2, 2015.

Exercise 3-9 Adjustments and subsequent cash entries for accrued expenses LO⁴

The following three situations require adjusting journal entries to prepare financial statements as of April 30, 2014. For each situation, present the adjusting entry and the entry that would be made to record the payment of the accrued liability during May 2014.

a. The company has a $460,000 note payable that requires 0.3% interest to be paid each month on the 20th of the month. The interest was last paid on April 20 and the next payment is due on May 20.

b. The total weekly salaries expense for all employees is $14,500. This amount is paid at the end of the day on Friday of each week with five working days. April 30 falls on a Wednesday this year, which means that the employees had worked three days since the last payday. The next payday is May 2.

c. On April 1, the company retained a lawyer at a flat monthly fee of $4,500. This amount is payable on the 12th of the following month.

Exercise 3-10 Identifying the effects of adjusting entries LO⁴,⁵

Following are two income statements for Javelin Company for the month ended December 31, 2014. Column B was prepared before any adjusting entries were recorded and column D includes the effects of adjusting entries. The company records cash receipts and disbursements related to unearned and prepaid items in balance sheet accounts. Analyze the statements and prepare the adjusting entries that must have been recorded. (Note: Of the $12,000 increase in *Fees earned*, 30% represents additional fees earned but not billed. The other 70% was earned by performing services that the customers had paid for in advance.)

	Javelin Company Income Statements.xls		
	Home Insert Page Layout Formulas Data Review View		
	P18 *fx*		

	A	B	C	D
1	**Javelin Company**			
2	**Income Statements**			
3	**For Month Ended December 31, 2014**			
4		**Before**		**After**
5		**Adjustments**	**Adjustments**	**Adjustments**
6	Revenues:			
7	Fees earned	$ 48,000		$ 60,000
8	Commissions earned	85,000		85,000
9	Total revenues	$133,000		$145,000
10	Operating expenses:			
11	Depreciation expense, computers	$ -0-		$ 3,000
12	Depreciation expense, office furniture	-0-		3,500
13	Salaries expense	25,000		29,900
14	Insurance expense	-0-		2,600
15	Rent expense	9,000		9,000
16	Office supplies expense	-0-		960
17	Advertising expense	6,000		6,000
18	Utilities expense	2,500		2,640
19	Total operating expenses	$ 42,500		$ 57,600
20	**Net Income**	$ 90,500		$ 87,400

Analysis Component: Identify and explain which GAAP requires that adjusting entries be recorded. By how much would revenues, expenses, and net income be overstated/understated if adjustments were *not* recorded at December 31, 2014, for Javelin Company?

Exercise 3-11 Adjusting entries LO[4,6]

	Nuna Music Trial Balances.xls						
Home Insert Page Layout Formulas Data Review View							
P18 fx							

Nuna Music
Trial Balances
February 28, 2014

		Unadjusted Trial Balance		Adjustments		Adjusted Trial Balance	
		Dr.	Cr.	Dr.	Cr.	Dr.	Cr.
7	Cash	$ 14,000					
8	Accounts receivable	32,000					
9	Prepaid insurance	16,800					
10	Equipment	102,000					
11	Accumulated depreciation, equipment		$ 23,000				
12	Accounts payable		19,000				
13	Abraham Nuna, capital		213,000				
14	Abraham Nuna, withdrawals	102,000					
15	Revenues		214,000				
16	Depreciation expense, equipment	-0-					
17	Salaries expense	187,700					
18	Insurance expense	14,500					
19	**Totals**	$ 469,000	$ 469,000				

Additional information:

a. Annual depreciation of the equipment; $11,500.

b. $12,000 of the Prepaid Insurance balance has expired.

c. Unbilled and unrecorded revenues at year-end totalled $31,000.

Required Referring to Exhibit 3.22, use the information provided to complete the columns.

Exercise 3-12 Preparing financial statements LO[7]

Using the completed adjusted trial balance columns from Exercise 3-11, prepare an income statement, a statement of changes in equity, and a balance sheet for the year ended February 28, 2014. Assume that the owner made no investments during the year.

Analysis Component: Which GAAP requires the preparation of financial statements?

*Exercise 3-13 Journalizing correcting entries LO[8]

For each of the following incorrect entries, journalize the appropriate correcting entry(ies).

a. The purchase of office supplies on credit for $1,800 was recorded as:

Office Supplies	1,800	
Cash		1,800

b. A credit customer paid her account in full: $4,500. This was recorded as:

Cash	4,500	
Revenue		4,500

An asterisk (*) identifies assignment material based on Appendix 3A or Appendix 3B.

c. The owner withdrew cash of $1,500. This was recorded as:

Salaries Expense...	1,500	
Cash...		1,500

d. Work was performed for a customer today and cash of $750 was received. This was recorded as:

Cash	750	
Accounts Receivable		750

Analysis Component: If the error in (b) is not corrected, what is the effect on the income statement and balance sheet?

*Exercise 3-14 Entering adjustments for prepaid items recorded in expense and revenue accounts LO⁹

Classic Customs began operations on December 1, 2014. In setting up the bookkeeping procedures, the company decided to debit expense accounts when the company prepays its expenses and to credit revenue accounts when customers pay for services in advance. Prepare journal entries for items (a) through (c) and adjusting entries as of December 31, 2014, for items (d) through (f):

a. Supplies were purchased on December 1 for $8,000.

b. The company prepaid insurance premiums of $3,200 on December 2.

c. On December 15, the company received an advance payment of $16,100 from one customer for remodelling work.

d. By counting the supplies on December 31, Classic Customs determined that $1,450 was on hand.

e. An analysis of the insurance policies in effect on December 31 showed that $800 of insurance coverage had expired.

f. As of December 31, it was determined that $8,500 of the amount received in advance on December 15 had been earned.

*Exercise 3-15 Alternative procedures for revenues received in advance LO⁹

Pavillion Company experienced the following events and transactions during July:

July	1	Received $4,000 in advance of performing work for Andrew Renking.
	6	Received $16,800 in advance of performing work for Matt Swarbuck.
	12	Completed the job for Andrew Renking.
	18	Received $15,000 in advance of performing work for Drew Sayer.
	27	Completed the job for Matt Swarbuck.
	31	The job for Drew Sayer has not been started.

a. Give journal entries (including any adjusting entry as of the end of the month) to record these items using the procedure of initially crediting the Unearned Fees account when a payment is received from a customer in advance of performing services.

b. Give journal entries (including any adjusting entry as of the end of the month) to record these items using the procedure of initially crediting the Fees Earned account when a payment is received from a customer in advance of performing services.

c. Under each method, determine the amount of earned fees that should be reported on the income statement for July and the amount of unearned fees that should appear on the balance sheet as of July 31.

Problem 3-1A Preparing adjusting entries—prepaid expenses LO⁴

Impala Window Washing Services prepares adjustments monthly and shows the following selected accounts on its December 31, 2014, unadjusted trial balance:

Account	Debit	Credit
Prepaid insurance..........................	$ 3,600	
Prepaid office rent.........................	21,000	
Prepaid subscriptions	1,260	
Prepaid equipment rental...............	25,200	

Required Prepare the required monthly adjusting entries at December 31, 2014, based on the following additional information:

a. The remaining balance in Prepaid Insurance was for a six-month insurance policy purchased for $7,200 and in effect on September 1, 2014.

b. $4,800 of the balance in Prepaid Office Rent had not been used as at December 31, 2014.

c. $1,100 of the balance in Prepaid Subscriptions had been used as at December 31, 2014.

d. The company paid $32,400 on April 1, 2014, to rent equipment for a three-year period beginning April 1, 2014.

Analysis Component: If the above adjustments were not recorded, identify the types of accounts that would be affected and if they would be over- or understated.

Problem 3-2A Preparing adjusting entries—depreciation expense LO⁴

Details regarding Leroux Steel's purchases of plant and equipment items during 2014 follow:

Date of Purchase	Plant and Equipment Item	Cost	Estimated Useful Life	Estimated Sales Value at End of Estimated Useful Life
a. Jan. 1	Machine A	$102,000	5 years	$ -0-
b. Apr. 1	Machine B	61,000	4 years	3,400
c. Nov. 1	Machine C	30,500	2 years	2,900

Required Prepare the annual adjusting entry at December 31, 2014, Leroux's year-end, for each plant and equipment item.

Analysis Component: What is the purpose of recording depreciation? If depreciation is not recorded, how would the income statement be affected?

Problem 3-3A Preparing adjusting entries—unearned revenues LO⁴

Outdoor's Best pre-sells yard maintenance packages for the gardening season. During October, the company collects cash from clients for Christmas trees to be delivered in December. Snow removal services are also provided. Outdoor's Best prepares adjusting entries monthly. The following selected accounts appear on the November 30, 2014, unadjusted trial balance:

Account	Debit	Credit
Unearned lawn services..................		$102,000
Unearned garden services		36,400
Unearned snow removal services....		11,800
Unearned Christmas tree sales........		21,200

Required Prepare the monthly adjusting journal entries at November 30, 2014, using the following additional information.

a. $86,000 of the Unearned Lawn Services account represents payments received from customers for the 2015 season. The remainder represents fall lawn services actually performed during November 2014.

b. $31,950 of the Unearned Garden Services account had been earned by November 30, 2014.

c. $9,200 of the Unearned Snow Removal Services account remained unearned at November 30, 2014.

d. Outdoor's arranges with its customers to deliver trees from December 5 to December 20. As a result, the Unearned Christmas Tree Sales account will be earned in total by December 20.

Analysis Component: If the Unearned Lawn Services of $102,000 had been recorded as a revenue when received instead of as a liability, what would the effect have been on the November 30, 2014, financial statements assuming no adjustment was made on November 30, 2014?

Problem 3-4A Preparing adjusting and subsequent cash entries—accrued expenses LO⁴

Mannix Resources prepares adjusting entries monthly. In reviewing the accounts on March 31, Mannix Resources discovered the following:

a. Interest of $1,050 had accrued on the note payable as at March 31. It is to be paid on April 2.

b. Unpaid and unrecorded salaries at March 31 totalled $32,850. The $32,850 plus salaries of $21,900 for the first four days of April were paid on April 4.

c. The March telephone bill for $440 is unpaid and unrecorded at March 31. It is to be paid on April 15.

d. Mannix normally pays rent in three-month installments. At March 31, rent of $4,200 per month had not been paid for February, March, or April. Rent of $4,200 was correctly accrued at the end of February. The balance owing plus rent for May, June, and July was paid on April 26.

e. Mannix pays commissions to the technicians at the rate of 4% of services performed. During March, total services performed were $410,000. Commissions are unrecorded and unpaid at March 31. Commissions are paid on the 15th of the following month.

Required Using the information provided above, prepare the monthly adjusting journal entries at March 31 along with the appropriate subsequent cash entries.

Problem 3-5A Preparing adjusting and subsequent cash entries—accrued revenues LO⁴

In reviewing the accounts on March 31 for the year just ended, DigiTech discovered the following:

a. DigiTech owns the building that it occupies. Part of the building is rented to E-Quip Company for $4,150 per month. E-Quip had not paid the March rent as at March 31. On April 3, DigiTech collected the rent accrued on March 31.

b. Services performed but unrecorded at March 31 totalled $8,400. This amount was collected on April 7.

c. Interest for the month of March had accrued on a note receivable in the amount of $640. The interest accrued on March 31 was collected on April 1.

d. On February 1, DigiTech signed a $34,500 six-month contract to perform services for a client. DigiTech has been providing the services but as of March 31 no cash had been received. On April 2, DigiTech collected the revenue accrued on March 31.

Required Using the information provided above, prepare the annual adjusting journal entries at March 31 along with the appropriate subsequent cash entries.

Problem 3-6A Adjusting entries; adjusted trial balance LO^{4,6}

PacRim Careers provides training to individuals who pay tuition directly to the business. The business also offers extension training to groups in off-site locations. Additional information available at the December 31, 2014, year-end follows:

a. An analysis of the company's policies shows that $1,250 of insurance coverage has expired.

b. An inventory shows that teaching supplies costing $450 are on hand at the end of the year.

c. The estimated annual depreciation on the equipment is $8,000.

d. The estimated annual depreciation on the professional library is $4,500.

e. The school offers off-campus services for specific employers. On November 1, the company agreed to do a special six-month course for a client. The contract calls for a monthly fee of $950, and the client paid the first five months' fees in advance. When the cash was received, the Unearned Extension Fees account was credited.

PacRim Careers Trial Balances.xls

Home   Insert   Page Layout   Formulas   Data   Review   View

P18   fx

	A	B	C	D	E	F	G
1		**PacRim Careers**					
2		**Trial Balances**					
3		**December 31, 2014**					
4		**Unadjusted**				**Adjusted**	
5		**Trial Balance**		**Adjustments**		**Trial Balance**	
6	**Account**	**Dr.**	**Cr.**	**Dr.**	**Cr.**	**Dr.**	**Cr.**
7	Cash	$ 18,000					
8	Accounts receivable	-0-					
9	Teaching supplies	6,500					
10	Prepaid insurance	1,400					
11	Prepaid rent	7,200					
12	Professional library	60,000					
13	Accumulated depreciation, professional library		$ 18,000				
14	Equipment	96,000					
15	Accumulated depreciation, equipment		32,000				
16	Accounts payable		2,500				
17	Salaries payable		-0-				
18	Unearned extension fees		6,300				
19	Karoo Ashevak, capital		229,000				
20	Karoo Ashevak, withdrawals	92,000					
21	Tuition fees earned		196,000				
22	Extension fees earned		72,500				
23	Depreciation expense, equipment	-0-					
24	Depreciation expense, professional library	-0-					
25	Salaries expense	206,000					
26	Insurance expense	-0-					
27	Rent expense	44,000					
28	Teaching supplies expense	-0-					
29	Advertising expense	14,000					
30	Utilities expense	11,200					
31	**Totals**	$ 556,300	$ 556,300				

f. On October 15, the school agreed to teach a four-month class for an individual for $1,200 tuition per month payable at the end of the class. The services to date have been provided as agreed, but no payment has been received.

g. The school's two employees are paid weekly. As of the end of the year, three days' wages have accrued at the rate of $120 per day for each employee.

h. The balance in the Prepaid Rent account represents the rent for three months: December, January, and February.

Required

   1. Prepare the necessary annual adjusting journal entries at December 31, 2014, based on (a) to (h) above.

Analysis Component:

   2. Refer to the format presented in Exhibit 3.22 and complete the adjusted trial balance using the information in (a) through (h) above.

   3. If the adjustments were *not* recorded, calculate the over- or understatement of income.

   4. Is it ethical to ignore adjusting entries?

Problem 3-7A Adjusting entries LO⁴

Wedona Energy Consultants prepares adjusting entries monthly. Based on an analysis of the unadjusted trial balance at January 31, 2014, the following information was available for the preparation of the January 31, 2014, month-end adjusting entries:

a. Equipment purchased on November 1 of this accounting period for $21,600 is estimated to have a useful life of three years. After three years of use, it is expected that the equipment will be scrapped due to technological obsolescence.

b. Of the $11,400 balance in Unearned Consulting Fees, $8,700 had been earned.

c. The Prepaid Rent account showed a balance of $13,500. This was paid on January 1 of this accounting period and represents six months of rent commencing on the same date.

d. Accrued wages at January 31 totalled $18,500.

e. One month of interest had accrued at the rate of 4% per year on a $42,000 note payable.

f. Unrecorded and uncollected consulting fees at month-end were $6,150.

g. A $3,510 insurance policy was purchased on April 1 of the current accounting period and debited to the Prepaid Insurance account. Coverage began April 1 for 18 months.

h. The monthly depreciation on the office furniture was $625.

i. Repair revenues accrued at month-end totalled $3,400.

j. The Store Supplies account had a balance of $800 at the beginning of January. During January, $1,780 of supplies were purchased and debited to the Store Supplies account. At month-end, a count of the supplies revealed a balance of $650.

Required Prepare adjusting journal entries for the month ended January 31, 2014, based on the above.

Problem 3-8A Adjusting and subsequent cash journal entries LO⁴

The following information concerns the adjusting entries to be recorded on November 30, 2014, for RaiLink's year just ended.

a.   The Office Supplies account started the year with a $4,800 balance. During 2014, the company purchased supplies at a cost of $24,800, which was added to the Office Supplies account. The inventory of supplies on hand at November 30 had a cost of $6,300.

b.   An analysis of the company's insurance policies provided these facts:

Policy	Date of Purchase	Years of Coverage	Total Cost
1	March 1, 2013	2	$ 5,760
2	March 1, 2014	3	22,320
3	July 1, 2014	1	3,780

The total premium for each policy was paid in full at the purchase date, and the Prepaid Insurance account was debited for the full cost. *Appropriate adjusting entries have been made to November 30, 2013.*

c.   The company has 15 employees who earn a total of $4,800 in salaries for every working day. They are paid each Monday for their work in the five-day workweek ending on the preceding Friday. November 30, 2014, falls on a Sunday, and all 15 employees worked November 24 to 28 inclusive. They will be paid salaries for five full days on Monday, December 1, 2014.

d.   The company purchased a building on July 1, 2014. The building cost $306,000 and is expected to have a $25,000 residual value at the end of its predicted 30-year life.

e.   Because the company is not large enough to occupy the entire building, it arranged to rent some space to a tenant at $3,100 per month, starting on October 1, 2014. The rent was paid on time on October 1, and the amount received was credited to the Rent Earned account. However, the tenant has not paid the November rent. The company has worked out an agreement with the tenant, who has promised to pay both November's and December's rent in full on December 15.

f.   On October 1, the company also rented space to another tenant for $3,650 per month. The tenant paid five months' rent in advance on that date. The payment was recorded with a credit to the Unearned Rent account.

Required

1. Use the information to prepare the annual adjusting entries as of November 30, 2014.

2. Prepare journal entries to record the subsequent cash transactions in December 2014 described in parts (c) and (e).

Problem 3-9A Adjusting entries LO⁴

Rainmaker Environmental Consultants is just finishing its second year of operations. The company's unadjusted trial balance at October 31, 2014, follows:

Rainmaker prepares adjustments each October 31. The following additional information is available on October 31, 2014.

a.   It was determined that $12,000 of the unearned consulting fees had not yet been earned.

b.   It was discovered that $14,000 of the balance in the Consulting Fees Earned account was for services to be performed in November.

c.   The balance in the Prepaid Rent account represents three months of rent beginning September 1, 2014.

d.   Accrued wages at October 31 totalled $6,800.

e.   The office furniture was purchased on March 1, 2013, and has an estimated useful life of two years. After two years of use, it is expected that the furniture will be worthless.

f.   Accrued consulting fees at year-end totalled $4,200.

Acct. No.	Account	Debit	Credit
	Rainmaker Environmental Consultants		
	Unadjusted Trial Balance		
	October 31, 2014		
101	Cash..	$ 26,000	
106	Accounts receivable......................................	61,000	
109	Interest receivable	-0-	
111	Notes receivable...	50,000	
126	Supplies...	5,300	
128	Prepaid insurance...	3,400	
131	Prepaid rent	27,000	
161	Office furniture...	84,000	
162	Accumulated depreciation, office furniture		$ 28,000
201	Accounts payable		18,000
210	Wages payable		-0-
233	Unearned consulting fees		26,000
301	Jeff Moore, capital		223,000
302	Jeff Moore, withdrawals................................	28,000	
401	Consulting fees earned		232,020
409	Interest revenue...		480
601	Depreciation expense, office furniture	-0-	
622	Wages expense...	192,000	
637	Insurance expense..	-0-	
640	Rent expense..	44,000	
650	Supplies expense..	6,800	
	Totals	$527,500	$527,500

g. Interest of $85 had accrued on the note receivable for the month of October.

h. The balance in the Prepaid Insurance account represents the remaining balance of a two-year policy purchased on April 1, 2013.

i. A count of the supplies on October 31 revealed a balance remaining of $620.

Required Prepare the annual adjusting journal entries for October 31, 2014, based on the above.

CHECK FIGURES:
3. Adjusted trial balance, debits = $580,585
4. Net loss = $79,895

Problem 3-10A Posting, adjusted trial balance, and preparing financial statements LO6,7

Required Using the information in Problem 3-9A, complete the following:

1. Set up balance column accounts for Rainmaker Environmental Consultants and enter the balances listed in the unadjusted trial balance.

2. Post the adjusting entries prepared in Problem 3-9A to the accounts.

3. Prepare an adjusted trial balance.

4. Use the adjusted trial balance to prepare an income statement, a statement of changes in equity, and a balance sheet. Assume that the owner, Jeff Moore, made no owner investments during the year.

Analysis Component: Assume that total revenues and expenses reported for the year ended October 31, 2013, were $189,000 and $157,600, respectively. Compare the business's financial performance for the years ended October 31, 2013 and 2014.

Note

For Part 1, your instructor may ask you to set up T-accounts instead of balance column accounts. The solution is available in both formats.

Problem 3-11A Adjusting entries LO⁴

Arrow Hospitality prepares adjustments monthly and showed the following at September 30, 2014:

	Arrow Hospitality Trial Balances.xls						
Home Insert Page Layout Formulas Data Review View							
P18	fx						
	A	B	C	D	E	F	G
1	**Arrow Hospitality**						
2	Trial Balances						
3	September 30, 2014						
4		**Unadjusted**				**Adjusted**	
5		**Trial Balance**		**Adjustments**		**Trial Balance**	
6	**Account**	**Dr.**	**Cr.**	**Dr.**	**Cr.**	**Dr.**	**Cr.**
7	Cash	$ 6,000					
8	Accounts receivable	11,200					
9	Repair supplies	2,200					
10	Prepaid rent	14,000					
11	Office furniture	26,000					
12	Accounts payable		$ 8,000				
13	Notes payable		21,600				
14	Eli Arrow, capital		67,758				
15	Eli Arrow, withdrawals	5,000					
16	Hospitality revenues		128,000				
17	Salaries expense	144,000					
18	Wages expense	16,958					
19	**Totals**	$ 225,358	$ 225,358				

Additional information available for the month ended September 30, 2014:

a. Interest of $162 had accrued on the notes payable for the month of September.

b. The office furniture was acquired on September 1, 2014, and has an estimated four-year life. The furniture will be sold for about $2,000 at the end of its four-year life.

c. A count of the Repair Supplies revealed a balance on hand of $700.

d. A review of the Prepaid Rent account showed that $10,000 had been used during September.

e. Accrued wages of $2,800 had not been recorded at month-end.

f. The September Internet bill for $100 had been received and must be paid by October 14.

g. Accrued revenues of $6,200 were not recorded at September 30.

Required Prepare adjusting entries for the month ended September 30, 2014, for each of (a) through (g) above.

CHECK FIGURES:
1. Adjustments columns = $21,262;
Adjusted trial balance columns = $235,120
2. Net loss = $41,820

Problem 3-12A Preparation of financial statements LO⁶,⁷

Required

1. Using the format presented in Problem 3-11A, complete the adjusted trial balance by including the adjusting entries prepared in Problem 3-11A.

2. Prepare an income statement, a statement of changes in equity and a balance sheet based on the adjusted trial balance completed in Part 1. Assume that the owner, Eli Arrow, made an investment during September of $3,600.

Analysis Component: Assume that total assets reported at August 31, 2014, were $76,900. Determine what total liabilities and equity were on that date and comment on the change in the financial position from August to September.

Problem 3-13A Preparing financial statements from the adjusted trial balance LO[7]

This alphabetized adjusted trial balance is for GalaVu Entertainment as of its December 31, 2014, year-end:

	Debit	Credit
Accounts payable...		$ 44,000
Accounts receivable	$ 18,700	
Accumulated depreciation, automobiles.........		69,000
Accumulated depreciation, equipment...........		20,500
Advertising expense	9,000	
Automobiles..	140,000	
Cash	11,000	
Depreciation expense, automobiles...............	13,200	
Depreciation expense, equipment..................	4,100	
Equipment..	65,000	
Fees earned..		240,000
Interest earned...		150
Interest expense...	3,500	
Interest payable..		75
Interest receivable..	300	
John Conroe, capital		23,000
John Conroe, withdrawals	19,000	
Land	35,000	
Long-term notes payable		115,000
Notes receivable (due in 90 days)	80,000	
Office supplies..	4,000	
Office supplies expense..................................	13,000	
Repairs expense, automobiles........................	8,400	
Salaries expense	76,225	
Salaries payable..		5,500
Unearned fees..		11,000
Wages expense	27,800	
Totals..	$528,225	$528,225

Required Use the information in the trial balance to prepare:

a. The income statement for the year ended December 31, 2014.

b. The statement of changes in equity for the year ended December 31, 2014, assuming that the owner made additional investments of $15,000 during the year.

c. The balance sheet as of December 31, 2014.

Analysis Component: The owner, John Conroe, is very pleased with the change in the business's financial position. Specifically, he noted that his equity increased. "My banker told me that as long as equity is increasing, my business is doing great." Comment.

Problem 3-14A Journalizing, posting, adjusted trial balance, adjusting entries, financial statements LO^{4,5,6,7}

On August 1, 2014, Delanie Tugut began a tour company in the Northwest Territories called Tugut Arctic Tours. The following occurred during the first month of operations:

Aug.	1	Purchased office furniture on account; $5,200.
	1	Delanie Tugut invested $7,000 cash into her new business.
	2	Collected $3,900 in advance for a three-week guided caribou hunt beginning the last week of August.
	3	Paid $6,000 for six months' rent for office space effective August 1.
	4	Received $3,000 for a four-day northern lights viewing tour just completed.
	7	Paid $1,500 for hotel expenses regarding the August 4 tour.
	15	Delanie withdrew cash of $500 for personal use.
	22	Met with a Japanese tour guide to discuss a $150,000 tour contract.
	31	Paid wages of $1,300.

Required

1. Prepare General Journal entries to record the August transactions.

2. Set up the following T-accounts: Cash (101); Prepaid Rent (131); Office Furniture (161); Accumulated Depreciation, Office Furniture (162); Accounts Payable (201); Unearned Revenue (233); Delanie Tugut, Capital (301); Delanie Tugut, Withdrawals (302); Revenue (401); Depreciation Expense, Office Furniture (602); Wages Expense (623); Rent Expense (640); Telephone Expense (688); and Hotel Expenses (696).

3. Post the entries to the accounts; calculate the ending balance in each account.

4. Prepare an unadjusted trial balance at August 31, 2014.

5. Use the following information to prepare and post adjusting entries on August 31:

   a. The office furniture has an estimated life of four years and a $208 residual value.

   b. Two-thirds of the August 2 advance has been earned.

   c. One month of the Prepaid Rent has been used.

   d. The August telephone bill was not received as of August 31 but amounted to $320.

6. Prepare an adjusted trial balance.

7. Prepare an income statement, a statement of changes in equity, and a balance sheet.

Analysis Component: When a company shows revenue on its income statement, does this mean that cash equal to revenues was received during the period in which the revenues were reported?

*Problem 3-15A Correcting entries LO^8

The accountant for Karma Counselling Services found several errors in reviewing the unadjusted trial balance on September 30. You are to prepare correcting entries based on the following information:

a. The Counselling Fees Earned account included an entry debiting cash for $7,000 that should have been debited to Accounts Receivable.

b. Utilities Expense was debited $1,680 that should have been recorded as Telephone Expense.

c. The *Office* Supplies account shows a credit of $2,800 regarding the use of *Cleaning* Supplies.

d. A transaction involving $19,600 of service revenue performed on account was incorrectly recorded as a debit to Accounts Payable and a credit to Unearned Service Revenue.

e. Equipment was incorrectly debited for $1,200 with a corresponding credit to Accounts Payable regarding supplies that were sold to a neighbouring store on credit.

Required Journalize the correcting entries required on September 30.

Analysis Component: The error in (b) shows that an incorrect expense account was debited. Since the net effect on the financial statements is nil after recording the correction, is it necessary to prepare a correcting entry for this type of error?

An asterisk (*) identifies assignment material based on Appendix 3A or Appendix 3B.

CHECK FIGURE:
Adjusted trial balance,
debits = $136,400

*Problem 3-16A Recording prepaid expenses and unearned revenues LO[9]

Willis Consulting follows the approach of recording prepaid expenses as expenses and unearned revenues as revenues. Willis's unadjusted trial balance for the year ended March 31, 2014, follows.

Willis Consulting Trial Balances.xls

Home   Insert   Page Layout   Formulas   Data   Review   View

P18   fx

Willis Consulting
Trial Balances
March 31, 2014

	Account	Unadjusted Trial Balance Dr.	Unadjusted Trial Balance Cr.	Adjustments Dr.	Adjustments Cr.	Adjusted Trial Balance Dr.	Adjusted Trial Balance Cr.
7	Cash	$ 32,000					
8	Accounts receivable	63,000					
9	Prepaid rent	-0-					
10	Prepaid insurance	-0-					
11	Accounts payable		$ 16,000				
12	Unearned consulting fees		-0-				
13	Bruce Willis, capital		38,400				
14	Consulting fees earned		82,000				
15	Rent expense	38,990					
16	Insurance expense	2,410					
17	**Totals**	$ 136,400	$ 136,400				

Additional information:

a. A review of the Consulting Fees Earned account showed that $6,400 of the balance has not yet been earned.

b. The balance in the Rent Expense account was paid on January 15, 2014, and represents seven months of rent beginning February 1, 2014.

c. It was determined that $1,900 of the balance in the Insurance Expense account was used by March 31, 2014.

Required Refer to Exhibit 3.22 and use the information provided to complete the columns above.

*Problem 3-17A Recording prepaid expenses and unearned revenues LO[4,9]

The following events occurred for a company during the last two months of its fiscal year ended December 31, 2014:

Nov.	1	Paid $4,500 for future newspaper advertising.
	1	Paid $7,800 for insurance through October 31 of the following year.
	30	Received $6,600 for future services to be provided to a customer.
Dec.	1	Paid $5,850 for the services of a consultant, to be received over the next three months.
	15	Received $12,100 for future services to be provided to a customer.
	31	Of the advertising paid for on November 1, $1,780 worth had not yet been published by the newspaper.
	31	Part of the insurance paid for on November 1 had expired.
	31	Services worth $1,650 had not yet been provided to the customer who paid on November 30.
	31	One-third of the consulting services paid for on December 1 had been received.
	31	The company had performed $2,750 of the services that the customer had paid for on December 15.

Required

1. Prepare the November and December entries for the above activities under the approach that records prepaid expenses as assets and records unearned revenues as liabilities. Also, prepare adjusting entries at the end of the year.

2. Prepare the November and December entries under the approach that records prepaid expenses as expenses and records unearned revenues as revenues. Also, prepare adjusting entries at the end of the year.

Analysis Component: Explain why the alternative sets of entries in requirements 1 and 2 do not result in different financial statement amounts.

An asterisk (*) identifies assignment material based on Appendix 3A or Appendix 3B.

Problem 3-1B Preparing adjusting entries—prepaid expenses LO⁴

Domino's Cleaning Services is gathering information for its year-end, April 30, 2014. Selected accounts on the April 30, 2014, unadjusted trial balance are reproduced below:

Account	Debit	Credit
Prepaid equipment rental...............	$24,750	
Prepaid warehouse rental...............	7,800	
Prepaid insurance..........................	8,160	
Cleaning supplies..........................	3,100	

Required Prepare the required annual adjusting entries at April 30, 2014, based on the following additional information:

a. The balance in the Prepaid Equipment Rental account is for 18 months of equipment rental that began December 1, 2013.

b. $6,000 of the balance in the Prepaid Warehouse Rental account had been used as of April 30, 2014.

c. The balance in the Prepaid Insurance account represents six months of insurance effective February 1, 2014.

d. A count of the cleaning supplies revealed that $2,400 had been used.

Analysis Component: Which GAAP require the recording of adjusting entries and why?

Problem 3-2B Preparing adjusting entries—depreciation expense LO⁴

Zebra Consulting prepares adjusting entries and financial statements monthly. Details regarding Zebra Consulting's plant and equipment items follow:

Date of Purchase	Plant and Equipment Item	Cost	Estimated Useful Life	Estimated Sales Value at End of Estimated Useful Life
a. Dec. 1, 2013	Furniture	$ 27,000	3 years	$ -0-
b. Mar. 1, 2014	Equipment	171,600	10 years	24,000
c. Nov. 1, 2014	Building	491,000	15 years	140,000

Required Prepare the monthly adjusting entry to record depreciation for each plant and equipment item at November 30, 2014.

Analysis Component: What is the purpose of recording depreciation? If depreciation is not recorded, how would each of the components of the accounting equation be affected?

Problem 3-3B Preparing adjusting entries—unearned revenues LO⁴

Blackfeather Tours sells scuba diving and kayaking excursions, along with a number of unique sightseeing packages. The company requires a 50% payment from the customer at the time of booking. The following selected accounts appear on Blackfeather's January 31, 2014, year-end unadjusted trial balance:

Account	Debit	Credit
Unearned heli-tour revenue		$ 38,000
Unearned tour package revenue		652,000
Unearned scuba diving revenue		290,000
Unearned kayaking tour revenue ...		116,000

Required Prepare the annual adjusting journal entries at January 31, 2014, using the following additional information:

a. Blackfeather Tours has custom helicopter packages in which groups are flown in and out of island retreats. The balance in this unearned account is for a group scheduled for early March 2014.

b. Three-quarters of the Unearned Tour Package Revenue account had been earned by January 31, 2014.

c. $72,000 of the Unearned Scuba Diving Revenue account remained unearned at January 31, 2014.

d. $15,500 of the Unearned Kayaking Tour Revenue account represents payments received from customers for February and March 2014. The balance in the account is for tours provided in January 2014.

Analysis Component: Using your understanding of GAAP, explain how and why unearned revenues are adjusted at the end of the accounting period.

Problem 3-4B Preparing adjusting and subsequent cash entries—accrued expenses LO⁴

In reviewing the accounts on September 30, 2014, for the year just ended, Geek Designers discovered the following:

a. Interest of $1,500 had accrued on the bank loan as at September 30. It is to be paid on October 2.

b. Accrued wages at September 30 totalled $80,500. On October 3, the first biweekly payday of October, $115,000 was paid to employees representing the seven days accrued on September 30 plus the first three working days in October.

c. The September cell phone bill for $215 was unpaid and unrecorded at September 30. It will be paid on October 5.

d. On September 30, $1,150 of cable charges were accrued regarding the past two months of usage that were not recorded or paid. This amount was paid on October 2.

e. $1,140 of property taxes covering September were accrued on September 30. This amount was paid on October 15.

Required Using the information provided above, prepare the annual adjusting journal entries at September 30 along with the appropriate subsequent cash entries.

Problem 3-5B Preparing adjusting and subsequent cash entries—accrued revenues LO⁴

WonderWeb prepares adjusting entries monthly. In reviewing the accounts on March 31, 2014, WonderWeb discovered the following:

a. Interest of $450, representing 25 days in March, had accrued on the note receivable as of March 31. The accrual of $450 plus an additional five days in April was collected on April 5.

b. Accrued consulting fees totalling $5,600 were not recorded on March 31. This amount was collected on April 6.

c. Web design work totalling $8,750 was completed on March 31 but not recorded. This amount was collected on April 13.

d. WonderWeb rents the basement of its building to a student. The student has not paid the March rent of $950 as at March 31. On April 27, the March rent plus the rent for April was collected.

Required Using the information provided above, prepare the March 31 month-end adjusting journal entries along with the appropriate subsequent cash entries.

Problem 3-6B Adjusting entries; adjusted trial balance LO^{4,6}

Fawcett Institute provides one-on-one training to individuals who pay tuition directly to the business and also offers extension training to groups in off-site locations. Fawcett prepares adjusting entries monthly. Additional information available on December 31, 2014:

a. An analysis of the company's policies shows that $31,000 of insurance coverage has expired.

b. An inventory shows that teaching supplies costing $13,400 are on hand at the end of the month.

c. The estimated monthly depreciation on the equipment is $650.

d. The estimated monthly depreciation on the professional library is $320.

e. The school offers off-campus services for specific operators. On December 1, the company agreed to do a special four-month course for a client. The contract calls for a $5,400 monthly fee, and the client paid the first two months' fees in advance. When the cash was received, the Unearned Extension Fees account was credited.

f. On December 15, the school agreed to teach a four-month class to an individual for $1,600 tuition per month payable at the end of the class. The services have been provided as agreed, and no payment has been received.

g. The school's only employee is paid weekly. As of the end of the month, wages of $1,200 have accrued.

h. The balance in the Prepaid Rent account represents the rent for December, January, February, and March.

	Fawcett Institute Trial Balance.xls
Home Insert Page Layout Formulas Data Review View	
P18 fx	

	A	B	C	D	E	F	G
1		**Fawcett Institute**					
2		**Trial Balance**					
3		**December 31, 2014**					
4		**Unadjusted**				**Adjusted**	
5		**Trial Balance**		**Adjustments**		**Trial Balance**	
6	**Account**	**Dr.**	**Cr.**	**Dr.**	**Cr.**	**Dr.**	**Cr.**
7	Cash	$ 25,000					
8	Accounts receivable	-0-					
9	Teaching supplies	107,200					
10	Prepaid insurance	36,000					
11	Prepaid rent	11,600					
12	Professional library	20,000					
13	Accumulated depreciation, professional library		$ 3,000				
14	Equipment	141,400					
15	Accumulated depreciation, equipment		32,000				
16	Accounts payable		24,400				
17	Salaries payable		-0-				
18	Unearned extension fees		55,200				
19	Jay Fawcett, capital		62,000				
20	Jay Fawcett, withdrawals	40,000					
21	Tuition fees earned		285,000				
22	Extension fees earned		124,000				
23	Depreciation expense, equipment	-0-					
24	Depreciation expense, professional library	-0-					
25	Salaries expense	143,600					
26	Insurance expense	-0-					
27	Rent expense	-0-					
28	Teaching supplies expense	-0-					
29	Advertising expense	36,000					
30	Utilities expense	24,800					
31	**Totals**	$ 585,600	$ 585,600				

Required

1. Prepare the necessary December 31, 2014, month-end adjusting journal entries based on (a) through (h) above.

Analysis Component:

2. Refer to the format presented in Exhibit 3.22 and prepare an adjusted trial balance using the information in (a) through (h) above.

3. If the adjustments were *not* recorded, calculate the over- or understatement of income.

4. Is it ethical to ignore adjusting entries?

Problem 3-7B Adjusting entries LO⁴

Kazz Industries' year-end is May 31. Based on an analysis of the unadjusted trial balance at May 31, 2014, the following information was available:

a. Machinery costing $65,500 was acquired on September 1 of this accounting period. It is estimated to have a useful life of six years. The machinery is estimated to have a $7,000 value at the end of its six-year life.

b. It was determined that $6,000 of completed work was included in the $9,200 Unearned Revenue account balance at year-end.

c. The Prepaid Insurance account showed a balance of $23,040. This was paid and takes effect on March 1 of this accounting period and represents a two-year policy.

d. Accrued salaries at year-end were $17,300.

e. $2,160 of interest had accrued on the $144,000 note payable.

f. Accrued revenues at year-end totalled $16,800.

g. $11,340 worth of advertising was prepaid on January 1 of the current accounting period and debited to the Prepaid Advertising account. This covered four months of advertising beginning on the same date.

h. The annual depreciation on the office equipment was $4,100.

i. Interest revenue accrued at year-end totalled $620.

j. The Office Supplies account had a balance of $4,000 at the beginning of the accounting period. During the year, $27,500 of supplies were purchased and debited to the Office Supplies account. At year-end, a count of the supplies revealed that $29,400 had been used.

Required Prepare adjusting journal entries for the year ended May 31, 2014, based on the above.

Problem 3-8B Identifying adjusting and subsequent cash journal entries LO[4]

Valor Ventures prepares adjusting entries monthly. The following information concerns the adjusting entries that need to be recorded on October 31, 2014, for the month just ended.

a. The Office Supplies account had a $1,000 balance on October 1. During October, the company purchased supplies at a cost of $9,100, which was added to the Office Supplies account. The inventory of supplies on hand at October 31 had a cost of $600.

b. An analysis of the company's insurance policies provided these facts:

Policy	Date of Purchase	Years of Coverage	Total Cost
1	April 1, 2013	2	$8,400
2	April 1, 2014	3	6,660
3	August 1, 2014	1	1,500

The total premium for each policy was paid in full at the purchase date, and the Prepaid Insurance account was debited for the full cost. *Appropriate adjusting entries have been made to September 30, 2014.*

c. The company has 10 employees who earn a total of $3,250 for every working day. They are paid each Monday for their work in the five-day workweek ending on the preceding Friday. October 31, 2014, falls on a Friday, and all 10 employees worked the five days that week. They will be paid salaries for five full days on Monday, November 3, 2014.

d. The company purchased a building on August 1, 2012. The building cost $250,000, and is expected to have a $40,000 residual value at the end of its predicted 25-year life.

e. Because the company is not large enough to occupy the entire building, it arranged to rent some space to a tenant at $2,600 per month, starting on September 1, 2014. The rent was paid on time on September 1, and the amount received was credited to the Rent Earned account. However, the tenant has not paid the October rent. The company has worked out an agreement with the tenant, who has promised to pay both October's and November's rent in full on November 15.

f. On October 1, the company also rented space to another tenant for $2,350 per month. The tenant paid five months' rent in advance on that date. The payment was recorded with a credit to the Unearned Rent account.

Required

1. Use the information to prepare the October 31, 2014, month-end adjusting entries.
2. Prepare journal entries to record the subsequent cash transactions described in items (c) and (e).

Problem 3-9B Adjusting journal entries LO[4]

Ben Hallmark, the owner of Hallmark Surveying Services, has been in business for two years. The unadjusted trial balance at December 31, regarding the month just ended, follows:
The following additional information is available on December 31, 2014:

a. Depreciation on the equipment for the month was $430.

b. $9,600 of the balance in Unearned Surveying Fees is unearned at December 31.

c. The balance in Prepaid Rent is for six months of rent beginning December 1.

d. Accrued wages at month-end were $12,400.

e. December's interest in the amount of $120 had accrued on the notes payable.

f. Accrued surveying fees at month-end totalled $21,800.

g. The balance in Prepaid Advertising covers four months of advertising beginning December 15.

h. A count of the supplies on December 31 showed $1,320 had been used.

i. The December electricity bill for $2,340 was received on December 31. It is unrecorded and unpaid.

Required Prepare adjusting journal entries for the month ended December 31, 2014, based on the above.

Analysis Component: Explain the differences between *Accumulated Depreciation* and *Depreciation Expense*.

	Hallmark Surveying Services Unadjusted Trial Balance December 31, 2014		
Acct. No.	**Account**	**Debit**	**Credit**
101	Cash..	$ 15,600	
106	Accounts receivable	29,200	
126	Supplies	1,640	
128	Prepaid advertising......................................	1,280	
131	Prepaid rent	17,880	
167	Surveying equipment	58,000	
168	Accumulated depreciation, surveying equipment		$ 7,348
201	Accounts payable		13,800
203	Interest payable..		-0-
210	Wages payable		-0-
233	Unearned surveying fees		14,800
251	Notes payable		36,000
301	Ben Hallmark, capital.................................		28,652
302	Ben Hallmark, withdrawals	24,300	
401	Surveying fees earned		170,948
601	Depreciation expense, surveying equipment	-0-	
622	Salaries expense	56,000	
623	Wages expense	39,726	
633	Interest expense	-0-	
637	Insurance expense.......................................	6,000	
640	Rent expense...	-0-	
650	Supplies expense...	2,958	
655	Advertising expense	-0-	
671	Gas and oil expense	6,564	
684	Repairs expense...	12,400	
690	Utilities expense	-0-	
	Totals	$271,548	$271,548

Problem 3-10B Posting, adjusted trial balance, and preparing financial statements LO[6,7]

Required Using the information in Problem 3-9B, complete the following:

1. Set up balance column accounts for Hallmark Surveying Services and enter the balances listed in the unadjusted trial balance.

2. Post the adjusting entries prepared in Problem 3-9B to the balance column accounts.

3. Prepare an adjusted trial balance.

4. Use the adjusted trial balance to prepare an income statement, a statement of changes in equity, and a balance sheet. Assume that the owner, Ben Hallmark, made owner investments of $4,000 during the month.

Analysis Component: At December 31, 2014, how much of the business's assets are financed by the owner? by debt? Assuming total assets at the end of the previous month totalled $84,200, did equity financing increase or decrease during December? Generally speaking, is this a favourable or unfavourable change?

Note
For Part 1, your instructor may ask you to set up T-accounts instead of balance column accounts. The solution is available in both formats.

Problem 3-11B Adjusting entries LO[4]

B52 Skate Training prepares adjustments annually and showed the following on its June 30, 2014, year-end:

	B52 Skate Training Unadjusted Trial Balance.xls						
	Home Insert Page Layout Formulas Data Review View						
	P18 _fx_						
	A	B	C	D	E	F	G
1	**B52 Skate Training**						
2	Unadjusted Trial Balance						
3	June 30, 2014						
4		**Unadjusted**				**Adjusted**	
5		**Trial Balance**		**Adjustments**		**Trial Balance**	
6	**Account**	**Dr.**	**Cr.**	**Dr.**	**Cr.**	**Dr.**	**Cr.**
7	Cash	$ 112,000					
8	Accounts receivable	28,000					
9	Repair supplies	2,800					
10	Prepaid arena rental	182,000					
11	Skate equipment	428,000					
12	Accumulated depreciation, skate equipment		$ 164,000				
13	Accounts payable		5,400				
14	Unearned training fees		19,600				
15	Notes payable		160,000				
16	Ben Gibson, capital		451,400				
17	Ben Gibson, withdrawals	72,000					
18	Training fees earned		550,000				
19	Salaries expense	350,000					
20	Arena rental expense	168,000					
21	Other expenses	7,600					
22	**Totals**	$1,350,400	$1,350,400				

Additional information available at year-end:

a. The Prepaid Arena Rental of $182,000 was paid on February 1, 2014. It represents seven months of rent on the arena.

b. A count of the Repair Supplies at year-end revealed that $1,900 had been used.

c. Annual depreciation of the skate equipment was $82,000.

d. A review of the Unearned Training Fees account at year-end showed that included in the balance was $12,600 that had not yet been earned.

e. Accrued salaries of $58,000 had not been recorded at year-end.

f. Interest of $1,800 had accrued regarding the Notes Payable.

g. On June 5, 2014, cash of $92,000 was received for 2014/2015 training sessions (lessons begin in October). This amount is included in the Training Fees Earned balance.

Required Prepare the annual adjusting entries on June 30, 2014, for each of (a) through (g) above.

Problem 3-12B Preparing financial statement LO^6,7

Required

1. Using the format presented in Problem 3-11B, complete the adjusted trial balance by including the adjusting entries prepared in Problem 3-11B.

2. Prepare an income statement, a statement of changes in equity, and a balance sheet based on the adjusted trial balance completed in Part 1. Assume that the owner, Ben Gibson, made an investment during the year of $20,000.

Analysis Component: Assume that total liabilities reported at June 30, 2013, were $90,000. Determine what equity and total assets were on that date and comment on the change in the financial position from 2013 to 2014.

Problem 3-13B Preparing financial statements from the adjusted trial balance LO^7

This alphabetized adjusted trial balance is for Mad Catz Courier as of its December 31, 2014, month-end:

	Debit	Credit
Accounts payable.....................................		$ 37,000
Accounts receivable	$ 25,000	
Accumulated depreciation, equipment		95,000
Accumulated depreciation, trucks		24,000
Advertising expense	9,800	
Cash	14,000	
Delivery fees earned		190,000
Depreciation expense, equipment	23,000	
Depreciation expense, trucks	12,000	
Equipment	130,000	
Interest earned..		250
Interest expense......................................	650	
Interest payable		325
Interest receivable	125	
Land	60,000	
Long-term notes payable		100,000
Madison Catz, capital...............................		152,500
Madison Catz, withdrawals	5,000	
Notes receivable (due in 90 days)	100,000	
Office supplies	1,800	
Office supplies expense...........................	5,400	
Repairs expense	17,300	
Salaries expense......................................	41,000	
Salaries payable		15,000
Trucks..	62,000	
Unearned delivery fees............................		55,000
Wages expense	162,000	
Totals..	$669,075	$669,075

Required Use the information in the trial balance to prepare:

1. The income statement for the month ended December 31, 2014.

2. The statement of changes in equity for the month ended December 31, 2014, assuming the owner invested $127,000 during December.

3. The balance sheet as of December 31, 2014.

Problem 3-14B Journalizing, posting, adjusted trial balance, adjusting entries, financial statements LO^{4,5,6,7}

On July 1, 2014, Melanie Thornhill began her third month of operating an electronics repair shop called MT Repairs out of her dad's garage. The following occurred during the third month of operations:

July	1	Collected $3,600 as a deposit for work to be done at the local college in the fall.
	1	Melanie Thornhill withdrew $4,000 cash for personal expenses.
	2	Paid $2,200 for repair supplies purchased on account last month.
	3	Did work for a client and immediately collected $1,400.
	4	Performed services for a customer and collected $3,600.
	7	Hired a new technician to start next week on a casual basis at $400 per day.
	15	Melanie withdrew cash of $1,000 for personal use.
	22	Purchased repair supplies for cash; $1,600.
	31	Paid wages of $2,800.

Required

1. Prepare General Journal entries to record the July transactions.

2. Set up the following T-accounts with June 30 adjusted balances: Cash (101), $6,400; Repair Supplies (131), $3,000; Tools (161), $16,800; Accumulated Depreciation, Tools (162), $560; Accounts Payable (201), $3,200; Unearned Revenue (233), $700; Melanie Thornhill, Capital (301) $?; Melanie Thornhill, Withdrawals (302), $0; Revenue (401), $25,800; Depreciation Expense, Tools (602), $560; Wages Expense (623), $1,960; Rent Expense (640), $8,000; and Repair Supplies Expense (696), $2,700.

3. Post the entries to the accounts; calculate the ending balance in each account.

4. Prepare an unadjusted trial balance at July 31, 2014.

5. Use the following information to prepare and post adjusting entries for the month of July:

    a. The tools have an estimated life of five years with no residual value.

    b. One-quarter of the repair supplies balance remained on hand at July 31.

    c. Accrued the July rent expense of $4,000; it will be paid in August.

    d. $3,800 of the unearned revenues remained unearned as at July 31.

6. Prepare an adjusted trial balance.

7. Prepare an income statement and a statement of changes in equity for the three months ended July 31, 2014, and a July 31, 2014, balance sheet.

Analysis Component: When a company shows expenses on its income statement, does this mean that cash equal to the expenses was paid during the period in which the expenses were reported?

*Problem 3-15B Correcting entries LO^8

As the accountant for Jasper's Telemarketing Services, you discovered the following errors in the May 31 unadjusted trial balance that require correction:

a. Advertising Expense was debited and Accounts Receivable was credited on May 17 for $16,200 of repairs paid for by Jasper's.

b. On May 18, Computer Equipment was debited and Accounts Payable was credited, each for $8,100 regarding the purchase of office furniture in exchange for a promissory note.

c. On May 28, Cash was debited and Telemarketing Fees Earned was credited for $15,000 cash received in advance from a client.

d. The Telephone Expense account included $6,300 of delivery expense.

e. The Telemarketing Fees Earned account was credited for $1,200 of interest revenue.

Required Journalize the correcting entries required on May 31.

Analysis Component: The error in (e) shows that an incorrect revenue account was credited. Since the net effect on the financial statements is nil after recording the correction, is it necessary to prepare a correcting entry for this type of error?

*Problem 3-16B Recording prepaid expenses and unearned revenues LO[9]

Rainbow Janitorial Services follows the approach of recording prepaid expenses as expenses and unearned revenues as revenues. Rainbow's unadjusted trial balance for the year ended October 31, 2014, follows.

	Rainbow Janitorial Services Trial Balances.xls						

	A	B	C	D	E	F	G
1	**Rainbow Janitorial Services**						
2	**Trial Balances**						
3	**October 31, 2014**						
4		**Unadjusted**				**Adjusted**	
5		**Trial Balance**		**Adjustments**		**Trial Balance**	
6	**Account**	**Dr.**	**Cr.**	**Dr.**	**Cr.**	**Dr.**	**Cr.**
7	Cash	$ 3,500					
8	Accounts receivable	7,200					
9	Prepaid advertising	-0-					
10	Cleaning supplies	-0-					
11	Equipment	29,000					
12	Accumulated depreciation, equipment		$ 3,200				
13	Unearned window washing fees		-0-				
14	Unearned office cleaning fees		-0-				
15	William Nahanee, capital		9,150				
16	Window washing fees earned		23,800				
17	Office cleaning fees earned		71,500				
18	Advertising expense	2,900					
19	Salaries expense	56,900					
20	Depreciation expense, equipment	-0-					
21	Cleaning supplies expense	8,150					
22	**Totals**	$ 107,650	$ 107,650				

Additional information:

a. On October 31, a physical count revealed cleaning supplies on hand of $6,150.

b. Annual depreciation on the equipment is $3,200.

c. It was determined that $6,900 of the balance in Office Cleaning Fees Earned had not yet been earned as of October 31.

d. A review of the Window Washing Fees Earned account showed that only $21,400 had been earned as of October 31.

e. $1,500 of the total recorded in the Advertising Expense account had not yet been used.

Required Refer to Exhibit 3.22 and use the information provided to complete the columns above.

An asterisk (*) identifies assignment material based on Appendix 3A or Appendix 3B.

*Problem 3-17B Recording prepaid expenses and unearned revenues LO^{4,9}

The following occurred for a company during the last two months of its fiscal year ended May 31, 2014:

Apr.	1	Paid $7,200 for future consulting services.
	1	Paid $1,920 for insurance through March 31 of the following year.
	30	Received $7,500 for future services to be provided to a customer.
May	1	Paid $1,200 for future newspaper advertising.
	23	Received $9,200 for future services to be provided to a customer.
	31	Of the consulting services paid for on April 1, $5,000 worth had been received.
	31	Part of the insurance paid for on April 1 had expired.
	31	Services worth $7,200 had not yet been provided to the customer who paid on April 30.
	31	Of the advertising paid for on May 1, $340 worth had not been published yet.
	31	The company had performed $9,000 of the services that the customer had paid for on May 23.

Required

1. Prepare entries for April and May under the approach that records prepaid expenses and unearned revenues in balance sheet accounts. Also, prepare adjusting entries at the end of the year.

2. Prepare entries for April and May under the approach that records prepaid expenses and unearned revenues in income statement accounts. Also, prepare adjusting entries at the end of the year.

Analysis Component: Explain why the alternative sets of entries in requirements 1 and 2 do not result in different financial statement amounts.

ANALYTICAL AND REVIEW PROBLEM

A & R Problem 3-1

The Salaries Payable account of James Bay Company Limited appears below:

Salaries Payable			
		22,520	Bal. Jan. 1, 2014
Entries during 2014	398,120	388,400	Entries during 2014

The company records the salary expense and related liability at the end of each week and pays the employees on the last Friday of the month.

Required

1. What was the salary expense for 2014?
2. How much was paid to employees in 2014 for work done in 2013?
3. How much was paid to employees in 2014 for work done in 2014?
4. How much will be paid to employees in 2015 for work done in 2014?

ETHICS CHALLENGE

EC 3-1

Jackie Houston is a new accountant for Seitzer Company. She is learning on the job from Bob Welch, who has already worked several years for Seitzer. Jackie and Bob are preparing the year-end adjusting entries. Jackie has calculated that depreciation expense for the fiscal year should be recorded as:

Depreciation Expense, Equipment..................	123,546	
Accum. Dep., Equipment......................		123,546

Bob is rechecking the numbers and says that he agrees with her computation. However, he says that the credit entry should be made directly to the Equipment account. He argues that while accumulated depreciation is taught in the classroom, "It is easier to ignore the contra account and just credit the Equipment account directly for the annual depreciation. Besides, the balance sheet shows the same amount for total assets under both methods."

Required

1. How should depreciation be recorded? Do you support Jackie or Bob?
2. Evaluate the strengths and weaknesses of Bob's reasons for preferring his method.
3. Indicate whether the situation faced by Jackie is an ethical problem.

An asterisk (*) identifies assignment material based on Appendix 3A or Appendix 3B.

FOCUS ON FINANCIAL STATEMENTS

FFS 3-1

eXcel

You have been given the following information for RPE Consulting for the year ended July 31, 2014.

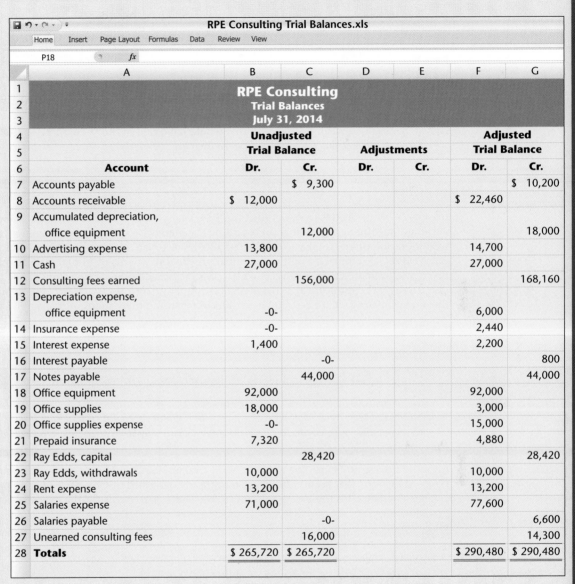

Account	Unadjusted Trial Balance Dr.	Unadjusted Trial Balance Cr.	Adjustments Dr.	Adjustments Cr.	Adjusted Trial Balance Dr.	Adjusted Trial Balance Cr.
Accounts payable		$ 9,300				$ 10,200
Accounts receivable	$ 12,000				$ 22,460	
Accumulated depreciation, office equipment		12,000				18,000
Advertising expense	13,800				14,700	
Cash	27,000				27,000	
Consulting fees earned		156,000				168,160
Depreciation expense, office equipment	-0-				6,000	
Insurance expense	-0-				2,440	
Interest expense	1,400				2,200	
Interest payable		-0-				800
Notes payable		44,000				44,000
Office equipment	92,000				92,000	
Office supplies	18,000				3,000	
Office supplies expense	-0-				15,000	
Prepaid insurance	7,320				4,880	
Ray Edds, capital		28,420				28,420
Ray Edds, withdrawals	10,000				10,000	
Rent expense	13,200				13,200	
Salaries expense	71,000				77,600	
Salaries payable		-0-				6,600
Unearned consulting fees		16,000				14,300
Totals	**$ 265,720**	**$ 265,720**			**$ 290,480**	**$ 290,480**

RPE Consulting — Trial Balances — July 31, 2014

Required

1. Prepare the company's income statement, statement of changes in equity, and balance sheet. Assume that the owner, Ray Edds, invested $20,000 during the year ended July 31, 2014.

Analysis Component:

2. Analyze the unadjusted and adjusted trial balances and identify the adjustments that must have been made by inserting them in the two middle columns. Label each entry with a letter.

3. If the adjustments had not been recorded, identify the net overstatement/understatement of each component of the accounting equation.

FFS 3-2

Part 1

Refer to WestJet's income statement in Appendix II at the end of the textbook.

a. Prepare two possible adjusting entries that would have caused 2011 *Guest revenues* to increase.

b. Prepare two possible adjusting entries that would have caused 2011 *Aircraft leasing expenses* to increase.

Part 2

Refer to WestJet's balance sheet in Appendix II at the end of the textbook.

c. Prepare the possible adjusting entry that would have caused the December 31, 2011, balance in *Prepaid expenses and deposits* to decrease.

d. Prepare a possible adjusting entry that would have caused the December 31, 2011, balance in *Accounts payable and accrued liabilities* to increase.

CRITICAL THINKING MINI CASE

It's a week before Scotiabank's October 31, 2014, year-end. You are the personnel director and are reviewing some financial information regarding the March 1, 2012, purchase of office furniture for the western region offices totalling $700,000 ($300,000 was paid in cash and the balance was financed over four years at 4% annual interest with annual principal payments of $100,000). The useful life of the furniture was estimated to be five years with a projected resale value at that time of $20,000. Insurance was purchased on the furniture at a cost of $8,000 annually, payable each March 1. You leave the office for the day wondering what needs to be considered regarding these items in preparation for year-end.

Required Using the elements of critical thinking described on the inside front cover, respond.

SERIAL PROBLEM

Echo Systems

(This comprehensive problem was introduced in Chapter 2 and continues in Chapters 4 and 5. If the Chapter 2 segment has not been completed, the assignment can begin at this point. You need to use the facts presented in Chapter 2. Because of its length, this problem is most easily solved if you use the Working Papers[10] that accompany this book.)

After the success of its first two months, Mary Graham has decided to continue operating Echo Systems. (The transactions that occurred in these months are described in Chapter 2.) Before proceeding in December, Graham adds these new accounts to the chart of accounts for the ledger:

Account	No.
Accumulated Depreciation, Office Equipment	164
Accumulated Depreciation, Computer Equipment	168
Wages Payable	210
Unearned Computer Services Revenue	236
Depreciation Expense, Office Equipment	612
Depreciation Expense, Computer Equipment	613
Insurance Expense	637
Rent Expense	640
Computer Supplies Expense	652

---

10 If students have not purchased the Working Papers package, the Working Papers for the Serial Problem are available on Connect.

Required

1. Prepare journal entries to record each of the following transactions for Echo Systems. Post the entries to the accounts in the ledger.

Dec.   3   Paid $2,100 to the Lakeshore Mall for the company's share of mall advertising costs.
        3   Paid $1,200 to repair the company's computer.
        4   Received $7,500 from Alamo Engineering Co. for the receivable from the prior month.
       10   Paid Carly Smith for six days' work at the rate of $200 per day.
       14   Notified by Alamo Engineering Co. that Echo's bid of $12,000 on a proposed project was accepted. Alamo paid an advance of $3,000.
       17   Purchased $2,310 of computer supplies on credit from Abbott Office Products.
       18   Sent a reminder to Fostek Co. to pay the fee for services originally recorded on November 8.
       20   Completed a project for Elite Corporation and received $11,250 cash.
    24–28   Took the week off for the holidays.
       31   Received $5,700 from Fostek Co. on its receivable.
       31   Reimbursed Mary Graham's business automobile expenses of 600 kilometres at $1.00 per kilometre.
       31   Mary Graham withdrew $3,600 cash from the business.

2. Prepare adjusting entries to record the following additional information collected on December 31, 2014. Post the entries to the accounts in the ledger.

   a. The December 31 inventory of computer supplies was $1,440.

   b. Three months have passed since the annual insurance premium was paid.

   c. As of the end of the year, Carly Smith has not been paid for four days of work at the rate of $200 per day.

   d. The computer is expected to have a four-year life with no residual value.

   e. The office equipment is expected to have a three-year life with no residual value.

   f. Prepaid rent for three of the four months has expired.

3. Prepare an adjusted trial balance as of December 31, 2014.

4. Prepare an income statement and statement of changes in equity for the three months ended December 31, 2014.

5. Prepare a balance sheet as of December 31, 2014.

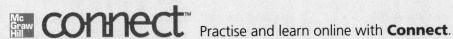 Practise and learn online with **Connect**.

Completing the Accounting Cycle and Classifying Accounts

LEAKY LEDGER

Econnics, based in Victoria, British Columbia, was founded by Kirk Stinchcombe in 2009. His business's goal is to help communities significantly reduce their demand for water in ways that are not only cost effective but also customer friendly. Kirk has a Master's in Environmental Studies from the University of Waterloo in Ontario as well as a Master's of Business Administration from Griffith University in Australia. He believes that setting the right price for water is one tool we should use to help us conserve it and value it appropriately.

Kirk was co-author of *Worth Every Penny*, a handbook sponsored in part by the POLIS Project at the University of Victoria. The handbook identifies Canadians as among the greatest per capita consumers of water globally. It also explains that water service providers often do not recover the full costs of providing services from their customers through the water bill. In accounting terms, this translates into expenses being greater than revenues! Instead, costs are subsidized from other public revenue sources, or we let our infrastructure decay due to underfunding.

The underlying problem is that accounting for water needs rethinking: we need accounting for consumption, accounting for costs, as well as billing and metering practices. As Kirk says, "Price can be used as a way not only to control consumption but also to improve the financial performance of water service providers because revenue can be reinvested to replace and maintain infrastructure. This means it is reinvested in the community. The starting point for this has to be accurately recording how we use water and the full costs we incur to provide services."

Canadian communities have improved metering and billing over the last few decades but more can be done. Accurate accounting can help preserve this natural resource.

Econnics: www.econnics.com
Worth Every Penny: http://poliswaterproject.org/publication/344

www.econnics.com

LEARNING OBJECTIVES

LO¹ Describe and prepare a work sheet and explain its usefulness.

LO² Describe the closing process and explain why temporary accounts are closed each period.

LO³ Prepare closing entries.

LO⁴ Explain and prepare a post-closing trial balance.

LO⁵ Complete the steps in the accounting cycle.

LO⁶ Explain and prepare a classified balance sheet.

*Appendix 4A

LO⁷ Prepare reversing entries and explain their purpose.

*Appendix 4B

LO⁸ Calculate the current ratio and describe what it reveals about a company's financial condition.

CRITICAL THINKING CHALLENGE What type of current and non-current assets might Econnics show on its balance sheet? If your job was to review bank loan applications for a bank, what financial statement information would you examine (and why) if Kirk Stinchcombe submitted a loan application to purchase office space? What does it mean when revenues are "reinvested to replace and maintain infrastructure"?

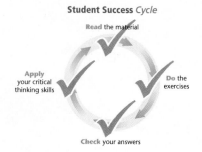

CHAPTER PREVIEW

This chapter begins with the introduction of the work sheet, an optional tool useful in preparing financial statements. Chapter 4 also describes the final steps in the accounting cycle (Exhibit 4.1), Steps 8 and 9, involving the closing process that prepares revenue, expense, and withdrawals accounts for the next reporting period and updates the owner's capital account. We also explain how accounts are classified on a balance sheet to give more useful information to decision makers. These tools for managing data are the kind Kirk Stinchcombe in the opening article uses to improve decision making.

WORK SHEET AS A TOOL

LO¹ Describe and prepare a work sheet and explain its usefulness.

EXHIBIT 4.1

Steps in the Accounting Cycle Introduced in Chapter 4

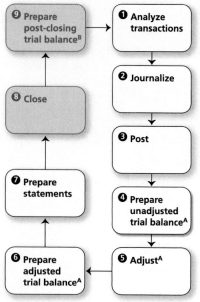

❾ Prepare post-closing trial balance^B

❶ Analyze transactions

❷ Journalize

❽ Close

❸ Post

❼ Prepare statements

❹ Prepare unadjusted trial balance^A

❻ Prepare adjusted trial balance^A

❺ Adjust^A

^ASteps 4, 5, and 6 can be done on a *work sheet*.
^BReversing entries are optional and, if prepared, are done between Steps 9 and 1. Reversing entries are covered in Appendix 4A.

When organizing the information presented in formal reports to internal and external users accountants prepare numerous analyses and informal documents. These informal documents, called **working papers**, are important tools for accountants. The **work sheet** is an *optional* working paper that can simplify the accountant's efforts in preparing financial statements. It is not distributed to decision makers. The work sheet is prepared before making adjusting entries at the end of a reporting period. It gathers information about the accounts, the needed adjustments, and the financial statements. When it is finished, the work sheet contains information that is recorded in the journal and then presented in the statements.

Benefits of a Work Sheet (Spreadsheet)

Computerized accounting systems prepare financial statements without the need for a work sheet. Yet there are several potential benefits to using a manual or electronic work sheet:

1. It is useful in preparing interim (monthly or quarterly) financial statements when journalizing and posting of adjusting entries are postponed until the year-end.

2. It captures the entire accounting process, linking economic transactions to their effects in financial statements.

3. Auditors of financial statements often use a work sheet for planning and organizing the audit. It can also be used to reflect any additional adjustments necessary as a result of the audit.

4. It helps preparers to avoid errors when working with a lot of information in accounting systems involving many accounts and adjustments.

DECISION INSIGHT

High-Tech Work Sheet

Electronic work sheets using spreadsheet software such as Excel make it easy to change numbers, assess the impact of alternative strategies, and prepare financial statements quickly and at less cost. This can also increase the time available for analysis and interpretation. Several of the end-of-chapter exercises and problems include the symbol shown to the right, which means that an Excel template is available to help in the preparation of a solution.

eXcel

Using a Work Sheet

Exhibit 4.2 shows a blank work sheet. Notice that it has five sets of double columns for the:

EYK
4-1

1. Unadjusted trial balance.
2. Adjustments.
3. Adjusted trial balance.
4. Income statement.
5. Balance sheet and statement of changes in equity.

EXHIBIT 4.2

Preparing the Work Sheet at the End of the Accounting Period

	Vertically Inclined Rock Gym Work Sheet.xls

| Home | Insert | Page Layout | Formulas | Data | Review | View |

P18   fx

	A	B	C	D	E	F	G	H	I	J	K
1		**Vertically Inclined Rock Gym**						The heading should identify the entity, the document, and the time period.			
2		**Work Sheet**									
3		**For Month Ended March 31, 2014**									
	Account	**Unadjusted Trial Balance**		**Adjustments**		**Adjusted Trial Balance**		**Income Statement**		**Balance Sheet & Statement of Changes in Equity**	
		Dr.	Cr.	Dr.	Cr.	Dr.	Cr.	Dr.	Cr.	Dr.	Cr.

The work sheet can be prepared manually or with a computer spreadsheet program.

The work sheet collects and summarizes the information used to prepare adjusting entries, financial statements, and closing entries.

The purpose of double columns is to accommodate both debits and credits. Because the statement of changes in equity includes only a few items, they are simply listed with the balance sheet items.

The work sheet can be completed by following five steps.

Enter Unadjusted Trial Balance

To begin the work sheet, we list the number and title of each account from the ledger along with the account's unadjusted debit or credit balance as shown in Exhibit 4.3.[1] We use the information of Vertically Inclined Rock Gym to describe and interpret the work sheet.

Enter Adjustments

Step 2 begins with the entry of adjustments in the adjustment columns. The adjustments shown in Exhibit 4.3 are the same as those discussed in Chapter 3. They are as follows:

> **a.** Expiration of $100 of prepaid insurance.
>
> **b.** Used $1,050 of supplies.
>
> **c.** Depreciation on equipment of $200.
>
> **d.** Earned $250 of revenue received in advance.
>
> **e.** Accrued interest of $35 on the note payable.
>
> **f.** Accrued $70 of salaries owed to an employee.
>
> **g.** Accrued $1,800 of revenue owed by a customer.

To help you correctly match the debit and credit of each adjusting entry, notice that an identifying letter is used for each adjustment. In entering adjustments, we sometimes find additional accounts that need to be inserted on the work sheet. Additional accounts are inserted below the initial list. ***After entering adjustments on a work sheet, we still must enter adjusting entries in the journal and post them to the ledger.***

Prepare Adjusted Trial Balance

The adjusted trial balance is prepared by combining the adjustments with the unadjusted balances for each account. As an example, in Exhibit 4.3, the Supplies account has a $3,600 debit balance in the Unadjusted Trial Balance columns. This $3,600 debit is combined with the $1,050 credit in the Adjustments columns to give Supplies a $2,550 debit in the Adjusted Trial Balance columns. The totals of the Adjusted Trial Balance columns confirm the equality of debits and credits.

Extend Adjusted Trial Balance Amounts to Financial Statement Columns

This step involves sorting adjusted amounts to their proper financial statement columns. Expense items go to the Income Statement Debit column, and revenues to the Income Statement Credit column. Assets and withdrawals go to the Balance Sheet and Statement of Changes in Equity Debit column. Liabilities and owner's capital go to the Balance Sheet and Statement of Changes in Equity Credit column. Recall that accumulated depreciation is a contra asset account, so it also goes to the Balance Sheet and Statement of Changes in Equity Credit column as shown in Exhibit 4.3. Each statement column is totalled. Notice in Exhibit 4.3 that the debits do not equal the credits (explained in Step Five).

---

1   In practice, accounts with a zero balance that are likely to require an adjusting entry would also be listed.

EXHIBIT 4.3
Work Sheet

NOTE: The steps for completing a work sheet are colour coded to follow the description.

Vertically Inclined Rock Gym Work Sheet.xls

Home Insert Page Layout Formulas Data Review View

P18   fx

	Account	Unadjusted Trial Balance Dr.	Cr.	Adjustments Dr.	Cr.	Adjusted Trial Balance Dr.	Cr.	Income Statement Dr.	Cr.	Balance Sheet & Statement of Changes in Equity Dr.	Cr.
8 101	Cash	8,070				8,070				8,070	
9 125	Supplies	3,600			b) 1,050	2,550				2,550	
10 128	Prepaid insurance	2,400			a) 100	2,300				2,300	
11 167	Equipment	6,000				6,000				6,000	
12 168	Accumulated depreciation, equipment				c) 200		200				200
13 201	Accounts payable		200				200				200
14 236	Unearned teaching revenue		3,000	d) 250			2,750				2,750
15 240	Notes payable		6,000				6,000				6,000
16 301	Virgil Klimb, capital		10,000				10,000				10,000
17 302	Virgil Klimb, withdrawals	600				600				600	
18					d) 250						
19 403	Teaching revenue		3,800		g) 1,800		5,850		5,850		
20 406	Equipment rental revenue		300				300		300		
21 622	Salaries expense	1,400		f) 70		1,470		1,470			
22 641	Rent expense	1,000				1,000		1,000			
23 690	Utilities expense	230				230		230			
24	Totals	23,300	23,300								
25 637	Insurance expense			a) 100		100		100			
26 651	Supplies expense			b) 1,050		1,050		1,050			
27 614	Depreciation expense, equipment			c) 200		200		200			
28 209	Salaries payable				f) 70		70				70
29 633	Interest expense			e) 35		35		35			
30 203	Interest payable				e) 35		35				35
31 106	Accounts receivable			g) 1,800		1,800				1,800	
32	Totals			3,505	3,505	25,405	25,405	4,085	6,150	21,320	19,255
33	Net income							2,065			2,065
34	Totals							6,150	6,150	21,320	21,320

1. When entering the unadjusted trial balances, include all accounts that have balances or that are expected to have balances after adjustments.

2. Adjustments may create the need for additional accounts. Add new accounts to the existing list as required.

Add two new lines for the net income (or loss) and the totals.

These two columns must show equal totals.

Enter the drafts of the adjusting entries and find the total debits and credits.

These two columns must show equal totals.

3. Sum the unadjusted trial balance accounts with the adjustments, and enter them in the adjusted trial balance.

These two columns must show equal totals.

Extend revenues and expenses from the adjusted trial balance columns to these columns.

The totals are not equal because the debit and the credit balances in the revenue and expense accounts are not equal.

4. Extend assets, liabilities, and the owner's capital and withdrawals from the adjusted trial balance columns to these columns.

The totals are not equal because the net income component of equity is missing.

5. Enter the net income amount as the difference between the debits and the credits in the income statement columns.

Also enter the net income amount in the credit column to include in equity the change caused by net income.

Step Five

Enter Net Income (or Loss) and Balance the Financial Statement Columns

The difference between the Debit and Credit totals of the Income Statement columns is net income or net loss. If the Credit total exceeds the Debit total, there is a net income. If the Debit total exceeds the Credit total, there is a net loss. In Exhibit 4.3, Vertically Inclined's work sheet shows the Credit total to exceed the Debit total, resulting in net income of $2,065. The difference is added to the *Income Statement* and *Balance Sheet & Statement of Changes in Equity* columns for balancing. In the case of Vertically Inclined where a net income of $2,065 has been calculated, the $2,065 is listed as a *debit* in the Income Statement columns. It is also listed in the Balance Sheet & Statement of Changes in Equity columns, but as a *credit*. The new totals are entered for both sets of columns, showing that the Income Statement columns and Balance Sheet & Statement of Changes in Equity columns now balance. If they do not balance, an error has occurred in the completion of the work sheet.[2] The term *Net income* (or *Net loss*) is listed in the Account column to label the $2,065.

Adding net income to the last Credit column implies that it is to be added to owner's capital. If a loss occurs, it is listed in the last Debit column, implying that it is to be subtracted from owner's capital.

Step Six

Prepare Financial Statements From Work Sheet Information

A work sheet is not a substitute for financial statements. The completed work sheet is used to prepare the financial statements. While the ending balance of owner's capital does not appear in the last two columns as a single amount, it is calculated as the owner's capital account balance plus net income (or minus net loss) minus the withdrawals account balance. The opening capital balance for the period would be determined by subtracting any owner investments made during the period from the owner's capital account balance, as shown in the last credit column on the work sheet. Exhibit 4.4 shows the statements for Vertically Inclined as prepared from the work sheet.[3]

DECISION MAKER   Answer—End of chapter

Analyzing Results

You make a printout of the electronic work sheet used to prepare financial statements. There is no depreciation adjustment, yet you own a large amount of equipment. Does the absence of a depreciation adjustment concern you?

CHECKPOINT

1. Where do we get the amounts entered in the Unadjusted Trial Balance columns of a work sheet?
2. What are the advantages of using a work sheet to prepare adjusting entries?
3. What are the benefits of a work sheet?

Do Quick Study questions: QS 4-1, QS 4-2, QS 4-3, QS 4-4

---

2   If the columns balance, an error(s) could still be present. For example, the columns would still balance if Accounts Payable were listed as a credit, but in the Income Statement columns. Net income would be incorrect, but the columns would still balance.

3   Notice that the $21,320 balance of the last two columns in the work sheet in Exhibit 4.3 does not agree with the balance of $20,520 on the balance sheet; there is a difference of $800 (= $21,320 − $20,520). *This is not an error!* Notice that accumulated depreciation of $200 is subtracted on the balance sheet to arrive at total assets; it is *added* in the last Credit column on the work sheet. Also, withdrawals of $600 are *subtracted* on the statement of changes in equity to arrive at ending capital; on the work sheet, they are *added* in the last Debit column. These two items account for the difference of $800 (= $200 + $600).

Vertically Inclined Rock Gym
Income Statement
For Month Ended March 31, 2014

Revenues:

Teaching revenue	$5,850	
Equipment rental revenue	300	
Total revenues		$6,150

Operating expenses:

Salaries expense	$1,470	
Supplies expense	1,050	
Rent expense	1,000	
Utilities expense	230	
Depreciation expense, equipment	200	
Insurance expense	100	
Interest expense	35	
Total operating expenses		4,085
Net income		$2,065

Vertically Inclined Rock Gym
Statement of Changes in Equity
For Month Ended March 31, 2014

Virgil Klimb, capital, March 1		$ -0-
Add: Investments by owner	$10,000	
Net income	2,065	12,065
Total		$12,065
Less: Withdrawals by owner		600
Virgil Klimb, capital, March 31		$11,465

Vertically Inclined Rock Gym
Balance Sheet
March 31, 2014

Assets

Cash		$ 8,070
Accounts receivable		1,800
Supplies		2,550
Prepaid insurance		2,300
Equipment	$ 6,000	
Less: Accumulated depreciation	200	5,800
Total assets		$20,520

Liabilities

Accounts payable	$ 200	
Interest payable	35	
Salaries payable	70	
Unearned teaching revenue	2,750	
Notes payable	6,000	
Total liabilities		$ 9,055

Equity

Virgil Klimb, capital		11,465
Total liabilities and equity		$20,520

CLOSING PROCESS

LO² Describe the closing process and explain why temporary accounts are closed each period.

The **closing process** is an important step of the accounting cycle that is performed at the end of an accounting period after financial statements are prepared. It prepares accounts for recording the transactions of the next period.

An income statement aims to report revenues earned and expenses incurred during one accounting period. We know that the net income (or loss) from the income statement is shown on the statement of changes in equity, along with withdrawals, to show the change caused to the owner's capital account during one period. Because revenues, expenses, and withdrawals are a part of equity, their balances need to be transferred to the owner's capital account at the end of the period. This transfer of account balances is accomplished by using closing entries.

Therefore, closing entries are a necessary step because we want the:

EYK
4-2

1. Revenue, expense, and withdrawals accounts to begin with zero balances to measure the results from the period just ending.
2. Owner's capital account to reflect:
   a. Increases from net income (or decreases from net losses), and
   b. Decreases from withdrawals from the period just ending.

In the closing process, we must:

1. Identify accounts for closing,
2. Record and post the closing entries, and
3. Prepare the post-closing trial balance.

Identify Accounts for Closing—Temporary and Permanent Accounts

Temporary (or nominal) accounts accumulate data related to one accounting period. They include all income statement accounts, withdrawals accounts, and the *Income Summary*. They are temporary because the accounts are opened at the beginning of a period, used to record transactions for that period, and then closed at the end of the period by transferring their balances to the owner's capital account. They are *temporary* because the accounts describe transactions or changes that have occurred rather than the financial position that exists at the end of the period. **Only temporary accounts are closed.**

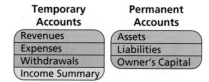

Temporary Accounts	Permanent Accounts
Revenues	Assets
Expenses	Liabilities
Withdrawals	Owner's Capital
Income Summary	

Permanent (or real) accounts report on transactions related to one or more future accounting periods. They carry their ending balances into the next period, and include all balance sheet accounts. *Asset, liability, and owner's capital accounts are not closed* as long as a company continues to own the assets, owe the liabilities, and have equity. They are permanent because they describe the existing financial position.

Recording and Posting Closing Entries

Recording and posting **closing entries** transfers the end-of-period balances in the revenue, expense, and withdrawals to the permanent owner's capital account.

LO³ Prepare closing entries.

To close revenue and expense accounts, we transfer their balances first to an account called *Income Summary*. **Income Summary** is a temporary account that contains a credit for the sum of all revenues and a debit for the sum of all expenses. Its balance equals net income or net loss, and is transferred to the owner's capital account. Next, we transfer the withdrawals account balance to the owner's capital account. After these closing entries are posted, the revenue, expense, Income Summary, and withdrawals accounts have zero balances. These accounts are then said to be closed or cleared. The four-step closing process is illustrated in Exhibit 4.5.

Four-Step Closing Process

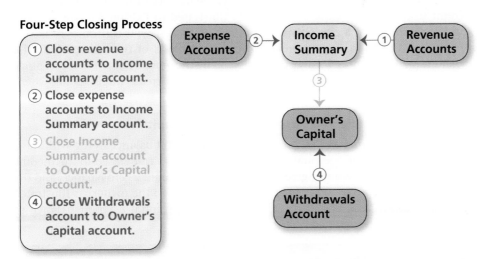

① Close revenue accounts to Income Summary account.

② Close expense accounts to Income Summary account.

③ Close Income Summary account to Owner's Capital account.

④ Close Withdrawals account to Owner's Capital account.

EXHIBIT 4.5

Closing Process for a Proprietorship

Vertically Inclined's adjusted trial balance on March 31, 2014, is shown in Exhibit 4.6. Exhibit 4.7 shows the four closing entries necessary to close Vertically Inclined's revenue, expense, Income Summary, and withdrawals accounts. We explain each of these four entries.

Entry 1: Close Credit Balances in Revenue Accounts to Income Summary

The first closing entry in Exhibit 4.7 transfers credit balances in revenue accounts to the Income Summary account. We get accounts with credit balances to zero by debiting them as shown in Exhibit 4.8. This prepares each account to record new revenues for the next period. The Income Summary account is created and used only for the closing process. The $6,150 total credit balance in Income Summary equals the total revenues for the year.

Entry 2: Close Debit Balances in Expense Accounts to Income Summary

The second closing entry in Exhibit 4.7 transfers debit balances in expense accounts to the Income Summary account. We get the debit balances in the expense accounts to zero by crediting them as shown in Exhibit 4.8. This prepares each account for expense entries for the next period. The entry makes the balance of Income Summary equal to March's net income of $2,065. All debit and credit balances related to expense and revenue accounts have now been collected in the Income Summary account.

Entry 3: Close Income Summary to Owner's Capital

The third closing entry in Exhibit 4.7 transfers the balance of the Income Summary account to the owner's capital account. As illustrated in Exhibit 4.8, the Income Summary account has a zero balance after posting this entry. It continues to have a zero balance until the closing process occurs at the end of the next period. The owner's capital account has now been increased by the amount of net income. Since we know that the normal balance of owner's capital is a credit, increases to owner's capital from net income are credits.

Entry 4: Close Withdrawals Account to Owner's Capital

The fourth closing entry in Exhibit 4.7 transfers any debit balance in the withdrawals account to the owner's capital account (withdrawals *is not* closed to the Income Summary account). This entry gives the withdrawals account a zero balance, and the account is ready to accumulate next period's payments to the owner. As illustrated in Exhibit 4.8, this entry reduces the Virgil Klimb, Capital account balance to $11,465, the amount reported on the balance sheet.

EXHIBIT 4.6

Adjusted Trial Balance

Vertically Inclined Rock Gym Adjusted Trial Balance March 31, 2014		
	Debit	**Credit**
Cash	$ 8,070	
Accounts receivable	1,800	
Supplies	2,550	
Prepaid insurance	2,300	
Equipment	6,000	
Accumulated depreciation, equipment		$ 200
Accounts payable		200
Interest payable		35
Notes payable		6,000
Salaries payable		70
Unearned teaching revenue		2,750
Virgil Klimb, capital		10,000
Virgil Klimb, withdrawals	600	
Teaching revenue		5,850
Equipment rental revenue		300
Depreciation expense, equipment	200	
Salaries expense	1,470	
Interest expense	35	
Insurance expense	100	
Rent expense	1,000	
Supplies expense	1,050	
Utilities expense	230	
Totals	$25,405	$25,405

Entry 1:	**Close revenue accounts**		
Mar. 31	Teaching Revenue..	5,850	
	Equipment Rental Revenue	300	
	Income Summary		6,150
	To close the revenue accounts.		
Entry 2:	**Close expense accounts**		
31	Income Summary..	4,085	
	Depreciation Expense, Equipment.........		200
	Salaries Expense....................................		1,470
	Interest Expense....................................		35
	Insurance Expense		100
	Rent Expense		1,000
	Supplies Expense		1,050
	Utilities Expense...................................		230
	To close expense accounts.		
Entry 3:	**Close Income Summary to owner's capital**		
31	Income Summary..	2,065	
	Virgil Klimb, Capital.............................		2,065
	To close the Income Summary account.		
Entry 4:	**Close withdrawals account to owner's capital**		
31	Virgil Klimb, Capital	600	
	Virgil Klimb, Withdrawals......................		600
	To close the withdrawals account.		

EXHIBIT 4.7

Closing Entries for Vertically Inclined

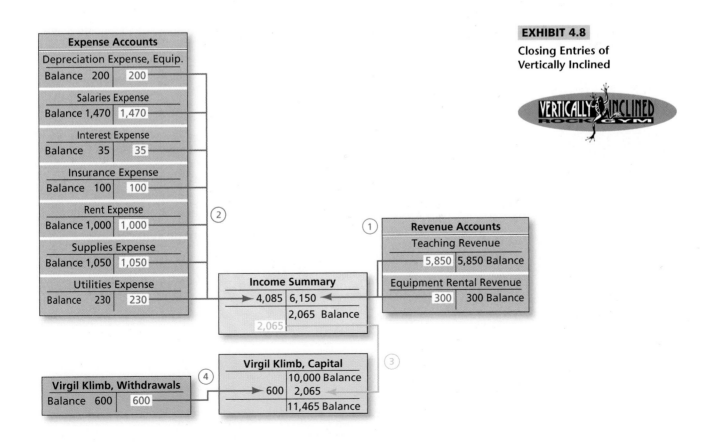

EXHIBIT 4.8

Closing Entries of Vertically Inclined

Sources of Closing Entry Information

We can identify the accounts that need to be closed and the amounts in the closing entries by looking to individual revenue, expense, and withdrawals accounts in the ledger.[4] If we prepare an adjusted trial balance after the adjusting process, the information for closing entries is available on the trial balance as illustrated in Exhibit 4.6.

Exhibit 4.9 highlights the posting of closing entries of Exhibit 4.7 in the ledger accounts for Vertically Inclined. Notice that all of the temporary accounts (revenues, expenses, and withdrawals) have a zero balance. The closing process transferred the balances of the temporary accounts to the Virgil Klimb, Capital account. The capital account balance of $11,465 includes owner investment of $10,000 and net income of $2,065, less withdrawals of $600.

EXHIBIT 4.9 Ledger After the Closing Process for Vertically Inclined

Ledger

Asset Accounts

Cash			101
Mar. 1	10,000	2,500	Mar. 1
10	2,200	2,400	1
25	1,900	1,000	10
26	3,000	700	14
		900	25
		600	26
		230	26
		700	28
Bal.	8,070		

Accounts Receivable			106
Mar.15	1,900	1,900	Mar. 25
31	1,800		
Bal.	1,800		

Supplies			125
Mar. 1	2,500	1,050	Mar. 31
1	1,100		
Bal.	2,550		

Prepaid Insurance			128
Mar. 1	2,400	100	Mar. 31
Bal.	2,300		

Equipment			167
Mar. 1	6,000		
Bal.	6,000		

Accumulated Depreciation, Equipment			168
		200	Mar. 31
		200	Bal.

Liability and Equity Accounts

Accounts Payable			201
Mar. 25	900	1,100	Mar. 1
		200	Bal.

Interest Payable			203
		35	Mar. 31
		35	Bal.

Salaries Payable			209
		70	Mar. 31
		70	Bal.

Unearned Teaching Revenue			236
Mar. 31	250	3,000	Mar. 26
		2,750	Bal.

Notes Payable			240
		6,000	Mar. 1
		6,000	Bal.

Virgil Klimb, Capital			301
Mar. 31	600	10,000	Mar. 1
		2,065	31
		11,465	Bal.

Virgil Klimb, Withdrawals			302
Mar. 26	600	600	Mar. 31
Bal.	-0-		

---

4   When accounting software is in use, closing entries are done automatically.

EXHIBIT 4.9 (continued)

Ledger After the Closing Process for Vertically Inclined

Revenues and Expense Accounts (including Income Summary)			

Teaching Revenue		403	
Mar. 31	5,850	2,200	Mar. 10
		1,600	15
		250	31
		1,800	31
		-0-	Bal.

Equipment Rental Revenue		406	
Mar. 31	300	300	Mar. 15
		-0-	Bal.

Depreciation Expense, Equipment		614	
Mar. 31	200	200	Mar. 31
Bal.	-0-		

Salaries Expense		622	
Mar. 14	700	1,470	Mar. 31
28	700		
31	70		
Bal.	-0-		

Interest Expense		633	
Mar. 31	35	35	Mar. 31
Bal.	-0-		

Insurance Expense		637	
Mar. 31	100	100	Mar. 31
Bal.	-0-		

Rent Expense		641	
Mar. 10	1,000	1,000	Mar. 31
Bal.	-0-		

Supplies Expense		651	
Mar. 31	1,050	1,050	Mar. 31
Bal.	-0-		

Utilities Expense		690	
Mar. 26	230	230	Mar. 31
Bal.	-0-		

Income Summary		901	
Mar. 31	4,085	6,150	Mar. 31
31	2,065	2,065	Bal.
		-0-	Bal.

CHECKPOINT

4. What are the four major closing entries?
5. Why are revenue and expense accounts called temporary? Are there other temporary accounts?

Do Quick Study questions: QS 4-5, QS 4-6, QS 4-7

Preparing a Post-Closing Trial Balance

A **post-closing trial balance** is a list of permanent accounts and their balances from the ledger after all closing entries are journalized and posted. It is a list of balances for accounts not closed. These accounts are a company's assets, liabilities, and equity at the end of a period. They are identical to those in the balance sheet. The aim of a post-closing trial balance is to verify that (1) total debits equal total credits for permanent accounts, and (2) all temporary accounts have zero balances.

LO⁴ Explain and prepare a post-closing trial balance.

Vertically Inclined's post-closing trial balance is shown in Exhibit 4.10 and is the last step in the accounting process. The post-closing trial balance in Exhibit 4.10 was created by listing the account balances found in Exhibit 4.9. Like the trial balance, the post-closing trial balance does not prove that all transactions are recorded or that the ledger is correct.

EXHIBIT 4.10

Post-Closing Trial Balance

Vertically Inclined Rock Gym Post-Closing Trial Balance March 31, 2014		
	Debit	**Credit**
Cash	$ 8,070	
Accounts receivable	1,800	
Supplies	2,550	
Prepaid insurance	2,300	
Equipment	6,000	
Accumulated depreciation, equipment		$ 200
Accounts payable		200
Interest payable		35
Salaries payable		70
Unearned teaching revenue		2,750
Notes payable		6,000
Virgil Klimb, capital		11,465
Totals	$20,720	$20,720

Closing Entries After Period-End Date

We are not usually able to make closing entries on the last day of each period. This is because information about certain transactions that require *adjusting* is not always available until several days or even weeks later. Because some adjusting entries are recorded later, closing entries are recorded later, but both are dated as of the last day of the period. Financial statements therefore reflect what is known on the date they are prepared instead of what was known as of the last day of the period.

One example is a company that receives a utility bill on February 14 for costs incurred for the month of January. When the bill is received, the company records the expense and the payable as of January 31. The January income statement then reflects expenses incurred in January and the January 31 balance sheet includes the payable, even though the amounts are not actually known on January 31.

CHECKPOINT

6. What accounts are listed on the post-closing trial balance?

Do Quick Study question: QS 4-8

COMPLETING THE ACCOUNTING CYCLE

We have now completed the steps in the accounting cycle which have been the focus in this and the previous chapters. Let's now briefly summarize these steps in Exhibit 4.11 to emphasize their importance in providing users with information for decision making.

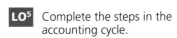 Complete the steps in the accounting cycle.

1.	Analyze transactions	Analyze transactions in preparation for journalizing.
2.	Journalize	Record debits and credits with explanations in a journal.
3.	Post	Transfer debits and credits from journal entries to the ledger accounts.
4.	Unadjusted trial balance[A]	Summarize ledger accounts and amounts.
5.	Adjust[A]	Record adjustments to bring account balances up to date; journalize and post adjusting entries to the accounts.
6.	Adjusted trial balance[A]	Summarize adjusted ledger accounts and amounts.
7.	Prepare statements	Use adjusted trial balance to prepare: income statement, statement of changes in equity, balance sheet, and statement of cash flows (details of preparing the statement of cash flows are in Chapter 17).
8.	Close	Journalize and post entries to close temporary accounts (revenue, expense, and withdrawals) and update the owner's capital account.
9.	Post-closing trial balance[B]	Test clerical accuracy of adjusting and closing steps.

[A] Steps 4, 5, and 6 can be done on a work sheet.
[B] *Reversing entries* are optional and, if prepared, are done between Steps 9 and 1. Reversing entries are covered in Appendix 4A.

EXHIBIT 4.11

Summary of Steps in the Accounting Cycle

EYK
4-3

 CHECKPOINT

7. What steps in the accounting cycle are optional?

Do Quick Study question: QS 4-9

The closing process just demonstrated using account information for Vertically Inclined was a case where revenues were greater than expenses, thus creating net income. The closing process is applied in an identical manner when a net loss occurs, as illustrated in the following Mid-Chapter Demonstration Problem.

MID-CHAPTER DEMONSTRATION PROBLEM

Using the account information in the following adjusted trial balance for Booster's Towing Service:

1. Prepare the closing entries for December 31, 2014.
2. Post the closing entries.
3. Prepare the post-closing trial balance at December 31, 2014.

Analysis Component:
Rather than closing temporary accounts, it would be more efficient to record all transactions affecting temporary accounts (revenues, expenses, and owner withdrawals) directly into capital. Explain why this would be problematic.

Booster's Towing Service Adjusted Trial Balance December 31, 2014		
	Debit	Credit
Cash...	$ 7,000	
Accounts receivable..	3,000	
Tow truck..	31,000	
Accumulated depreciation, tow truck................................		$27,000
Salaries payable..		700
Terry Booster, capital...		17,200
Terry Booster, withdrawals..	2,300	
Towing revenue		38,000
Salaries expense	30,000	
Depreciation expense, tow truck.......................................	5,000	
Utilities expense	4,600	
Totals..	$82,900	$82,900

Planning the Solution

1. Journalize the four closing entries.
2. Post the closing entries.
3. Prepare the post-closing trial balance.
4. Prepare a response to the analysis question.

SOLUTION

Part 1

Entry 1:	**Close the revenue account:**		
Dec. 31	Towing Revenue	38,000	
	Income Summary		38,000
	To close the revenue account.		

Entry 2:	**Close the expense accounts:**		
31	Income Summary..	39,600	
	Salaries Expense......................................		30,000
	Depreciation Expense, Tow Truck		5,000
	Utilities Expense......................................		4,600
	To close the expense accounts.		

Entry 3:	**Close Income Summary to owner's capital:**		
31	Terry Booster, Capital......................................	1,600	
	Income Summary		1,600
	To close the net loss in the Income Summary account to capital.		

Entry 4:	**Close withdrawals account to owner's capital:**		
31	Terry Booster, Capital......................................	2,300	
	Terry Booster, Withdrawals		2,300
	To close the withdrawals account.		

Part 2

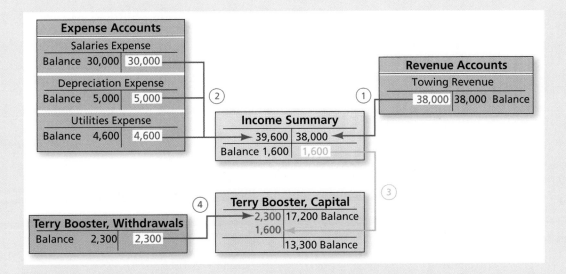

Part 3

Booster's Towing Service Post-Closing Trial Balance December 31, 2014		
	Debit	Credit
Cash..	$ 7,000	
Accounts receivable..	3,000	
Tow truck...	31,000	
Accumulated depreciation, tow truck...........................		$27,000
Salaries payable...		700
Terry Booster, capital..		13,300
Totals	$41,000	$41,000

Analysis Component:

It might be more efficient to record all transactions affecting temporary accounts directly in capital, but the result would be that the information needed by decision makers regarding the business's performance would be *hidden* within the capital account balance. The purpose of using temporary accounts is to have revenues and expenses appear on the income statement to detail the business's performance for the period. The resulting net income or loss is then combined with owner withdrawals and owner investments as part of capital to show the business's equity position at a specific point in time.

CLASSIFIED BALANCE SHEET

LO⁶ Explain and prepare a classified balance sheet.

Our discussion to this point has been limited to unclassified financial statements. An **unclassified balance sheet** is one in which items are broadly grouped into assets, liabilities, and equity. One example is Vertically Inclined's balance sheet in Exhibit 4.4. A **classified balance sheet** organizes assets and liabilities into important subgroups to provide users with more useful information for making decisions. One example is information to differentiate liabilities that are due shortly from those not due for several years. Information in this case helps us assess a company's ability to meet liabilities when they come due.

Classification Scheme

EYK

4-4

EXHIBIT 4.12

Sections of a Classified Balance Sheet

There is no required layout for a classified balance sheet.⁵ Yet a classified balance sheet often contains common groupings, including those shown in Exhibit 4.12:

Assets	Liabilities and Equity
Current Assets	Current Liabilities
Long-Term Investments*	Long-Term Liabilities
Property, Plant and Equipment*	Equity
Intangible Assets*	
*Noncurrent assets	

One of the more important classifications is the separation between current and noncurrent items for both assets and liabilities. Current items are those that are expected to come due within the longer of one year or the company's normal *operating cycle*. An **operating cycle** is the average length of time between (1) paying employees who perform services and receiving cash from customers (for a service company) or (2) paying for merchandise and receiving cash from customers (for a company that sells goods).⁶

Exhibit 4.13 shows the steps of an operating cycle for both service and merchandising companies.

EXHIBIT 4.13

Operating Cycles for a Service Company and a Merchandising Company

Most operating cycles are less than one year. This means that most companies use a one-year period in deciding which assets and liabilities are current. Yet there are companies with an operating cycle that is longer than one year. One example is a company that routinely allows customers to take more than one year to pay for purchases. Another example is a producer of beverages and other products that require aging for several years. These companies use their operating cycle in deciding which balance sheet items are current.⁷

---

5   IFRS 2012, IAS 1, para. 57.
6   IFRS 2012, IAS 1, para. 68.
7   In these uncommon situations, companies provide supplemental information about their current assets and liabilities to allow users to compare them with other companies.

A balance sheet lists current assets before long-term assets, and current liabilities before long-term liabilities. This highlights assets that are most easily converted to cash, and liabilities that are shortly coming due. Items in the current group are usually listed in the order of how quickly they could be converted to or paid in cash.

Classification Example

The balance sheet for Music Components is shown in Exhibit 4.14. It shows the most commonly used groupings. Its assets are classified into (1) current assets, (2) long-term investments, (3) property, plant and equipment, and (4) intangible assets. Its liabilities are classified as either current or long-term. Not all companies use

EXHIBIT 4.14

A Classified Balance Sheet

Music Components Balance Sheet* January 31, 2014		
Assets		
Current assets:		
Cash	$ 6,500	
Short-term investments	2,100	
Accounts receivable	4,400	
Merchandise inventory	29,000	
Prepaid expenses	2,400	
Total current assets		$ 44,400
Long-term investments:		
Notes receivable, due March 31, 2016	$ 18,000	
Land not currently used in operations	48,000	
Total investments		66,000
Property, plant and equipment:		
Land	$ 73,200	
Buildings	$170,000	
Less: Accumulated depreciation	45,000	125,000
Store equipment	$ 33,200	
Less: Accumulated depreciation	8,000	25,200
Total property, plant and equipment		223,400
Intangible assets:		
Trademark		10,000
Total assets		$343,800
Liabilities		
Current liabilities:		
Accounts payable	$ 15,300	
Wages payable	3,200	
Notes payable	3,000	
Current portion of long-term liabilities	7,500	
Total current liabilities	$ 29,000	
Long-term liabilities:		
Notes payable (less current portion)	150,000	
Total liabilities		$179,000
Equity		
Donald Bowie, capital		164,800
Total liabilities and equity		$343,800

*The classified balance sheet is labelled "*Balance Sheet*"; it is *not* labelled "*Classified Balance Sheet,*" a common error made by students.

the same categories of assets and liabilities on their balance sheets. For example, **TransCanada PipeLines Limited's** December 31, 2011, balance sheet lists five asset classes: current assets; property, plant and equipment; goodwill; regulatory assets; and intangible and other assets.

Classification Groups

Current Assets

Current assets are cash and other resources that are expected to be sold, collected, or used within the longer of one year or the company's operating cycle.[8] Examples are cash, short-term investments, accounts receivable, notes receivable, goods for sale to customers (called *merchandise inventory* or *inventory*), and prepaid expenses. As of December 31, 2011, **Barrick Gold Corporation's** current assets were reported as shown in Exhibit 4.15.

EXHIBIT 4.15

Current Assets Section

Barrick Gold Corporation	
Current assets (in millions of United States dollars)	
Cash and equivalents	$2,745
Accounts receivable	426
Inventories	2,498
Other current assets	876
Total current assets...	$6,545

A company's prepaid expenses are usually small compared to other assets, and are often combined and shown as a single item. It is likely that prepaid expenses in Exhibit 4.14 include such items as prepaid insurance, prepaid rent, office supplies, and store supplies. Prepaid expenses are usually listed last because they will not be converted to cash.

Long-Term Investments

Long-term investments are held for more than one year or the operating cycle. Notes receivable and investments in shares and bonds are in many cases long-term assets. Note that the *short-term* investments in Exhibit 4.14 are current assets and not shown as long-term investments. We explain the differences between short- and long-term investments later in this book. Long-term investments also often include land that is not being used in operations.

Property, Plant and Equipment (PPE)

Property, plant and equipment (PPE) are tangible assets used for more than one accounting period to produce or sell products and services.[9] Examples of PPE are equipment, vehicles, buildings, and land. Land held for future expansion is generally a long-term investment and not a PPE asset since it is not used to produce or sell products and services. The order of listing PPE assets within this category varies.

Intangible Assets

Intangible assets are long-term resources used to produce or sell products and services; they lack physical form.[10] Examples are patents, trademarks, copyrights, and franchises. Their value comes from the privileges or rights granted to or held by

---

8   IFRS 2012, IAS 1, para. 66.
9   IFRS 2012, IAS 16, para. 6–7.
10 IFRS 2012, IAS 38, para. 8–12. Intangible assets are subject to *amortization* in a way similar to how plant and equipment are depreciated. *Amortization* is discussed in Chapter 10.

the owner. **Danier Leather Inc.** lists intangible assets at June 25, 2011, as shown in Exhibit 4.16.

Danier Leather Inc. (in thousands)	
Intangible assets	$1,054

EXHIBIT 4.16
Intangible Assets Section

Current Liabilities

Current liabilities are obligations due to be paid or settled within the longer of one year or the operating cycle. They are usually settled by paying out current assets. Current liabilities include accounts payable, notes payable, wages payable, taxes payable, interest payable, and unearned revenues. Any portion of a long-term liability due to be paid within the longer of one year or the operating cycle is a current liability. Exhibit 4.14 shows how the current portion of long-term liabilities is usually reported. Unearned revenues are current liabilities when they will be settled by delivering products or services within the longer of the year or the operating cycle. While practice varies, current liabilities are often reported in the order of those to be settled first.

Long-Term Liabilities

Long-term liabilities are obligations due beyond the longer of one year or the operating cycle. Notes payable, mortgages payable, bonds payable, and lease obligations are often long-term liabilities. If a portion of a long-term liability is to be paid within the period immediately following the balance sheet date, it must be separated and shown as a current liability on the balance sheet. For example, assume the Long-Term Notes Payable account at December 31, 2014, shows a balance of $150,000. We know that $25,000 of this amount will be paid during 2015. On the December 31, 2014, balance sheet, the $25,000 current portion is disclosed as a current liability and the balance of $125,000 ($150,000 − $25,000) is listed as a long-term liability as follows:

EYK
4-5

Liabilities	
Current liabilities:	
Current portion of long-term notes payable	$ 25,000
Long-term liabilities:	
Long-term notes payable (less current portion)	125,000

Equity

Equity is the owner's claim on the assets of a company. In a sole proprietorship, it is reported in the equity section with an owner's capital account. The equity sections of a partnership and corporation are discussed in detail in later chapters.

CHECKPOINT

8. Identify which of the following assets are classified as (1) current assets, (2) property, plant and equipment, or (3) intangible assets: (a) land used in operations; (b) office supplies; (c) receivables from customers due in 10 months; (d) insurance protection for the next nine months; (e) trucks used to provide services to customers; (f) trademarks used in advertising the company's services.
9. Name two examples of assets classified as long-term investments on the balance sheet.
10. Explain an operating cycle for a service company, and identify its importance to the classified balance sheet.

Do Quick Study questions: QS 4-10, QS 4-11, QS 4-12

CRITICAL THINKING CHALLENGE   Refer to the Critical Thinking Challenge questions at the beginning of the chapter. Compare your answers to those suggested on Connect.

IFRS AND ASPE—THE DIFFERENCES

Difference	International Financial Reporting Standard (IFRS)	Accounting Standards for Private Enterprises (ASPE)
Depreciation vs. amortization	• IFRS use the term *depreciation** (although they use *amortization* for intangible assets**)	• ASPE use the term *amortization****

* IFRS 2012, IAS 16, para. 6.
**IFRS 2012, IAS 38, para. 8.
*** ASPE, Accounting Standards, Section 3061.16.

SUMMARY

LO¹ **Describe and prepare a work sheet and explain its usefulness.** A work sheet is optional and can be a useful tool when preparing and analyzing financial statements. It is helpful at the end of a period for preparing adjusting entries, an adjusted trial balance, and financial statements. A work sheet often contains five pairs of columns for an unadjusted trial balance, the adjustments, an adjusted trial balance, an income statement, and the balance sheet and statement of changes in equity.

LO² **Describe the closing process and explain why temporary accounts are closed each period.** The closing process is the final step of the accounting cycle; it closes temporary accounts at the end of each accounting period: (1) to update the owner's capital account for revenue, expense, and withdrawals transactions recorded for the period; and (2) to prepare revenue, expense, and withdrawals accounts for the next reporting period by giving them zero balances.

LO³ **Prepare closing entries.** Closing entries involve four steps: (1) close credit balances in revenue accounts to Income Summary, (2) close debit balances in expense accounts to Income Summary, (3) close Income Summary to owner's capital, and (4) close the withdrawals account to owner's capital.

LO⁴ **Explain and prepare a post-closing trial balance.** A post-closing trial balance is a list of permanent accounts and their balances after all closing entries are journalized and posted. Permanent accounts are asset, liability, and equity accounts. The purpose of a post-closing trial balance is to verify that (1) total debits equal total credits for permanent accounts and (2) all temporary accounts have zero balances.

LO⁵ **Complete the steps in the accounting cycle.** The accounting cycle consists of nine steps: (1) analyze transactions, (2) journalize, (3) post, (4) prepare unadjusted trial balance, (5) adjust, (6) prepare adjusted trial balance, (7) prepare statements, (8) close, and (9) prepare post-closing trial balance. If a work sheet is prepared, it covers Steps 4 to 6. Reversing entries are an optional step that is done between Steps 9 and 1.

LO⁶ **Explain and prepare a classified balance sheet.** Classified balance sheets usually report four groups of assets: current assets; long-term investments; property, plant and equipment; and intangible assets. Also, they include at least two groups of liabilities: current and long-term. The equity section on the balance sheet for a proprietorship reports the capital account balance.

GUIDANCE ANSWER TO **DECISION MAKER**

Analyzing Results
Yes, you are concerned about the absence of a depreciation adjustment. Equipment does depreciate, and financial statements must recognize this occurrence. Its absence suggests an error or a misrepresentation (there is also the possibility that equipment is fully depreciated or that it was scrapped).

GUIDANCE ANSWERS TO **CHECKPOINT**

1. Amounts in the Unadjusted Trial Balance columns are taken from account balances in the ledger.

2. A work sheet offers the advantage of listing on one page all of the necessary information to make adjusting entries.

3. A work sheet can help in: (a) preparing interim financial statements, (b) linking transactions and events to their effects in financial statements, (c) showing adjustments for audit purposes, (d) avoiding errors, and (e) showing effects of proposed or "what-if" transactions.

4. The four major closing entries consist of closing:
   (1) credit balances in revenue accounts to Income Summary,
   (2) debit balances in expense accounts to Income Summary,
   (3) Income Summary to owner's capital, and
   (4) withdrawals account to owner's capital.

5. Revenue and expense accounts are called temporary because they are opened and closed every reporting period. The Income Summary and owner's withdrawals accounts are also temporary accounts.

6. Permanent accounts are listed on the post-closing trial balance. These accounts are the asset, liability, and equity accounts.

7. Making reversing entries is an optional step in the accounting cycle. Also, a work sheet is an optional tool for completing Steps 4 to 6.

8. Current assets: b, c, d. Property, plant and equipment: a, e. Intangible assets: f.

9. Notes receivable, land not currently used in business operations.

10. An operating cycle for a service company is the average time between (1) paying employees who do the services and (2) receiving cash from customers. Knowing the operating cycle allows current versus long-term assets and liabilities to be disclosed appropriately on the balance sheet.

DEMONSTRATION PROBLEM

The partial adjusted trial balance for Westside Appliance Repair shows the following account balances as at December 31, 2014.

			Debit	Credit
_____	101	Cash	$ 15,000	
_____	106	Accounts receivable	22,665	
_____	124	Spare parts supplies	5,800	
_____	128	Prepaid insurance	8,700	
_____	141	Notes receivable[A]	36,900	
_____	163	Office equipment	12,510	
_____	164	Accumulated depreciation, office equipment		$ 2,825
_____	173	Building	129,000	
_____	174	Accumulated depreciation, building		33,000
_____	183	Land	55,000	
_____	191	Patent	11,500	
_____	193	Franchise	26,000	
_____	201	Accounts payable		16,500
_____	209	Salaries payable		26,300
_____	230	Unearned fees		7,600
_____	251	Long-term notes payable[B]		142,000
_____	301	Brian Westside, capital[C]		104,000
_____	302	Brian Westside, withdrawals	72,000	

[A]The note receivable is due to be collected May 1, 2016.
[B]$22,000 of the December 31, 2014, balance in notes payable will be paid during 2015.
[C]Brian Westside, the owner, invested $5,000 during the accounting period.

Required

Using the information provided above for Westside Appliance Repair,

1. Prepare a classified balance sheet at December 31, 2014. For simplicity, Westside Appliance lists accounts on the balance sheet in account order.
2. Prepare a statement of changes in equity for the year ended December 31, 2014.

Analysis Component:

Has Brian Westside, the owner of Westside Appliance Repair, financed growth by reinvesting profits? Explain.

Planning the Solution

1. Prepare a classified balance sheet by first listing all of the classification headings under each of assets and liabilities. Then, sort the accounts by listing them under the appropriate heading. *Hint: Place an 'X' in the column provided to the left of the account number column on the adjusted trial balance as you transfer account information from the adjusted trial balance to the balance sheet. This process will help you determine whether all of the appropriate accounts have been transferred to the balance sheet.*

2. Prepare a statement of changes in equity. *Hint: Revenue and expense information has not been provided from which to calculate net income or net loss. However, you will be able to determine what the net income or loss was by taking into consideration the balance sheet prepared in Step 1 and the other elements of equity that have been provided.*

3. Review the information and prepare an answer to the analysis component question.

SOLUTION

1. Prepare a classified balance sheet.

Westside Appliance Repair Balance Sheet December 31, 2014			
Assets			
Current assets:			
Cash..		$ 15,000	
Accounts receivable...		22,665	
Spare parts supplies...		5,800	
Prepaid insurance...		8,700	
Total current assets..			$ 52,165
Long-term investments:			
Notes receivable..			36,900
Property, plant and equipment:			
Land..		$ 55,000	
Building	$129,000		
Less: Accumulated depreciation......................	33,000	96,000	
Office equipment	$ 12,510		
Less: Accumulated depreciation......................	2,825	9,685	
Total property, plant and equipment..................			160,685
Intangible assets:			
Patent		$ 11,500	
Franchise..		26,000	
Total intangible assets			37,500
Total assets			$287,250
Liabilities			
Current liabilities:			
Accounts payable	$ 16,500		
Salaries payable...	26,300		
Unearned fees	7,600		
Current portion of long-term notes payable	22,000		
Total current liabilities		$ 72,400	
Long-term liabilities:			
Long-term notes payable (less current portion)...		120,000	
Total liabilities..			$192,400
Equity			
Brian Westside, capital			94,850
Total liabilities and equity.................................			$287,250

2. Prepare a statement of changes in equity.

Westside Appliance Repair
Statement of Changes in Equity
For Year Ended December 31, 2014

Brian Westside, capital December 31, 2013		$ 99,000[1]
Add: Net income	$62,850[3]	
Investment by owner	5,000	67,850[4]
Total..		$166,850[2]
Less: Withdrawals by owner		72,000
Brian Westside, capital, December 31, 2014		$ 94,850

[1]Adjusted capital balance on December 31, 2014 = $104,000; $104,000 − $5,000 owner investment during 2014 = $99,000 capital balance on December 31, 2013.
[2]$94,850 post-closing balance per December 31, 2014, balance sheet + $72,000 owner withdrawals = $166,850
[3]$166,850 − $5,000 − $99,000 = $62,850
[4]$62,850 + $5,000 = $67,850

---

3. Brian Westside is not reinvesting profits. This is evident from the amount of his withdrawals, $72,000, which represents 115% of net income ($72,000/$62,850 × 100% = 115%). Reinvesting profits means that as net income causes equity to increase, assets are retained by the business for the purpose of growth rather than being withdrawn, which depletes assets.

APPENDIX 4A

Reversing Entries

REVERSING ENTRIES

LO7 Prepare reversing entries and explain their purpose.

Reversing entries are optional entries used to simplify recordkeeping. They are prepared on the first day of the new accounting period. Reversing entries are prepared for those adjusting entries that created accrued assets and liabilities (such as interest receivable and salaries payable).

Exhibit 4A.1 shows how reversing entries work for Vertically Inclined. The top of the exhibit shows the adjusting entry recorded by Vertically Inclined on March 31, 2014, for earned but unpaid salary. The entry recorded one day's salary to increase March's total salary expense to $1,470. The entry also recognized a liability of $70. The expense is reported on March's income statement and the expense account is closed. As a result, the ledger on April 1, 2014, reflects a $70 liability and a zero balance in the Salaries Expense account. At this point, April 1, the choice is made to use reversing entries or not.

Accounting *Without* Reversing Entries

The path down the left side of Exhibit 4A.1 is described in Chapter 3. That is, when the next payday occurs on April 1, we record payment with a compound entry that debits both the expense and liability accounts. Posting that entry creates a $630 balance in the expense account and reduces the liability account balance to zero because the debt has been settled.

The disadvantage of this approach is the complex entry required on April 1. Paying the accrued liability means that this entry differs from the routine entries made on all other paydays. To construct the proper entry on April 1, we must recall the effect of the adjusting entry. Reversing entries overcome this disadvantage.

Accounting *With* Reversing Entries

The right side of Exhibit 4A.1 shows how a reversing entry on April 1 overcomes the disadvantage of the complex April 11 entry. The reversing entry is the exact opposite of the adjusting entry recorded on March 31. The Salaries Payable liability is debited for $70, meaning that this account now has a zero balance after the entry is posted. Technically, the Salaries Payable account now understates the liability, but this is not a problem since financial statements are not prepared before the liability is settled on April 11. The credit to the Salaries Expense account is unusual because it gives the account an *abnormal credit balance*.

Because of the reversing entry, the April 11 entry to record payment is simple. This entry debits the Salaries Expense account for the full $700 paid. It is the same as all other entries made to record 10 days' salary for the employee.

Accrue salaries expense on March 31, 2014:

| Salaries Expense | . . . . 70 | |
| Salaries Payable | . . . . 70 | |

Salaries Expense

Mar. 12	700	
26	700	
31	70	

Salaries Payable

| | 70 | Mar. 31 |

No reversing entry recorded on April 1, 2014:

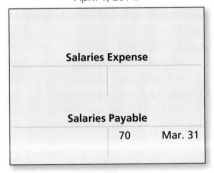

Salaries Expense

Salaries Payable

| | 70 | Mar. 31 |

Reversing entry recorded on April 1, 2014:

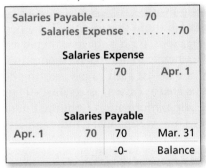

| Salaries Payable | . . . . 70 | |
| Salaries Expense | . . . . 70 | |

Salaries Expense

| | 70 | Apr. 1 |

Salaries Payable

| Apr. 1 | 70 | 70 | Mar. 31 |
| | | -0- | Balance |

Pay the accrued and current salaries on April 11, the first payday in April 2014:

Salaries Expense	 630	
Salaries Payable	 70	
Cash	 700	

Salaries Expense

| Apr. 11 | 630 | |

Salaries Payable

| Apr. 11 | 70 | 70 | Mar. 31 |
| | | -0- | Balance |

| Salaries Expense | . . . . 700 | |
| Cash | . . . . 700 | |

Salaries Expense

| Apr. 11 | 700 | 70 | Apr. 1 |
| Balance | 630 | | |

Salaries Payable

| Apr. 1 | 70 | 70 | Mar. 31 |
| | | -0- | Balance |

After the payment entry is posted, the expense and liability accounts have exactly the same balances whether reversing occurs or not.

CHECKPOINT

11. How are financial statements affected by a decision to make reversing entries?

Do Quick Study question: *QS 4-13

APPENDIX 4B

Using the Information

CURRENT RATIO

EXHIBIT 4B.1

Current Ratio

$$\text{Current ratio} = \frac{\text{Current assets}}{\text{Current liabilities}}$$

Financial statements are important tools for helping decision makers to determine a company's ability to pay its debts in the near future.

The **current ratio** is one important measure used to evaluate a company's ability to pay its short-term obligations. The *ability to pay* day-to-day obligations (current liabilities) with existing *liquid assets* is commonly referred to as **liquidity**. **Liquid assets** are those that can easily be converted to cash or used to pay for services or obligations. Cash is the most liquid asset. The current ratio helps us to make decisions like whether or not to lend money to a company or allow a customer to buy on credit, or how to use cash to pay existing debts when they come due. The current ratio is calculated as current assets divided by current liabilities, as shown in Exhibit 4B.1.

Using information from the financial statements of **High Liner Foods Incorporated**, we calculate and compare its current ratios at December 31, 2011, and January 1, 2011 (rounded to two decimal places):

December 31, 2011	January 1, 2011
$\dfrac{\$357{,}432{,}000}{\$236{,}598{,}000} = 1.51$	$\dfrac{\$186{,}510{,}000}{\$114{,}302{,}000} = 1.63$

High Liner's current ratio at December 31, 2011, can also be expressed as 1.51:1, meaning that there are $1.51 of current assets available to cover each $1.00 of current debt. This tells us that High Liner is in a good position to pay its day-to-day obligations but it decreased from January 1, 2011, to December 31, 2011. Although it varies between industries, generally speaking, an acceptable (favourable) current ratio falls between 1.5 and 2.0. When the current ratio is less than this, a company would likely face challenges in covering current liabilities with current assets. A current ratio greater than 2:1 may signal that an excess of current assets exists. Excessive current assets represent an inefficient use of assets.

DECISION MAKER   Answer—End of appendix

Analyst
You are analyzing the financial condition of a company to assess its ability to meet upcoming loan payments. You calculate its current ratio as 1.2. You also find that a major portion of accounts receivable is due from one client who has not made any payments in the past 12 months. Removing this receivable from current assets lowers the current ratio to 0.7. What do you conclude?

CHECKPOINT

12. If a company misclassifies a portion of liabilities as long-term when they are short-term, how does this affect its current ratio?

Do Quick Study question: *QS 4-14

SUMMARY OF APPENDIX 4A AND APPENDIX 4B

LO⁷ Prepare reversing entries and explain their purpose. Reversing entries are an optional step. They are applied to accrued assets and liabilities. The purpose of reversing entries is to simplify subsequent journal entries. Financial statements are unaffected by the choice to use reversing entries or not.

LO⁸ Calculate the current ratio and describe what it reveals about a company's financial condition. A company's current ratio is defined as current assets divided by current liabilities. We use it to evaluate a company's ability to pay its current liabilities out of current assets.

GUIDANCE ANSWER TO **DECISION MAKER**

Analyst
A current ratio of 1.2 suggests that current assets are sufficient to cover current liabilities, but it implies a minimal buffer in case of errors in measuring current assets or current liabilities.

Removing the past due receivable reduces the current ratio to 0.7. Your assessment is that the company will have some difficulty meeting its loan payments.

GUIDANCE ANSWERS TO **CHECKPOINT**

11. Financial statements are unchanged by the choice of using reversing entries or not.
12. Since the current ratio is defined as current assets divided by current liabilities, then ignoring a portion of current liabilities

(1) decreases the reported amount of current liabilities and (2) increases the current ratio because current assets are now divided by a smaller number.

GLOSSARY

Classified balance sheet A balance sheet that presents the assets and liabilities in relevant subgroups.

Closing entries Journal entries recorded at the end of each accounting period that transfer the end-of-period balances in revenue, expense, and withdrawals accounts to the permanent owner's capital account in order to prepare for the upcoming period and update the owner's capital account for the period just finished.

Closing process A step at the end of the accounting period that prepares accounts for recording the transactions of the next period.

Current assets Cash or other assets that are expected to be sold, collected, or used within the longer of one year or the company's operating cycle.

Current liabilities Obligations due to be paid or settled within the longer of one year or the operating cycle.

Current ratio A ratio that is used to evaluate a company's ability to pay its short-term obligations, calculated by dividing current assets by current liabilities.

Equity The owner's claim on the assets of a company.

Income Summary A temporary account used only in the closing process to which the balances of revenue and expense accounts are transferred; its balance equals net income or net loss and is transferred to the owner's capital account.

Intangible assets Long-lived assets that lack physical form and are used to produce or sell products or services.

Liquid assets Assets that can easily be converted to cash or used to pay for services or obligations; cash is the most liquid asset.

Liquidity The ability to pay day-to-day obligations (current liabilities) with existing liquid assets.

Long-term investments Assets not used in day-to-day operating activities that are held for more than one year or the operating cycle, such as a long-term note receivable.

Long-term liabilities Obligations that are not due to be paid within the longer of one year or the operating cycle.

Nominal accounts See *temporary accounts*.

Operating cycle For a business, the average time between paying cash for employee salaries or merchandise and receiving cash from customers.

Permanent accounts Accounts that are used to report on activities related to one or more future accounting periods; their balances are carried into the next period, and include all balance sheet accounts; permanent account balances are not closed as long as the company continues to own the assets, owe the liabilities, and have equity; also called *real accounts*.

Post-closing trial balance A list of permanent accounts and their balances from the ledger after all closing entries are journalized and posted; a list of balances for all accounts not closed.

PPE See *property, plant and equipment*.

Property, plant and equipment (PPE) Long-lived tangible assets used to produce or sell products and services; abbreviated *PPE*.

Real accounts See *permanent accounts*.

Reversing entries Optional entries recorded at the beginning of a new period that prepare the accounts for simplified journal entries subsequent to accrual adjusting entries.

Temporary accounts Accounts that are used to describe revenues, expenses, and owner's withdrawals for one accounting period; they are closed at the end of the reporting period; also called *nominal accounts*.

Unclassified balance sheet A balance sheet that broadly groups the assets, liabilities, and equity.

Working papers Internal documents that are used to assist the preparers in doing the analyses and organizing the information for reports to be presented to internal and external decision makers.

Work sheet A 10-column spreadsheet used to draft a company's unadjusted trial balance, adjusting entries, adjusted trial balance, and financial statements; an optional step in the accounting process.

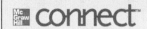 Visit **Connect** for additional study tools, practice quizzes, to search an interactive eBook, and much more.

CONCEPT REVIEW QUESTIONS

1. What tasks are performed with the work sheet?

2. Why are the debit and credit entries in the Adjustments columns of the work sheet identified with letters?

3. What two purposes are accomplished by recording closing entries?

4. What are the four closing entries?

5. What accounts are affected by closing entries? What accounts are not affected?

6. Describe the similarities and differences between adjusting and closing entries.

7. What is the purpose of the Income Summary account?

8. Explain whether an error has occurred if a post-closing trial balance includes a Depreciation Expense, Building account.

9. Refer to Danier's income statement in Appendix II at the end of the book. What journal entry was recorded as of June 25, 2011, to close the interest account?

10. What is a company's operating cycle?

11. How is an unearned revenue classified on the balance sheet?

12. What classes of assets and liabilities are shown on a typical classified balance sheet?

13. What are the characteristics of property, plant and equipment?

14. Refer to the December 31, 2011, balance sheet for WestJet in Appendix II at the end of the book. What amount of WestJet's long-term debt is coming due before December 31, 2012?

*15. How do reversing entries simplify a company's bookkeeping efforts?

*16. If a company had accrued unpaid salaries expense of $500 at the end of a fiscal year, what reversing entry could be made? When would it be made?

QUICK STUDY

QS 4-1 Applying a work sheet LO¹

In preparing a work sheet, indicate the financial statement debit column to which a normal balance of each of the following accounts should be extended. Use *IS* for the Income Statement Debit column and *BS* for the Balance Sheet or Statement of Changes in Equity Debit column.

1. Equipment

2. Owner, withdrawals

3. Insurance expense

4. Prepaid insurance

5. Accounts receivable

6. Depreciation expense, equipment

An asterisk (*) identifies assignment material based on Appendix 4A or Appendix 4B.

QS 4-2 Completing a work sheet LO¹

Enter the following unadjusted trial balance and adjustment information onto a work sheet. Complete the work sheet.

	Trial Balance.xls				
	Home Insert Page Layout Formulas Data Review View				
	P18 *fx*				
	A	B	C	D	E
1					
2	Trial Balance				
3		Unadjusted			
4		Trial Balance		Adjustments	
5	**Account**	**Dr.**	**Cr.**	**Dr.**	**Cr.**
6	Cash	15			
7	Accounts receivable	22			
8	Supplies	25			8
9	Ed Wolt, capital		40		
10	Ed Wolt, withdrawals	12			
11	Fees earned		48		
12	Supplies expense	14		8	
13	**Totals**	88	88	8	8

QS 4-3 Work sheet information LO¹

The following information is from the work sheet for Pursley Company as of December 31, 2014. Using this information, determine the amount that should be reported for Alice Pursley, Capital on the December 31, 2014, balance sheet.

	Income Statement		Balance Sheet and Statement of Changes in Equity	
	Debit	**Credit**	**Debit**	**Credit**
Cash			7,000	
Alice Pursley, capital				50,000
Alice Pursley, withdrawals			32,000	
Totals	125,000	184,000		

QS 4-4 Interpreting a work sheet LO¹

The following information is from the work sheet for Hascal Company as of December 31, 2014. Using this information, determine the amount for Sam Hascal, Capital that should be reported on the December 31, 2014, balance sheet.

	Income Statement		Balance Sheet and Statement of Changes in Equity	
	Debit	**Credit**	**Debit**	**Credit**
Cash			4,500	
Sam Hascal, capital				165,000
Sam Hascal, withdrawals			32,000	
Totals	115,000	74,000		

QS 4-5 Effects of closing entries LO[2,3]

Jontil Co. began the current period with a $14,000 balance in the Peter Jontil, Capital account. At the end of the period, the company's adjusted account balances include the following temporary accounts with normal balances:

Service fee earned	$35,000	Interest earned	$3,500
Salaries expense	19,000	Peter Jontil, withdrawals	6,000
Depreciation expense	4,000	Utilities expense	2,300

a. After closing the revenue and expense accounts, what will be the balance of the Income Summary account?

b. After all of the closing entries are journalized and posted, what will be the balance of the Peter Jontil, Capital account?

QS 4-6 Closing entries LO[3]

Jaspur Rentals showed the following adjusted account balances on April 30, 2014. Prepare and post the closing entries.

Assets		Liabilities		Capital	
250			30		200

Withdrawals		Revenue		Expenses		Income Summary	
20			100	60			

QS 4-7 Closing entries LO[3]

Warden Repairs showed the following adjusted account balances on October 31, 2014. Prepare and post the closing entries.

Assets		Liabilities		Capital	
250			110		200

Withdrawals		Revenue		Expenses		Income Summary	
20			100	140			

QS 4-8 Post-closing trial balance LO[4]

SilverStar Automotive showed the following account balances at October 31, 2014, after posting the closing entries. Prepare the post-closing trial balance.

Cash		Accounts Receivable		Unearned Revenue	
Bal.	40	Bal.	20		10 Bal.

Capital		Withdrawals		Revenues		Expenses	
	5 40	5	5	23	23	8	8
	15						
	50 Bal.	Bal.	-0-		-0- Bal.	Bal.	-0-

QS 4-9 Explaining the accounting cycle LO[5]

List the following steps of the accounting cycle in the proper order:

a. Preparing the unadjusted trial balance.

b. Preparing the post-closing trial balance.

c. Journalizing and posting adjusting entries.

d. Journalizing and posting closing entries.

e. Preparing the financial statements.

f. Journalizing transactions.

g. Posting the transaction entries.

h. Completing the work sheet.

QS 4-10 Classifying balance sheet items LO[6]

The following are categories on a classified balance sheet:

a. Current assets

b. Long-term investments

c. Property, plant and equipment

d. Intangible assets

e. Current liabilities

f. Long-term liabilities

For each of the following items, select the letter that identifies the balance sheet category in which the item should appear.

_____ **1.** Store equipment

_____ **2.** Wages payable

_____ **3.** Cash

_____ **4.** Notes payable (due in three years)

_____ **5.** Land not currently used in business operations

_____ **6.** Accounts receivable

_____ **7.** Trademarks

QS 4-11 Balance sheet classifications LO[6]

In the blank space beside each numbered balance sheet item, enter the letter of its balance sheet classification. If the item should not appear on the balance sheet, enter an *h* in the blank.

a. Current assets

b. Long-term investments

c. Property, plant and equipment

d. Intangible assets

e. Current liabilities

f. Long-term liabilities

g. Equity

h. Does not appear on balance sheet

_____ **1.** Depreciation expense, trucks

_____ **2.** Lee Hale, capital

_____ **3.** Interest receivable

_____ **4.** Lee Hale, withdrawals

_____ **5.** Automobiles

_____ **6.** Notes payable (due in three years)

_____ **7.** Accounts payable

_____ **8.** Prepaid insurance

_____ **9.** Land not currently used in business operations

_____ **10.** Unearned services revenue

_____ **11.** Accumulated depreciation, trucks

_____ **12.** Cash

_____ **13.** Building

_____ **14.** Patent

_____ **15.** Office equipment

_____ **16.** Land (used in operations)

_____ **17.** Repairs expense

_____ **18.** Prepaid property taxes

_____ **19.** Notes payable (due in two months)

_____ **20.** Notes receivable (due in two years)

QS 4-12 Classifying liabilities LO⁶

Use the following March 31, 2014, year-end adjusted balances to prepare Jardine Servicing's liabilities section on its March 31, 2014, classified balance sheet.

Accounts payable	$ 14,000
Unearned fees	26,000
Notes payable, due February 1, 2015	45,000
Mortgage payable*	115,000

*$56,000 of this amount will be paid by March 31, 2015.

*QS 4-13 Reversing entries LO⁷

On December 31, 2014, Ace Management Co. prepared an adjusting entry to accrue $9,800 of earned but unrecorded rent revenue. On January 20, 2015, Ace received rent payments in the amount of $15,500. Assuming Ace uses reversing entries, prepare the 2015 entries pertaining to the rent transactions.

*QS 4-14 Calculating current ratio LO⁸

Calculate Tucker Company's current ratio, given the following information about its assets and liabilities (round to two decimal places) and compare it to the industry average current ratio of 2.2.

Accounts receivable	$15,000	Long-term notes payable*	$20,000
Accounts payable	10,000	Office supplies	1,800
Buildings	42,000	Prepaid insurance	2,500
Cash	6,000	Unearned services revenue	4,000

*Due in three years.

Exercise 4-1 Extending adjusted account balances on a work sheet LO¹

These accounts are from the Adjusted Trial Balance columns in a company's 10-column work sheet. In the blank space beside each account, write the letter of the appropriate financial statement column to which a normal account balance should be extended.

a. Debit column for the income statement.

b. Credit column for the income statement.

c. Debit column for the balance sheet and statement of changes in equity.

d. Credit column for the balance sheet and statement of changes in equity.

_____ **1.** Roberta Jefferson, withdrawals	_____ **9.** Cash
_____ **2.** Interest earned	_____ **10.** Office supplies
_____ **3.** Accumulated depreciation, machinery	_____ **11.** Roberta Jefferson, capital
_____ **4.** Service fees revenue	_____ **12.** Wages payable
_____ **5.** Accounts receivable	_____ **13.** Machinery
_____ **6.** Rent expense	_____ **14.** Insurance expense
_____ **7.** Depreciation expense, machinery	_____ **15.** Interest expense
_____ **8.** Accounts payable	_____ **16.** Interest receivable

An asterisk (*) identifies assignment material based on Appendix 4A or Appendix 4B.

CHECK FIGURE:
Net loss = $8,150

Exercise 4-2 Extending accounts in the work sheet LO[1]

The Adjusted Trial Balance columns of a 10-column work sheet for Webber Co. follow. Complete the work sheet by extending the account balances into the appropriate financial statement columns and by entering the amount of net income or loss for the reporting period.

		Webber Co. Work Sheet.xls		
		Home Insert Page Layout Formulas Data Review View		
		P18 fx		
		A	B	C
1		**Webber Co.**		
2		**Work Sheet**		
3		**December 31, 2014**		
4			**Adjusted**	
5			**Trial Balance**	
6		**Account**	**Debit**	**Credit**
7	101	Cash	$ 21,000	
8	106	Accounts receivable	8,200	
9	153	Trucks	48,000	
10	154	Accumulated depreciation, trucks		$ 31,250
11	193	Franchise	6,500	
12	201	Accounts payable		13,000
13	209	Salaries payable		14,600
14	233	Unearned fees		2,450
15	301	Bo Webber, capital		37,750
16	302	Bo Webber, withdrawals	7,200	
17	401	Plumbing fees earned		31,600
18	611	Depreciation expense, trucks	12,100	
19	622	Salaries expense	17,800	
20	640	Rent expense	6,000	
21	677	Miscellaneous expense	3,850	
22		**Totals**	$ 130,650	$ 130,650

Exercise 4-3 Preparing a work sheet LO[1]

The December 31, 2014, unadjusted trial balance for Musical Sensations after its second year of operations follows:

	Musical Sensations Work Sheet.xls		
	Home Insert Page Layout Formulas Data Review View		
	P18	fx	
	A	B	C
1 2 3	**Musical Sensations** **Work Sheet** **December 31, 2014**		
4 5		**Unadjusted** **Trial Balance**	
6	**Account**	**Debit**	**Credit**
7	Cash	$ 7,500	
8	Accounts receivable	14,200	
9	Office supplies	790	
10	Musical equipment	125,000	
11	Accumulated depreciation, musical equipment		$ 21,600
12	Accounts payable		4,200
13	Unearned performance revenue		12,400
14	Jim Daley, capital		154,300
15	Jim Daley, withdrawals	52,000	
16	Performance revenue		138,000
17	Salaries expense	86,000	
18	Travelling expense	45,010	
19	**Totals**	$ 330,500	$ 330,500

Required

1. Enter the unadjusted trial balance onto a work sheet.

2. Using the following additional information, enter the adjustments into the work sheet:

    a. A review of the Unearned Performance Revenue account revealed a balance remaining of $9,225.

    b. Annual depreciation on the musical equipment is $21,600.

    c. Accrued salaries at December 31 totalled $6,100.

    d. It was determined that $650 of the balance in the Office Supplies account had been used.

3. Complete the work sheet.

4. Calculate the balance in the capital account as it would appear on the December 31, 2014, balance sheet.

Exercise 4-4 Work sheet interpretation and closing entries LO[1,3]

Below are excerpts from the work sheets of two businesses as at March 31, 2014. Those rows that calculate totals are at the bottom of the last two sets of columns.

Required Do the following for each business:

1. Identify the net income or net loss for the year ended March 31, 2014.

2. Prepare the entry to close the Income Summary account to capital.

3. Calculate the post-closing balance in capital at March 31, 2014.

a.

	Income Statement		Balance Sheet and Statement of Changes in Equity	
	Debit	Credit	Debit	Credit
	263,700	300,500	357,300	320,500
	36,800			36,800
	300,500	300,500	357,300	357,300

*The adjusted balances in withdrawals and capital were $17,000 and $63,000, respectively.

b.

	Income Statement		Balance Sheet and Statement of Changes in Equity	
	Debit	Credit	Debit	Credit
	540,000	480,000	945,000	1,005,000
		60,000	60,000	
	540,000	540,000	1,005,000	1,005,000

*The adjusted balances in withdrawals and capital were $0 and $114,000, respectively.

Exercise 4-5 Completing the income statement columns and preparing closing entries LO[1,3]

These partially completed Income Statement columns from a 10-column work sheet are for the Winston Sail'em Boat Rental Company for the year ended December 31, 2014. Use the information to determine the amount that should be entered on the net income line of the work sheet. In addition, prepare closing entries for the company. The owner's name is Carl Winston, and the preclosing balance of the withdrawals account is $18,000.

	Debit	Credit
Rent earned		99,000
Salaries expense	35,300	
Insurance expense..........................	4,400	
Dock rental expense......................	12,000	
Boat supplies expense	6,220	
Depreciation expense, boats	21,500	
Totals..		
Net income...................................		
Totals..		

CHECK FIGURE:
Post-closing trial
balance columns =
$51,300

Exercise 4-6 Preparing closing entries and the post-closing trial balance LO[2,3,4]

The adjusted trial balance at April 30, 2014, for Willard Co. follows. Prepare the four closing entries and the post-closing trial balance.

		Debit	Credit
101	Cash	$ 3,600	
106	Accounts receivable	8,500	
153	Trucks	26,000	
154	Accumulated depreciation, trucks		$ 8,250
193	Franchise...	13,200	
201	Accounts payable..		9,600
209	Salaries payable...		3,200
233	Unearned fees...		1,300
301	Sid Willard, capital		29,100
302	Sid Willard, withdrawals	9,600	
401	Plumbing fees earned...		42,050
611	Depreciation expense, trucks	4,900	
622	Salaries expense..	17,800	
640	Rent expense	3,000	
677	Advertising expense	6,900	
901	Income summary		
	Totals...	$93,500	$93,500

Exercise 4-7 Closing entries LO²,³

Following is the adjusted trial balance, with accounts in alphabetical order, for TRN Magazine as at January 31, 2014:

	Debit	Credit
Accounts receivable	$ 21,000	
Accumulated depreciation, equipment		$ 12,000
Cash	8,500	
Depreciation expense, equipment	1,500	
Equipment	19,000	
Interest revenue		450
Rent expense	17,500	
Salaries expense	61,000	
Subscription revenues		71,000
Trish Norris, capital		45,450
Trish Norris, withdrawals	19,400	
Unearned subscription revenue		19,000
Totals	$147,900	$147,900

Required Prepare the closing entries.

Exercise 4-8 Closing entries LO²,³

The following adjusted trial balance contains the accounts and balances of Stilz Co. as of December 31, 2014, the end of its fiscal year:

No.	Title	Debit	Credit
101	Cash	$ 36,000	
126	Supplies	4,000	
128	Prepaid insurance	6,500	
167	Equipment	46,000	
168	Accumulated depreciation, equipment		$ 13,000
301	Nick Stilz, capital		110,100
302	Nick Stilz, withdrawals	43,000	
404	Services revenue		131,000
612	Depreciation expense, equipment	4,000	
622	Salaries expense	42,000	
637	Insurance expense	3,000	
640	Rent expense	61,000	
652	Supplies expense	8,600	
	Totals	$254,100	$254,100

Required Prepare the closing entries for the company.

Exercise 4-9 Closing entries LO²,³

Following is the adjusted trial balance, with accounts in alphabetical order, for eSOFT as at September 30, 2014:

	Debit	Credit
Accounts payable		$ 14,500
Accumulated depreciation, office equipment		10,500
Cash	$ 14,000	
Consulting fees earned		123,000
Depreciation expense, office equipment	3,500	
Office equipment	31,500	
Prepaid rent	6,800	
Sandra Sloley, capital		20,350
Sandra Sloley, withdrawals	69,000	
Unearned consulting fees		21,700
Rent expense	51,750	
Wages expense	13,500	
Totals	$190,050	$190,050

Required Prepare the closing entries.

CHECK FIGURE:
Post-closing balance,
Marcy Jones, Capital =
$91,000

Exercise 4-10 Preparing and posting closing entries LO²,³

Set up the following T-accounts for Jones's Consulting with the balances provided. Prepare closing entries at December 31, 2014, and post them to the accounts.

Assets				Liabilities	
Dec. 31	142,000			51,000	Dec. 31

Marcy Jones, Capital			Rent Expense	
	71,800	Dec. 31	Dec. 31	9,100

Marcy Jones, Withdrawals			Salaries Expense	
Dec. 31	38,000		Dec. 31	27,000

Income Summary			Insurance Expense	
			Dec. 31	1,500

Services Revenue			Depreciation Expense	
	103,000	Dec. 31	Dec. 31	8,200

Exercise 4-11 Post-closing trial balance LO⁴

Required Using your answer from Exercise 4-10, prepare a post-closing trial balance.

Exercise 4-12 Post-closing trial balance LO²,³,⁴

Bill's Roofing Services showed the following post-closing trial balance after the posting of the closing entries on June 30, 2014:

	Debit	Credit
Cash	$ 21,000	
Accounts receivable	36,000	
Equipment	59,500	
Accumulated depreciation, equipment		$ 12,000
Trucks	138,000	
Accumulated depreciation, trucks		66,000
Accounts payable		19,200
Bill Duggan, capital		216,200
Bill Duggan, withdrawals	59,900	
Interest revenue		1,150
Other expenses	150	
Totals	$314,550	$314,550

Required

1. Identify the error(s) in the post-closing trial balance.
2. What entry is required to correct the error?
3. Calculate the correct balance at June 30, 2014, for Bill Duggan, Capital.

CHECK FIGURE:
b. = $200,150

Exercise 4-13 Post-closing trial balance LO²,³,⁴

The March 31, 2014, adjusted trial balance for Sopik Refrigeration Repairs is shown below with accounts in alphabetical order.

		Debit	Credit
_____	Accounts payable		$ 31,000
_____	Accounts receivable	$ 48,000	
_____	Accumulated depreciation, equipment		9,000
_____	Accumulated depreciation, truck		21,000
_____	Cash	14,400	
_____	Depreciation expense	3,800	
_____	Equipment	19,000	
_____	Franchise	21,000	
_____	Gas and oil expense	7,500	
_____	Interest expense	450	
_____	Interest payable		750
_____	Land not currently used in business operations	148,000	
_____	Long-term notes payable[1]		35,000
_____	Notes payable, due February 1, 2015		7,000
_____	Notes receivable[2]	6,000	
_____	Patent	7,000	
_____	Prepaid rent	14,000	
_____	Rent expense	51,000	
_____	Repair revenue		266,000
_____	Repair supplies	13,100	
_____	Repair supplies expense	29,000	
_____	Truck	26,000	
_____	Unearned repair revenue		12,600
_____	Vic Sopik, capital		74,900
_____	Vic Sopik, withdrawals	49,000	
	Totals	$457,250	$457,250

[1]$5,000 of the long-term note payable is due during the year ended March 31, 2015.
[2]$2,000 of the notes receivable will be collected by March 31, 2015.

Required
Preparation Component:

a. Place an 'X' in the space provided beside each *account balance* that would *not* appear on the post-closing trial balance.

b. Calculate the post-closing balance in the owner's capital.

Analysis Component: Explain why the account balances identified in part (a) would not appear on the post-closing trial balance.

Exercise 4-14 Classified balance sheet LO6

Using the information in Exercise 4-13, calculate each of the following:

a. Current assets
b. Property, plant and equipment
c. Intangible assets
d. Long-term investments
e. Total assets

f. Current liabilities
g. Long-term liabilities
h. Total liabilities
i. Total liabilities and equity

Exercise 4-15 Classified balance sheet LO6

A partial alphabetized list of adjusted account balances for Dover Pacific Tours as at November 30, 2014, is shown (all accounts have normal balances). Pat Dover, the owner, uses the following account classification system:

101–149 Current assets
150–169 Property, plant and equipment
170–189 Intangible assets

190–199 Long-term investments
201–249 Current liabilities
250–299 Long-term liabilities

Acct. No.	Account Title	Adjusted Account Balance
201	Accounts payable	$41,000
106	Accounts receivable	19,000
155	Accumulated depreciation, office furniture	4,100
153	Accumulated depreciation, vehicles	15,800
101	Cash	7,200
172	Copyright	9,000
240	Notes payable	14,000
270	Notes payable[1]	21,600
195	Notes receivable[2]	20,500
154	Office furniture	6,500
110	Prepaid insurance	4,600
112	Prepaid rent	9,000
205	Salaries payable	12,100
118	Supplies	2,250
206	Unearned touring revenue	23,000
152	Vehicles	64,000

[1]$10,000 of this note payable is to be paid by November 30, 2015.
[2]$7,500 of the notes receivable is to be collected by November 30, 2015.

Required Prepare a classified balance sheet.

Exercise 4-16 Preparing a classified balance sheet LO⁶

Use the following adjusted trial balance of Hanson Trucking Company to prepare a classified balance sheet as of December 31, 2014.

Account Title	Debit	Credit
Cash	$ 13,000	
Accounts receivable	29,600	
Office supplies	3,100	
Trucks	170,000	
Accumulated depreciation, trucks		$ 46,000
Land	275,000	
Accounts payable		31,000
Interest payable		400
Long-term notes payable (due in 4 years)		152,000
Stanley Hanson, capital		206,200
Stanley Hanson, withdrawals	19,000	
Trucking fees earned		168,000
Depreciation expense, trucks	22,500	
Salaries expense	58,000	
Office supplies expense	6,500	
Repairs expense, trucks	6,900	
Total	$603,600	$603,600

Exercise 4-17 Comprehensive accounting cycle LO²,³,⁴,⁵,⁶

After five years of operations, Svenson's Tutoring Clinic showed the following post-closing balances at December 31, 2013.

Cash		Accounts Receivable		Prepaid Rent		Office Equipment	
2,000		5,000		3,000		20,000	

Accumulated Depreciation, Office Equipment		Unearned Fees		Leda Svenson, Capital		Leda Svenson, Withdrawals	
	10,000		2,900		17,100	-0-	

Tutoring Fees Earned		Rent Expense		Depreciation Expense		Advertising Expense	
	-0-	-0-		-0-		-0-	

Required

Analysis Component:

a.   Explain why Leda Svenson, Withdrawals, Tutoring Fees Earned, Rent Expense, Depreciation Expense, and Advertising Expense have zero balances.

Preparation Component:

b. Journalize and post the following transactions that occurred during 2014.

Jan 15	Provided $8,000 of tutoring services on account.
Feb. 20	Paid $2,000 for advertising that appeared in today's newspaper.
Jul. 7	Collected $9,000 from credit customers.
Dec. 10	The owner withdrew $3,000 cash for personal use.

c. Prepare an unadjusted trial balance as at December 31, 2014.

d. Journalize and post the adjusting entries on December 31, 2014, based on the following additional information:
  – Annual depreciation on the office equipment is $2,000.
  – $2,400 of the balance in unearned fees has been earned.
  – The entire balance in prepaid rent has expired.

e. Prepare an adjusted trial balance at December 31, 2014.

f. Prepare an income statement, statement of changes in equity, and classified balance sheet.

g. Journalize and post the closing entries.

h. Prepare a post-closing trial balance.

*Exercise 4-18 Reversing entries LO⁷

Breaker Corporation records prepaid assets and unearned revenues in balance sheet accounts. The following information was used to prepare adjusting entries for Breaker Corporation as of August 31, 2014, the end of the company's fiscal year:

a. The company has earned $5,000 of unrecorded service fees.

b. The expired portion of prepaid insurance is $2,700.

c. The earned portion of the Unearned Fees account balance is $1,900.

d. Depreciation expense for the office equipment is $2,300.

e. Employees have earned but have not been paid salaries of $2,400.

Required Prepare the appropriate reversing entries that would simplify the bookkeeping effort for recording subsequent cash transactions related to these adjustments.

*Exercise 4-19 Reversing entries LO⁷

The following conditions existed for Maxit Co. on October 31, 2014, the end of its fiscal year:

a. Maxit rents a building for $3,200 per month. By a prearrangement, the company delayed paying October's rent until November 5. On this date, the company paid the rent for both October and November.

b. Maxit rents space in a building it owns to a tenant for $750 per month. By prearrangement, the tenant delayed paying the October rent until November 8. On this date, the tenant paid the rent for both October and November.

Required

1. Prepare the adjusting entries that Maxit should record for these situations as of October 31.

2. Assuming that Maxit does not use reversing entries, prepare journal entries to record Maxit's payment of rent on November 5 and the collection of rent on November 8 from Maxit's tenant.

3. Assuming that Maxit does use reversing entries, prepare those entries and the journal entries to record Maxit's payment of rent on November 5 and the collection of rent on November 8 from Maxit's tenant.

*Exercise 4-20 Calculating the current ratio LO⁸

Calculate (to two decimal places) the current ratio in each of the following cases and indicate whether it is *Favourable* (F) or *Unfavourable* (U) (assuming that the current ratio for the industry is an average of 1.1):

	Case 1	Case 2	Case 3	Case 4
Current Assets	$78,000	$104,000	$44,000	$84,500
Current Liabilities	31,000	75,000	48,000	80,600

An asterisk (*) identifies assignment material based on Appendix 4A or Appendix 4B.

PROBLEMS   connect™

Problem 4-1A Completing a work sheet LO¹

The March 31, 2014, unadjusted trial balance for Nanimahoo Rentals after its first year of operations is shown below:

No.	Account	Dr.	Cr.
	Nanimahoo Rentals		
	Unadjusted Trial Balance		
	March 31, 2014		
		Unadjusted Trial Balance	
		Dr.	Cr.
101	Cash	$ 7,000	
110	Rent receivable	31,000	
124	Office supplies	2,250	
141	Notes receivable, due 2017	46,000	
161	Furniture	16,000	
173	Building	216,000	
183	Land	41,000	
191	Patent	9,600	
201	Accounts payable		$ 13,750
252	Long-term note payable		175,000
301	Joan Nanimahoo, capital		90,250
302	Joan Nanimahoo, withdrawals	92,000	
406	Rent earned		328,800
620	Office salaries expense	52,000	
633	Interest expense	5,250	
655	Advertising expense	14,600	
673	Janitorial expense	41,000	
690	Utilities expense	34,100	
	Totals	$ 607,800	$ 607,800

Required

1. Enter the unadjusted trial balance onto a work sheet.

2. Using the following additional information, enter the adjustments into the work sheet (the Chart of Accounts at the back of the textbook may be useful when additional accounts are required):

   a. It was determined that the balance in the Rent Receivable account at March 31 should be $36,000.

   b. A count of the office supplies showed $1,830 of the balance had been used.

   c. Annual depreciation on the building is $25,000 and $3,500 on the furniture.

   d. The two part-time office staff members each get paid $1,600 bi-weekly. The last bi-weekly pay period ended Friday, March 21. At March 31, six days' salary had accrued.

   e. A review of the balance in Advertising Expense showed that $2,400 was for advertisements to appear in the April issue of *Canadian Business* magazine.

   f. Accrued utilities at March 31 totalled $2,620.

   g. March interest of $425 on the long-term note payable is unrecorded and unpaid as of March 31.

3. Complete the work sheet.

Problem 4-2A Completing a work sheet LO[1]

The June 30, 2014, unadjusted trial balance for Trenton Consulting after its first year of operations follows:

	Trenton Consulting Trial Balance.xls		
	A	**B**	**C**
1	**Trenton Consulting**		
2	**Unadjusted Trial Balance**		
3	**June 30, 2014**		
4		**Unadjusted**	
5		**Trial Balance**	
6	**Account**	**Dr.**	**Cr.**
7	Cash	680	
8	Accounts receivable	2,900	
9	Prepaid rent	3,660	
10	Equipment	9,600	
11	Accounts payable		1,730
12	Toni Trenton, capital		26,650
13	Toni Trenton, withdrawals	6,880	
14	Consulting fees earned		30,200
15	Wages expense	24,920	
16	Insurance expense	1,620	
17	Rent expense	8,320	
18	**Totals**	58,580	58,580

Required

1. Enter the unadjusted trial balance onto a work sheet.
2. Using the following additional information, enter the adjustments onto the work sheet:
   a. Annual depreciation on the equipment is $1,500.
   b. The balance in the Prepaid Rent account is for six months of rent commencing March 1, 2014.
   c. Unpaid and unrecorded wages at June 30 totalled $3,200.
   d. Accrued revenues at June 30 totalled $4,100.
3. Complete the work sheet.
4. Calculate the balance in the capital account as it would appear on the June 30, 2014, balance sheet.

Analysis Component: What effect does a net loss have on the accounting equation?

Problem 4-3A Work sheet, journal entries, and financial statements LO^{1,6}

This unadjusted trial balance is for Challenger Construction at the end of its fiscal year, September 30, 2014. The beginning balance of the owner's capital account was $46,000 and the owner invested another $25,000 cash in the company during the year.

	Challenger Construction Trial Balance.xls		
	Home Insert Page Layout Formulas Data Review View		
	P18 *fx*		
	A	B	C

		Challenger Construction	
1			
2		**Unadjusted Trial Balance**	
3		**September 30, 2014**	
4		**Unadjusted**	
5		**Trial Balance**	
6	**No.** **Account**	**Dr.**	**Cr.**
7	101 Cash	$ 22,000	
8	126 Supplies	17,200	
9	128 Prepaid insurance	9,600	
10	149 Land not currently used in operations	50,000	
11	167 Equipment	106,000	
12	168 Accumulated depreciation, Equipment		$ 40,500
13	191 Copyright	6,000	
14	201 Accounts payable		8,100
15	203 Interest payable		-0-
16	210 Wages payable		-0-
17	251 Long-term notes payable		50,000
18	301 Chris Challenger, capital		71,000
19	302 Chris Challenger, withdrawals	68,000	
20	401 Construction fees earned		255,620
21	612 Depreciation expense, equipment	-0-	
22	623 Wages expense	96,000	
23	633 Interest expense	1,200	
24	637 Insurance expense	-0-	
25	640 Rent expense	26,400	
26	652 Supplies expense	-0-	
27	683 Business taxes expense	10,000	
28	684 Repairs expense	5,020	
29	690 Utilities expense	7,800	
30	**Totals**	**$ 425,220**	**$ 425,220**

Required

1. Prepare a 10-column work sheet for fiscal 2014, starting with the unadjusted trial balance and including these additional facts:

   a. The inventory of supplies at the end of the year had a cost of $3,200.

   b. The cost of expired insurance for the year is $8,400.

   c. Annual depreciation of the equipment is $17,600.

   d. The September utilities expense was not included in the trial balance because the bill arrived after it was prepared. Its $750 amount needs to be recorded.

   e. The company's employees have earned $4,200 of accrued wages.

   f. The interest expense of $120 for September has not yet been paid or recorded.

2. Use the work sheet to prepare the adjusting and closing entries.

3. Prepare an income statement, a statement of changes in equity, and a classified balance sheet. $16,000 of the long-term note payable is to be paid by September 30, 2015.

Analysis Component: Analyze the following potential errors and describe how each would affect the 10-column work sheet. Explain whether the error is likely to be discovered in completing the work sheet and, if not, the effect of the error on the financial statements.

a. The adjustment to record used supplies was credited to Supplies for $3,200 and debited the same amount to Supplies Expense.

b. When completing the adjusted trial balance in the work sheet, the $22,000 cash balance was incorrectly entered in the Credit column.

CHECK FIGURE:
2. Post-closing trial balance = $122,000

Problem 4-4A Closing entries LO²,³,⁴

MY Autobody's adjusted trial balance on December 31, 2014, appears in the work sheet as follows:

No.	Account	Debit	Credit
101	Cash	$ 28,000	
124	Shop supplies	1,800	
128	Prepaid insurance	4,200	
167	Equipment	88,000	
168	Accumulated depreciation, equipment		$ 7,500
201	Accounts payable		19,000
210	Wages payable		8,860
301	Mike Yang, capital		140,000
302	Mike Yang, withdrawals	36,000	
401	Repair fees earned		157,630
612	Depreciation expense, equipment	8,500	
623	Wages expense	104,500	
637	Insurance expense	1,900	
640	Rent expense	52,350	
650	Office supplies expense	4,800	
690	Utilities expense	2,940	
	Totals	$332,990	$332,990

Required

1. Prepare closing entries.

2. Prepare the post-closing trial balance at December 31, 2014.

CHECK FIGURES:
Net loss = $17,360;
Total assets = $114,500

Problem 4-5A Financial statements LO⁶

Using the information from Problem 4-4A, prepare an income statement and a statement of changes in equity for the year ended December 31, 2014, and a classified balance sheet at December 31, 2014. There were no investments by the owner during the year.

Analysis Component: MY Autobody experienced a loss during 2014. If you were one of the business's creditors, should this loss cause you to be concerned about being paid in 2015?

Problem 4-6A Closing entries LO²,³

The adjusted trial balance for Lloyd Construction as of December 31, 2014, follows:

No.	Account	Debit	Credit
101	Cash	$ 16,000	
104	Short-term investments...	21,000	
126	Supplies	7,600	
149	Notes receivable	42,000	
167	Equipment...	78,000	
168	Accumulated depreciation, equipment.............................		$ 38,000
173	Building	260,000	
174	Accumulated depreciation, building.................................		141,000
183	Land	86,000	
193	Franchise..	31,000	
201	Accounts payable..		17,000
203	Interest payable		130
233	Unearned professional fees..		27,000
251	Long-term notes payable		132,000
301	Sig Lloyd, capital..		92,000
302	Sig Lloyd, withdrawals	3,000	
401	Professional fees earned		206,480
406	Rent earned		26,000
606	Depreciation expense, building....................................	20,000	
612	Depreciation expense, equipment...............................	8,000	
623	Wages expense	64,000	
633	Interest expense...	610	
637	Insurance expense..	18,000	
652	Supplies expense..	12,800	
688	Telephone expense	4,400	
690	Utilities expense	7,200	
	Totals	$679,610	$679,610

An analysis of other information reveals that Lloyd Construction is required to make a $45,000 payment on the long-term notes payable during 2015. The notes receivable are due May 1, 2016. Also, Sig Lloyd invested $75,000 cash early in 2014.

Required Prepare the closing entries made at the end of the year.

CHECK FIGURES:
Net income = $97,470;
Total assets = $362,600

Problem 4-7A Financial statements LO⁶

Using the adjusted trial balance in Problem 4-6A, prepare the income statement and statement of changes in equity for the year ended December 31, 2014, and the classified balance sheet at December 31, 2014.

Analysis Component: Why must liabilities be separated on the balance sheet between *current* and *long-term*? What effect would it have had on Lloyd's balance sheet if the long-term note was not separated?

Problem 4-8A Closing entries LO²,³

The March 31, 2014, adjusted trial balance for Brenner Climbing Adventures has been alphabetized as follows:

No.	Account	Debit	Credit
201	Accounts payable		$ 2,600
103	Accounts receivable	$ 7,100	
168	Accumulated depreciation, equipment		7,000
300	Becky Brenner, capital		34,700
301	Becky Brenner, withdrawals	31,200	
101	Cash	9,600	
194	Copyright	6,500	
606	Depreciation expense, equipment	1,100	
167	Equipment	22,000	
633	Insurance expense	1,875	
623	Interest expense	120	
141	Notes receivable, due January 1, 2017	10,000	
233	Long-term notes payable		19,000
610	Rent expense	7,500	
402	Revenues		64,515
126	Supplies	270	
637	Supplies expense	1,800	
652	Telephone expense	2,300	
203	Unearned revenues		9,100
688	Utilities expense	2,150	
612	Wages expense	33,400	
	Totals	$136,915	$136,915

Required Journalize the closing entries.

CHECK FIGURES:
Net income = $14,270;
Total assets = $48,470

Problem 4-9A Financial statements LO⁶

Using the information in Problem 4-8A, prepare an income statement and a statement of changes in equity for the year ended March 31, 2014, and a classified balance sheet at March 31, 2014. The owner made an additional investment during the year of $15,000. A $6,500 payment on the long-term notes payable will be made during the year ended March 31, 2015.

Analysis Component: Why might Brenner Climbing Adventures be tempted to report the notes receivable as a current asset on the March 31, 2014, balance sheet?

Problem 4-10A Analyzing closing entries LO^{2,3,4}

The following closing entries were prepared for Apex Architectural Designs regarding its year just ended June 30, 2014:

2014				
June 30	Design Fees Earned..	136,000	
	Income Summary		136,000
	To close the revenue account.		
30	Income Summary...	75,200	
	Depreciation Expense, Office Equipment ...		1,750
	Depreciation Expense, Office Furniture		950
	Insurance Expense		1,200
	Interest Expense...		350
	Supplies Expense		2,150
	Telephone Expense.....................................		1,600
	Utilities Expense...		2,700
	Salaries Expense...		64,500
	To close expense accounts.		
June 30	Income Summary...	60,800	
	Noel Apex, Capital.....................................		60,800
	To close Income Summary to capital.		
30	Noel Apex, Capital...	35,000	
	Noel Apex, Withdrawals.............................		35,000
	To close withdrawals to capital.		

Required

1. Prepare an income statement based on the information provided.

2. Calculate the post-closing balance in the capital account at June 30, 2014, given that the adjusted balance on June 30, 2013, was $86,000.

Problem 4-11A Preparing financial statements LO^6

The adjusted trial balance for Impressions Dance School has been provided for the year ended September 30, 2014. The new bookkeeper alphabetized the accounts.

Account	Debit	Credit
Accounts payable..		$ 22,680
Accounts receivable	$ 13,500	
Accumulated depreciation, automobiles...........................		39,360
Accumulated depreciation, building.................................		164,000
Alisha Bjorn, capital...		168,960
Alisha Bjorn, withdrawals	10,000	
Automobiles...	71,000	
Building	236,000	
Cash	11,600	
Copyright	6,900	
Depreciation expense, automobiles.................................	7,100	
Depreciation expense, building......................................	28,400	
Fees earned...		154,680
Gas, oil, and repairs expense...	29,600	
Land	32,900	
Land for future expansion	50,000	
Notes payable*..		90,000
Patents..	8,800	
Rent earned		21,000
Salaries expense...	174,000	
Store supplies..	4,380	
Unearned fees..		23,500
Totals	$684,180	$684,180

*The notes payable plus interest are due in 18 months.

Required Prepare an income statement and a statement of changes in equity for the year ended September 30, 2014, plus a September 30, 2014, classified balance sheet. The owner made no investments during the year.

Analysis Component: Alisha wants to buy a new car for the business. As her bank manager, what do you advise?

CHECK FIGURES:
1. Capital = $520,775
2. Total assets = $895,400

Problem 4-12A Preparing a classified balance sheet LO⁶

An alphabetical list of the adjusted trial balance accounts for North Country Rentals after its first year of operations ending March 31, 2014, is shown below:

Account	Adjusted Account Balance*
Accounts payable	$ 9,100
Accumulated depreciation, building	25,000
Accumulated depreciation, furniture	3,500
Advertising expense	16,200
Building	591,000
Cash	17,000
Depreciation expense, building	25,000
Depreciation expense, furniture	3,500
Furniture	42,800
Interest expense	10,260
Interest payable	900
Janitorial expense	41,000
Land	110,000
Long-term notes payable	362,000
Notes receivable, due 2017	143,000
Office salaries expense	126,625
Office supplies	700
Office supplies expense	6,100
Patent	3,000
Prepaid advertising	400
Rent earned	398,400
Rent receivable	16,000
Salaries payable	2,625
Utilities expense	36,720
Wyett North, capital	415,780
Wyett North, withdrawals	28,000

*Assume all accounts have a normal balance.

Required

1. Calculate the capital balance as it would appear on the March 31, 2014, balance sheet.

2. Prepare a classified balance sheet. Assume that $215,000 of the Long-Term Notes Payable will be paid during the year ended March 31, 2015. Also, $55,000 of the notes receivable will be collected by March 31, 2015.

Analysis Component: North Country shows an adjusted balance in the *Long-Term Notes Payable* account of $362,000 at March 31, 2014. Review the balance sheet just prepared and make a reasonable assumption about what the $362,000 was most logically used for by North Country. Explain whether or not this is generally considered a good use of borrowed funds and why.

Problem 4-13A Performing the steps in the accounting cycle LO^{2,3,4,5,6}

On June 1, 2014, Sam Near created a new travel agency called Tours-For-Less. These activities occurred during the company's first month:

June	1	Near created the new company by investing $40,000 cash, $5,000 of furniture, and computer equipment worth $60,000.
	2	The company rented furnished office space by paying $3,200 rent for the first month.
	3	The company purchased $2,400 of office supplies for cash.
	10	The company paid $7,200 for the premium on a one-year insurance policy.
	14	The owner's assistant was paid $3,600 for two weeks' salary.
	24	The company collected $13,600 of commissions from airlines on tickets obtained for customers.
	28	The assistant was paid another $3,600 for two weeks' salary.
	29	The company paid the month's $3,500 phone bill.
	30	The company repaired its computer for $700 on account.
	30	The owner withdrew $2,850 cash from the business for personal use.

The company's chart of accounts included these accounts:

101	Cash		302	Sam Near, Withdrawals
106	Accounts Receivable		405	Commissions Earned
124	Office Supplies		610	Depreciation Expense, Furniture
128	Prepaid Insurance		612	Depreciation Expense,
160	Furniture			Computer Equipment
161	Accumulated Depreciation, Furniture		622	Salaries Expense
167	Computer Equipment		637	Insurance Expense
168	Accumulated Depreciation,		640	Rent Expense
	Computer Equipment		650	Office Supplies Expense
201	Accounts Payable		684	Repairs Expense
209	Salaries Payable		688	Telephone Expense
301	Sam Near, Capital		901	Income Summary

Required

1. Set up each of the listed accounts. *Note: Your instructor will tell you to use either the balance column format or T-accounts.*

2. Prepare journal entries to record the transactions for June and post them to the accounts.

3. Use the following information to journalize and post the adjustments for the month:

   a. Two-thirds of one month's insurance coverage was consumed.

   b. There were $1,600 of office supplies on hand at the end of the month.

   c. Depreciation on the computer equipment was estimated to be $1,650 and $400 on the furniture.

   d. The assistant had earned $320 of unpaid and unrecorded salary.

   e. The company had earned $3,500 of commissions that had not yet been billed.

4. Prepare an income statement, a statement of changes in equity, and a classified balance sheet.

5. Prepare journal entries to close the temporary accounts and post them to the accounts.

6. Prepare a post-closing trial balance.

*Problem 4-14A Adjusting, reversing, and subsequent cash entries LO[7]

The unadjusted trial balance for Lewis Fitness Centre as of December 31, 2014, follows:

Account	Debit	Credit
Cash	$ 22,000	
Accounts receivable	-0-	
Supplies	9,000	
Equipment	300,000	
Accumulated depreciation, equipment		$ 30,000
Interest payable		-0-
Salaries payable		-0-
Unearned membership fees		48,000
Notes payable		100,000
Bev Lewis, capital		116,500
Bev Lewis, withdrawals	60,000	
Membership fees earned		180,000
Depreciation expense, equipment	-0-	
Salaries expense	76,000	
Interest expense	7,500	
Supplies expense	-0-	
Totals	$474,500	$474,500

Information necessary to prepare adjusting entries is as follows:

a. As of December 31, employees have earned $1,600 of unpaid and unrecorded wages. The next payday is January 4, and the total wages to be paid will be $2,400.

b. The cost of supplies on hand at December 31 is $3,600.

c. The note payable requires an interest payment to be made every three months. The amount of unrecorded accrued interest at December 31 is $2,500, and the next payment is due on January 15. This payment will be $3,000.

d. An analysis of the unearned membership fees shows that $32,000 remains unearned at December 31.

e. In addition to the membership fees included in the revenue account, the company has earned another $24,000 in fees that will be collected on January 21. The company is also expected to collect $14,000 on the same day for new fees earned during January.

f. Depreciation expense for the year is $30,000.

Required

1. Prepare adjusting journal entries.
2. Prepare journal entries to reverse the effects of the adjusting entries that involve accruals.
3. Prepare journal entries to record the cash payments and collections that are described for January.

ALTERNATE PROBLEMS

Problem 4-1B Completing a work sheet LO[1]

The July 31, 2014, unadjusted trial balance for Daimler Tours after its first month of operations is shown below:

No.	Account	Dr.	Cr.
	Daimler Tours		
	Unadjusted Trial Balance		
	July 31, 2014		
		Unadjusted Trial Balance	
		Dr.	Cr.
101	Cash	$ 9,100	
106	Accounts receivable	18,700	
111	Notes receivable, due Feb. 2015	16,000	
128	Prepaid insurance	5,100	
161	Furniture	6,750	
201	Accounts payable		$ 6,925
230	Unearned tour revenue		12,430
301	Jan Rider, capital		60,975
302	Jan Rider, withdrawals	-0-	
403	Tour revenue		16,700
623	Wages expense	41,380	
	Totals	$ 97,030	$ 97,030

Required

1. Enter the unadjusted trial balance onto a work sheet.

2. Using the following additional information, enter the adjustments into the work sheet (the Chart of Accounts at the back of the textbook may be useful when additional accounts are required):

   a. Interest of $40 had accrued on the note receivable by month-end.

   b. The July utility bill for $175 was received in the mail on July 31. It is unpaid and unrecorded.

   c. Depreciation on the furniture for the month of July is $210.

   d. The balance in Prepaid Insurance is from a six-month policy that went into effect on July 1, 2014.

   e. The company has two part-time employees, each of whom gets paid $315 every Friday for a five-day part-time workweek. July 31 falls on a Tuesday, therefore two days of accrued wages need to be recorded.

   f. At July 31, it was determined that $4,900 of the balance in Unearned Tour Revenue was not yet earned.

   g. Accrued tour revenue of $1,600 was unrecorded and uncollected at July 31.

3. Complete the work sheet.

Problem 4-2B Completing a work sheet—net income LO[1]

The December 31, 2014, unadjusted trial balance for Tucker Photographers after the first month of operations is shown below:

		Tucker Photographers Trial Balance.xls	
	Home Insert Page Layout Formulas Data Review View		
	P18	fx	
	A	**B**	**C**

	Account	Unadjusted Trial Balance Dr.	Cr.
1	**Tucker Photographers**		
2	**Unadjusted Trial Balance**		
3	**December 31, 2014**		
4		**Unadjusted**	
5		**Trial Balance**	
6	**Account**	**Dr.**	**Cr.**
7	Cash	$ 9,100	
8	Accounts receivable	13,000	
9	Prepaid equipment rental	3,860	
10	Automobile	49,000	
11	Accumulated depreciation, automobile		$ -0-
12	Accounts payable		1,920
13	Unearned fees		5,740
14	Jim Tucker, capital		65,700
15	Jim Tucker, withdrawals	2,600	
16	Fees earned		8,400
17	Depreciation expense, automobile	-0-	
18	Equipment rental expense	4,200	
19	**Totals**	$ 81,760	$ 81,760

Required

1. Enter the unadjusted trial balance onto a work sheet.

2. Using the following additional information, enter the adjustments into the work sheet.

   a. It was determined that $2,000 of the balance in the Prepaid Equipment Rental account had been used during December.

   b. Depreciation on the automobile for the month of December was $610.

   c. Accrued utilities expense of $940 was unrecorded at December 31.

   d. $460 of the Unearned Fees account had been earned by December 31.

3. Complete the work sheet.

4. Calculate the balance in the capital account as it would appear on the December 31, 2014, balance sheet.

Analysis Component: What effect does a net income have on the balance sheet?

Problem 4-3B Work sheet, journal entries, financial statements LO[1,6]

Presented below is the unadjusted trial balance of Webster Demolition Company as of June 30, 2014, the end of its fiscal year. The owner invested $17,500 cash in the company during the year.

Webster Demolition Company Trial Balance.xls

Home   Insert   Page Layout   Formulas   Data   Review   View

P18   fx

	A	B	C
1	**Webster Demolition Company**		
2	**Unadjusted Trial Balance**		
3	**June 30, 2014**		
4		**Unadjusted**	
5		**Trial Balance**	
6	**No.** **Account**	**Dr.**	**Cr.**
7	101 Cash	$ 4,500	
8	126 Supplies	8,200	
9	128 Prepaid insurance	7,300	
10	167 Equipment	72,000	
11	168 Accumulated depreciation, equipment		$ 5,000
12	201 Accounts payable		9,100
13	203 Interest payable		-0-
14	210 Wages payable		-0-
15	251 Long-term notes payable		45,000
16	301 Rusty Webster, capital		21,400
17	302 Rusty Webster, withdrawals	2,100	
18	401 Demolition fees earned		83,300
19	612 Depreciation expense, equipment	-0-	
20	623 Wages expense	27,400	
21	633 Interest expense	1,100	
22	637 Insurance expense	-0-	
23	640 Rent expense	24,400	
24	652 Supplies expense	-0-	
25	683 Business tax expense	4,200	
26	684 Repairs expense	4,200	
27	690 Utilities expense	8,400	
28	**Totals**	**$ 163,800**	**$ 163,800**

Required

Preparation Component:

1. Prepare a 10-column work sheet for 2014, starting with the unadjusted trial balance and including these additional facts:

   a. The inventory of supplies at the end of the year had a cost of $6,800.

   b. The cost of expired insurance for the year is $5,750.

   c. Annual depreciation on the equipment is $8,700.

   d. The June utilities expense of $375 was not included in the trial balance because the bill arrived after it was prepared. The $375 amount owed needs to be recorded.

   e. The company's employees have earned $1,100 of accrued wages.

   f. Interest of $110 for June has not yet been paid or recorded. In addition, the company is required to make a $2,000 payment on the note on August 30, 2014.

2. Use the work sheet to journalize the adjusting and closing entries.

3. Prepare an income statement, a statement of changes in equity, and a classified balance sheet.

Analysis Component: Analyze the following independent errors and describe how each would affect the 10-column work sheet. Explain whether the error is likely to be discovered in completing the work sheet and, if not, the effect of the error on the financial statements.

    a. The adjustment for consumption of the insurance coverage credited the Prepaid Insurance account for $5,750 and debited the same amount to the Insurance Expense account.

    b. When completing the adjusted trial balance in the work sheet, the $4,200 Repairs Expense account balance was extended to the Debit column for the balance sheet.

Problem 4-4B Closing entries LO²,³,⁴

CHECK FIGURE:
2. Post-closing trial
balance = $86,800

Dillan's Tailoring Services' adjusted trial balance on December 31, 2014, appears as follows:

No.	Account	Debit	Credit
101	Cash	$ 15,500	
125	Store supplies..	6,500	
128	Prepaid insurance..	3,800	
167	Equipment	61,000	
168	Accumulated depreciation, equipment..........................		$ 19,700
201	Accounts payable...		39,400
210	Wages payable...		6,400
301	Vy Dillan, capital		23,300
302	Vy Dillan, withdrawals..	32,000	
401	Sewing fees earned		109,920
612	Depreciation expense, equipment.................................	5,400	
623	Wages expense	61,200	
637	Insurance expense..	2,200	
640	Rent expense	4,800	
651	Store supplies expense	2,600	
690	Utilities expense...	3,720	
	Totals...	$198,720	$198,720

Required

    1. Prepare closing entries.

    2. Prepare a post-closing trial balance.

Problem 4-5B Financial statements LO⁶

CHECK FIGURES:
Net income = $30,000;
Total assets = $67,100

Using the information from Problem 4-4B, prepare an income statement and a statement of changes in equity for the year ended December 31, 2014, and a classified balance sheet at December 31, 2014. The owner made no investments during the year.

Analysis Component: Dillan's Tailoring Services experienced a net income during 2014. If you were one of the business's creditors, would you conclude that because of this net income Dillan's Tailoring will pay its obligations in 2015?

Problem 4-6B Closing entries LO^{2,3}

The adjusted trial balance for Warren's Photo Studio as of December 31, 2014, follows:

No.	Account	Debit	Credit
101	Cash	$ 4,100	
104	Short-term investments	6,800	
126	Supplies	2,250	
149	Notes receivable, due May 1, 2016	41,000	
167	Equipment	27,000	
168	Accumulated depreciation, equipment		$ 14,600
173	Building	69,400	
174	Accumulated depreciation, building		58,000
183	Land	47,000	
193	Franchise	8,900	
201	Accounts payable		5,000
203	Unearned professional fees		1,300
233	Long-term notes payable		64,000
251	Warren Jones, capital		31,000
301	Warren Jones, withdrawals	1,500	
302	Photography fees earned		86,342
401	Interest earned		240
605	Depreciation expense, building	4,000	
606	Depreciation expense, equipment	3,000	
612	Wages expense	34,000	
623	Interest expense	2,400	
633	Insurance expense	2,850	
637	Supplies expense	1,800	
652	Telephone expense	842	
688	Utilities expense	3,640	
	Totals	$260,482	$260,482

An analysis of other information reveals that Warren's Photo Studio is required to make a $25,000 payment on the long-term notes payable during 2015. Also, Warren Jones invested $15,000 cash early in the year.

Required Prepare the closing entries made at the end of the year.

Problem 4-7B Financial statements LO^6

Using the adjusted trial balance in Problem 4-6B, prepare the income statement, statement of changes in equity, and classified balance sheet.

Analysis Component: Why must liabilities be separated on the balance sheet between *current* and *long-term*? What effect would it have had on Warren's balance sheet if the long-term notes were not separated?

Problem 4-8B Closing entries LO²,³

The December 31, 2014, adjusted trial balance for Eagle Consulting Services has been alphabetized as follows:

No.	Account	Debit	Credit
201	Accounts payable..		$ 720
168	Accumulated depreciation, equipment..........................		8,250
184	Accumulated depreciation, office furniture....................		3,100
101	Cash	$ 1,500	
302	Consulting fees earned..		45,000
194	Copyright	4,200	
251	Dan Eagle, capital		24,715
301	Dan Eagle, withdrawals...	3,500	
406	Depreciation expense, equipment.................................	1,000	
606	Depreciation expense, office furniture..........................	700	
167	Equipment..	16,000	
633	Insurance expense..	600	
401	Interest earned...		70
623	Interest expense...	30	
233	Long-term notes payable		4,000
145	Notes receivable	5,000	
183	Office furniture	5,100	
104	Short-term investments...	4,000	
126	Supplies	750	
637	Supplies expense..	2,150	
652	Telephone expense	470	
203	Unearned consulting fees..		375
688	Utilities expense...	3,230	
612	Wages expense	38,000	
	Totals..	$86,230	$86,230

Required Prepare the closing entries.

Problem 4-9B Financial statements LO⁶

Using the information in Problem 4-8B, prepare an income statement and a statement of changes in equity for the year ended December 31, 2014, and a classified balance sheet at December 31, 2014. The owner made no additional investments during the year. A $2,500 payment on the long-term notes payable will be made during 2015. Also, $1,500 of the notes receivable will be collected by December 31, 2015.

Analysis Component: Eagle Consulting's equity decreased by $4,610 during 2014. What effect does a decrease in equity have on the other major components of the balance sheet?

Problem 4-10B Analyzing closing entries LO²,³,⁴

The following closing entries were prepared for Greenway Gardening Services regarding the year ended October 31, 2014:

	2014			
Oct.	31	Service Revenue	136,000	
		Income Summary		136,000
		To close the revenue account.		
	31	Income Summary...	177,290	
		Depreciation Expense,		
		Gardening Equipment		9,950
		Depreciation Expense, Vehicles		10,600
		Insurance Expense		6,900
		Interest Expense..		340
		Supplies Expense		24,800
		Telephone Expense....................................		1,700
		Utilities Expense..		1,800
		Fuel Expense..		9,200
		Wages Expense..		112,000
		To close expense accounts.		
Oct.	31	Grant Greenway, Capital............................	41,290	
		Income Summary		41,290
		To close the Income Summary to capital.		
	31	Grant Greenway, Capital............................	10,000	
		Grant Greenway, Withdrawals		10,000
		To close withdrawals to capital.		

Required

1. Prepare an income statement based on the information provided.

2. Calculate the post-closing balance in the capital account at October 31, 2014, given that the adjusted balance on October 31, 2013, was $76,000.

Problem 4-11B Preparing financial statements LO⁶

Required Using the adjusted trial balance below, for FairQuest Drill Servicing for the year ended August 31, 2014, prepare an income statement, statement of changes in equity, and classified balance sheet. The owner made a $50,000 investment into the business during the year.

No.	Account	Debit	Credit
101	Cash	$ 7,500	
106	Accounts receivable	16,000	
109	Interest receivable..	280	
124	Office supplies	1,700	
141	Long-term investment in Nova shares	35,000	
161	Furniture...	81,000	
162	Accumulated depreciation, furniture		$ 21,400
193	Franchise...	16,500	
201	Accounts payable..		4,300
205	Notes payable, due in 7 months		3,200
230	Unearned servicing revenue.............................		5,000
251	Long-term notes payable*.................................		31,000
301	Jade Fairquest, capital		61,400
302	Jade Fairquest, withdrawals...........................	4,000	
403	Drill servicing revenue.....................................		171,080
409	Interest earned..		2,600
601	Depreciation expense, furniture	2,060	
623	Wages expense	116,000	
637	Insurance expense...	16,680	
688	Telephone expense	2,800	
690	Utilities expense..	460	
	Totals	$299,980	$299,980

*An $18,000 payment will be made on the long-term notes payable during the year ended August 31, 2015.

Analysis Component: Why might FairQuest Drill Servicing be tempted to report the investment in Nova shares as a current asset on the August 31, 2014, balance sheet?

Problem 4-12B Preparing a classified balance sheet LO[6]

An alphabetical list of the adjusted trial balance accounts at July 31, 2014, for Delta Tours after its first month of operations is shown below:

Account	Adjusted Account Balance*
Accounts payable	$ 27,000
Accounts receivable	21,300
Accumulated depreciation, furniture	700
Cash	25,300
Depreciation expense, furniture	700
Furniture	29,000
Insurance expense	5,250
Interest receivable	100
Interest revenue	700
Jan Delta, capital	95,434
Jan Delta, withdrawals	10,700
Notes receivable (due in 6 months)	56,000
Prepaid insurance	2,100
Tour revenue	146,000
Unearned tour revenue	19,600
Utility expense	1,300
Wages expense	139,700
Wages payable	2,016

*Assume all accounts have a normal balance.

Required

1. Calculate the capital balance as it would appear on the July 31, 2014, balance sheet.
2. Prepare a classified balance sheet.

Problem 4-13B Performing the steps in the accounting cycle LO²,³,⁴,⁵,⁶

On July 1, 2014, Amy Young created a new self-storage business called Young Co. These events occurred during the company's first month:

July	1	Young invested $40,000 cash and land and buildings worth $320,000 and $240,000, respectively.
	2	Rented equipment by paying $3,600 rent for the first month.
	5	Purchased $4,600 of office supplies for cash.
	10	Paid $10,800 for the premium on a one-year insurance policy effective today.
	14	Paid an employee $1,800 for two weeks' salary.
	24	Collected $17,600 of storage fees from customers.
	28	Paid another $1,800 for two weeks' salary.
	29	Paid the month's $600 phone bill.
	30	Repaired leaking roof for $1,700 on account.
	31	Young withdrew $3,200 cash from the business for personal use.

The company's chart of accounts included these accounts:

101	Cash	201	Accounts Payable	637	Insurance Expense
106	Accounts Receivable	209	Salaries Payable	640	Equipment Rental Expense
124	Office Supplies	301	Amy Young, Capital	650	Office Supplies Expense
128	Prepaid Insurance	302	Amy Young, Withdrawals	684	Repairs Expense
170	Land	401	Storage Fees Earned	688	Telephone Expense
173	Buildings	606	Depreciation Expense, Buildings	901	Income Summary
174	Accumulated Depreciation, Buildings	622	Salaries Expense		

Required

1. Set up each of the listed accounts. *Note: Your instructor will tell you to use either the balance column format or T-accounts.*

2. Prepare journal entries to record the transactions for July and post them to the accounts. Record prepaid and unearned items in balance sheet accounts.

3. Use the following information to journalize and post the adjustments for the month:

   a. Two-thirds of one month's insurance coverage was consumed.

   b. There were $3,100 of office supplies on hand at the end of the month.

   c. Depreciation on the buildings was estimated to be $2,400 per month.

   d. The employee had earned $360 of unpaid and unrecorded salary.

   e. The company had earned $1,900 of storage fees that had not yet been billed.

4. Prepare an income statement, a statement of changes in equity, and a classified balance sheet.

5. Prepare journal entries to close the temporary accounts and post them to the accounts.

6. Prepare a post-closing trial balance.

*Problem 4-14B Adjusting, reversing, and subsequent cash entries LO⁷

IBS Company's unadjusted trial balance on December 31, 2014, the end of its annual accounting period, is as follows:

Account	Debit	Credit
Cash	$ 73,725	
Note receivable..	37,500	
Office supplies..	4,200	
Land	45,000	
Unearned service fees..		$ 18,000
Note payable		90,000
Jean Boat, capital		37,500
Jean Boat, withdrawals	60,000	
Service fees earned..		267,000
Interest revenue		2,550
Rent revenue..		12,375
Salaries expense	193,500	
Insurance expense..	4,950	
Interest expense...	8,550	
Totals	$427,425	$427,425

Information necessary to prepare adjusting entries is as follows:

a. Employees, who are paid $7,500 every two weeks, have earned $5,250 since the last payment. The next payment of $7,500 will be on January 4.

b. IBS rents office space to a tenant who has paid only $450 of the $1,125 rent for December. On January 12, the tenant will pay the remainder along with the rent for January.

c. An inventory of office supplies discloses $675 of unused supplies.

d. Premiums for insurance against injuries to employees are paid monthly. The $450 premium for December will be paid January 12.

e. IBS owes $90,000 on a note payable that requires quarterly payments of accrued interest. The quarterly payments of $2,700 each are made on the 15th of January, April, July, and October.

f. An analysis of IBS's service contracts with customers shows that $6,300 of the amount customers have prepaid remains unearned.

g. IBS has a $37,500 note receivable on which interest of $175 has accrued. On January 22, the note and the total accrued interest of $575 will be repaid to IBS.

h. IBS has earned but unrecorded revenue for $8,250 for services provided to a customer who will pay for the work on January 24. At that time, the customer will also pay $3,100 for services IBS will perform in early January.

Required

1. Prepare adjusting journal entries.
2. Prepare reversing entries.
3. Prepare journal entries to record the January 2015 cash receipts and cash payments identified in the above information.

An asterisk (*) identifies assignment material based on Appendix 4A or Appendix 4B.

ANALYTICAL AND REVIEW PROBLEM

A & R Problem 4-1 The owner of Dynamo Stores has come to you for assistance because his bookkeeper has just moved to another city. The following is the only information his bookkeeper left him.

1. Balance sheets as of December 31, 2014 and 2015.

2. The owner withdrew $105,000 in 2015 for his personal use.

3. The business incurred total expenses of $168,000 for 2015, of which $126,000 was for wages and $42,000 was for advertising.

	2015	2014
Assets..	$168,000	$210,000
Liabilities.....................................	$ 42,000	$ 63,000
Capital	126,000	147,000
	$168,000	$210,000

Required

1. Calculate the net income and total revenue for 2015.

2. Prepare closing entries for 2015.

A & R Problem 4-2 The partially completed work sheet for the current fiscal year of Sandy's Delivery Service appears below:

Sandy's Delivery Service Work Sheet.xls

Home   Insert   Page Layout   Formulas   Data   Review   View

P18   fx

Sandy's Delivery Service
Work Sheet
For the Year Ended December 31, 2014

Account	Unadjusted Trial Balance Dr.	Cr.	Adjustments Dr.	Cr.	Adjusted Trial Balance Dr.	Cr.	Income Statement Dr.	Cr.	Balance Sheet & Statement of Changes in Equity Dr.	Cr.
8 Cash	10,650									
9 Accounts receivable	7,000				9,000					
10 Supplies	4,200								1,600	
11 Prepaid insurance	2,400									
12 Prepaid rent	1,800									
13 Delivery trucks	40,000				40,000					
14 Accounts payable		3,130				3,130				
15 Unearned delivery fees		4,500								2,000
16 Sandra Berlasty, capital		50,000								
17 Sandra Berlasty, withdrawals	3,000									
18 Delivery service revenue		18,500								
19 Advertising expense	600									
20 Gas and oil expense	680									
21 Salaries expense	5,600									
22 Utilities expense	200									
23 **Totals**	76,130	76,130								
24 Insurance expense					800					
25 Rent expense					900					
26 Supplies expense										
27 Dep. expense, delivery trucks										
28 Accumulated dep., delivery trucks										2,000
29 Salaries payable										400
30 Net income										

Required

1. Complete the work sheet.

2. Journalize the adjusting and closing entries (omit narratives).

ETHICS CHALLENGE

EC 4-1

On January 20, 2014, Jennifer Nelson, the staff accountant for Newby Enterprises, is feeling pressure to complete the preparation of the annual financial statements. The president of the company has said he needs up-to-date financial statements to share with several bankers on January 21 at a dinner meeting that has been called to discuss the possibility of Newby's obtaining loan financing for a special building project. Jennifer knows that she won't be able to gather all the needed information in the next 24 hours to prepare the entire set of adjusting entries that must be posted before the financial statements will accurately portray the company's performance and financial position for the fiscal period just ended December 31, 2013. Jennifer ultimately decides to estimate several expense accruals at the last minute. When deciding on estimates for the expenses Jennifer uses low estimates as she doesn't want to make the financial statements look worse than they possibly are in reality. Jennifer finishes the financial statements before the deadline and gives them to the president without mentioning that several accounts could only be estimated as to their balance on December 31, 2013.

Required

1. List several courses of action that Jennifer could have taken instead of the one on which she ultimately decided.

2. If you had been in Jennifer's situation, what would you have done? Briefly justify your response.

FOCUS ON FINANCIAL STATEMENTS

FFS 4-1

CHECK FIGURES:
1. Net income = $70,575; Total assets = $95,850
3. Post-closing trial balance = $121,350

Sarda Electrical Servicing began operations two years ago. Its adjusted account balances at December 31, 2014, are listed alphabetically below. The owner, Nymeth Sarda, made a $20,000 investment early in the year just ended December 31, 2014.

Required

1. Prepare an income statement, statement of changes in equity, and classified balance sheet based on the information provided.

2. Prepare the closing entries.   3. Prepare the post-closing trial balance.

Account	Account Balance*
Accounts payable	$ 21,000
Accounts receivable	10,500
Accumulated depreciation, tools	4,500
Accumulated depreciation, truck	21,000
Cash	5,000
Copyright	5,100
Depreciation expense, tools	2,250
Depreciation expense, truck	3,600
Electrical fees earned	126,600
Electrical supplies	19,000
Insurance expense	1,275
Interest expense	900
Notes receivable**	12,000
Nymeth Sarda, capital	27,825
Nymeth Sarda, withdrawals	61,500
Notes payable, due August 31, 2016	27,000
Notes payable, due June 1, 2015	2,550
Prepaid insurance	1,050
Prepaid rent	7,200
Rent expense	21,000
Salaries expense	27,000
Salaries payable	3,150
Tools	21,000
Truck	40,500
Unearned electrical fees	5,250

*Assume all account balances are normal.
**$2,000 of the note is due September 15, 2015.

Analysis Component: Refer to the chapter opening vignette. Kirk Stinchcombe financed growth by reinvesting profits. Is Nymeth Sarda, the owner of Sarda Electrical Servicing, following a similar practice? Explain.

FFS 4-2   **ClubLink Enterprises Limited**, headquartered in King City, Ontario, is Canada's largest owner, operator, and developer of golf courses and resorts. An excerpt from its comparative balance sheet at December 31, 2011, shows the following assets and liabilities, in alphabetical order:

(thousands of dollars)	2011	2010
Accounts payable and accrued liabilities	$ 20,706	$ 17,755
Accounts receivable	3,743	3,238
Cash	1,567	1,447
Goodwill	26,689	26,689
Income taxes receivable	1,322	176
Intangible assets	24,234	24,653
Inventories and prepaid expenses	5,848	5,289
Long-term borrowings	317,767	331,917
Mortgages and loans receivable	4,113	5,744
Mortgages and loans receivable, current portion	1,411	61
Other long-term assets	3,329	3,037
Other long-term liabilities	93,335	91,988
Prepaid annual dues and deposits*	12,965	6,037
Property, plant and equipment	589,876	582,913
Short-term borrowings	27,817	24,839

*These are dues and deposits collected in advance from ClubLink's golf club and resort members.

Required

Part 1

    a.   Calculate total current assets at December 31, 2011, and December 31, 2010.

    b.   Calculate total current liabilities at December 31, 2011, and December 31, 2010.

*Part 2

    c.   Calculate the current ratio for December 31, 2011 and December 31, 2010 (round to two decimal places).

    d.   Explain the meaning of ClubLink's current ratio results calculated in part (c). Also indicate whether the change in the ratio was favourable or unfavourable.

CRITICAL THINKING MINI CASE

The owner of Delton Property Rentals, Teal Delton, has requested an emergency meeting with you, a representative from the bank. "Our accountant has been on leave for the past several months and her replacement has resigned suddenly. I'm told we can't pay our employees this month and your bank won't lend us any money. I don't understand. We have lots of assets that can be used to pay expenses, as you can see from our balance sheet."

Delton Property Rentals Balance Sheet March 31		
	2014	**2013**
Assets	$2,850,000	$750,000
Liabilities	2,780,000	240,000
Equity	70,000	510,000

An asterisk (*) identifies assignment material based on Appendix 4A or Appendix 4B.

You explain to Mr. Delton that you will need to obtain some additional information. He faxes you the following:

Delton Property Rentals Post-Closing Trial Balance March 31		
	2014	**2013**
Accounts payable	$ 340,000	$ 7,000
Accounts receivable	75,000	215,000
Accumulated depreciation, buildings	165,000	150,000
Accumulated depreciation, equipment	35,000	30,000
Buildings	2,112,000	430,000
Cash	15,000	40,000
Equipment	45,000	45,000
Land	675,000	150,000
Notes payable*	2,440,000	204,000
Notes receivable, due Nov. 30, 2018	120,000	-0-
Supplies	8,000	50,000
Teal Delton, capital**	70,000	510,000
Unearned fees	-0-	29,000

*$200,000 principal is due annually each February 1.
**No withdrawals were made during 2013 or 2014.

Required Using the elements of critical thinking described on the inside front cover, comment.

SERIAL PROBLEM

Echo Systems

CHECK FIGURE:
2. Total credits in post-closing trial balance = $155,720

(The first two segments of this comprehensive problem were in Chapters 2 and 3, and the final segment is presented in Chapter 5. If the Chapter 2 and 3 segments have not been completed, the assignment can begin at this point. It is recommended that you use the Working Papers[12] that accompany this book because they reflect the account balances that resulted from posting the entries required in Chapters 2 and 3.)

The transactions of Echo Systems for October through December 2014 have been recorded in the problem segments in Chapters 2 and 3, as well as the year-end adjusting entries. Prior to closing the revenue and expense accounts for 2014, the accounting system is modified to include the Income Summary account, which is given the number 901.

Required

1. Record and post the appropriate closing entries.

2. Prepare a post-closing trial balance.

---

12 If students have not purchased the Working Papers package, the Working Papers for the serial problem are available on Connect.

Accounting for Merchandising Activities

MECING MILLIONS

Mountain Equipment Co-op, more commonly referred to as just MEC, is Canada's leading retailer of outdoor merchandise including clothing and gear for self-propelled sports like cycling, hiking, paddling, and climbing. MEC was founded in 1971 in Vancouver by six individuals interested in providing mountain climbers with reasonably priced, quality wilderness gear. This isn't your usual store, however: MEC is a members-only cooperative and before you can buy or rent from MEC, you have to purchase a $5 membership that is good for your lifetime. This investment in the store hasn't put people off, and in fact, the idea of membership is obviously appealing to many: Membership has grown from 57,000 in 1981 to 330,000 in 1991, to 3.5 million in 2011 when annual sales hit $270 million. MEC now has 15 outlets in six provinces across Canada as well as its online store at www.mec.ca.

MEC carries a huge variety of merchandise inventory and, to minimize its ecological impact, it promotes sustainable products. This means in part that MEC-brand contract manufacturing centres are required to follow MEC's Social Compliance Program designed to improve the human condition in factories. Also, to the greatest extent possible, the components of MEC's products are organic (cotton), recycled (polyester), and PVC-free.

Clearly, implementing the many facets of MEC's philosophy in such a massive business is no simple task. But MEC seeks simplicity wherever it can be found, and inventory management is one such area. MEC's Tim Southam says that "Continually balancing supply against demand is the crux of MEC's inventory management practices. A perpetual inventory system allows us to replenish stock in a timely manner to best meet the needs of our members. It also enables us to respond quickly to discrepancies and gives us a high level of control over our inventory. At any given time—in real time—we are able to access the current inventory levels in our stores and our distribution centre."

MEC celebrated its fortieth year of operation in 2011. As a member of *1% For The Planet* and through its community grants program, MEC is widely recognized for its commitment to sustainable outdoor recreation and environmental initiatives. MEC has raised the bar in terms of how a business can meet social and environmental goals and make millions at the same time.

http://www.mec.ca

LEARNING OBJECTIVES

LO¹ Describe merchandising and identify and explain the important income statement and balance sheet components for a merchandising company.

LO² Describe both perpetual and periodic inventory systems.

LO³ Analyze and record transactions for merchandise purchases and sales using a perpetual system.

LO⁴ Prepare adjustments for a merchandising company.

LO⁵ Define, prepare, and use merchandising income statements.

LO⁶ Prepare closing entries for a merchandising company.

*Appendix 5A

LO⁷ Record and compare merchandising transactions using both periodic and perpetual inventory systems.

*Appendix 5B

LO⁸ Explain and record Provincial Sales Tax (PST) and Goods and Services Tax (GST).

CRITICAL THINKING CHALLENGE | Why would MEC choose a perpetual inventory system over periodic? Is the periodic inventory system acceptable under GAAP?

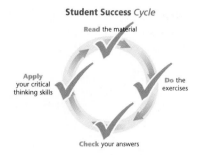

CHAPTER PREVIEW

Our emphasis in previous chapters was on the accounting and reporting activities of companies providing services. Chapter 5 emphasizes merchandising, a major part of modern business. Consumers expect a wealth of products, discount prices, inventory on demand, and high quality. This chapter introduces us to the business and accounting practices used by companies engaged in merchandising activities. These companies buy products and then resell them to customers. We show how financial statements capture merchandising transactions. The new financial statement elements created by merchandising transactions are demonstrated using fictitious information from MEC, the company introduced in the opening article. We also analyze and record merchandise purchases and sales and explain adjusting entries and the closing process for merchandising companies. An understanding of these important topics is what MEC in the opening article knows is necessary to ensure continued success.

MERCHANDISING ACTIVITIES

LO¹ Describe merchandising and identify and explain the important income statement and balance sheet components for a merchandising company.

A merchandising company's activities are different from those of a service company. A **merchandiser** earns net income by buying and selling merchandise. **Merchandise** consists of products, also called *goods*, that a company acquires for the purpose of reselling them to customers. The cost of these goods is an expense called **cost of goods sold (COGS)**.[1]

Merchandisers are often identified as either *wholesalers* or *retailers*. A **wholesaler** is a company that buys products from manufacturers or other wholesalers and sells them to retailers or other wholesalers. Wholesalers include companies such as **Tricana**, **Western Family Foods**, and **Westfair Foods**. A **retailer** is an *intermediary* that buys products from manufacturers or wholesalers and sells them to consumers. Examples of retailers include **Danier Leather**, **Loblaw**, **Canadian Tire**, and **The Gap**. Some retailers, such as **Bell Canada**, often sell both products and services.

Reporting Financial Performance

Net income to a merchandiser results when revenue from selling merchandise exceeds both the cost of merchandise sold to customers and the cost of other operating expenses for the period (see Exhibit 5.1). The usual accounting term for revenues from selling merchandise is *sales*. **Net sales** refers to the result of subtracting *sales discounts*[2] and *sales returns and allowances*[2] from total or gross sales. The term used for the cost of merchandise sold to customers is an expense called *cost of goods sold*.[3] A merchandiser's other expenses are often called *operating expenses*.

EXHIBIT 5.1

Calculating Income for Both a Service Company and a Merchandising Company

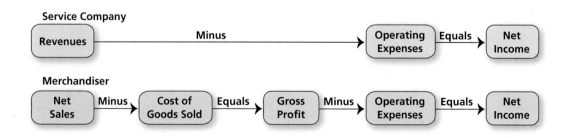

---

1 *Cost of goods sold* is also commonly called **cost of sales**.
2 *Sales discounts* and *sales returns and allowances* are discussed in more detail later in this chapter.
3 When preparing the income statement using the "function of expense" method per IFRS 2012, IAS 1, para. 103, cost of goods sold must be shown separately from other expenses.

MEC Summarized Income Statement Information For Year Ended December 31, 2014	
Net sales...	$314,700
Cost of goods sold..	230,400
Gross profit from sales	$ 84,300
Total operating expenses and other revenues and expenses...................	68,960
Net income	$ 15,340

EXHIBIT 5.2

Summarized Income Statement Information for a Merchandiser

The summarized fictitious income statement information for MEC in Exhibit 5.2 shows us how net sales, gross profit, and income are related. This statement shows that MEC sold products to customers for $314,700. MEC acquired these goods at a cost of $230,400. This yields an $84,300 gross profit. **Gross profit**, also called **gross margin**, equals net sales less cost of goods sold. Changes in gross profit often greatly impact a merchandiser's operations since gross profit must cover all other expenses and yield a return for the owner. MEC, for instance, used gross profit to cover $68,960 of operating and other revenues and expenses. This left $15,340 in net income for the year 2014.

Reporting Financial Position

A merchandising company's balance sheet includes an item not on the balance sheet of a service company. This item is a current asset called *merchandise inventory*. **Merchandise inventory**, or **inventory**, refers to products a company owns for the purpose of selling to customers. Exhibit 5.3 shows the fictitious classified balance sheet for MEC, highlighting merchandise inventory of $21,000. The cost of this asset includes the cost incurred to buy the goods, ship them to the store, and

EXHIBIT 5.3

Classified Balance Sheet for a Merchandiser

MEC Balance Sheet December 31, 2014			
Assets			
Current assets:			
Cash		$ 8,200	
Accounts receivable		11,200	
Merchandise inventory.................................		21,000	
Prepaid expenses		1,100	
Total current assets			$41,500
Plant and equipment:			
Office equipment	$ 4,200		
Less: Accumulated depreciation....................	1,400	$ 2,800	
Store equipment	$30,000		
Less: Accumulated depreciation	6,000	24,000	
Total plant and equipment			26,800
Total assets			$68,300
Liabilities			
Current liabilities:			
Accounts payable		$ 16,000	
Salaries payable		800	
Total liabilities..			$16,800
Equity			
David Wingate*, capital			51,500
Total liabilities and equity.................................			$68,300

*It will be assumed that the owner is David Wingate, one of the six original founders of MEC.

otherwise make them ready for sale. Although companies usually hold inventories of other items such as supplies, *most companies simply refer to merchandise inventory as inventory*. We will use both terms in reference to merchandise inventory.

Operating Cycle

A merchandising company's operating cycle[4] begins with the purchase of merchandise and ends with the collection of cash from the sale of merchandise.

Exhibit 5.4 graphically shows an operating cycle for a merchandiser with (1) cash sales and (2) credit sales. Credit sales delay the receipt of cash until the account receivable is paid by the customer. Companies try to shorten their operating cycles to increase income. Assets tied up in the form of merchandise inventory or receivables are not productive assets. Merchandise inventory is not productive (earning income) until it is sold. Receivables need to be collected so that the resulting cash can be used to earn income. The length of an operating cycle differs across the types of businesses. Department stores such as **Sears** commonly have operating cycles of three to five months, but operating cycles for grocery merchants such as **Loblaw** and **Safeway** usually range from one to two months.

EXHIBIT 5.4

Operating Cycle of a Merchandiser

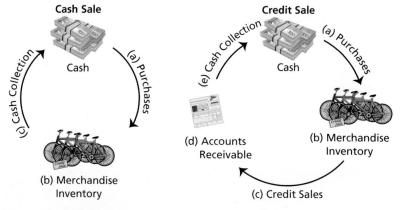

Inventory Systems

Exhibit 5.5 shows that a company's merchandise available for sale is a combination of what it begins with (beginning inventory) and what it purchases (net cost of purchases). The merchandise available is either sold (cost of goods sold) or kept for future sales (ending inventory).

EXHIBIT 5.5

Merchandising Cost Flow

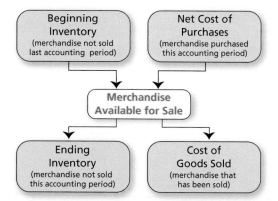

Two inventory accounting systems are used to collect information about cost of goods sold and cost of inventory on hand: *perpetual* and *periodic*. Both inventory systems are generally accepted, therefore, companies have a choice. We introduce these systems in this section.

---

4   IFRS 2012, IAS 1, para. 68.

Perpetual Inventory System

A **perpetual inventory system** gives a continuous record of the amount of inventory on hand. A perpetual system accumulates the net cost of merchandise purchases in the inventory account and transfers the cost of each sale from the inventory account to the Cost of Goods Sold account (COGS) when an item is sold, as shown in the illustration to the right. With a perpetual system, we can find out the cost of merchandise on hand at any time by looking at the balance of the inventory account. We can also find out the cost of goods sold to date during a period by looking at the balance in the Cost of Goods Sold account.

Before advancements in computing technology, a perpetual system was often limited to businesses making a small number of daily sales, such as automobile dealers and major appliance stores. Because there were relatively few transactions, a perpetual system was feasible. Today, with widespread use of computing technology, the use of a perpetual system has dramatically grown to include merchandisers with high-volume sales as well, such as **Wal-Mart**, **Canadian Tire**, **Superstore**, **Staples**, **Leon's**, and **London Drugs**. The number of companies that use a perpetual system continues to increase.

Because perpetual inventory systems give users more timely information and are widely used in practice, our discussion in this chapter emphasizes a perpetual system.

Periodic Inventory System

A **periodic inventory system** requires updating the inventory account only at the *end of a period* to reflect the quantity and cost of both goods on hand and goods sold. It does not require continual updating of the inventory account. The company records the cost of new merchandise in a temporary expense account called *Purchases*. When merchandise is sold, revenue is recorded but the cost of the merchandise sold is *not* recorded as a cost at this time. When financial statements are prepared, the company takes a *physical count of inventory* by counting the quantities of merchandise on hand. Cost of merchandise on hand is determined by relating the quantities on hand to records showing each item's original cost. This cost of merchandise on hand is used to calculate cost of goods sold as shown to the right. The inventory account is then adjusted to reflect the amount from the physical count of inventory.

Periodic systems were historically used by companies such as hardware, drug, and department stores that sold large quantities of low-value items. Before computers and scanners, it was not feasible for accounting systems to track such small items as nails, pencils, toothpaste, paper clips, and socks through inventory and into customers' hands. *We analyze and record merchandising transactions using both periodic and perpetual inventory systems in Appendix 5A.*

LO² Describe both perpetual and periodic inventory systems.

Merchandise Inventory (MI)

Beginning MI 10	LESS	
PLUS	COGS	COGS
Purchases 50	55 ---→55	
EQUALS		
Ending MI 5		

Under a perpetual system, the MI account is updated continually for purchases and goods sold. The balance in MI and COGS is always up to date.

Merchandise Inventory (MI)

| Beginning MI 10 | |

PLUS

Purchases

| Purchases   50 | |

LESS
Ending MI (per a physical count)
5
EQUALS
COGS
55

Under a periodic system, the MI account is updated when a physical count is performed. COGS is *calculated* once ending MI is known.

DECISION INSIGHT

From Periodic to Perpetual to Virtual Inventory Systems
"Traditional models . . . are going away," according to Keyur Patel, a KPMG partner. Web businesses are changing the way inventory is managed and accounted for. Rather than risk having too little or too much in inventory along with all of the related costs, e-businesses are turning to the manufacturers to package and ship products direct to consumers. The result is that these merchants maintain zero inventory. Instead, they take customer orders and transmit that information directly to the respective manufacturer, who fulfills the distribution obligation to the customer. Therefore, for these merchants, discussion of an inventory costing system has become redundant.

SOURCE: www.planetit.com

CHECKPOINT

1. Describe a company's cost of goods sold.
2. What is gross profit for a merchandising company?
3. Explain why use of the perpetual inventory system has grown dramatically.

Do Quick Study questions: QS 5-1, QS 5-2, QS 5-3, QS 5-4

ACCOUNTING FOR MERCHANDISE TRANSACTIONS—PERPETUAL INVENTORY SYSTEM

LO³ Analyze and record transactions for merchandise purchases and sales using a perpetual system.

Recording merchandise transactions involves issues regarding the purchase and sale of merchandise inventory. In this first section, we will examine purchase transactions and associated items. Then, in the next section, transactions related to sales will be examined.

Accounting for Merchandise Purchases—Perpetual Inventory System

With a perpetual inventory system, the cost of merchandise bought for resale is recorded in the Merchandise Inventory account. MEC records a $1,200 credit purchase of merchandise on November 2 with this entry:

Nov.	2	Merchandise Inventory	1,200	
		Accounts Payable.................................		1,200
		Purchased merchandise on credit.		

Note that neither GST (Goods and Services Tax) nor PST (Provincial Sales Tax) has been considered in this transaction. The accounting for GST and PST is deferred to Appendix 5B. Although GST and PST affect merchandising transactions, they are specifically a tax issue. To include discussion of GST and PST at this point would complicate merchandising transactions for the introductory student.

The invoice for this merchandise is shown in Exhibit 5.6. The buyer usually receives the original, while the seller keeps a copy. This single source document serves as the purchase invoice of MEC (buyer) and the sales invoice for Trex (seller). The amount recorded for merchandise inventory includes its purchase cost, shipping fees, taxes, and any other costs necessary to make it ready for sale.

To calculate the total cost of merchandise purchases, we must adjust the invoice cost for:

(1) Any returns and allowances for unsatisfactory items received from a supplier;

(2) Any discounts given to a purchaser by a supplier for early payment; and

(3) Any required freight costs paid by a purchaser.

This section explains these items in more detail.

Purchase Returns and Allowances

Purchase returns are merchandise received by a purchaser but returned to the supplier. Reasons for returns vary. Perhaps the merchandise received was the wrong colour or size. A *purchase allowance* is a reduction in the cost of defective merchandise received by a purchaser from a supplier. Purchasers will often keep defective merchandise that is still marketable if the supplier grants an acceptable allowance. For

TREX

9797 Cherry Rd.
Windsor, ON N9G 2P5

Sold to

Firm Name __MEC__ ③	
Attention of __Tom Novak,__ Purchasing Agent	
Address __MEC Street__	
__Winnipeg__ __MB__ __R3J 1G9__	
City Province Postal Code	

Invoice	
Date ②	Number
Nov. 2/14	4657-2

④	⑤		⑥	
P.O. Date Oct. 30/14	Salesperson #141	Terms 2/10, n/30	Freight FOB Destination	Ship Via FedEx
Model No.	Description		Quantity	Price	Amount

Model No.	Description	Quantity	Price	Amount
⑦ CH015	Challenger X7	1	490	490
SD099	Speed Demon	1	710	710

See reverse for terms of sale and returns.

SubTotal	1,200
Ship. Chg.	—
Tax	—
⑧ Total	1,200

①	Seller
②	Invoice date
③	Purchaser
④	Order date
⑤	Credit terms
⑥	Freight terms
⑦	Goods
⑧	Total invoice amount

EXHIBIT 5.6

Invoice

example, assume that the merchandise received by the purchaser was furniture scratched during shipment. The purchaser may repair the furniture if the supplier provides an allowance.

The purchaser usually informs the supplier in writing of any returns and allowances. This is done with a letter or a **debit memorandum**, a form issued by the purchaser to inform the supplier of a debit made to the supplier's account, including the reason for a return or allowance. The purchaser sends the debit memorandum to the supplier and also keeps a copy.

To illustrate how a buyer accounts for an allowance, we assume that the Speed Demon mountain bike purchased by MEC on November 2 was discovered to be defective when received on November 5. Exhibit 5.7 shows the debit memorandum prepared by MEC requesting an allowance from Trex. The November 5 entry by MEC for the purchase allowance is:

Nov. 5	Accounts Payable..	300	
	Merchandise Inventory		300
	Purchase allowance re debit memo dated November 5.		

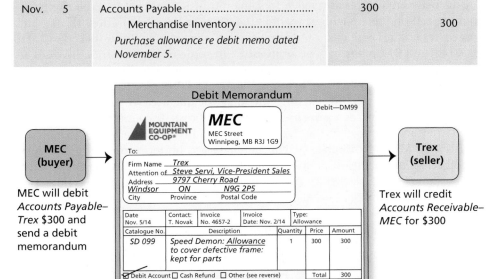

MEC will debit *Accounts Payable– Trex* $300 and send a debit memorandum

Trex will credit *Accounts Receivable– MEC* for $300

EXHIBIT 5.7

Debit Memorandum: MEC proposes $300 allowance from Trex

The entry reduces the Merchandise Inventory account to reflect the allowance. The Accounts Payable account is debited to reduce the liability to the supplier, hence the term *debit memorandum*.

If this had been a return, then the recorded cost[5] of the defective merchandise would be entered. If there is a refund of cash, then the Cash account is debited for $300 instead of Accounts Payable as follows:

Nov.	5	Cash	300	
		Merchandise Inventory		300
		Cash refund for return of defective merchandise.		

Trade Discounts

When a manufacturer or wholesaler prepares a catalogue of items that it has for sale, each item is usually given a **list price**, also called a **catalogue price**. Often the intended selling price equals list price minus a given percentage called a **trade discount**. The amount of trade discount usually depends on the quantities purchased and on whether a buyer is a wholesaler, retailer, or final consumer. For example, a wholesaler buying 50,000 pens might be granted a 35% trade discount, while a retailer purchasing 500 pens might be granted a 5% trade discount.

Trade discounts are commonly used by manufacturers and wholesalers to change selling prices without republishing their catalogues. When a seller wants to change selling prices, it can notify its customers merely by sending them a new table of trade discounts that they can apply to catalogue prices.

Because a list price is not intended to reflect the actual selling price of merchandise, a buyer records the net amount of list price minus trade discount rather than accounting separately for the discount. For example, on November 2, MEC purchased inventory that was listed at $2,000 in the catalogue. Since MEC receives a 40% trade discount, the company records the transaction at $1,200 [= $2,000 − (40% × $2,000)].

Purchase Discounts

The purchase of goods on credit requires a clear statement of the *credit terms* to avoid misunderstanding. **Credit terms** are a listing of the amounts and timing of payments between a buyer and seller. In some industries, purchasers expect terms requiring full or "net" payment within 10 days after the end of a month in which purchases occur. These credit terms are entered on sales invoices or tickets as "n/10 EOM." The **EOM** refers to "end of month." In some other industries, invoices are often due and payable 30 calendar days after the invoice date. These credit terms are entered as "n/30," meaning "net amount due in 30 days." The 30-day period is called the **credit period**. Credit terms may include a **cash discount**. A buyer views a cash discount as a **purchase discount**. If cash discounts for early payment exist, they are described in the credit terms on an invoice. Referring to Exhibit 5.6, notice that MEC's November 2 credit purchase was on terms of 2/10, n/30. These credit terms mean there is a 30-day credit period before full payment is due. The seller allows MEC to deduct 2% of the invoice amount from the payment if it is paid within 10 days of the invoice date. Sellers do this to encourage early payment. The 10 days are the **discount period**, the period in which the reduced payment can be made. Exhibit 5.8 explains these credit terms.

---

5   Recorded cost is the cost reported in a Merchandise Inventory account minus any discounts.

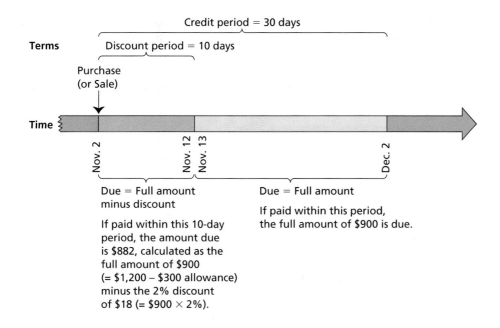

EXHIBIT 5.8

Credit Terms Illustration—
2/10, n/30

When MEC takes advantage of the discount and pays the amount due on November 12, the entry to record payment is:

Nov.	12	Accounts Payable	900	
		Merchandise Inventory		18
		Cash		882
		Paid for the purchase of November 2		
		less the allowance of November 5 and		
		the discount; $1,200 − $300 = $900;		
		2% × $900 = $18; $900 − $18 = $882.		

Notice that this entry shows that when goods are returned within the discount period, a buyer will take the discount only on the remaining balance of the invoice.

MEC's Merchandise Inventory account now reflects the net cost of merchandise purchased. Its Accounts Payable account also shows the debt to be satisfied.

Merchandise Inventory				
Nov. 2	1,200	300	Nov. 5	
		18	Nov. 12	
Balance	882			

Accounts Payable				
Nov. 5	300	1,200	Nov. 2	
Nov. 12	900			
		-0-	Balance	

Managing Discounts

A buyer's failure to pay within a discount period is often quite expensive. If MEC does not pay within the 10-day discount period, it delays the payment by 20 more days. This delay costs MEC an added 2%. Most buyers try to take advantage of purchase discounts. For MEC's terms of 2/10, n/30, missing the 2% discount for an additional 20 days is equal to an annual interest rate of 36.5%, calculated as (365 days ÷ 20 days × 2%).

Most companies set up a system to pay invoices with favourable discounts within the discount period. Careful cash management means that no invoice is paid until the last day of a discount period. Computerized systems achieve this goal by using a code that identifies the last date in the discount period. When that date occurs, the system automatically identifies accounts to be paid.[6]

Transfer of Ownership

The point where ownership of merchandise inventory transfers from the buyer to the seller must be identified on the invoice because it determines who pays transportation costs and other incidental costs of transit such as insurance. The party responsible for paying shipping costs is also responsible for insuring the merchandise during transport. The point of transfer is called the **FOB** point, where FOB stands for *free on board*.

Exhibit 5.9 identifies two alternative points of transfer. *FOB shipping point*, also called *FOB factory*, means the buyer accepts ownership at the seller's place of business. The buyer is then responsible for paying shipping costs and bears the risk of

EXHIBIT 5.9

Identifying Transfer of Ownership

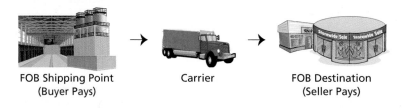

FOB Shipping Point (Buyer Pays)   Carrier   FOB Destination (Seller Pays)

	Ownership transfers when goods:	Transportation costs paid by:
FOB Shipping Point	Leave the seller's warehouse	Buyer
FOB Destination	Arrive at buyer's warehouse	Seller

---

6 Companies that automatically take advantage of favourable discounts use the *net method* to record merchandise purchases as opposed to using the gross invoice amount when debiting Merchandise Inventory and crediting Accounts Payable (as illustrated in the textbook; known as the *gross method*). Under the net method, both Merchandise Inventory and Accounts Payable are debited/credited for the gross purchase amount *less* the discount. If payment is not made within the discount period, the payment would debit Accounts Payable for the net amount originally recorded, debit *Discounts Lost* for the amount of the lost discount, and credit Cash for the gross amount of the invoice. The gross method more strictly adheres to the revenue recognition principle than the net method, hence its inclusion in the textbook.

damage or loss when goods are in transit. The goods are part of the buyer's inventory when they are in transit since ownership has transferred to the buyer.

FOB destination means ownership of the goods transfers to the buyer at the buyer's place of business. The seller is responsible for paying shipping charges and bears the risk of damage or loss in transit. The seller does not record revenue from this sale until the goods arrive at the destination because this transaction is not complete before that point.

There are situations when the party not responsible for shipping costs pays the carrier. In these cases, the party paying these costs either bills the party responsible or, more commonly, adjusts its account payable or receivable with the other party.

Transportation Costs

Shipping costs on purchases are called **transportation-in** or **freight-in** costs. MEC's $1,200 purchase on November 2 is on terms of FOB destination. This means that MEC is not responsible for paying transportation costs.

A different situation arises when a company is responsible for paying transportation costs. The cost principle requires these transportation costs to be included as part of the cost of merchandise inventory. This means that a separate entry is necessary when they are not listed on the invoice. For example, MEC's entry to record a $75 freight charge to an independent carrier for merchandise purchased FOB shipping point is:

Nov.	2	Merchandise Inventory	75	
		Cash		75
		Paid freight charges on purchased merchandise.		

The costs of shipping goods to customers are different from transportation-in costs. **Transportation-out** or **freight-out** costs regarding the shipping of goods to customers are debited to the Delivery Expense account when the seller is responsible for these costs, and are reported as a selling expense in the income statement.

Recording Purchases Information

We have explained how purchase returns and allowances, purchase discounts, and transportation-in are included in calculating the total cost of merchandise inventory. MEC's 2014 net cost of merchandise purchases is summarized in Exhibit 5.10.

EXHIBIT 5.10

Net Cost of Merchandise Purchases Calculation— Perpetual

Net Cost of Purchases during 2014 = $232,400

Merchandise Inventory			
Dec. 31, 2013, balance 19,000			
Reflects entries to record **purchases of merchandise** during 2014................................. 235,800		Reflects entries to record **purchase discounts** 4,200 ....during 2014	
Reflects **transportation-in** costs incurred during 2014 2,300		Reflects entries to record **purchase returns and** 1,500 .... **allowances** during 2014	

CHECKPOINT

4. Refer to Exhibit 5.6. When the merchandise inventory is shipped by Trex to MEC, identify when ownership transfers.
5. How long are the credit and discount periods when credit terms are 2/10, n/60?
6. Identify items subtracted from the list amount when calculating purchase price: (a) freight-in, (b) trade discount, (c) purchase discount, (d) purchase return and/or allowance.

Do Quick Study questions: QS 5-5, QS 5-6, QS 5-7

Accounting for Merchandise Sales—Perpetual Inventory System

Merchandising companies also must account for sales, sales discounts, sales returns and allowances, and cost of goods sold. A merchandising company such as MEC reports these items in an income statement, as shown in Exhibit 5.11.

EXHIBIT 5.11

Gross Profit Section of Income Statement

MEC Calculation of Gross Profit For Year Ended December 31, 2014		
Sales		$321,000
Less: Sales discounts	$4,300	
Sales returns and allowances	2,000	6,300
Net sales		$314,700
Cost of goods sold		230,400
Gross profit from sales		$ 84,300

This section explains how information in this calculation is derived from transactions involving sales, sales discounts, and sales returns and allowances.

Sales Transactions

Accounting for a sales transaction for a seller of merchandise involves capturing information about two related parts:

1. Receiving revenue in the form of an asset from a customer, and

2. Recognizing the cost of merchandise sold to a customer.

As an example, MEC sold $2,400 of merchandise on credit on November 3. The revenue part of this transaction is recorded as:

Nov.	3	Accounts Receivable	2,400	
		Sales		2,400
		Sold merchandise on credit.		

This entry reflects an increase in MEC's assets in the form of an account receivable. It also shows the revenue from the credit sale. If the sale is for cash, the debit is to Cash instead of Accounts Receivable.

The expense or cost of the merchandise sold by MEC on November 3 is $1,600. We explain in Chapter 6 how the cost of this merchandise is calculated.

The entry to record the cost part of this sales transaction (under a perpetual inventory system) is:

Nov.	3	Cost of Goods Sold	1,600	
		Merchandise Inventory		1,600
		To record the cost of Nov. 3 sale and reduce inventory.		

This entry records the cost of the merchandise sold as an expense and reduces the Merchandise Inventory account to reflect the remaining balance of inventory on hand.

Sales Discounts

When sellers offer credit terms that include a cash discount, the cash discount is referred to as a **sales discount**. Sales discounts can encourage prompt payments, improve cash flow, and also reduce future efforts and costs of billing customers.

A seller does not know whether a customer will pay within the discount period and take advantage of a cash discount at the time of a credit sale, so a sales discount is usually not recorded until a customer pays within the discount period. As an example, MEC completed a credit sale for $1,000 on November 12, subject to terms of 2/10, n/60 (the cost of the inventory sold was $600). The entry to record this sale is:

Nov.	12	Accounts Receivable..	1,000	
		Sales		1,000
		Sold merchandise under terms of 2/10, n/60.		
	12	Cost of Goods Sold	600	
		Merchandise Inventory		600
		To record the cost of the Nov. 12 sale and reduce inventory.		

This entry records the receivable and the revenue as if the full amount will be paid by the customer.

The customer has two options. One option is to wait 60 days until January 11 and pay the full $1,000. In this case, MEC records the payment as:

Jan.	11	Cash	1,000	
		Accounts Receivable		1,000
		Received payment for November 12 sale.		

The customer's second option is to pay $980 within a 10-day period that runs through November 22. If the customer pays on or before November 22, MEC records the payment as:

Nov.	22	Cash	980	
		Sales Discounts	20	
		Accounts Receivable		1,000
		Received payment for November 12 sale less the discount; $1,000 × 2% = $20.		

Sales discounts are recorded in a *contra revenue* account called Sales Discounts. This is so management can monitor sales discounts to assess their effectiveness and cost. The Sales Discounts account is deducted from the Sales account when calculating a company's net sales (refer to Exhibit 5.11). While information about sales discounts is useful internally, it is seldom reported on income statements distributed to external users.

Sales Returns and Allowances

Sales returns refer to merchandise that customers return to the seller after a sale. Customers return merchandise for a variety of reasons, such as having received an incorrect item or one of poor quality. Many companies allow customers to return merchandise for a full refund. *Sales allowances* refer to reductions in the selling price of merchandise sold to customers. This can occur with damaged merchandise that a customer is willing to purchase if the selling price is decreased. **Sales returns and allowances** involve dissatisfied customers and the possibility of lost future sales. To monitor these problems managers need detailed information, so many accounting systems record returns and allowances in a separate contra revenue account.

Recall MEC's sale of merchandise on November 3. As already recorded, the merchandise is sold for $2,400 and cost $1,600, but what if the customer returns part of the merchandise on November 6, when returned items sell for $800 and cost $600? The revenue part of this transaction must reflect the decrease in sales from the customer's return:

Nov.	6	Sales Returns and Allowances........................	800	
		Accounts Receivable		800
		Customer returned merchandise.		

MEC can record this return with a debit to the Sales account instead of Sales Returns and Allowances. This method provides the same net sales, but does not provide information needed by managers to monitor returns and allowances. By using the Sales Returns and Allowances contra account, this information is available. Published income statements usually omit this detail and show only net sales.

If the merchandise returned to MEC is not defective and can be resold to another customer, then MEC returns these goods to its inventory. The entry necessary to restore the cost of these goods to the Merchandise Inventory account is:

Nov.	6	Merchandise Inventory	600	
		Cost of Goods Sold.............................		600
		Returned goods to inventory.		

If the merchandise returned is defective, however, the seller may discard the returned items. In this case, the cost of returned merchandise is not restored to the Merchandise Inventory account. Instead, most companies leave the cost of defective merchandise in the Cost of Goods Sold account.[7]

Another possibility is that $800 of the merchandise sold by MEC on November 3 is defective but the customer decides to keep it because MEC grants the customer a price reduction of $500. The only entry that MEC must make in this case is one to reflect the decrease in revenue:

Nov.	6	Sales Returns and Allowances........................	500	
		Accounts Receivable		500
		To record sales allowance.		

---

7   When managers want to monitor the cost of defective merchandise, a better method is to remove the cost from Cost of Goods Sold and charge it to a *Loss From Defective Merchandise* account.

As shown in Exhibit 5.12, the seller prepares a **credit memorandum** to confirm a customer's return or allowance. A credit memorandum informs a customer of a credit to his or her account receivable, hence the term *credit memorandum*.

EXHIBIT 5.12

Credit Memorandum

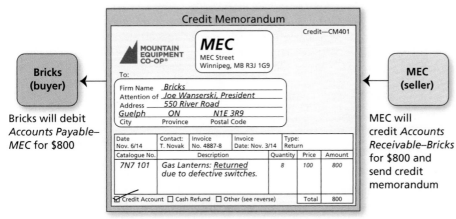

**Case: MEC (seller) accepts $800
of returned merchandise from Bricks (buyer)**

Bricks will debit *Accounts Payable–MEC* for $800

MEC will credit *Accounts Receivable–Bricks* for $800 and send credit memorandum

The information in a credit memorandum is similar to that of a debit memorandum. The following table summarizes what debit and credit memoranda (memos) are and why they arise:

Debit Memo	Credit Memo
What is a debit memo? • A document prepared by the purchaser to "debit" or reduce the purchaser's account payable	What is a credit memo? • A document prepared by the seller to "credit" or reduce the customer's account receivable
Why is a debit memo issued? • To reduce the purchaser's account payable because of: 1. Return of unsatisfactory goods 2. Allowance 3. Error	Why is a credit memo issued? • To reduce the seller's account receivable because of: 1. Return of unsatisfactory goods 2. Allowance 3. Error

CHECKPOINT

7. Why are sales discounts and sales returns and allowances recorded in contra revenue accounts instead of directly in the Sales account?

8. Under what conditions are two entries necessary to record a sales return?

9. When merchandise is sold on credit and the seller notifies the buyer of a price reduction, does the seller send a credit memorandum or a debit memorandum?

Do Quick Study questions: QS 5-8, QS 5-9, QS 5-10, QS 5-11

MID-CHAPTER DEMONSTRATION PROBLEM

Beta Company, a retail store, had the following transactions in March:

March	2	Purchased merchandise from Alfa Company under the following terms: $1,800 invoice price, 2/15, n/60, FOB factory. (The cost of the merchandise to Alfa Company was $990.)
	3	Paid CanPar Shipping $125 for shipping charges on the purchase of March 2.
	4	Returned to Alfa Company unacceptable merchandise that had an invoice price of $300 (and a cost to Alfa of $165). Alfa returned the merchandise to inventory.
	17	Sent a cheque to Alfa Company for the March 2 purchase, net of the discount and the returned merchandise.

Required

Assuming both Beta and Alfa use a perpetual inventory system:

a.   Present the journal entries Beta Company should record for these transactions.

b.   Present the journal entries Alfa Company should record for these transactions.

Analysis Component:

Who should be insuring the merchandise during shipping: Beta or Alfa? Explain.

SOLUTION

a.

Beta Company (the buyer)		
March 2	Merchandise Inventory....................... 1,800	
	Accounts Payable—Alfa Company	1,800
	Purchased merchandise on credit.	
3	Merchandise Inventory....................... 125	
	Cash..	125
	Paid shipping charges on purchased merchandise.	
4	Accounts Payable—Alfa Company 300	
	Merchandise Inventory	300
	Returned unacceptable merchandise.	
17	Accounts Payable—Alfa Company 1,500	
	Merchandise Inventory	30
	Cash...	1,470
	Paid balance within the discount period and took a 2% discount.	

b.

Alfa Company (the seller)		
Accounts Receivable—Beta Company 1,800	
Sales	1,800
Sold merchandise under terms 2/15, n/60.	
Cost of Goods Sold............................... 990	
Merchandise Inventory	990
Recorded cost of sales.	
No entry	
Sales Returns and Allowances 300	
Accounts Receivable—Beta Company	300
Customer returned merchandise.	
Merchandise Inventory 165	
Cost of Goods Sold.......................................	165
Merchandise returned to inventory.	
Cash... 1,470	
Sales Discounts.. 30	
Accounts Receivable—Beta Company	1,500
Received payment for March 2 sale less the return and discount.	

Analysis Component:

Beta should be insuring the merchandise during shipping because the terms, FOB factory, transfer ownership to Beta the moment the merchandise leaves Alfa.

ADDITIONAL MERCHANDISING ISSUES— PERPETUAL INVENTORY SYSTEM

This section identifies and explains how merchandising activities affect other accounting processes. We address preparing adjusting entries, and relations between important accounts.

Adjusting Entries

Most adjusting entries are the same for merchandising companies and service companies and involve prepaid expenses, unearned revenues, depreciation, accrued expenses, and accrued revenues.

LO⁴ Prepare adjustments for a merchandising company.

A merchandising company using a perpetual inventory system needs one additional adjustment to update the Merchandise Inventory account for any losses of merchandise. Merchandising companies can lose merchandise in several ways, including theft and deterioration, referred to as **shrinkage**.

While a perpetual inventory system tracks all goods as they move into and out of the company, a perpetual system is unable to measure shrinkage directly. Yet we can calculate shrinkage by comparing the recorded quantities of inventory with a physical count, usually performed at least once annually to verify the Merchandise Inventory account. Most companies record any necessary adjustment due to shrinkage by charging it to Cost of Goods Sold, assuming that shrinkage is not abnormally large.

As an example, MEC's Merchandise Inventory account at the end of 2014 had an unadjusted balance of $21,250, but a physical count of inventory revealed only $21,000 of inventory on hand. The adjusting entry to record this $250 shrinkage is:

Dec.	31	Cost of Goods Sold	250	
		Merchandise Inventory		250
		To adjust for $250 shrinkage disclosed by physical count of inventory.		

DECISION INSIGHT

A study by GPI Atlantic reports that businesses have to build the cost of security systems, guards, shoplifting, and employee theft—all related to shrinkage—into their product pricing. The average Nova Scotian household, according to the study, pays $800 more per year because of shrinkage.

SOURCE: eda.gov.ns.ca/press

CHECKPOINT

10. When a merchandising company uses a perpetual inventory system, why is it often necessary to adjust the Merchandise Inventory balance with an adjusting entry?

Do Quick Study question: QS 5-12

Summary of Merchandising Cost Flows

The Merchandise Inventory account balance at the end of one period is the amount of beginning inventory in the next period.

To summarize the effects of merchandising transactions on the Merchandise Inventory and Cost of Goods Sold accounts, MEC's merchandising activities during 2014 are illustrated in Exhibit 5.13. Most amounts in these T-accounts are summary representations of several entries during the year 2014. Notice that the Cost of Goods Sold balance of $230,400 is the amount reported in the income statement information in Exhibit 5.2. The Merchandise Inventory balance of $21,000 is the amount reported as a current asset on the balance sheet in Exhibit 5.3. These amounts also appear on MEC's adjusted trial balance in Exhibits 5.14 and 5.20.

EXHIBIT 5.13

Summary of MEC's Merchandising Activities for 2014 Reflected in T-Accounts

Merchandise Inventory			
Dec. 31, 2013, balance	19,000		
Reflects entries to record **purchases of merchandise** during 2014	235,800	4,200	Reflects entries to record **purchase discounts** during 2014
Reflects **transportation-in** costs incurred during 2014	2,300	1,500	Reflects entries to record **purchase returns and allowances** during 2014
Reflects entries to record **merchandise returned by customers** and restored to inventory during 2014	1,400	231,550	Reflects **cost of sales** transactions during 2014
Dec. 31, 2014, unadjusted balance	21,250	250	Dec. 31, 2014, adjustment for **shrinkage**
Dec. 31, 2014, adjusted balance ...	21,000		

Net cost of purchases

Cost of goods sold transferred from inventory account.

Cost of Goods Sold			
Reflects entries to record the **cost of sales** for 2014	231,550	1,400	Reflects entries to record **merchandise returned** by customers and restored to inventory during 2014
Dec. 31, 2014, unadjusted balance	230,150		
Dec. 31, 2014, adjustment for **shrinkage**	250		
Dec. 31, 2014 adjusted balance	230,400		

INCOME STATEMENT FORMATS—PERPETUAL INVENTORY SYSTEM

LO⁵ Define, prepare, and use merchandising income statements.

Companies have flexibility as to what format can be used for the presentation of financial statements. As a result, there will be many different formats in practice. However, there are minimum classification requirements regarding how expenses are to be shown on the income statement. The first part of this section looks at formulating a draft income statement through the preparation of a work sheet. The second part of this section describes the classification requirements for expenses and illustrates three presentation formats using MEC's data.

A Work Sheet for a Merchandising Company

Exhibit 5.14, based on fictitious data, presents a work sheet that could be prepared in the process of developing MEC's 2014 financial statements.

EXHIBIT 5.14

Work Sheet (Perpetual) for MEC for Year Ended December 31, 2014

MEC Work Sheet.xls

MEC
Work Sheet
For the Year Ended December 31, 2014

No.	Account	Unadjusted Trial Balance Dr.	Cr.	Adjustments Dr.	Cr.	Adjusted Trial Balance Dr.	Cr.	Income Statement Dr.	Cr.	Balance Sheet & Statement of Changes in Equity Dr.	Cr.
101	Cash	8,200				8,200				8,200	
106	Accounts receivable	11,200				11,200				11,200	
119	Merchandise inventory	21,250			g) 250	21,000				21,000	
124	Office supplies	2,350			c) 1,800	550				550	
125	Store supplies	1,450			b) 1,200	250				250	
128	Prepaid insurance	900			a) 600	300				300	
163	Office equipment	4,200				4,200				4,200	
164	Accum. dep., office equipment		700		e) 700		1,400				1,400
165	Store equipment	30,000				30,000				30,000	
166	Accum. dep., store equipment		3,000		d) 3,000		6,000				6,000
201	Accounts payable		16,000				16,000				16,000
209	Salaries payable				f) 800		800				800
301	David Wingate, capital		40,160				40,160				40,160
302	David Wingate, withdrawals	4,000				4,000				4,000	
406	Rent revenue		2,800				2,800		2,800		
413	Sales		321,000				321,000		321,000		
414	Sales returns and allowances	2,000				2,000		2,000			
415	Sales discounts	4,300				4,300		4,300			
502	Cost of goods sold	230,150		g) 250		230,400		230,400			
612	Dep. expense, store equipment			d) 3,000		3,000		3,000			
613	Dep. expense, office equipment			e) 700		700		700			
620	Office salaries expense	25,000		f) 300		25,300		25,300			
621	Sales salaries expense	18,000		f) 500		18,500		18,500			
633	Interest expense	360				360		360			
637	Insurance expense			a) 600		600		600			
641	Rent expense, office space	900				900		900			
642	Rent expense, selling space	8,100				8,100		8,100			
650	Office supplies expense			c) 1,800		1,800		1,800			
651	Store supplies expense			b) 1,200		1,200		1,200			
655	Advertising expense	11,300				11,300		11,300			
	Totals	383,660	383,660	8,350	8,350	388,160	388,160	308,460	323,800	79,700	64,360
	Net income							15,340			15,340
	Totals							323,800	323,800	79,700	79,700

The adjustments in the work sheet reflect the following:

a. Expiration of $600 of prepaid insurance.

b. Use of $1,200 of store supplies.

c. Use of $1,800 of office supplies.

d. Depreciation of the store equipment for $3,000.

e. Depreciation of the office equipment for $700.

f. Accrual of $300 of unpaid office salaries and $500 of unpaid store salaries.

g. Physical count of merchandise inventory revealed $21,000 on hand.

The financial statement columns in Exhibit 5.14 are used to develop the company's financial statements.

Expense Classification Requirements

Expenses are to be shown on an income statement based on either their *nature* or their *function*.[8] In previous chapters, expenses were listed on the income statement based on their *nature*. The **nature of an expense** is determined by its basic characteristics or what it is. For example, when expenses are identified on the income statement as depreciation, rent, property tax, and salaries, the nature of each expense is being identified. The **function of an expense** describes the grouping of expenses based on their purpose or what they relate to. For example, an income statement that shows cost of goods sold, *selling expenses*, and *general and administrative expenses* has grouped expenses by their function. When expenses are grouped by function, additional information must be *disclosed* to show the nature of expenses within each group.[9] The **full disclosure principle** is the generally accepted accounting principle that requires financial statements to report all relevant information about the operations and financial position of the entity. Information that is relevant but not included in the body of the statements is provided in **notes to financial statements** such as those for **WestJet** in Appendix II of the text.

Multiple-Step Income Statement

There are two general types of multiple-step income statements: the *multiple-step* format and the *classified, multiple-step* format. Both formats can be used in either a perpetual or periodic inventory system.

Classified, Multiple-Step Format (for internal reporting)

Exhibit 5.15 shows a **classified, multiple-step income statement** using fictitious data for MEC. This format is useful for internal reporting because of the detail it includes, such as the calculation of net sales. The difference between net sales and cost of goods sold is MEC's gross profit.

Exhibit 5.15 shows operating expenses, a broad function or category. Operating expenses are divided into two additional functions: *selling expenses* and *general and administrative expenses*. **Selling expenses** include the expenses of promoting sales through displaying and advertising merchandise, making sales, and delivering goods to customers. In Exhibit 5.15, the selling expenses are disclosed within the body of the statement by providing detailed information on the nature of expenses, including sales salaries, advertising, rent expense allocated to selling, depreciation on the store equipment, and store supplies. **General and administrative expenses** support the overall operations of a company and include expenses related to accounting, human resource management, and financial management. In Exhibit 5.15, the

---

8   IFRS 2012, IAS 1, para. 99–105.
9   IFRS 2012, IAS 1, para. 104. Although students at the introductory level should understand the concept of disclosure, the actual preparation of notes is left to a more advanced accounting course.

general and administrative expenses section provides detail on the nature of these expenses by including office salaries, office supplies, rent expense allocated to the general and administrative category, depreciation on the office equipment, and insurance expense.

Notice that an expense may be divided between categories when it contributes to more than one activity. For example, Exhibit 5.15 shows that MEC allocates rent expense of $9,000 for its store building between two categories: $8,100 is a selling expense, while $900 is listed as a general and administrative expense based on relative rental values.[10]

Revenues and expenses that are **not** part of normal operating activities are reported under the functional heading *Other revenues and expenses* of the income statement. MEC's main operating activity is merchandising, therefore rent revenue—not a merchandising activity—is added under *Other revenues and expenses*. Another example, interest expense, arises because of a financing (or borrowing) activity and not because of MEC's merchandising (or operating) activities. It is subtracted under *Other revenues and expenses* as highlighted in Exhibit 5.15. Other examples of *Other revenues and expenses* include dividend income and gains and losses on the sale of property, plant and equipment assets.

EXHIBIT 5.15

Classified, Multiple-Step Income Statement—Perpetual Inventory System

MEC Income Statement For Year Ended December 31, 2014			
Sales			$321,000
Less: Sales discounts		$ 4,300	
Sales returns and allowances		2,000	6,300
Net sales			$314,700
Cost of goods sold			230,400
Gross profit from sales			$ 84,300
Operating expenses:			
Selling expenses:			
Sales salaries expense	$18,500		
Advertising expense	11,300		
Rent expense, selling space	8,100		
Depreciation expense, store equipment	3,000		
Store supplies expense	1,200		
Total selling expenses		$42,100	
General and administrative expenses:			
Office salaries expense	$25,300		
Office supplies expense	1,800		
Rent expense, office space	900		
Depreciation expense, office equipment	700		
Insurance expense	600		
Total general and administrative expenses		29,300	
Total operating expenses			71,400
Income from operations			$ 12,900
Other revenues and expenses:			
Rent revenue		$ 2,800	
Interest expense		360	2,440
Net income			$ 15,340

‹-- Rent revenue is added
‹-- Interest expense is subtracted
‹-- to get total *Other revenues and expenses.*

---

10 These expenses can be recorded in a single ledger account or in two separate accounts. If they are recorded in one account, we allocate its balance between the two expenses when preparing statements.

Multiple-Step Format (for external reporting)

Exhibit 5.16 shows a multiple-step income statement format that can be used in external reports. In comparison to Exhibit 5.15, a multiple-step statement leaves out the detailed calculation of net sales. The functional categories of *selling expenses* and *general and administrative expenses* are not included on a multiple-step income statement; operating expenses are listed by nature only on a multiple-step income statement.

EXHIBIT 5.16

Multiple-Step Income Statement—Perpetual Inventory System

MEC Income Statement For Year Ended December 31, 2014		
Net sales		$314,700
Cost of goods sold		230,400
Gross profit from sales		$ 84,300
Operating expenses:		
Salaries expense	$43,800	
Advertising expense	11,300	
Rent expense	9,000	
Depreciation expense	3,700	
Supplies expense	3,000	
Insurance expense	600	
Total operating expenses		71,400
Income from operations		$ 12,900
Other revenues and expenses:		
Rent revenue	$ 2,800	
Interest expense	360	2,440
Net income		$ 15,340

Single-Step Income Statement

A **single-step income statement** is another format for external reporting. It shows items based on their function only and is shown in Exhibit 5.17 for MEC. This simple format includes cost of goods sold as an operating expense and shows only one subtotal for total expenses. Because operating expenses are highly summarized on a single-step income statement, additional information regarding the nature of expenses included in each function must be disclosed in the notes to the financial statements.

EXHIBIT 5.17

Single-Step Income Statement—Perpetual Inventory System

MEC Income Statement For Year Ended December 31, 2014		
Revenues:		
Net sales	$314,700	
Rent revenue	2,800	
Total revenues		$317,500
Expenses:		
Cost of goods sold	$230,400	
Selling expenses	42,100	
General and administrative expense	29,300	
Interest expense	360	
Total expenses		302,160
Net income		$ 15,340

Companies can use formats that combine features of both the single- and multiple-step statements for external reporting. As long as income statement items are shown sensibly and minimum requirements are satisfied, management can choose the presentation format.

Gross Profit Ratio

Gross profit, also called gross margin, is the relation between sales and cost of goods sold. A merchandising company needs sufficient gross profit to cover operating expenses or it will likely fail. To focus on gross profit, users often calculate a gross profit ratio. The **gross profit ratio**, or **gross margin ratio**, is defined as shown in Exhibit 5.18.

$$\text{Gross profit ratio} = \frac{\text{Gross profit from sales}}{\text{Net sales}} \times 100\%$$

EXHIBIT 5.18
Gross Profit Ratio

Exhibit 5.19 shows the gross profit ratios of MEC based on fictitious data for the years 2012, 2013, and 2014.

	2014	2013	2012
Units sold	214,000	160,000	100,000
Gross profit from sales	$84,300	$69,440	$46,400
Net sales	$314,700	$248,000	$160,000
Gross profit ratio	26.8%	28.0%	29.0%

EXHIBIT 5.19
MEC's Gross Profit Ratio

This ratio represents the gross profit in each dollar of sales. For example, Exhibit 5.19 shows that MEC's gross profit ratio in 2012 was 29.0%. This means that each $1 of sales yielded 29¢ in gross profit to cover all other expenses. Exhibit 5.19 shows that MEC's gross profit ratio decreased from 2012 to 2014, reflecting an unfavourable trend. How is this possible given that net sales and gross profit in dollars are both increasing? If net sales are increasing but at a slower rate than the increase in cost of goods sold, gross profit on sales will grow but at a decreasing rate.[11] Success for companies such as MEC depends on a gross profit that adequately covers operating expenses.

CHECKPOINT

11. What income statement format shows detailed calculations for net sales? What format gives no subtotals except total expenses?
12. K-One Merchandising shows gross profit ratios of 39%, 39.5%, and 41% for 2012, 2013, and 2014 respectively. Assuming that all other factors have remained constant, does this reflect a favourable (good) or unfavourable (bad) trend?

Do Quick Study questions: QS 5-13, QS 5-14

---

11 A more detailed analysis of the information in Exhibit 5.19 shows that net sales are increasing but at a slower rate than the increases in cost of goods sold. This has caused gross profit to shrink as a percentage of sales (an unfavourable trend). This conclusion is supported by the following:

	2014	% Change	2013	% Change	2012
Units sold	214,000	33.8	160,000	60.0	100,000
Net sales	$314,700	26.9	$248,000	55.0	$160,000
COGS	230,400	29.0	178,560	57.2	113,600
Gross profit from sales	$ 84,300	21.4	$ 69,440	49.7	$ 46,400
Gross profit ratio	26.8%	−4.3	28.0%	−3.4	29.0%

CLOSING ENTRIES FOR A MERCHANDISING COMPANY—PERPETUAL INVENTORY SYSTEM

LO⁶ Prepare closing entries for a merchandising company.

When using a perpetual system, closing entries are similar for merchandising companies and service companies. Both use an adjusted trial balance to prepare closing entries. The one difference is that we must close the additional temporary accounts related to merchandising activities.

These accounts are bolded in the adjusted trial balance in Exhibit 5.20 and include: Sales, Sales Discounts, Sales Returns and Allowances, and Cost of Goods Sold. The closing process for a merchandiser is identical to that described in Chapter 4 for a service company. The closing entries for MEC are shown in Exhibit 5.21. Notice that the temporary accounts unique to a merchandiser are highlighted for you in these closing entries.

EXHIBIT 5.20

Adjusted Trial Balance

The temporary accounts unique to a merchandiser are highlighted here and in the closing entries shown in Exhibit 5.21.

MEC Adjusted Trial Balance December 31, 2014	Debit	Credit
Cash	$ 8,200	
Accounts receivable	11,200	
Merchandise inventory	21,000	
Office supplies	550	
Store supplies	250	
Prepaid insurance	300	
Office equipment	4,200	
Accumulated depreciation, office equipment		$ 1,400
Store equipment	30,000	
Accumulated depreciation, store equipment		6,000
Accounts payable		16,000
Salaries payable		800
David Wingate, capital		40,160
David Wingate, withdrawals	4,000	
Rent revenue		2,800
Sales		**321,000**
Sales returns and allowances	**2,000**	
Sales discounts	**4,300**	
Cost of goods sold	**230,400**	
Depreciation expense, store equipment	3,000	
Depreciation expense, office equipment	700	
Office salaries expense	25,300	
Sales salaries expense	18,500	
Interest expense	360	
Insurance expense	600	
Rent expense, office space	900	
Rent expense, selling space	8,100	
Office supplies expense	1,800	
Store supplies expense	1,200	
Advertising expense	11,300	
Totals	$388,160	$388,160

Entry 1: **Close Credit Balances in Temporary Accounts to Income Summary.**
MEC has two temporary accounts with credit balances and they are closed with the entry:

EXHIBIT 5.21

Dec.	31	Rent Revenue...	2,800	
		Sales	321,000	
		Income Summary		323,800
		To close temporary accounts having credit balances.		

Posting this entry to the ledger gives a zero balance to the Rent Revenue and Sales accounts and opens the Income Summary account.

Entry 2: **Close Debit Balances in Temporary Accounts to Income Summary.**
Temporary accounts having debit balances include Cost of Goods Sold, Sales Discounts, and Sales Returns and Allowances. This second entry yields the amount of net income as the balance in the Income Summary account. MEC's second closing entry is:

Dec.	31	Income Summary...	308,460	
		Sales Discounts		4,300
		Sales Returns and Allowances		2,000
		Cost of Goods Sold		230,400
		Depreciation Expense, Store Equipment		3,000
		Depreciation Expense, Office Equipment		700
		Office Salaries Expense.....................		25,300
		Sales Salaries Expense		18,500
		Interest Expense................................		360
		Insurance Expense		600
		Rent Expense, Office Space..................		900
		Rent Expense, Selling Space.................		8,100
		Office Supplies Expense		1,800
		Store Supplies Expense		1,200
		Advertising Expense............................		11,300
		To close temporary accounts having debit balances.		

As contra revenue accounts, these are income statement accounts and must be closed.

Entry 3: **Close Income Summary to Owner's Capital.**
The third closing entry is the same for a merchandising company and a service company. It closes the Income Summary account and updates the owner's capital account for income or loss. MEC's third closing entry is:

Dec.	31	Income Summary...	15,340	
		David Wingate, Capital		15,340
		To close the income summary account.		

Notice that the $15,340 amount in the entry is net income reported on the income statement in Exhibits 5.15 to 5.17.

Entry 4: **Close Withdrawals Account to Owner's Capital.**
The fourth closing entry for a merchandising company is the same as the fourth closing entry for a service company. It closes the withdrawals account and reduces the owner's capital account balance to the amount shown on the balance sheet. The fourth closing entry for MEC is:

Dec.	31	David Wingate, Capital	4,000	
		David Wingate, Withdrawals.................		4,000
		To close the withdrawals account.		

When this entry is posted, all temporary accounts are closed and ready to record events for the year 2015. The owner's capital account is also updated and reflects transactions of 2014.

CHECKPOINT

13. What temporary accounts do you expect to find in a merchandising business but not in a service business?

14. Describe the closing entries normally made by a merchandising company.

Do Quick Study question: QS 5-15

CRITICAL THINKING CHALLENGE   Refer to the Critical Thinking Challenge questions at the beginning of the chapter. Compare your answers to those suggested on Connect.

IFRS AND ASPE—THE DIFFERENCES

Difference	International Financial Reporting Standards (IFRS)	Accounting Standards for Private Enterprises (ASPE)
Expense classification	• Must be classified by nature or by function	• Can be classified in way most useful for the company

SUMMARY

LO¹ Describe merchandising and identify and explain the important income statement and balance sheet components for a merchandising company. Operations of merchandising companies involve buying products and reselling them. A merchandiser's costs on an income statement include an amount for cost of goods sold. Gross profit, or gross margin, equals net sales minus cost of goods sold. The current assets section of the balance sheet includes merchandise inventory, which refers to the products a merchandiser sells and has on hand at the balance sheet date.

LO² Describe both perpetual and periodic inventory systems. A perpetual inventory system continuously tracks the cost of goods on hand and the cost of goods sold. A periodic system accumulates the cost of goods *purchased* during the period and does not compute the amount of inventory on hand or the cost of goods sold until the end of a period.

LO³ Analyze and record transactions for merchandise purchases and sales using a perpetual system. For a perpetual inventory system, purchases net of trade discounts are added (debited) to the Merchandise Inventory account. Purchase discounts and purchase returns and allowances are subtracted from (credited to) Merchandise Inventory, and transportation-in costs are added (debited) to Merchandise Inventory. A merchandiser records sales at list price less any trade discounts. The cost of items sold is transferred from

Merchandise Inventory to Cost of Goods Sold. Refunds or credits given to customers for unsatisfactory merchandise are recorded (debited) in Sales Returns and Allowances, a contra account to Sales. If merchandise is returned and restored to inventory, the cost of this merchandise is removed from Cost of Goods Sold and transferred back to Merchandise Inventory. When cash discounts from the sales price are offered and customers pay within the discount period, the seller records (debits) discounts in Sales Discounts, a contra account to Sales. Debit and credit memoranda are documents sent between buyers and sellers to communicate that the sender is either debiting or crediting an account of the recipient.

LO⁴ Prepare adjustments for a merchandising company. With a perpetual inventory system, it is often necessary to make an adjustment for inventory shrinkage. This is calculated by comparing a physical count of inventory with the Merchandise Inventory account balance. Shrinkage is normally charged to Cost of Goods Sold.

LO⁵ Define, prepare, and use merchandising income statements. Multiple-step income statements show items by both function and nature. Classified multiple-step income statements are usually limited to internal use and show the calculation of net sales, and report expenses by function—such as selling and general and administrative—supported by a list of expenses by nature. The format of income statements published for external parties is flexible and includes the multiple-step or single-step format. The single-step format shows expenses by function with supporting note disclosure about the nature of the expenses. The gross profit ratio is calculated as gross profit divided by net sales. It is an indicator of a company's profitability before deducting operating expenses. A gross profit ratio must be large

enough to cover operating expenses and give an adequate net income.

LO⁶ Prepare closing entries for a merchandising company. Temporary accounts of merchandising companies include Sales, Sales Discounts, Sales Returns and Allowances, and Cost of Goods Sold. Each is closed to Income Summary.

GUIDANCE ANSWER TO **DECISION MAKER**

Accounts Payable Manager

Your decision is whether to comply with prior policy or create new policy not to abuse discounts offered by suppliers. Your first step should be to meet with your superior to find out if the automatic late payment policy is the actual policy and, if so, its rationale. It is possible that the prior employee was reprimanded because of this behaviour. If it is the policy to pay late, then you must apply your own sense of right and wrong.

One point of view is that the late payment policy is unethical. A deliberate plan to make late payments means that the company lies when it pretends to make purchases within the

credit terms. There is the potential that your company could lose its ability to get future credit.

Another view is that the late payment policy is acceptable. There may exist markets in which attempts to take discounts through late payments are accepted as a continued phase of price negotiation. Also, your company's suppliers can respond by billing your company for the discounts not accepted because of late payments. This is a dubious viewpoint, especially given the old employee's proposal to cover up late payments as computer or mail problems, and given that some suppliers have previously complained.

GUIDANCE ANSWERS TO **CHECKPOINT**

1. Cost of goods sold is the cost of merchandise sold to customers during a period.
2. Gross profit is the difference between net sales and cost of goods sold.
3. Widespread use of computing and related technology has dramatically increased use of the perpetual inventory system in practice.
4. The invoice indicates that the shipping terms are FOB destination, which means that Trex maintains ownership until the merchandise inventory reaches MEC. Trex must therefore bear the freight costs and is responsible for insuring the merchandise inventory during transport.
5. Under credit terms of 2/10, n/60, the credit period is 60 days and the discount period is 10 days.
6. *b*
7. Recording sales discounts and sales returns and allowances separately from sales gives useful information to managers for internal monitoring and decision making.
8. When a customer returns merchandise and the seller restores the merchandise to inventory, two entries are necessary. One entry records the decrease in revenue and credits the customer's account. The second entry debits inventory and reduces cost of goods sold.

9. There will be a credit memorandum showing the *credit* to the seller's account receivable.
10. Merchandise Inventory balance may need adjusting to reflect shrinkage.
11. Classified, multiple-step income statement. Single-step income statement.
12. All other factors remaining constant, this reflects a favourable trend because K-One is showing an increase in gross profit per $1 of net sales over time (from 39¢ of gross profit per $1 of net sales in 2012 to 41¢ of gross profit per $1 of net sales in 2014). This indicates that K-One is generating more gross profit to cover operating expenses, which appears to be favourable.
13. Sales, Sales Discounts, Sales Returns and Allowances, and Cost of Goods Sold.
14. Four closing entries (the same for merchandising and service companies): (1) close credit balances in temporary accounts to income summary, (2) close debit balances in temporary accounts to income summary, (3) close income summary to owner's capital, and (4) close withdrawals account to owner's capital.

DEMONSTRATION PROBLEM

Use the following adjusted trial balance and additional information to complete the requirements:

Ingersoll Antiques Adjusted Trial Balance December 31, 2014		
Cash	$ 19,300	
Merchandise inventory..	50,000	
Store supplies...	1,000	
Equipment	44,600	
Accumulated depreciation, equipment		$ 16,500
Accounts payable..		8,000
Salaries payable..		1,000
Dee Rizzo, capital...		69,000
Dee Rizzo, withdrawals...	8,000	
Interest revenue		300
Sales		325,000
Sales discounts...	6,000	
Sales returns and allowances	5,000	
Cost of goods sold	148,000	
Depreciation expense, store equipment	4,000	
Depreciation expense, office equipment	1,500	
Sales salaries expense	28,000	
Office salaries expense	32,000	
Insurance expense...	12,000	
Rent expense (70% is store, 30% is office)	24,000	
Store supplies expense	6,000	
Advertising expense	30,400	
Totals	$419,800	$419,800

Ingersoll Antiques showed the following additional information regarding merchandising activities for 2014:

Invoice cost of merchandise purchases.....................	$140,000
Purchase discounts......................................	3,500
Purchase returns and allowances	2,600
Transportation-in	4,000

Required

1. Use the additional information to calculate the total cost of merchandise purchases.
2. Prepare a 2014 classified, multiple-step income statement for internal use similar to Exhibit 5.15.
3. Present a single-step income statement for 2014 similar to the one in Exhibit 5.17.
4. Prepare closing entries.

Analysis Component:

Calculate the gross profit ratio for Ingersoll and for **Danier Leather** (refer to Appendix II at the back of the textbook). Round calculations to two decimal places. Can you compare the gross profit ratios for these two companies? Explain.

Planning the Solution

- Calculate the total cost of merchandise purchases.
- Calculate net sales. Subtract cost of goods sold from net sales to get gross profit. Then, classify the operating expenses as selling expenses and general and administrative expenses.
- To prepare the single-step income statement, begin with the net sales and interest earned. Then, subtract the cost of goods sold and operating expenses.
- The first closing entry debits all temporary accounts with credit balances and opens the Income Summary account. The second closing entry credits all temporary accounts with debit balances. The third entry closes the Income Summary account to the owner's capital account, and the fourth closing entry closes the withdrawals account to the capital account.
- Prepare an answer to the analysis component.

SOLUTION

1.

Invoice cost of merchandise purchases.....................	$140,000
Less: Purchase discounts	3,500
Purchase returns and allowances.....................	2,600
Add: Transportation-in.....................................	4,000
Total cost of merchandise purchases	$137,900

2. Classified, multiple-step income statement

Ingersoll Antiques Income Statement For Year Ended December 31, 2014			
Sales			$325,000
Less: Sales discounts		$ 6,000	
Sales returns and allowances		5,000	11,000
Net sales..			$314,000
Cost of goods sold			148,000
Gross profit from sales...................................			$166,000
Operating expenses:			
Selling expenses:			
Advertising expense	$30,400		
Sales salaries expense	28,000		
Rent expense, selling space	16,800		
Store supplies expense	6,000		
Depreciation expense, store equipment	4,000		
Total selling expenses............................		$85,200	
General and administrative expenses:			
Office salaries expense	$32,000		
Insurance expense	12,000		
Rent expense, office space	7,200		
Depreciation expense, office equipment	1,500		
Total general and administrative expenses...........		52,700	
Total operating expenses			137,900
Income from operations...............................			$ 28,100
Other revenues and expenses:			
Interest revenue..			300
Net income..			$ 28,400

3. Single-step income statement

Ingersoll Antiques Income Statement For Year Ended December 31, 2014		
Revenues:		
Net sales...		$314,000
Interest revenue..		300
Total revenues..		$314,300
Expenses:		
Cost of goods sold..	$148,000	
Selling expenses	85,200	
General and administrative expense	52,700	
Total expenses..		285,900
Net income..		$ 28,400

4.

Dec.	31	Sales	325,000	
		Interest Revenue	300	
		Income Summary		325,300
		To close temporary accounts with credit balances to Income Summary.		
	31	Income Summary...	296,900	
		Sales Discounts		6,000
		Sales Returns and Allowances.................		5,000
		Cost of Goods Sold...............................		148,000
		Depreciation Expense, Store Equipment		4,000
		Depreciation Expense, Office Equipment		1,500
		Sales Salaries Expense		28,000
		Office Salaries Expense..........................		32,000
		Insurance Expense		12,000
		Rent Expense		24,000
		Store Supplies Expense		6,000
		Advertising Expense..............................		30,400
		To close temporary accounts with debit balances to Income Summary.		
	31	Income Summary...	28,400	
		Dee Rizzo, Capital.................................		28,400
		To close the income summary account to capital.		
	31	Dee Rizzo, Capital	8,000	
		Dee Rizzo, Withdrawals.........................		8,000
		To close the withdrawals account to capital.		

Analysis Component:

The gross profit ratio for Ingersoll is 52.87% ($166,000/$314,000 × 100%) and 54.74% ($86,288,000/$157,621,000 × 100%) for **Danier**'s year ended June 25, 2011. You cannot compare the gross profit ratios for these two companies because they are in different industries: antiques vs. clothing.

APPENDIX 5A

Periodic and Perpetual Inventory Systems Compared

ACCOUNTING COMPARISONS

Recall that under a perpetual system, the Merchandise Inventory account is updated after each purchase and each sale. The Cost of Goods Sold account is also updated after each sale so that during the period the account balance reflects the period's total cost of goods sold to date. At the end of the period, a physical count of the merchandise inventory is performed to adjust Merchandise Inventory and Cost of Goods Sold.

Under a periodic inventory system, the Merchandise Inventory account is updated only once each accounting period. This update occurs at the *end* of the period based on a physical count of the merchandise inventory. During the next period, the Merchandise Inventory balance remains unchanged. It reflects the beginning inventory balance until it is updated again at the end of the period. In a periodic inventory system, cost of goods sold is *not* recorded as each sale occurs. Instead, the total cost of goods sold during the period is calculated at the end of the period.

LO7 Record and compare merchandising transactions using both periodic and perpetual inventory systems.

RECORDING MERCHANDISE TRANSACTIONS

Under a perpetual system, each purchase, purchase return and allowance, purchase discount, and transportation-in transaction is recorded in the Merchandise Inventory account. Under a periodic system, a separate temporary account is set up for each of these items. At the end of a period, each of these temporary accounts is closed and the Merchandise Inventory account is updated. To illustrate the differences, we use parallel columns to show journal entries for the most common transactions using both periodic and perpetual inventory systems (we drop explanations for simplicity).

Purchases

MEC purchases merchandise for $1,200 on credit with terms of 2/10, n/30, and records this purchase as:

Periodic		
Purchases	1,200	
Accounts Payable		1,200

Perpetual		
Merchandise Inventory	1,200	
Accounts Payable		1,200

The periodic system debits all merchandise purchases to an expense account called *Purchases*.

Purchase Returns and Allowances

MEC returns merchandise because of defects. If the recorded cost[12] of the defective merchandise is $300, MEC records the return with this entry:

Periodic		
Accounts Payable	300	
Purchase Returns and Allowances		300

Perpetual		
Accounts Payable	300	
Merchandise Inventory		300

---

12 Recorded cost is the cost recorded in the account after any discounts.

This entry is the same if MEC is granted a price reduction (allowance) instead of returning the merchandise. In the periodic system, the entry credits a contra expense account called **Purchase Returns and Allowances** that accumulates the cost of all returns and allowances transactions during a period. Because Purchase Returns and Allowances is a contra expense account related to the Purchases account, it is subtracted from Purchases when determining net purchases as shown in Exhibit 5A.1.

EXHIBIT 5A.1

Calculation of Net Purchases and Cost of Goods Purchased Under a Periodic Inventory System

Purchases		$235,800
Less: Purchase discounts	$4,200	
Purchase returns and allowances	1,500	5,700
Net purchases		$230,100
Add: Transportation-in		2,300
Cost of goods purchased		$232,400

Purchase Discount

When MEC pays the supplier for the previous purchase within the discount period, the required payment is $882 (= $1,200 − $300 = $900 × 98% = $882) and is recorded as:

Periodic				Perpetual		
Accounts Payable	900			Accounts Payable	900	
Purchase Discounts		18		Merchandise Inventory		18
Cash		882		Cash		882

The periodic system credits a contra expense account called *Purchase Discounts* that accumulates discounts taken on purchase transactions during the period. Purchase Discounts, like Purchase Returns and Allowances, is subtracted from the Purchases account balance as shown in Exhibit 5A.1. If payment is delayed until after the discount period expires, the entry under both the periodic and perpetual methods is to debit Accounts Payable and credit Cash for $900 each.

Transportation-In

MEC paid a $75 freight charge to haul merchandise to its store. In the periodic system, this cost is charged to an expense account known as *Transportation-In*. Transportation-in is included as part of the $232,400 total cost of merchandise purchased as shown in Exhibit 5A.1.

Periodic				Perpetual		
Transportation-In	75			Merchandise Inventory	75	
Cash		75		Cash		75

Sales

MEC sold $2,400 of merchandise on credit and MEC's cost of this merchandise is $1,600:

Periodic				Perpetual		
Accounts Receivable	2,400			Accounts Receivable	2,400	
Sales		2,400		Sales		2,400
				Cost of Goods Sold	1,600	
				Merchandise Inventory		1,600

Under the periodic system, the cost of goods sold is *not* recorded at the time of sale. We later show how the periodic system calculates total cost of goods sold at the end of a period.

Sales Returns

A customer returns part of the merchandise from the previous transaction, where returned items sell for $800 and cost $600. MEC restores the merchandise to inventory and records the return as:

Periodic	
Sales Returns and Allowances............	800
Accounts Receivable	800

Perpetual	
Sales Returns and Allowances............	800
Accounts Receivable	800
Merchandise Inventory.....................	600
Cost of Goods Sold......................	600

The periodic system records only the revenue reduction.

CHECKPOINT

15. Identify those accounts included in a periodic system that are not included in a perpetual system.
16. The perpetual system has a Cost of Goods Sold account. Explain why the periodic system does not have a Cost of Goods Sold account.

Do Quick Study questions: *QS 5-16, *QS 5-17

ADJUSTING ENTRIES

The adjusting entries recorded under a periodic and a perpetual inventory system are identical except for the treatment of merchandise inventory. Under a perpetual inventory system, recall that the adjusting entry shown below was recorded to reflect shrinkage of $250 (the difference between the $21,250 unadjusted balance in Merchandise Inventory and the $21,000 physical count). Under a periodic inventory system, there is no corresponding adjustment to update the $19,000 unadjusted balance in Merchandise Inventory. Instead, we use closing entries to update the Merchandise Inventory account. We show the closing entry approach to update Merchandise Inventory in the next section.

Periodic
No entry

Perpetual	
Cost of Goods Sold	250
Merchandise Inventory	250

A WORK SHEET AND AN INCOME STATEMENT FOR A MERCHANDISING COMPANY— PERIODIC INVENTORY

Exhibit 5A.2 presents a version of the work sheet that the accountant for MEC could prepare in the process of developing its financial statements. Note the differences (bolded) from the work sheet in Exhibit 5.14.

In particular, the unadjusted trial balance includes the beginning inventory balance of $19,000. The beginning inventory balance is entered in the Debit column for the income statement. The ending inventory balance of $21,000 is entered in the Credit column of the income statement **and** the Debit column of the balance sheet. This step allows the calculation of cost of goods sold to be included in net income while the correct ending inventory balance is included on the balance sheet. Recall that cost of goods sold is calculated as:

Beginning merchandise inventory	$ 19,000
Plus: Net cost of purchases..	232,400
Less: Ending merchandise inventory...........................	21,000
Equals: Cost of goods sold	$230,400

EXHIBIT 5A.2
Work Sheet for MEC for the Year Ended December 31, 2014

MEC Work Sheet.xls

Home   Insert   Page Layout   Formulas   Data   Review   View

P18   fx

MEC
Work Sheet
For the Year Ended December 31, 2014

No.	Account	Unadjusted Trial Balance Dr.	Cr.	Adjustments Dr.	Cr.	Adjusted Trial Balance Dr.	Cr.	Income Statement Dr.	Cr.	Balance Sheet & Statement of Changes in Equity Dr.	Cr.
101	Cash	8,200				8,200				8,200	
106	Accounts receivable	11,200				11,200				11,200	
119	Merchandise inventory	19,000				19,000		19,000	21,000	21,000	
124	Office supplies	2,350			c) 1,800	550				550	
125	Store supplies	1,450			b) 1,200	250				250	
128	Prepaid insurance	900			a) 600	300				300	
163	Office equipment	4,200				4,200				4,200	
164	Accum. dep., office equipment		700		e) 700		1,400				1,400
165	Store equipment	30,000				30,000				30,000	
166	Accum. dep., store equipment		3,000		d) 3,000		6,000				6,000
201	Accounts payable		16,000				16,000				16,000
209	Salaries payable				f) 800		800				800
301	David Wingate, capital		40,160				40,160				40,160
302	David Wingate, withdrawals	4,000				4,000				4,000	
406	Rent revenue		2,800				2,800		2,800		
413	Sales		321,000				321,000		321,000		
414	Sales returns and allowances	2,000				2,000		2,000			
415	Sales discounts	4,300				4,300		4,300			
505	**Purchases**	235,800				235,800		235,800			
506	**Purchase returns and allow.**		1,500				1,500		1,500		
507	**Purchase discounts**		4,200				4,200		4,200		
508	**Transportation-in**	2,300				2,300		2,300			
612	Dep. expense, store equipment			d) 3,000		3,000		3,000			
613	Dep. expense, office equipment			e) 700		700		700			
620	Office salaries expense	25,000		f) 300		25,300		25,300			
621	Sales salaries expense	18,000		f) 500		18,500		18,500			
633	Interest expense	360				360		360			
637	Insurance expense			a) 600		600		600			
641	Rent expense, office space	900				900		900			
642	Rent expense, selling space	8,100				8,100		8,100			
650	Office supplies expense			c) 1,800		1,800		1,800			
651	Store supplies expense			b) 1,200		1,200		1,200			
655	Advertising expense	11,300				11,300		11,300			
	Totals	389,360	389,360	8,100	8,100	393,860	393,860	335,160	350,500	79,700	64,360
	Net income							15,340			15,340
	Totals							350,500	350,500	79,700	79,700

Note: Notice that **both beginning and ending inventory appear in the income statement** columns of the work sheet. This is because both amounts are part of the cost of goods sold calculation in a periodic inventory system (Beginning MI = Net cost of purchases − Ending MI = COGS). Be alert to the fact that **ending inventory appears on the balance sheet** since that is the actual balance on hand at December 31, 2014.

The adjustments in the work sheet reflect the following:

a. Expiration of $600 of prepaid insurance.

b. Use of $1,200 of store supplies.

c. Use of $1,800 of office supplies.

d. Depreciation of the store equipment for $3,000.

e. Depreciation of the office equipment for $700.

f. Accrual of $300 of unpaid office salaries and $500 of unpaid store salaries.

Once the adjusted amounts are extended into the financial statement columns, the accountant uses the information to develop the company's financial statements.

The classified, multiple-step income statement under a periodic inventory system is shown in Exhibit 5A.3.

EXHIBIT 5A.3

Classified, Multiple-Step Income Statement—Periodic

MEC Income Statement For Year Ended December 31, 2014			
Sales			$321,000
Less: Sales discounts		$ 4,300	
Sales returns and allowances		2,000	6,300
Net sales			$314,700
Cost of goods sold			
Merchandise inventory, Dec. 31, 2013		$ 19,000	
Purchases	$235,800		
Less: Purchase returns and allowances	$1,500		
Purchase discounts	4,200	5,700	
Net purchases		$230,100	
Add: Transportation-in		2,300	
Cost of goods purchased		232,400	
Goods available for sale		$251,400	
Less: Merchandise inventory, Dec. 31, 2014		21,000	
Cost of goods sold			230,400
Gross profit from sales			$ 84,300
Operating expenses:			
Selling expenses:			
Sales salaries expense	$ 18,500		
Advertising expense	11,300		
Rent expense, selling space	8,100		
Depreciation expense, store equipment	3,000		
Store supplies expense	1,200		
Total selling expenses		$ 42,100	
General and administrative expenses			
Office salaries expense	$ 25,300		
Office supplies expense	1,800		
Rent expense, office space	900		
Depreciation expense, office equipment	700		
Insurance expense	600		
Total general and administrative expense		29,300	
Total operating expenses			71,400
Income from operations			$ 12,900
Other revenues and expenses:			
Rent revenue		$ 2,800	
Interest expense		360	2,440
Net income			$ 15,340

CLOSING ENTRIES

The closing entries under a periodic system are the same as for a perpetual system except for the differences highlighted in Exhibit 5A.4. In a periodic system, notice that the temporary accounts for Purchases, Purchase Discounts, Purchase Returns and Allowances, and Transportation-In must be closed. Because the transactions reflected by these accounts are included in the Cost of Goods Sold account under a perpetual inventory system, the closing entries under a perpetual system involve fewer accounts.

The closing entries under a periodic system also involve the Merchandise Inventory account. The $19,000 unadjusted balance in the Merchandise Inventory account shown in Exhibit 5A.2 is beginning inventory. Therefore, the Merchandise Inventory account needs to be updated to reflect the ending merchandise inventory actually on hand of $21,000. Different approaches can be used to update the balance in Merchandise

EXHIBIT 5A.4

Comparison of Closing Entries—Periodic and Perpetual

Periodic — Closing Entries		
(1)		
Rent Revenue	2,800	
Sales	321,000	
Merchandise Inventory†	21,000	
Purchase Discounts	4,200	
Purchase Returns and Allowances	1,500	
Income Summary		350,500
(2)		
Income Summary	335,160	
Sales Discounts		4,300
Sales Returns and Allowances		2,000
Merchandise Inventory‡		19,000
Purchases		235,800
Transportation-In		2,300
Depreciation Expense, Store Equipment		3,000
Depreciation Expense, Office Equipment		700
Office Salaries Expense		25,300
Sales Salaries Expense		18,500
Interest Expense		360
Insurance Expense		600
Rent Expense, Office Space		900
Rent Expense, Selling Space		8,100
Office Supplies Expense		1,800
Store Supplies Expense		1,200
Advertising Expense		11,300
(3)		
Income Summary	15,340	
David Wingate, Capital		15,340
(4)		
David Wingate, Capital	4,000	
David Wingate, Withdrawals		4,000

Perpetual — Closing Entries		
(1)		
Rent Revenue	2,800	
Sales	321,000	
Income Summary		323,800
(2)		
Income Summary	308,460	
Sales Discounts		4,300
Sales Returns and Allowances		2,000
Cost of Goods Sold		230,400
Depreciation Expense, Store Equipment		3,000
Depreciation Expense, Office Equipment		700
Office Salaries Expense		25,300
Sales Salaries Expense		18,500
Interest Expense		360
Insurance Expense		600
Rent Expense, Office Space		900
Rent Expense, Selling Space		8,100
Office Supplies Expense		1,800
Store Supplies Expense		1,200
Advertising Expense		11,300
(3)		
Income Summary	15,340	
David Wingate, Capital		15,340
(4)		
David Wingate, Capital	4,000	
David Wingate, Withdrawals		4,000

†This is the *ending* merchandise inventory balance being **added** to the account.
‡This is the *beginning* merchandise inventory balance being **subtracted** from the account.

Inventory. We will update Merchandise Inventory using the closing entry approach. The closing entry approach removes the beginning inventory amount (by crediting Merchandise Inventory) and replaces it with the correct ending inventory value (by debiting Merchandise Inventory). These entries are highlighted in Exhibit 5A.4.

By updating Merchandise Inventory and closing Purchases, Purchase Discounts, Purchase Returns and Allowances, and Transportation-In, the periodic system transfers the cost of goods sold amount to Income Summary. Review the periodic side of Exhibit 5A.4 and notice that the boldface items affect Income Summary, as shown in Exhibit 5A.5.

EXHIBIT 5A.5

Merchandising Cost Flows Across Periods

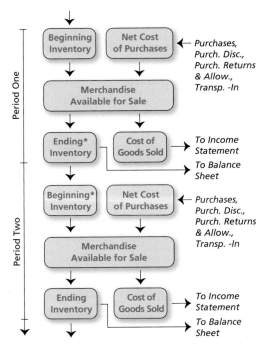

*One period's ending inventory is the next period's beginning inventory.

Credited to Income Summary in the first closing entry:	
Merchandise Inventory (ending balance)	$ 21,000
Purchase Discounts	4,200
Purchase Returns and Allowances	1,500
Debited to Income Summary in the second closing entry:	
Merchandise Inventory (beginning balance)	(19,000)
Purchases	(235,800)
Transportation-in	(2,300)
Net effect on Income Summary	$(230,400)

This $230,400 effect on Income Summary is the cost of goods sold amount. This figure is confirmed as follows:

Beginning inventory		$ 19,000
Purchases	$235,800	
Less: Purchase discounts	4,200	
Less: Purchase returns and allowances	1,500	
Add: Transportation-in	2,300	
Net cost of goods purchased		232,400
Cost of goods available for sale		$251,400
Less: Ending inventory		21,000
Cost of goods sold		$230,400

The periodic system transfers cost of goods sold to the Income Summary account but does not use a Cost of Goods Sold account. Exhibit 5A.5 shows the relation between inventory, purchases, and cost of goods sold across periods.

The periodic system does not measure shrinkage. Instead it calculates cost of goods available for sale, subtracts the cost of ending inventory, and defines the difference as cost of goods sold, which includes shrinkage.

CHECKPOINT

17. Why does the Merchandise Inventory account on the periodic unadjusted trial balance differ from the Merchandise Inventory balance on the perpetual unadjusted trial balance?

18. What account is used in a perpetual inventory system but not in a periodic system?

19. Which of the following accounts are temporary accounts? (a) Merchandise Inventory, (b) Purchases, (c) Transportation-In

20. How is cost of goods sold calculated under a periodic inventory accounting system?

Do Quick Study questions: *QS 5-18, *QS 5-19, *QS 5-20

APPENDIX 5B

Sales Tax

LO8 Explain and record Provincial Sales Tax (PST) and Goods and Services Tax (GST).

This section looks at the additional issue of recording sales tax. Most provinces and the federal government require retailers to collect sales tax from customers and to send these taxes periodically to the appropriate agency.

PROVINCIAL SALES TAX

Provincial Sales Tax (PST) is a tax applied on sales to the final consumers of products and/or services. All provinces except Alberta (and the territories) require retailers to collect PST from their customers and to remit this tax periodically to the appropriate provincial authority. It should be noted that not all sales are subject to PST.[13] PST collected is credited to a separate account, as shown in the following example where JC Sales sells merchandise on January 5 costing $600 for $900 on account (assuming PST of 7%).

As well as being collected, PST may be *paid* on items purchased for use or on long-term assets acquired. In these cases, the PST paid is part of the expense or asset cost associated with the purchase.

GOODS AND SERVICES TAX

The **Goods and Services Tax (GST)** is a 5%[14] tax on almost all goods and services provided in Canada. It is a federal tax on the consumer. However, unlike the PST, businesses pay GST up front but generally receive a full credit or refund for all GST paid. Ultimately only the final consumer pays this tax. This is because businesses collect GST on sales, but since they receive full credit for GST paid on their purchases, they only remit the difference to the appropriate federal authority. The **Harmonized Sales Tax (HST)** is a combined GST and PST rate applied to taxable supplies. At the time of writing, New Brunswick, Nova Scotia, Newfoundland and Labrador, and Ontario apply HST of 13%.

PST and GST are accounted for under both perpetual and periodic inventory systems. To illustrate, assume JC Sales, a merchandiser located in Manitoba, purchases $600 of merchandise inventory on January 3 with terms n/10. These items are then sold for $900 on January 5 with terms of n/15. JC Sales records these transactions as follows:[15]

Jan.	3	Merchandise Inventory	600	
		GST Receivable[16]...	30	
		Accounts Payable....................................		630
		To record the purchase of merchandise on account; $600 × 5% = $30 GST.		

---

13 A detailed discussion of the liabilities created by PST and GST is found in Chapter 11.

14 Effective since January 1, 2008.

15 Assume that all amounts here and in related end-of-chapter materials are before PST and GST.

16 Some businesses will debit GST Payable instead of GST Receivable because they use only one account for GST. In such a case, when the account has a credit balance, cash must be paid to the Receiver General for Canada. When the account has a debit balance, a refund is applied for.

Jan.	5	Accounts Receivable.................................	1,008	
		Sales		900
		PST Payable		63
		GST Payable.............................		45
		To record the sale of merchandise on account; $900 × 7% = $63 PST; $900 × 5% = $45 GST; $900 + $63 + $45 = $1,008.		
	5	Cost of Goods Sold	600	
		Merchandise Inventory		600
		To record the cost of sales.		

PST and GST are calculated as a percentage of the selling price, except in Quebec and PEI, where GST is initially calculated as a percentage of the selling price and PST is calculated as a percentage of the total of the selling price plus the GST. It should also be noted that while GST is a 5% federal tax, and thus is uniform in all of the provinces, PST is a provincial tax and differs in percentage from province to province. The detailed rates for each province are provided in Exhibit 5B.1.

To continue the example, assume the January 3 purchase is paid on January 13 and the sale of January 5 is collected on January 20. Assuming no other purchases and sales during the month, the January sales taxes are paid to the appropriate government bodies on February 28. The entries to record these transactions are:

Jan.	13	Accounts Payable	630	
		Cash		630
		To record payment of January 3 purchase.		
	20	Cash	1,008	
		Accounts Receivable		1,008
		To record collection of January 5 sale.		
Feb.	28	PST Payable	63	
		Cash		63
		To record payment of PST to provincial government authority.		
	28	GST Payable..	45	
		Cash		15
		GST Receivable		30
		To record payment of GST to Receiver General for Canada.		

Examples demonstrating PST/GST for each region in Canada can be found online in Extend Your Knowledge 5-1, along with reinforcement exercises.

EYK

EXHIBIT 5B.1

Sales Tax Rates

	PST Rate	GST Rate	HST Rate*
Alberta	-0-	5%	—
British Columbia***	7%	5%	
Manitoba	7%	5%	—
Northwest Territories	-0-	5%	—
Nunavut	-0-	5%	—
Prince Edward Island**	10%	5%	—
Quebec**	9.5%	5%	—
Saskatchewan	5%	5%	—
Yukon	-0-	5%	—
New Brunswick*	—	—	13%
Nova Scotia*	—	—	15%
Newfoundland and Labrador*	—	—	13%
Ontario*	—	—	13%

*A Harmonized Sales Tax (HST) is applied in place of PST and GST. HST is the combination of the PST with
the GST for a total sales tax. For New Brunswick, Nova Scotia, Newfoundland and Labrador, and Ontario,
the PST of 8% is combined with the GST of 5% for HST of 13%.
**In Quebec and Prince Edward Island, PST = PST% × (Sales price + GST).
***Effective April 1, 2013.

CHECKPOINT

21. What is the difference between PST, GST, and HST?

Do Quick Study questions: *QS 5-21, *QS 5-22, *QS 5-23, *QS 5-24

SUMMARY OF APPENDIX 5A AND APPENDIX 5B

**LO⁷   Record and compare merchandising transactions
using both periodic and perpetual inventory systems.**
Transactions involving the sale and purchase of merchandise
are recorded and analyzed under both inventory systems.
Adjusting and closing entries for both inventory systems are
also illustrated and explained.

**LO⁸   Explain and record Provincial Sales Tax (PST) and
Goods and Services Tax (GST).** PST is a tax applied on sales
to final consumers that varies in percent between provinces.
GST is a 5% tax collected on most sales but full credit is
received for GST paid by a GST registrant (business).
Harmonized Sales Tax (HST) is a combined GST and PST rate
applied to taxable supplies.

GUIDANCE ANSWERS TO CHECKPOINT

15. The beginning Merchandise Inventory balance is included
on the periodic unadjusted trial balance and not the perpetual along with Purchases, Purchase Discounts, Purchase
Returns and Allowances, and Transportation-In.

16. Cost of Goods Sold is calculated under the periodic system using the account balances of Merchandise Inventory
(beginning inventory balance), Purchases, Purchase Discounts, Purchase Returns and Allowances, Transportation-
In, and subtracting the ending inventory amount
determined through a physical count.

17. The Merchandise Inventory account on the periodic
unadjusted trial balance represents the balance at the
beginning of the period. The Merchandise Inventory
account on the perpetual unadjusted trial balance has
been adjusted regularly during the accounting period

for all transactions affecting inventory, such as
purchases, returns, discounts, transportation-in,
and cost of sales, and therefore represents the balance
at the end of the period.

18. Cost of Goods Sold.

19. (b) Purchases and (c) Transportation-In.

20. Under a periodic inventory system, the cost of goods sold
is determined at the end of an accounting period by adding the net cost of goods purchased to the beginning inventory and subtracting the ending inventory.

21. PST is Provincial Sales Tax and varies across Canada. GST is
the Goods and Services Tax of 5% that is constant across
Canada. HST is Harmonized Sales Tax that is a combination of the Provincial Sales Tax applicable in the jurisdic-
tions and the 5% Goods and Services Tax.

GLOSSARY

Cash discount A reduction in the price of merchandise that is granted by a seller to a purchaser in exchange for the purchaser paying within a specified period of time called the *discount period*.

Catalogue price See *list price*.

Classified, multiple-step income statement An income statement format that shows intermediate totals between sales and net income and detailed computations of net sales and cost of goods sold.

Cost of goods sold (COGS) The cost of merchandise sold to customers during a period; also commonly referred to as *cost of sales*.

Cost of sales See *cost of goods sold*.

Credit memorandum A notification that the sender has entered a credit in the recipient's account maintained by the sender.

Credit period The time period that can pass before a customer's payment is due.

Credit terms The description of the amounts and timing of payments that a buyer agrees to make in the future.

Debit memorandum A notification that the sender has entered a debit in the recipient's account maintained by the sender.

Discount period The time period in which a cash discount is available and a reduced payment can be made by the buyer.

EOM The abbreviation for *end of month*, used to describe credit terms for some transactions.

FOB The abbreviation for *free on board*, the designated point at which ownership of goods passes to the buyer; *FOB shipping point* (or *factory*) means that the buyer pays the shipping costs and accepts ownership of the goods at the seller's place of business; *FOB destination* means that the seller pays the shipping costs and the ownership of the goods transfers to the buyer at the buyer's place of business.

Freight-in See *transportation-in*.

Freight-out See *transportation-out*.

Full disclosure principle The generally accepted accounting principle that requires financial statements to report all relevant information about the operations and financial position of the entity; disclosure of items not contained in the body of financial statements is often accomplished by providing notes to financial statements such as those for WestJet in Appendix II of the text.

Function of an expense A method of classifying or grouping expenses based on their purpose or what the expenses relate to, such as cost of goods sold, selling expenses, and general and administrative expenses; this method must also provide additional information to show the nature of expenses within each group.

General and administrative expenses Expenses that support the overall operations of a business and include the expenses of such activities as providing accounting services, human resource management, and financial management.

Goods and Services Tax (GST) A federal tax on almost all goods and services provided in Canada.

Gross margin The difference between net sales and the cost of goods sold; also called *gross profit*.

Gross margin ratio See *gross profit ratio*.

Gross profit The difference between net sales and the cost of goods sold; also called *gross margin*.

Gross profit ratio Gross profit from sales (net sales minus cost of goods sold) divided by net sales; also called *gross margin ratio*.

Harmonized Sales Tax (HST) A combined GST and PST rate applied to taxable supplies.

Inventory See *merchandise inventory*.

List price The catalogue price of an item before any trade discount is deducted.

Merchandise Products, also called *goods*, that a company acquires for the purpose of reselling them to customers.

Merchandise inventory Products that a company owns for the purpose of selling them to customers. Also called *inventory*.

Merchandiser Earns net income by buying and selling merchandise.

Nature of an expense A method of classifying an expense based on its basic characteristics or what it is. For example, when expenses are identified on the income statement as depreciation, rent, property tax, and salaries, the nature of the expense is being identified.

Net sales Calculated as gross sales less sales discounts and sales returns and allowances.

Notes to financial statements An integral part of financial statements that provides relevant information about the operations and financial position of the entity in addition to that contained in the financial statements; providing notes complies with the full disclosure principle; for an example, see the notes for WestJet in Appendix II of the text.

Periodic inventory system A method of accounting that records the cost of inventory purchased but does not track the quantity on hand or sold to customers; the records are updated at the end of each period to reflect the results of physical counts of the items on hand.

Perpetual inventory system A method of accounting that maintains continuous records of the cost of inventory on hand and the cost of goods sold.

Provincial Sales Tax (PST) A tax applied on sales to the final consumers of products and/or services.

Purchase discount A term used by a purchaser to describe a cash discount granted to the purchaser for paying within the discount period.

Purchase Returns and Allowances A contra expense account used when a periodic inventory system is in place in which purchase returns and/or purchase allowances are recorded.

Retailer An intermediary that buys products from manufacturers or wholesalers and sells them to consumers.

Sales discount A term used by a seller to describe a cash discount granted to customers for paying within the discount period.

Sales returns and allowances A contra revenue account in which sales returns and/or sales allowances are recorded.

Selling expenses The expenses of promoting sales by displaying and advertising the merchandise, making sales, and delivering goods to customers.

Shrinkage Inventory losses that occur as a result of theft or deterioration.

Single-step income statement An income statement format that includes cost of goods sold as an operating expense and shows only one subtotal for total expenses.

Trade discount A reduction below a list or catalogue price that may vary in amount for wholesalers, retailers, and final consumers.

Transportation-in The cost to the purchaser to transport merchandise purchased to the purchaser; transportation-in is part of Cost of Goods Sold.

Transportation-out The cost to the seller to transport merchandise sold to the customer; transportation-out is a selling expense.

Wholesaler A company that buys products from manufacturers or other wholesalers and sells them to retailers or other wholesalers.

Connect Visit **Connect** for additional study tools, practice quizzes, to search an interactive eBook, and much more.

CONCEPT REVIEW QUESTIONS

1. Refer to the income statement for 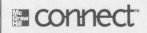 WestJet in Appendix II. Is WestJet a merchandiser?

2. Refer to the income statement for  Danier in Appendix II. Is a detailed calculation of the cost of goods sold presented?

3. In comparing the accounts of a merchandising company with those of a service company, what additional accounts would the merchandising company be likely to use, assuming it employs a perpetual inventory system?

4. What items appear in the financial statements of merchandising companies but not in the statements of service companies?

5. Explain how a business can earn a gross profit on its sales and still have a net loss.

6. Distinguish between cash discounts and trade discounts. Is the amount of a trade discount on purchased merchandise recorded in the accounts?

7. Why would a company's manager be concerned about the quantity of its purchase returns if its suppliers allow unlimited returns?

8. Danier needs to be skillful in negotiating purchase contracts with suppliers. What shipping terms should Danier negotiate to minimize its freight-in costs?

9. Does the sender of a debit memorandum record a debit or a credit in the account of the recipient? Which does the recipient record?

10. What is the difference between a sales discount and a purchase discount?

11. Why would a company offer a cash discount?

12. Briefly explain why a company's manager would want the accounting system to record a customer's return of unsatisfactory goods in the Sales Returns and Allowances account instead of the Sales account. In addition, explain whether the information would be useful for external decision makers.

13. How does a company that uses a perpetual inventory system determine the amount of inventory shrinkage?

14. What is the difference between single-step and multiple-step income statement formats?

QUICK STUDY

QS 5-1 Components of income for a merchandiser LO¹

Referring to the format presented in Exhibit 5.2, calculate gross profit and the net income or net loss for each of the following.

	A	B	C	D	E
Net sales	$14,000	$102,000	$68,000	$540,000	$398,000
Cost of goods sold	8,000	64,000	31,000	320,000	215,000
Operating expenses	9,000	31,000	22,000	261,000	106,000

QS 5-2 Contrasting periodic and perpetual systems LO²

For each description below, identify the inventory system as either periodic or perpetual.

a. Requires a physical count of inventory to determine the amount of inventory to report on the balance sheet.

b. Records the cost of goods sold each time a sales transaction occurs.

c. Provides more timely information to managers.

d. Was traditionally used by companies such as drug and department stores that sold large quantities of low-valued items.

e. Requires an adjusting entry to record inventory shrinkage.

QS 5-3 Perpetual and periodic inventory systems LO²

For each situation given, calculate cost of goods sold and identify if the information provided reflects a perpetual or periodic inventory system.

a.

Merchandise Inventory			Cost of Goods Sold	
Beginning Inventory	150	?	?	
Purchases	340			
Ending Inventory	60			

b.

Merchandise Inventory*		Purchases	
Beginning Inventory	150	340	

*A physical inventory count at year-end showed a balance on hand of $60.

QS 5-4 Perpetual and periodic inventory systems LO²

For each situation given, calculate cost of goods sold and identify if the information provided reflects a perpetual or periodic inventory system.

a. Merchandise Inventory shows a balance at January 1, 2014, of $170, the Purchases account has a balance of $700 at December 31, 2014, and a physical count of merchandise inventory on the same date reveals a balance of $120 on hand.

b. Merchandise Inventory shows a $200 balance at January 1, 2014, purchases during the period of $1,000, and a balance of $75 at December 31, 2014, after the adjustment for shrinkage.

QS 5-5 Merchandise purchase transactions—perpetual LO³

Journalize each of the following transactions assuming a perpetual inventory system.

May	1	Purchased $1,200 of merchandise inventory; terms 1/10, n/30.
	14	Paid for the May 1 purchase.
	15	Purchased $3,000 of merchandise inventory; terms 2/15, n/30.
	30	Paid for the May 15 purchase, less the applicable discount.

QS 5-6 Merchandise purchase: allowance—perpetual LO³

Journalize each of the following transactions assuming a perpetual inventory system.

Aug.	2	Purchased $14,000 of merchandise inventory; terms 1/5, n/15.
	4	Received a credit memorandum from the supplier confirming a $1,500 allowance regarding the August 2 purchase.
	17	Paid for the August 2 purchase, less the allowance.

QS 5-7 Merchandise purchase: trade discount, return—perpetual LO³

Prepare journal entries to record each of the following transactions of a merchandising company. Show any supporting calculations. Assume a perpetual inventory system.

Mar. 5 Purchased 500 units of product with a list price of $5 per unit. The purchaser was granted a trade discount of 20% and the terms of the sale were 2/10, n/60.
7 Returned 50 defective units from the March 5 purchase and received full credit.
15 Paid the amount due resulting from the March 5 purchase, less the return on March 7 and applicable discount.

QS 5-8 Sale of merchandise transactions—perpetual LO³

Journalize each of the following transactions assuming a perpetual inventory system.

Sept. 1 Sold merchandise to JenAir for $6,000 (cost of sales $4,200); terms 2/10, n/30.
14 Collected the amount owing regarding the September 1 sale to JenAir.
15 Sold merchandise costing $1,500 to Dennis Leval for $1,800; terms 2/10, n/30.
25 Collected the amount owing from the September 15 sale to Dennis Leval, less the applicable discount.

QS 5-9 Sale of merchandise: allowance—perpetual LO³

Journalize each of the following transactions assuming a perpetual inventory system.

Oct. 15 Sold merchandise to Leslie Garth for $900 (cost of sales $600); terms 1/5, n/20.
16 Issued a $100 credit memorandum to Leslie Garth regarding an allowance on the October 15 sale.
25 Collected the amount owing regarding the October 15 sale to Leslie Garth, less the allowance granted on October 16.

QS 5-10 Sale of merchandise: return—perpetual LO³

Prepare journal entries to record each of the following transactions of a merchandising company. Show any supporting calculations. Assume a perpetual inventory system.

Apr. 1 Sold merchandise for $2,000, granting the customer terms of 2/10, EOM. The cost of the merchandise was $1,400.
4 The customer in the April 1 sale returned merchandise and received credit for $500. The merchandise, which had cost $350, was returned to inventory.
11 Received payment for the amount due resulting from the April 1 sale, less the return and applicable discount, on April 4.

QS 5-11 Profitability LO¹,³,⁵

Using a format similar to Exhibit 5.11, calculate net sales, gross profit from sales, and the gross profit ratio (round to two decimal places).

	a	b	c	d
Sales	$130,000	$512,000	$35,700	$245,700
Sales discounts	4,200	16,500	400	3,500
Sales returns and allowances	17,000	5,000	5,000	700
Cost of goods sold	76,600	326,700	21,300	125,900

QS 5-12 Shrinkage LO⁴

Beamer Company's unadjusted ledger on July 31, the end of the fiscal year, includes the following accounts, which have normal balances (assume a perpetual inventory system):

Merchandise inventory	$ 34,800
Joy Beamer, capital	115,300
Joy Beamer, withdrawals	4,000
Sales	157,200
Sales discounts	1,700
Sales returns and allowances	3,500
Cost of goods sold	102,000
Depreciation expense	7,300
Salaries expense	29,500
Miscellaneous expenses	2,000

A physical count of the inventory discloses that the cost of the merchandise on hand is $32,900. Prepare the entry to record this information and calculate gross profit.

QS 5-13 Classified multi-step vs. single-step income statements LO⁵

Use the following adjusted trial balance information for JetCo's December 31, 2014, year-end to prepare (a) a classified multi-step income statement, and (b) a single-step income statement.

Account	Debit	Credit
Advertising expense	$ 6	
Assets	120	
Cost of goods sold	60	
Interest revenue		$ 5
Liabilities		90
Lisa Jet, capital		31
Lisa Jet, withdrawals	8	
Office salaries expense	10	
Office supplies expense	3	
Sales		100
Sales discounts	4	
Sales salaries expense	15	

QS 5-14 Gross profit ratio LO⁵

Willaby Company had net sales of $248,000 and cost of goods sold of $114,080. Calculate and interpret the gross profit ratio, assuming the gross profit ratio for the industry is an average of 53%.

QS 5-15 Closing entries LO⁶

Use the following adjusted trial balance information to prepare closing entries for TI Company at December 31, 2014.

Account	Debit	Credit
Accounts payable		$ 6
Accumulated depreciation, building		8
Advertising expense	$ 7	
Depreciation expense	2	
Building	50	
Cash	5	
Cost of goods sold	25	
Merchandise inventory	10	
Sales		70
Sales discounts	3	
Sales returns and allowances	4	
Tony Ingram, capital		23
Tony Ingram, withdrawals	1	

*QS 5-16 Merchandise purchase transactions—periodic LO⁷

Using the information in QS 5-5 through QS 5-7, prepare journal entries to record each of the transactions of the merchandising companies assuming a periodic inventory system.

*QS 5-17 Sale of merchandise transactions—periodic LO⁷

Using the information in QS 5-8 through QS 5-10, prepare journal entries to record each of the transactions of the merchandising companies assuming a periodic inventory system.

*QS 5-18 Cost of goods sold—periodic LO⁷

Using the following information, calculate cost of goods sold for the year ended December 31, 2014.

Merchandise inventory (January 1, 2014)	$ 40,000
Kay Bondar, capital	102,000
Kay Bondar, withdrawals	65,000
Sales	450,000
Sales returns and allowances	27,000
Purchases	180,000
Purchase discounts	1,400
Transportation-in	14,000
Merchandise inventory (December 31, 2014)	22,000
Salaries expense	120,000
Depreciation expense	31,000

*QS 5-19 Closing entries—periodic LO⁷

Using the information in *QS 5-18, prepare the closing entries.

*QS 5-20 Profitability—periodic LO⁵,⁷

Calculate net sales, cost of goods sold, gross profit, and the gross profit ratio (round to two decimal places) in each of the following situations.

	a	b	c	d
Sales	$130,000	$512,000	$35,700	$245,700
Sales discounts	4,200	16,500	400	3,500
Merchandise inventory, Jan. 1, 2014	8,000	21,000	1,500	4,300
Purchases	120,000	350,000	29,000	131,000
Purchase returns and allowances	4,000	14,000	750	3,100
Merchandise inventory, Dec. 1, 2014	7,500	22,000	900	4,100

*QS 5-21 Sales tax on purchases—perpetual LO³,⁸

On March 1, Dolomite Sales purchased $5,000 of merchandise on account. Record the entry on March 1 including 5% GST. Assume a perpetual inventory system.

*QS 5-22 Sales tax on sales—perpetual LO³,⁸

On March 17, Dolomite Sales sold merchandise on credit for $5,800 (cost of sales $5,000). Assuming 7% PST and 5% GST, record the entries on March 17. Assume a perpetual inventory system.

*QS 5-23 Sales tax on purchases—periodic LO⁷,⁸

On March 1, Dolomite Sales purchased $5,000 of merchandise on account. Record the entry on March 1 including 5% GST. Assume a periodic inventory system.

*QS 5-24 Sales tax on sales—periodic LO⁷,⁸

On March 17, Dolomite Sales sold merchandise on credit for $5,800 (cost of sales $5,000). Assuming 7% PST and 5% GST, record the entry on March 17. Assume a periodic inventory system.

An asterisk (*) identifies assignment material based on Appendix 5A or Appendix 5B.

Exercise 5-1 Calculating income statement components LO¹

Referring to Exhibit 5.2, calculate the missing amounts.

	a	b	c	d	e
Sales	$210,000	$165,000	$75,000	$?	$?
Cost of goods sold	?	?	42,000	303,000	206,000
Gross profit from sales	109,000	?	?	?	76,000
Operating expenses	92,000	93,000	?	106,000	?
Net income (loss).............	?	(31,000)	(5,500)	57,000	(28,000)

Exercise 5-2 Recording journal entries for merchandise purchase transactions—perpetual LO³

Journalize each of the following transactions assuming a perpetual inventory system.

Feb.	1	Purchased $17,000 of merchandise inventory; terms 1/10, n/30.
	5	Purchased for cash $8,200 of merchandise inventory.
	6	Purchased $22,000 of merchandise inventory; terms 2/15, n/45.
	9	Purchased $1,900 of office supplies; terms n/15.
	10	Contacted a major supplier to place an order for $200,000 of merchandise in exchange for a 30% trade discount to be shipped on April 1 FOB destination.
	11	Paid for the merchandise purchased on February 1.
	24	Paid for the office supplies purchased on February 9.
Mar.	23	Paid for the February 6 purchase.

Exercise 5-3 Recording journal entries for merchandise purchase transactions—perpetual LO³

Prepare journal entries for March 2014 to record the following transactions for a retail store. Assume a perpetual inventory system.

Mar.	2	Purchased merchandise from Blanton Company under the following terms: $4,200 invoice price, 2/15, n/60, FOB factory.
	3	Paid $350 for shipping charges on the purchase of March 2.
	4	Returned to Blanton Company unacceptable merchandise that had an invoice price of $400.
	17	Sent a cheque to Blanton Company for the March 2 purchase, net of the returned merchandise and applicable discount.
	18	Purchased merchandise from Fleming Corp. under the following terms: $9,600 invoice price, 2/10, n/30, FOB destination.
	21	After brief negotiations, received from Fleming Corp. a $2,100 allowance on the purchase of March 18.
	28	Sent a cheque to Fleming Corp. paying for the March 18 purchase, net of the discount and the allowance.

Exercise 5-4 Recording journal entries for merchandise sales transactions—perpetual LO³

Journalize each of the following transactions assuming a perpetual inventory system.

Jan.	5	Sold merchandise to a customer for $6,800; terms 1/10, n/30 (cost of sales $4,080).
	7	Made a cash sale of $5,100 of merchandise to a customer today (cost of sales $3,060).
	8	Sold merchandise for $12,400; terms 1/10, n/30 (cost of sales $7,440).
	15	Collected the amount owing from the credit customer of January 5.
Feb.	4	The customer of January 8 paid the balance owing.

Exercise 5-5 Recording journal entries for merchandise sales transactions—perpetual LO³

Journalize each of the following transactions assuming a perpetual inventory system.

Feb.	1	Sold merchandise with a cost of $1,500 for $2,100; terms 2/10, n/30, FOB destination.
	2	Paid $225 to ship the merchandise sold on February 1.
	3	The customer of February 1 returned half of the amount purchased because it was the incorrect product; it was returned to inventory.
	4	Sold merchandise to a customer for $3,800 (cost of sales $2,280); terms 2/10, n/30, FOB destination.
	11	Collected the amount owing from the customer of February 1.
	23	Sold merchandise to a customer for cash of $1,200 (cost of sales $720).
	28	The customer of February 4 paid the amount owing.

Exercise 5-6 Analyzing and recording merchandise transactions—perpetual LO³

On March 1, 2014, Sundown Company purchased merchandise for resale from Raintree with an invoice price of $10,000 and credit terms of 3/10, n/60. The merchandise had cost Raintree $8,000. Sundown paid on March 11. Assume that both the buyer and seller use perpetual inventory systems.

Required

a. Prepare the entries that the purchaser should record for the purchase and payment.

b. Prepare the entries that the seller should record for the sale and collection.

Analysis Component: Assume that the buyer borrowed enough cash to pay the balance on the last day of the discount period at an annual interest rate of 3% and paid it back on the last day of the credit period. Calculate how much the buyer saved by following this strategy. *Use a 365-day year and round all calculations to the nearest whole cent.*

Exercise 5-7 Analyzing and recording merchandise transactions—perpetual LO³

On May 11, 2014, Wilson Purchasing purchased $25,000 of merchandise from Hostel Sales; terms 3/10, n/90, FOB Hostel Sales. The cost of the goods to Hostel was $20,000. Wilson paid $1,500 to Express Shipping Service for the delivery charges on the merchandise on May 11. On May 12, Wilson returned $4,000 of goods to Hostel Sales, which restored them to inventory. The returned goods had cost Hostel $3,200. On May 20, Wilson mailed a cheque to Hostel for the amount owed on that date. Hostel received and recorded the cheque on May 21.

Required

a. Present the journal entries that Wilson Purchasing should record for these transactions. Assume that Wilson uses a perpetual inventory system.

b. Present the journal entries that Hostel Sales should record for these transactions. Assume that Hostel uses a perpetual inventory system.

Analysis Component: Assume that the buyer, Wilson Purchasing, borrowed enough cash to pay the balance on the last day of the discount period at an annual interest rate of 4% and paid it back on the last day of the credit period. Calculate how much the buyer saved by following this strategy. *Use a 365-day year and round all calculations to the nearest whole cent.*

Exercise 5-8 Merchandising terms LO^{1,2,3}

Insert the letter for each term in the blank space beside the definition that it most closely matches:

a. Cash discount
e. FOB shipping point
h. Purchase discount

b. Credit period
f. Gross profit
i. Sales discount

c. Discount period
g. Merchandise inventory
j. Trade discount

d. FOB destination

_____ **1.** An agreement that ownership of goods is transferred at the buyer's place of business.

_____ **2.** The time period in which a cash discount is available.

_____ **3.** The difference between net sales and the cost of goods sold.

_____ **4.** A reduction in a receivable or payable that is granted if it is paid within the discount period.

_____ **5.** A purchaser's description of a cash discount received from a supplier of goods.

_____ **6.** An agreement that ownership of goods is transferred at the seller's place of business.

_____ **7.** A reduction below a list or catalogue price that is negotiated in setting the selling price of goods.

_____ **8.** A seller's description of a cash discount granted to customers in return for early payment.

_____ **9.** The time period that can pass before a customer's payment is due.

_____ **10.** The goods that a company owns and expects to sell to its customers.

Exercise 5-9 Effects of merchandising activities on the accounts—perpetual LO^{3,4}

The following amounts summarize Transeer Company's merchandising activities during 2014. Set up T-accounts for Merchandise Inventory and Cost of Goods Sold (see Exhibit 5.13). Then record the activities directly in the accounts and calculate the account balances.

Cost of merchandise sold to customers in sales transactions	$180,000
Merchandise inventory balance, Dec. 31, 2013	35,000
Invoice cost of merchandise purchases	186,000
Shrinkage determined on Dec. 31, 2014	31,000
Cost of transportation-in	1,900
Cost of merchandise returned by customers and restored to inventory	2,200
Purchase discounts received	1,600
Purchase returns and allowances received	4,100

Analysis Component: You are the inventory manager and have reviewed these numbers. Comment on the shrinkage.

Exercise 5-10 Calculating expenses and cost of goods sold—perpetual LO^{1,3,5}

Westlawn Company discloses the following for the year ended May 31, 2014:

Sales	$495,000
Sales discounts	5,900
Sales returns	13,000
Gross profit from sales	124,000
Net loss	28,000

Required Calculate (a) net sales, (b) total operating expenses, (c) cost of goods sold, and (d) gross profit ratio (round to two decimal places).

Analysis Component: Refer to your answer in part (d). Westlawn experienced a gross profit ratio for the year ended May 31, 2013, of 23%. Is the change in the ratio favourable or unfavourable?

Exercise 5-11 Calculating income statement components LO^{1,5}

Referring to Exhibit 5.15, calculate the missing amounts (round to two decimal places).

	Company A		Company B	
	2014	2013	2014	2013
Sales	$256,000	$180,000	$?	$45,000
Sales discounts	2,560	?	1,100	500
Sales returns and allowances	?	16,000	5,500	?
Net sales	?	163,000	?	42,000
Cost of goods sold	153,600	?	57,000	?
Gross profit from sales	51,000	?	48,400	20,000
Selling expenses	17,920	19,000	25,000	?
Administrative expenses	25,600	?	29,700	9,000
Total operating expenses	?	46,000	?	?
Net income (loss)	?	14,400	?	2,000
Gross profit ratio	?	?	?	?

Analysis Component: Company A and Company B are in similar industries. Comment on their comparative performances.

*Exercise 5-12 Calculating cost of goods sold LO^{2,3,7}

Refer to Exhibit 5A.3 and determine each of the missing numbers in the following situations:

	a	b	c
Purchases	$92,000	$158,000	$120,000
Purchase discounts	4,000	?	2,600
Purchase returns and allowances	3,000	6,000	4,400
Transportation-in	?	14,000	16,000
Beginning inventory	5,000	?	34,000
Cost of goods purchased	89,400	156,000	?
Ending inventory	4,400	30,000	?
Cost of goods sold	?	166,400	136,520

*Exercise 5-13 Calculating expenses and income LO^{1,2,3,5,7}

Referring to Exhibit 5A.3, fill in the following blanks. Identify any losses by putting the amount in brackets.

	Company A		Company B	
	2014	2013	2014	2013
Sales	$110,000	$178,000	$90,000	$?
Cost of goods sold:				
Merchandise inventory (beginning)	8,700	27,300	8,875	6,000
Net cost of merchandise purchases	82,000	?	?	26,100
Merchandise inventory (ending)	?	(22,000)	(8,920)	(9,875)
Cost of goods sold	82,300	106,000	?	?
Gross profit from sales	?	?	39,545	19,775
Operating expenses	26,000	54,000	27,000	?
Net income (loss)	1,700	18,000	?	6,275
Gross profit ratio	?	?	?	?

Analysis Component: Company A and Company B are in similar industries. Comment on their gross profit ratios.

An asterisk (*) identifies assignment material based on Appendix 5A or Appendix 5B.

*Exercise 5-14 Components of cost of goods sold LO1,2,3,5,7

Referring to Exhibit 5A.3, use the data provided to determine each of the missing numbers in the following situations:

	a	b	c
Invoice cost of merchandise purchases.........................	$44,000	$21,000	$16,250
Purchase discounts..	2,000	?	325
Purchase returns and allowances.................................	1,500	750	550
Cost of transportation-in	?	1,750	2,000
Merchandise inventory (beginning of period)	4,500	?	3,500
Net cost of merchandise purchases	44,700	19,750	?
Merchandise inventory (end of period)	2,200	3,750	?
Cost of goods sold	?	20,800	17,065

CHECK FIGURE:
a. Net income
= $7,815

Exercise 5-15 Preparing an income statement and closing entries—perpetual LO5,6

The following account information, in alphabetical order, was taken from the work sheet of Compu-Soft for the month ended November 30, 2014.

Required

a. Prepare a multiple-step income statement for the month ended November 30, 2014.

b. Prepare closing entries.

c. Calculate the post-closing balance in the capital account at November 30, 2014.

	Account	Adjusted Trial Balance	
		Debit	Credit
201	Accounts payable		$ 750
106	Accounts receivable	$ 1,200	
166	Accumulated depreciation, store equipment..........................		4,600
101	Cash	2,100	
502	Cost of goods sold..	14,800	
612	Depreciation expense, store equipment................................	120	
301	Peter Delta, capital		1,935
302	Peter Delta, withdrawals	4,600	
406	Rent revenue		2,500
413	Sales...		29,400
415	Sales discounts	45	
414	Sales returns and allowances....., ...	720	
165	Store equipment...	7,200	
690	Utilities expense...	2,100	
623	Wages expense...	6,300	
	Totals	$39,185	$39,185

Analysis Component: Assume that for the month ended October 31, 2014, net sales were $32,000, cost of goods sold was $19,200, and income from operations was $8,000. Calculate and compare the company's gross profit ratios for October and November.

An asterisk (*) identifies assignment material based on Appendix 5A or Appendix 5B.

Exercise 5-16 Adjusting and closing entries, preparing a work sheet and income statement—perpetual LO[5,6]

The following list of accounts is taken from the December 31, 2014, unadjusted trial balance of Perdu Sales, a business that is owned by Eldon Perdu.

	Debit	Credit
Cash	$ 8,000	
Merchandise inventory	9,800	
Prepaid selling expense	8,000	
Store equipment	40,000	
Accumulated depreciation, store equipment		$ 9,800
Accounts payable		14,840
Salaries payable		-0-
Eldon Perdu, capital		25,360
Eldon Perdu, withdrawals	3,600	
Sales		858,000
Sales returns and allowances	33,000	
Sales discounts	8,000	
Cost of goods sold	431,000	
Sales salaries expense	94,000	
Utilities expense, store	12,600	
Other selling expenses	70,000	
Other administrative expenses	190,000	

Additional information:

Accrued sales salaries amount to $3,200. Prepaid selling expenses of $5,200 have expired. Depreciation for the period is $2,500.

Required Assuming a perpetual inventory system:

a. Prepare a work sheet.

b. Prepare a classified multiple-step income statement for the year ended December 31, 2014.

c. Journalize the closing entries.

Analysis Component: Assume that for the year ended December 31, 2013, net sales were $600,000; operating expenses were $344,000; and there was a net loss of $14,000. Calculate and compare the company's gross profit ratios for 2013 and 2014.

Exercise 5-17 Preparing reports from closing entries—perpetual LO[5,6]

The following closing entries for Sabba Co. were made on January 31, 2014, the end of its annual accounting period:

Jan.	31	Sales	642,000	
		Income Summary		642,000
		To close temporary accounts with credit balances.		
	31	Income Summary	588,950	
		Cost of Goods Sold		332,000
		Sales Returns and Allowances		21,000
		Sales Discounts		9,500
		Selling Expenses		117,000
		General and Administrative Expenses		109,000
		Interest Expense		450
		To close temporary accounts with debit balances.		

Required Use the information in the closing entries to prepare:

a. A calculation of net sales.

b. A single-step income statement for the year.

*Exercise 5-18 Journal entries to contrast the periodic and perpetual systems LO[3,7]

Journalize the following merchandising transactions for Scout Systems assuming: (a) a periodic system, and (b) a perpetual system.

Nov.	1	Scout Systems purchases merchandise for $4,400 on credit with terms of 2/10, n/30.
	5	Scout Systems pays for the previous purchase.
	7	Scout Systems receives payment for returned defective merchandise of $500 that was purchased on November 1.
	10	Scout Systems pays $400 to transport merchandise to its store.
	13	Scout Systems sells merchandise for $6,500 on account. The cost of the merchandise was $4,200.
	16	A customer returns merchandise from the November 13 transaction. The returned item sold for $1,200 and cost $780. The item will be returned to inventory.

*Exercise 5-19 Recording journal entries for merchandise purchase transactions—periodic LO[7]

Using the information in Exercise 5-2, prepare journal entries to record the transactions assuming a periodic inventory system.

*Exercise 5-20 Recording journal entries for merchandise purchase transactions—periodic LO[7]

Using the information in Exercise 5-3, prepare journal entries to record the March transactions assuming a periodic inventory system.

*Exercise 5-21 Recording journal entries for merchandise sales transactions—periodic LO[7]

Using the information in Exercise 5-4, prepare journal entries to record the transactions assuming a periodic inventory system.

*Exercise 5-22 Recording journal entries for merchandise sales transactions—periodic LO[7]

Using the information in Exercise 5-5, prepare journal entries to record the transactions assuming a periodic inventory system.

*Exercise 5-23 Analyzing and recording merchandise transactions and discounts—periodic LO[7]

Using the information in Exercise 5-6, and assuming instead a periodic inventory system:

a. Prepare the entries that the purchaser should record for the purchase and payment.

b. Prepare the entries that the seller should record for the sale and collection.

*Exercise 5-24 Analyzing and recording merchandise transactions and returns—periodic LO[7]

Using the information in Exercise 5-7:

a. Present the journal entries that Wilson Purchasing should record for these transactions assuming a periodic inventory system.

b. Present the journal entries that Hostel Sales should record for these transactions assuming a periodic inventory system.

CHECK FIGURE:
c. $16,900

*Exercise 5-25 Calculating expenses and cost of goods sold—periodic LO[5,7]

Friar Company discloses the following information for the year ended October 31, 2014:

Sales	$355,000
Sales discounts	5,500
Sales returns	14,000
Merchandise inventory (beginning of period)	31,000
Invoice cost of merchandise purchases	178,000
Purchase discounts	3,600
Purchase returns and allowances	6,000
Cost of transportation-in	11,000
Gross profit from sales	142,000
Net income	65,000

Required Calculate (a) total operating expenses, (b) cost of goods sold, (c) merchandise inventory (end of period), and (d) gross profit ratio (round to two decimal places).

Analysis Component: Assuming that the gross profit ratio for the year ended October 31, 2013, was 47%, compare Friar Company's performance from 2013 to 2014.

An asterisk (*) identifies assignment material based on Appendix 5A or Appendix 5B.

*Exercise 5-26 Preparing a work sheet—periodic LO⁷

The following unadjusted trial balance relates to Dewer's Stop'n Shop at the end of its fiscal year, December 31, 2014.

No.	Title	Debit	Credit
101	Cash	$ 1,400	
106	Accounts receivable	3,600	
119	Merchandise inventory	2,700	
125	Store supplies	1,350	
201	Accounts payable		$ 280
209	Salaries payable		-0-
301	Mi Dewer, capital		7,220
302	Mi Dewer, withdrawals	1,750	
413	Sales		12,000
414	Sales returns and allowances	290	
505	Purchases	6,400	
506	Purchase discounts		250
507	Transportation-in	160	
622	Salaries expense	1,600	
640	Rent expense	500	
651	Store supplies expense	-0-	
	Totals	$19,750	$19,750

Required Use the preceding information and the following additional facts to complete a work sheet for the company.

a. The ending inventory of store supplies was $900.

b. Accrued salaries at the end of the year were $120.

c. The ending merchandise inventory was $1,720.

*Exercise 5-27 Preparing reports from closing entries—periodic LO⁷

The following closing entries for Fox Fixtures Co. were made on March 31, 2014, the end of its annual accounting period:

1.	Interest Revenue	1,200	
	Merchandise Inventory	8,500	
	Sales	445,000	
	Purchase Returns and Allowances	22,000	
	Purchase Discounts	5,300	
	Income Summary		482,000
	To close temporary accounts with credit balances and record the ending inventory.		
2.	Income Summary	438,400	
	Merchandise Inventory		17,000
	Sales Returns and Allowances		25,000
	Sales Discounts		4,100
	Purchases		281,000
	Transportation-In		8,800
	Selling Expenses		69,000
	General and Administrative Expenses		33,500
	To close temporary accounts with debit balances and to remove the beginning inventory balance.		

Required Use the information in the closing entries to prepare:

a. A calculation of net sales.

b. A calculation of cost of goods purchased.

c. A calculation of cost of goods sold.

d. A multiple-step income statement for the year.

An asterisk (*) identifies assignment material based on Appendix 5A or Appendix 5B.

*Exercise 5-28 Preparing an income statement and closing entries—periodic LO[7]

The following adjusted account information, in alphabetical order, was taken from the work sheet of John's Electronics for the month ended April 30, 2014. A physical count on April 30, 2014, revealed a merchandise inventory balance actually on hand of $2,460.

	Account	Debit	Credit
201	Accounts payable		$ 2,118
154	Accumulated depreciation, trucks		15,600
101	Cash	$ 1,600	
611	Depreciation expense, delivery trucks	640	
633	Interest expense	130	
301	John Yu, capital		26,964
302	John Yu, withdrawals	9,200	
119	Merchandise inventory	5,700	
507	Purchase discounts		28
506	Purchase returns and allowances		110
505	Purchases	16,140	
413	Sales		33,700
414	Sales returns and allowances	1,740	
688	Telephone expense, office	150	
689	Telephone expense, store	340	
508	Transportation-in	380	
153	Trucks	29,600	
623	Wages expense, office	4,900	
624	Wages expense, selling	8,000	
	Totals	$78,520	$78,520

Required

a. Calculate net sales.   b. Calculate cost of goods sold.

c. Prepare a classified multiple-step income statement for the month ended April 30, 2014.

d. Prepare closing entries.

e. Calculate the post-closing balance in the capital account at April 30, 2014.

*Exercise 5-29 Sales taxes—perpetual LO[3,8]

Journalize each of the following transactions assuming a perpetual inventory system and PST at 8% along with 5% GST.

June	1	Purchased $2,000 of merchandise; terms 1/10, n/30.
	5	Sold $1,000 of merchandise for $1,400; terms n/15.

*Exercise 5-30 Sales taxes—periodic LO[7,8]

Journalize each of the transactions in *Exercise 5-29 assuming a periodic inventory system and PST at 8% along with 5% GST.

PROBLEMS

Problem 5-1A Journal entries for merchandising activities—perpetual LO[3]

Part 1

Prepare General Journal entries to record the following perpetual system merchandising transactions of Belton Company. *Use a separate account for each receivable and payable; for example, record the sale on June 1 in Accounts Receivable—Avery & Wiest.*

June	1	Sold merchandise to Avery & Wiest for $9,500; terms 2/5, n/15, FOB destination (cost of sales $6,650).
	2	Purchased $4,900 of merchandise from Angolac Suppliers; terms 1/10, n/20, FOB shipping point.
	4	Purchased merchandise inventory from Bastille Sales for $11,400; terms 1/15, n/45, FOB Bastille Sales.
	5	Sold merchandise to Gelgar for $11,000; terms 2/5, n/15, FOB destination (cost of sales $7,700).
	6	Collected the amount owing from Avery & Wiest regarding the June 1 sale.
	12	Paid Angolac Suppliers for the June 2 purchase.
	20	Collected the amount owing from Gelgar regarding the June 5 sale.
	30	Paid Bastille Sales for the June 4 purchase.

Part 2

Based on the information provided above, calculate: (a) net sales, (b) cost of goods sold, and (c) gross profit for the month ended June 30, 2014.

An asterisk (*) identifies assignment material based on Appendix 5A or Appendix 5B.

Problem 5-2A Journal entries for merchandising activities—perpetual LO³

Prepare General Journal entries to record the following perpetual system merchandising transactions of Belton Company. *Use a separate account for each receivable and payable; example, record the purchase July 1 in Accounts Payable—Jones Company.* Do the analysis component.

July	1	Purchased merchandise from Jones Company for $14,800 under credit terms of 1/15, n/30, FOB factory.
	2	Sold merchandise to Terra Co. for $2,600 under credit terms of 2/10, n/60, FOB shipping point. The merchandise had cost $1,950.
	3	Paid $450 for freight charges on the purchase of July 1.
	8	Sold merchandise that cost $3,825 for $5,100 cash.
	9	Purchased merchandise from Keene Co. for $9,100 under credit terms of 2/15, n/60, FOB destination.
	12	Received a $1,500 credit memorandum acknowledging the return of merchandise purchased on July 9.
	12	Received the balance due from Terra Co. for the credit sale dated July 2.
	13	Purchased office supplies from EastCo on credit, $960, n/30.
	16	Paid the balance due to Jones Company.
	19	Sold merchandise that cost $2,850 to Urban Co. for $3,800 under credit terms of 2/15, n/60, FOB shipping point.
	21	Issued a $300 credit memorandum to Urban Co. for an allowance on goods sold on July 19.
	22	Received a debit memorandum from Urban Co. for an error that overstated the total invoice by $200.
	29	Paid Keene Co. the balance due.
	30	Received the balance due from Urban Co. for the credit sale dated July 19.
	31	Sold merchandise that cost $7,500 to Terra Co. for $10,000 under credit terms of 2/10, n/60, FOB shipping point.

Analysis Component: As the senior purchaser for Belton Company, you are concerned that the purchase discounts you have negotiated are not being taken advantage of by the accounts payable department. Calculate the cost of the lost discount regarding the July 9 purchase and explain to accounts payable when to take advantage of discounts (assume a 6% interest rate; round calculations to four decimal places).

Problem 5-3A Journal entries for merchandising activities—perpetual LO³

Prepare General Journal entries to record the following perpetual system merchandising transactions of Hanifin Company. *Use a separate account for each receivable and payable; for example, record the purchase on August 1 in Accounts Payable—Dickson Company.*

Aug.	1	Purchased merchandise from Dickson Company for $4,000 under credit terms of 1/10, n/30, FOB destination.
	4	At Dickson's request, paid $350 for freight charges on the August 1 purchase, reducing the amount owed to Dickson.
	5	Sold merchandise to Griften Corp. for $3,800 under credit terms of 2/10, n/60, FOB destination. The merchandise had cost $2,470.
	8	Purchased merchandise from Kendall Corporation for $5,200 under credit terms of 1/10, n/45, FOB shipping point.
	9	Paid $325 shipping charges related to the August 5 sale to Griften Corp.
	10	Griften returned merchandise from the August 5 sale that had cost $440 and been sold for $800. The merchandise was restored to inventory.
	12	After negotiations with Kendall Corporation concerning problems with the merchandise purchased on August 8, received a credit memorandum from Kendall granting a price reduction of $400.
	15	Received balance due from Griften Corp. for the August 5 sale.
	17	Purchased office equipment from WestCo on credit, $6,000, n/45.
	18	Paid the amount due Kendall Corporation for the August 8 purchase.
	19	Sold merchandise to Farley for $1,800 under credit terms of 1/10, n/30, FOB shipping point. The merchandise had cost $990.
	22	Farley requested a price reduction on the August 19 sale because the merchandise did not meet specifications. Sent Farley a credit memorandum for $300 to resolve the issue.
	29	Received Farley's payment of the amount due from the August 19 purchase.
	30	Paid Dickson Company the amount due from the August 1 purchase.

Problem 5-4A Work sheet and income statement—perpetual LO⁵

Information from the unadjusted trial balance of Jumbo's on December 31, 2014, the end of the annual accounting period, is as follows:

	Debit	Credit
Cash	$ 8,100	
Accounts receivable	22,665	
Merchandise inventory	34,600	
Store supplies	2,415	
Office supplies	775	
Prepaid insurance	3,255	
Equipment	74,490	
Accumulated depreciation, equipment		$ 13,655
Accounts payable		8,000
Salaries payable		-0-
Sally Fowler, capital		168,965
Sally Fowler, withdrawals	62,000	
Interest revenue		310
Sales		529,000
Sales returns and allowances	5,070	
Cost of goods sold	381,160	
Salaries expense	96,300	
Rent expense	29,100	
Supplies expense	-0-	
Depreciation expense, equipment	-0-	
Insurance expense	-0-	
Totals	$719,930	$719,930

Required

1. Copy the unadjusted trial balance on a work sheet form and complete the work sheet using the information that follows:

   a. A review of the store supplies on December 31, 2014, revealed a balance on hand of $2,000; a similar examination of the office supplies showed that $640 had been used.

   b. The balance in the Prepaid Insurance account was reviewed and it was determined that $255 was unused at December 31, 2014.

   c. The records show that the equipment was estimated to have a total estimated useful life of 10 years with a resale value at the end of its life of $14,490.

   d. Accrued salaries payable, $1,800.

   e. A count of the merchandise inventory revealed a balance on hand December 31, 2014, of $33,800.

2. Prepare a multiple-step income statement showing the expenses in detail.

Analysis Component: Explain why *Interest Revenue* is shown under *Other revenues and expenses* on the multiple-step income statement.

CHECK FIGURE:
1. Income from operations = $55,000

Problem 5-5A Income statement calculations and formats—perpetual LO[5]

The following amounts appeared on Davison Company's adjusted trial balance as of October 31, 2014, the end of its fiscal year:

	Debit	Credit
Merchandise inventory	$ 16,000	
Other assets	256,800	
Liabilities		$ 78,400
Brenda Davison, capital		203,280
Brenda Davison, withdrawals	65,000	
Interest revenue		1,120
Sales		424,000
Sales discounts	6,500	
Sales returns and allowances	28,000	
Cost of goods sold	169,300	
Sales salaries expense	52,000	
Rent expense, selling space	19,000	
Store supplies expense	5,000	
Advertising expense	29,400	
Office salaries expense	53,000	
Rent expense, office space	5,200	
Office supplies expense	1,600	
Totals	$706,800	$706,800

Required

1. Prepare a classified, multiple-step income statement for internal use (see Exhibit 5.15) that lists the company's net sales, cost of goods sold, and gross profit, as well as the components and amounts of selling expenses and general and administrative expenses.

2. Present a condensed single-step income statement (see Exhibit 5.17) that lists these costs: cost of goods sold, selling expenses, and general and administrative expenses.

Problem 5-6A Closing entries—perpetual LO[6]

Use the data for Davison Company in Problem 5-5A to prepare compound closing entries for the company as of October 31.

CHECK FIGURE:
1. Income from
operations = $13,590

Problem 5-7A Income statements—perpetual LO[5]

On December 31, 2014, the end of Plymouth Electronics' annual accounting period, the financial statement columns of its work sheet appeared as follows:

	Plymouth Electronics Work Sheet.xls			
	Home Insert Page Layout Formulas Data Review View			
	P18 fx			
	A	H	I	J	K
1	**Plymouth Electronics**				
2	**Work Sheet**				
3	**For the Year Ended December 31, 2014**				
4				**Balance Sheet**	
5		**Income**		**& Statement of**	
6		**Statement**		**Changes in Equity**	
7	**Account**	**Dr.**	**Cr.**	**Dr.**	**Cr.**
8	Merchandise inventory			19,500	
9	Other assets			487,785	
10	Celine Plymouth, capital				247,605
11	Liabilities				312,370
12	Celine Plymouth, withdrawals			67,000	
13	Interest earned		720		
14	Sales		942,000		
15	Sales returns and allowances	5,715			
16	Sales discounts	14,580			
17	Cost of goods sold	719,000			
18	Sales salaries expense	79,200			
19	Rent expense, selling space	33,000			
20	Store supplies expense	1,620			
21	Depreciation expense, store equipment	8,910			
22	Office salaries expense	56,500			
23	Rent expense, office space	3,000			
24	Office supplies expense	735			
25	Insurance expense	3,390			
26	Depreciation expense, office equipment	2,760			
27	Totals	928,410	942,720	574,285	559,975
28	Net income	14,310			14,310
29	**Totals**	942,720	942,720	574,285	574,285

Required

1. Prepare a 2014 classified, multiple-step income statement for Plymouth Electronics, like Exhibit 5.15.

2. Prepare a single-step income statement, like Exhibit 5.17.

Analysis Component: The gross profit ratio for Plymouth Electronics' year ended December 31, 2013, was 32%. Calculate this ratio for the year ended December 31, 2014, and compare it to the prior year, commenting on whether the change was favourable or unfavourable.

Problem 5-8A Closing entries—perpetual LO[6]

Using the information in Problem 5-7A, prepare compound closing entries for Plymouth Electronics.

Problem 5-9A Income statements—perpetual LO[5]

The following adjusted trial balance for Bell Servicing was prepared at the end of the fiscal year, December 31, 2014:

		Debit	Credit
101	Cash	$ 8,000	
119	Merchandise inventory	16,200	
125	Supplies	10,000	
128	Prepaid insurance	4,000	
165	Store equipment	51,000	
166	Accumulated depreciation, store equipment		$ 46,800
167	Office equipment	69,000	
168	Accumulated depreciation, office equipment		34,200
201	Accounts payable		16,000
301	Jonah Bell, capital		29,000
302	Jonah Bell, withdrawals	41,000	
413	Sales		291,800
415	Sales discounts	2,000	
505	Cost of goods sold	74,800	
612	Depreciation expense, store equipment	5,200	
613	Depreciation expense, office equipment	3,800	
622	Sales salaries expense	46,000	
623	Office salaries expense	32,000	
637	Insurance expense, store	2,000	
638	Insurance expense, office	1,600	
640	Rent expense, office space	13,000	
641	Rent expense, selling space	17,000	
651	Office supplies expense	1,200	
652	Store supplies expense	2,400	
655	Advertising expense	17,600	
	Totals	$417,800	$417,800

Required

1. Prepare a classified multiple-step income statement that would be used by the business's owner (like Exhibit 5.15).

2. Prepare a multiple-step income statement that would be used by external users (like Exhibit 5.16).

3. Prepare a single-step income statement that would be provided to decision makers outside the company (like Exhibit 5.17).

Analysis Component: If you were a decision maker external to Bell Servicing, which income statement format would you prefer and why, if you had a choice? Which income statement format(s) could you expect as an external user? Why?

*Problem 5-10A Journal entries for merchandising activities—periodic LO[7]

Using the information provided in Part 1 of Problem 5-1A, journalize each of the transactions assuming a periodic inventory system.

An asterisk (*) identifies assignment material based on Appendix 5A or Appendix 5B.

*Problem 5-11A Journal entries for merchandising transactions—periodic LO[7]

Prepare General Journal entries to record the following periodic system merchandising transactions for Schafer Merchandising. *Use a separate account for each receivable and payable:*

Oct.		
	1	Purchased merchandise from Zeon Company on credit, terms 2/10, n/30, $15,800.
	2	Sold merchandise for cash, $2,100.
	7	Purchased merchandise on credit from Billings Co., terms 2/10, n/30, $11,600, FOB the seller's factory.
	7	Paid $450 cash for freight charges on the merchandise shipment of the previous transaction.
	8	Purchased delivery equipment from Finlay Supplies on credit, $24,000.
	12	Sold merchandise on credit to Comry Holdings, terms 2/15, 1/30, n/60, $5,800.
	13	Received a $1,500 credit memorandum for merchandise purchased on October 7 and returned for credit.
	13	Purchased office supplies on credit from Staples, $620, n/30.
	15	Sold merchandise on credit to Tom Willis, terms 2/10, 1/30, n/60, $4,650.
	15	Paid for the merchandise purchased on October 7.
	16	Received a credit memorandum for unsatisfactory office supplies purchased on October 13 and returned, $120.
	19	Issued a $420 credit memorandum to the customer who purchased merchandise on October 15 and returned a portion for credit.
	25	Received payment for the merchandise sold on October 15.
	29	The customer of October 12 paid for the purchase of that date.
	31	Paid for the merchandise purchased on October 1.

CHECK FIGURES:
3. $34,300
4. Loss from operations = $18,265;
Net loss = $18,115

*Problem 5-12A Income statement calculations and formats—periodic LO[7]

The following amounts appeared on the Mendelstein Company's adjusted trial balance as of October 31, 2014, the end of its fiscal year:

	Debit	Credit
Merchandise inventory	$ 1,400	
Other assets	40,000	
Liabilities		$ 36,340
Joe Mendelstein, capital		37,375
Joe Mendelstein, withdrawals	3,000	
Interest revenue		150
Sales		96,400
Sales returns and allowances	7,500	
Sales discounts	1,125	
Purchases	43,500	
Purchase returns and allowances		2,150
Purchase discounts		900
Transportation-in	5,050	
Sales salaries expense	17,800	
Rent expense, selling space	9,200	
Store supplies expense	3,200	
Advertising expense	9,000	
Office salaries expense	22,000	
Rent expense, office space	7,600	
Office supplies expense	2,940	
Totals	$173,315	$173,315

A physical count shows that the cost of the ending inventory is $12,600.

Required

1. Calculate the company's net sales for the year.

2. Calculate the company's cost of goods purchased for the year.

3. Calculate the company's cost of goods sold for the year.

4. Present a multiple-step income statement that lists the company's net sales, cost of goods sold, and gross profit from sales.

5. Present a condensed single-step income statement that lists these expenses: cost of goods sold, selling expenses, and general and administrative expenses.

An asterisk (*) identifies assignment material based on Appendix 5A or Appendix 5B.

*Problem 5-13A Closing entries—periodic LO⁷

Use the data for the Mendelstein Company in *Problem 5-12A to prepare compound closing entries for the company as of October 31.

CHECK FIGURE:
1. Balance sheet
columns = $137,590

*Problem 5-14A Work sheet and closing entries—periodic LO⁷

Information from the December 31, 2014, year-end, unadjusted trial balance of Woodstock Store is as follows:

	Debit	Credit
Cash	$ 3,500	
Merchandise inventory	31,400	
Store supplies	1,715	
Office supplies	645	
Prepaid insurance	3,960	
Store equipment	57,615	
Accumulated depreciation, store equipment		$ 6,750
Office equipment	13,100	
Accumulated depreciation, office equipment		6,550
Accounts payable		4,000
Zen Woodstock, capital		52,000
Zen Woodstock, withdrawals	31,500	
Rental revenue		14,600
Sales		501,520
Sales returns and allowances	2,915	
Sales discounts	5,190	
Purchases	331,315	
Purchase returns and allowances		2,140
Purchase discounts		4,725
Transportation-in	3,690	
Sales salaries expense	34,710	
Rent expense, selling space	24,000	
Advertising expense	6,400	
Store supplies expense	-0-	
Depreciation expense, store equipment	-0-	
Office salaries expense	27,630	
Rent expense, office space	13,000	
Office supplies expense	-0-	
Insurance expense	-0-	
Depreciation expense, office equipment	-0-	
Totals	$592,285	$592,285

Required

1. Copy the unadjusted trial balance on a work sheet form and complete the work sheet using the following information:

   a. The balance on January 1, 2014, in the Store Supplies account was $480. During the year, $1,235 of store supplies were purchased and debited to the Store Supplies account. A physical count on December 31, 2014, shows an ending balance of $180.

   b. The balance on January 1, 2014, in the Office Supplies account was $50. Office supplies of $595 were bought in 2014 and added to the Office Supplies account. An examination of the office supplies at year-end revealed that $590 had been used.

   c. The balance in the Prepaid Insurance account represents a policy purchased on September 1, 2014; it was valid for 12 months from that date.

   d. The store equipment was originally estimated to have a useful life of 12 years and a residual value of $3,615.

   e. When the office equipment was purchased, it was estimated that it would last four years and have no residual value.

   f. Ending merchandise inventory, $29,000.

An asterisk (*) identifies assignment material based on Appendix 5A or Appendix 5B.

2. Journalize closing entries for the store. Use page 10 for your journal.

3. Open a balance column Merchandise Inventory account (110) and enter a December 31, 2013, balance of $31,400. Then post those portions of the closing entries that affect the account.

*Problem 5-15A Classified, multi-step income statement—periodic LO⁷

Using the information in *Problem 5-14A, prepare a classified multi-step income statement, like Exhibit 5A.3.

*Problem 5-16A Sales taxes—perpetual LO³,⁸

Journalize each of the following transactions assuming a perpetual inventory system and PST at 8% along with 5% GST. *Note: Any available cash discount is taken only on the sale price before taxes.*

Aug.	1	Purchased $2,000 of merchandise for cash.
	2	Purchased $6,800 of merchandise; terms 2/10, n/30.
	5	Sold merchandise costing $3,600 for $5,200; terms 1/10, n/30.
	12	Paid for the merchandise purchased on August 2.
	15	Collected the amount owing from the customer of August 5.
	17	Purchased $6,000 of merchandise; terms n/15.
	19	Recorded $7,000 of cash sales (cost of sales $5,800).

*Problem 5-17A Sales taxes—periodic LO⁷,⁸

Journalize each of the transactions in *Problem 5-16A assuming a periodic inventory system and PST at 7% along with 5% GST.

ALTERNATE PROBLEMS

CHECK FIGURE:
2c. = $21,280

Problem 5-1B Journal entries for merchandising activities—perpetual LO³

Part 1

Prepare General Journal entries to record the following perpetual system merchandising transactions of Lyryx Company. *Use a separate account for each receivable and payable; for example, record the sale on March 6 in Accounts Receivable—Tessier & Welsh.*

Mar.	5	Purchased $48,000 of merchandise from Delton Suppliers paying cash.
	6	Sold merchandise for $36,000 to Tessier & Welsh; terms 2/10, n/30, FOB destination (cost of sales $27,100).
	7	Purchased merchandise from Janz Company for $71,000; terms 1/10, n/45, FOB shipping point.
	8	Paid $1,540 shipping costs regarding the purchase of March 7.
	9	Sold merchandise for $46,000 to Parker Company; terms 2/10, n/30, FOB destination (cost of sales $32,900).
	10	Purchased $17,800 of merchandise from Delton Suppliers; terms 2/10, n/45, FOB destination.
	16	Collected the balance owing from Tessier & Welsh regarding the March 6 sale.
	17	Paid for the March 7 purchase from Janz Company.
	30	Paid for the March 10 purchase from Delton Suppliers.
	31	Collected the balance owing from Parker Company regarding the sale of March 9.

Part 2

Based on the information provided above, calculate: (a) net sales, (b) cost of goods sold, and (c) gross profit for the month ended March 31, 2014.

An asterisk (*) identifies assignment material based on Appendix 5A or Appendix 5B.

Problem 5-2B Journal entries for merchandising activities—perpetual LO³

Prepare General Journal entries to record the following perpetual system merchandising transactions of Lyryx Company. *Use a separate account for each receivable and payable; for example, record the purchase on May 2 in Accounts Payable—Mobley Co.*

May	2	Purchased merchandise from Mobley Co. for $18,000 under credit terms of 1/15, n/30, FOB factory.
	4	Sold merchandise to Cornerstone Co. for $3,400 under credit terms of 2/10, n/60, FOB shipping point. The merchandise had cost $2,100.
	4	Paid $750 for freight charges on the purchase of May 2.
	9	Sold merchandise that cost $3,600 for $5,200 cash.
	10	Purchased merchandise from Richter Co. for $7,300 under credit terms of 2/15, n/60, FOB destination.
	12	Received a $600 credit memorandum acknowledging the return of merchandise purchased on May 10.
	14	Received the balance due from Cornerstone Co. for the credit sale dated May 4.
	15	Sold for cash a piece of office equipment at its original cost, $1,200.
	17	Paid the balance due to Mobley Co.
	18	Purchased $1,750 of cleaning supplies from A & Z Suppliers; terms n/15.
	20	Sold merchandise that cost $2,700 to Harrill Co. for $3,900 under credit terms of 2/15, n/60, FOB shipping point.
	22	Issued a $500 credit memorandum to Harrill Co. for an allowance on goods sold on May 20.
	23	Received a debit memorandum from Harrill Co. for an error that overstated the total invoice by $150.
	25	Paid Richter Co. the balance due.
	31	Received the balance due from Harrill Co. for the credit sale dated May 20.
	31	Sold merchandise that cost $10,200 to Cornerstone Co. for $15,000 under credit terms of 2/10, n/60, FOB shipping point.

Analysis Component: You are working in Lyryx's accounts payable department and have been instructed to pay the Richter account on the last day of the discount period even though the money will have to be borrowed at 6% interest. Why would the company borrow to pay within the discount period? Show your calculations (round to two decimal places).

Problem 5-3B Journal entries for merchandising activities—perpetual LO³

Prepare General Journal entries to record the following perpetual system merchandising transactions of Goodfish Lake Company. *Use a separate account for each receivable and payable; for example, record the purchase on July 3 in Accounts Payable—CMP Corp.*

July	3	Purchased merchandise from CMP Corp. for $32,000 under credit terms of 1/10, n/30, FOB destination.
	4	At CMP's request, paid $1,500 for freight charges on the July 3 purchase, reducing the amount owed to CMP.
	7	Sold merchandise to Harbison Co. for $21,000 under credit terms of 2/10, n/60, FOB destination. The merchandise had cost $17,500.
	10	Purchased merchandise from Cimarron Corporation for $29,300 under credit terms of 1/10, n/45, FOB shipping point.
	11	Paid $1,200 shipping charges related to the July 7 sale to Harbison Co.
	12	Harbison returned merchandise from the July 7 sale that had cost $2,500 and been sold for $3,500. The merchandise was restored to inventory.
	14	After negotiations with Cimarron Corporation concerning problems with the merchandise purchased on July 10, received a credit memorandum from Cimarron granting a price reduction of $4,100.
	17	Received balance due from Harbison Co. for the July 7 sale.
	18	Sold for cash a piece of vacant land for its original cost of $62,000.
	19	Purchased a used van for the business, $28,000; paid cash of $10,000 and borrowed the balance from the bank.
	20	Paid the amount due Cimarron Corporation for the July 10 purchase.
	21	Sold merchandise to Hess for $18,000 under credit terms of 1/10, n/30, FOB shipping point. The merchandise had cost $13,100.
	24	Hess requested a price reduction on the July 21 sale because the merchandise did not meet specifications. Sent Hess a credit memorandum for $3,000 to resolve the issue.
	31	Received Hess's payment of the amount due from the July 21 purchase.
	31	Paid CMP Corp. the amount due from the July 3 purchase.

Analysis Component: Regarding the July 24 transaction, what alternative is there to granting a credit memorandum? Be sure to identify and explain an advantage and disadvantage of the alternative.

Problem 5-4B Adjusting entries and income statements—perpetual LO[5]

The following information is from the unadjusted trial balance for Journey's End Company prepared at October 31, 2014, the end of the fiscal year:

	Debit	Credit
Cash	$ 12,800	
Merchandise inventory	41,500	
Store supplies	16,700	
Prepaid insurance	5,700	
Store equipment	167,600	
Accumulated depreciation, store equipment		$ 60,000
Accounts payable		34,700
Dallas End, capital		172,100
Dallas End, withdrawals	12,000	
Sales		391,000
Sales discounts	3,500	
Sales returns and allowances	8,000	
Cost of goods sold	149,600	
Depreciation expense, store equipment	-0-	
Salaries expense	144,000	
Interest expense	800	
Insurance expense	-0-	
Rent expense	56,000	
Store supplies expense	-0-	
Advertising expense	39,600	
Totals	$657,800	$657,800

Rent and salaries expense are equally divided between the selling and administrative functions. Journey's End Company uses a perpetual inventory system.

Required

1. Copy the unadjusted trial balance on a work sheet form and complete the work sheet using the following information:

   a. Store supplies on hand at year-end amount to $6,600.

   b. The balance in the Prepaid Insurance account represents 12 months of insurance that was in effect starting November 1, 2013.

   c. The store equipment was purchased several years ago, when it was estimated to have a 20-year useful life and a resale value at the end of its life of $47,600.

   d. A physical count of the ending merchandise inventory shows $29,800 of goods on hand.

2. Prepare a multiple-step income statement (see Exhibit 5.16).

Analysis Component: Explain why *Interest Expense* is shown under *Other revenues and expenses* on the multiple-step income statement.

Problem 5-5B Income statement calculations and formats—perpetual LO[5]

The following amounts appeared on Excel Company's adjusted trial balance as of May 31, 2014, the end of its fiscal year:

	Debit	Credit
Merchandise inventory	$ 21,000	
Other assets	385,200	
Liabilities		$ 105,000
Reena Excel, capital		339,150
Reena Excel, withdrawals	48,000	
Sales		636,000
Sales discounts	9,750	
Sales returns and allowances	42,000	
Cost of goods sold	296,000	
Sales salaries expense	87,000	
Rent expense, selling space	30,000	
Store supplies expense	7,500	
Advertising expense	54,000	
Office salaries expense	79,500	
Rent expense, office space	17,800	
Office supplies expense	2,400	
Totals	$1,080,150	$1,080,150

Required

1. Present a classified multiple-step income statement for internal users (see Exhibit 5.15) that lists the company's net sales, cost of goods sold, and gross profit, as well as the components and amounts of selling expenses and general and administrative expenses.

2. Present a condensed single-step income statement (see Exhibit 5.17) that lists these costs: cost of goods sold, selling expenses, and general and administrative expenses.

Problem 5-6B Closing entries—perpetual LO[6]

Use the data for Excel Company in Problem 5-5B to prepare compound closing entries for the company as of May 31.

Problem 5-7B Income statements—perpetual LO[5]

On December 31, 2014, the end of Ucore Sales' annual accounting period, the financial statement columns of its work sheet appeared as follows in alphabetical order:

		Ucore Sales Work Sheet.xls			
		Home Insert Page Layout Formulas Data Review View			
		P18 fx			

Ucore Sales
Work Sheet
For the Year Ended December 31, 2014

	Account	Income Statement Dr.	Income Statement Cr.	Balance Sheet & Statement of Changes in Equity Dr.	Balance Sheet & Statement of Changes in Equity Cr.
8	Cost of goods sold	129,964			
9	Depreciation expense, office equipment	690			
10	Depreciation expense, store equipment	3,204			
11	Insurance expense	1,240			
12	Liabilities				84,000
13	Lyle Ucore, capital				46,547
14	Lyle Ucore, withdrawals			20,500	
15	Merchandise inventory			3,400	
16	Other assets			102,952	
17	Rent expense (80% sales)	19,950			
18	Salaries expense (70% sales)	71,000			
19	Sales		226,500		
20	Sales discounts	278			
21	Sales returns and allowances	1,469			
22	Supplies expense (35% sales)	2,400			
23	Totals	230,195	226,500	126,852	130,547
24	Net loss		3,695	3,695	
25	**Totals**	230,195	230,195	130,547	130,547

Required

1. Prepare a classified, multiple-step income statement for Ucore Sales, like Exhibit 5.15.

2. Prepare a single-step income statement, like Exhibit 5.17.

Analysis Component: The gross profit ratio for Ucore Sales' year ended December 31, 2013, was 28%. Calculate this ratio for the year ended December 31, 2014, and compare it to the prior year, commenting on whether the change was favourable or unfavourable (round to two decimal places).

Problem 5-8B Closing entries—perpetual LO[6]

Using the information in Problem 5-7B, prepare compound closing entries for Ucore Sales.

Problem 5-9B Income statements—perpetual LO[5]

The following adjusted trial balance information was taken from the end of the July 31, 2014, fiscal year for Brilliant Sales:

		Debit	Credit
101	Cash	$ 6,500	
119	Merchandise inventory	12,220	
125	Supplies	2,400	
128	Prepaid insurance	1,150	
165	Store equipment	29,400	
166	Accumulated depreciation, store equipment		$ 7,500
167	Office equipment	15,600	
168	Accumulated depreciation, office equipment		8,100
201	Accounts payable		6,400
301	Ty Brilliant, capital		107,920
302	Ty Brilliant, withdrawals	61,000	
413	Sales		395,400
415	Sales discounts	1,200	
505	Cost of goods sold	261,800	
612	Depreciation expense, store equipment	1,500	
613	Depreciation expense, office equipment	1,250	
622	Sales salaries expense	39,000	
623	Office salaries expense	32,000	
637	Insurance expense, store	4,100	
638	Insurance expense, office	2,800	
640	Rent expense, office space	13,100	
641	Rent expense, selling space	21,000	
651	Office supplies expense	2,600	
652	Store supplies expense	1,800	
655	Advertising expense	14,900	
	Totals	$525,320	$525,320

Brilliant Sales uses a perpetual inventory system.

Required

1. Prepare a classified multiple-step income statement for use by internal users (like Exhibit 5.15).
2. Prepare a multiple-step income statement for external users (like Exhibit 5.16).
3. Prepare a single-step income statement (like Exhibit 5.17).

*Problem 5-10B Journal entries for merchandising activities—periodic LO[7]

Using the information provided in Part 1 of Problem 5-1B, journalize each of the transactions assuming a periodic inventory system.

*Problem 5-11B Journal entries for merchandising transactions—periodic LO[7]

Prepare General Journal entries to record the following periodic system transactions of Inter-Cap Merchandising. *Use a separate account for each receivable and payable.*

March	1	Purchased merchandise on credit from Zender Holdings, terms 1/10, n/15, $40,000.
	2	Sold merchandise for cash, $5,100.
	7	Purchased merchandise on credit from Red River Co., terms 2/10, n/30, $29,500, FOB the seller's factory.
	8	Incurred freight charges for $1,750 on credit to Dan's Shipping regarding the merchandise shipment of the previous transaction.
	12	Sold merchandise on credit to Bev Dole, terms 2/10, n/45, $26,000.
	13	Received a $1,000 credit memorandum for merchandise purchased on March 7 and returned for credit.
	14	Purchased furniture for the office on credit from Wilson Supplies, $3,200.
	15	Sold merchandise on credit to Ted Smith, terms 2/10, n/45, $24,000.
	16	Paid for the merchandise purchased on March 7.
	17	Issued a credit memorandum to the customer of March 15 granting an allowance of $2,000 due to damage during shipment.
	19	The supplier issued a credit memorandum for $1,500 regarding unsatisfactory furniture purchased on March 14 and returned.
	24	Received payment for the merchandise sold on March 15.
	27	The customer of March 12 paid for the purchase of that date.
	31	Paid for the merchandise purchased on March 1.

*Problem 5-12B Income statement calculations and formats—periodic LO[7]

The following amounts appeared on the Mullen Company's adjusted trial balance in alphabetical order as of November 30, 2014, the end of its fiscal year:

	Debit	Credit
Advertising expense	$ 3,000	
Interest expense	350	
Liabilities		$ 31,000
Merchandise inventory	5,600	
Mitsy Mullen, capital		113,800
Mitsy Mullen, withdrawals	10,000	
Other assets	144,650	
Purchase discounts		1,150
Purchase returns and allowances		4,050
Purchases	120,000	
Rent expense (75% selling)	38,000	
Salaries expense (60% selling)	62,000	
Sales		276,000
Sales discounts	2,350	
Sales returns and allowances	28,500	
Supplies expense (80% selling)	6,700	
Transportation-in	4,850	
Totals	$426,000	$426,000

A physical count shows that the cost of the ending inventory is $6,100.

Required

1. Calculate the company's net sales for the year.

2. Calculate the company's cost of goods purchased for the year.

3. Calculate the company's cost of goods sold for the year.

4. Present a multiple-step income statement (like Exhibit 5.16) that lists the company's net sales, cost of goods sold, and gross profit, as well as the components and amounts of selling expenses and general and administrative expenses.

5. Present a single-step income statement (like Exhibit 5.17) that lists these expenses: cost of goods sold, selling expenses, general and administrative expenses, and interest expense.

An asterisk (*) identifies assignment material based on Appendix 5A or Appendix 5B.

*Problem 5-13B Closing entries—periodic LO⁷

Use the data for the Mullen Company in *Problem 5-12B to prepare compound closing entries for the company as of November 30, 2014.

CHECK FIGURE:
1. Balance sheet columns = $175,950

*Problem 5-14B Work sheet and closing entries—periodic LO⁷

Information from the March 31, 2014, year-end, unadjusted trial balance of The Online Store is as follows:

	Debit	Credit
Cash	$ 7,000	
Merchandise inventory	39,500	
Supplies	1,600	
Prepaid rent	19,200	
Store equipment	60,000	
Accumulated depreciation, store equipment		$ 14,000
Office equipment	23,000	
Accumulated depreciation, office equipment		6,500
Accounts payable		16,000
Lucy Baker, capital		134,600
Lucy Baker, withdrawals	34,000	
Sales		506,750
Sales returns and allowances	13,800	
Sales discounts	6,000	
Purchases	346,000	
Purchase returns and allowances		4,600
Purchase discounts		7,150
Transportation-in	16,000	
Salaries expense (60% selling, 40% office)	58,000	
Rent expense (80% selling space; 20% office space)	49,000	
Advertising expense	7,000	
Supplies expense (30% selling supplies; 70% office supplies)	9,500	
Depreciation expense, store equipment	-0-	
Depreciation expense, office equipment	-0-	
Totals	$689,600	$689,600

Required

1. Copy the unadjusted trial balance on a work sheet form and complete the work sheet using the following information:

   a. Supplies inventory at year-end, $920.

   b. The balance in the Prepaid Rent account represents a six-month contract effective November 1, 2013.

   c. Depreciation on the store equipment, $1,600.

   d. The useful life and trade-in value of the office equipment were originally estimated to be seven years and $250, respectively.

   e. Ending merchandise inventory, $19,200.

2. Journalize closing entries for the store. Use page 14 for your journal.

3. Open a balance column Merchandise Inventory account (110) and enter the March 31, 2013, balance of $39,500. Then post those portions of the closing entries that affect the account.

*Problem 5-15B Classified, multi-step income statement—periodic LO⁷

Using the information in *Problem 5-14B, prepare a classified multi-step income statement (like Exhibit 5A.3).

*Problem 5-16B Sales taxes—perpetual LO[3,8]

Journalize each of the following transactions assuming a perpetual inventory system and PST at 8% along with 5% GST. *Note: Any available cash discount is taken only on the sale price before taxes.*

Sept.	2	Recorded $9,000 of cash sales (cost of sales $6,200).
	3	Purchased $11,000 of merchandise inventory for cash.
	7	Purchased $6,500 of merchandise; terms 1/10, n/45.
	8	Sold merchandise costing $13,200 for $16,200; terms 2/10, n/30.
	17	Paid for the merchandise purchased on September 7.
	18	Collected the amount owing from the customer of September 8.

*Problem 5-17B Sales taxes—periodic LO[7,8]

Journalize each of the transactions in *Problem 5-16B assuming a periodic inventory system and PST at 8% along with 5% GST.

ANALYTICAL AND REVIEW PROBLEM

A & R Problem 5-1—perpetual

The following income statement was prepared by an office clerk hired for July. As the accounting supervisor, you recognize that it is incorrect and prepare a corrected multi-step income statement.

EYK
5-2

Demo Sales Income Statement For Month Ended July 31, 2014		
Sales		$562,140
Accounts receivable		37,000
Unearned sales		18,000
Net sales...		$617,140
Operating expenses:		
Accumulated depreciation, equipment.........................	$ 30,000	
Advertising expense	14,000	
Cost of goods sold	394,000	
Depreciation expense, equipment...............................	3,000	
Insurance expense..	2,500	
Interest expense...	1,700	
Interest payable..	250	
Jen Conway, withdrawals...	14,000	
Office supplies..	9,000	
Prepaid insurance...	14,000	
Prepaid rent	25,000	
Rent expense..	5,000	
Salaries payable..	175,000	
Sales discounts	2,800	690,250
Net loss		$ 73,110

ETHICS CHALLENGE

EC 5-1

Claire Phelps is a popular high school student who attends approximately four dances a year at her high school. Each dance requires a new dress and accessories that necessitate a financial outlay of $100 to $200 per event. Claire's parents inform her that she is "on her own" with respect to financing the dresses. After incurring a major hit to her savings for the first dance in her second year, Claire developed a different approach. She buys the dress on credit the week before the dance, wears it to the dance, and returns the dress the next week to the store for a full refund on her charge card.

Required

1. Comment on the ethics exhibited by Claire and possible consequences of her actions.

2. How does the store account for the dresses that Claire returns?

An asterisk (*) identifies assignment material based on Appendix 5A or Appendix 5B.

FOCUS ON FINANCIAL STATEMENTS

FFS 5-1

CHECK FIGURES:
Net loss = $154;
Total current
assets = $430;
Total assets = $562;
Total current
liabilities = $74

Colombia Textiles began operations several years ago. Its post-closing trial balance at December 31, 2014, is shown below (with accounts listed in alphabetical order):

Account	Account Balance[1] ($000s)
Accounts payable	17
Accounts receivable	106
Accumulated depreciation, office furniture	38
Accumulated depreciation, store fixtures	61
Brandy Colombia, capital[2]	308
Cash	48
Franchise	62
Merchandise inventory	236
Notes payable[3]	225
Notes receivable[4]	14
Office furniture	52
Office supplies	5
Prepaid rent	32
Store fixtures	106
Unearned sales	12

[1] Assume all accounts have a normal balance.
[2] The owner, Brandy Colombia, made no investments during 2014.
[3] $180,000 of the note is due after December 31, 2015.
[4] $3,000 of the notes receivable will be collected during 2015.

Additional information: The following closing entries were recorded on December 31, 2014, for the year just ended.

2014			
Dec. 31	Sales	640	
	Interest Earned	2	
	Income Summary		642
	To close temporary credit balance accounts to the Income Summary account.		
31	Income Summary	796	
	Depreciation Expense, Office Furniture		13
	Depreciation Expense, Store Fixtures		6
	Cost of Goods Sold		459
	Delivery Expense		21
	Interest Expense		4
	Office Salaries Expense		63
	Office Supplies Expense		17
	Rent Expense, Office		21
	Rent Expense, Sales		46
	Sales Discounts		7
	Sales Returns and Allowances		19
	Sales Salaries Expense		120
	To close temporary debit balance accounts to the Income Summary account.		
31	Brandy Colombia, Capital	154	
	Income Summary		154
	To close the Income Summary account to Capital.		
31	Brandy Colombia, Capital	78	
	Brandy Colombia, Withdrawals		78
	To close Withdrawals to Capital.		

Required Using the information provided, prepare a single-step income statement, statement of changes in equity, and classified balance sheet.

Analysis Component: Refer to **Danier Leather**'s June 25, 2011, balance sheet in Appendix II at the back of the textbook. Compare Danier's liabilities to those of Colombia Textiles. Ignoring the balance sheet dates, which company has the stronger balance sheet? *(A balance sheet is considered to be stronger the fewer liabilities it has as a percentage of total assets.)*

FFS 5-2

Required Answer the following questions.

DANIER

a. Based on a review of the income statement for **Danier** in Appendix II at the end of the textbook, determine if Danier sells products or services. Explain your answer.

b. Based on a review of **WestJet**'s income statement in Appendix II at the end of the textbook, determine if WestJet sells products or services. Explain your answer.

c. The income statement for Danier shows a gross profit of $86,288 (thousand) for the year ended June 25, 2011. Explain what this gross profit represents.

d. Did Danier have sufficient gross profit to cover operating expenses for the year ended June 25, 2011?

e. Is the income statement format used by Danier a classified multi-step, a multi-step, or a single-step? (Compare the income statement for Danier to those in Exhibits 5.15, 5.16, and 5.17)

f. Refer to the balance sheets for Danier and WestJet in Appendix II at the end of the textbook. Both balance sheets include *Inventory*. Explain how *Inventory* is unique for each of these companies.

CRITICAL THINKING MINI CASE

You have just graduated with a business diploma in management and have been hired as the inventory manager for a local sporting goods store. Your first task is to review and assess the following information:

	2014	2013
Cost of merchandise sold to customers in sales transactions.............	$480,000	$320,000
Merchandise inventory balance, beginning of year...........................	?	84,000
Invoice cost of merchandise purchases...	510,000	240,000
Shrinkage determined at end of year..	2,500	14,000
Cost of transportation-in	25,500	12,000
Cost of merchandise returned by customers and restored to inventory	115,000	22,400
Purchase discounts received..	5,100	2,400
Purchase returns and allowances received	2,550	1,200

Required Using the elements of critical thinking described on the inside front cover, comment.

SERIAL PROBLEMS

Echo Systems—perpetual or *periodic

Note: Solutions are available for both perpetual and *periodic.

CHECK FIGURES:
4. Net income = $23,198
6. Total current assets = $162,358; Total assets = $208,858

(The first three segments of this comprehensive problem were presented in Chapters 2, 3, and 4. If those segments have not been completed, the assignment can begin at this point. However, you should use the Working Papers[17] that accompany this text because they reflect the account balances that resulted from posting the entries required in Chapters 2, 3, and 4.)

Earlier segments of this problem have described how Mary Graham created Echo Systems on October 1, 2014. The company has been successful, and its list of customers has started to grow. To accommodate the growth, the accounting system is ready to be modified to set up separate accounts for each customer. The following list of customers includes the account number used for each account and any balance as of the end of 2014. Graham decided to add a fourth digit with a decimal point to the 106 account number that had been used for the single Accounts Receivable account. This modification allows the existing chart of accounts to continue being used. The list also shows the balances that two customers owed as of December 31, 2014:

Customer Account	No.	Dec. 31 Balance
Alamo Engineering Co.	106.1	-0-
Buckman Services	106.2	-0-
Capital Leasing	106.3	-0-
Decker Co.	106.4	$2,700
Elite Corporation	106.5	-0-
Fostek Co.	106.6	$3,000
Grandview Co.	106.7	-0-
Hacienda, Inc.	106.8	-0-
Images, Inc.	106.9	-0-

In response to frequent requests from customers, Graham has decided to begin selling computer software. The company will extend credit terms of 1/10, n/30 to customers who purchase merchandise. No cash discount will be available on consulting fees. The following additional accounts were added to the General Ledger to allow the system to account for the company's new merchandising activities:

Account (Periodic)	No.		Account (Perpetual)	No.
Merchandise Inventory	119		Merchandise Inventory	119
Sales	413		Sales	413
Sales Discounts	414	**OR**	Sales Discounts	414
Sales Returns and Allowances	415		Sales Returns and Allowances	415
Purchases	505		Cost of Goods Sold	502
Purchase Returns and Allowances	506			
Purchase Discounts	507			
Transportation-In	508			

Because the accounting system does not use reversing entries, all revenue and expense accounts have zero balances as of January 1, 2015.

---

17 If students have not purchased the Working Papers package, the Working Papers for the Serial Problem are available on Connect.

Required

1. Prepare journal entries to record each of the following transactions for Echo Systems, assuming either a perpetual system or a periodic system.

2015

Jan.	4	Paid Carly Smith for five days at the rate of $200 per day, including one day in addition to the four unpaid days from the prior year.
	5	Mary Graham invested an additional $48,000 cash in the business.
	7	Purchased $11,200 of merchandise from Shephard Corp. with terms of 1/10, n/30, FOB shipping point.
	9	Received $3,000 from Fostek Co. as final payment on its account.
	11	Completed five-day project for Alamo Engineering Co. and billed them $9,000, which is the total price of $12,000 less the advance payment of $3,000.
	13	Sold merchandise with a retail value of $8,400 and a cost of $6,720 to Elite Corporation with terms of 1/10, n/30, FOB shipping point.
	15	Paid $1,400 for freight charges on the merchandise purchased on January 7.
	16	Received $6,000 cash from Grandview Co. for computer services.
	17	Paid Shephard Corp. for the purchase on January 7.
	20	Elite Corporation returned $800 of defective merchandise from its purchase on January 13. The returned merchandise, which had a cost of $640, was scrapped.
	22	Received the balance due from Elite Corporation.
	24	Returned defective merchandise to Shephard Corp. and accepted credit against future purchases. Its cost, net of the discount, was $792.
	26	Purchased $16,000 of merchandise from Shephard Corp. with terms of 1/10, n/30, FOB destination.
	26	Sold merchandise with a cost of $9,280 for $11,600 on credit to Hacienda, Inc.
	29	Received a $792 credit memo from Shephard Corp. concerning the merchandise returned on January 24.
	31	Paid Carly Smith for 10 days' work at $200 per day.
Feb.	1	Paid $6,750 to the Lakeshore Mall for another three months' rent in advance.
	3	Paid Shephard Corp. for the balance due.
	5	Paid $1,600 to the local newspaper for advertising.
	11	Received the balance due from Alamo Engineering Co. for fees billed on January 11.
	15	Mary Graham withdrew $9,600 cash for personal use.
	23	Sold merchandise with a cost of $5,120 for $6,400 on credit to Grandview Co.; terms 1/10, n/30.
	26	Paid Carly Smith for eight days' work at $200 per day.
	27	Reimbursed Mary Graham's business automobile expenses for 600 kilometres at $1.00 per kilometre.
Mar.	8	Purchased $4,800 of computer supplies from Abbott Office Products on credit.
	9	Received the balance due from Grandview Co. for merchandise sold on February 23.
	11	Repaired the company's computer paying cash of $1,720.
	16	Received $8,520 cash from Images, Inc. for computing services.
	19	Paid the full amount due to Abbott Office Products, including amounts created on December 17 and March 8.
	24	Billed Capital Leasing for $11,800 of computing services.
	25	Sold merchandise with a cost of $2,004 for $3,600 on credit to Buckman Services.
	30	Sold merchandise with a cost of $2,200 for $4,440 on credit to Decker Company.
	31	Reimbursed Mary Graham's business automobile expenses for 400 kilometres at $1.00 per kilometre.

2. Post the journal entries to the accounts in the company's General Ledger. (Use asset, liability, and equity accounts that start with balances as of December 31, 2014.)

3. Prepare a partial work sheet consisting of the first six columns showing the unadjusted trial balance, the March 31 adjustments described in (a) through (g) below, and the adjusted trial balance. *Do not prepare closing entries and do not journalize the adjusting entries or post them to the ledger.*

   a. The March 31 computer supplies on hand is $4,230.

   b. Three more months have passed since the company purchased the annual insurance policy at the cost of $4,320.

   c. Carly Smith has not been paid for seven days of work.

   d. Three months have passed since any prepaid rent cost has been transferred to expense. The monthly rent is $2,250.

   e. Depreciation on the computer for January through March is $2,250.

   f. Depreciation on the office equipment for January through March is $1,500.

   g. The March 31 inventory of merchandise is $1,960.

4. Prepare an interim single-step income statement for the three months ended March 31, 2015. List all expenses without differentiating between selling expenses and general and administrative expenses.

5. Prepare an interim statement of changes in equity for the three months ended March 31, 2015.

6. Prepare an interim classified balance sheet as of March 31, 2015.

Merchandise Inventory and Cost of Sales

THE INVENTORY CHALLENGE

Inventory management is a priority for merchandisers given today's economic downturn, especially for a business as highly competitive as **Rona**'s. With its head office in Boucherville, Quebec, Rona offers services and products to consumers of housing and home improvement products. It operates a network of more than 950 stores under banners such as Totem, TruServe, Botanix, and, Dick's Lumber. To help meet consumer demand as efficiently as possible, Rona has nine distribution centres across Canada with a total of 197,976 square metres of indoor space and 143,071 square metres of outdoor lumberyard—that's a combined total of about 42 football fields to handle all the inventory! For the year ended December 25, 2011, those distribution centres moved more than $3.41 billion of inventory that retailed for $4.80 billion. Rona's December 25, 2011, balance sheet shows inventory of $840 million representing 67% of total current assets on the same date. To cost its 90,000 products efficiently and effectively, Rona has implemented a state of the art, real-time inventory management system that incorporates the weighted average method. To optimize inventory processes and decisions, Rona's goals for 2011 included refining its inventory demand planning; reducing inventory levels and improving inventory turnover to reduce inventory holding costs; reviewing the distribution alternatives regarding Chinese imports; and investigating cost saving strategies regarding transportation services and routes and warehousing. Rona sees the economic downturn as an opportunity to get creative and offer consumers more for less.

www.rona.ca

ENTRANCE

LEARNING OBJECTIVES

LO1 Identify the components and costs included in merchandise inventory.

LO2 Calculate cost of goods sold and merchandise inventory using specific identification, moving weighted average, and FIFO—perpetual.

LO3 Analyze the effects of the costing methods on financial reporting.

LO4 Calculate the lower of cost and net realizable value of inventory.

LO5 Analyze the effects of inventory errors on current and future financial statements—perpetual.

LO6 Apply both the gross profit and retail inventory methods to estimate inventory.

*APPENDIX 6A

LO7 Calculate cost of goods sold and merchandise inventory using FIFO—periodic, weighted average, and specific identification.

LO8 Analyze the effects of inventory errors on current and future financial statements—periodic.

*APPENDIX 6B

LO9 Assess inventory management using both merchandise turnover and days' sales in inventory.

CRITICAL THINKING CHALLENGE Would Rona have a merchandise turnover similar to **Danier Leather**'s? Explain why or why not. What does "inventory demand planning" refer to? What would the effect of cost saving strategies be on the weighted average cost of inventory?

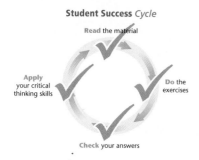

Student Success *Cycle*

Read the material

Do the exercises

Check your answers

Apply your critical thinking skills

CHAPTER PREVIEW

Activities of merchandising companies involve the purchase and resale of products. We explained accounting for merchandisers in the last chapter and explained how perpetual and periodic inventory systems account for merchandise inventory. In this chapter, we extend our study and analysis of inventory by identifying the items that make up inventory and how they are evaluated. We also explain methods used to assign costs to merchandise inventory and to cost of goods sold. These methods include those that differ from historical cost. The principles and methods we describe are used in department stores, grocery stores, and many other merchandising companies that purchase products for resale. These principles and methods affect reported amounts of income, assets, and equity. Understanding these fundamental concepts of inventory accounting increases our ability to analyze and interpret financial statements. As is the case for Rona in the opening article, an understanding of these topics also helps in managing inventory.

Accounting for inventory affects both the balance sheet and income statement. A major goal in accounting for inventory is matching relevant costs against revenues. This is important in order to calculate income properly.[1] We use the matching principle when accounting for inventory to decide how much of the cost of the goods available for sale is deducted from sales and how much is carried forward as inventory and matched against future sales. Management must make this decision and several others when accounting for inventory. These decisions include selecting the:

- Items included and their costs
- Costing method (specific identification, moving weighted average, or FIFO)
- Inventory system (perpetual or periodic)
- Use of net realizable value or other estimates.

These selections affect the reported amounts for inventory, cost of goods sold, gross profit, income, current assets, and other accounts. This chapter discusses all of these important issues and their reporting effects.

INVENTORY ITEMS AND COSTS

Items in Merchandise Inventory

LO1 Identify the components and costs included in merchandise inventory.

Merchandise inventory includes all goods owned by a company and held for sale. This rule holds regardless of where goods are located at the time inventory is counted. Most inventory items are no problem when applying this rule, but certain items require special attention. These include goods in transit, goods on consignment, and goods damaged or obsolete.

Goods in Transit

Do we include in a purchaser's inventory the goods in transit from a supplier? Our answer depends on whether the rights and risks of ownership have passed from the supplier to the purchaser: whether the goods are FOB shipping point or FOB destination. If ownership has passed to the purchaser, they are included in the purchaser's inventory.

---

1   IFRS 2012, IAS 2, par. 1.

Goods on Consignment

Goods on consignment are goods shipped by their owner, called the **consignor**, to another party called the **consignee.** A consignee is to sell goods for the owner without ever having legal title to the goods. Consigned goods are owned by the consignor and are reported in the consignor's inventory.

Goods Damaged or Obsolete

Damaged goods and obsolete (or deteriorated) goods are not counted in inventory if they are unsaleable. If these goods are saleable at a reduced price, they are included in inventory at a conservative estimate of their *net realizable value.* **Net realizable value (NRV)** is sales price minus the cost of making the sale. The period when damage or obsolescence (or deterioration) occurs is the period where the loss is reported.

Costs of Merchandise Inventory

Costs included in merchandise inventory are those expenditures necessary, directly or indirectly, in bringing an item to a saleable condition and location.[2] This means the cost of an inventory item includes its invoice price minus any discount, plus any added or incidental costs necessary to put it in a place and condition for sale. Added or incidental costs can include import duties, transportation-in, storage, insurance, and costs incurred in an aging process (for example, aging of wine and cheese).

Accounting principles imply that incidental costs are assigned to every unit purchased. This is so that all inventory costs are properly matched against revenue in the period when inventory is sold. The **materiality principle**[3] states that an amount may not be ignored if its effect on the financial statements is important to their users. The *materiality principle* is used by some companies not to assign incidental costs of acquiring merchandise to inventory. These companies argue either that incidental costs are immaterial or that the effort in assigning these costs to inventory outweighs the benefits. Such companies price inventory using invoice prices only. When this is done, the incidental costs are allocated to cost of goods sold in the period when they are incurred.

Physical Count of Merchandise Inventory

To help determine the value of inventory included on financial statements, units on hand need to be confirmed through a **physical count** (also known as **taking an inventory**). This often occurs at the end of the fiscal year or when inventory amounts are low. The physical count is used to adjust the Merchandise Inventory account balance to the actual inventory on hand. In a perpetual inventory system, this is done by debiting Cost of Goods Sold and crediting Merchandise Inventory if the physical count is less than the unadjusted balance in the Merchandise Inventory account. If the count is more than the unadjusted balance, the entry is the opposite. Differences occur because of events including theft, loss, damage, and errors. This means that nearly all companies take a physical count of inventory at least once each year regardless of whether a perpetual or periodic inventory system is in place.

When performing a physical count of inventory, *internal controls* should be followed to minimize errors. **Internal controls,** discussed in more detail in Chapter 8, are the policies and procedures used to protect assets, ensure reliable

---

2   IFRS 2012, IAS 2, par. 10–22.
3   IFRS 2012, "Framework," para. QC 11.

EXHIBIT 6.1

Inventory Ticket

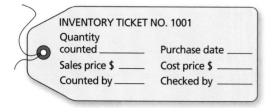

INVENTORY TICKET NO. 1001

Quantity
counted _____   Purchase date _____

Sales price $ _____   Cost price $ _____

Counted by _____   Checked by _____

accounting, promote efficient operations, and urge adherence to company policies. An example of an internal control technique is the use of prenumbered inventory tickets, one for each product on hand, to reduce the risk of items being counted more than once or omitted. We show a typical inventory ticket in Exhibit 6.1. By multiplying the number of units counted for each product by its unit cost, we get the dollar amount for each product in inventory. The sum total of all products is the dollar amount reported for inventory on the balance sheet.

In lieu of inventory tickets, the merchandise inventory items of many businesses are labelled with UPC (Universal Product Code) bar codes. The UPC bar codes not only are used for the pricing and costing of sales, but also make physical counts easier.

DECISION INSIGHT

If you look at any grocery product, you will find a UPC bar code printed on the package. Universal Product Codes were created in 1973 to assist in the checkout and inventory process of grocery stores, and UPC bar codes have since spread to nearly every item in the retail world. The Uniform Code Council (UCC) is responsible for issuing the manufacturer's portion of the code. The manufacturer's UPC coordinator assigns the next digits as the item number. The retailer can then assign a price to each individual UPC code along with costing information. In this way, inventory and sales records can be updated instantly when the bar code is scanned.

0   67350 91649   8

CHECKPOINT

1. If General Electric sells goods to The Bay with terms FOB General Electric's factory, does General Electric or The Bay report these goods in its inventory when they are in transit?

2. An art gallery purchases a painting for $11,400. Additional costs in obtaining and offering the artwork for sale include $130 for transportation-in, $150 for import duties, $100 for insurance during shipment, $180 for advertising, $400 for framing, and $800 for sales salaries. For calculating inventory cost, what is assigned to the painting?

Do Quick Study questions: QS 6-1, QS 6-2, QS 6-3, QS 6-4

ASSIGNING COSTS TO INVENTORY

LO² Calculate cost of goods sold and merchandise inventory using specific identification, moving weighted average, and FIFO—perpetual.

One of the most important decisions in accounting for inventory is determining the per unit costs assigned to inventory items. When all units are purchased at the same unit cost, this process is simple, but when identical items are purchased at different costs, a question arises as to what amounts are recorded in cost of goods sold when sales occur and what amounts remain in inventory. When using a perpetual inventory system, we must record cost of goods sold and reductions in inventory as sales occur. A periodic inventory system determines cost of goods sold and inventory amounts at the end of a period. How we assign these costs to inventory and cost of goods sold affects the reported amounts for both systems, as shown in Exhibit 6A.5.

Three methods are often used in assigning costs to inventory and cost of goods sold:

- First-in, first-out (FIFO)
- Moving weighted average
- Specific identification

Each method assumes a particular pattern for how costs flow through inventory. All three methods are accepted under GAAP and are described in this section.[4] The last-in, first-out (LIFO) method is another way to assign costs to inventory and is popular in the United States, but it is not permitted under GAAP or the Canadian *Income Tax Act*.[5]

If a business has inventory items that are ordinarily interchangeable, either the FIFO or moving weighted average method may be used. A business is required to use the specific identification method for inventory items that are not ordinarily interchangeable. Examples of inventory that would be costed using specific identification might include custom furniture where each piece produced is different or cars at an automobile dealership, each with a unique serial number and unique options. **Loblaw Companies Limited** and **Canadian Tire** both chose to use weighted average cost as per their 2011 annual reports. **Maple Leaf Foods Inc.** and **Perlite Canada Inc.** use FIFO according to each company's 2011 annual report. Some companies use different methods for different types of inventory. In its 2011 statements, **Bombardier Inc.** disclosed the use of two methods: specific identification and moving weighted average, depending on the inventory item.

We use fictitious information from MEC, the sporting goods store introduced in the Chapter 5 opening article, to illustrate the three methods. Among its many products, MEC carries one type of mountain bike. Its mountain bike ("unit") inventory at the beginning of August 2014 and its purchases during August are shown in Exhibit 6.2.

MOUNTAIN EQUIPMENT CO-OP®

		Units		Cost Per Unit		Total Cost
Aug. 1	Beginning inventory.............	10	@	$ 91	=	$ 910
3	Purchased	15	@	$106	=	$1,590
17	Purchased	20	@	$115	=	$2,300
Total goods available for sale..................		45 Units available for sale				$4,800
						Total cost of goods that were available for sale

EXHIBIT 6.2

Cost of Goods Available for Sale

MEC had two sales of mountain bikes to two different biking clubs in August, as shown in Exhibit 6.3. MEC ends August with 11 bikes in inventory (45 units available for sale less 34 units sold).

		Units		Selling Price Per Unit		Total Sales
Aug. 14	Sales..	20	@	$133	=	$2,660
28	Sales..	14	@	$150	=	$2,100
		34 Units				$4,760

EXHIBIT 6.3

Retail Sales of Goods

---

4 Physical flow of goods depends on the type of product and the way it is used. Perishable goods such as fresh fruit demand that a business attempt to sell them in a first-in, first-out pattern. Other products such as canned food can often be sold in a random pattern.

5 IFRS 2012, IAS 2, par. 23–25.

In this section, we will determine how much of the cost of goods available for sale is to be assigned to cost of goods sold and to ending merchandise inventory using the three different cost flow assumptions.

We explained in the last chapter how use of a perpetual inventory system is increasing dramatically due to advances in information and computing technology. Widespread use of electronic scanners and product bar codes further encourages its use. Accordingly, we discuss the assignment of costs to cost of goods sold and merchandise inventory in a perpetual system. The assignment of costs to inventory using a periodic system is discussed in Appendix 6A.

First-In, First-Out

The **first-in, first-out (FIFO)** method of assigning cost to inventory and the goods sold assumes that inventory items are sold in the order acquired. When sales occur, costs of the earliest units purchased are charged to cost of goods sold. This leaves the costs from the most recent purchases in inventory. Use of FIFO for MEC means the costs of mountain bikes are assigned to inventory and goods sold as shown in Exhibit 6.4.

EXHIBIT 6.4

FIFO Calculations—Perpetual

Date	Purchases			Sales (at cost)			Inventory Balance		
	Units	Unit Cost	Total Cost	Units	Unit Cost	Cost of Goods Sold	Units	Unit Cost	Total Cost
Aug. 1	Beginning inventory 10 @ $ 91 = $ 910						10 @	$ 91 = $ 910	
3	15 @	$106	= $1,590		① ②		10 @ 15 @	$ 91 = $ 910 $106 = $1,590	
14				10 @ 10 @	$ 91 $106	= $ 910 = $1,060	③ 5 @	$106 = $ 530	
17	20 @	$115	= $2,300				5 @ 20 @	$106 = $ 530 $115 = $2,300	
28				5 @ 9 @	$106 $115	= $ 530 = $1,035	11 @	$115 = $1,265	
Totals	45		$4,800	34		$3,535	11		$1,265

Cost of goods available for sale   =   Cost of goods sold   +   Ending inventory

① Under FIFO, units are assumed to be sold in the order acquired; therefore, of the 20 units sold on August 14, the first 10 units come from beginning inventory.

② The remaining 10 units sold on August 14 come from the next purchase, August 3.

③ All of the units from beginning inventory have been sold but 5 units remain from the August 3 purchase.

MEC's cost of goods sold on the income statement is $3,535 (= $910 + $1,060 + $530 + $1,035) and its ending inventory reported on the balance sheet is $1,265.

Moving Weighted Average

The **moving weighted average** inventory costing method (*weighted average* when a periodic inventory system is in place) requires calculating the average cost per unit of merchandise inventory at the time of each purchase. The average is calculated by dividing the cost of goods available for sale by the units on hand. Using the moving weighted average method for MEC means the costs of mountain bikes are assigned to inventory and goods sold as shown in Exhibit 6.5.

EXHIBIT 6.5

Moving Weighted Average Calculations—Perpetual

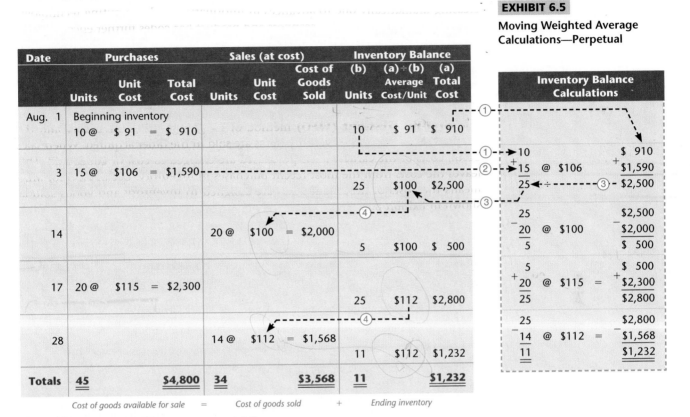

Cost of goods available for sale = Cost of goods sold + Ending inventory

① August 1 beginning inventory in units and dollars.

② August 1 beginning inventory is added to the purchase of August 3 to determine the total cost of the units in inventory on August 3.

③ The total cost of all units is divided by the total number of units to get the average cost per unit of $100 on August 3.

④ The most current average cost is assigned as the cost per unit sold.

MEC's cost of goods sold reported on the income statement is $3,568 (= $2,000 + $1,568) and its ending inventory reported on the balance sheet is $1,232. The moving weighted average perpetual system often raises a rounding problem in the calculations because the currency figures are limited to two decimal places. The typical solution is to adjust or "plug" the inventory figure after calculating the cost of goods sold amount at the moving weighted average cost.

Specific Identification

When each item sold and remaining in inventory can be directly identified with a specific purchase and its invoice, we can use **specific identification** to assign costs. MEC's internal documents reveal that on August 14, 20 units were sold; specifically, these were 8 units from beginning inventory and 12 units from the August 3 purchase. On August 28, 14 units were sold; specifically, these were 2 units from beginning inventory and 12 units from the August 17 purchase.

Specific identification assigns costs to the goods sold and to ending inventory based on specific items identified, as shown in Exhibit 6.6.

EXHIBIT 6.6

Specific Identification Calculations—Perpetual

Date	Purchases			Sales (at cost)			Inventory Balance		
	Units	Unit Cost	Total Cost	Units	Unit Cost	Cost of Goods Sold	Units	Unit Cost	Total Cost
Aug. 1	Beginning inventory 10 @	$ 91	= $ 910				10 @	$ 91 =	$ 910
3	15 @	$106	= $1,590				10 @ 15 @	$ 91 = $106 =	$ 910 $1,590
14				8 @ 12 @	$ 91 $106	= $ 728 = $1,272	2 @ 3 @	$ 91 = $106 =	$ 182 $ 318
17	20 @	$115	= $2,300				2 @ 3 @ 20 @	$ 91 = $106 = $115 =	$ 182 $ 318 $2,300
28				2 @ 12 @	$ 91 $115	= $ 182 = $1,380	3 @ 8 @	$106 = $115 =	$ 318 $ 920
Totals	45		$4,800	34		$3,562	11		$1,238

Cost of goods available for sale　=　Cost of goods sold　+　Ending inventory

① Of the 10 units from beginning inventory, 8 were specifically identified as being sold.

② Of the 10 units from beginning inventory, 2 remain in ending inventory.

③ Of the 15 units purchased on August 3, 12 were specifically identified as being sold.

④ Of the 15 units purchased on August 3, 3 remain in ending inventory.

When using specific identification, MEC's cost of goods sold reported on the income statement is $3,562 (= $728 + $1,272 + $182 + $1,380) and its ending inventory reported on the balance sheet is $1,238.

The specific identification method works best when each item of inventory is unique or different, as in an antique store, an art gallery, or a custom furniture manufacturer. For example, a car dealership would use specific identification because each car has a unique serial number, known as the vehicle identification number (VIN). In all cases where specific identification is used, each inventory item needs to be identified separately.

When inventory items are similar (such as bags of sugar, pallets of concrete blocks, or loaves of bread), specific units being purchased and sold cannot be easily traced; large quantities are often purchased at different times, possibly with different costs. When the cost is greater than the benefit of tracking the sale of individual units that are similar, one of the other methods may be better conceptually and more efficient to use.

Notice in Exhibit 6.7 that the total units and cost of the goods available for sale are the same regardless of the method used. What is different is the dollar amount assigned to the ending inventory and the cost of goods sold.

EXHIBIT 6.7

Comparison of Inventory Methods

	FIFO		Moving Weighted Average		Specific Identification	
	Units	$	Units	$	Units	$
Cost of Goods Sold (or Cost of Sales)	34	$3,535	34	$3,568	34	$3,562
Ending Inventory	11	1,265	11	1,232	11	1,238
Goods Available for Sale	45	$4,800	45	$4,800	45	$4,800

Inventory Costing and Technology

A perpetual inventory system can be kept in either electronic or manual form. A manual form is often too costly for businesses, especially those with many purchases and sales or many units in inventory. Advances in information and computing technology have greatly reduced the cost of an electronic perpetual inventory system, and many companies are now asking whether they can afford not to have one. This is because timely access to information is being used strategically by companies to gain a competitive advantage. Scanned sales data, for instance, can reveal crucial information on buying patterns, and can also help companies target promotional and advertising activities. These and other applications have greatly increased the use of the perpetual system. Maintaining inventory records is discussed in Chapter 7.

CHECKPOINT

3. What accounting principle most governs allocations of cost of goods available for sale between ending inventory and cost of goods sold?

Do Quick Study questions: QS 6-5, QS 6-6, QS 6-7, QS 6-8

MID-CHAPTER DEMONSTRATION PROBLEM

Tale Company uses a perpetual inventory system and had the following beginning inventory and purchases during January 2014:

Date		Units	Item X			Total Cost
			Unit Cost			
Jan. 1	Inventory..............................	300	@	$14	=	$ 4,200
16	Purchase..............................	200	@	15	=	3,000
20	Purchase..............................	300	@	16	=	4,800
	Total units and cost of goods available for sale.........	800				$12,000

Sales of units were as follows (all on credit):

Jan. 15..............................	200 units at $30
28..............................	460 units at $35
Total units sold......................	660

Additional data for use in applying the specific identification method:
   The specific units sold were:

Jan. 15	200 units from the January 1 units on hand
28	75 units from the January 1 units on hand
	150 units from the January 16 purchase, and
	235 units from the January 20 purchase

Required

1. Calculate the ending inventory and the cost of goods sold under a perpetual inventory system by applying each of the three different methods of inventory costing:
   a. FIFO
   b. Moving weighted average
   c. Specific identification

2. Using your calculations from Part 1, record the purchase on January 16 and the sale on January 28 for each of:
   a. FIFO
   b. Moving weighted average
   c. Specific identification

Analysis Component:

A new supplier has approached Tale Company, offering the merchandise inventory to Tale at $11 per unit. What should Tale consider when deciding whether or not to change to the new supplier?

Planning the Solution

- Prepare a perpetual FIFO schedule showing the composition of beginning inventory and how the composition of inventory changes after each purchase of inventory and after each sale.
- Make a schedule of purchases and sales, recalculating the average cost of inventory after each purchase to arrive at the moving weighted average cost of ending inventory. Add up the average costs associated with each sale to determine the cost of goods sold using the moving weighted average method.
- Prepare a schedule showing the calculation of the cost of goods sold and ending inventory using the specific identification method. Use the information provided to determine the cost of the specific units sold and which specific units remain in inventory.
- Journalize the purchase on January 16 and the sale on January 28 by taking the relevant information from the schedules prepared in Part 1 for each method.
- Prepare an answer to the analysis question.

SOLUTION

1a. FIFO Perpetual

Date	Purchases			Sales (at cost)			Inventory Balance		
	Units	Unit Cost	Total Cost	Units	Unit Cost	Cost of Goods Sold	Units	Unit Cost	Total Cost
Jan. 1	Beginning inventory								
	300 @	$14	= $4,200	----①----			300 @	$14 =	$4,200
15				200 @	$14	= $2,800	② 100 @	$14 =	$1,400
							100 @	$14 =	$1,400
16	200 @	$15	= $3,000				200 @	$15 =	$3,000
						③	100 @	$14 =	$1,400
							200 @	$15 =	$3,000
20	300 @	$16	= $4,800		③	③	300 @	$16 =	$4,800
28				100 @	$14 =	$1,400	④		
				200 @	$15	= $3,000			
				160 @	$16	= $2,560	140 @	$16 =	$2,240
Totals	**800**		**$12,000**	**660**		**$9,760**	**140**		**$2,240**

Cost of goods available for sale = Cost of goods sold + Ending inventory

① Under FIFO, units are assumed to be sold in the order acquired; therefore the 200 units sold on January 15 come from beginning inventory.
② The 100 units remaining in inventory after the January 15 sale are from beginning inventory.
③ The 460 units sold on January 28 are assumed to be the 100 units from beginning inventory, plus the 200 units purchased on January 16, plus 160 units from the January 20 purchase.
④ All of the units remaining in inventory after the January 28 sale are from the January 20 purchase.

1b. Moving Weighted Average Perpetual

Date		Purchases			Sales (at cost)			Inventory Balance				Inventory Balance Calculations	
Total	Units	Unit Cost	Total Cost	Units	Unit Cost	Cost of Goods Sold	(b) Units	(a) ÷ (b) Average Cost/Unit	(a) Total Cost			
Jan. 1	Beginning inventory 300 @ $14 = $4,200						300 @ $14.00 = $4,200.00						
15				200 @ $14.00		= $2,800.00	100 @ $14.00 = $1,400.00				300	$ 4,200.00
											200 @ $14.00 =	$ 2,800.00
											100	$ 1,400.00
16	200 @	$15	= $3,000				300 @ $14.67 = $4,400.00				100	$ 1,400.00
											+ 200 @ $15.00 =	+ $ 3,000.00
											300	$ 4,400.00
20	300 @	$16	= $4,800				600 @ $15.33 = $9,200.00				300	$ 4,400.00
											+ 300 @ $16.00 =	+ $ 4,800.00
											600	$ 9,200.00
28				460 @ $15.33		= $7,051.80	140 @ $15.34* = $2,148.20				600	$ 9,200.00
											− 460 @ $15.33 =	− $ 7,051.80
											140	$ 2,148.20
Totals	**800**		**$12,000**	**660**		**$9,851.80**	**140**		**2,148.20**			

Cost of goods available for sale   =   Cost of goods sold   +   Ending inventory

*Cost/unit changed due to rounding
① The most current average cost per unit is assigned to the units sold.
② The beginning balance less the units sold equals the remaining inventory.
③ The total cost remaining in inventory divided by the total units remaining equals the average unit cost. Notice that the average unit cost does not change because of a sale.

1c. Specific Identification

Date		Purchases			Sales (at cost)			Inventory Balance	
	Units	Unit Cost	Total Cost	Units	Unit Cost	Cost of Goods Sold	Units	Unit Cost	Total Cost
Jan. 1	Beginning inventory 300 @ $14 = $4,200						300 @	$14 =	$4,200
15				200 @	$14	= $2,800	100 @	$14 =	$1,400
16	200 @	$15	= $3,000				100 @	$14 =	$1,400
							200 @	$15 =	$3,000
20	300 @	$16	= $4,800				100 @	$14 =	$1,400
							200 @	$15 =	$3,000
							300 @	$16 =	$4,800
28				75 @	$14	= $1,050	25 @	$14 =	$ 350
				150 @	$15	= $2,250	50 @	$15 =	$ 750
				235 @	$16	= $3,760	65 @	$16 =	$1,040
Totals	**800**		**$12,000**	**660**		**$9,860**	**140**		**$2,140**

Cost of goods available for sale   =   Cost of goods sold   +   Ending inventory

① 200 of the beginning inventory units were specifically identified as being sold on January 15. Therefore, the 100 units remaining on January 15 are identified as units from beginning inventory.
② The units sold on January 28 are specifically identified. The units sold determines exactly which units are remaining.

2.

		a.	b.	c.
		FIFO	**Moving Weighted Average**	**Specific Identification**
2014 Jan. 16	Merchandise Inventory	3,000	3,000	3,000
	Accounts Payable	3,000	3,000	3,000
	To record purchase of *merchandise on credit.*			
28	Accounts Receivable	16,100	16,100	16,100
	Sales...	16,100	16,100	16,100
	To record credit sales; *460 units × $35 = $16,100.*			
28	Cost of Goods Sold.......................................	6,960	7,052*	7,060
	Merchandise Inventory.......................	6,960	7,052*	7,060
	To record the sale of merchandise.			

*Rounded to nearest whole dollar for simplicity

Analysis Component:

Tale should consider the following (as well as other possibilities):

- The quality of the merchandise inventory offered by the new supplier
- Whether the new supplier can meet Tale's merchandise inventory quantity needs
- Whether the new supplier will deliver merchandise when required (dependable)
- The payment/delivery terms
- What kind of service the new supplier provides (customer support)
- Whether the new supplier can provide references (from satisfied customers; reputation)
- The duration of the $11 per unit offer and potential price increases

FINANCIAL REPORTING AND INVENTORY

LO³ Analyze the effects of the costing methods on financial reporting.

This section reviews the financial reporting issues related to inventory, including inventory disclosure, consistency, and prudence. As well, we look at the effects of inventory errors.

Financial Reporting

In our analysis of financial statements, it is important to know and understand inventory costing methods because the method used can have a material impact on the income statement and balance sheet, as illustrated in Exhibit 6.8. For this reason, the inventory costing method used must be *disclosed* in the notes to the financial statements.

MEC Income Statement—Mountain Bikes For Month Ended August 31, 2014			
	FIFO	**Moving Weighted Average**	**Specific Identification**
Sales...	$4,760	$4,760	$4,760
Cost of goods sold*	3,535	3,568	3,562
Gross profit from sales	$1,225	$1,192	$1,198
Operating expenses.................................	374	374	374
Income from operations	$ 851	$ 818	$ 824
*From Exhibit 6.7			
Partial Balance Sheet			
Assets			
Current assets:			
Merchandise inventory*..................	$1,265	$1,232	$1,238
*From Exhibit 6.7			

EXHIBIT 6.8

Income Statement and Balance Sheet Effects of Inventory Costing Methods

MOUNTAIN EQUIPMENT CO-OP®

When purchase prices do not change, the choice of an inventory costing method is unimportant. All methods assign the same cost amounts when prices remain constant. When purchase prices are rising or falling, however, the methods are likely to assign different cost amounts.

Because MEC's purchase prices rose in August, FIFO assigned the least amount to cost of goods sold. This led to the highest gross profit and the highest income. This result will always occur in times of rising prices because the most recent and therefore most costly units are in ending inventory, leaving the least expensive units in cost of goods sold.[6]

Because inventory costing methods can materially affect amounts on financial statements, a manager would want to use the method that gave the most favourable results. For example, if management bonus plans were based on net income, managers might pick the method that gave them the highest bonus each period. If managers were allowed to change methods each period, it would be more difficult for users of financial statements to compare a company's financial statements from one period to the next. If income increased, for instance, a user would need to decide whether it resulted from successful operations or from the accounting method change. The *consistency principle* is used to avoid this problem.

The **consistency principle** requires a company to use the same accounting methods period after period so that the financial statements are comparable across periods.[7] The consistency principle applies to all accounting methods.

The consistency principle *does not* require a company to use one method exclusively. It can use different methods to value different categories of inventory. As mentioned earlier, **Bombardier Inc.** uses two methods (specific identification and weighted average) to assign costs to various types of inventory. Also, the consistency principle does not mean that a company can never change from one accounting method to another. Instead, it means a company must argue that the method to which it is changing will improve its financial reporting. Under this circumstance, a change is acceptable; yet, when such a change is made, the full disclosure principle requires that the notes to the statements report the type of change, its justification, and its effect on net income.[8]

---

6   The moving weighted average amount can be higher or lower than the FIFO amount depending on whether prices steadily increase or decrease.

7   IFRS 2012, IAS 1, par. 45.

8   IFRS 2012, IAS 8, par. 14–18 and 28–31.

Inventory Manager

You are the inventory manager for a merchandiser. Your compensation includes a bonus plan based on the amount of gross profit reported in the financial statements. Your superior comes to you and asks your opinion about changing the inventory costing method from moving weighted average to FIFO. Since costs have been rising and are expected to continue to rise, your superior predicts the company will be more attractive to investors because of the reported higher income using FIFO. You realize this proposed change will likely increase your bonus as well. What do you recommend?

Exhibit 6.9 summarizes advantages and disadvantages for the cost flow assumptions discussed.

EXHIBIT 6.9

Advantages and Disadvantages of Cost Flow Assumptions

	FIFO	Moving Weighted Average	Specific Identification
Advantages:	Most current values are on the balance sheet as ending inventory	Smooths out purchase price changes	Exactly matches costs and revenues
Disadvantages:	Cost of goods sold does not reflect current costs, so does not accurately match expenses to revenue	Averaging does not accurately match expenses to revenues	Relatively more costly to implement and maintain

CHECKPOINT

4. Give examples of types of businesses that might use specific identification despite the disadvantage indicated in Exhibit 6.9. Explain why these businesses might choose to use specific identification.
5. When costs and prices are rising, what effect does moving weighted average have on a balance sheet compared to FIFO?

Do Quick Study question: QS 6-9

Lower of Cost and Net Realizable Value (LCNRV)

LO4 Calculate the lower of cost and net realizable value of inventory.

The cost of inventory is not necessarily the amount always reported on a balance sheet. The *principle of faithful representation* provides the guidance in reporting inventory at net realizable value (NRV) when NRV is lower than cost.[9] Merchandise inventory is then said to be reported on the balance sheet at the **lower of cost and net realizable value (LCNRV)**. **Faithful representation** requires that information be complete, neutral, and free from error so that assets and income are not overstated and liabilities and expenses are not understated.[10] Why? If, for example, the December 31, 2014, inventory of a music store included eight-track tapes that cost the merchandiser a total of $100,000 but had an NRV on that date of $500, which value is *most realistic*—cost or NRV? Because we know that eight-track tapes are essentially

9 IFRS 2012, IAS 2, par. 28.
10 IFRS 2012, "Framework," par. QC 12.

obsolete, inventory should be written down and reported at the NRV of $500 to ensure that assets and income are not overstated. If the NRV of the inventory were to recover after the balance sheet date, the inventory write-down would be reversed. The reversal is limited to the amount of the write-down to ensure that inventory is always reported at the lower of cost and NRV. The concept of inventory write-downs and reversals will be demonstrated in the next section.

Calculating the Lower of Cost and Net Realizable Value (LCNRV)

The decline in merchandise inventory from cost to NRV is recorded in an adjusting entry at the end of the period. LCNRV is applied in one of two ways:

(1) Usually item by item, or, when not practicable,
(2) To groups of similar or related items.[11]

We show in Exhibit 6.10 how LCNRV is applied to the ending inventory of MEC.

EXHIBIT 6.10

LCNRV Calculations

Inventory Items	No. of Units	Cost/ Unit	Total Cost	NRV/ Unit	Total NRV	LCNRV applied to: Items	Groups
Bicycles:							
Roadster	25	$ 750	$ 18,750	$ 790	$19,750	$ 18,750	
Sprint	60	1,100	66,000	1,100	66,000	66,000	
Group subtotal			$ 84,750		$85,750		$ 84,750
Kayaks:							
A1 Series	21	$1,800	$ 37,800	$1,300	$27,300	$ 27,300	
Trax-4	29	2,200	63,800	2,250	65,250	63,800	
Group subtotal			$101,600		$92,550		$ 92,550
Totals			$186,350			$175,850	$177,300

Using the information in Exhibit 6.10 to demonstrate the application of LCNRV on an item-by-item basis, we see that total LCNRV is $175,850. Therefore, $175,850 must be reported on the balance sheet. To achieve this, inventory needs to be reduced by $10,500, which is the difference between the total cost of $186,350 and total LCNRV of $175,850. The entry is:

Cost of Goods Sold	10,500	
Merchandise Inventory		10,500
To write inventory down to LCNRV;		
$186,350 − $175,850 = $10,500.		

After posting this entry, merchandise inventory would appear on the balance sheet as:

Current assets:	
Cash	$ ×,×××
Accounts receivable	×,×××
Merchandise inventory, at LCNRV	**175,850**

---

11 IFRS 2012, IAS 2, par. 29.

Assume that the A1 Series kayaks in Exhibit 6.10 are still on hand at the end of the next accounting period. There is evidence that their NRV has increased to $1,450 per unit. The original write-down can be reversed (but is limited to the amount of the original write-down).[12] The entry is:

Merchandise Inventory	3,150	
Cost of Goods Sold...............................		3,150
To reverse the inventory write-down;		
$1,450 − $1,300 = $150;		
$150 × 21 units = $3,150.		

DANIER

Either of the two applications of LCNRV—to items or to groups—is acceptable in practice. **Danier Leather** reports that its inventories are valued at the lower of cost and NRV.

To demonstrate the application of LCNRV to groups, refer to the information in Exhibit 6.10. The entry to write inventory down to LCNRV applied to groups is:

Cost of Goods Sold	9,050	
Merchandise Inventory		9,050
To write inventory down to LCNRV;		
$186,350 − $177,300 = $9,050.		

CHECKPOINT

6. Refer to the information in Exhibit 6.10. Assume that LCNRV was applied to inventory on an item-by-item basis. In the next accounting period, the NRV of the A1 Series kayaks increased to $1,900 per unit because the factory burned down, causing a shortage in the marketplace. MEC had four of the previously written down A1 Series kayaks left in ending inventory a year after the original write-down. What entry, if any, is required in applying LCNRV to the remaining four units?

7. A company's ending inventory includes the following items:

Product	Units on Hand	Unit Cost	NRV Per Unit
A	20	$ 6	$ 5
B	40	9	8
C	10	12	15

Using LCNRV applied separately to individual items, calculate the reported amount for inventory.

Do Quick Study question: QS 6-10

Errors in Reporting Inventory

LO⁵ Analyze the effects of inventory errors on current and future financial statements—perpetual.

Companies must take care in calculating and taking a physical count of inventory. If inventory is reported in error, it causes misstatements of cost of goods sold, gross profit, net income, current assets, and equity. It also means misstatements will exist in the next period's statements. This is because ending inventory of one period is the beginning inventory of the next. An error carried forward causes misstatements of the next period's cost of goods sold, gross profit, and net income. Since the inventory amount often is large, misstatements can reduce the usefulness of financial statements.

---

12 IFRS 2012, IAS 2, par. 33.

Income Statement Effects

The income statement effects of an inventory error are evident when looking at the components of cost of goods sold in each of the alternative presentations in Exhibit 6.11.

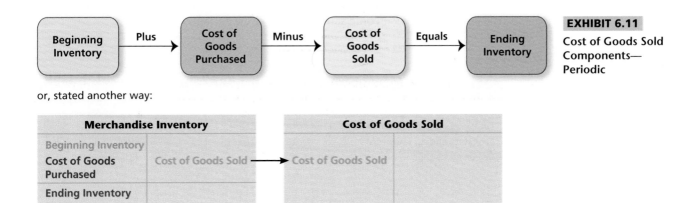

EXHIBIT 6.11

Cost of Goods Sold Components—Periodic

or, stated another way:

Merchandise Inventory		Cost of Goods Sold	
Beginning Inventory			
Cost of Goods Purchased	Cost of Goods Sold ⟶	Cost of Goods Sold	
Ending Inventory			

The effect of an inventory error on cost of goods sold is determined by calculating the inventory correctly and comparing the result to the result of the calculation when using the incorrect amount, as in Exhibit 6.12.

EXHIBIT 6.12

Effects of $2,000 Overstatement in Ending Inventory for 2014 on Three Periods' Income Statement Information—Perpetual

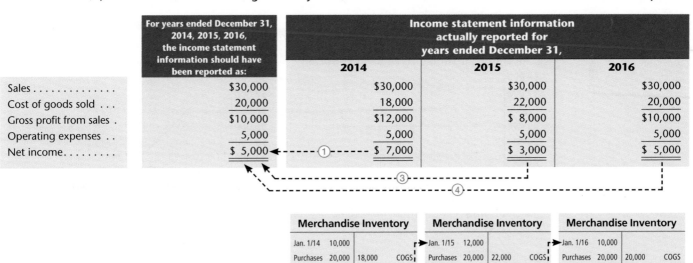

	For years ended December 31, 2014, 2015, 2016, the income statement information should have been reported as:	Income statement information actually reported for years ended December 31,		
		2014	**2015**	**2016**
Sales	$30,000	$30,000	$30,000	$30,000
Cost of goods sold . . .	20,000	18,000	22,000	20,000
Gross profit from sales .	$10,000	$12,000	$ 8,000	$10,000
Operating expenses . .	5,000	5,000	5,000	5,000
Net income.	$ 5,000	$ 7,000	$ 3,000	$ 5,000

Merchandise Inventory				Merchandise Inventory				Merchandise Inventory			
Jan. 1/14	10,000			Jan. 1/15	12,000			Jan. 1/16	10,000		
Purchases	20,000	18,000	COGS	Purchases	20,000	22,000	COGS	Purchases	20,000	20,000	COGS
Dec. 31/14	12,000			Dec. 31/15	10,000			Dec. 31/16	10,000		

① 2014 net income and gross profit are overstated (too high) and cost of goods sold is understated (too low) when ending inventory is overstated (too high).

② Ending inventory for one period becomes the beginning inventory for the next period, carrying forward any errors that existed.

③ 2015 net income and gross profit are understated (too low) and cost of goods sold is overstated (too high) when beginning inventory is overstated (too high). Notice that the error has reversed itself in 2015, the second year.

④ An inventory error in the year 2014 does not affect 2016.

Exhibit 6.12 assumes that $2,000 of merchandise sold but awaiting delivery was incorrectly included in ending inventory on December 31, 2014. This ending inventory error carries over to the next period as a beginning inventory error yielding a reverse effect. We can see that overstating ending inventory will understate cost of goods sold. An understatement of cost of goods sold yields an overstatement of net income. We can do the same analysis with understating ending inventory and for an error in beginning inventory. Exhibit 6.13 shows the effects of inventory errors on the current period's income statement amounts.

EXHIBIT 6.13

Effect of Inventory Errors on This Period's Income Statement

Inventory Error	Cost of Goods Sold	Net Income
Understate ending inventory	Overstated	Understated
Understate beginning inventory	Understated	Overstated
Overstate ending inventory	Understated	Overstated
Overstate beginning inventory	Overstated	Understated

Notice that inventory errors yield opposite effects in cost of goods sold and net income.

Because an inventory error causes an offsetting error in the next period, it is sometimes said to be *self-correcting*. Do not think, however, that this makes inventory errors less serious. Managers, lenders, owners, and other users make important decisions on changes in net income and cost of goods sold. Imagine how a lender's decision would be affected by each of the graphs presented in Exhibit 6.14. Inventory errors must be avoided.

EXHIBIT 6.14

Graphing the Effects of Inventory Errors on Net Income

Net Income As It Should Have Been Reported

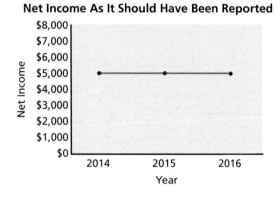

Net Income As Incorrectly Reported

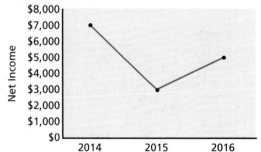

Balance Sheet Effects

Balance sheet effects of an inventory error are made evident by looking at the components of the accounting equation in Exhibit 6.15.

EXHIBIT 6.15

Accounting Equation

$$Assets = Liabilities + Equity$$

We can see, for example, that understating ending inventory will understate both current and total assets. An understatement of ending inventory also yields an understatement in equity because of the understatement of net income. We can do the same analysis with overstating ending inventory. Exhibit 6.16 shows the effects of inventory errors on the current period's balance sheet amounts.

Inventory Error	Assets	Equity
Understate ending inventory	Understated	Understated
Overstate ending inventory	Overstated	Overstated

EXHIBIT 6.16

Effects of Inventory Errors on This Period's Balance Sheet

Errors in beginning inventory do not yield misstatements in the balance sheet, but they do affect the income statement.

CHECKPOINT

8. During 2015, a company discovered that the merchandise inventory reported on the 2014 balance sheet was overstated by $10,000. Did this error cause cost of goods sold to be overstated or understated in 2014? in 2015? By how much?

Do Quick Study question: QS 6-11

ESTIMATING INVENTORY

This section describes methods to estimate inventory. Knowledge of these methods is important for preparers and users in understanding and analyzing financial information.

Gross Profit Method

The **gross profit method** estimates the cost of ending inventory by applying the *gross profit ratio* to net sales (at *retail*). Recall that the **gross profit ratio** measures how much of each sales dollar is gross profit. A need for the gross profit estimate can arise when inventory is destroyed, lost, or stolen. These cases need an estimate of inventory so a company can file a claim with its insurer. Users also apply this method to see if inventory amounts from either management or a physical count are reasonable. This method uses the historical relation between cost of goods sold and net sales to estimate the proportion of cost of goods sold making up current sales. This cost of goods sold estimate is then subtracted from cost of goods available for sale to give us an estimate of ending inventory at cost.

To illustrate, assume the following in March of 2014 when the company's inventory is destroyed by fire:

 LO6 Apply both the gross profit and retail inventory methods to estimate inventory.

Sales	$31,500
Sales returns	1,500
Inventory, January 1, 2014	12,000
Net cost of goods purchased	20,500
Gross profit ratio	30%

To estimate the inventory loss, we first need to recognize that each dollar of net sales is made up of gross profit and cost of goods sold. If this company's gross profit ratio is 30% as given, then 30% of each net sales dollar is gross profit and 70% is cost of goods sold. We show in Exhibit 6.17 how this 70% is used to estimate lost inventory.

EXHIBIT 6.17

Calculating Inventory Using the Gross Profit Method

In Step 1 we use income statement relationships to calculate the dollar value of the estimated cost of goods sold. In Step 2 we use our understanding of the cost of goods sold components as described earlier in Exhibit 6.11 to determine the estimated March inventory.

Step 1:

Sales	$31,500
Less: Sales returns..	1,500
Net sales	$30,000
Less: COGS*	**21,000**
Gross profit from sales	30%
	or $9,000

Step 2:

Inventory, January 1, 2014......................	$ 12,000
Add: Net cost of goods purchased........	20,500
Less: COGS..	**21,000**
Estimated March inventory	**$11,500**

*If gross profit equals 30% of net sales or $9,000 (30% × $30,000), then COGS must equal 70% of net sales or $21,000 (70% × $30,000).

Retail Inventory Method

Many companies prepare financial statements on a quarterly or monthly basis. The cost of goods sold information needed to prepare these interim financial reports is readily available if a perpetual inventory system is used. A periodic system, however, requires a physical inventory to determine cost of goods sold. To avoid the time-consuming and expensive process of taking a physical inventory each month or quarter, some companies use the **retail inventory method** to estimate cost of goods sold and ending inventory. Some companies even use the retail inventory method to prepare the annual statements since it is acceptable for income tax purposes. **Reitman's (Canada) Limited**, for instance, reports in its January 28, 2012, annual report that:

Merchandise inventories are accounted for by the retail method.

EXHIBIT 6.18

Inventory Estimation Using Retail Inventory Method

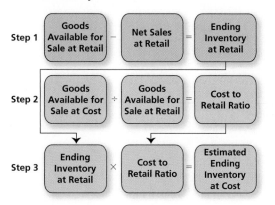

All companies should take a physical inventory at least once each year to identify any errors or shortages.

Calculating the Retail Inventory Estimate

When the retail inventory method is used to estimate inventory, we need to know the amount of inventory a company had at the beginning of the period in both *cost* and *retail* amounts. The **retail** amount of inventory refers to its dollar amount measured using selling prices of inventory items. We also need the net amount of goods purchased (minus returns, allowances, and discounts) during the period, both at cost and at retail. The amount of net sales at retail is also needed.

A three-step process is used to estimate ending inventory after we calculate the amount of goods available for sale during the period both at cost and at retail. This process is shown in Exhibit 6.18.

The reasoning behind the retail inventory method is that if we can get a good estimate of the cost to retail ratio, then we can multiply ending inventory at retail by this ratio to estimate ending inventory at cost. We show in Exhibit 6.19 how these steps are applied to estimate ending inventory.

		At Cost	At Retail
	Goods available for sale:		
	Beginning inventory...	$20,500	$ 34,500
	Cost of goods purchased	39,500	65,500
	Goods available for sale......................................	$60,000	$100,000
Step 1:	Less: Net sales at retail		70,000
	Ending inventory at retail....................................		$ 30,000
Step 2:	Cost to retail ratio: ($60,000 ÷ $100,000)..........		× 60%
Step 3:	Estimated ending inventory at cost		$ 18,000

EXHIBIT 6.19

Calculating Ending Inventory Using the Retail Inventory Method

Estimating Physical Inventory at Cost

Items for sale by retailers usually carry price tags listing selling prices. When a retailer takes a physical inventory, it commonly totals inventory using selling prices of items on hand. It then reduces the dollar total of this inventory to a cost basis by applying the cost to retail ratio. This is done because selling prices are readily available and using the cost to retail ratio eliminates the need to look up invoice prices of items on hand.

Let's assume that the company in Exhibit 6.19 estimates its inventory by the retail method and takes a physical inventory using selling prices. If the retail value of this physical inventory is $29,600, then we can calculate the cost of this inventory by applying its cost to retail ratio as follows: $29,600 × 60% = $17,760. The $17,760 cost figure for ending physical inventory is an acceptable number for annual financial statements. It is also acceptable to CRA for tax reporting.

Estimating Inventory Shortage at Cost

The inventory estimate in Exhibit 6.19 is an estimate of the amount of goods on hand (at cost). Since it is calculated by deducting sales from goods available for sale (at retail), it does not reveal any shrinkage due to breakage, loss, or theft. However, we can estimate the amount of shrinkage by comparing the inventory calculated in Exhibit 6.19 with the amount from taking a physical inventory. In Exhibit 6.19, for example, we estimated ending inventory at retail as $30,000, but a physical inventory revealed only $29,600 of inventory on hand (at retail). The company has an inventory shortage (at retail) of $400, calculated as $30,000 − $29,600. The inventory shortage (at cost) is $240, calculated as $400 × 60%.

CHECKPOINT

9. The following data pertain to a company's inventory during 2014:

	Cost	Retail
Beginning inventory...	$324,000	$530,000
Cost of goods purchased.................................	195,000	335,000
Net sales		320,000

Using the retail method, estimate the cost of ending inventory.

Do Quick Study questions: QS 6-12, QS 6-13, QS 6-14, QS 6-15

CRITICAL THINKING CHALLENGE Refer to the Critical Thinking Challenge questions at the beginning of the chapter. Compare your answers to those suggested on Connect.

IFRS AND ASPE—THE DIFFERENCES

Difference	International Financial Reporting Standards (IFRS)	Accounting Standards for Private Enterprises (ASPE)
There are no significant differences between IFRS and ASPE related to this chapter.		

SUMMARY

LO¹ Identify the components and costs included in merchandise inventory. Merchandise inventory comprises goods owned by a company and held for resale. Goods in transit are reported in inventory of the company that holds ownership rights. Goods out on consignment are reported in inventory of the consignor. Goods damaged or obsolete are reported in inventory at a conservative estimate of their net realizable value, calculated as sales price minus the selling costs. Costs of merchandise inventory include expenditures necessary, directly or indirectly, in bringing an item to a saleable condition and location (in other words, the invoice price minus any discount, plus any added or incidental costs necessary to put it in a place and condition for sale).

LO² Calculate cost of goods sold and merchandise inventory using specific identification, moving weighted average, and FIFO—perpetual. Costs are assigned to the cost of goods sold account each time that a sale occurs in a perpetual system. Specific identification assigns cost by referring to the actual cost of the unit sold. Moving weighted average assigns a weighted average cost per unit calculated by taking the current balance in the merchandise inventory account and dividing it by the total items available for sale to determine the weighted average cost per unit. FIFO assigns cost assuming units purchased earliest are the first units sold.

LO³ Analyze the effects of the costing methods on financial reporting. When purchase prices are rising or falling, the inventory methods are likely to assign different cost amounts. Specific identification exactly matches costs and revenues. Moving weighted average smooths out price changes. FIFO assigns an amount to inventory closely approximating

current replacement cost. The method(s) used must be disclosed in the notes to the financial statements and be consistent from period to period.

LO⁴ Calculate the lower of cost and net realizable value of inventory. Inventory is reported at net realizable value (NRV) when NRV is lower than cost. This is called the lower of cost and net realizable value (LCNRV) of inventory. LCNRV can be applied by item or by categories of similar or related items.

LO⁵ Analyze the effects of inventory errors on current and future financial statements—perpetual. An error in the amount of ending inventory affects assets (inventory), net income (cost of goods sold), and equity of that period. Since ending inventory is next period's beginning inventory, an error in ending inventory affects next period's cost of goods sold and net income. The financial statement effects of errors in one period are offset (reversed) in the next.

LO⁶ Apply both the gross profit and retail inventory methods to estimate inventory. The gross profit method involves two calculations: (1) net sales at retail multiplied by the gross profit ratio gives estimated cost of goods sold; and (2) goods available at cost minus estimated cost of goods sold gives estimated ending inventory at cost. The retail inventory method involves three calculations: (1) goods available at retail minus net sales at retail gives ending inventory at retail; (2) goods available at cost divided by goods available at retail gives the cost to retail ratio; and (3) ending inventory at retail is multiplied by the cost to retail ratio to give estimated ending inventory at cost.

Inventory Manager

Your recommendation is a difficult one. Increased profits may attract investors but they will also increase your bonus. The question becomes one of motivation. That is, would the change really be better for the investors, or would the change take place only because your bonus would increase? This presents the classic conflict of interests. Another problem is that profits can be manipulated by changing accounting methods, and if this is the motivation the profession would frown on the change.

1. The Bay.
2. Total cost is $12,180, calculated as:
   $11,400 + $130 + $150 + $100 + $400.
3. The matching principle.
4. Businesses that sell unique, high dollar value merchandise in relatively low volume levels might choose specific identification. Car dealerships are a good example because each car received as merchandise inventory is unique in terms of both features and identification number. Using specific identification allows the business to accurately tag each item coming in and going out.
5. Moving weighted average gives a lower inventory figure on the balance sheet as compared to FIFO. FIFO's inventory amount will approximate current replacement costs. Moving weighted average costs increase but more slowly because of the effect of averaging.

6. Because these units are the same ones that were originally written down, a reversal is appropriate and would be recorded as:

Merchandise Inventory	2,000	
Cost of Goods Sold		2,000

   $1,800 − $1,300 = $500/unit original write-down; $500 × 4 = $2,000 maximum reversal

7. The reported inventory amount is $540, calculated as (20 × $5) + (40 × $8) + (10 × $12).
8. Cost of goods sold is understated by $10,000 in 2014 and overstated by $10,000 in 2015.
9. The estimated ending inventory (at cost) is $327,000 and is calculated as:

   Step 1: ($530,000 + $335,000) − $320,000
          = $545,000

   Step 2: $\dfrac{\$324,000 + \$195,000}{\$530,000 + \$335,000} = 60\%$

   Step 3: $545,000 × 60% = $327,000

DEMONSTRATION PROBLEM

Part 1

Lipke Sales prepared the following schedule comparing the total cost and NRV of its December 31, 2014, ending inventory:

	Total Cost	Total NRV	LCNRV applied to: Products	LCNRV applied to: Group*
Product A	$ 29,000	$ 28,000		
Product B	46,000	36,000		
Product C	17,000	17,000		
Product D	31,000	30,000		
Product E	3,000	7,000		
Totals	$126,000	$118,000		

*Assume that all products are similar.

Required

a. Calculate the merchandise inventory value that should appear on Lipke Sales' December 31, 2014, balance sheet. Apply LCNRV to each product and to inventory as a group by completing the schedule provided.

b. Based on your calculations in part (a), prepare the appropriate adjusting entry at year-end assuming LCNRV is applied to inventory as a group.

Analysis Component:

Assuming the adjustment in part (b) is not recorded, identify the over- or understatement of net income, assets, and equity.

Part 2

Coe Company had $435,000 of sales during each of three consecutive years, and it purchased merchandise costing $300,000 during each of the years. It also maintained a $105,000 inventory from the beginning to the end of the three-year period. However, $15,000 of merchandise inventory purchased FOB shipping point on December 31, 2014, was accidentally excluded from the December 31, 2014, inventory. This error caused the company's ending 2014 inventory to appear on the statements at $90,000 rather than at the correct $105,000.

Required

1. Calculate the actual amount of the company's gross profit in each of the years.
2. Prepare a comparative income statement like Exhibit 6.12 to show the effect of this error on the company's cost of goods sold and gross profit in 2014, 2015, and 2016.

SOLUTION

Part 1

a.

	Total Cost	Total NRV	LCNRV applied to: Products	LCNRV applied to: Group*
Product A	$ 29,000	$ 28,000	$ 28,000	
Product B	46,000	36,000	36,000	
Product C	17,000	17,000	17,000	
Product D	31,000	30,000	30,000	
Product E	3,000	7,000	3,000	
Totals	$126,000	$118,000	$114,000	$118,000

*Assume that all products are similar.

b.

2014			
Dec. 31	Cost of Goods Sold	8,000	
	Merchandise Inventory		8,000
	To write inventory down to LCNRV.		

Analysis Component:

If the adjusting entry in part (b) is not recorded, net income would be overstated, assets would be overstated, and equity would also be overstated, each by $8,000.

Part 2

1. $435,000 − ($105,000 + $300,000 − $105,000) = $135,000
2.

	For years ended December 31, 2014, 2015, 2016, the income statement information should have been reported as:	Income statement information actually reported for years ended December 31, 2014	Income statement information actually reported for years ended December 31, 2015	Income statement information actually reported for years ended December 31, 2016
Sales	$435,000	$435,000	$435,000	$435,000
Cost of goods sold	300,000	315,000	285,000	300,000
Gross profit from sales ..	$135,000	$120,000	$150,000	$135,000

Merchandise Inventory			
Jan. 1/14 105,000			
Purchases 300,000	315,000		COGS
Dec. 31/14 90,000			

Merchandise Inventory			
Jan. 1/15 90,000			
Purchases 300,000	285,000		COGS
Dec. 31/15 105,000			

Merchandise Inventory			
Jan. 1/16 105,000			
Purchases 300,000	300,000		COGS
Dec. 31/16 105,000			

APPENDIX 6A

Assigning Costs to Inventory and Inventory Errors–Periodic System

LO7 Calculate cost of goods sold and merchandise inventory using FIFO—periodic, weighted average, and specific identification.

The aim of the periodic system is the same as the perpetual system: to assign costs to the inventory and the goods sold. The same three methods are used in assigning costs: first-in, first-out; weighted average; and specific identification. We use information from MEC to describe how we assign costs using these three methods with a periodic system. Data for sales and purchases are reported in the chapter in Exhibits 6.2 and 6.3 and are not repeated here.

FIRST-IN, FIRST-OUT

The first-in, first-out (FIFO) method of assigning cost to inventory and goods sold using the periodic system is shown in Exhibit 6A.1.

EXHIBIT 6A.1

FIFO Calculations—Periodic

Total cost of 45 units available for sale	$4,800
Less: **Ending inventory** priced using FIFO:	
11 units from August 17 purchase at $115 each	**1,265**
Cost of goods sold	**$3,535**

MEC's ending inventory reported on the balance sheet is $1,265 and its cost of goods sold reported on the income statement is $3,535. The assignment of costs to cost of goods sold and inventory using FIFO is the same for both the perpetual and periodic systems, as summarized in Exhibit 6A.4. This will always occur because the most recent purchases are in ending inventory under both systems.

WEIGHTED AVERAGE

The **weighted average** inventory costing method involves three important steps, as illustrated in Exhibits 6A.2 and 6A.3. First, we multiply the per unit cost for beginning inventory and each particular purchase by their corresponding number of units. Second, we add these amounts and divide by the total number of units available for sale to find the *weighted average cost per unit.*

Step 1:

Aug.	1	Beginning inventory	10 units	@	$ 91	=	$ 910
	3	Purchased	15 units	@	106	=	1,590
	17	Purchased	20 units	@	115	=	2,300
			45 units available for sale				$4,800 Total cost of goods available for sale

Step 2: $4,800/45 = **$106.67** weighted average cost per unit

EXHIBIT 6A.2

Weighted Average Cost Per Unit—Periodic

The third step is to use the weighted average cost per unit to assign costs to inventory and to units sold:

Step 3:

Total cost of 45 units available for sale	$4,800
Less: **Ending inventory** priced on a weighted average cost basis:	
11 units at $106.67 each	**1,173***
Cost of goods sold (= 34 units × $106.67)	**$3,627***

*Rounded to nearest whole dollar.

EXHIBIT 6A.3

Weighted Average Calculations—Periodic

The assignment of costs to cost of goods sold and inventory using weighted average usually gives different results depending on whether a perpetual or periodic system is used, as shown in Exhibit 6A.4. This is because weighted average under a perpetual system recalculates the per unit cost at the time of each purchase. Under the periodic system, the per unit cost is only calculated at the end of a period.

SPECIFIC IDENTIFICATION

The amounts of cost assigned to inventory and cost of goods sold are the same under the perpetual and periodic systems as detailed in Exhibit 6A.4. This is because specific identification precisely defines which units are in inventory and which are sold.

Exhibit 6A.4 compares the inventory methods for both the periodic and perpetual systems.

EXHIBIT 6A.4

Comparison of Inventory Methods—Periodic and Perpetual

	FIFO		Weighted Average		Specific Identification	
	Perpetual	Periodic	Perpetual	Periodic*	Perpetual	Periodic
COGS	$3,535	$3,535	$3,568	$3,627	$3,562	$3,562
Ending Inventory...........................	1,265	1,265	1,232	1,173	1,238	1,238
Cost of Goods Available for Sale...........................	$4,800	$4,800	$4,800	$4,800	$4,800	$4,800

*Rounded to the nearest whole dollar for simplicity

Exhibit 6A.4 shows that the figures for specific identification and FIFO are identical under periodic and perpetual systems. However, the figures for weighted average will differ between the perpetual and periodic systems.

CHECKPOINT

10. A company uses a periodic inventory system and reports the following beginning inventory and purchases (and ends the period with 30 units on hand):

	Units	Cost Per Unit
Beginning Inventory...	100	$10
Purchases #1	40	12
#2	20	14

a. Calculate ending inventory using FIFO
b. Calculate cost of goods sold using weighted average.

Do Quick Study question: *QS 6-16

Errors in Reporting Inventory

LO⁸ Analyze the effects of inventory errors on current and future financial statements—periodic.

Exhibits 6.11 and 6.12 were based on a perpetual inventory system. Those exhibits are reflected below under the assumption of a periodic inventory system.

Income Statement Effects of Inventory Errors

The income statement effects of an inventory error are evident when looking at the components of cost of goods sold in Exhibit 6A.5.

EXHIBIT 6A.5

Cost of Goods Sold Components—Periodic

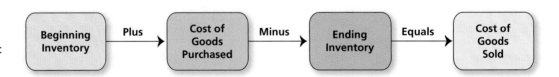

The effect of an inventory error on cost of goods sold is determined by calculating the inventory correctly and comparing it to the result of the calculation when using the incorrect amount, as in Exhibit 6A.6.

Exhibit 6A.6 assumes that $2,000 of merchandise sold but awaiting delivery was incorrectly included in ending inventory on December 31, 2014.

EXHIBIT 6A.6

Effects of $2,000 Overstatement in Ending Inventory for 2014 on Three Periods' Income Statement Information—Periodic

	For years ended December 31, 2014, 2015, 2016, the income statement information should have been reported as:	Income statement information actually reported for years ended December 31,		
		2014	**2015**	**2016**
Sales	$30,000	$30,000	$30,000	$30,000
Cost of goods sold:				
Beginning inventory	$10,000	$10,000	$12,000	$10,000
Add: Purchases	20,000	20,000	20,000	20,000
Less: Ending inventory	10,000	12,000	10,000	10,000
Cost of goods sold.............	20,000	18,000	22,000	20,000
Gross profit	$10,000	$12,000	$ 8,000	$10,000
Operating expenses	5,000	5,000	5,000	5,000
Net income............................	$ 5,000	$ 7,000	$ 3,000	$ 5,000

① 2014 net income and gross profit are overstated (too high) and cost of goods sold is understated (too low) when ending inventory is overstated (too high).

② Ending inventory for one period becomes the beginning inventory for the next period, carrying forward any errors that existed.

③ 2015 net income and gross profit are understated (too low) and cost of goods sold is overstated (too high) when beginning inventory is overstated (too high). Notice that the error has reversed itself in 2015, the second year.

④ An inventory error in the year 2014 does not affect 2016.

DEMONSTRATION PROBLEM

Tale Company uses a periodic inventory system and had the following beginning inventory and purchases during January 2014:

		Units		Cost Per Unit		Total Cost
Jan. 1	Beginning inventory	300	@	$ 14	=	$ 4,200
16	Purchased.............................	200	@	15	=	3,000
20	Purchased.............................	300	@	16	=	4,800
	Total goods available for sale	800				$12,000

Sales of units were as follows:

Jan. 15	200	units at $30
28	460	units at $35
Total units sold	660	

Additional data for use in applying the specific identification method:
The specific units sold were:

Jan. 15	200 units from the January 1 units on hand
28	75 units from the January 1 units on hand
	150 units from the January 16 purchase, and
	235 units from the January 20 purchase

Required

Using the preceding information, calculate the ending inventory and the cost of goods sold under a periodic inventory system by applying each of the three different methods of inventory costing:

a.   FIFO
b.   Weighted average, and
c.   Specific identification

Planning the Solution

- Prepare a periodic FIFO schedule similar to Exhibit 6A.1 (recall that although the calculations differ, the results are the same under each of the periodic and perpetual systems for FIFO).
- Prepare a periodic weighted average schedule similar to Exhibits 6A.2 and 6A.3.
- Prepare a specific identification schedule similar to Exhibit 6.6 (recall that specific identification is calculated in the same manner under each of the perpetual and periodic systems for specific identification).

SOLUTION

a.   FIFO

Cost of goods available for sale..	$12,000
Less: Ending inventory of 140 units:	
140 @ $16 =...	2,240
Equals: Cost of goods sold	$ 9,760

b.   Weighted Average

Cost of goods available for sale..	$12,000
Less: Ending inventory of 140 units:	
140 × $15 avg. cost/unit*......................	2,100
Equals: Cost of goods sold	$ 9,900
*$12,000 ÷ 800 units = $15/unit avg. cost	

c.   Specific Identification

Cost of goods available for sale...		$12,000
Less: Ending inventory of 140 units:		
25 @ $14 = $ 350		
50 @ $15 = 750		
65 @ $16 = 1,040............................		2,140
Equals: Cost of goods sold		$ 9,860

APPENDIX 6B

Using the Information

Merchandise Turnover and Days' Sales in Inventory

This section describes how we use information about inventory to assess a company's short-term liquidity and its management of inventory. Two measures useful for these assessments are defined and explained in this section.

LO⁹ Assess inventory management using both merchandise turnover and days' sales in inventory.

Merchandise Turnover

A company's ability to pay its short-term obligations depends, in part, on how quickly it sells its merchandise inventory. The **merchandise turnover**, also called **inventory turnover**, is one ratio used to help analyze short-term liquidity. It is also used to assess whether management is doing a good job of controlling the amount of inventory on hand. The merchandise turnover is defined as shown in Exhibit 6B.1.

$$\text{Merchandise turnover} = \frac{\text{Cost of goods sold}}{\text{Average merchandise inventory}}$$

EXHIBIT 6B.1

Merchandise Turnover

Average merchandise inventory is usually calculated by adding beginning and ending inventory amounts and dividing the total by 2. If a company's sales vary within the year, it is often better to take an average of inventory amounts at the end of each quarter or month.

The merchandise turnover ratio tells us how many *times* a company turns its inventory over during a period. For example, Exhibit 6B.2 shows the merchandise turnover for **Loblaw Companies Limited** for its year ended December 31, 2011, in comparison to **Danier Leather** for its year ended June 25, 2011.

As Exhibit 6B.2 illustrates, Loblaw's turnover ratio suggests that the amount of inventory on hand is low and that it is sold more quickly than that of Danier Leather. However, Loblaw sells foodstuffs, and is a different type of business than Danier Leather. Loblaw is part of an industry where it is critical to move merchandise quickly because of the perishable nature of foodstuffs. Danier Leather is in a different industry where merchandise turnovers of 2.57 times per year are typical. Ratio comparisons such as the preceding must be based on companies that are similar in order to be meaningful. There is no simple rule with merchandise turnover, except to say that a high ratio is preferable provided inventory is adequate to meet demand.

EXHIBIT 6B.2

Merchandise Turnovers Compared for Loblaw Companies Limited and Danier Leather

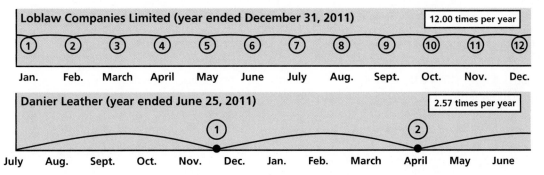

Days' Sales in Inventory

To better interpret merchandise turnover, many users want a measure to determine if inventory levels can meet sales demand. **Days' sales in inventory** is a ratio that estimates how many days it will take to convert inventory on hand into accounts receivable or cash. Days' sales in inventory is calculated as shown in Exhibit 6B.3.

EXHIBIT 6B.3

Days' Sales in Inventory

$$\text{Days' sales in inventory} = \frac{\text{Ending inventory}}{\text{Cost of goods sold}} \times 365$$

Notice the different focuses of days' sales in inventory and merchandise turnover. Days' sales in inventory focuses on ending inventory, whereas merchandise turnover focuses on average inventory.

 CHECKPOINT

11. Company A and Company B sell similar merchandise. Company A has a merchandise turnover of 4.8, while this same ratio is 5.2 for Company B. Which company is more efficient at selling its inventory?

Do Quick Study questions: *QS 6-17, *QS 6-18

SUMMARY OF APPENDIX 6A AND APPENDIX 6B

LO⁷   Calculate cost of goods sold and merchandise inventory using FIFO—periodic, weighted average, and specific identification. Periodic systems allocate the cost of goods available for sale between cost of goods sold and ending inventory *at the end of a period*. Specific identification and FIFO give identical results whether the periodic or perpetual system is used. Weighted average cost calculates cost per unit by taking the total cost of both beginning inventory and net purchases and dividing by the total number of units available. It then multiplies cost per unit by the number of units sold to give cost of goods sold.

LO⁸   Analyze the effects of inventory errors on current and future financial statements—periodic. An error in the amount of ending inventory affects assets (inventory), net income (cost of goods sold), and equity of that period. Since ending inventory is next period's beginning inventory, an error in ending inventory affects next period's cost of goods sold and net income. The financial statement effects of errors in one period are offset (reversed) in the next.

LO⁹   Assess inventory management using both merchandise turnover and days' sales in inventory. We prefer a high merchandise turnover provided inventory is not out of stock and customers are not being turned away. We use days' sales in inventory to assess the likelihood of inventory being out of stock. Together, these ratios help us assess inventory management and evaluate a company's short-term liquidity.

GUIDANCE ANSWERS TO **CHECKPOINT**

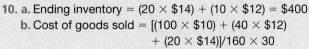

10. a. Ending inventory = (20 × $14) + (10 × $12) = $400
    b. Cost of goods sold = [(100 × $10) + (40 × $12)
                               + (20 × $14)]/160 × 30
                            = $11 × 30
                            = $330

11. Company B is more efficient at selling its inventory because it has higher merchandise turnover.

GLOSSARY

Consignee One who receives and holds goods owned by another party for the purpose of selling the goods for the owner.

Consignor An owner of goods who ships them to another party who will then sell the goods for the owner.

Consistency principle The accounting requirement that a company use the same accounting methods period after period so that the financial statements of succeeding periods will be comparable.

Days' sales in inventory An estimate of how many days it will take to convert the inventory on hand into accounts receivable or cash; calculated by dividing the ending inventory by cost of goods sold and multiplying the result by 365.

Faithful representation The accounting principle that requires information to be complete, neutral, and free from error.

First-in, first-out (FIFO) The pricing of an inventory under the assumption that inventory items are sold in the order acquired; the first items received were the first items sold.

Gross profit method A procedure for estimating an ending inventory in which the past gross profit rate is used to estimate cost of goods sold, which is then subtracted from the cost of goods available for sale to determine the estimated ending inventory.

Gross profit ratio Measures how much of net sales is gross profit; calculated as gross profit divided by net sales; also known as the *gross margin ratio*.

Internal controls The policies and procedures used to protect assets, ensure reliable accounting, promote efficient operations, and urge adherence to company policies.

Inventory turnover See *merchandise turnover.*

Lower of cost and net realizable value (LCNRV) The required method of reporting merchandise inventory in the balance sheet where net realizable value is reported when net realizable value is lower than cost.

Materiality principle This GAAP states that an amount may be ignored if its effect on the financial statements is not important to their users.

Merchandise turnover The number of times a company's average inventory was sold during an accounting period, calculated by dividing cost of goods sold by the average merchandise inventory balance; also called *inventory turnover.*

Moving weighted average A perpetual inventory pricing system in which the unit cost in inventory is recalculated at the time of each purchase by dividing the total cost of goods available for sale at that point in time by the corresponding total units available for sale. The most current moving weighted average cost per unit is multiplied by the units sold to determine cost of goods sold.

Net realizable value (NRV) The expected sales price of an item minus the cost of making the sale.

Physical count To count merchandise inventory for the purpose of reconciling goods actually on hand to the inventory control account in the General Ledger; also called *taking an inventory.*

Retail The selling price of merchandise inventory.

Retail inventory method A method for estimating an ending inventory cost based on the ratio of the amount of goods for sale at cost to the amount of goods for sale at marked selling prices.

Specific identification The pricing of an inventory where the purchase invoice of each item in the ending inventory is identified and used to determine the cost assigned to the inventory.

Taking an inventory See *physical count.*

Weighted average A periodic inventory pricing system in which the total cost of goods available for sale is divided by the total units available for sale. The resulting weighted average unit cost is multiplied by the units in ending inventory and then by the units that were sold.

McGraw Hill **connect**™   Visit **Connect** for additional study tools, practice quizzes, to search an interactive eBook, and much more.

CONCEPT REVIEW QUESTIONS

1. Why are incidental costs often ignored in pricing an inventory? Under what accounting principle is this permitted?

2. Give the meanings of the following when applied to inventory: (a) FIFO, and (b) cost.

3. If prices are falling, will the moving weighted average or the FIFO method of inventory valuation result in the lower cost of goods sold?

4. Where is merchandise inventory disclosed in the financial statements?

5. May a company change its inventory pricing method each accounting period?

6. Does the accounting principle of consistency disallow any changes from one accounting method to another?

7. What effect does the full disclosure principle have if a company changes from one acceptable accounting method to another?

8. What guidance for accountants is provided by faithful representation?

9. What is the usual meaning of NRV as it is used in determining the LCNRV for merchandise inventory?

10. What is meant when it is said that inventory errors correct themselves?

11. If inventory errors correct themselves, why be concerned when such errors are made?

12. Refer to WestJet's financial statements in Appendix II. On December 31, 2011, what percentage of WestJet's assets was represented by what would be WestJet's inventory? Is this merchandise inventory?

13. Refer to Danier's financial statements in Appendix II. Is it possible to determine a cost of goods sold figure for Danier? What is the cost of goods sold figure for Danier?

QUICK STUDY

QS 6-1 Inventory ownership LO¹

1. At year-end Carefree Company has shipped, FOB destination, $500 of merchandise that is still in transit to Stark Company. Which company should include the $500 as part of inventory at year-end?

2. Carefree Company has shipped goods to Stark and has an arrangement that Stark will sell the goods for Carefree. Identify the consignor and the consignee. Which company should include any unsold goods as part of inventory?

QS 6-2 Inventory ownership LO¹

Crafts and More, a distributor of handmade gifts, operates out of owner Scott Arlen's home. At the end of the accounting period, Arlen tells us he has 1,500 units of products in his basement, 30 of which were damaged by water leaks and cannot be sold. He also has another 250 units in his van, ready to deliver to fill a customer order, terms FOB destination, and another 70 units out on consignment to a friend who owns a stationery store. How many units should be included in the end-of-period inventory?

QS 6-3 Inventory costs LO¹

A car dealer acquires a used car for $3,000. Additional costs in obtaining and offering the car for sale include $150 for transportation-in, $200 for import duties, $50 for insurance during shipment, $25 for advertising, and $250 for sales staff salaries. For calculating inventory, what cost is assigned to the used car acquired?

QS 6-4 Inventory costs LO¹

Rigby & Son, antique dealers, purchased the contents of an estate for a bulk bid price of $37,500. The terms of the purchase were FOB shipping point, and the cost of transporting the goods to Rigby & Son's warehouse was $1,200. Rigby & Son insured the shipment at a cost of $150. Prior to placing the goods in the store, they cleaned and refurbished some merchandise at a cost of $490 for labour and parts. Determine the cost of the inventory acquired in the purchase of the estate's contents.

QS 6-5 Calculating cost of goods available for sale LO²

A company has beginning inventory of 10 units at $50. Every week for four weeks an additional 10 units are purchased at respective costs of $51, $52, $55, and $60. 38 units were sold for $72 each. Calculate the total cost of goods that were available for sale and the total units that were available for sale.

QS 6-6 Inventory costing methods—perpetual LO²

A company had the following beginning inventory and purchases during January for a particular item. On January 28, 345 units were sold. What is the cost of the 140 units that remain in the ending inventory, assuming:

a. FIFO

b. Moving weighted average?

Round numbers to the nearest cent. Assume a perpetual inventory system.

	Units	Unit Cost	Total Cost
Beginning inventory on January 1	310	$3.00	$ 930.00
Purchase on January 9	75	3.20	240.00
Purchase on January 25	100	3.35	335.00
Total available for sale	485		$1,505.00

QS 6-7 Specific identification inventory method LO²

Refer to the information in QS 6-6. Recall that 345 units were sold on January 28. The units specifically sold were:

- 250 units from beginning inventory
- 50 units from the January 9 purchase
- 45 units from the purchase on January 25.

Calculate cost of goods sold and the cost of ending inventory.

QS 6-8 Inventory costing methods—perpetual LO²

Bishr Company uses the moving weighted average method for inventory costing. You are to complete the following inventory sheet regarding Product XJ23789 (round calculations to two decimal places):

Date		Purchases/Transportation-In/ (Purchase Returns/Discounts)			Cost of Goods Sold/ (Returns to Inventory)			Balance in Inventory		
		Units	Cost/Unit	Total $	Units	Cost/Unit	Total $	Units	Avg Cost/Unit	Total $
Jan.	1		Brought Forward					10	$15.00	$150.00
	3				6					
	7	25	$18.50	$462.50						
	8			50.00						
	17			(46.25)						
	18				14					

Note: January 8 reflects transportation costs regarding the January 7 purchase. The $46.25 on January 17 represents the discount taken regarding payment of the January 7 purchase within the discount period.

QS 6-9 Contrasting inventory costing methods LO³

Identify the inventory costing method most closely related to each of the following statements, assuming a period when the cost per unit is increasing:

a. Current cost of inventory not reflected on income statement.

b. Results in a balance sheet inventory closest to replacement costs.

c. Is best when each unit of product has unique features that affect cost.

QS 6-10 Applying LCNRV to inventories LO[4]

Thrifty Trading Co. has the following products in its ending inventory at December 31, 2014:

Product	Quantity	Per Unit Cost	Per Unit NRV
Aprons	9	$6.00	$5.50
Bottles	12	3.50	4.25
Candles	25	8.00	7.00

a. Calculate LCNRV for the inventory as a whole, if applicable.

b. Calculate LCNRV applied separately to each product.

c. Prepare the appropriate adjusting entry, if any, assuming your calculations in (b).

QS 6-11 Inventory errors LO[5,8]

The Weston Company performed a physical inventory count at the end of 2014. It was later determined that certain units were counted twice. Explain how this error affects the following:

a. 2014 cost of goods sold

b. 2014 gross profit

c. 2014 net income

d. 2015 net income

e. The combined two-year income

f. Income in years after 2015.

QS 6-12 Estimating inventories—gross profit method LO[6]

The inventory of Bell Department Store was destroyed by a fire on September 10, 2014. The following 2014 data were found in the accounting records:

Jan. 1 inventory..	$180,000
Jan. 1–Sept. 10 purchases (net)................	$342,000
Jan. 1–Sept. 10 sales.................................	$675,000
2014 estimated gross profit rate................	42%

Estimate the cost of the inventory destroyed in the fire using the gross profit method.

QS 6-13 Estimating inventories—gross profit method LO[6]

During the past two months, management of Wallace Lake Computing Supplies was closely watching inventory levels due to suspected shrinkage caused by unknown factors. The physical count on July 31, the end of the current month, shows $48,000 of merchandise actually on hand. The accounting records for prior periods indicate that gross profit should be 30% of the $565,000 net sales for July. Inventory at June 30 was actually $65,000 and July purchases were $385,500. Calculate the estimated:

a. Ending inventory

b. Shrinkage.

QS 6-14 Estimating ending inventory—retail method LO[6]

Best Stereo Centre showed the following selected information on August 31, 2014:

	Cost	Retail
Cost of goods available for sale	$67,600	$104,000
Net sales		82,000

Using the retail method, estimate the cost of the ending inventory.

QS 6-15 Estimating ending inventory—retail method LO[6]

Complete the following schedule by using the retail method to estimate ending inventory for September and October.

	September		October	
	Cost	Retail	Cost	Retail
Beginning inventory..............................	$ 74,950	$112,000		
Cost of goods purchased.......................	395,000	611,000	461,590	674,000
Goods available for sale				
Less: Net sales at retail...........................		614,000		700,000
Ending inventory at retail				
Cost to retail ratio				
Estimated ending inventory				

*QS 6-16 Inventory costing methods—periodic LO[7]

Refer to the information in QS 6-6. Determine the cost of the 140 units that remain in ending inventory, assuming:

a. FIFO

b. Weighted average.

Round numbers to the nearest cent and use a periodic inventory system.

*QS 6-17 Merchandise turnover LO[9]

Huff Company and Mesa Company are similar firms that operate within the same industry. The following information is available.

	Huff			Mesa		
	2014	2013	2012	2014	2013	2012
Merchandise turnover	23.2	20.9	16.1	13.5	12.0	11.6

Required Based on the information provided, which company is managing inventory more efficiently? Explain.

*QS 6-18 Merchandise turnover and days' sales in inventory LO[9]

Mixon Company showed the following selected information for the years ended December 31, 2014, 2013, and 2012:

	2014	2013	2012
Cost of goods sold	$410,225	$344,500	$312,600
Merchandise inventory (December 31)	56,195	82,500	111,500

For the years ended 2014 and 2013, calculate:

a. Days' sales in inventory

b. Merchandise turnover.

Indicate if the change in the ratio from 2013 to 2014 is generally considered to be favourable (good) or unfavourable (not good). Round calculations to two decimal places.

An asterisk (*) identifies assignment material based on Appendix 6A or Appendix 6B.

EXERCISES   connect™

Exercise 6-1 Alternative cost flow assumptions—perpetual LO[2]

Parfour made purchases of a particular product in the current year as follows:

Jan. 1	Beginning inventory..................	75 units	@	$12.00	=	$ 900
Mar. 14	Purchased	250 units	@	$13.00	=	3,250
July 30	Purchased	500 units	@	$14.00	=	7,000
	Units available for sale..............................	825 units				
	Cost of goods available for sale					$11,150

Parfour made sales on the following dates at a selling price of $35 per unit:

Jan. 10..	70 units
Mar. 15..	180 units
Oct. 5..	450 units
Total	700 units

Required The business uses a perpetual inventory system. Determine the costs that should be assigned to the ending inventory and to goods sold under:

a. FIFO

b. Moving weighted average (round to the nearest whole cent)

Also calculate the gross profit under each method.

Exercise 6-2 Specific identification cost flow assumption LO[2]

Refer to the data in Exercise 6-1. Assume that Parfour uses the specific identification method to cost inventory. The 700 units were specifically sold as follows:

Jan. 10:	70	units from beginning inventory
Mar. 15:	3	units from beginning inventory, and
	177	units from the March 14 purchase
Oct. 5:	50	units from the March 14 purchase, and
	400	units from the July 30 purchase

Calculate cost of goods sold and the gross profit.

Exercise 6-3 Alternative cost flow assumptions—perpetual inventory system LO[2]

Trout Company uses a perpetual inventory system and made purchases and sales of a particular product in 2014 as follows:

Jan. 1	Beginning inventory..................	120 units	@	$6.50	=	$ 780
Jan. 10	Sold	70 units	@	$15.00	=	1,050
Mar. 7	Purchased	250 units	@	$5.80	=	1,450
Mar. 15	Sold	125 units	@	$15.00	=	1,875
July 28	Purchased	500 units	@	$5.60	=	2,800
Oct. 3	Purchased	450 units	@	$5.50	=	2,475
Oct. 5	Sold	600 units	@	$15.00	=	9,000

Required

1. Calculate the total goods available for sale (in units and cost).

2. Calculate the number of units sold and units remaining in ending inventory.

3. Determine the share of the cost of goods available for sale calculated in Part 1 that should be assigned to ending inventory and to goods sold under:

a. FIFO

b. Moving weighted average

Exercise 6-4 Specific identification cost flow assumption LO²

Use the information in Exercise 6-3. Assume that Trout Company specifically sold the following units:

Jan. 10:   70   units from beginning inventory

Mar. 15:   25   units from beginning inventory, and
          100   units from the March 7 purchase

Oct.   5: 320   units from the July 28 purchase, and
          280   units from the October 3 purchase

Calculate cost to be assigned to ending inventory and cost of goods sold.

Exercise 6-5 Income statement effects of alternative cost flow assumptions LO³

Use the data in Exercises 6-3 and 6-4 to construct comparative income statements for Trout Company (year-end December 31, 2014), similar to those shown in Exhibit 6.8 in the chapter. Assume that operating expenses are $1,250.

1. Which method results in the highest net income?

2. If costs were rising instead of falling, which method would result in the highest net income?

Exercise 6-6 Moving weighted average cost flow assumption—perpetual LO²,³

Telamark Company uses the moving weighted average method for inventory costing. The following incomplete inventory sheet regarding Product W506 is available for the month of March 2014:

| Date | Purchases/Transportation-In/ (Purchase Returns/Discounts) | | | Cost of Goods Sold/ (Returns to Inventory) | | | Balance in Inventory | | |
	Units	Cost/Unit	Total $	Units	Cost/Unit	Total $	Units	AvgCost/Unit	Total $
Mar. 1		Brought Forward					60	$94.00	$5,640.00
2	35	$96.00							
3				22					
4				(2)					
7				65					
17	40	97.00							
28				43					

Note: March 4 reflects a return made by a customer of incorrect items shipped on March 3; these items were returned to inventory.

Required Complete the inventory sheet. Round all calculations to two decimal places.

Analysis Component: The gross profit realized on the sale of Product W506 during February 2014 was 32.16%. The selling price was $148 during both February and March. Calculate the gross profit ratio for Product W506 for March 2014 and determine whether the change is favourable or unfavourable from February. Identify the most probable cause of the change.

Exercise 6-7 Lower of cost and net realizable value LO⁴

Showtime Company's ending inventory at December 31, 2014, includes the following items: Calculate LCNRV for the inventory:

Product	Units on Hand	Unit Cost	Net Realizable Value Per Unit
BB	22	$110	$115
FM	15	145	138
MB	36	186	172
SL	40	78	92

a.   As a whole (assuming the items are similar), and

b.   Applied separately to each product.

c.   Prepare the appropriate adjusting entry, if required, based on your calculations in (b).

Exercise 6-8 Analysis of inventory errors LO5,8

Assume that The John Henry Company had $900,000 of sales during each of three consecutive years, and it purchased merchandise costing $500,000 during each of the years. It also maintained a $200,000 inventory from the beginning to the end of the three-year period. However, it made an error at the end of the first year, 2014, that caused its ending 2014 inventory to appear on its statements at $180,000 rather than the correct $200,000.

Required

1. Calculate the actual amount of the company's gross profit in each of the years.

2. Prepare a comparative income statement like Exhibit 6.12 (or Exhibit 6A.6) to show the effect of this error on the company's cost of goods sold and gross profit in 2014, 2015, and 2016.

Exercise 6-9 Estimating ending inventory—gross profit method LO6

On January 1, The Parts Store had a $450,000 inventory at cost. During the first quarter of the year, it purchased $1,590,000 of merchandise, returned $23,100, and paid freight charges on purchased merchandise totalling $37,600. During the past several years, the store's gross profit on sales has averaged 30%. Under the assumption the store had $2,000,000 of sales during the first quarter of the year, use the gross profit method to estimate its inventory at the end of the first quarter.

CHECK FIGURE:
$71,941.68

Exercise 6-10 Estimating ending inventory—retail method LO6

During 2014, Harmony Co. sold $520,000 of merchandise at marked retail prices. At the end of 2014, the following information was available from its records:

	At Cost	At Retail
Beginning inventory	$127,600	$256,800
Net purchases	231,240	393,600

Use the retail method to estimate Harmony's 2014 ending inventory at cost. Round all calculations to two decimal places.

Exercise 6-11 Reducing physical inventory to cost—retail method LO6

Assume that in addition to estimating its ending inventory by the retail method, Harmony Co. of Exercise 6-10 also took a physical inventory at the marked selling prices of the inventory items at the end of 2014. Assume further that the total of this physical inventory at marked selling prices was $109,200.

a. Determine the amount of this inventory at cost.

b. Determine Harmony's 2014 inventory shrinkage from breakage, theft, or other causes at retail and at cost.

Round all calculations to two decimal places.

CHECK FIGURE:
a. COGS = $12,672

*Exercise 6-12 Alternative cost flow assumptions—periodic LO7

Paddington Gifts made purchases of a particular product in the current year as follows:

Jan.	1	Beginning inventory	240 units	@	$6.00	=	$ 1,440
Mar.	7	Purchased	500 units	@	$5.60	=	2,800
July	28	Purchased	1,000 units	@	$5.00	=	5,000
Oct.	3	Purchased	900 units	@	$4.40	=	3,960
		Totals	2,640 units				$13,200

Required The business uses a periodic inventory system. Ending inventory consists of 120 units. Calculate the costs to be assigned to the ending inventory and to goods sold under:

a. FIFO

b. A weighted average cost basis

Which method provides the lower net income and why?

CHECK FIGURE:
b. Ending inventory
= $350.30

*Exercise 6-13 Alternative cost flow assumptions—periodic LO[7]

Jasper & Williams made purchases of a particular product in the current year as follows:

Jan.	1	Beginning inventory................	120 units	@	$2.10	=	$ 252
Mar.	7	Purchased	250 units	@	$2.20	=	550
July	28	Purchased	500 units	@	$2.30	=	1,150
Oct.	3	Purchased	60 units	@	$2.45	=	147
		Totals......................................	930 units				$2,099

Required Ending inventory consists of 155 units. Assuming a periodic system, determine the costs to be assigned to cost of goods sold and ending inventory under:

a. FIFO

b. Weighted average cost basis.

Which method provides the lower net income, and why?

CHECK FIGURE:
COGS = $1,761.20

*Exercise 6-14 Specific identification cost flow assumption—periodic LO[7]

Use the information in *Exercise 6-13. Assume that the specific identification method is used to assign costs to cost of goods sold ending inventory. The units in ending inventory were specifically identified as follows:

- 80 units from beginning inventory
- 27 units from the March 7 purchase, and
- 48 units from the July 28 purchase.

Required Determine the cost to be assigned to ending inventory and cost of goods sold.

*Exercise 6-15 Merchandise turnover and days' sales in inventory LO[9]

From the following information for Russo Merchandising Co., calculate merchandise turnover for 2015 and 2014 and days' sales in inventory at December 31, 2015 and 2014. Round answers to one decimal place.

	2015	2014	2013
Cost of goods sold	$643,825	$426,650	$391,300
Merchandise inventory (December 31)	96,400	86,750	91,500

Comment on Russo's efficiency in using its assets to support increasing sales from 2014 to 2015.

connect

Problem 6-1A Alternative cost flows—perpetual LO[2]

The Stilton Company has the following inventory and credit purchases during the fiscal year ended December 31, 2014.

Beginning	500 units	@	$85/unit
Feb. 10	250 units	@	$82/unit
Aug. 21	130 units	@	$95/unit

Stilton Company has two credit sales during the period. The units have a selling price of $145.00 per unit.

Sales	
Mar. 15	330 units
Sept. 10	235 units

Stilton Company uses a perpetual inventory system.

Required

1. Calculate the dollar value of cost of goods sold and ending inventory using:
   a. FIFO
   b. Moving weighted average. Round to two decimal places.

2. Calculate the dollar value of cost of goods sold and ending inventory using specific identification, assuming the sales were specifically identified as follows:

   Mar. 15: 170 units from beginning inventory, and
            160 units from the February 10 purchase

   Sept. 10: 165 units from beginning inventory, and
             20 units from the February 10 purchase, and
             50 units from the August 21 purchase

3. Using information from your answers in Parts 1 and 2, journalize the credit purchase on February 10 and the credit sale on September 10 for each of:
   a. FIFO
   b. Moving weighted average
   c. Specific identification.

*Problem 6-2A Alternative cost flows—periodic LO[7]

Use the data from Problem 6-1A and do Part 1, assuming Stilton Company uses a periodic inventory costing system. Round calculations to two decimal places.

An asterisk (*) identifies assignment material based on Appendix 6A or Appendix 6B.

Problem 6-3A Gross profit comparisons and cost flow assumptions—perpetual LO[2,3]

The Gale Company has the following inventory and purchases during the fiscal year ended December 31, 2014.

Beginning inventory	280 units	@	$80/unit
Feb. 10 purchased	195 units	@	$84/unit
Feb. 20 sold	360 units	@	$160/unit
Mar. 13 purchased	290 units	@	$78/unit
Sept. 5 purchased	255 units	@	$64/unit
Oct. 10 sold	510 units	@	$160/unit

Gale Company employs a perpetual inventory system.

Required

1. Calculate the dollar value of ending inventory and cost of goods sold using:

   a. FIFO

   b. Moving weighted average. Round all unit costs to two decimal places.

2. Using your calculations from Part 1, complete the following schedule:

	FIFO	Moving Weighted Average
Sales		
Cost of goods sold		
Gross profit		

Analysis Component: How would the gross profits calculated in Part 2 above change if Gale Company had been experiencing increasing prices in the acquisition of additional inventory?

*Problem 6-4A Alternative cost flows—periodic LO[7]

Use the data from Problem 6-3A and do Part 1 assuming Gale Company uses a periodic inventory costing system.

Problem 6-5A Income statement comparisons and cost flow assumptions—perpetual LO[2,3]

During 2014, Fresh Express Company sold 2,500 units of its product on September 20 and 3,000 units on December 22, all at a price of $90 per unit. Incurring operating expenses of $14 per unit sold, it began the year with and made successive purchases of the product as follows:

January 1 beginning inventory	600 units	@	$35 per unit
Purchases:			
February 20	1,500 units	@	$37 per unit
May 16	700 units	@	$41 per unit
December 11	3,300 units	@	$42 per unit
Total	6,100 units		

Required Prepare a comparative income statement for the company, showing in adjacent columns the net incomes earned from the sale of the product, assuming the company uses a perpetual inventory system and prices its ending inventory on the basis of:

a. FIFO

b. Moving weighted average cost. Round all unit costs to two decimal places.

Analysis Component: If the manager of Fresh Express Company earns a bonus based on a percentage of gross profit, which method of inventory costing will she prefer?

An asterisk (*) identifies assignment material based on Appendix 6A or Appendix 6B.

CHECK FIGURE:
Net income weighted
average = $198,182

*Problem 6-6A Income statement comparisons and cost flow assumptions—periodic LO[7]

Use the data from Problem 6-5A and do the question assuming Fresh Express Company uses a periodic inventory costing system.

Problem 6-7A Analysis of inventory errors LO[5,8]

Shockley Co. reported the following amounts in its financial statements:

	Financial Statements for Year Ended December 31		
	2014	2015	2016
(a) Cost of goods sold	$ 715,000	$ 847,000	$ 770,000
(b) Net income	220,000	275,000	231,000
(c) Total current assets	1,155,000	1,265,000	1,100,000
(d) Equity	1,287,000	1,430,000	1,232,000

In making the physical counts of inventory, the following errors were made:

- Inventory on December 31, 2014: understated $70,000
- Inventory on December 31, 2015: overstated $32,000

Required For each of the preceding financial statement items—(a), (b), (c), and (d)—prepare a schedule similar to the following and show the adjustments that would have been necessary to correct the reported amounts.

	2014	2015	2016
Cost of goods sold:			
Reported	————	————	————
Adjustments: Dec. 31/14 error	————	————	————
Dec. 31/15 error	————	————	————
Corrected	————	————	————

Analysis Component: What is the error in the aggregate net income for the three-year period that resulted from the inventory errors? Explain why this result occurs. Also explain why the understatement of inventory by $70,000 at the end of 2014 resulted in an understatement of equity by the same amount that year.

Problem 6-8A Analysis of inventory errors LO[5,8]

While performing a detailed review of its financial records, Doors Unlimited noted the following ending inventory errors:

2014	2015	2016
Understated $52,000	Overstated $14,000	No errors

	2014	2015	2016
Ending inventory as reported	$ 345,000	$ 420,000	$ 392,000
Cost of goods sold as reported	1,300,000	1,750,000	2,100,000
Net income as reported	340,000	516,000	652,000

Required Calculate the corrected ending inventory and cost of goods sold amounts for each year by completing the following schedule:

	2014	2015	2016
Corrected ending inventory			
Corrected cost of goods sold			
Corrected net income			

An asterisk (*) identifies assignment material based on Appendix 6A or Appendix 6B.

Problem 6-9A Lower of cost and net realizable value LO⁴

The following information pertains to the physical inventory of Electronics Unlimited taken at December 31:

Product	Units on Hand	Per Unit Cost	Per Unit NRV
Audio equipment:			
Wireless audio receivers	335	$185	$196
Touchscreen MP3 players	250	220	200
Audio mixers	316	174	190
Audio stands	194	100	82
Video equipment:			
Televisions	470	295	250
1GB video cards	281	180	168
Satellite video recorders.............................	202	615	644
Car audio equipment:			
In-dash GPS navigators...............................	175	142	168
Double-DIN CD/bluetooth/USB receivers ...	160	195	210

Required

1. Calculate the LCNRV:

    a. For the inventory by major group

    b. For the inventory, applied separately to each product.

2. Prepare the appropriate entry, if any, for (a) and (b).

Problem 6-10A Estimating ending inventory—gross profit method LO⁶

The Navarre Company had a fire on February 10, 2014, that destroyed a major portion of its inventory. The salvaged accounting records contained the following information:

Sales, January 1 to February 10	$ 350,600
Net merchandise purchased Jan. 1 to Feb. 10	182,400
Additional information was determined from the 2013 annual report:	
Income statement:	
Sales...	$3,200,225
Cost of goods sold..	1,760,575
Balance sheet:	
Merchandise inventory	294,100

Navarre was able to salvage inventory with a cost of $106,200.

Required Determine the amount of inventory lost by Navarre as a result of the fire. Navarre has a December 31 year-end. *Round the gross profit ratio to the nearest whole percentage point.*

Problem 6-11A Gross profit method LO⁶

Alanood Company wants to prepare interim financial statements for the first quarter of 2014 but would like to avoid making a physical count of inventory. During the last five years, the company's gross profit rate has averaged 36%. The following information for the year's first quarter is available from its records:

January 1 beginning inventory	$300,260
Purchases..	945,200
Purchase returns..	13,050
Transportation-in...	6,900
Sales	1,191,150
Sales returns...	9,450

Required Use the gross profit method to prepare an estimate of the company's March 31 inventory.

Problem 6-12A Retail inventory method LO[6]

The records of Earthly Goods provided the following information for the year ended December 31, 2014.

	At Cost	At Retail
January 1 beginning inventory	$ 471,350	$ 927,150
Purchases	3,328,830	6,398,700
Purchase returns	52,800	119,350
Sales		5,495,700
Sales returns		44,600

Required

1. Prepare an estimate of the company's year-end inventory by the retail method. Round all calculations to two decimal places.

2. Under the assumption the company took a year-end physical inventory at marked selling prices that totalled $1,675,800, prepare a schedule showing the store's loss from theft or other causes at cost and at retail.

Problem 6-13A Retail inventory method LO[6]

Petcetera had a robbery on the weekend in which a large amount of inventory was taken. The loss is totally covered by insurance. A physical inventory count determined that the cost of the remaining merchandise is $58,500. The following additional information is available:

	At Cost	At Retail
Beginning merchandise inventory	$ 75,000	$ 93,750
Purchase returns and allowances	15,000	20,000
Purchases	1,275,000	1,731,250
Transportation-in	18,750	
Sales		1,642,500
Sales returns and allowances		18,000

Required

1. Prepare an estimate of ending merchandise inventory using the retail method.

2. Calculate the cost of the stolen inventory.

*Problem 6-14A Alternative cost flows—periodic LO[7]

Synergy Company began 2014 with 19,000 units of Product X in its inventory that cost $7.50 per unit, and it made successive purchases of the product as follows:

Mar.	7	26,000 units	@	$9.00 each
May	25	31,000 units	@	$11.00 each
Aug.	1	21,500 units	@	$12.00 each
Nov.	10	31,000 units	@	$13.50 each

The company uses a periodic inventory system. On December 31, 2014, a physical count disclosed that 15,000 units of Product X remained in inventory.

An asterisk (*) identifies assignment material based on Appendix 6A or Appendix 6B.

Required

1. Prepare a calculation showing the number and total cost of the units available for sale during 2014.

2. Prepare calculations showing the amounts that should be assigned to the 2014 ending inventory and to cost of goods sold, assuming:

   a. FIFO

   b. Weighted average cost basis (round the average cost per unit to two decimal places).

ALTERNATE PROBLEMS

CHECK FIGURES:
1. Ending inventory
a. $56,625.00
b. $55,309.25
2. Ending inventory
   = $54,025.00

Problem 6-1B Alternative cost flows—perpetual LO²

The Obama Company has the following inventory purchases during the fiscal year ended December 31, 2014.

Beginning	600 units	@	$105/unit
Feb. 13	200 units	@	$109/unit
Aug. 5	345 units	@	$112/unit

Obama Company has two sales during the period. The units have a selling price of $165 per unit.

Sales	
Feb. 15	300 units
Aug. 10	335 units

Obama Company uses a perpetual inventory system.

Required

1. Calculate the dollar value of cost of goods sold and ending inventory using

   a. FIFO

   b. Moving weighted average method (round the average cost per unit to two decimal places).

2. Calculate the dollar value of cost of goods sold and ending inventory using specific identification assuming the sales were specifically identified as follows:

Feb. 15:	175	units from beginning inventory
	125	units from the February 13 purchase
Aug. 10:	15	units from beginning inventory
	320	units from the August 5 purchase

3. Using information from your answers in Parts 1 and 2, journalize the credit sale on February 15, and the credit purchase on August 5 for each of:

   a. FIFO

   b. Moving weighted average

   c. Specific identification

CHECK FIGURES:
Cost of goods sold
a. $66,815.00
b. $68,456.90

*Problem 6-2B Alternative cost flows—periodic LO⁷

Use the data from Problem 6-1B and do Part 1, assuming Obama Company uses a periodic inventory costing system. Round calculations to two decimal places.

An asterisk (*) identifies assignment material based on Appendix 6A or Appendix 6B.

Problem 6-3B Gross profit comparisons and cost flow assumptions—perpetual LO[2,3]

The Manson Company has the following sales, inventory, and purchases during the fiscal year ended December 31, 2014.

Beginning inventory	180 units	@	$30/unit
Feb. 20 sold	145 units	@	$40/unit
Apr. 30 purchased	315 units	@	$29/unit
Oct. 5 purchased	225 units	@	$25/unit
Oct. 10 sold	540 units	@	$40/unit

Manson Company employs a perpetual inventory system.

Required

1. Calculate the dollar value of ending inventory and cost of goods sold using:

   a. FIFO

   b. Moving weighted average method. Round all unit costs to two decimal places.

2. Using your calculations from Part 1, complete the following schedule:

	FIFO	Moving Weighted Average
Sales		
Cost of goods sold		
Gross profit		

Analysis Component: How would the gross profits calculated in Part 2 above change if Manson Company had been experiencing increasing prices in the purchase of additional inventory?

*Problem 6-4B Alternative cost flows—periodic LO[7]

Use the data from Problem 6-3B and do Part 1 assuming Manson Company uses a periodic inventory costing system. Round calculations to two decimal places.

Problem 6-5B Income statement comparisons and cost flow assumptions—perpetual LO[2,3]

During 2014, the Blizzard Company sold 1,350 units of its product on May 20 and 1,700 units on October 25, all at a price of $51 per unit. Incurring operating expenses of $7 per unit in selling the units, it began the year with, and made successive purchases of, units of the product as follows:

January 1 Beginning inventory		610 units costing $29 per unit	
Purchases:			
April 2	810 units	@	$28 per unit
June 14	320 units	@	$27 per unit
Aug. 29	1,340 units	@	$26 per unit
Total	3,080 units		

Required Prepare a comparative income statement for the company for 2014, showing in adjacent columns the net incomes earned from the sale of the product, assuming the company uses a perpetual inventory system and prices its ending inventory on the basis of:

a. FIFO

b. Moving weighted average cost. Round unit costs to two decimal places.

Analysis Component: If the Blizzard Company's manager earns a bonus based on a percentage of gross profit, which method of inventory costing will she prefer?

An asterisk (*) identifies assignment material based on Appendix 6A or Appendix 6B.

*Problem 6-6B Income statement comparisons and cost flow assumptions—periodic LO[7]

Use the data from Problem 6-5B and do the question assuming Blizzard Company uses a periodic inventory costing system.

Problem 6-7B Analysis of inventory errors LO[5,8]

Fireplace Company reported the following amounts in its financial statements:

	Financial Statements For Year Ended December 31		
	2014	2015	2016
(a) Cost of goods sold	$102,600	$106,400	$ 98,015
(b) Net income	87,400	105,635	91,955
(c) Total current assets	133,000	138,250	131,475
(d) Equity	152,000	158,000	168,000

In making the physical counts of inventory, the following errors were made:

- Inventory on December 31, 2014: overstated $8,100
- Inventory on December 31, 2015: understated $10,800

Required For each of the preceding financial statement items—(a), (b), (c), and (d)—prepare a schedule similar to the following and show the adjustments that would have been necessary to correct the reported amounts.

	2014	2015	2016
Cost of goods sold:			
Reported	————	————	————
Adjustments: Dec. 31/14 error	————	————	————
Dec. 31/15 error	————	————	————
Corrected	————	————	————

Analysis Component: What is the error in the aggregate net income for the three-year period that resulted from the inventory errors?

Problem 6-8B Analysis of inventory errors LO[5,8]

	Incorrect Income Statement Information For Years Ended December 31				Corrected Income Statement Information For Years Ended December 31			
	2014	%	2015	%	2014	%	2015	%
Sales	$671,000	100	$835,000	100				
Cost of goods sold	402,600	60	417,500	50				
Gross profit	$268,400	40	$417,500	50				

In comparing income statement information for the years ended December 31, 2014 and 2015, the owner noticed an increase in the gross profit. He was puzzled because he knew that inventory costs were increasing.

A detailed review of the records showed the following:

a. Goods with a cost of $37,500 were on consignment at another location. Through an error, they were not included in the inventory of December 31, 2014.

b. $16,000 of merchandise inventory purchased on December 25, 2015, was shipped *FOB Shipping Point* and received on January 6, 2016. It was not included in inventory on December 31, 2015, in error.

c. While performing the physical inventory count on December 31, 2015, a calculation error was discovered that caused inventory on hand to be overstated by $24,500.

Required

1. Using the information provided, complete the schedule showing the corrected income statement information (round percentages to the nearest whole number).

2. Does the new gross profit information reflect the owner's knowledge of increasing inventory costs?

An asterisk (*) identifies assignment material based on Appendix 6A or Appendix 6B.

Problem 6-9B Lower of cost and net realizable value LO⁴

The following information pertains to the physical inventory of Geo Furniture Company taken at December 31:

Product	Units on Hand	Per Unit Cost	Per Unit NRV
Office furniture:			
Desks....................................	430	$261	$305
Credenzas.............................	290	227	256
Chairs...................................	585	49	43
Bookshelves..........................	320	93	82
Filing cabinets:			
Two-drawer..........................	215	81	70
Four-drawer..........................	400	135	122
Lateral	178	104	118
Office equipment:			
Fax machines........................	415	168	200
Copiers.................................	544	317	288
Typewriters...........................	355	125	117

Required

1. Calculate the LCNRV for the:

   a.   Inventory by major category

   b.   Inventory, applied separately to each product.

2. Prepare the appropriate entry, if any, for (a) and (b).

Problem 6-10B Estimating ending inventory—gross profit method LO⁶

The Zeon Company had a flood on July 5, 2014, that destroyed all of its inventory. The salvaged accounting records contained the following information:

Sales, January 1 to July 5	$ 737,650
Net merchandise purchased Jan. 1 to July 5	414,900
Additional information was determined from the 2013 annual report:	
Income statement:	
Sales...	$2,122,550
Cost of goods sold..	1,337,175
Balance sheet:	
Merchandise inventory	131,200

Zeon was unable to salvage any usable inventory after the water subsided.

Required Determine the amount of inventory lost by Zeon as a result of the flood. Zeon has a December 31 year-end. Round the gross profit ratio to the nearest whole percentage point.

Problem 6-11B Gross profit method LO⁶

Belle Equipment Co. wants to prepare interim financial statements for the first quarter of 2014. The company uses a periodic inventory system but would like to avoid making a physical count of inventory. During the last five years, the company's gross profit rate has averaged 30%. The following information for the year's first quarter is available from its records:

January 1 beginning inventory	$ 376,440
Purchases..	1,066,050
Purchase returns...	19,185
Transportation-in..	32,950
Sales	1,855,125
Sales returns..	37,100

Required Use the gross profit method to prepare an estimate of the company's March 31, 2014, inventory.

Problem 6-12B Retail inventory method LO⁶

The records of The Wilke Co. provided the following information for the year ended December 31, 2014:

	At Cost	At Retail
January 1 beginning inventory	$ 40,835	$ 57,305
Purchases	251,945	383,530
Purchase returns..	5,370	7,665
Sales		393,060
Sales returns...		2,240

Required

1. Prepare an estimate of the company's year-end inventory by the retail method. Round all calculations to two decimal places.

2. Under the assumption the company took a year-end physical inventory at marked selling prices that totalled $39,275, prepare a schedule showing the store's loss from theft or other causes at cost and at retail.

Problem 6-13B Retail inventory method LO⁶

Poundmaker Company just had a fire in its warehouse that destroyed all of its merchandise inventory. The insurance company covers 80% of the loss. The following information is available regarding the year ended March 31, 2014:

	At Cost	At Retail
Beginning merchandise inventory	$ 75,000	$ 125,000
Purchases	1,050,000	1,750,000
Purchase returns and allowances	125,000	200,000
Transportation-in..	5,000	
Sales		1,357,500
Sales returns and allowances		17,500

Required Prepare an estimate of the company's loss using the retail method.

*Problem 6-14B Alternative cost flows—periodic LO⁷

Bonaire Co. began 2014 with 6,300 units of Product B in its inventory that cost $68 each, and it made successive purchases of the product as follows:

Jan. 4	10,500 units	@	$65 each
May 18	13,000 units	@	$62 each
July 9	12,000 units	@	$59 each
Nov. 21	15,500 units	@	$56 each

The company uses a periodic inventory system. On December 31, 2014, a physical count disclosed that 16,500 units of Product B remained in inventory.

Required

1. Prepare a calculation showing the number and total cost of the units available for sale during the year.

2. Prepare calculations showing the amounts that should be assigned to the ending inventory and to cost of goods sold assuming:

   a. FIFO

   b. Weighted average cost basis (round the average unit cost to two decimal places).

An asterisk (*) identifies assignment material based on Appendix 6A or Appendix 6B.

ANALYTICAL AND REVIEW PROBLEM

A & R Problem 6-1

The records of Thomas Company as of December 31, 2014, show the following:

	Net Purchases	Net Income	Accounts Payable	Inventory
Balance per company's books	$325,000	$25,000	$31,000	$18,400
(a)				
(b)				
(c)				
(d)				
(e)				
Correct balances				

The accountant of Thomas Company discovers in the first week of January 2015 that the following errors were made by his staff.

a. Goods costing $4,500 were in transit (FOB shipping point) and were not included in the ending inventory. The invoice had been received and the purchase recorded.

b. Damaged goods (cost $4,100) that were being held for return to the supplier were included in inventory. The goods had been recorded as a purchase and the entry for the return of these goods had also been made.

c. Inventory items costing $3,900 were incorrectly excluded from the final inventory. These goods had not been recorded as a purchase and had not been paid for by the company.

d. Goods that were shipped FOB destination had not yet arrived and were not included in inventory. However, the invoice had arrived on December 30, 2014, and the purchase for $2,700 was recorded.

e. Goods that cost $2,400 were segregated and not included in inventory because a customer expressed an intention to buy the goods. The sale of the goods for $4,200 had been recorded in December 2014.

Required Using the format provided above, show the correct amount for net purchases, net income, accounts payable, and inventory for Thomas Company as at December 31, 2014.

ETHICS CHALLENGE

EC 6-1   Diversion Inc. is a retail sports store carrying primarily women's golf apparel and equipment. The store is at the end of its second year of operations and, as new businesses often do, is struggling a bit to be profitable. The cost of inventory items has increased just in the short time the store has been in business. In the first year of operations the store accounted for inventory costs using the moving weighted average method. A loan agreement the store has with Dollar Bank, its prime source of financing, requires that the store maintain a certain gross profit and current ratio. The store's owner, Cindy Foor, is looking over Diversion's annual financial statements after year-end inventory has been taken. The numbers are not very favourable and the only way the store can meet the required financial ratios agreed upon with the bank is to change from the moving weighted average to the FIFO method of inventory. Cindy originally decided upon moving weighted average for inventory costing because she felt that moving weighted average yielded a better matching of costs to revenues. Cindy recalculates the ending inventory using FIFO and submits her income statement and balance sheet to the loan officer at the bank for the required bank review of the loan. As Cindy mails the financial statements to the bank, she thankfully reflects on the latitude she has as manager in choosing an inventory costing method.

Required

1. Why does Diversion's use of FIFO improve the gross profit ratio and current ratio?
2. Is the action by Diversion's owner ethical?

FOCUS ON FINANCIAL STATEMENTS

FFS 6-1

The owner of Fardan Stereo Sales showed the following adjusted trial balance at December 31, 2014:

Account	Account Balance*
Cash	16,000
Accounts receivable	27,000
Merchandise inventory...	?
Prepaid rent	36,000
Store fixtures..	117,000
Accumulated depreciation, store fixtures..	82,000
Trademark...	3,000
Accounts payable..	18,000
Unearned sales revenue..	4,000
Notes payable, due in 2017	22,000
Mikel Fardan, capital	61,000
Mikel Fardan, withdrawals..	44,000
Sales	449,000
Sales discounts...	6,000
Cost of goods sold	?
Delivery expense...	5,000
Rent expense	92,000
Salaries expense...	109,000
Interest expense..	2,000
Depreciation expense..	8,000

*Assume normal account balances.

The owner, Mikel Fardan, is analyzing the effect of the various merchandise inventory costing methods on his financial statements and has prepared the following schedule:

	FIFO	Moving Weighted Average
Merchandise inventory, December 31, 2013	12,000	12,000
Purchases..	159,000	159,000
Merchandise inventory, December 31, 2014	?	?
Cost of goods sold	152,000	148,000

Required

1. Calculate the merchandise inventory values at December 31, 2014, under each inventory costing method shown in the schedule above.

2. Prepare a single-step income statement (showing one line each for net sales, cost of goods sold, operating expenses, and interest expense) for the year ended December 31, 2014, along with a balance sheet at December 31, 2014, assuming:

   a. FIFO

   b. Moving weighted average.

Analysis Component:

3. Does the schedule above reflect rising costs for merchandise inventory or falling costs? Explain how you know.

4. Based on your results in Part 2, which method should the owner use if he wants to:

   a. Maximize net income?

   b. Maximize assets?

FFS 6-2

DANIER

Required Answer the following questions.

a. Refer to the balance sheets for **WestJet** and **Danier** in Appendix II at the end of the textbook. Both balance sheets include *Inventory*. Explain how *Inventory* is unique for each of these companies.

b. What method does Danier use to value its inventory? (Refer to the notes to Danier's financial statements in Appendix II at the end of the textbook.)

c. *Inventory* is classified on Danier's balance sheet as what type of asset?

d. Did the balance in inventory for Danier increase or decrease from June 26, 2010, to June 25, 2011?

CRITICAL THINKING MINI CASE

The former CEO of Benton Beverages retired and you have been hired in her place. In reviewing the selected financial data shown below, you are puzzled given that industry information clearly shows that the cost of beverages has been on the rise. As you walk about the warehouse area for the first time, you observe that, as pallets of beverages are being moved to the loading dock, empty areas appear behind various rows. You question the forklift driver, who says that the CEO told him always to leave alternating empty rows when stacking pallets. You climb a ladder to get a better view of the inventory layout, gasp, climb down, and determine that an emergency report to the board of directors is required.

	Years Ended December 31,							
	2014		**2013**		**2012**		**2011**	
Sales	$900,000	100%	$750,000	100%	$690,000	100%	$640,000	100%
Cost of goods sold...	459,000	51%	390,000	52%	372,600	54%	352,000	55%

Merchandise Inventory		Merchandise Inventory		Merchandise Inventory		Merchandise Inventory	
85,000[1]		73,000[1]		63,000[1]		45,000[1]	
345,000[2]	396,000[3]	306,000[2]	342,000[3]	312,600[2]	337,600[3]	330,000[2]	332,000[3]
63,000[4]		48,000[4]		35,000[4]		20,000[4]	
97,000[5]		85,000[5]		73,000[5]		63,000[5]	

1. Beginning inventory
2. Purchases during the period
3. Cost of goods sold
4. Year-end adjusting entry
5. Ending inventory

Required Incorporating the elements of critical thinking on the inside front cover, comment.

Accounting Information Systems

PRETTY IN PINK!

Marissa McTasney, founder of **Moxie Trades**, the maker of the infamous pink work boot, was successful in capturing $600,000 of financing and 50 percent equity from Brett Wilson, one of 'The Dragons'—a panel of successful Canadian venture capitalists on *Dragons' Den*, a reality television program where entrepreneurs pitch their business ideas in an attempt to secure investment dollars. Marissa acted on a niche marketing opportunity when she discovered that there were no female-specific clothing and safety items available for women working in construction and the trades. Moxie Trades products are designed for women, by women, and provide comfort, safety, and, yes, fashion!

In its first two years, Moxie Trades realized $1 million in revenue ... and then 2009 hit ... when the economic downturn slowed annual revenues to $150,000. Moxie Trades lost major clients like **WalMart** and **Zellers** because Marissa couldn't forecast sales and deliver product—her accounting information system was failing her. Rather than walk away from the business, she sub-contracted responsibility for delivery and accounts payable to a distribution company so that she could focus on marketing, her specialty. In 2010, sales recovered to $1.5 million and Moxie Trades has a strong relationship with one of Canada's largest retailers, **Mark's Work Wearhouse**. So next time you're at a Mark's, check out that stylish pink work gear!

www.moxietrades.com

LEARNING OBJECTIVES

LO¹ Explain the relationship of the accounting information system (AIS) to the management information system (MIS) and identify the components of an AIS.

LO² Explain the goals and uses of special journals.

LO³ Describe the use of controlling accounts and subledgers.

LO⁴ Journalize and post transactions using special journals.

*Appendix 7A

LO⁵ Journalize and post transactions using special journals in a periodic inventory system.

CRITICAL THINKING CHALLENGE Where in the accounting information system would Marissa have looked to monitor how many units of a particular product were on hand? What about to find out the balance owing to suppliers?

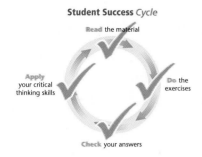

CHAPTER PREVIEW

An organization collects and processes a wide range of information. The accounting information system is part of a larger system, the management information system. Accounting information systems must be efficient and effective in meeting the demands of the increasing complexity and volume of financial transactions. In this chapter, we take a brief look at where the accounting information system is positioned in the organization's total information system and how it is structured. We learn about fundamental standards guiding information systems, and we study components of these systems. We also explain procedures that use special journals and subsidiary ledgers to make accounting information systems more efficient. Our understanding of where the details of accounting reports come from makes us better decision makers when using financial information, and it improves our ability to analyze and interpret financial statements. Just as for Marissa McTasney in the opening article, knowledge of these topics helps in running a company successfully.

INFORMATION SYSTEMS

Management Information Systems

LO¹ Explain the relationship of the accounting information system (AIS) to the management information system (MIS) and identify the components of an AIS.

A **management information system (MIS)** is designed to collect and process data within an organization for the purpose of providing users with information. Within the MIS are subsystems[1]: sales and marketing, production, finance, human resources, and accounting. These subsystems and their relationship to the MIS and external and internal users are shown in Exhibit 7.1. The arrows illustrate the exchange of information. Notice that each subsystem is both a user and a provider of information.

EXHIBIT 7.1

Accounting Information System in Relation to Other Information Systems

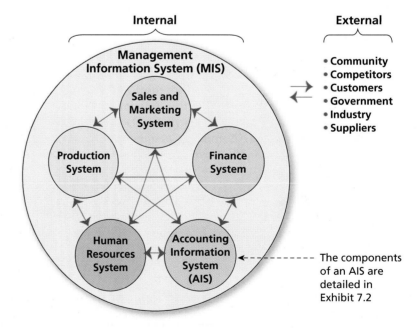

---

1   There is discussion as to whether the accounting information system is a subsystem of the MIS or whether the two systems simply overlap. That discussion is beyond the scope of this textbook. Therefore, for the sake of brevity, the position taken here will be that the accounting information system is a subsystem of the MIS.

Accounting Information Systems

An **accounting information system (AIS)** is a group of components that collect and process raw *financial* data into timely, accurate, relevant, and cost-effective information to meet the purposes of internal and external users. The primary components within an AIS are Accounts Payable, Accounts Receivable, and Payroll. Specialty components, such as Property, Plant and Equipment Assets, are often added dependent on the needs of the business. Exhibit 7.2 illustrates these components within the AIS.

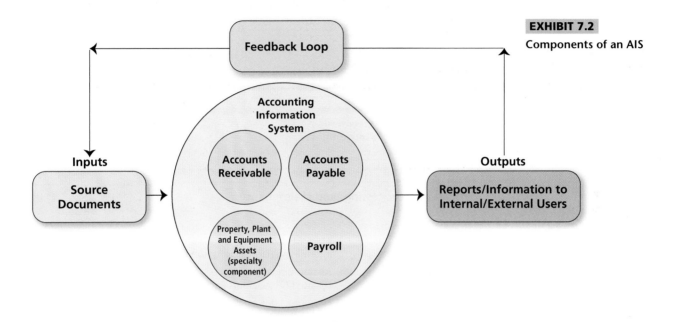

EXHIBIT 7.2
Components of an AIS

Other components of an AIS include people, data (inputs), software (accounting programs), hardware (computers), and reports (outputs).

Structure of an AIS

How the AIS is structured depends on the requirements of the users. A bank will have different needs than a restaurant or a steel manufacturer; however, the basic structure is similar for any AIS.

The journals and the accounts in the General Ledger form the foundation of the process that produces user reports. The General Ledger system represents the primary database. Because the journal is the book of original entry, it serves as a check to the entries posted in the General Ledger accounts. The accounting components used for operating and financial controls are developed based on the journal and General Ledger systems. For example, the component used for accounts receivable control is related to sales and cash receipts.

Exhibit 7.3 shows the basic structural relationships. The sale of inventory (1) decreases inventory (requiring purchases to replenish stock), and (2) when on credit, creates accounts receivable and initiates the billing process. Accounts receivable are collected (cash receipts) and inventory purchases on account need to be paid (payment of accounts payable). These transactions, plus payroll activity, are posted into the General Ledger.

Source documents provide the basic information processed by an accounting system. Examples are bank statements, cheques received for deposit, invoices from suppliers, billings to customers, and employee earnings records, to name a few. Source documents are often paper-based, but they are increasingly taking electronic

EXHIBIT 7.3

Accounting Information System Processing Cycle

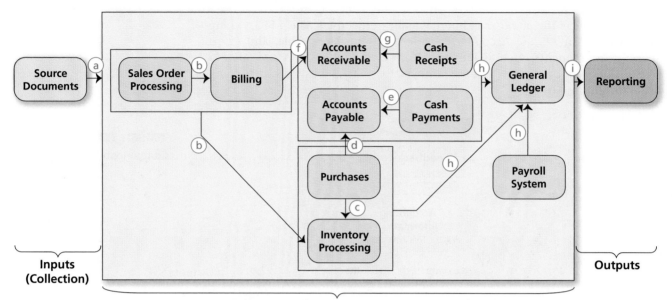

Explanation (not necessarily performed in this sequence):

(a) Source documents enter the Accounting Information System (AIS)

(b) Sales information is used to update records for both billing (Dr Accounts Receivable) and merchandise inventory (Cr Merchandise Inventory)

(c) Purchases are made based on sales information to maintain appropriate levels (Dr Merchandise Inventory)

(d) Purchases information is used to update Accounts Payable (Cr Accounts Payable)

(e) Purchases are paid when due and Accounts Payable is updated (Dr Accounts Payable)

(f) Accounts Receivable records are updated based on sales information (Dr Accounts Receivable)

(g) As cash is received from customers, Accounts Receivable is updated (Cr Accounts Receivable)

(h) All transactions are posted into the General Ledger, including payroll transactions

(i) The AIS generates financial statements at the end of the accounting period in addition to special purpose reports created as needed

form, such as those created by consumers using debit cards in lieu of cash to pay for goods purchased.

Computer hardware is the physical equipment in a computerized system. **Computer software** is the programs that direct the operations of computer hardware. QuickBooks® and Simply Accounting® are examples of accounting software used for small to medium-sized businesses. **Enterprise-application software** (such as SAP® and Oracle®) is an integrated program that manages a company's vital operations from order-taking to manufacturing to accounting, and is commonly used by companies around the world.

 CHECKPOINT

1. Explain the difference between an MIS and an AIS.
2. Name the four basic components of an AIS.

Do Quick Study questions: QS 7-1, QS 7-2

Public Accountant
You are a public accountant consulting with a client. This client's business has grown to the point where the accounting system must be updated to handle both the volume of transactions and management's information needs. Your client requests your advice in purchasing new software for the accounting system. You have been offered a 10% commission by a software company for each purchase of its system by one of your clients. Do you think your evaluation of software alternatives is affected by this commission arrangement? Do you think this commission arrangement is appropriate? Do you tell your client about the commission arrangement before making a recommendation?

SPECIAL JOURNALS IN ACCOUNTING

This section focuses on the underlying operations of accounting systems: *special journals* and *subsidiary ledgers* (commonly referred to as *subledgers*). These operations are set up to be efficient in processing transactions and are done almost exclusively using technology. ***The manual approach described in this section has the advantage of clearly illustrating how accounting information moves through a computerized environment. If we do not understand how the information enters and is processed through a computerized system, how can we fully understand the information it creates?***

LO² Explain the goals and uses of special journals.

This section uses selected transactions of Outdoors Unlimited to illustrate special journals and subledgers. Since Outdoors Unlimited uses a *perpetual inventory* system, the special journals are set up using this system. The special journals in a *periodic* inventory system are shown in Appendix 7A.

Basics of Special Journals— Perpetual Inventory System

A General Journal is an all-purpose journal where we can record any transaction. A **special journal** is used in recording and posting transactions of similar type. Most transactions of a merchandiser, for instance, fall into four groups: sales on credit, purchases on credit, cash receipts, and cash disbursements. Exhibit 7.4 shows the special journals for these groups. This section assumes the use of these special journals along with the General Journal.

Sales Journal	Cash Receipts Journal	Purchases Journal	Cash Disbursements Journal	General Journal
For recording credit sales	For recording cash receipts	For recording credit purchases	For recording cash payments	For transactions not in special journals

EXHIBIT 7.4

Using Special Journals With a General Journal

The General Journal continues to be used for transactions not covered by special journals and for adjusting, closing, and correcting entries.

Subledgers

Accounting information systems must provide several detailed listings of amounts. One of the most important listings is the amounts due from customers, called *accounts receivable*, and amounts owed to creditors, called *accounts payable*. The Accounts Receivable account in the General Ledger (also known as Accounts Receivable Control) shows the total accounts receivable but it is difficult to get

LO³ Describe the use of controlling accounts and subledgers.

information regarding a particular customer. To collect this information we often create a separate ledger called a *subledger* (*subsidiary ledger*).

A **subledger** (or **subsidiary ledger**) is a listing of individual accounts with a common characteristic. Using subledgers removes unnecessary details from the General Ledger. Two common subledgers are:

- **Accounts Receivable Subledger** for storing transaction data with individual customers.
- **Accounts Payable Subledger** for storing transaction data with individual creditors.

Accounts Receivable Subledger

When we recorded credit sales in prior transaction analysis, we debited Accounts Receivable. Yet when a company has more than one credit customer, the accounts receivable records must show how much *each* customer purchased, paid, and still owes. This information is collected by keeping a separate account receivable for each customer in a subledger called the Accounts Receivable Subledger.

The General Ledger continues to keep a single Accounts Receivable account, called the **controlling account** because it is a summary of the *Accounts Receivable Subledger*. Like a General Ledger, a subledger can exist in electronic or paper form. Customer accounts in a subledger are kept separate from the Accounts Receivable account in the General Ledger.

Exhibit 7.5 shows the relation between the Accounts Receivable controlling account and its related accounts in the subledger. After all items are posted, the Accounts Receivable controlling account must equal the sum of balances in the customers' accounts in the Accounts Receivable Subledger.

EXHIBIT 7.5

Accounts Receivable Controlling Account and Subledger

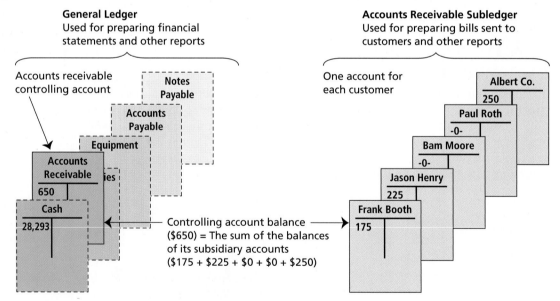

Accounts Payable Subledger

There are other controlling accounts and subledgers. We know, for example, that many companies buy on credit from several suppliers. This means a company must keep a separate account for each creditor by keeping an Accounts Payable controlling account in the General Ledger and a separate account for each creditor in an Accounts Payable Subledger.

Inventory Subledger

Merchandisers often have more than one type of item in inventory. **Canadian Tire,** for example, stocks thousands of different items from teapots to tents to tires.

To manage such extensive stocks of inventory, companies using a perpetual inventory system record transactions affecting each type of inventory in a separate record. This group of individual inventory records makes up the *Inventory Subledger*. By keeping inventory information in separate records, detailed information about quantity, for example, is readily available. Exhibit 7.6 illustrates a typical Inventory Subledger record. This subledger is based on a FIFO cost flow assumption.

EXHIBIT 7.6

Inventory Subledger Record

Item		Leather Sports Bags						Location code	W18C2	
Catalogue No.		LSB-117				Units: Maximum	25	Minimum	5	

		Purchases			Sales (at cost)			Balance		
Date	PR	Units	Unit Cost	Total Cost	Units	Unit Cost	Total Cost	Total Units	Unit Cost	Total Cost
2014 Aug. 1								10	$100	$1,000
12	S2				4	$100	$400	6	100	600
								6	100	
18	P3	20	$110	$2,200				20	110	2,800
30	S2				6	100	600			
					2	110	220	18	110	1,980
Totals		20		$2,200	12		$1,220			

Reitmans (Canada) Limited showed inventory on its January 28, 2012, balance sheet of $78 million. The $78 million is the balance in the Inventory account in the General Ledger and represents the total of the hundreds of individual inventory records in the Inventory Subledger. The total in the General Ledger is known as the controlling account. The balance of the Inventory controlling account must agree with the sum of the balances of the inventory records in the Inventory Subledger.

DECISION INSIGHT

Accounting Information in Real Time

A new generation of accounting support is available. With the touch of a key, users can create real-time inventory reports showing all payments, charges, and credit limits at any point in the accounting cycle. Many services also include "alert signals" notifying the company when, for example, a large order exceeds a customer's credit limit or when purchases need to be made or when a bank balance is running low. These alerts occur via email, fax, PDA, or phone.

Other Subledgers

Subledgers are also common for several other accounts. A company with many items of equipment, for example, might keep only one Equipment account in its General Ledger. But this company's Equipment account would control a subledger in which each item of equipment is recorded in a separate account. Similar treatment is common with investments and other large accounts needing separate detailed records.

ClubLink Enterprises Limited is Canada's largest owner and operator of golf club and resort operations. In Note 19 of its 2011 annual report, ClubLink discloses detailed information by operating segment (as shown in Exhibit 7.7). Yet ClubLink's accounting system most certainly keeps more detailed operating records than reflected in its annual report. ClubLink for instance, has numerous resorts and is likely able to analyze the operating performance of each one of them. This detail can be captured by many different General Ledger sales and expense accounts. But it is likely captured by using supplementary records that function like subledgers. The concept of a subledger can be applied in many different ways to ensure that our accounting system captures sufficient details to support analyses that decision makers need.

EXHIBIT 7.7

ClubLink Enterprises Limited's Results by Operating Segment

(thousands of Canadian dollars)	For the Year Ended December 31, 2011			
	Golf Club and Resort Operations	Rail, Tourism and Port Operations	Corporate Operations	Total
Canadian operating revenue	$ 151,580	$ -	$ -	$ 151,580
US operating revenue	13,094	35,572	-	48,666
Costs of sales and operating expenses	(128,136)	(18,105)	(2,700)	(148,941)
Net operating income (loss)	36,538	17,467	(2,700)	51,305
Net membership fee income	14,353	-	-	14,353
Earnings before other items and income taxes	50,891	17,467	(2,700)	65,658
Depreciation and amortization	(17,266)	(5,961)	-	(23,227)
Land lease rent	(5,281)	(185)	-	(5,466)
Segment earnings (loss) before interest, other income and income taxes	$ 28,344	$ 11,321	$ (2,700)	36,965
Interest, net (unallocated)				(21,114)
Other income, net (unallocated)				6,182
Provision for income taxes (unallocated)				(5,645)
Net earnings				$ 16,388
Capital expenditures	$ 8,080	$ 7,046	$ -	$ 15,126

CHECKPOINT

3. When special journals are used, where are all cash payments by cheque recorded?

Do Quick Study questions: QS 7-3, QS 7-4, QS 7-5, QS 7-6

MID-CHAPTER DEMONSTRATION PROBLEM

Indicate in which journal each of the following transactions should be recorded. Also, assuming three subledgers are maintained—Accounts Receivable, Accounts Payable, and Merchandise Inventory—identify which subledger(s) if any would be affected by each transaction.

a.   Purchase of office supplies for cash.
b.   Sale of merchandise on account.
c.   Entry to record depreciation expense for the period.
d.   Purchase of merchandise on account.
e.   Sale of old equipment for cash.
f.   Collection of the amount of the sale in (b).

SOLUTION

a.   Cash Disbursements Journal; no subledger
b.   Sales Journal; both the Accounts Receivable and Merchandise Inventory Subledgers
c.   General Journal; no subledger
d.   Purchases Journal; both the Accounts Payable and Merchandise Inventory Subledgers
e.   Cash Receipts Journal; no subledger
f.   Cash Receipts Journal; Accounts Receivable Subledger

The next sections demonstrate the four common special journals: Sales, Cash Receipts, Purchases, and Cash Disbursements. While all of the transactions take place during the month of February, you will note that some of the General Ledger accounts have opening balances as of January 31. These balances are included for demonstration purposes only and to provide some continuity, where necessary. For simplicity, it has been assumed that the Accounts Receivable and Accounts Payable balances are zero at the beginning of February.

LO⁴ Journalize and post transactions using special journals.

Sales Journal

A **Sales Journal** is used to record sales of merchandise on credit. Sales of merchandise for cash are not recorded in a Sales Journal, but instead are recorded in a Cash Receipts Journal. Sales of nonmerchandise assets on credit are recorded in the General Journal.

Journalizing

Credit sale transactions are recorded with information about each sale entered separately in a Sales Journal. This information is often taken from a copy of the sales ticket or invoice prepared at the time of sale. The top of Exhibit 7.8 shows a Sales

EXHIBIT 7.8

Sales Journal With Posting

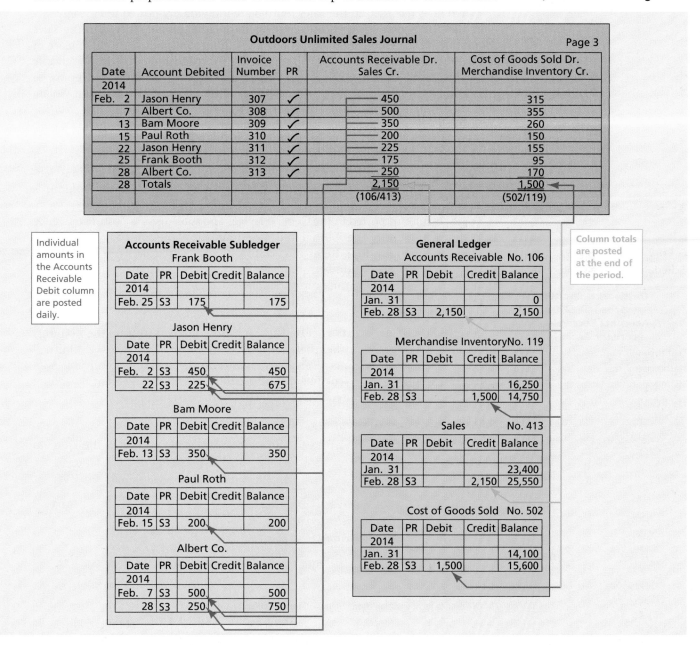

Journal from a sporting goods merchandiser, Outdoors Unlimited. The Sales Journal in this exhibit is called a **columnar journal** because it has more than one column for recording the date, customer's name, invoice number, amount of each credit sale, and cost of the merchandise sold.[2]

Each transaction results in a debit to Accounts Receivable and a credit to Sales, and a debit to Cost of Goods Sold and a credit to Merchandise Inventory. We only need two columns for these four accounts. More columns can be added to include information about taxes, returns, departments, and other details of transactions described later in this section. The Posting Reference (PR) column is *not* used until posting is completed.

Posting

A Sales Journal is posted as shown by following the arrows in Exhibit 7.8. Individual transactions in the Sales Journal are typically posted each day to customer accounts in the Accounts Receivable Subledger to keep customer accounts up to date. This is important for the person granting credit to customers, who needs to know the amount owed by credit-seeking customers to be sure a correct decision can be made.

When sales recorded in the Sales Journal are individually posted to customer accounts in the Accounts Receivable Subledger, check marks are entered in the Sales Journal's Posting Reference column. Customer account numbers are used in place of check marks if available. Note that when debits (or credits) to Accounts Receivable are posted twice (once to the Accounts Receivable controlling account and once to the customer's account in the Accounts Receivable Subledger) this does not violate the accounting equation of debits equal credits. *The equality of debits and credits is always maintained in the General Ledger.* The Accounts Receivable Subledger is a duplicate record with detailed information for each customer.

The Sales Journal's *amount* columns are totalled at the end of the period and posted to the General Ledger accounts. The total of the first amount column is debited to Accounts Receivable and credited to Sales. The second amount column is debited to Cost of Goods Sold and credited to Merchandise Inventory.

For each amount posted in the General Ledger and subledgers, a posting reference is included to identify the journal and page number of the source. We identify a journal by using an initial. Items posted from the Sales Journal carry the initial *S* before their journal page numbers in the Posting Reference columns. Likewise, items from the Cash Receipts Journal carry the initials *CR*, items from the Cash Disbursements Journal carry the initials *CD*, items from the Purchases Journal carry the initial *P*, and items from the General Journal carry the initial *G*.

A **schedule of accounts receivable** is a listing of accounts from the Accounts Receivable Subledger with their balances and the sum of all balances. Exhibit 7.9 shows a schedule of accounts receivable drawn from the Accounts Receivable Subledger of Exhibit 7.8. The schedule can be useful in credit management by adding information about the time each receivable has been outstanding.

Sales Returns and Allowances

A company with sales returns and allowances can record them in the General Journal as:

Mar.	7	Sales Returns and Allowances..........................	414	10.00	
		Accounts Receivable—Robert Moore	106/✓		10.00
		Customer returned merchandise.			
	7	Merchandise Inventory	119	6.00	
		Cost of Goods Sold	502		6.00
		The merchandise was returned to inventory.			

EXHIBIT 7.9

Schedule of Accounts Receivable

Outdoors Unlimited Schedule of Accounts Receivable February 28, 2014	
Frank Booth........................	$ 175
Jason Henry	675
Bam Moore	350
Paul Roth..........................	200
Albert Co.	750
Total accounts receivable.........................	$2,150

---

2   We do not record explanations in any of our special journals for brevity purposes.

The debit in this entry is posted to the Sales Returns and Allowances account. The credit is posted both to the Accounts Receivable controlling account and to the customer's account in the subledger (posted daily). We also include the account number and the check mark, 106/✓, in the PR column on the credit line. This means both the Accounts Receivable controlling account in the General Ledger and the Robert Moore account in the Accounts Receivable Subledger are credited for $10.00. Both are credited because the balance of the controlling account in the General Ledger does not equal the sum of the customer account balances in the subledger unless *both* are credited.

CHECKPOINT

4. How do debits and credits remain equal when credit sales to customers are posted twice (once to the Accounts Receivable controlling account and once to the customer's account in the subledger)?
5. How do we identify the journal from which an amount in a ledger account was posted?

Do Quick Study question: QS 7-7

Cash Receipts Journal

A **Cash Receipts Journal** records *all* receipts of cash. A Cash Receipts Journal must be a columnar journal because different accounts are credited when cash is received from different sources.

Journalizing

Cash receipts usually fall into one of three groups: (1) cash from credit customers in payment of their accounts, (2) cash from cash sales, and (3) cash from other sources. The Cash Receipts Journal in Exhibit 7.10 has a special column for credits when cash is received from one or more of these three sources.

Cash From Credit Customers

To record cash received in payment of a customer's account, the customer's name is first entered in the Cash Receipts Journal's Accounts Credited column. Then the amounts debited to Cash and Sales Discounts, if any, are entered in their respective journal columns, and the amount credited to the customer's account is entered in the Accounts Receivable Credit column. Note that the Accounts Receivable Credit column contains only credits to customer accounts.

   To post, individual amounts are posted daily to subledger accounts. Column totals are posted at the end of the period to General Ledger accounts.

Cash Sales

When cash sales are collected and totalled at the end of a day, the daily total is recorded in the Cash Receipts Journal with a debit to Cash and a credit to Sales.[3] At the same time, the cost of sales is accumulated and recorded as a debit to Cost of Goods Sold and a credit to Merchandise Inventory. Cash sales are journalized weekly in Exhibit 7.10 for brevity. By using a separate Sales Credit column, we can post the total cash sales for a month as a single amount, the column total.

---

3 Remember that in practice under a perpetual system these cash sales are recorded at the point of sale. To do that here would make this journal extremely lengthy since Outdoors Unlimited is a retailer with many cash sales every day.

EXHIBIT 7.10

Cash Receipts Journal With Posting

Outdoors Unlimited Cash Receipts Journal

Page 2

Date	Accounts Credited	PR	Explanation	Cash Dr.	Sales Discount Dr.	Accounts Receivable Cr.	Sales Cr.	Other Accounts Cr.	Cost of Goods Sold Dr. Merchandise Inventory Cr.
2014									
Feb. 7	Sales		Cash sales	4,450			4,450		3,150
12	Jason Henry	✓	Invoice, Feb. 2	441	9	450			
14	Sales		Cash sales	3,925			3,925		2,950
17	Albert Co.	✓	Invoice, Feb. 7	490	10	500			
20	Notes Payable	245	Note to bank	750				750	
21	Sales		Cash sales	4,700			4,700		3,400
22	Interest Revenue	409	Bank account	250				250	
23	Bam Moore	✓	Invoice, Feb. 13	343	7	350			
25	Paul Roth	✓	Invoice, Feb.15	196	4	200			
28	Sales		Cash sales	4,225			4,225		3,050
28	Totals			19,770	30	1,500	17,300	1,000	12,550
				(101)	(415)	(106)	(413)	(X)	(502/119)

Accounts Receivable Subledger

Frank Booth

Date	PR	Debit	Credit	Balance
2014				
Feb. 25	S3	175		175

Jason Henry

Date	PR	Debit	Credit	Balance
2014				
Feb. 2	S3	450		450
12	CR2		450	-0-
22	S3	225		225

Bam Moore

Date	PR	Debit	Credit	Balance
2014				
Feb. 13	S3	350		350
23	CR2		350	-0-

Paul Roth

Date	PR	Debit	Credit	Balance
2014				
Feb. 15	S3	200		200
25	CR2		200	-0-

Albert Co.

Date	PR	Debit	Credit	Balance
2014				
Feb. 7	S3	500		500
17	CR2		500	-0-
28	S3	250		250

Individual amounts in the Accounts Receivable Credit and Other Accounts Credit columns are posted daily.

General Ledger

Cash No. 101

Date	PR	Debit	Credit	Balance
2014				
Jan. 31				9,450
Feb. 28	CR2	19,770		29,220

Accounts Receivable No. 106

Date	PR	Debit	Credit	Balance
2014				
Jan. 31				-0-
Feb. 28	S3	2,150		2,150
28	CR2		1,500	650

Merchandise Inventory No. 119

Date	PR	Debit	Credit	Balance
2014				
Jan. 31				16,250
Feb. 28	S3		1,500	14,750
28	CR2		12,550	2,200

Notes Payable No. 245

Date	PR	Debit	Credit	Balance
2014				
Jan. 31				-0-
Feb. 20	CR2		750	750

Sales No. 413

Date	PR	Debit	Credit	Balance
2014				
Jan. 31				23,400
Feb. 28	S3		2,150	25,550
28	CR2		17,300	42,850

Sales Discounts No. 415

Date	PR	Debit	Credit	Balance
2014				
Jan. 31				35
Feb. 28	CR2	30		65

Interest Revenue No. 409

Date	PR	Debit	Credit	Balance
2014				
Jan. 31				260
Feb. 22	CR2		250	510

Cost of Goods Sold No. 502

Date	PR	Debit	Credit	Balance
2014				
Jan. 31				14,100
Feb. 28	S3	1,500		15,600
28	CR2	12,550		28,150

Column totals except for Other Accounts columns are posted at the end of the period.

The total of the Cost of Goods Sold and Merchandise Inventory amount column is posted to *both* of their General Ledger accounts at the end of the period.

Cash From Other Sources

Other sources of cash include borrowing money from a bank, interest on account, or selling unneeded assets. The Other Accounts Credit column is for receipts that do not occur often enough to warrant a separate column. This means items entered in this column are posted to a variety of General Ledger accounts. These individual items are posted. Therefore, the total in this column is not posted. The Cash Receipts Journal's PR column is used only for postings from the Other Accounts and Accounts Receivable columns. The account numbers in the PR column refer to items that are posted to General Ledger accounts.

Posting

At the end of a period, the amounts in the Cash, Sales Discounts, Accounts Receivable, Sales, Cost of Goods Sold, and Merchandise Inventory columns of the Cash Receipts Journal are posted as column totals. The transactions recorded in all journals must result in equal debits and credits to General Ledger accounts. To be sure that total debits and credits in a columnar journal are equal, we often *crossfoot* column totals before posting them. To **foot** a column of numbers is to add it. To **crossfoot** we add the debit column totals and the credit column totals and compare the two sums for equality. Footing and crossfooting of the numbers in Exhibit 7.11 are as follows:

Debit Columns		Credit Columns	
Cash Debit	$19,770	Accounts Receivable Credit	$ 1,500
Cost of Goods Sold Debit	12,550	Sales Credit	17,300
Sales Discounts Debit	30	Other Accounts Credit	1,000
		Inventory Credit	12,550
Total	$32,350	Total	$32,350

EXHIBIT 7.11

Footing and Crossfooting Journal Amounts

After crossfooting the journal to confirm that debits equal credits, we post the totals of all but the Other Accounts column as indicated by their column headings. Because items in the Other Accounts column are posted individually, this column total is not posted. We place an 'X' below the Other Accounts column to indicate that this *column total* is not posted. The account numbers of the accounts where the remaining column totals are posted are in parentheses below each column.

DECISION MAKER   Answer—End of chapter

Retailer

You are a retailer in computer equipment and supplies. You want to know how promptly customers are paying their bills. This information can help you in deciding whether to extend credit and in planning your own cash payments. Where might you look for this information?

Purchases Journal

A **Purchases Journal** is used to record *all* purchases on credit. Purchases for cash are recorded in the Cash Disbursements Journal.

Journalizing

A Purchases Journal with one column for dollar amounts can be used to record purchases of merchandise on credit. But a Purchases Journal usually is more useful if it is a multicolumn journal in which all credit purchases, not only merchandise, are recorded. Exhibit 7.12 shows a multicolumn Purchases Journal.

Purchase invoices or other source documents are used in recording transactions in the Purchases Journal. Journalizing is similar to the Sales Journal. We use the invoice date and terms to calculate the date when payment for each purchase is due. The Merchandise Inventory Debit column is used for recording merchandise purchases. When a purchase involves an amount recorded in the Other Accounts Debit

EXHIBIT 7.12

Purchases Journal With Posting

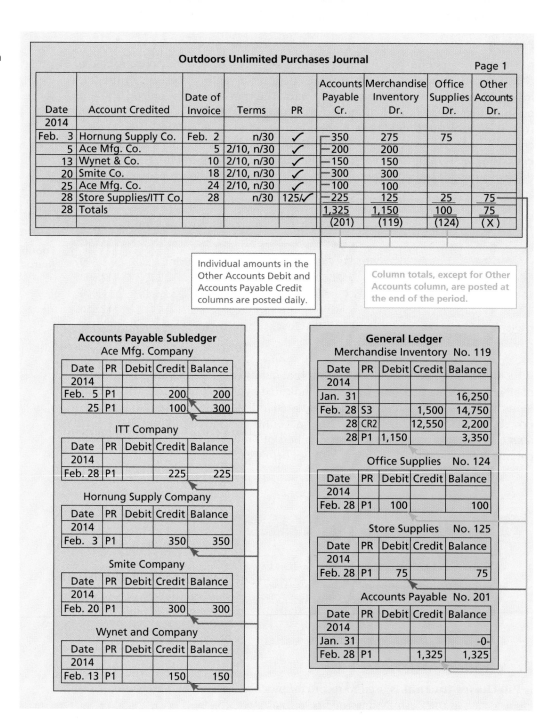

column, we use the Account column to identify the General Ledger account debited. Outdoors Unlimited also includes a separate column for credit purchases of office supplies. A separate column such as this is useful whenever several transactions involve debits to a specific account. Each company uses its own judgement in deciding on the number of separate columns necessary. The Other Accounts Debit column allows the Purchases Journal to be used for all purchase transactions involving credits to Accounts Payable. The Accounts Payable Credit column is used to record the amounts credited to each creditor's account.

Posting

The amounts in the Accounts Payable Credit column are posted daily to individual creditor accounts in the Accounts Payable Subledger. Individual amounts in the Other Accounts Debit column are posted to their General Ledger accounts. All column totals except the Other Accounts Debit column are posted to their General Ledger accounts. The balance in the Accounts Payable controlling account must equal the sum of the account balances in the Accounts Payable Subledger after posting.

Cash Disbursements Journal

A **Cash Disbursements Journal,** also called a *Cash Payments Journal*, is used to record *all* payments of cash. It is a multicolumn journal because cash payments are made for several different purposes.

Journalizing

A Cash Disbursements Journal is similar to a Cash Receipts Journal except that it has repetitive cash payments instead of receipts. Exhibit 7.13 shows the Cash Disbursements Journal for Outdoors Unlimited. We see repetitive credits to the Cash column of this journal. We also commonly see credits to Merchandise Inventory for purchase discounts and debits to the Accounts Payable account. Many companies purchase merchandise on credit and, therefore, a Merchandise Inventory Debit column is not often needed. Instead, the occasional cash purchase is recorded in the Other Accounts Debit column and Cash Credit column as shown for the February 5 transaction of Exhibit 7.13.

The Cash Disbursements Journal has a column titled Cheque Number (Ch. No.). For control over cash disbursements, all payments except for very small amounts are made by cheque.[4] Cheques should be prenumbered and entered in the journal in numerical order with each cheque's number in the column headed Ch. No. This makes it possible to scan the numbers in the column for omitted cheques. When a Cash Disbursements Journal has a column for cheque numbers, it is sometimes called a **Cheque Register**.

Consistent with the treatment of purchase discounts and transportation-in in Chapter 5 under a perpetual system, Exhibit 7.13 posts these directly to the Merchandise Inventory account.

Posting

Individual amounts in the Accounts Payable Debit column are posted daily to the specific creditors' accounts in the Accounts Payable Subledger. Individual amounts in the Other Accounts Debit column of a Cash Disbursements Journal are posted to their General Ledger accounts. We also crossfoot column totals and post the Accounts Payable Debit column total to the Accounts Payable controlling account. The Merchandise Inventory Credit column total is posted to the Merchandise Inventory account and the Cash Credit column total is posted to the Cash account.

---

4 We describe a system for controlling small cash payments in Chapter 8.

EXHIBIT 7.13

Cash Disbursements Journal With Posting

Outdoors Unlimited Cash Disbursements Journal

Page 2

Date	Ch. No.	Payee	Account Debited	PR	Cash Cr.	Merchandise Inventory Cr.	Other Accounts Dr.	Accounts Payable Dr.
2014								
Feb. 3	105	L & N Railroad	Inventory re transp-in	119	15		15	
5	106	East Sales Co.	Inventory	119	25		25	
13	107	Ace Mfg. Co.	Ace Mfg. Co.	✓	196	4		200
20	108	Jerry Hale	Salaries Expense	622	250		250	
25	109	Wynet & Co.	Wynet & Co.	✓	147	3		150
28	110	Smite Co.	Smite Co.	✓	294	6		300
28		Totals			927	13	290	650
					(101)	(119)	(X)	(201)

Column totals, except for Other Accounts column, are posted at the end of the period.

Individual amounts in the Other Accounts column and Accounts Payable column are posted daily.

General Ledger

Cash   No. 101

Date	PR	Debit	Credit	Balance
2014				
Jan. 31	CR2			9,450
Feb. 28	CR2	19,770		29,220
28	CD2		927	28,293

Merchandise Inventory No. 119

Date	PR	Debit	Credit	Balance
2014				
Jan. 28				16,250
Feb. 3	CD2	15		16,265
5	CD2	25		16,290
28	S3		1,500	14,790
28	CR2		12,550	2,240
28	P1	1,150		3,390
28	CD2		13	3,377

Accounts Payable   No. 201

Date	PR	Debit	Credit	Balance
2014				
Jan. 31				-0-
Feb. 28	P1		1,325	1,325
28	CD2	650		675

Salaries Expense   No. 622

Date	PR	Debit	Credit	Balance
2014				
Feb. 20	CD2	250		250

Accounts Payable Subledger

Ace Mfg. Company

Date	PR	Debit	Credit	Balance
2014				
Feb. 5	P1		200	200
13	CD2	200		-0-
25	P1		100	100

ITT Company

Date	PR	Debit	Credit	Balance
2014				
Feb. 28	P1		225	225

Hornung Supply Company

Date	PR	Debit	Credit	Balance
2014				
Feb. 3	P1		350	350

Smite Company

Date	PR	Debit	Credit	Balance
2014				
Feb. 20	P1		300	300
28	CD2	300		-0-

Wynet & Company

Date	PR	Debit	Credit	Balance
2014				
Feb. 13	P1		150	150
25	CD2	150		-0-

Exhibit 7.14 shows a schedule of accounts payable drawn from the Accounts Payable Subledger of Exhibit 7.13. A **schedule of accounts payable** is a listing of accounts from the Accounts Payable Subledger with their balances and the sum of all balances. This schedule is useful in the management of payables by adding additional information such as when the accounts are due.

DECISION MAKER   Answer—End of chapter

Controller
You are a controller for a merchandising company. You want to analyze your company's cash payments to suppliers, including an analysis of purchase discounts. Where might you look for this information?

General Journal Transactions

When special journals are used, we still need a General Journal for adjusting, closing, and correcting entries, and for special transactions not recorded in special journals. These special transactions include purchase returns and allowances, purchases of plant assets by issuing a note payable, sales returns, and receiving a note receivable from a customer.

The process to follow when using special journals is based on the first four steps of the accounting cycle: analyze, record, post, and prepare an unadjusted trial balance. The last section described this process in detail. A summary of the steps to follow when working with special journals is to:

1. Analyze
2. Record transactions in the appropriate journal
3. Post
   - Post to the subledger account, if any is affected
   - Post individual amounts in the Other Accounts column to the General Ledger
   - Foot and crossfoot the journals
   - Post column totals from the journals to the General Ledger (except Other Accounts)
4. Prepare a trial balance
   - Agree the total of the accounts in each subledger to the respective controlling account on the trial balance

CHECKPOINT

6. What is the normal recording and posting procedure when using special journals and controlling accounts with subledgers?
7. Why does a company need a General Journal when using special journals for sales, purchases, cash receipts, and cash disbursements?

Do Quick Study questions: QS 7-8, QS 7-9, QS 7-10

CRITICAL THINKING CHALLENGE   Refer to the Critical Thinking Challenge questions at the beginning of the chapter. Compare your answers to those suggested on Connect.

Difference	International Financial Reporting Standards (IFRS)	Accounting Standards for Private Enterprises (ASPE)
There are no significant differences between IFRS and ASPE related to this chapter.		

SUMMARY

LO¹ Explain the relationship of the accounting information system (AIS) to the management information system (MIS) and identify the components of an AIS. The MIS includes the subsystems of Finance, Sales and Marketing, Human Resources, Production, and Accounting. Information systems collect and process data based on inputs for the purpose of generating useful information for both internal and external users. An AIS collects financial data and processes it through the relevant component: Accounts Payable, Accounts Receivable, Payroll, or a specialty component such as Property, Plant and Equipment Assets. Source documents have evolved from paper-based to technology-based. General purpose accounting software is available for small to medium-sized businesses, whereas large businesses purchase enterprise-application software programs that can be customized to fit their specific needs.

LO² Explain the goals and uses of special journals. Special journals are used for recording and posting transactions of similar type, with each meant to cover one kind of transaction. Four of the most common special journals are the Sales Jour-

nal, Cash Receipts Journal, Purchases Journal, and Cash Disbursements Journal.

LO³ Describe the use of controlling accounts and subledgers. A General Ledger keeps controlling accounts such as Accounts Receivable or Accounts Payable, but details on individual accounts making up the controlling account are kept in a subledger (such as an Accounts Receivable Subledger).

LO⁴ Journalize and post transactions using special journals. Special journals are devoted to similar kinds of transactions. Transactions are journalized on one line of a special journal, with columns devoted to specific accounts, dates, names, posting references, explanations, and other necessary information. Posting is threefold: (1) individual amounts in a column that is posted in total to a controlling account at the end of a period (month) are posted regularly (daily) to its account in the subledger, (2) total amounts for all columns except the Other Accounts column are posted at the end of a period (month) to their column's account title, and (3) individual amounts in the Other Accounts column are posted to their General Ledger accounts.

GUIDANCE ANSWERS TO DECISION MAKER

Public Accountant

As a professional accountant, you are guided by the Professional Codes of Conduct detailed in Extend Your Knowledge 1-5. You should recognize the main issue: whether commissions have an actual or perceived impact on the integrity and objectivity of your advice. The code says that you should not accept a commission if you perform either an audit or a review of the client's financial statements or if you review prospective financial information for the client. The code also precludes a commission if you compile the client's statements, unless the compilation report discloses a lack of independence. Even in situations where a commission is allowed, the code requires you to tell the client of your commission arrangement. These suggested actions seem appropriate even if you are not bound by the code. Also, you need to seriously examine the merits of agreeing to a commission arrangement when you are in a position to exploit it.

Retailer

The Accounts Receivable Subledger has much of the information you need. It lists detailed information for each customer's account, including the amounts, dates for transactions, and dates of payments. It can be reorganized into an "aging schedule" to show how long customers wait in paying their bills. We describe an aging schedule in Chapter 9.

Controller

Much of the information you need is in the Accounts Payable Subledger. It contains information for each supplier, the amounts due, and when payments are made. This subledger, along with information on credit terms, should enable you to conduct your analyses.

1. An AIS is part of the MIS and collects and processes financial data for communication to users. The MIS collects and processes data from sales and marketing, finance, production, human resources, and accounting and provides information to these in turn and also to external users.

2. The four basic components of an AIS are Accounts Payable, Accounts Receivable, Payroll, and specialty components such as Property, Plant and Equipment Assets.

3. All cash payments by cheque are recorded in the Cash Disbursements Journal.

4. The equality of debits and credits is kept within the General Ledger. The subledger keeps the customer's individual account and is used only for supplementary information.

5. An initial and page number of the journal from which the amount was posted is entered in the Posting Reference column of the ledger account next to the amount.

6. The normal recording and posting procedures are three-fold. First, transactions are entered in a special journal column if applicable. Second, individual amounts are posted to the subledger accounts. Third, column totals are posted to General Ledger accounts.

7. The General Journal is still needed for adjusting, closing and correcting entries, and for special transactions such as sales returns, purchases returns, plant asset purchases, and sales on credit of assets other than merchandise inventory.

DEMONSTRATION PROBLEM

The Pepper Company completed these transactions during March 2014:

Mar.	1	Merchandise inventory on hand was $28,400.
	1	Adrian Pepper, Capital has an opening balance of $28,400.
	4	Sold merchandise on credit to Jennifer Nelson, invoice #954, $16,800. Cost, $10,100. (Terms of all credit sales are 2/10, n/30.)
	6	Purchased office supplies on credit from Mack Company, $1,220. Invoice dated March 3, terms n/30.
	6	Sold merchandise on credit to Dennie Hoskins, invoice #955, $10,200. Cost, $6,200.
	11	Received merchandise and an invoice dated March 11, terms 2/10, n/30, from Defore Industries, $52,600.
	12	Borrowed $26,000 by giving Commerce Bank a long-term promissory note payable.
	14	Received payment from Jennifer Nelson for the March 4 sale.
	16	Received a credit memorandum from Defore Industries for unsatisfactory merchandise received on March 11 and returned for credit, $200.
	16	Received payment from Dennie Hoskins for the March 6 sale.
	18	Purchased store equipment on credit from Schmidt Supply, invoice dated March 15, terms n/30, $22,850.
	20	Sold merchandise on credit to Marjorie Allen, invoice #956, $5,600. Cost, $3,400.
	21	Sent Defore Industries cheque #516 in payment of its March 11 invoice less returns.
	22	Received merchandise and an invoice dated March 18, terms 2/10, n/30, from the Welch Company, $41,625.
	26	Issued a credit memorandum to Marjorie Allen for defective merchandise sold on March 22 and returned for credit, $600. The merchandise was scrapped and not returned to inventory.
	31	Issued cheque #517, payable to Payroll, in payment of sales salaries for the month, $15,900. For simplicity, we assume one cheque.
	31	Cash sales for the month were $134,680. (Normally, cash sales are recorded daily; however, they are recorded only once in this problem to reduce the repetitive entries.) Cost, $80,800.
	31	Foot and crossfoot the journals and make the month-end postings.

Required

1. Open the following General Ledger accounts: Cash (101), Accounts Receivable (106), Merchandise Inventory (119), Office Supplies (124), Store Equipment (165), Accounts Payable (201), Long-Term Notes Payable (251), Adrian Pepper, Capital (301), Sales (413), Sales Returns and Allowances (414), Sales Discounts (415), Cost of Goods Sold (502), and Sales Salaries Expense (621).
2. Open the following Accounts Receivable Subledger accounts: Marjorie Allen, Dennie Hoskins, and Jennifer Nelson.
3. Open the following Accounts Payable Subledger accounts: Defore Industries, Mack Company, Schmidt Supply, and Welch Company.
4. Enter the transactions in a Purchases Journal, a Sales Journal, a Cash Receipts Journal, a Cash Disbursements Journal, and a General Journal similar to the ones illustrated in the chapter. Post at the end of the month.
5. Prepare a trial balance and prepare schedules of accounts receivable and payable.

Planning the Solution

- Set up the required General Ledger and subledger accounts and the five required journals as illustrated in the chapter.
- First read and analyze each transaction and decide in which special journal (or General Journal) the transaction would be recorded.
- Now record each transaction in the proper journal, posting to the subledgers as appropriate. Also, post transactions affecting the *Other Accounts* column to the corresponding ledger account.
- Once you have recorded all the transactions, total the journal columns.
- Now post column totals from each journal to the appropriate ledger accounts.
- After you have completed posting, prepare a trial balance to prove the equality of the debit and credit balances in your General Ledger.
- Finally, prepare schedules of accounts receivable and accounts payable.

SOLUTION

Sales Journal					**Page 2**
Date	Account Debited	Invoice No.	PR	Accounts Receivable Dr. Sales Cr.	Cost of Goods Sold/Dr. Merchandise Inventory/Cr.
2014 Mar. 4	Jennifer Nelson	954	✓	16,800	10,100
6	Dennie Hoskins	955	✓	10,200	6,200
20	Marjorie Allen	956	✓	5,600	3,400
31	Totals			32,600	19,700
				(106/413)	(502/119)

Cash Receipts Journal   Page 3

Date	Account Credited	Explanation	PR	Cash Dr.	Sales Discount Dr.	Accounts Receivable Cr.	Sales Cr.	Other Accounts Cr.	Cost of Goods Sold/Dr Merchandise Inventory/Cr.
2014 Mar. 12	L.T. Notes Payable	Note to bank	251	26,000				26,000	
14	Jennifer Nelson	Invoice, Mar. 4	✓	16,464	336	16,800			
16	Dennie Hoskins	Invoice, Mar. 6	✓	9,996	204	10,200			
31	Sales	Cash sales		134,680	—	—	134,680	—	80,800
31	Totals			187,140	540	27,000	134,680	26,000	80,800
				(101)	(415)	(106)	(413)	(X)	(502/119)

Purchases Journal   Page 3

Date	Account Credited	Date of Invoice	Terms	PR	Accounts Payable Cr.	Merchandise Inventory Dr.	Office Supplies Dr.	Other Accounts Dr.
2014 Mar. 6	Office Supplies/Mack Co.	Mar. 3	n/30	✓	1,220		1,220	
11	Defore Industries	Mar. 11	2/10, n/30	✓	52,600	52,600		
18	Store Equipment/Schmidt Supp.	Mar. 15	n/30	165/✓	22,850			22,850
22	Welch Company	Mar. 18	2/10, n/30	✓	41,625	41,625	—	—
31	Totals				118,295	94,225	1,220	22,850
					(201)	(119)	(124)	(X)

Cash Disbursements Journal   Page 4

Date	Ch. No.	Payee	Account Debited	PR	Cash Cr.	Merchandise Inventory Cr.	Other Accounts Dr.	Accounts Payable Dr.
2014 Mar. 21	516	Defore Industries	Defore Industries	✓	51,352	1,048		52,400
31	517	Payroll	Sales Salaries Expense	621	15,900	—	15,900	—
31		Totals			67,252	1,048	15,900	52,400
					(101)	(119)	(X)	(201)

General Journal   Page 2

Mar. 16	Accounts Payable—Defore Industries	201/✓	200	
	Merchandise Inventory	119		200
	Credit memo regarding merchandise returned.			
26	Sales Returns and Allowances.........................	414	600	
	Accounts Receivable—Marjorie Allen	106/✓		600
	Issued credit memo regarding merchandise returned and scrapped.			

Accounts Receivable Subledger

Marjorie Allen

Date	PR	Debit	Credit	Balance
2014 Mar. 20	S2	5,600		5,600
26	G2		600	5,000

Dennie Hoskins

Date	PR	Debit	Credit	Balance
2014 Mar. 6	S2	10,200		10,200
16	CR3		10,200	-0-

Jennifer Nelson

Date	PR	Debit	Credit	Balance
2014 Mar. 4	S2	16,800		16,800
14	CR3		16,800	-0-

Accounts Payable Subledger

Defore Industries

Date	PR	Debit	Credit	Balance
2014 Mar. 11	P3		52,600	52,600
16	G2	200		52,400
21	CD4	52,400		-0-

Mack Company

Date	PR	Debit	Credit	Balance
2014 Mar. 6	P3		1,220	1,220

Schmidt Supply

Date	PR	Debit	Credit	Balance
2014 Mar. 18	P3		22,850	22,850

Welch Company

Date	PR	Debit	Credit	Balance
2014 Mar. 22	P3		41,625	41,625

General Ledger

Cash — Acct. No. 101

Date	Explanation	PR	Debit	Credit	Balance
2014 Mar. 31		CR3	187,140		187,140
31		CD4		67,252	119,888

Accounts Receivable — 106

Date	Explanation	PR	Debit	Credit	Balance
2014 Mar. 26		G2		600	(600)
31		S2	32,600		32,000
31		CR3		27,000	5,000

Merchandise Inventory — 119

Date	Explanation	PR	Debit	Credit	Balance
2014 Mar. 1	Opening Balance				28,400
16		G2		200	28,200
31		S2		19,700	8,500
31		CR3		80,800	(72,300)
31		P3	94,225		21,925
31		CD4		1,048	20,877

Office Supplies — 124

Date	Explanation	PR	Debit	Credit	Balance
2014 Mar. 31		P3	1,220		1,220

Store Equipment — 165

Date	Explanation	PR	Debit	Credit	Balance
2014 Mar. 18		P3	22,850		22,850

Accounts Payable — 201

Date	Explanation	PR	Debit	Credit	Balance
2014 Mar. 16		G2	200		(200)
31		P3		118,295	118,095
31		CD4	52,400		65,695

Long-Term Notes Payable — Acct. No. 251

Date	Explanation	PR	Debit	Credit	Balance
2014 Mar. 12		CR3		26,000	26,000

Adrian Pepper, Capital — 301

Date	Explanation	PR	Debit	Credit	Balance
2014 Mar. 1	Opening Balance				28,400

Sales — 413

Date	Explanation	PR	Debit	Credit	Balance
2014 Mar. 31		S2		32,600	32,600
31		CR3		134,680	167,280

Sales Returns and Allowances — 414

Date	Explanation	PR	Debit	Credit	Balance
2014 Mar. 26		G2	600		600

Sales Discounts — 415

Date	Explanation	PR	Debit	Credit	Balance
2014 Mar. 31		CR3	540		540

Cost of Goods Sold — 502

Date	Explanation	PR	Debit	Credit	Balance
2014 Mar. 31		S2	19,700		19,700
31		CR3	80,800		100,500

Sales Salaries Expense — 621

Date	Explanation	PR	Debit	Credit	Balance
2014 Mar. 31		CD4	15,900		15,900

Pepper Company
Trial Balance
March 31, 2014

Acct.	Title	Debit	Credit
101	Cash	$119,888	
106	Accounts receivable	5,000	
119	Merchandise inventory	20,877	
124	Office supplies	1,220	
165	Store equipment	22,850	
201	Accounts payable		$ 65,695
251	Long-term notes payable		26,000
301	Adrian Pepper, capital		28,400
413	Sales		167,280
414	Sales returns and allowances	600	
415	Sales discounts	540	
502	Cost of goods sold	100,500	
621	Sales salaries expense	15,900	
	Totals	$287,375	$287,375

Pepper Company
Schedule of Accounts Receivable
March 31, 2014

Marjorie Allen	$5,000
Total accounts receivable	$5,000

Pepper Company
Schedule of Accounts Payable
March 31, 2014

Mack Company	$ 1,220
Schmidt Supply	22,850
Welch Company	41,625
Total accounts payable	$65,695

Notice how the totals for both the Schedule of Accounts Receivable and Schedule of Accounts Payable agree to the respective controlling account balances in the trial balance.

APPENDIX 7A

Special Journals Under a Periodic System

LO⁵ Journalize and post transactions using special journals in a periodic inventory system.

This appendix shows the special journals under a periodic inventory system. The Sales Journal and the Cash Receipts Journal each require one column fewer. The Purchases Journal replaces the *Merchandise Inventory Dr.* column with a *Purchases Dr.* column in a periodic system. The Cash Disbursements Journal replaces the *Inventory Cr.* column with a *Purchases Discounts Cr.* column in a periodic system. These changes are illustrated below.

Sales Journal

The Sales Journal for Outdoors Unlimited using the periodic inventory system is shown in Exhibit 7A.1. The difference in the Sales Journal between the perpetual and periodic system is the deletion of the cost of goods sold and merchandise inventory amounts for each sale. The periodic system does not record the increase in cost of goods sold and decrease in inventory at the time of sale.

EXHIBIT 7A.1

Sales Journal—Periodic System

Outdoors Unlimited Sales Journal				Page 3
Date	Account Debited	Invoice Number	PR	Accounts Receivable Dr. Sales Cr.
2014				
Feb. 2	Jason Henry	307	✓	450
7	Albert Co.	308	✓	500
13	Bam Moore	309	✓	350
15	Paul Roth	310	✓	200
22	Jason Henry	311	✓	225
25	Frank Booth	312	✓	175
28	Albert Co.	313	✓	250
28	Total			2,150
				(106/413)

Posting from journals to General Ledger accounts and subledgers in a periodic system is identical to the posting process in a perpetual system.

Cash Receipts Journal

The Cash Receipts Journal under the periodic system is shown in Exhibit 7A.2. Note the deletion of the column on the far right side to record debits to Cost of Goods Sold and credits to Merchandise Inventory for the cost of merchandise sold.

Consistent with the Cash Receipts Journal shown under the perpetual system in the chapter, we only show the weekly cash sale entries.

EXHIBIT 7A.2

Cash Receipts Journal—Periodic System

								Page 2
					Sales	Accounts		Other
	Accounts			Cash	Discount	Receivable	Sales	Accounts
Date	Credited	PR	Explanation	Dr.	Dr.	Cr.	Cr.	Cr.
2014								
Feb. 7	Sales		Cash sales	4,450			4,450	
12	Jason Henry	✓	Invoice, Feb. 2	441	9	450		
14	Sales		Cash sales	3,925			3,925	
17	Albert Co.	✓	Invoice, Feb. 7	490	10	500		
20	Notes Payable	245	Note to bank	750				750
21	Sales		Cash sales	4,700			4,700	
22	Interest Revenue	409	Bank account	250				250
23	Bam Moore	✓	Invoice, Feb. 13	343	7	350		
25	Paul Roth	✓	Invoice, Feb.15	196	4	200		
28	Sales		Cash sales	4,225			4,225	
28	Totals			19,770	30	1,500	17,300	1,000
				(101)	(415)	(106)	(413)	(X)

Outdoors Unlimited Cash Receipts Journal

Purchases Journal

The Purchases Journal under the periodic system is shown in Exhibit 7A.3. This journal in a perpetual system includes the Merchandise Inventory column where the periodic system has the Purchases column. All else is identical under the two systems.

EXHIBIT 7A.3

Purchases Journal—Periodic System

								Page 1
					Accounts		Office	Other
		Date of			Payable	Purchases	Supplies	Accounts
Date	Account Credited	Invoice	Terms	PR	Cr.	Dr.	Dr.	Dr.
2014								
Feb. 3	Hornung Supply Co.	Feb. 2	n/30	✓	350	275	75	
5	Ace Mfg. Co.	5	2/10, n/30	✓	200	200		
13	Wynet & Co.	10	2/10, n/30	✓	150	150		
20	Smite Co.	18	2/10, n/30	✓	300	300		
25	Ace Mfg. Co.	24	2/10, n/30	✓	100	100		
28	Store Supplies/ITT Co.	28	n/30	125/✓	225	125	25	75
28	Totals				1,325	1,150	100	75
					(201)	(505)	(124)	(X)

Outdoors Unlimited Purchases Journal

Cash Disbursements Journal

The Cash Disbursements Journal in a periodic system is shown in Exhibit 7A.4. This journal includes the Purchases Discounts column where the perpetual system had the Merchandise Inventory column. All else is identical under the two systems. When a company has several cash purchases of inventory, it often adds a new column for Purchases Debit entries.

EXHIBIT 7A.4

Cash Disbursements Journal—Periodic System

Outdoors Unlimited Cash Disbursements Journal								Page 2
Date	Ch. No.	Payee	Account Debited	PR	Cash Cr.	Purchases Discounts Cr.	Other Accounts Dr.	Accounts Payable Dr.
2014								
Feb. 3	105	L & N Railroad	Transportation-In	508	15		15	
5	106	East Sales Co.	Purchases	505	25		25	
13	107	Ace Mfg. Co.	Ace Mfg. Co.	✓	196	4		200
20	108	Jerry Hale	Salaries Expense	622	250		250	
25	109	Wynet & Co.	Wynet & Co.	✓	147	3		150
28	110	Smite Co.	Smite Co.	✓	294	6		300
28		Totals			927	13	290	650
					(101)	(507)	(X)	(201)

SUMMARY OF APPENDIX 7A

LO⁵ Journalize and post transactions using special journals in a periodic inventory system. Transactions are journalized and posted using special journals in a periodic system. The methods are similar to those in a perpetual system. The primary difference is that cost of goods sold and inventory do not need adjusting at the time of each sale. This normally results in the deletion of one or more columns in each special journal devoted to these accounts.

GLOSSARY

Accounting information system (AIS) The people, records, methods, and equipment that collect and process data from transactions, organize them in useful forms, and communicate results to decision makers.

Accounts Payable Subledger A subsidiary ledger listing individual credit supplier accounts.

Accounts Receivable Subledger A subsidiary ledger listing individual credit customer accounts.

Cash Disbursements Journal The special journal that is used to record all payments of cash; also called *Cash Payments Journal*.

Cash Receipts Journal The special journal that is used to record all receipts of cash.

Cheque Register Another name for a Cash Disbursements Journal when the journal has a column for cheque numbers.

Columnar journal A journal with more than one column.

Computer hardware The physical equipment in a computerized accounting information system.

Computer software The programs that direct the operations of computer hardware.

Controlling account A General Ledger account, the balance of which (after posting) equals the sum of the balances of the accounts in a related subsidiary ledger.

Crossfoot To add debit and credit column totals and compare the sums for equality.

Enterprise-application software Programs that manage a company's vital operations, which range from order-taking programs to manufacturing to accounting.

Foot To add a column of numbers.

Management information system (MIS) Designed to collect and process data within an organization for the purpose of providing users with information.

Purchases Journal A journal that is used to record all purchases on credit.

Sales Journal A journal used to record sales of merchandise on credit.

Schedule of accounts payable A list of the balances of all the accounts in the Accounts Payable Subledger that is summed to show the total amount of accounts payable outstanding.

Schedule of accounts receivable A list of the balances of all the accounts in the Accounts Receivable Subledger that is summed to show the total amount of accounts receivable outstanding.

Special journal Any journal that is used for recording and posting transactions of a similar type.

Subledger See *subsidiary ledger*.

Subsidiary ledger A listing of individual accounts with a common characteristic.

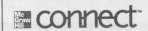 Visit **Connect** for additional study tools, practice quizzes, to search an interactive eBook, and much more.

CONCEPT REVIEW QUESTIONS

1. Refer to the chapter opening story. Identify all of the special journals and subledgers that Marissa McTasney could likely be using for Moxie Trades.

2. When special journals are used, separate special journals normally record each of four different types of transactions. What are these four types of transactions?

3. Why should sales to and receipts of cash from credit customers be recorded and posted daily?

4. Both credits to customer accounts and credits to miscellaneous accounts are individually posted from a Cash Receipts Journal similar to the one in Exhibit 7.10. Why not put both kinds of credits in the same column?

5. When a General Journal entry is used to record a returned credit sale, the credit of the entry must be posted twice. Does this cause the trial balance to be out of balance? Why or why not?

6. What notations are entered into the Posting Reference column of a ledger account?

Note 1: *End-of-chapter items do not include consideration of GST/PST unless stated otherwise.*
Note 2: *When setting up General Ledger accounts, recall that a Chart of Accounts is provided at the end of the textbook, in Appendix III, to assist you in numbering your accounts.*

QS 7-1 AIS and source documents LO¹

Refer to Exhibit 7.2. Identify which component of the AIS would process each of the following source documents:

	Accounts Payable (AP) Accounts Receivable (AR) Payroll (P)
1. Time cards from employees	_____
2. Sales invoice; terms 2/10, n/30	_____
3. Deposit slip regarding cash collections from credit customers	_____
4. Cheque written to pay account with supplier	_____

QS 7-2 Inputs and outputs of AIS LO¹

Refer to Exhibit 7.3. Identify each of the following as an *input to* or an *output from* an AIS:

	Input (I) or Output (O)
1. Bank statement	_____
2. Sales invoice issued to customer	_____
3. Schedule of accounts payable	_____
4. Income statement	_____
5. Purchase order issued to supplier	_____
6. Schedule detailing property, plant and equipment	_____
7. Report detailing employee absences/minutes late	_____
8. Memorandum issued by supplier regarding defective merchandise	_____

QS 7-3 Special journal identification LO²

Trenton Iron Works uses a Sales Journal, a Purchases Journal, a Cash Receipts Journal, a Cash Disbursements Journal, and a General Journal. Trenton recently completed the following transactions. List the transaction letters and, next to each letter, give the name of the journal in which the transaction should be recorded.

a. Sold merchandise on credit.
b. Purchased shop supplies on credit.
c. Paid an employee's salary.
d. Paid a creditor.
e. Purchased merchandise on credit.
f. Borrowed money from the bank.
g. Sold merchandise for cash.

QS 7-4 Entries belonging to the General Journal—perpetual LO²

The Nostalgic Book Shop uses a Sales Journal, a Purchases Journal, a Cash Receipts Journal, a Cash Disbursements Journal, and a General Journal. The following transactions occurred during the month of November. Journalize the November transactions that should be recorded in the General Journal, assuming a perpetual inventory system.

Nov.	2	Purchased merchandise on credit for $2,900 from the Ringdol Co., terms 2/10, n/30.
	12	The owner, Jesse Cooke, contributed an automobile worth $15,000 to the business.
	16	Sold merchandise on credit to R. Wyder for $1,100, terms n/30; cost, $700.
	19	R. Wyder returned $150 (cost, $95) of merchandise originally purchased on November 16. The merchandise was returned to inventory.
	28	Returned $170 of defective merchandise to the Ringdol Co. from the November 2 purchase.

QS 7-5 Accounts Receivable Subledger LO3

Identify the effect caused by each of the following transactions on the Accounts Receivable Subledger:

	Debit (DR), Credit (CR), or No Effect (NE)
1. Sale of merchandise on credit.	_____
2. Purchase of merchandise on credit.	_____
3. Closing of revenue accounts at year-end.	_____
4. Receipt of cash from credit customer.	_____
5. Payment to supplier.	_____
6. Credit memo issued to customer regarding defective merchandise returned.	_____
7. Accrued wages payable at month-end.	_____

QS 7-6 Accounts Payable Subledger LO3

Identify the effect caused by each of the following transactions on the Accounts Payable Subledger:

	Debit (DR), Credit (CR), or No Effect (NE)
1. Purchase of merchandise on credit.	_____
2. Sale of merchandise on credit.	_____
3. Purchase of office supplies on credit.	_____
4. Receipt of cash from credit customer.	_____
5. Payment to supplier.	_____
6. Memorandum issued by supplier regarding defective merchandise returned.	_____
7. Closing of Income Summary to Capital at year-end.	_____

QS 7-7 Sales Journal—perpetual LO4

On a sheet of notebook paper, draw a Sales Journal like the one that appears in Exhibit 7.8 and journalize the following March 2014 sales transactions for Suttleton Company.

Mar.	3	Sold $3,000 of merchandise to Tim Edson (cost $2,040); terms 2/15, n/30; invoice #1103.
	10	$10,800 of merchandise was sold to Willis Company (cost $7,344); terms 2/15, n/30; invoice #1104.
	11	Ellton Kingston purchased $7,400 of merchandise (cost $5,032); terms 2/15, n/30; invoice #1105.

QS 7-8 Cash Receipts Journal—perpetual LO⁴

On a sheet of notebook paper, draw a Cash Receipts Journal like the one in Exhibit 7.10 and journalize the following March 2014 cash receipts transactions for Suttleton Company.

Mar.	18	Collected the amount owing regarding the $3,000 of merchandise sold to Tim Edson on March 3; terms 2/15, n/30; invoice #1103.
	30	Willis Company paid for the $10,800 of merchandise purchased on March 10; terms 2/15, n/30; invoice #1104.
	31	Sold $6,200 of merchandise to ABC Company for cash (cost $4,216).

QS 7-9 Purchases Journal—perpetual LO⁴

On a sheet of notebook paper, draw a Purchases Journal like the one that appears in Exhibit 7.12 and journalize the following March 2014 transactions for Suttleton Company.

Mar.	2	Purchased $4,800 of merchandise from Tex Company; terms 3/10, n/20.
	12	$14,000 of merchandise was purchased from Littleton; terms 2/15, n/30.
	13	Worsley Company sold Suttleton $9,400 of office furniture; terms 2/15, n/45.

QS 7-10 Cash Disbursements Journal—perpetual LO⁴

On a sheet of notebook paper, draw a Cash Disbursements Journal like the one that appears in Exhibit 7.13 and journalize the following March 2014 payments for Suttleton Company (assume the first cheque is #101).

Mar.	14	Paid for the $4,800 March 2 purchase from Tex Company; terms 3/10, n/20.
	27	Paid for the $14,000 purchase of merchandise from Littleton on March 12; terms 2/15, n/30.
	31	Paid Thorn Real Estate Management for the March rent; $6,500.

EXERCISES

Exercise 7-1 Sales Journal—perpetual LO⁴

Spindle Company uses a Sales Journal, a Purchases Journal, a Cash Receipts Journal, a Cash Disbursements Journal, and a General Journal. The following transactions occurred during the month of February 2014:

Feb.	2	Sold merchandise to S. Mayer for $450 cash, invoice #5703. Cost, $200.
	5	Purchased merchandise on credit from Camp Corp., $2,300.
	7	Sold merchandise to J. Eason for $1,150, terms 2/10, n/30, invoice #5704. Cost, $700.
	8	Borrowed $8,000 by giving a note to the bank.
	12	Sold merchandise to P. Lathan for $320, terms n/30, invoice #5705. Cost, $170.
	16	Received $1,127 from J. Eason to pay for the purchase of February 7.
	19	Sold used store equipment to Whiten, Inc., for $900 cash.
	25	Sold merchandise to S. Summers for $550, terms n/30, invoice #5706. Cost, $300.

Required On a sheet of notebook paper, draw a Sales Journal like the one that appears in Exhibit 7.8. Journalize the February transactions that should be recorded in the Sales Journal.

*Exercise 7-2 Sales Journal—periodic LO⁵

Using the information in Exercise 7-1, complete the requirements assuming a periodic inventory system.

An asterisk (*) identifies assignment material based on Appendix 7A.

Exercise 7-3 Cash Receipts Journal—perpetual LO⁴

StickUps Company uses a Sales Journal, a Purchases Journal, a Cash Receipts Journal, a Cash Disbursements Journal, and a General Journal. The following transactions occurred during the month of September 2014:

Sept.	3	Purchased merchandise on credit for $6,200 from Pacer Co.
	7	Sold merchandise on credit to J. Namal for $1,800, subject to a 2% sales discount if paid by the end of the month. Cost, $1,000.
	9	Borrowed $5,500 by giving a note to the bank.
	13	The owner, Dale Trent, invested an additional $7,000 cash into the business.
	18	Sold merchandise to B. Baird for $460 cash. Cost, $280.
	22	Paid Pacer Co. $6,200 for the merchandise purchased on September 3.
	27	Received $1,764 from J. Namal in payment of the September 7 purchase.
	30	Paid salaries of $3,200.

Required On a sheet of notebook paper, draw a multicolumn Cash Receipts Journal like the one that appears in Exhibit 7.10. Journalize the September transactions that should be recorded in the Cash Receipts Journal.

*Exercise 7-4 Cash Receipts Journal—periodic LO⁵

Using the information in Exercise 7-3, complete the requirements assuming a periodic inventory system.

Exercise 7-5 Purchases Journal—perpetual LO⁴

Chem Company uses a Sales Journal, a Purchases Journal, a Cash Receipts Journal, a Cash Disbursements Journal, and a General Journal. The following transactions occurred during the month of July 2014:

July	1	Purchased merchandise on credit for $8,100 from Angler, Inc., terms n/30.
	8	Sold merchandise on credit to B. Harren for $1,500, subject to a $30 sales discount if paid by the end of the month. Cost, $820.
	10	The owner of Chem Company, Pat Johnson, invested $2,000 cash.
	14	Purchased store supplies from Steck Company on credit for $240, terms 2/10, n/30.
	17	Purchased merchandise inventory on credit from Marten Company for $2,600, terms n/30.
	24	Sold merchandise to W. Winger for $630 cash. Cost, $350.
	28	Purchased merchandise inventory from Hadley's for $9,000 cash.
	29	Paid Angler, Inc., $8,100 for the merchandise purchased on July 1.

Required On a sheet of notebook paper, draw a multicolumn Purchases Journal like the one that appears in Exhibit 7.12. Journalize the July transactions that should be recorded in the Purchases Journal.

*Exercise 7-6 Purchases Journal—periodic LO⁵

Using the information in Exercise 7-5, complete the requirements assuming a periodic inventory system.

Exercise 7-7 Cash Disbursements Journal—perpetual LO⁴

Xion Supply uses a Sales Journal, a Purchases Journal, a Cash Receipts Journal, a Cash Disbursements Journal, and a General Journal. The following transactions occurred during the month of March 2014:

Mar.	3	Purchased merchandise for $5,500 on credit from Pace, Inc., terms 2/10, n/30.
	9	Issued cheque #210 to Narlin Corp. to buy store supplies for $900.
	12	Sold merchandise on credit to K. Camp for $1,340, terms n/30. Cost, $800.
	17	Issued cheque #211 for $3,000 to repay a note payable to City Bank.
	20	Purchased merchandise for $7,000 on credit from LeBaron, terms 2/10, n/30.
	29	Issued cheque #212 to LeBaron to pay the amount due for the purchase of March 20, less the discount.
	31	Paid salary of $3,400 to E. Brandon by issuing cheque #213.
	31	Issued cheque #214 to Pace, Inc., to pay the amount due for the purchase of March 3.

Required On a sheet of notebook paper, draw a multicolumn Cash Disbursements Journal like the one that appears in Exhibit 7.13. Journalize the March transactions that should be recorded in the Cash Disbursements Journal.

An asterisk (*) identifies assignment material based on Appendix 7A.

*Exercise 7-8 Cash Disbursements Journal—periodic LO[5]

Using the information in Exercise 7-7, complete the requirements assuming a periodic inventory system.

Exercise 7-9 Special journal transactions—perpetual LO[4]

On May 11, 2014, Wilson Purchasing purchased $30,000 of merchandise from Hostel Sales; terms 3/10, n/90, FOB Hostel Sales. The cost of the goods to Hostel was $20,000. Wilson issued cheque #84 in the amount of $335 to pay Express Shipping Service for the delivery charges on the merchandise on May 11. On May 12, Wilson returned $1,200 of goods to Hostel Sales, which restored them to inventory. The returned goods had cost Hostel $800. On May 20, Wilson mailed cheque #85 to Hostel for the amount owed on that date. Hostel received and recorded the cheque on May 21.

Required

1. Record the transactions for Wilson Purchasing in a Purchases Journal, Cash Disbursements Journal, and General Journal as appropriate.

2. Record the transactions for Hostel Sales in a Sales Journal, Cash Receipts Journal, and General Journal as appropriate. Assume invoice #1601 for the May 11 sale.

*Exercise 7-10 Special journal transactions—periodic LO[5]

Using the information in Exercise 7-9, complete the requirements assuming a periodic inventory system.

Required

1. Record the transactions for Wilson Purchasing in a Purchases Journal, Cash Disbursements Journal, and General Journal as appropriate.

2. Record the transactions for Hostel Sales in a Sales Journal, Cash Receipts Journal, and General Journal as appropriate.

Exercise 7-11 Special journal transactions—perpetual LO[4]

Simon Pharmacy uses the following journals: Sales Journal, Purchases Journal, Cash Receipts Journal, Cash Disbursements Journal, and General Journal. On June 5, Simon purchased merchandise priced at $24,000, subject to credit terms of 2/10, n/30. On June 14, the pharmacy paid the net amount due. However, in journalizing the payment, the bookkeeper debited Accounts Payable for $24,000 and failed to record the cash discount. Cash was credited for the actual amount paid. In what journals would the transactions of June 5 and June 14 have been recorded? What procedure is likely to discover the error in journalizing the June 14 transaction?

Exercise 7-12 Errors related to the Purchases Journal—perpetual LO[4]

A company that records credit purchases in a Purchases Journal and records purchase returns in its General Journal made the following errors. List each error by letter and, opposite each letter, tell when the error should be discovered:

a. Made an addition error in determining the balance of a creditor's account.

b. Made an addition error in totalling the Office Supplies column of the Purchases Journal.

c. Posted a purchase return to the Accounts Payable account and to the creditor's account but did not post to the Merchandise Inventory account.

d. Posted a purchase return to the Merchandise Inventory account and to the Accounts Payable account but did not post to the creditor's account.

e. Correctly recorded a $4,000 purchase in the Purchases Journal but posted it to the creditor's account as a $400 purchase.

Exercise 7-13 Posting to subledger accounts—perpetual LO⁴

At the end of May 2014, the Sales Journal of Value-Mart Goods appeared as follows:

	Sales Journal				Page 4
Date	Account Debited	Invoice Number	PR	A/R Dr. Sales Cr.	Cost of Goods Sold Dr. Merchandise Inventory Cr.
2014 May 6	Brad Smithers	190		5,760.00	3,200.00
10	Dan Holland	191		3,880.00	2,200.00
17	Sanders Farrell	192		1,700.00	1,000.00
25	Dan Holland	193		680.00	260.00
31	Totals			12,020.00	6,660.00

Value-Mart had also recorded the return of merchandise with the following General Journal entry:

May 20	Sales Returns and Allowances	500	
	Accounts Receivable—Sanders Farrell ...		500
	Merchandise Inventory	260	
	Cost of Goods Sold		260
	Customer returned merchandise.		

Required

1. On a sheet of notebook paper, open an Accounts Receivable Subledger that has a T-account for each customer listed in the Sales Journal. Post to the customer accounts the entries in the Sales Journal and any portion of the General Journal entry that affects a customer's account.

2. Open a General Ledger that has T-accounts for Accounts Receivable, Sales, and Sales Returns and Allowances. Post the Sales Journal and any portion of the General Journal entry that affects these accounts. Calculate the ending balance for each account.

3. Prepare a schedule of the accounts in the Accounts Receivable Subledger and add their balances to show that the total equals the balance in the Accounts Receivable controlling account.

*Exercise 7-14 Posting from special journals and subledgers to T-accounts—periodic system LO⁵

Following are the condensed journals of Wilson Bakery Supplies. The journal column headings are incomplete in that they do not indicate whether the columns are debit or credit columns. Assume a periodic inventory system.

Sales Journal	
Account	Amount
Jack Hertz..................................	7,400
Trudy Stone	16,800
Dave Waylon............................	2,000
Total	26,200

Purchases Journal	
Account	Amount
Grass Corp.	10,800
Sulter, Inc..................................	9,000
McGrew Company..................	3,400
Total	23,200

Sales Returns and Allowances..........................	600	
Accounts Receivable—Jack Hertz...........		600
Customer returned merchandise.		
Accounts Payable—Grass Corp.......................	1,500	
Purchase Returns and Allowances..........		1,500
Returned merchandise.		

Cash Receipts Journal					
Account	Other Accounts	Accounts Receivable	Sales	Sales Discounts	Cash
Jack Hertz..................................		6,800		136	6,664
Sales			4,500		4,500
Notes Payable	9,000				9,000
Sales			1,250		1,250
Trudy Stone		16,800		336	16,464
Store Equipment	1,000				1,000
Totals..	10,000	23,600	5,750	472	38,878

Cash Disbursements Journal				
Account	Other Accounts	Accounts Payable	Purchase Discounts	Cash
Prepaid Insurance......................	1,700			1,700
Sulter, Inc.		9,000	270	8,730
Grass Corp................................		9,300	186	9,114
Store Equipment......................	3,500			3,500
Totals..	5,200	18,300	456	23,044

Required

1. Prepare T-accounts on notebook paper for the following General Ledger and subledger accounts. Separate the accounts of each ledger group as follows:

General Ledger Accounts
   Cash
   Accounts Receivable
   Prepaid Insurance
   Store Equipment
   Accounts Payable
   Notes Payable
   Sales
   Sales Discounts
   Sales Returns and Allowances
   Purchases

   Purchase Discounts
   Purchase Returns and Allowances

Accounts Receivable Subledger Accounts
   Jack Hertz
   Trudy Stone
   Dave Waylon

Accounts Payable Subledger Accounts
   Grass Corp.
   McGrew Company
   Sulter, Inc.

2. Without referring to any of the illustrations in the chapter that show complete column headings for the journals, post the journals to the proper T-accounts. Ignore dates.

An asterisk (*) identifies assignment material based on Appendix 7A.

Problem 7-1A Special journals and subledgers—perpetual LO^{2,3,4}

Moore Corporation is a major distributor of office supplies. *All sales are on terms 1/10, n/15.* During March, the following selected transactions occurred. For each transaction, identify into which special journal it should be journalized. Also indicate which subledger(s) is (are) affected. Use the list of codes to label your answers. Moore Corporation uses a perpetual inventory system.

Special Journals	
Sales	S
Purchases	P
Cash Receipts	CR
Cash Disbursements	CD
General Journal	G

Subledgers	
Accounts Receivable	AR
Accounts Payable	AP
Merchandise Inventory	MI
No Effect	NE

Date		Transaction	Special Journal	Subledger(s)
Mar.	1	Sold merchandise on credit.		
	2	Defective merchandise sold on March 1 was returned by the customer. It was scrapped.		
	3	Purchased office equipment on credit terms n/30.		
	5	Received payment regarding the March 1 sale.		
	10	Received a credit memorandum from the supplier regarding defective equipment purchased on March 3.		
	14	Sold merchandise for cash.		
	16	Purchased merchandise inventory on credit; terms 1/5, n/30.		
	17	Paid the balance owing on the March 3 transaction.		
	18	Purchased merchandise inventory for cash.		
	21	Paid for the merchandise purchased on March 16.		
	22	Sold old equipment for cash.		
	30	Paid salaries for the month of March.		
	30	Accrued utilities for the month of March.		
	30	Closed the credit balance in the Income Summary to Capital.		

Problem 7-2A Special journals—perpetual LO⁴

Janish Supplies completed the transactions listed below during April 2014. *All sales are on terms 2/10, n/30.*

April	2	Sold merchandise to Tim Bennett for $35,000 on credit; invoice #306 (cost $22,750).
	3	Cash sales for the day totalled $15,000; invoices #307 to #310 (cost $9,750).
	4	Purchased $48,000 of merchandise from Wallace Brothers; terms 1/10, n/30.
	5	Sold merchandise to Brian Kennedy for $42,000 on credit; invoice #311 (cost $27,300).
	6	Returned $4,200 of defective merchandise purchased on April 4.
	9	Purchased $230 of office supplies; cheque #620.
	11	Purchased $56,000 of merchandise from McKinley & Sons; terms n/30.
	12	Received payment from Tim Bennett regarding the sale of April 2.
	13	Paid for the merchandise purchased on April 4; cheque #621.
	16	Sold merchandise to Wynne Walsh for $14,000 on credit; invoice #312 (cost $9,100).
	19	Issued a credit memo regarding a $3,000 allowance granted to Wynne Walsh to cover defective merchandise sold on April 16.
	20	Received payment from Brian Kennedy for the sale of April 5.
	23	Purchased $3,800 of equipment from Zardon Company; terms 1/15, n/30.
	24	Sold merchandise to Brian Kennedy for $18,000 on credit; invoice #313 (cost $11,700).
	26	Paid for the purchase of April 11; cheque #622.
	27	Received payment from Wynne Walsh regarding the sale of April 16.
	30	Paid April salaries; $36,000; cheque #623. For simplicity, we assume one cheque.

Required

1. Prepare a Sales Journal, Cash Receipts Journal, Purchases Journal, Cash Disbursements Journal, and General Journal like the ones illustrated in this chapter.

2. Journalize the April transactions into the appropriate journal *(do not post to the subledgers or the General Ledger)*.

Problem 7-3A Special journals, subledgers—perpetual LO⁴

Newton Company completed these transactions during April 2014. *The terms of all credit sales are 2/10, n/30.*

Apr.	2	Purchased merchandise on credit from Baskin Company, invoice dated April 2, terms 2/10, n/60, $12,800.
	3	Sold merchandise on credit to Linda Hobart, invoice #760, $3,200. Cost, $1,900.
	3	Purchased office supplies on credit from Eau Claire Inc., $1,340. Invoice dated April 2, terms n/10 EOM.
	4	Issued cheque #587 to *The Record* for advertising expense, $1,020.
	5	Sold merchandise on credit to Paul Abrams, invoice #761, $9,400. Cost, $5,600.
	6	Received an $85 credit memorandum from Eau Claire Inc. for office supplies received on April 3 and returned for credit.
	9	Purchased store equipment on credit from Frank's Supply, invoice dated April 9, terms n/10 EOM, $10,500.
	11	Sold merchandise on credit to Kelly Schaefer, invoice #762, $10,000. Cost, $6,000.
	12	Issued cheque #588 to Baskin Company in payment of its April 2 invoice.
	13	Received payment from Linda Hobart for the April 3 sale.
	13	Sold merchandise on credit to Linda Hobart, invoice #763, $5,200. Cost, $3,100.
	14	Received payment from Paul Abrams for the April 5 sale.
	16	Issued cheque #589, payable to Payroll, in payment of the sales salaries for the first half of the month, $9,500. For simplicity, we assume one cheque.
	16	Cash sales for the first half of the month were $54,000. Cost, $32,400. *Cash sales are usually recorded daily from the cash register readings. However, they are recorded only once in this problem to reduce the repetitive transactions.*

Required

1. Set up Accounts Receivable Subledger accounts for Paul Abrams, Linda Hobart, and Kelly Schaefer.

2. Set up Accounts Payable Subledger accounts for Frank's Supply, Baskin Company, Sprocket Company, and Eau Claire Inc.

3. Journalize the transactions of Newton Company into the appropriate special journal, posting to the subledgers where required. Use page 3 for all journals.

CHECK FIGURE:
5. Trial balance
= $506,105

Problem 7-4A Special journals, subledgers, schedules of accounts receivable and accounts payable, and trial balance—perpetual LO⁴

This is a continuation of Problem 7-3A. You must complete Problem 7-3A before attempting this problem. Additional transactions for April follow:

Apr.	17	Purchased merchandise on credit from Sprocket Company, invoice dated April 16, terms 2/10, n/30, $12,750.
	18	Borrowed $50,000 from First Bank by giving a long-term note payable.
	20	Received payment from Kelly Schaefer for the April 11 sale.
	20	Purchased store supplies on credit from Frank's Supply, invoice dated April 19, terms n/10 EOM, $650.
	23	Received a $400 credit memorandum from Sprocket Company for defective merchandise received on April 17 and returned.
	23	Received payment from Linda Hobart for the April 13 sale.
	25	Purchased merchandise on credit from Baskin Company, invoice dated April 24, terms 2/10, n/60, $10,900.
	26	Issued cheque #590 to Sprocket Company in payment of its April 16 invoice.
	27	Sold merchandise on credit to Paul Abrams, invoice #764, $3,800. Cost, $2,300.
	27	Sold merchandise on credit to Kelly Schaefer, invoice #765, $6,200. Cost, $3,800.
	30	Issued cheque #591, payable to Payroll, in payment of the sales salaries for the last half of the month, $9,500. For simplicity, we assume one cheque.
	30	Cash sales for the last half of the month were $69,000. Cost, $41,400.

Required

1. Set up the following General Ledger accounts: Cash (101); Accounts Receivable (106); Merchandise Inventory (119); Office Supplies (124); Store Supplies (125); Store Equipment (165); Accounts Payable (201); Long-Term Notes Payable (251); Jeff Newton, Capital (301); Sales (413); Sales Discounts (415); Cost of Goods Sold (502); Sales Salaries Expense (621); and Advertising Expense (655). Enter the March 31 balances of $167,000 for Cash; $105,000 for Merchandise Inventory; $105,000 for Jeff Newton, Capital; and $167,000 for Long-Term Notes Payable.

2. Continuing from Problem 7-3A, journalize the remaining April transactions for Newton Company into the appropriate special journal, posting to the subledgers as required.

3. Post the items that should be posted as individual amounts from the journals.

4. Foot and crossfoot the journals and make the month-end postings.

5. Prepare a trial balance of the General Ledger and prepare schedules of accounts receivable and accounts payable.

Analysis Component: Assume that the sum of the account balances on the schedule of accounts receivable does not equal the balance of the controlling amount in the General Ledger. Describe the steps you would go through to discover the error(s).

(If the Working Papers that accompany this textbook are not being used, the forms needed to complete this problem are available on Connect.)

CHECK FIGURE:
4. Trial balance =
$221,073

Problem 7-5A Special journals, subledgers, schedules of accounts receivable and accounts payable, and trial balance—perpetual LO⁴

It is October 16, 2014, and you have just taken over the accounting work of Saskan Enterprises, whose annual accounting period ends each October 31. The company's previous accountant journalized its transactions through October 15 and posted all items that required posting as individual amounts, as an examination of the journals and ledgers in the Working Papers will show.

The company completed these transactions beginning on October 16, 2014:

Oct. 16   Sold merchandise on credit to Vickie Foresman, invoice #916, $7,500. Cost, $3,750. *Terms of all credit sales are 2/10, n/30.*
      17   Received a $1,090 credit memorandum from Shore Company for merchandise received on October 15 and returned for credit.
      17   Purchased office supplies on credit from Brown Supply Company, $580. Invoice dated October 16, terms n/10 EOM.
      18   Received a $40 credit memorandum from Brown Supply Company for office supplies received on October 17 and returned for credit.
      20   Issued a credit memorandum to Amy Ihrig for defective merchandise sold on October 15 and returned for credit, $500. The returned merchandise was scrapped.
      21   Purchased store equipment on credit from Brown Supply Company, invoice dated October 21, terms n/10 EOM, $7,200.
      22   Received payment from Vickie Foresman for the October 12 sale.
      23   Issued cheque #623 to Sunshine Company in payment of its October 15 invoice.
      24   Sold merchandise on credit to Bill Grigsby, invoice #917, $1,400. Cost, $750.
      24   Issued cheque #624 to Shore Company in payment of its October 15 invoice.
      25   Received payment from Amy Ihrig for the October 15 sale.
      26   Received merchandise and an invoice dated October 25, terms 2/10, n/60, from Sunshine Company, $7,900.
      29   Sold a neighbouring merchant five boxes of file folders (office supplies) for cash at cost, $50.
      30   Ken Shaw, the owner of Saskan Enterprises, used cheque #625 to withdraw $2,500 cash from the business for personal use.
      31   Issued cheque #626 to Jamie Green, the company's only sales employee, in payment of her salary for the last half of October, $2,200.
      31   Issued cheque #627 to Countywide Electric Company in payment of the October electric bill, $680.
      31   Cash sales for the last half of the month were $31,000. Cost, $15,500. *Cash sales are usually recorded daily but are recorded only twice in this problem to reduce the repetitive transactions.*

Required

1. Record the transactions in the journals provided.

2. Post to the customer and creditor accounts and also post any amounts that should be posted as individual amounts to the General Ledger accounts. (Normally, these amounts are posted daily, but they are posted only once by you in this problem because they are few in number.)

3. Foot and crossfoot the journals and make the month-end postings.

4. Prepare an October 31 trial balance and prepare schedules of accounts receivable and accounts payable.

CHECK FIGURE:
Total COGS for
January = $727.00

Problem 7-6A Inventory Subledger—perpetual LO⁴

The Turner Company sells a product called TurnUp for $25 each and uses a perpetual inventory system to account for its merchandise. The beginning balance of TurnUps and transactions during January 2014 were as follows:

Jan. 1   Balance: 25 units costing $8 each.
      3   Purchased from Curtis & Sons 50 units costing $9 each.
      7   Sold to G. Little 20 units, invoice #103.
      19 Sold to B. Moore 15 units, invoice #104.
      20 Purchased from Norton Industries 30 units costing $11 each.
      24 Sold to C. Woudstra 15 units, invoice #105.
      29 Sold to D. Isla 32 units, invoice #106.

Required Journalize the January transactions in the Sales and Purchases Journal. Use page 1 for each journal. *Assume all sales and purchases are on credit; terms n/30.* Under the assumption that the company keeps its records on a FIFO basis, you will need to enter the beginning balances and post each transaction on an inventory subledger record like the one illustrated in Exhibit 7.6 in order to determine cost of goods sold for each sale.

*Problem 7-7A Special journals, subledgers—periodic LO[5]

Using the information in Problem 7-3A, complete the requirements assuming a periodic inventory system.

*Problem 7-8A Special journals, subledgers, schedules of accounts receivable and accounts payable, and trial balance—periodic LO[5]

*You must complete *Problem 7-7A before attempting this problem.* Using the information in Problem 7-4A, complete the following requirements assuming a periodic inventory system:

1. Set up the following General Ledger accounts: Cash (101); Accounts Receivable (106); Merchandise Inventory (119); Office Supplies (124); Store Supplies (125); Store Equipment (165); Accounts Payable (201); Long-Term Notes Payable (251); Jeff Newton, Capital (301); Sales (413); Sales Discounts (415); Purchases (505); Purchase Discounts (506); Purchase Returns and Allowances (507); Sales Salaries Expense (621); and Advertising Expense (655). Enter the March 31 balances of $167,000 for Cash; $105,000 for Merchandise Inventory; $105,000 for Jeff Newton, Capital; and $167,000 for Long-Term Notes Payable.

2. Continuing from *Problem 7-7A, journalize the remaining April transactions for Newton Company into the appropriate special journals, posting to the subledgers where required.

3. Post the items that should be posted as individual amounts from the journals.

4. Foot and crossfoot the journals and make the month-end postings.

5. Prepare a trial balance of the General Ledger and prepare schedules of accounts receivable and accounts payable.

ALTERNATE PROBLEMS

Problem 7-1B Special journals and subledgers—perpetual LO[2,3]

Lavender Gifts and Novelties uses a perpetual inventory system. *All sales are on terms of 2/15, n/30.* During May, the following selected transactions occurred. Identify into which special journal each transaction should be journalized. Also indicate which subledger(s) is (are) affected. Use the list of codes to label your answers. Assume a perpetual inventory system.

Special Journals		Subledgers	
Sales	S	Accounts Receivable...........................	AR
Purchases..	P	Accounts Payable	AP
Cash Receipts......................................	CR	Merchandise Inventory......................	MI
Cash Disbursements.........................	CD	No Effect..	NE
General Journal	G		

Date	Transaction	Special Journal	Subledger(s)
May 1	The owner invested an automobile into the business.		
2	Sold merchandise and received cash.		
3	Purchased merchandise inventory on credit; terms 1/5, n/30.		
4	Sold merchandise on credit.		
5	The customer of May 4 returned defective merchandise; the merchandise was scrapped.		
6	Regarding the May 3 purchase, received a credit memorandum from the supplier granting an allowance.		
15	Paid mid-month salaries.		
17	Purchased office supplies on credit; terms n/30.		
19	Paid for the balance owing on the May 3 purchase.		
22	Received payment on the May 4 sale.		
25	Borrowed money from the bank.		
29	Purchased merchandise inventory; paid cash.		
30	Accrued interest revenue.		
30	Closed all revenue accounts to the Income Summary account.		

An asterisk (*) identifies assignment material based on Appendix 7A.

Problem 7-2B Special journals—perpetual LO⁴

Fraser Antiques completed the transactions listed below during June 2014. *All sales are on terms 2/10, n/30.*

June	1	Purchased equipment costing $22,500 from Exeter Equipment; terms n/30.
	4	Purchased a collection of antiques for $42,500 from Whitby Co.; terms 1/5, n/15.
	5	Sold a group of antiques to Martha Stohart for $51,000 on credit; invoice #347 (cost $25,500).
	6	Sold an antique to Carol Larson for $4,100 on credit; invoice #348 (cost $2,850).
	7	Received an allowance of $2,400 regarding the June 4 purchase due to damages that occurred during delivery.
	8	Purchased office supplies of $900 from Suppliers Unlimited; terms 2/10, n/30.
	11	Paid for the purchase of June 4; cheque #101.
	12	Received payment from Carol Larson regarding the sale of June 6.
	14	Paid mid-month salaries of $7,500; cheque #102.
	18	Sold an antique to Lars Wilson for $3,000 on credit; invoice #349 (cost $2,450).
	24	Received payment regarding the sale of June 5.
	25	Sold a group of antiques to Nathan Blythe for $12,000 on credit; invoice #350 (cost $7,250).
	26	Nathan Blythe returned one of the antiques purchased on June 25 for $1,400 because it was not suited to his home (cost $1,100). The item was returned to inventory.
	27	Received payment on the sale of June 18.
	28	Paid for the purchase of June 1; cheque #103.
	29	Paid month-end salaries of $7,500; cheque #104.

Required

1. Prepare a General Journal, Sales Journal, Purchases Journal, Cash Receipts Journal, and Cash Disbursements Journal like the ones illustrated in this chapter.

2. Journalize the June transactions into the appropriate journal. *Do not post to the subledgers or General Ledger.*

Problem 7-3B Special journals, subledgers—perpetual LO⁴

Duncan Industries completed these transactions during July 2014. *The terms of all credit sales are 2/10, n/30.*

July	1	Purchased merchandise on credit from Beech Company, invoice dated June 30, terms 2/10, n/30, $14,500.
	3	Issued cheque #300 to *The Weekly Journal* for advertising expense, $1,075.
	5	Sold merchandise on credit to Karen Harden, invoice #918, $35,000. Cost, $19,250.
	6	Sold merchandise on credit to Paul Kane, invoice #919, $16,000. Cost, $8,800.
	7	Purchased store supplies on credit from Blackwater Inc., $2,300. Invoice dated July 7, terms n/10 EOM.
	8	Received a $300 credit memorandum from Blackwater Inc. for store supplies received on July 7 and returned for credit.
	9	Purchased store equipment on credit from Poppe's Supply, invoice dated July 8, terms n/10 EOM, $72,500.
	10	Issued cheque #301 to Beech Company in payment of its June 30 invoice.
	13	Sold merchandise on credit to Kelly Grody, invoice #920, $17,200. Cost, $9,460.
	14	Sold merchandise on credit to Karen Harden, invoice #921, $8,200. Cost, $4,500.
	15	Received payment from Karen Harden for the July 5 sale.
	15	Issued cheque #302, payable to Payroll, in payment of the sales salaries for the first half of the month, $60,400. For simplicity, we assume one cheque.
	15	Cash sales for the first half of the month were $242,740. Cost, $133,500. *Cash sales are usually recorded daily from the cash register readings. However, they are recorded only once in this problem to reduce the repetitive transactions.*

Required

1. Set up Accounts Receivable Subledger accounts for Kelly Grody, Karen Harden, and Paul Kane.

2. Set up Accounts Payable Subledger accounts for Beech Company, Blackwater Inc., Poppe's Supply, and Sprague Company.

3. Journalize the transactions of Duncan Industries into the appropriate special journal, posting to the subledgers where required. Use page 3 for all journals.

Problem 7-4B Special journals, subledgers, schedules of accounts receivable and accounts payable, and trial balance—perpetual LO^4

This is a continuation of Problem 7-3B. You must complete Problem 7-3B before attempting this problem. Additional transactions for July follow:

July	16	Received payment from Paul Kane for the July 6 sale.
	17	Purchased merchandise on credit from Sprague Company, invoice dated July 17, terms 2/10, n/30, $17,600.
	20	Purchased office supplies on credit from Poppe's Supply, $1,500. Invoice dated July 19, terms n/10 EOM.
	21	Borrowed $40,000 from College Bank by giving a long-term note payable.
	23	Received payment from Kelly Grody for the July 13 sale.
	24	Received payment from Karen Harden for the July 14 sale.
	24	Received a $4,800 credit memorandum from Sprague Company for defective merchandise received on July 17 and returned.
	26	Purchased merchandise on credit from Beech Company, invoice dated July 26, terms 2/10, n/30, $21,300.
	27	Issued cheque #303 to Sprague Company in payment of its July 17 invoice.
	29	Sold merchandise on credit to Paul Kane, invoice #922, $52,000. Cost, $28,600.
	30	Sold merchandise on credit to Kelly Grody, invoice #923, $33,000. Cost, $18,150.
	31	Issued cheque #304, payable to Payroll, in payment of the sales salaries for the last half of the month, $60,400. For simplicity, we assume one cheque.
	31	Cash sales for the last half of the month were $158,040. Cost, $86,900.

Required

1. Set up the following General Ledger accounts: Cash (101); Accounts Receivable (106); Merchandise Inventory (119); Office Supplies (124); Store Supplies (125); Store Equipment (165); Accounts Payable (201); Long-Term Notes Payable (251); Gene Duncan, Capital (301); Sales (413); Sales Discounts (415); Cost of Goods Sold (502); Sales Salaries Expense (621); and Advertising Expense (655). Enter the June 30 balances of $190,000 for Cash; $334,000 for Merchandise Inventory; $190,000 for Gene Duncan, Capital; and $334,000 for Long-Term Notes Payable.

2. Continuing from Problem 7-3B, journalize the remaining July transactions for Duncan Industries into the appropriate special journal, posting to the subledgers as required.

3. Post the items that should be posted as individual amounts from the journals.

4. Foot and crossfoot the journals and make the month-end postings.

5. Prepare a trial balance of the General Ledger and prepare schedules of accounts receivable and accounts payable.

Analysis Component: Assume that the sum of the account balances on the schedule of accounts payable does not equal the balance of the controlling account in the General Ledger. Describe the steps you would go through to discover the error(s).

(If the Working Papers that accompany this textbook are not being used, the forms needed to complete this problem are available on Connect.)

Problem 7-5B Special journals, subledgers, schedules of accounts receivable and accounts payable, and trial balance—perpetual LO⁴

It is October 16, 2014, and you have just taken over the accounting work of China Moon Products, whose annual accounting period ends October 31. The company's previous accountant journalized its transactions through October 15 and posted all items that required posting as individual amounts, as an examination of the journals and ledgers in the Working Papers will show.

The company completed these transactions beginning on October 16, 2014. *Terms of all credit sales are 2/10, n/30.*

Oct.	16	Purchased office supplies on credit from Green Supply Company, $1,470. Invoice dated October 16, terms n/10 EOM.
	16	Sold merchandise on credit to Heather Flatt, invoice #916, $9,100. Cost, $5,270.
	18	Issued a credit memorandum to Amy Izon for defective merchandise sold on October 15 and returned for credit, $400. The returned merchandise was scrapped.
	19	Received a $1,280 credit memorandum from Walters Company for merchandise received on October 15 and returned for credit.
	20	Received a $286 credit memorandum from Green Supply Company for office supplies received on October 16 and returned for credit.
	20	Purchased store equipment on credit from Green Supply Company, invoice dated October 19, terms n/10 EOM, $14,800.
	21	Sold merchandise on credit to Jan Wildman, invoice #917, $10,900. Cost, $6,320.
	22	Received payment from Heather Flatt for the October 12 sale.
	25	Received payment from Amy Izon for the October 15 sale.
	25	Issued cheque #623 to Walters Company in payment of its October 15 invoice.
	25	Issued cheque #624 to Sunshine Company in payment of its October 15 invoice.
	28	Received merchandise with an invoice dated October 28, terms 2/10, n/60, from Sunshine Company, $12,950.
	28	Sold a neighbouring merchant a carton of calculator tape (store supplies) for cash at cost, $116.
	29	Marlee Levin, the owner of China Moon Products, used cheque #625 to withdraw $8,000 cash from the business for personal use.
	30	Issued cheque #626 to Midwest Electric Company in payment of the October electric bill, $1,240.
	30	Issued cheque #627 to Jamie Ford, the company's only sales employee, in payment of her salary for the last half of October, $3,260.
	31	Cash sales for the last half of the month were $132,256. Cost, $76,700. *Cash sales are usually recorded daily but are recorded only twice in this problem to reduce the repetitive transactions.*

Required

1. Record the transactions in the journals provided.

2. Post to the customer and creditor accounts and also post any amounts that should be posted as individual amounts to the General Ledger accounts. *Normally, these amounts are posted daily, but they are posted only once by you in this problem because they are few in number.*

3. Foot and crossfoot the journals and make the month-end postings.

4. Prepare an October 31 trial balance and prepare schedules of accounts receivable and payable.

Problem 7-6B Inventory Subledger—perpetual LO[4]

The Digit-All Company sells a product called ReCord for $15 each and uses a perpetual inventory system to account for its merchandise. The beginning balance of ReCords and transactions during July 2014 were as follows:

July	1	Balance: 30 units costing $6 each.
	4	Purchased from Tulsco Supply 45 units costing $5 each.
	9	Sold to W. Tilden 10 units, invoice #213.
	15	Sold to J. Samuelson 25 units, invoice #214.
	18	Purchased from Gentry Holdings 30 units costing $4.50 each.
	22	Sold to V. Nels 20 units, invoice #215.
	30	Sold to M. Bains 27 units, invoice #216.

Required Journalize the July transactions in the Sales Journal and Purchases Journal. Use page 1 for each journal. *Assume all sales and purchases are on credit; terms n/30.* Under the assumption that the company keeps its records on a weighted average basis, you will need to enter the beginning balances and post each transaction on an Inventory Subledger record like the one illustrated in Exhibit 7.6 in order to determine cost of goods sold.

*Problem 7-7B Special journals, subledgers—periodic LO[5]

Using the information in Problem 7-3B, complete the requirements assuming a periodic inventory system.

*Problem 7-8B Special journals, subledgers, schedules of accounts receivable and accounts payable, and trial balance—periodic LO[5]

*You must complete *Problem 7-7B before attempting this problem.* Using the information in Problem 7-4B, complete the following requirements assuming a periodic inventory system:

1. Set up the following General Ledger accounts: Cash (101); Accounts Receivable (106); Merchandise Inventory (119); Office Supplies (124); Store Supplies (125); Store Equipment (165); Accounts Payable (201); Long-Term Notes Payable (251); Gene Duncan, Capital (301); Sales (413); Sales Discounts (415); Purchases (505); Purchase Discounts (506); Purchase Returns and Allowances (507); Sales Salaries Expense (621); and Advertising Expense (655). Enter the June 30 balances of $190,000 for Cash; $334,000 for Merchandise Inventory; $190,000 for Gene Duncan, Capital; and $334,000 for Long-Term Notes Payable.

2. Continuing from *Problem 7-7B, journalize the remaining July transactions for Duncan Industries into the appropriate special journal, posting to the subledgers as required.

3. Post the items that should be posted as individual amounts from the journals.

4. Foot and crossfoot the journals and make the month-end postings.

5. Prepare a trial balance of the General Ledger and prepare schedules of accounts receivable and accounts payable.

An asterisk (*) identifies assignment material based on Appendix 7A.

ANALYTICAL AND REVIEW PROBLEM—PERPETUAL

A & R Problem 7-1

The Williams Company sells a product called Mix-Right for $15 each and uses a perpetual inventory system to account for its merchandise. The beginning balance of Mix-Rights and transactions during October 2014 were as follows:

Oct.		
	1	Balance: 85 units costing $5 each.
	3	Purchased 100 units from Arnold Brothers costing $7.50 each.
	4	Returned 20 of the units purchased on October 3.
	9	Sold 75 units to Kitchen Club, invoice #210.
	15	Purchased 200 units from Arnold Brothers costing $7.75 each.
	18	Sold 150 units to Thorhild Co-op, invoice #211.
	19	Paid for the October 3 purchase; cheque #101.
	23	Paid for the October 15 purchase, cheque #102.
	24	Sold 50 units to Boyle Grocery, invoice #212.
	31	Purchased 75 units from Arnold Brothers costing $8.00 each.

Required Journalize the October transactions in the Sales, Purchases, and Cash Disbursements Journals. Use page 1 for all your journals. *Assume all sales and purchases are on credit; terms 2/10, n/30.* Under the assumption that the company keeps its records on a weighted average basis, you will need to enter the beginning balances and post each transaction on an Inventory Subledger record like the one illustrated below in order to determine cost of goods sold. Posting to other subledgers is not required.

(If the Working Papers that accompany this textbook are not available, the forms needed to complete this problem are available on Connect.)

Date	PR	Purchases (Returns, Allowances and Discounts)			Sales (At Cost)			Inventory Balance		
		Units	Cost	Total Cost	Units	Cost	Total Cost	(b) Total Units	(a) ÷ (b) Average Cost/Unit	(a) Total Cost

ETHICS CHALLENGE

EC 7-1

John Harris is a public accountant and a sole practitioner. He has been practising as an auditor for 10 years. Recently a longstanding audit client asked John to design and implement an integrated computerized accounting information system. The fees associated with this additional engagement with the client are very attractive. However, John wonders if he can remain objective in his evaluation of the client's accounting system and records on subsequent annual audits if he puts himself in the position of auditing a system he was responsible for installing. John knows that the professional auditing standards require him to remain independent in fact and appearance of all of his auditing clients.

Required

1. What do you think auditing standards mean when they require independence in fact? in appearance?
2. Why is it important that auditors remain independent of their clients?
3. Do you think John can accept this engagement and remain independent? Justify your response.

FOCUS ON FINANCIAL STATEMENTS

FFS 7-1

CHECK FIGURES:
Net income = $20,868
Total assets
= $286,988

Mango Designs began selling its custom furniture on June 1, 2014. At the end of the month, the special journals showed the following results. Other information you will need is as follows:

- Interest of $120 had accrued on the note payable as of June 30, 2014
- $13,200 of the office supplies had been used by June 30, 2014
- Depreciation on the store equipment was $550 for June

Sales Journal Page 3

Date	Account Debited	Invoice Number	PR	A/R Dr. Sales. Cr.	Cost of Goods Sold Dr. Merchandise Inventory Cr.
2014 June 5	Leslie Haverly	381	✓	9,100	6,800
6	Tomlinson Architects	382	✓	17,900	13,400
13	Dentures Galore	383	✓	38,400	28,800
14	Leslie Haverly	384	✓	2,900	2,175
27	Nelson Consulting	385	✓	22,700	17,025

Cash Receipts Journal Page 3

Date	Account Credited	Explanation	PR	Cash Debit	Sales Discount Debit	Accts. Rec. Credit	Sales Credit	Other Accts. Credit	Cost of Goods Sold Dr. Merchandise Inventory Cr.
2014 June 1	Tom Mandalay	Owner Invmt.	301	75,000				75,000	
10	Notes Payable	L.T. loan	251	50,000				50,000	
15	Leslie Haverly	Sale of June 5	✓	8,918	182	9,100			
20	Cash sales	Cash sales		121,370			121,370		66,700
29	Tomlinson	Sale of June 6	✓	17,900		17,900			

Purchases Journal Page 3

Date	Account Credited	Date of Invoice	Terms	PR	Accounts Payable Credit	Merchandise Inventory Debit	Office Supplies Debit	Other Accts. Debit
2014 June 2	Tenor Company	June 2	2/10, n/60	✓	72,000	72,000		
7	Indago Manufacturers	June 7	n/10 EOM	✓	18,000		18,000	
17	Penray Suppliers	June 17	1/10 EOM	✓	91,000	91,000		
18	Ego/Store Equipment	June 18	n/30	165/✓	32,000			32,000

Cash Disbursements Journal Page 3

Date	Ch. No.	Payee	Account Debited	PR	Cash Credit	Merchandise Inventory Credit	Other Accts. Debit	Accts. Payable Debit
2014 June 3	100	The Daily Gazette	Advertising Expense	655	550		550	
10	101	Tenor Company	Tenor Company	✓	70,560	1,440		72,000
30	102	Payroll	Sales Salaries Expense	621	42,000		42,000	

Required Using the information provided, prepare a single-step income statement, statement of changes in equity, and classified balance sheet. (*Hint: You may find it useful to use T-accounts.*)

Analysis Component: Does Mango Designs use a perpetual or periodic inventory system? Explain how you know.

FFS 7-2

Chapter 7 discusses the Accounts Payable Subledger, Accounts Receivable Subledger, and Inventory Subledger. It also briefly introduces other subledgers such as the Property, Plant and Equipment Asset Subledger.

DANIER

Required Review **Danier**'s financial statements in Appendix II at the end of the textbook. Which subledgers might Danier be using and why? Be sure to explain briefly what kind of information these subledgers might include that would be useful to decision makers.

CRITICAL THINKING MINI CASE

Northern Outposts Mining Company has 17 mines in various locations throughout Northern Quebec, Nunavut, and Yukon. You have just been hired as the assistant office manager in the head office, which is located in Whitehorse. Because of your computer expertise, one of your duties will be to generate special purpose reports from the accounting information system. The director of operations has asked you to prepare a report for an afternoon meeting that details all of the property, plant and equipment for each of the 17 mines. You are confident that this should be an easy task but, upon reviewing the accounting records, you discover that all of the information regarding the assets is maintained in only one location, a General Ledger account called Mining Assets!

Required Using the elements of critical thinking described on the inside front cover, comment.

COMPREHENSIVE PROBLEM 7.1—PERPETUAL

CHECK FIGURES:
3. Net income
= $23,856; Total
assets = $379,269

Alpine Company LO⁴

Assume it is Monday, May 1, 2014, the first business day of the month, and you have just been hired as the accountant for Alpine Company, which operates with monthly accounting periods. All of the company's accounting work has been completed through the end of April and its ledgers show April 30 balances. Alpine uses a perpetual system to account for inventory. *The terms of all credit sales are 2/10, n/30.* During your first month on the job, you record the following transactions on page 2 of each journal.

Note: If the Working Papers that accompany this textbook are not being used, the forms needed to complete this problem are available on Connect.

Required

1. Enter the transactions in the appropriate journals and post when instructed to do so.

2. Prepare a trial balance in the Trial Balance columns of the provided work sheet form and complete the work sheet using the following information.

   a. Expired insurance, $553.

   b. Ending store supplies inventory, $2,632.

   c. Ending office supplies inventory, $504.

   d. Estimated depreciation of store equipment, $567.

   e. Estimated depreciation of office equipment, $329.

   f. Ending merchandise inventory, $191,000.

3. Prepare a May classified, multiple-step income statement, a May statement of changes in equity, and a May 31 classified balance sheet.

4. Prepare and post adjusting and closing entries (omit explanations).

5. Prepare a post-closing trial balance. Also prepare a list of the Accounts Receivable Subledger accounts and a list of the Accounts Payable Subledger accounts.

May	1	Issued cheque #3410 to S&M Management Co. in payment of the May rent, $3,700. *Use two lines to record the transaction. Charge 80% of the rent to Rent Expense, Selling Space, and the balance to Rent Expense, Office Space.*
	2	Sold merchandise on credit to Essex Company, invoice #8785, $6,050. Cost $3,640.
	2	Issued a $130 credit memorandum to Nabors, Inc., for defective merchandise sold on April 28 and discarded when returned to inventory (cost $105) for credit. The total selling price was $4,730.
	3	Received a $350 credit memorandum from Parkay Products for merchandise received on April 29 and returned for credit.
	4	Purchased on credit from Thompson Supply Co.: merchandise, $37,100; store supplies, $580; and office supplies, $85. Invoice dated May 4, terms n/10 EOM.
	5	Received payment from Nabors, Inc. from the sale of April 28.
	8	Issued cheque #3411 to Parkay Products to pay for the $7,100 of merchandise received on April 29 (terms 2/10, n/30).
	9	Sold store supplies to the merchant next door at cost for cash, $325.
	10	Purchased office equipment on credit from Thompson Supply Co., invoice dated May 10, terms n/10 EOM, $4,200.
	11	Received payment from Essex Company for the May 2 sale.
	11	Received merchandise and an invoice dated May 10, terms 2/10, n/30, from Gale, Inc., $9,100.
	12	Received an $850 credit memorandum from Thompson Supply Co. for defective office equipment received on May 10 and returned for credit.
	15	Issued cheque #3412, payable to Payroll, in payment of sales salaries, $5,500, and office salaries, $3,600. For simplicity, we assume one cheque.
	15	Cash sales for the first half of the month, $61,000. Cost $36,600. *Such sales are normally recorded daily. They are recorded only twice in this problem to reduce the repetitive entries.*
	16	Sold merchandise on credit to Essex Company, invoice #8786, $3,700. Cost $2,220.
	17	Received merchandise and an invoice dated May 14, terms 2/10, n/60, from Chandler Corp., $14,700.
	19	Issued cheque #3413 to Gale, Inc. in payment of its May 10 invoice.
	22	Sold merchandise to Oscar Services, invoice #8787, $7,100. Cost $4,260.
	23	Issued cheque #3414 to Chandler Corp. in payment of its May 14 invoice.
	24	Purchased on credit from Thompson Supply Co.: merchandise, $9,200; store supplies, $630; and office supplies, $280. Invoice dated May 24, terms n/10 EOM.
	25	Received merchandise and an invoice dated May 23, terms 2/10, n/30, from Parkay Products, $3,100.
	26	Sold merchandise on credit to Deaver Corp., invoice #8788, $12,500. Cost $7,500.
	26	Issued cheque #3415 to Trinity Power in payment of the April electric bill, $1,350.
	29	The owner, Clint Barry, withdrew $7,000 from the business for personal use, using cheque #3416.
	30	Received payment from Oscar Services for the May 22 sale.
	30	Issued cheque #3417, payable to Payroll, in payment of sales salaries, $5,500, and office salaries, $3,600. For simplicity, we assume one cheque.
	31	Cash sales for the last half of the month were $61,000. Cost $36,600.
	31	*Post to the customer and creditor accounts. Also, post individual items that are not included in column totals at the end of the month to the General Ledger accounts. Normally, such items are posted daily, but you are asked to post them only once in this problem because they are few in number.*
	31	*Foot and crossfoot the journals and make the month-end postings.*

* C O M P R E H E N S I V E   P R O B L E M   7 . 2 — P E R I O D I C

CHECK FIGURES:
3. Net income
= $23,856
Total assets
= $379,269

Alpine Company LO[5]

Required Using information from Comprehensive Problem 7.1, complete the requirements assuming a periodic inventory system.

Note: If the Working Papers that accompany this textbook are not being used, the forms needed to complete this problem are available on Connect.

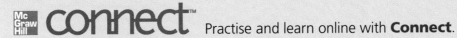 Practise and learn online with **Connect**.

An asterisk (*) identifies assignment material based on Appendix 7A.

Internal Control and Cash

LEARNING OBJECTIVES

LO¹ Define, explain the purpose, and identify the principles of internal control.

LO² Define cash and explain how it is reported.

LO³ Apply internal control to cash.

LO⁴ Explain and record petty cash fund transactions.

LO⁵ Explain and identify banking activities and the control features they provide.

LO⁶ Prepare a bank reconciliation and journalize any resulting adjustment(s).

*APPENDIX 8A

LO⁷ Calculate the acid-test ratio and explain its use as an indicator of a company's liquidity.

WILL THAT BE CASH OR *INTERAC* FLASH?

Not that long ago, cash transactions were conducted primarily using bills and coins as well as cheques. Today, because of the ubiquitous nature of technology, more and more cash transactions are processed through the use of debit cards, also known as "electronic cash."

For more than 20 years, Canadians have been able to access funds from their bank accounts by using *Interac** Debit at merchants and automated banking machines (ABMs). In 2008, the introduction of chip technology enabled card-holders to pay for items with even greater security by inserting their *Interac* Debit card into a merchant's point-of-sale reader and entering their PIN. Once again, *Interac* Debit has evolved with the introduction of *Interac* Flash—the contactless enhancement of traditional debit. Starting in 2011, **RBC**, **Scotiabank**, and **TD Canada Trust** began issuing *Interac* Flash debit cards that allow custom-ers to pay using contactless debit technology. By holding an *Interac* Flash card at the contactless reader, a purchase is quickly and securely processed.

The advantages? Convenience, for one: Merchants can serve customers more efficiently. The need for efficiency at the point of sale is significant because of the huge volumes of transactions now being handled electronically. The Con-sumers' Association of Canada reported that between 2008 and 2009, debit card transactions in Canada increased from $3.7 billion to $3.9 billion, and this number is continuing to grow.

Security is another advantage. Security is a growing concern given the increase in electronic payments and related increase in fraud. For example, in June of 2011, a bank machine gang located in the Greater Toronto area was charged with fraud that cost financial institutions $245,000. The RCMP reports that frauds like the preceding are on the rise with $119 million defrauded from Canadian debit card-holders in 2010 alone. The new *Interac* Flash card is reported to enhance protec-tion against security issues like skimming, counterfeiting, transaction replay types of fraud, and electronic pickpocketing. Electronic pickpocketing is based on radio frequency identification (RFID) technology, which allows a fraudster to walk by you in a crowd at a sports event, concert, or mall, and automatically upload the infor-mation on your debit card to a computerized device hidden on the fraudster ... they don't have to touch you, but just have to be close. *Interac* Flash is protected against electronic pickpocketing because it uses EMV-based secure chip processing instead of the less secure magnetic strip data chip processing. Controls have been put in place to limit the risk of other types of losses. For example, RBC requires that the cardholder enter their PIN after every $200 of Flash purchases to validate the cardholder's identity. In terms of additional security, the *Interac* Zero Liability Policy* automatically protects the debit card user from unauthorized transactions.

*   All *Interac* cardholders are protected from losses resulting from circumstances beyond their control under the *Interac* Zero Liability Policy. See your financial institution for details.

Note: *Interac, Interac* Flash, and *Interac* e-Transfer are trademarks of Interac Inc. Used under licence.

CRITICAL THINKING CHALLENGE | If a debit card is used instead of actual currency to purchase a $10 item, would the journal entry for the buyer/seller be affected? Explain.

CHAPTER PREVIEW

We are all aware of reports and experiences involving theft and fraud. These activities affect us and produce various actions, including locking doors, chaining bikes, reviewing sales receipts, and acquiring alarm systems. A business also takes action to safeguard, control, and manage what it owns. Experience tells us that small companies are most vulnerable, usually due to weak internal controls. It is management's responsibility to set up policies and procedures to safeguard a company's assets, especially cash. To do so, management and employees must understand and apply principles of internal control. This chapter introduces these principles to help us learn about the importance of internal control policies and procedures. We focus special attention on cash, because cash is easily transferable and is often at high risk of loss. Controls for cash are explained, including petty cash funds and reconciling bank accounts. Our understanding of these controls and procedures makes us more secure in carrying out business activities and in assessing those activities of companies. As was emphasized in the opening article, internal controls are crucial to protect the security of both businesses and consumers.

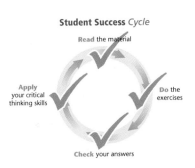

INTERNAL CONTROL

This section introduces internal control and its fundamental principles. We also discuss the impact of computing technology on internal control and the limitations of control procedures.

Purpose of Internal Control

Managers of small businesses often control the entire operation. They participate in all activities from hiring and managing employees to signing all cheques. These managers know from personal contact and observation whether the business is actually receiving the assets and services being paid for. The larger the operation, the more managers must delegate responsibilities and rely on formal procedures rather than personal contact in controlling and knowing all operations of the business.

LO¹ Define, explain the purpose, and identify the principles of internal control.

These managers place a high priority on internal control systems to monitor and control operations. This is because these systems can prevent avoidable losses, help managers plan operations, and monitor company and human performance. An **internal control system** is all policies and procedures used to:

- Protect assets,
- Ensure reliable accounting,
- Promote efficient operations, and
- Encourage adherence to company policies.

Principles of Internal Control

Internal control policies and procedures depend on the nature and size of the business. The fundamental **principles of internal control** are:

1. Ensure transactions and activities are authorized.

Establish responsibilities for each task clearly and for one person. Approvals must be made by authorized individuals. When two salesclerks share access to the same cash register, for instance, neither clerk can prove or disprove any alleged shortage. Instead, a company can use a register with a separate cash drawer for each clerk.

2. **Maintain records.**

Maintain adequate records to help protect assets by ensuring that employees use prescribed procedures. When detailed records of manufacturing equipment and tools are kept, for instance, lost or stolen items are readily noticed. Similarly, the use of a chart of accounts encourages the correct recording of transactions that improves the accuracy of reports.

Preprinted forms and internal business papers are also designed and properly used in a good internal control system. For example, when sales slips are prenumbered and accounted for, a salesperson is not able to pocket cash by making a sale and destroying the sales slip. Computerized point-of-sale systems achieve the same control results.

3. **Insure assets and bond key employees.**

Insure assets and *bond* key employees to reduce risk of loss from casualty and theft. To **bond** an employee is to purchase an insurance policy, or a bond, against losses from theft by that employee. Bonding reduces the risk of loss suffered from theft in addition to discouraging theft by the bonded employee.

4. **Separate recordkeeping and custody of assets.**

Recordkeeping should be separated from the custody of assets so a person who controls or has access to an asset is not responsible for the maintenance of that asset's accounting records. The risk of theft or waste is reduced since the person with control over the asset knows that records are kept by another person. The recordkeeper does not have access to the asset and has no reason to falsify records. In situations where recordkeeping is separate from the custody of assets, *collusion* is necessary to hide theft from the records. **Collusion** is not likely because it means two or more people must agree to commit a fraud.

5. **Establish a separation of duties.**

A **separation of duties** involves dividing responsibility for related transactions between two or more individuals or departments. This is not a call for duplication of work but instead ensures that the work of one acts as a check on the other. An example is requiring two signatures on cheques to verify that disbursements comply with policies and procedures. Other examples of transactions improved by dividing responsibility are issuing purchase orders and receiving merchandise. Having an independent person check incoming goods for quality and quantity encourages more care and attention to detail than when they are checked by the person who placed the order.

6. **Apply technological controls.**

Cash registers with a locked-in tape or electronic file make a record of each cash sale. A time clock registers the exact time an employee arrives at and departs from the job. Passwords limit access to sensitive information. Mechanical change and currency counters can quickly and accurately count amounts. Personal identification scanners can limit access to only those individuals who are authorized. All of these and other technological controls are effective parts of many internal control systems.

7. **Perform internal and external audits.**

Perform regular and independent reviews to ensure that internal control procedures are followed. No internal control system is entirely effective, for various reasons such as changes in personnel and time pressures. Reviews are preferably done by internal auditors who are employees not directly involved in operations and who report directly to senior management. Their independent perspective encourages an evaluation of the efficiency as well as the effectiveness of the internal control system.

Many companies also pay for audits by independent external auditors who are professional accountants. These external auditors test the company's financial records and then give an opinion as to whether the company's financial statements are presented fairly in accordance with generally accepted accounting principles. In the process of their evaluation, they often identify internal controls that need improvement.

Technology and Internal Control

The fundamental principles of internal control are relevant no matter what the technological state of the accounting system. This includes all systems from the purely manual to those that are fully automated with only electronic documentation. This section describes some technological impacts to which we must be alert.

Reduced Processing Errors

Provided the software and data entries are correct, the risk of mechanical and mathematical errors is nearly eliminated because of technology. Yet mistakes happen and one must be alert to that possibility. The decreasing human involvement in later data processing can cause data entry errors to go undiscovered. Similarly, errors in software can produce consistent erroneous processing of transactions.

More Extensive Testing

Auditors and others need to test not only samples of data from the electronic accounting system but also the controls over the system itself. The results of the review of the controls over the accounting system will affect the scope of the samples of data tested.

Limited Evidence of Processing

Because many data processing steps are increasingly done by computer, fewer "hard copy" items of documentary evidence are available for review. Yet technologically advanced systems can store additional evidence. They can, for instance, record information such as who made the entries, the date and time, and the source of their entry. Technology can also be designed to require use of passwords or other identification before access to the system is granted. This means that internal control depends more on the design and operation of the information system and less on analysis of the documents left behind by the system.

Crucial Separation of Duties

Technological advances in accounting information systems are so efficient that they often require fewer employees. This reduction in workforce carries a risk that separation of crucial responsibilities is lost. Companies that use advanced technology also need employees with special skills to operate programs and equipment. The duties of these employees must be controlled and monitored to minimize risk of error and fraud. Better control is maintained if, for instance, the person designing and programming the system does not serve as the operator. Also the control over programs and files related to cash receipts and disbursements must be separated. Cheque-writing activities should not be controlled by a computer operator in order to avoid risk of fraud. Yet achieving acceptable separation of duties can be especially difficult in small companies with few employees.

Increased Ecommerce

Technology has encouraged the growth of ecommerce. **Amazon.ca** and **Kijiji.ca** are examples of companies that have successfully exploited ecommerce, and most companies today have at least some ecommerce transactions. All such transactions involve at least three risks. (1) *Credit card number theft* is a risk of using, transmitting, and storing such data online. This increases the cost of ecommerce. (2) *Computer viruses* are malicious programs that attach themselves to innocent files for purposes of infecting and harming other files and programs. (3) *Impersonation* online can result in charges of sales to bogus accounts, purchases of inappropriate materials, and the inadvertent surrender of confidential information to hackers. To combat some of these risks, companies use both firewalls (points of entry to a system that require passwords to continue) and encryption (a mathematical process to rearrange contents that cannot be read without the process code).

DECISION INSIGHT

Warning Signs
There are clues to internal control violations. Warning signs from accounting include (1) an increase in customer refunds (could be fake), (2) missing documents (could be used for fraud), (3) differences between bank deposits and cash receipts (could be embezzled cash), and (4) delayed recording (could reflect fraudulent records). Warning signs from employees include (1) lifestyle changes (could be embezzlement), (2) too close with suppliers (could signal fraudulent transactions), and (3) failure to leave job, even for vacations (could conceal fraudulent activities).

Limitations of Internal Control

All internal control policies and procedures have limitations. Probably the most serious source of these limitations is the human element that we can categorize as either (1) human error, or (2) human fraud.

Human error is a factor whenever internal control policies and procedures are carried out by people. Human error can occur from negligence, fatigue, misjudgement, or confusion. Human fraud involves intent by people to defeat internal controls for personal gain. This human element highlights the importance of establishing an *internal control environment* that conveys management's attitude and commitment to internal control.

Another important limitation of internal control is the *cost–benefit standard*. This means the costs of internal controls must not exceed their benefits. Analysis of costs and benefits must consider all factors, including the impact on morale. Most companies, for instance, have a legal right to read employees' email. Yet companies seldom exercise that right unless confronted with evidence of potential harm to the company. The same holds for drug testing, phone tapping, and hidden cameras. The bottom line is that no internal control system is perfect and that managers must establish internal control policies and procedures with a net benefit to the company.

The preceding discussion is an introduction to internal controls. The study of *auditing* takes a detailed look at internal controls.

DECISION MAKER   Answer—End of chapter

Campaign Manager
You are leading a campaign to influence the government to improve the health care system. Your funding is limited and you try hiring people who are committed to your cause and will work for less. A systems analyst recently volunteered her services and put together a web strategy to attract supporters. She also strongly encouraged you to force all employees to take at least one week of vacation per year. Why does she feel so strongly about a "forced vacation" policy?

CASH

Cash is an important asset for every company and must be managed. Companies also need to carefully control access to cash by employees and others who are inclined to take it for personal use. Good accounting systems support both goals by managing how much cash is on hand and controlling who has access to it.

LO² Define cash and explain how it is reported.

Cash Defined

Cash consists of cash on hand and demand deposits.[1] For example, this would include currency, coins, and amounts on deposit in bank accounts, chequing accounts, and some savings accounts. Cash also includes items that are acceptable for deposit in these accounts, such as customers' cheques, cashier's cheques, certified cheques, money orders, and deposits made through electronic funds transfer (EFT).

Many companies invest idle cash in assets called *cash equivalents* or short-term investments to increase earnings. Because cash equivalents are similar to cash, many companies combine them with cash as a single item on the balance sheet. **WestJet Airlines Ltd.,** for instance, reports the following on its December 31, 2011, balance sheet:

Cash and cash equivalents.............$1,243,605 (thousand)

EYK
8-1

Liquidity

Cash is the usual means of payment when paying for other assets, services, or liabilities. **Liquidity** refers to how easily an asset can be converted into another asset or used in paying for services or obligations. Cash and similar assets are called **liquid assets** because they are converted easily into other assets or used in paying for services or liabilities. A company must own some liquid assets, for example, so that bills are paid on time and purchases are made for cash when necessary.

Control of Cash

It is important that we apply principles of good internal control to cash. Cash is the most liquid of all assets and is easily hidden and moved. A good system of internal control for cash provides adequate procedures for protecting both cash receipts and cash disbursements. These procedures should meet three basic guidelines:

LO³ Apply internal control to cash.

1. Separate handling of cash from recordkeeping of cash.
2. Deposit cash receipts promptly (daily) in a bank.
3. Make cash disbursements by cheque.

The first guideline aims to minimize errors and fraud by a division of duties. When duties are separated, it requires two or more people to collude for cash to be stolen

---

1   IFRS 2012, IAS 7, para. 6.

and the theft to be concealed in the accounting records. The second guideline aims to use immediate (daily) deposits of all cash receipts to produce a timely independent test of the accuracy of the count of cash received. It also reduces cash theft or loss, and it reduces the risk of an employee personally using the money before depositing it. The third guideline aims to use payments by cheque to develop a bank record of cash disbursements. This guideline also reduces the risk of cash theft. Often, two signatures are required to ensure that legitimate invoices are being paid.

One exception to the third guideline is to allow small disbursements of currency and coins from a petty cash fund. We describe a petty cash fund later in this section. Another important point is that the deposit of cash receipts and the use of cheques for cash disbursements allow a company to use bank records as a separate external record of cash transactions. We explain how to use bank records to confirm the accuracy of a company's own records later in this section.

Control of Cash Receipts

Internal control of cash receipts ensures that all cash received is properly recorded and deposited. Cash receipts arise from many transactions, including cash sales, collections of customers' accounts, receipts of interest and rent, bank loans, sale of assets, and owners' investments. This section explains internal control over two important types of cash receipts: over-the-counter and mail.

Over-the-Counter Cash Receipts

For purposes of internal control, over-the-counter cash sales should be recorded on a cash register at the time of each sale for internal control. To help ensure that correct amounts are entered, each register should be positioned so customers can read the amounts entered. The design of each cash register should provide a permanent, locked-in record of each transaction. Many software programs accept cash register transactions and enter them in accounting records. Less technology-dependent registers simply print a record of each transaction on a paper tape or electronic file locked inside the register.

Custody over cash should be separate from its recordkeeping; therefore the clerk who has access to cash in the register should not have access to its locked-in record. At the end of the clerk's work period, the clerk should count the cash in the register, record the amount, and turn over the cash and a record of its amount to an employee in the cashier's office. The employee in the cashier's office, like the clerk, has access to the cash and should not have access to accounting records (or the register tape or file). A third employee compares the record of total register transactions (or the register tape or file) with the cash receipts reported by the cashier's office. This record (or register tape or file) is the basis for a journal entry recording over-the-counter cash sales. Note that the third employee has access to the records for cash but not to the actual cash. The clerk and the employee from the cashier's office have access to cash but not to the accounting records. This means the accuracy of cash records and amounts is automatically checked. None of them can make a mistake or divert cash without the difference being revealed.

Cash Over and Short

Sometimes errors in making change are discovered when there is a difference between the cash in a cash register and the record of the amount of cash sales. This difference is reported in the **Cash Over and Short account**. This income statement account, shown under general and administrative expenses, records the income effects of cash overages and cash shortages from errors in making change and missing petty cash receipts. The journal entries to record cash over and short are illustrated later in this chapter.

Cash Receipts by Mail

Control of cash receipts[2] that arrive through the mail starts with the person who opens the mail. In a large business, two people are assigned the task and are present

---

2   Cash receipts by mail are normally in the form of cheques. Cheques are equivalent to cash and would therefore be recorded as cash.

when opening the mail. The person opening the mail makes a list of money received. This list should contain a record of each sender's name, the amount, and an explanation for what purpose the money is sent. Copies of the list are sent with the money to the cashier, and to the accounting area. The cashier deposits the money in the bank, and the recordkeeper records amounts received in the accounting records. In a small business, the owner should assume responsibility for cash.

Control of Cash Disbursements

Control of cash disbursements is especially important for companies. Most large thefts occur from payments of fictitious invoices. The key to controlling cash disbursements is to require that all expenditures be made by cheque, with two signatures if possible when not signed by the owner. The only exception is for small payments from petty cash. Another key is that when the authority to sign cheques is assigned to a person other than the owner, that person must not have access to the accounting records. This separation of duties helps prevent an employee from hiding fraudulent disbursements in the accounting records.

The manager of a small business often signs cheques and knows from personal contact that the items being paid for are actually received. This arrangement is impossible in large businesses. Instead, internal control procedures must be substituted for personal contact. These controls are achieved through a *voucher system*. Briefly, the voucher system of control requires that a number of procedures be performed and documents collected to support the validity of each disbursement. These procedures are designed to assure the cheque signer that the obligations recorded were properly incurred and should be paid.

EYK
8-2

The exact procedures used to achieve control over cash vary across companies. They depend on such factors as company size, number of employees, volume of cash transactions, and sources of cash. We must therefore view the procedures described in this section as illustrative of those in practice today.

DECISION INSIGHT

Fraud
What are the motivating factors that cause a person to perpetrate a fraud? "Profile of a Canadian Fraudster," published by KPMG in 2009, reports that the leading cause, as shown in the graph, is personal need, followed by opportunity, and then greed.

EYK
8-3

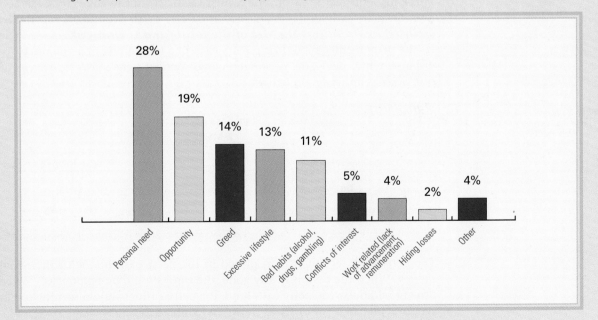

SOURCE: http://www.kpmg.com/Ca/en/IssuesAndInsights/ArticlesPublications/Press-Releases/Documents/ProfileofaCanadianFraudster_FNL.pdf

3. Good internal control procedures for cash receipts imply that (choose one):
   a. All cash disbursements, other than those for very small amounts, are made by cheque.
   b. An accounting employee should count cash received from sales and promptly deposit receipts.
   c. Cash receipts by mail should be opened by an accounting employee who is responsible for recording and depositing receipts.

Do Quick Study questions: QS 8-2, QS 8-3

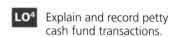 Explain and record petty cash fund transactions.

Petty Cash System of Control

A basic principle for controlling cash disbursements is that all payments are made by cheque. An exception to this rule is made for petty cash disbursements. Petty cash disbursements are the *small amount* payments required in most companies for items such as postage, courier fees, repairs, and supplies. To avoid writing cheques for small amounts, a company usually sets up a petty cash fund and uses the money in this fund to make small payments.

Operating a Petty Cash Fund

Establishing a petty cash fund requires estimating the total amount of small payments likely to be made during a short period such as a week or month. A cheque is then drawn by the company cashier's office for an amount slightly in excess of this estimate. To illustrate, assume Z-Mart established a petty cash fund on November 1, 2014, in the amount of $75. A $75 cheque was drawn, cashed, and its proceeds turned over to Jim Gibbs, an office employee designated as the *petty cashier* or *petty cash custodian*. The **petty cashier** is responsible for safekeeping of the cash, for making payments from this fund, and for keeping accurate records. The entry to record the set-up of this petty cash fund is:

Nov.	1	Petty Cash..	75	
		Cash		75
		To establish a petty cash fund.		

This entry transfers $75 from the regular Cash account to the Petty Cash account. After the petty cash fund is established, the ***Petty Cash account is not debited or credited again unless the size of the total fund is changed.***

The petty cashier should keep petty cash in a locked box in a safe place. As each disbursement is made, the person receiving payment signs a *petty cash receipt* or *petty cash ticket* as illustrated in Exhibit 8.1.

EXHIBIT 8.1

Petty Cash Receipt

	Petty Cash Receipt	No. 6
	Z-Mart	

For ____Delivery charges____   Date _____Nov.18/2014_____

Charge to____Delivery expense____   Amount_____$5.00_____

Approved by ___*Jim Gibbs*___   Received by ___*Dick Fitch*___

The petty cash receipt is then placed in the petty cash box with the remaining money. When the cash is nearly gone, the fund should be reimbursed. When it is time to reimburse the petty cash fund, the petty cashier should sort the receipts by type and prepare a summary as shown in Exhibit 8.2.

Z-Mart Petty Cash Payments Report			
Receipts:			
Office maintenance			
Nov. 2 Washing windows.....................................	$10.00		
17 Washing windows.....................................	10.00		
27 Computer repairs.....................................	26.50	$46.50	
Transportation-in			
Nov. 5 Delivery of merchandise purchased..........	$ 6.75		
20 Delivery of merchandise purchased..........	8.30	15.05	
Delivery expense			
Nov. 28 Customer's package delivered..................		5.00	
Office supplies			
Nov. 15 Purchased office supplies.........................		4.75	
Total receipts...			$71.30
Fund total...		$75.00	
Less: Cash remaining		2.20	
Equals: Cash required to replenish petty cash....................			$72.80
Cash over/(short)...			($ 1.50)

EXHIBIT 8.2

Petty Cash Payments Report

This summary and all petty cash receipts are presented to the company's cashier. The company's cashier stamps all receipts paid so they cannot be reused, files them for recordkeeping, records the reimbursement, and gives the petty cashier a cheque for a sum *equal to the fund size less the cash remaining*. In our example, Jim Gibbs had only $2.20 cash remaining in the fund at the end of November. Therefore, the reimbursement cheque is for $72.80 (= $75.00 − $2.20). Notice that Exhibit 8.2 shows total receipts for $71.30. The difference between the total receipts and the reimbursement cheque represents a cash shortage of $1.50 (= $71.30 − $72.80) due to an error. The reimbursement cheque is recorded as follows:

To replenish petty cash:

$$\begin{array}{c} \text{Cash required} \\ \text{to replenish} \\ \text{petty cash} \end{array} = \begin{array}{c} \text{Fund} \\ \text{size} \end{array} - \begin{array}{c} \text{Cash} \\ \text{remaining} \end{array}$$

To calculate cash over/(short):

$$\begin{array}{c} \text{Cash} \\ \text{over/(short)} \end{array} = \begin{array}{c} \text{Total of} \\ \text{petty cash} \\ \text{receipts} \end{array} - \begin{array}{c} \text{Cash required} \\ \text{to replenish} \\ \text{petty cash} \end{array}$$

Nov. 27	Office Maintenance Expenses.........................	46.50	
	Merchandise Inventory	15.05	
	Delivery Expense..	5.00	
	Office Supplies Expense	4.75	
	Cash Over and Short.......................................	1.50	
	Cash		72.80
	To reimburse petty cash.		

In the case of an overage in the petty cash fund, a credit to Cash Over and Short is recorded in the reimbursing entry.

When the reimbursement cheque is cashed and the money returned to the cash box, the total money in the box is restored to its original amount of $75.00 (= $72.80 + $2.20). The fund is now ready to begin a new cycle of operations.

Increasing or Decreasing Petty Cash Fund

A decision to increase or decrease a petty cash fund is often made when the fund is being reimbursed. To illustrate, let us assume that Z-Mart decides to increase the petty cash fund by $25, from $75 to $100, on November 27 when it reimburses the fund. This is recorded as follows:

Nov. 27	Petty Cash..	25.00	
	Office Maintenance Expenses.........................	46.50	
	Merchandise Inventory	15.05	
	Delivery Expense..	5.00	
	Office Supplies Expense	4.75	
	Cash Over and Short......................................	1.50	
	Cash		97.80
	To reimburse petty cash and increase it by $25.00.		

Internal Auditor
You just graduated and have been hired as an internal audit trainee for a company. As part of your training, your supervisor has instructed you to make surprise counts of three $200 petty cash funds. You arrive at the office of one of the petty cashiers while she is on the telephone. You explain the purpose of your visit, and the petty cashier asks politely that you come back after lunch so that she can finish the business she's conducting by long distance. You agree and return after lunch. The petty cashier opens the petty cash box and shows you nine new $20 bills with consecutive serial numbers plus receipts totalling $20. Do you take further action or comment on these events in your report to your supervisor?

CHECKPOINT

4. Why are some cash payments made from a petty cash fund?
5. Why should a petty cash fund be reimbursed at the end of an accounting period?
6. What are three results of reimbursing the petty cash fund?

Do Quick Study questions: QS 8-4, QS 8-5, QS 8-6

MID-CHAPTER DEMONSTRATION PROBLEM

Castillo Company established a $250 petty cash fund on February 10. On February 28, the fund had $180.14 remaining in cash and receipts for these expenditures: postage, $10.51; office supplies, $50.00; and repair expenses, $10.50. Prepare:

a. The February 10 entry to establish the fund,

b. The February 28 entry to record the fund transactions and replenish it, and

c. Independent of (b), the February 28 entry to record the fund transactions and reduce the fund to $100.

Analysis Component:
Assume that there was no receipt for the $50.00 of office supplies. Should this amount be reimbursed? Explain why or why not.

Planning the Solution

• Total petty cash receipts.
• Calculate cash required to replenish petty cash.
• Calculate cash over/(short), if any.
• Prepare journal entries as required.
• Prepare an answer to the analysis question.

SOLUTION

a.	Feb. 10	Petty Cash Fund...	250.00	
		Cash		250.00
		To establish petty cash fund.		
b.	28	Postage Expense	10.51	
		Office Supplies Expense	50.00	
		Repair Expense...	10.50	
		Cash		69.86[1]
		Cash Over and Short		1.15[2]
		To reimburse petty cash fund.		

Calculations:

[1]Total of petty cash receipts = $10.51 + $50.00 + $10.50 = $\underline{\underline{\$71.01}}$

$$
\begin{aligned}
\text{Cash required to replenish petty cash} &= \text{Fund size} - \text{Cash remaining} \\
&= \$250 - \$180.14 \\
&= \underline{\underline{\$69.86}}
\end{aligned}
$$

[2]$$
\begin{aligned}
\text{Cash over/(short)} &= \text{Receipt totals} - \text{Cash required} \\
&= \$71.01 - \$69.86 \\
&= \underline{\underline{\$1.15}}
\end{aligned}
$$

c.	28	Cash	80.14[3]	
		Postage Expense	10.51	
		Office Supplies Expense	50.00	
		Repair Expense	10.50	
		Petty Cash		150.00
		Cash Over and Short		1.15
		To reimburse petty cash fund and decrease it to $100.		

Calculation:

[3]$$
\begin{aligned}
\text{Cash required to replenish petty cash} &= \text{New fund size} - \text{Cash remaining} \\
&= \$100.00 - \$180.14 \\
&= \underline{\underline{-\$80.14}}\ \text{(therefore, instead of a credit to} \\
&\qquad\qquad\text{Cash, debit Cash)}
\end{aligned}
$$

Analysis Component:

The $50.00 should not be reimbursed without a receipt for two reasons. First, it is a basic internal control measure to ensure that only valid expenditures are reimbursed. If receipts were not required, individuals could request reimbursement for fictitious expenditures. Second, GAAP require that transactions be recorded based on verifiable evidence (which is related to internal controls).

BANKING ACTIVITIES AS CONTROLS

 Explain and identify banking activities and the control features they provide.

Banks are used by most companies for many different services. One of their most important services is helping companies control cash and cash transactions. Banks safeguard cash, provide detailed and independent records of cash transactions, and are a source of cash financing. This section describes services and documents provided by banking activities that increase managers' control over cash.

Basic Bank Services

This first section explains basic bank services. We include the bank account, bank deposits, and cheques. Each of these services contributes to the control or safeguarding of cash.

Bank Account

A bank account is a record set up by a bank for a customer, permitting this customer to deposit money for safeguarding and cheque withdrawals. To control access to a bank account, all persons authorized to use a bank account must sign a signature card. A **signature card** includes the signature of each person authorized to sign cheques from the account. Bank employees use signature cards to verify signatures on cheques. This lowers the risk of loss from forgery for both banks and customers. Many companies have more than one bank account for various reasons such as serving local needs and for special transactions.

EYK
8-4

Bank Deposit

Each bank deposit is supported by a *deposit slip*. A **deposit slip** lists the items such as currency, coins, and cheques deposited along with each of their dollar amounts. The bank gives the customer a copy of the deposit slip or a deposit receipt as proof of the deposit. Exhibit 8.3 shows a deposit slip.

Bank Cheque

To withdraw money from an account, a customer uses a *cheque*. A **cheque** is a document signed by the depositor instructing the bank to pay a specified amount of money to a designated recipient. A cheque involves three parties: a *maker* who signs the cheque, a *payee* who is the recipient, and a *bank* on which the cheque is drawn. The bank provides a depositor with cheques that are serially numbered and imprinted with the name and address of both the depositor and the bank. Both cheques and deposit slips are imprinted with identification codes in magnetic ink for

EXHIBIT 8.3

Deposit Slip

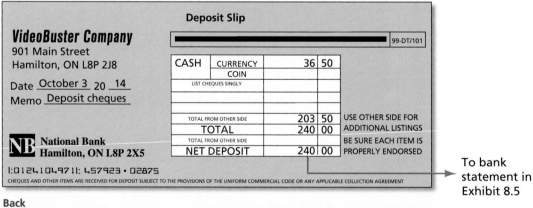

To bank statement in Exhibit 8.5

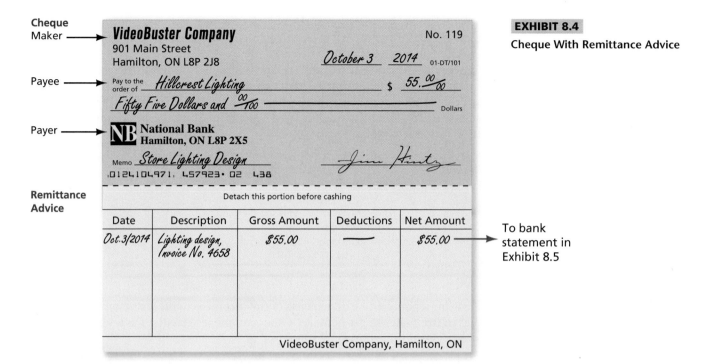

Cheque Maker ——→

Payee ——→

Payer ——→

Remittance Advice

EXHIBIT 8.4

Cheque With Remittance Advice

To bank statement in Exhibit 8.5

computer processing. Exhibit 8.4 shows a cheque. This cheque is accompanied by an optional *remittance advice* giving an explanation for the payment. When a remittance advice is unavailable, the memo line is often used for a brief explanation.

Electronic Funds Transfer

Electronic funds transfer (EFT) is the use of electronic communication to transfer cash from one party to another. No paper documents are necessary. Banks simply transfer cash from one account to another with a journal entry. Companies are increasingly using EFT because of its convenience and low cost. It can cost, for instance, up to a dollar to process a cheque through the banking system, whereas the EFT cost is near zero. We see items such as payroll, rent, utilities, insurance, and interest payments being handled by EFT. Technology has decreased the necessity for cheques for some businesses but for others, cheques are still required. For example, Alberta Blue Cross issues more than 110,000 cheques per month, but this number is declining as more payments are being made by direct deposit. The bank statement lists cash withdrawals by EFT with cheques and other deductions. Cash receipts by EFT are listed with deposits and other additions. A bank statement is sometimes a depositor's only notice of an EFT.

Credit Card Transactions

Many companies allow customers to use credit cards such as Visa or MasterCard or American Express to charge purchases. The customer has the convenience of using the credit card instead of using cash or cheques. The retailer enjoys the benefits of being paid by the credit card company. The payment to the retailer normally occurs faster than if the retailer had to collect credit sales personally and the risk of credit customers who do not pay is transferred to the credit card company. The credit card company issues the customer a monthly statement detailing the customer's transactions. The customer pays the credit card company monthly based on the credit terms on the statement.

The seller pays a fee for the services provided by the credit card company. The fee covers the credit card company's costs, which include credit checks on credit card customers, collecting cash, reimbursing retailers, and, of course, a profit margin. Therefore, when the fee is deducted, the cash received by the retailer is less than 100% of the sales value of the transaction. The fee charged by the credit card company can be calculated as a percent of sales or it may vary depending on the volume of sales. For simplicity, we will assume in this textbook that the credit card fee is based on a percent of the sales value.

When a credit card is used, the retailer receives cash, net of the credit card fee, immediately upon deposit of the credit card sales receipt at the bank or when the credit card is processed electronically at the point of sale. For instance, if TechCom has $100 of credit card sales with a 4% fee and cash is received immediately, the entry is (assume cost of sales is $40):

Aug.	15	Cash	96	
		Credit Card Expense	4	
		Sales		100
		To record credit card sales less a 4% credit card expense.		
	15	Cost of Goods Sold	40	
		Merchandise Inventory		40
		To record cost of sales.		

Some firms report credit card expense in the income statement as a type of discount deducted from sales to get net sales. Other companies classify it as a selling expense or even as an administrative expense.

DECISION MAKER
Answer—End of chapter

Entrepreneur
You are the owner of a small retail store. You are considering allowing customers to purchase merchandise using credit cards. Until now, your store only accepted cash and cheques. What forms of analysis do you use to make this decision?

Debit Card Transactions

The use of **debit cards** is common and popular with consumers. Payment for a purchase is electronically transferred from the customer's bank account to the vendor's bank account immediately at the point of sale. The customer authorizes the transaction by entering the Personal Identification Number (PIN). Normally, the bank charges the retailer a fee for this service. The entries are identical to a credit card sale. For example, assume a customer purchases a $100 service on October 1 and pays using a debit card. If the bank charges the retailer $0.40 per debit card transaction, the entry is:

Oct.	1	Cash	99.60	
		Debit Card Expense	0.40	
		Service Revenue		100.00
		To record a debit card transaction.		

CHECKPOINT

7. What is a benefit to the retailer of accepting credit and debit cards?

Do Quick Study questions: QS 8-7, QS 8-8

Bank Statement

At least once a month, the bank sends the depositor a bank statement showing the activity in the accounts during the month, or a company can access its banking activity online at any time. Different banks use a variety of formats for their bank statements. Yet all of them include the following items of information:

1. Beginning-of-month balance of the depositor's account.

2. Cheques and other debits decreasing the account during the month.

3. Deposits and other credits increasing the account during the month.

4. End-of-month balance of the depositor's account.

This information reflects the bank's records. Exhibit 8.5 shows a bank statement.

(A) Summarizes changes in the account.   (C) Lists deposits and credits (increases)
(B) Lists paid cheques in date order along   to the account.
    with other debits (or decreases).   (D) Shows the daily account balances.

EXHIBIT 8.5

Bank Statement

Member CDIC	**NB National Bank** Hamilton, ON L8P 2X5	Bank Statement

VideoBuster Company
901 Main Street
Hamilton, ON L8P 2J8

October 31, 2014
Statement Date

494 504 2
Account Number

(A)

Previous Balance	Total Cheques and Debits	Total Deposits and Credits	Current Balance
1,609.58	723.00	1,163.42	2,050.00

From deposit slip in Exhibit 8.3 →

Originally deposited as part of Oct. 3 deposit (see deposit slip in Exhibit 8.3) →

From cheque with remittance advice in Exhibit 8.4 →

(B) Cheques and Debits			(C) Deposits and Credits		(D) Daily Balance	
Date	No.	Amount	Date	Amount	Date	Amount
					OCT01	1,609.58
OCT03	119	55.00	OCT03	240.00	OCT03	1,794.58
OCT09	123	25.00	OCT09	180.00	OCT09	1,949.58
OCT15	127	50.00	OCT15	100.00	OCT15	1,999.58
OCT16		23.00 DM	OCT16	150.00	OCT16	2,126.58
OCT17	122	70.00	OCT17	485.00 CM	OCT17	2,541.58
OCT18	120	200.00			OCT18	2,341.58
OCT19	125	15.00			OCT19	2,326.58
OCT20		20.00 NSF			OCT20	2,306.58
		10.00 DM			OCT20	2,296.58
OCT26	121	120.00			OCT26	2,176.58
OCT29	128	135.00			OCT29	2,041.58
			OCT31	8.42 IN	OCT31	2,050.00

Symbols:	**CM**–Credit Memo	**EC**–Error Correction	**NSF**–Non-sufficient Funds	**SC**–Service Charge
	DM–Debit Memo	**IN**–Interest Earned	**OD**–Overdraft	

< Reconcile the account immediately. >

Notice that 'Deposits' are called credits and 'Cheques' are called debits on the bank statement. This is because the bank statement reports information from the bank's point of view—*that a depositor's account is a liability on the bank's records since the money belongs to the depositor and not the bank*. When a depositor, Smith, puts money into the bank, the bank debits cash and **credits** the bank's liability account to Smith. Hence, **credit memos** show the bank's increasing liability to Smith. When Smith withdraws money from the bank, the bank records it as a credit to cash and **debits** the bank's liability account for Smith. Therefore, **debit memos** reflect decreases in the bank's liability to Smith.[3]

---

3 Recall that a bank records transactions in an identical manner to any other business. For example, on October 3 the bank cashed a cheque written by VideoBuster. This was recorded by the bank as:

VideoBuster Customer Account (a liability to the bank) 55
    Cash (an asset to the bank) 55

Notice on the bank statement in Exhibit 8.5 that this cheque is reported to VideoBuster as a 'debit' because the bank has decreased its liability to VideoBuster. As a second example, on October 3 VideoBuster deposited $240 into its bank account; this was recorded by the bank as:

Cash 240
    VideoBuster Customer Account (a liability to the bank)................................. 240

The bank statement reports this deposit to VideoBuster as a 'credit' because the bank's liability to VideoBuster has increased.

Enclosed with a bank statement are the depositor's cancelled cheques and any debit or credit memoranda affecting the account. **Cancelled cheques** are cheques the bank has paid and deducted from the customer's account during the month. Other deductions also often appear on a bank statement and include: (1) service charges and fees assessed by the bank, (2) customers' cheques deposited that are uncollectible, (3) corrections of previous errors, (4) withdrawals through automated teller machines (ATMs)[4], and (5) periodic payments arranged in advance by a depositor such as insurance and lease payments. Except for service charges, the bank notifies the depositor of each deduction with a debit memorandum when the bank reduces the balance. A copy of each debit memorandum is usually sent with the monthly statement.

While deposits increase a depositor's bank balance, there are other transactions that increase the depositor's account. Examples are amounts the bank collects on behalf of the depositor and corrections of previous errors. Credit memoranda notify the depositor of all increases recorded by the bank. A copy of each credit memorandum is often sent with the bank statement. Another item added to the bank balance is interest earned by the depositor. Many chequing accounts pay the depositor interest based on the average cash balance maintained in the account. The bank computes the amount of interest earned and credits it to the depositor's account each month. In Exhibit 8.5, for instance, the bank credits $8.42 of interest to the account of VideoBuster. We describe the methods used to calculate interest in Chapter 9.

Bank Reconciliation

 LO⁶ Prepare a bank reconciliation and journalize any resulting adjustment(s).

When a company deposits all receipts intact and when all payments except petty cash payments are by cheque, the bank statement serves as a device for proving the accuracy of the depositor's cash records. We test the accuracy by preparing a *bank reconciliation*. A **bank reconciliation** is a form of internal control over cash that explains the difference between the balance of a chequing account according to the depositor's records and the balance reported on the bank statement.

Purpose of Bank Reconciliation

The balance of a chequing account reported on the bank statement is rarely equal to the balance in the depositor's accounting records. This is usually due to information that one party has that the other does not. We must therefore prove the accuracy of both the depositor's records and those of the bank. This means we must *reconcile* the two balances and explain or account for the differences in these two balances.

Among the factors causing the bank statement balance to differ from the depositor's book balance are:

1. *Unrecorded deposits* (also known as *deposits in transit* or *outstanding deposits*). These are deposits made and recorded by the depositor but not recorded on the bank statement. For example, companies often make deposits at the end of a business day, after the bank is closed. A deposit in the bank's night depository on the last day of the month is not recorded by the bank until the next business day and does not appear on the bank statement for that month. Also, deposits mailed to the bank near the end of a month may be in transit and unrecorded when the statement is prepared.

2. *Outstanding cheques.* These are cheques written (or drawn) by the depositor, deducted on the depositor's records, and sent to the payees. But they have not yet reached the bank for payment and deduction at the time of the bank statement.

3. *Additions for collections and for interest.* Banks sometimes act as collection agents for their depositors by collecting notes and other items. Banks can also receive electronic funds transfers to the depositor's account. When a bank collects an item, it adds it to the depositor's account, less any service fee. It also sends a credit memorandum to notify the depositor of the transaction. When the memorandum is received, it should be recorded by the depositor. Yet these sometimes remain unrecorded until the time of the bank reconciliation.

---

4 Because of a desire to make all disbursements by cheque, most business chequing accounts do not allow ATM withdrawals.

Many bank accounts earn interest on the average cash balance in the account during the month. If an account earns interest, the bank statement includes a credit for the amount earned during the past month. Notification of earned interest is provided by the bank statement.

4. *Deductions for uncollectible items and for services.* A company sometimes deposits a customer's cheque that is uncollectible. This usually is because the balance in the customer's account is not large enough to cover the cheque. This cheque is called a *non-sufficient funds (NSF)* cheque. The bank initially credited the depositor's account for the amount of the deposited cheque. When the bank learns that the cheque is uncollectible, it debits (reduces) the depositor's account for the amount of that cheque. The bank may also charge the depositor a fee for processing an uncollectible cheque and notify the depositor of the deduction by sending a debit memorandum. While each deduction should be recorded by the depositor when a debit memorandum is received, an entry is sometimes not made until the bank reconciliation is prepared.

Other possible bank charges to a depositor's account reported on a bank statement include the printing of new cheques and a service charge for maintaining the account. Notification of these charges is *not* provided until the statement is mailed.

5. *Errors.* Both banks and depositors can make errors. For example, a bank error might include a cheque written by *VideoBlaster* Company mistakenly charged against the account of *VideoBuster* Company or a deposit made by *VideoBuster* Company accidentally posted to the account of *Videon* Company. A depositor error might involve a cheque actually written for $102 but recorded in error in the Cash Disbursements Journal as $120. These kinds of errors might not be discovered until the depositor prepares a bank reconciliation.

Steps in Reconciling a Bank Balance

The employee who prepares the bank reconciliation should not be responsible for cash receipts, processing cheques, or maintaining cash records. This employee needs to gather information from the bank statement and from other records. A reconciliation requires this person to:

- Compare deposits on the bank statement with deposits in the accounting records (Cash Receipts Journal and last month's bank reconciliation). Identify any discrepancies and determine which is correct. List any errors or unrecorded deposits.

- Compare cancelled cheques on the bank statement with actual cheques returned with the statement. For each cheque, make sure the correct amount is deducted by the bank and the returned cheque is properly charged to the account. List any discrepancies or errors.

- Compare cancelled cheques on the bank statement with cheques recorded in the books (Cash Disbursements Journal). List any outstanding cheques. Also, while companies with good internal controls would rarely write a cheque without recording it, we should inspect and list any cancelled cheques that are unrecorded in the books.

- Identify any outstanding cheques listed on the previous month's bank reconciliation that are not included in the cancelled cheques on this month's bank statement. List these cheques that remain outstanding at the end of the current month. Send the list to the cashier's office for follow-up with the payees to see if the cheques were actually received.

- Inspect all additions (credits) on the bank statement and determine whether each is recorded in the books. These items include collections by the bank, correction of previous bank statement errors, and interest earned by the depositor. List any unrecorded items.

- Inspect all deductions (debits) to the account on the bank statement and determine whether each is recorded in the books. These include bank charges for newly printed cheques, NSF cheques, and monthly service charges. List items not yet recorded.

When this information is gathered, the employee can complete the reconciliation.

Illustrating a Bank Reconciliation

We illustrate a bank reconciliation by preparing one for VideoBuster as of October 31. We use the guidelines listed above and follow nine specific steps. Follow each step to the corresponding Exhibits 8.5 to 8.8 to see where the information comes from and how it is shown on the bank reconciliation in Exhibit 8.9.

① Identify the bank balance of the cash account at October 31 (balance per bank).
  – *Bank balance shown on the bank statement is $2,050 (from Exhibit 8.5).*

② Identify and list any unrecorded deposits[5] and any bank errors.[5] Add them to the bank balance on the bank reconciliation.
  – *A $145 deposit was placed in the bank's night depository on October 31 and is not recorded on the bank statement (from Exhibit 8.6).*

③ Identify and list any outstanding cheques[5] and any bank errors.[5] Deduct them from the bank balance on the bank reconciliation.
  – *A comparison of cancelled cheques with the company's books showed two cheques outstanding: #124 for $150 and #126 for $200 (from Exhibit 8.7).*

④ Calculate the *adjusted bank balance*, also called *corrected* or *reconciled* balance.
  – *See Exhibit 8.9.*

⑤ Identify the company's balance of the cash account (book balance).
  – *Cash balance shown in the accounting records is $1,404.58 (from Exhibit 8.8).*

⑥ Identify and list any unrecorded credit memoranda from the bank, such as interest earned and errors.[5] Add them to the book balance on the bank reconciliation.

  ⓐ *Enclosed with the bank statement is a credit memorandum showing that the bank collected a note receivable for the company on October 17. The note's proceeds of $500 (minus a $15 collection fee) were credited to the company's account. This credit memorandum is not yet recorded by the company (from Exhibit 8.5).*

  ⓑ *The bank statement shows a credit of $8.42 for interest earned on the average cash balance in the account. There was no prior notification of this item and it is not yet recorded on the company's books (from Exhibit 8.5).*

EXHIBIT 8.5

Bank Statement (repeated from earlier page for ease of reference)

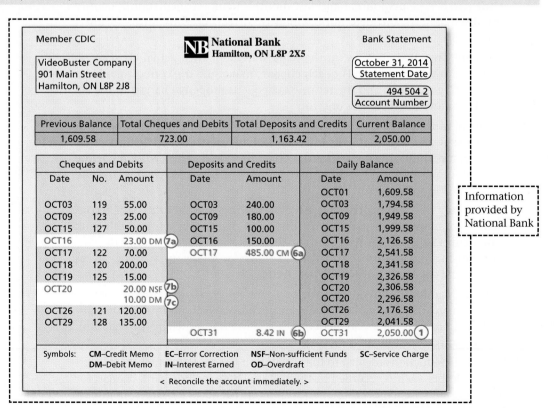

5   For simplicity, this example includes no errors and assumes that there were no outstanding cheques or
    deposits on last month's bank reconciliation. The End-of-Chapter Demonstration Problem illustrates
    these additional complexities.

⑦ Identify and list any unrecorded debit memoranda from the bank, such as service charges and errors.[5] Deduct them from the book balance on the bank reconciliation.

– *Debits on the bank statement that are not recorded on the books include:* ⓐ *a $23 charge for cheques printed by the bank, and* ⓑ *an NSF cheque for $20 plus* ⓒ *a related $10 processing fee. The NSF cheque is from a customer, Frank Heflin, and was originally included as part of the October 3 deposit (from Exhibit 8.5).*

⑧ Calculate the *adjusted book balance*, also called the *corrected* or *reconciled* balance.

– *See Exhibit 8.9.*

⑨ Verify that the two adjusted balances from Steps 4 and 8 are equal. If so, they are reconciled. If not, check for mathematical accuracy and missing data.

– *See Exhibit 8.9.*

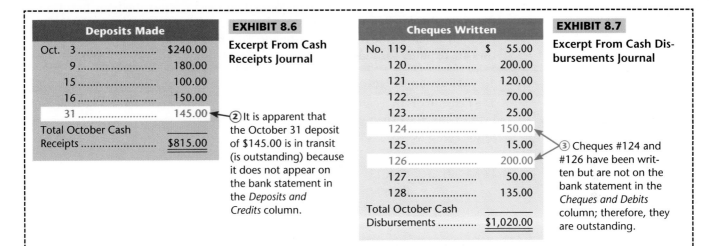

Deposits Made	
Oct. 3	$240.00
9	180.00
15	100.00
16	150.00
31	145.00
Total October Cash Receipts	$815.00

EXHIBIT 8.6

Excerpt From Cash Receipts Journal

② It is apparent that the October 31 deposit of $145.00 is in transit (is outstanding) because it does not appear on the bank statement in the *Deposits and Credits* column.

Cheques Written	
No. 119	$ 55.00
120	200.00
121	120.00
122	70.00
123	25.00
124	150.00
125	15.00
126	200.00
127	50.00
128	135.00
Total October Cash Disbursements	$1,020.00

EXHIBIT 8.7

Excerpt From Cash Disbursements Journal

③ Cheques #124 and #126 have been written but are not on the bank statement in the *Cheques and Debits* column; therefore, they are outstanding.

	Cash				Acct. No. 101
Date	Explanation	PR	Debit	Credit	Balance
2014					
Sept. 30	Balance				1,609.58
Oct. 31		CR6	815.00		⑤ 2,424.58
31		CD4		1,020.00	1,404.58

EXHIBIT 8.8

General Ledger Cash Account

Information provided by VideoBuster Company

EXHIBIT 8.9 Bank Reconciliation

VideoBuster Company
Bank Reconciliation
October 31, 2014

① Bank statement balance			$2,050.00	⑤ Book balance		$1,404.58
② Add:				⑥ Add:		
Deposit of Oct. 31 in transit			145.00	ⓐ Collection of $500 note less $15 collection fee	$485.00	
				ⓑ Interest earned	8.42	493.42
			$2,195.00			$1,898.00
③ Deduct:				⑦ Deduct:		
Outstanding cheques:				ⓐ Cheque printing charge	$ 23.00	
#124	$150.00			ⓑ+ⓒ NSF cheque plus service fee	30.00	53.00
#126	200.00	350.00				
④ Adjusted bank balance			$1,845.00	⑧ Adjusted book balance		$1,845.00

⑨ Balances are equal (reconciled)

When the reconciliation is complete, the employee sends a copy to the accounting department to record any needed journal entries. For instance, entries are needed to record any unrecorded debit and credit memoranda and any company mistakes. The entries resulting from VideoBuster's bank reconciliation are illustrated in the next section. Another copy goes to the cashier's office. This is especially important if the bank has made an error that needs correction.

Recording Adjusting Entries From the Bank Reconciliation

A bank reconciliation helps locate errors by either the bank or the depositor. It also identifies unrecorded items that need recording on the company's books. In Video-Buster's reconciliation, for instance, the adjusted balance of $1,845.00 is the correct balance as of October 31. But the company's accounting records show a $1,404.58 balance. We must prepare journal entries to adjust the book balance to the correct balance. It is important to remember that only the items reconciling the book balance side require adjustment. This means that the following four entries are required for VideoBuster:

1. Collection of Note

The first entry is to record the net proceeds of VideoBuster's note receivable collected by the bank, the expense of having the bank perform that service, and the reduction in the Notes Receivable account:

Oct.	31	Cash	485.00	
		Collection Expense	15.00	
		Notes Receivable		500.00
		To record collection fee and proceeds of a note collected by the bank.		

2. Interest Earned

The second entry records the interest credited to VideoBuster's account by the bank:

	31	Cash	8.42	
		Interest Revenue		8.42
		To record interest earned on the average Cash balance in the chequing account.		

Interest earned is a revenue, and the entry recognizes both the revenue and the related increase in Cash.

3. NSF Cheque

The third entry records the NSF cheque that is returned as uncollectible. The $20 cheque was received from Heflin in payment of his account and deposited. When the cheque cleared the banking system, Heflin's bank account was found to have insufficient funds to cover the cheque. The bank charged $10 for handling the NSF cheque and deducted $30 total from VideoBuster's account. The company must reverse the entry made when the cheque was received and also record the $10 fee:

	31	Accounts Receivable—Frank Heflin	30.00	
		Cash		30.00
		To charge Frank Heflin's account for his NSF cheque and the bank's fee.		

This entry reflects business practice by adding the NSF $10 fee to Heflin's account. The company will try to collect the entire $30 from Heflin.

4. Cheque Printing

The fourth entry debits Office Supplies Expense for the printing of cheques:

31	Office Supplies Expense	23.00	
	Cash		23.00
	Cheque printing charge.		

After these four entries are recorded, the balance of Cash is increased to the correct amount of $1,845 (= $1,404.58 + $485 + $8.42 − $30 − $23).

DECISION INSIGHT

The Financial Transactions and Reports Analysis Centre of Canada, or FINTRAC, is Canada's financial intelligence unit created to collect, analyze, and disclose financial information and intelligence on suspected money laundering and terrorist financing activities. Banks, among others identified in the Proceeds of Crime (Money Laundering) and Terrorist Financing Act and Regulations, are required to report certain transactions to FINTRAC. When there are reasonable grounds to suspect that the information is relevant to threats to the security of Canada, FINTRAC will disclose that information to the Canadian Security and Intelligence Service (CSIS).

SOURCE: http://www.fintrac.gc.ca/

CHECKPOINT

8. What is a bank statement?
9. What is the meaning of the phrase *to reconcile a bank balance*?
10. Why do we reconcile the bank statement balance of cash and the depositor's book balance of cash?
11. List items affecting the bank side of a reconciliation and indicate if the items are added or subtracted.
12. List items affecting the book side of a reconciliation and indicate if the items are added or subtracted.

Do Quick Study questions: QS 8-9, QS 8-10

CRITICAL THINKING CHALLENGE Refer to the Critical Thinking Challenge questions at the beginning of the chapter. Compare your answers to those suggested on Connect.

IFRS AND ASPE—THE DIFFERENCES

Difference	International Financial Reporting Standards (IFRS)	Accounting Standards for Private Enterprises (ASPE)
There are no significant differences between IFRS and ASPE related to this chapter.		

SUMMARY

LO¹   Define, explain the purpose, and identify the principles of internal control. An internal control system consists of the policies and procedures that managers use to protect assets, ensure reliable accounting, promote efficient operations, and encourage adherence to company policies. It is a key part of systems design, analysis, and performance. It can prevent avoidable losses and help managers both plan operations and monitor company and human performance. Principles of good internal control include establishing responsibilities, maintaining adequate records, insuring assets and bonding employees, separating recordkeeping from custody of assets, dividing responsibilities for related transactions, applying technological controls, and performing regular independent reviews.

LO²   Define cash and explain how it is reported. Cash consists of cash on hand and demand deposits, including currency and coins, and amounts on deposit in bank, chequing, and some savings accounts. It also includes items that are acceptable for deposit in these accounts. Cash equivalents or short-term investments are similar to cash, therefore most companies combine them with cash as a single item on the balance sheet. Cash and cash equivalents are liquid assets because they are converted easily into other assets or used in paying for services or liabilities.

LO³   Apply internal control to cash. Internal control of cash receipts ensures that all cash received is properly recorded and deposited. Cash receipts arise from cash sales, collections of customers' accounts, receipts of interest and rent, bank loans, sale of assets, and owner investments. Good internal control for cash receipts by mail includes at least two people being assigned to open the mail and prepare a list with each sender's name, amount of money received, and explanation.

LO⁴   Explain and record petty cash fund transactions. To avoid writing cheques for small amounts, a company sets up one or more petty cash funds to pay for items such as postage, courier fees, repairs, and supplies. A petty cashier is responsible for safekeeping of the cash, for making payments from this fund, and for keeping receipts and records. A Petty Cash account is debited when the fund is established or increased in size. The cashier presents all paid receipts to the company's cashier for reimbursement to restore petty cash to its full amount. Petty cash disbursements are recorded whenever the fund is replenished with debits to expense accounts reflecting receipts and a credit to cash.

LO⁵   Explain and identify banking activities and the control features they provide. Banks offer several services—such as the bank account, the bank deposit, and chequing—that promote the control or safeguarding of cash. A bank account is set up by a bank and permits a customer to deposit money for safeguarding and cheque withdrawals. A bank deposit is money added to the account with a deposit slip as proof. A cheque is a document signed by the depositor instructing the bank to pay a specified amount of money to a designated recipient. Sales resulting from debit card and credit card transactions are usually deposited into the bank account immediately, less a fee. Electronic funds transfer (EFT) uses electronic communication to transfer cash from one party to another, and it decreases certain risks. Companies increasingly use it because of its convenience and low cost.

LO⁶   Prepare a bank reconciliation and journalize any resulting adjustment(s). A bank reconciliation is prepared to prove the accuracy of the depositor's and the bank's records. In completing a reconciliation, the bank statement balance is adjusted for such items as outstanding cheques and unrecorded deposits made on or before the bank statement date but not reflected on the statement. The depositor's Cash account balance also often requires adjustment. These adjustments include items such as service charges, bank collections for the depositor, and interest earned on the account balance.

GUIDANCE ANSWERS TO **DECISION MAKER**

Campaign Manager
A forced vacation policy is part of a system of good internal controls. When employees are forced to take vacations, their ability to hide any fraudulent behaviour decreases. This is because someone must take on the responsibilities of the person on vacation, and the replacement employee potentially can uncover fraudulent behaviour or records. A forced vacation policy is especially important for employees in more sensitive positions of handling money or other easily transferable assets.

Internal Auditor
You inform your supervisor, who emphasizes that the purpose of the surprise visit was defeated because you allowed another

employee to interfere with and influence your actions; this was a valuable first lesson! Your problem is now whether to accept the situation or to dig further to see if the petty cashier is abusing petty cash. Since you were asked to postpone your count and the fund consists of new $20 bills, you have legitimate concerns about whether money is being borrowed for personal use. You should conduct a further investigation. One result might show that the most recent reimbursement of the fund was for $180 (= 9 × $20) or more. In that case, this reimbursement can leave the fund with sequentially numbered $20 bills. But if the most recent reimbursement was for less than $180, the presence of nine sequentially numbered $20 bills suggests that the $180 of new $20 bills was obtained from a bank as replacement for bills that had been removed. Neither situation shows that the cashier is stealing money. Yet the second case indicates that the cashier "borrowed" the cash and later replaced it after the auditor showed up. In writing your report, you must not conclude that the cashier is unethical unless evidence along with your knowledge of company policies supports it. Your report must present facts according to the evidence.

Entrepreneur
Your analysis of allowing credit card sales should estimate the benefits against the costs. The primary benefit is the potential to increase sales by attracting customers who prefer the convenience of credit cards. The primary cost is the fee charged by the credit card company for providing this service to your store. Your analysis should therefore estimate the expected increase in sales dollars from allowing credit card sales and then subtract (1) the normal costs and expenses, and (2) the credit card fees associated with this expected increase in sales dollars. If your analysis shows an increase in profit from allowing credit card sales, your store should probably allow them.

GUIDANCE ANSWERS TO **CHECKPOINT**

1. c
2. Technology reduces processing errors, allows more extensive testing of records, limits the amount of hard evidence of processing steps, and highlights the importance of maintaining separation of duties.
3. a
4. If all cash payments are made by cheque, numerous cheques for small amounts must be written. Because this practice is expensive and time consuming, a petty cash fund is established to make small cash payments.
5. If the petty cash fund is not reimbursed at the end of an accounting period, the transactions in petty cash are not yet recorded in the accounts and the petty cash asset is overstated. But these amounts are rarely large enough to affect users' decisions based on financial statements.
6. First, when the petty cash fund is reimbursed, the petty cash transactions are recorded in their proper accounts. Second, reimbursement also gives money that allows the fund to continue being used. Third, reimbursement identifies any cash shortage or overage in the fund.
7. The retailer receives payment faster than if it had to collect credit sales, and the risk of uncollectible customer

accounts is transferred to the credit card company and bank.
8. A bank statement is a report prepared by the bank describing the activities in a depositor's account.
9. To reconcile a bank balance means to explain the difference between the cash balance in the depositor's accounting records and the balance on the bank statement.
10. The purpose of the bank reconciliation is to determine if any errors have been made by the bank or by the depositor and to determine if the bank has completed any transactions affecting the depositor's account that the depositor has not recorded. It is also an internal control mechanism to ensure that the company's cash system is operating properly.
11. Outstanding cheques—subtracted
    Unrecorded deposits—added
12. Bank service charges—subtracted
    Debit memos—subtracted
    NSF cheques—subtracted
    Interest earned—added
    Credit memos—added

DEMONSTRATION PROBLEM

Required
Consider the following information and prepare a bank reconciliation, along with any resulting journal entries, for TJ Company at April 30, 2014.

Analysis Component:
Assume that you are the owner of TJ Company and have just read a newspaper article about employee accounting fraud. As a result, you have decided to review the bank reconciliation prepared for April 30. You notice that cheque #808 for $850 is not included with the cancelled cheques that are returned by the bank with the bank statement. Your office is small and is managed by one employee, Brent Wicker. When questioned, Brent cannot locate the missing cheque. What do you do, if anything? Explain.

The bank reconciliation prepared by TJ Company on March 31, 2014, follows:

TJ Company Bank Reconciliation March 31, 2014					
Bank statement balance		$7,670	Book balance		$8,590
Add:					
Deposit of March 31 in transit		1,100			
		$8,770			
Deduct:					
Outstanding cheques:					
#797:	$ 60				
#804:	120	180			
Adjusted bank balance		$8,590	Adjusted book balance		$8,590

The following bank statement is available for April:

Bank Statement					
To: TJ Company				April 30, 2014 Bank of Nova Scotia	
Cheques/Charges/Debits			Deposits/Credits		Balance
					7,670
#811	04/03	834	04/03	1,100	7,936
#807	04/07	375	04/07	810	8,371
#810	04/13	208	04/13	690	8,853
NSF	04/18	450	04/18	680	9,083
#808	04/23	850	04/23	355	8,588
#797	04/27	60	04/27	750	9,278
#814	04/30	550	04/30	620	9,348
#813	04/30	372	INT	47	9,023
#809	04/30	124			8,899
SC	04/30	32	04/30		8,867
NSF = Not Sufficient Funds		SC = Service Charge		INT = Interest	

A list of deposits made and cheques written during April, taken from the Cash Receipts Journal and Cash Disbursements Journal, is shown below:

Deposits Made	
April 7	$ 810
13	690
18	680
23	355
27	750
30	620
30	770
Total April Cash Receipts	$4,675

Cheques Written	
No. 807	$ 375
808	850
809	124
810	208
811	348
812	207
813	372
814	550
815	405
816	602
Total April Cash Disbursements	$4,041

General Ledger Cash Account:

Cash					Acct. No. 101
Date	Explanation	PR	Debit	Credit	Balance
2014					
March 31	Balance				8,590
April 30		CR12	4,675		13,265
30		CD14		4,041	9,224

In reviewing cheques returned by the bank, the bookkeeper discovered that cheque #811, for delivery expense, was recorded in the Cash Disbursements Journal incorrectly as $348. The NSF cheque for $450 was that of customer A. Hussain, deposited in April.

Planning the Solution
- Set up a schedule like Exhibit 8.9 with a bank side and a book side for the reconciliation.
- Follow the nine steps used in the chapter to prepare the bank reconciliation.
- For every reconciling item on the book side, prepare an entry, if required.
- Prepare an answer to the analysis component.

SOLUTION

TJ Company Bank Reconciliation April 30, 2014					
Bank statement balance		$8,867	Book balance		$9,224
Add:			Add:		
Deposit of April 30 in transit		770	Interest revenue		47
		$9,637			$9,271
Deduct:			Deduct:		
Outstanding cheques:			Error (cheque #811 for delivery exp)	$486	
#804:	$120		NSF cheque	450	
#812:	207		Service charge	32	968
#815:	405				
#816:	602	1,334			
Adjusted bank balance		$8,303	Adjusted book balance		$8,303

Required Entries

April	30	Cash	47	
		Interest Revenue		47
		To record interest earned.		
	30	Delivery Expense	486	
		Cash		486
		To correct accounting error on cheque #811.		
	30	Accounts Receivable—A. Hussain	450	
		Cash		450
		To reinstate customer account due to NSF cheque.		
	30	Bank Service Charges Expense	32	
		Cash		32
		To record bank service charges.		

Analysis Component:

Several things need to be done. A review of prior months' bank reconciliations needs to be conducted to determine if this is an anomaly or a recurring event. The journal entry regarding cheque #808 needs to be reviewed to determine the payee. The payee, if identifiable, needs to be contacted to verify the purchase. If this cannot be done, the bank needs to be contacted to determine if its records are able to verify the payee on the cheque. Hopefully, Brent made an honest mistake and misplaced the cheque. However, in the future, the owner of TJ Company should review each bank reconciliation and ensure that the cheques being paid are scrutinized to ensure they are for business-related payments.

APPENDIX 8A

Using the Information

ACID-TEST RATIO

LO⁷ Calculate the acid-test ratio and explain its use as an indicator of a company's liquidity.

We learned in Chapter 5 that merchandise inventory often makes up a large portion of current assets for merchandising companies. We know that merchandise inventory must be sold and any resulting accounts receivable need to be collected before cash is available. This often means that a large part of current assets is not readily available for paying liabilities because it is in the form of merchandise inventory.

We explained in Chapter 4 how the current ratio, calculated as total current assets divided by total current liabilities, is useful in assessing a company's ability to pay current liabilities. Because some current assets, specifically merchandise inventories and prepaids, are not readily available as a source of payment for current liabilities, we look to a measure other than the current ratio to obtain a stricter measure of a company's ability to cover current liabilities: the *acid-test ratio*.

The *acid-test ratio* differs from the current ratio by excluding current assets that are *less liquid*, such as inventory and prepaids. The **acid-test ratio**, also called the **quick ratio**, is defined as shown in Exhibit 8A.1.

EXHIBIT 8A.1

Acid-Test Ratio

$$\text{Acid-test ratio} = \frac{\text{Quick assets*}}{\text{Current liabilities}}$$

Quick assets are cash, short-term investments, and receivables.

Exhibit 8A.2 shows both the acid-test and current ratios of WestJet.

EXHIBIT 8A.2

Current and Acid-Test Ratios Compared

	At December 31,				
	2011	**2010**	**2009**	**2008**	**2007**
Current Ratio	1.51	1.53	1.48	1.25	1.22
Acid-Test Ratio	1.41	1.44	1.37	1.13	1.13

The acid-test ratio is interpreted in a similar manner as the current ratio. In Exhibit 8A.2, WestJet's current ratio at December 31, 2011, shows $1.51 of current assets available to cover each $1.00 of current liability as it comes due. As a stricter measure, the acid-test ratio tells us WestJet had $1.41 of quick assets to cover each $1.00 of current obligations at December 31, 2011. An acid-test ratio equal to or greater than 1 is generally considered favourable (good). Both WestJet's current and acid-test ratios are greater than 1 in all of the five years shown in Exhibit 8A.2, which indicates that, in the past, it was able to cover obligations as they came due. The current and acid-test ratios for 2011, 2010, and 2009 indicate a general improvement in WestJet's ability to pay short-term debt over 2008 and 2007.

CHECKPOINT

13. ABC Company had acid-test ratios of 1.4 and 1.6 for 2014 and 2013, respectively. Is the change in the ratio favourable or unfavourable?

Do Quick Study question: *QS 8-11

SUMMARY OF APPENDIX 8A

LO⁷ Calculate the acid-test ratio and explain its use as an indicator of a company's liquidity. The acid-test ratio is calculated as quick assets (cash, short-term investments, and receivables) divided by current liabilities. It is an indicator of a company's ability to pay its current liabilities with its existing quick assets. A ratio equal to or greater than 1 is often considered adequate.

GUIDANCE ANSWER TO CHECKPOINT

13. Unfavourable.

GLOSSARY

Acid-test ratio A ratio used to assess a company's ability to cover its current debts with existing assets calculated as quick assets (cash, short-term investments, and receivables) divided by current liabilities; also called *quick ratio*.

Bank reconciliation An analysis that explains the difference between the balance of a chequing account shown in the depositor's records and the balance reported on the bank statement.

Bond An insurance policy purchased by a company to protect against losses from theft by that employee.

Cancelled cheques Cheques that the bank has paid and deducted from the customer's account during the month.

Cash Consists of cash on hand and demand deposits, including currency, coins, and amounts on deposit in bank chequing or savings accounts.

Cash Over and Short account An income statement account used to record cash shortages and cash overages arising from omitted petty cash receipts and from errors in making change.

Cheque A document signed by the depositor instructing the bank to pay a specified amount of money to a designated recipient.

Collusion An act in which two or more people agree to commit a fraud.

Debit cards Cards used at point of sale to transfer payment for a purchase immediately from the customer's to the vendor's bank account.

Deposit slip Bank document that lists the items such as currency, coins, and cheques deposited along with each of their dollar amounts.

Electronic funds transfer (EFT) The use of electronic communication to transfer cash from one party to another.

Internal control system All the policies and procedures managers use to protect assets, ensure reliable accounting, promote efficient operations, and urge adherence to company policies.

Liquid assets Assets such as cash that are easily converted into other types of assets or used to buy services or to pay liabilities.

Liquidity A characteristic of an asset that refers to how easily the asset can be converted into cash or another type of asset or used in paying for services or obligations.

Petty cashier Employee responsible for safekeeping of the cash, making payments from this fund, and keeping accurate records.

Principles of internal control Fundamental principles of internal control that apply to all companies requiring management to ensure transactions and activities are authorized, maintain records, insure assets, separate record-keeping and custody of assets, establish a separation of duties, apply technological controls, and perform internal and external audits.

Quick assets Those current assets that are most liquid, specifically cash, short-term investments, and receivables.

Quick ratio See *acid-test ratio*.

Separation of duties An internal control principle requiring the division of responsibility for related transactions between two or more individuals or departments.

Signature card Bank document that includes the signature of each person authorized to sign cheques from the account.

 Visit **Connect** for additional study tools, practice quizzes, to search an interactive eBook, and much more.

CONCEPT REVIEW QUESTIONS

1. Which of the following assets is most liquid and which is least liquid: merchandise inventory, building, accounts receivable, cash?

2. List the seven broad principles of internal control.

3. Why should the person who keeps the record of an asset not be responsible for custody of the asset?

4. Internal control procedures are important in every business, but at what stage in the development of a business do they become critical?

5. Why should responsibility for a sequence of related transactions be divided among different departments or individuals?

6. Why should all receipts be deposited intact on the day of receipt?

7. When merchandise is purchased for a large store, why are department managers not permitted to deal directly with suppliers?

8. What is a petty cash receipt? Who signs a petty cash receipt?

9. Refer to **Danier**'s balance sheet in Appendix II. What is its cash balance as at June 25, 2011?   **DANIER**

10. **WestJet Airlines** showed cash and cash equivalents on December 31, 2011, of $1,243,605,000. What percentage is this of total assets?

QUICK STUDY

QS 8-1 Internal control objectives LO¹

You are currently part of a university work experience program. Your job placement is at the municipal transit centre. Your supervisor is responsible for the recording and distribution of monthly transit passes to authorized vendors throughout the city. The vendors pay $50 per bus pass and sell them for $55. Your work experience job is to prepare a monthly reconciliation of the transit passes including the quantity sold, the number actually distributed, the unsold passes, and the cash proceeds. You are unable to reconcile the past two months. The bus passes are sequentially numbered and, in checking the sequence, you notice that numbers 9750 to 9820, 11012 to 11750, and 22000 to 22440 cannot be accounted for. You bring this to the attention of the supervisor, who tells you that reconciliations are never done; the job was created by her superior "to give you something to do" so you are told not to worry about it.

a. What is the main objective of internal control and how is it accomplished?

b. Why should recordkeeping for assets be separated from custody over the assets?

c. Do you report your findings?

QS 8-2 Reporting cash and other current assets LO²

Prepare the current asset section based on the following alphabetized post-closing trial balance information at March 31, 2014, for Whiteagle Company:

Account	Debits	Credits
Accounts payable		$ 7,000
Accounts receivable	$ 4,500	
Accumulated depreciation		9,900
Cash	15,000	
Isaac Whiteagle, capital		25,800
Notes payable, due 2023		14,000
Petty cash	600	
Prepaid rent	3,200	
Property, plant and equipment	38,000	
Unearned revenue		4,600

QS 8-3 Internal controls for cash LO³

The treasurer of a local not-for-profit organization was found guilty today of defrauding the organization of thousands of dollars. Among the individual's many responsibilities were the recording of cash deposits, the writing of cheques, and the preparation of the bank reconciliation. A member of the organization suspected wrongdoing when the treasurer reported total cash collections of $2,800 regarding the sale of nonsequentially numbered raffle tickets; the member submitted $1,600 to the treasurer and knew that other members had collectively sold in excess of $3,000. The police were consulted and an investigation revealed that not only had the treasurer pocketed an undisclosed amount of cash over a two-year period but he had also made cash withdrawals from the bank and destroyed the debit memos when returned with the bank statement.

a. What three basic guidelines regarding a good system of internal control for cash were not observed?

b. What corrective action should the organization take in the future?

QS 8-4 Petty cash LO⁴

The petty cash fund of the Wee Ones Agency was established on May 1, 2014, at $75. At the end of the month, the fund contained $12.74 and had the following receipts: film rentals, $19.40; refreshments for meetings, $22.81 (both expenditures to be classified as Entertainment Expense); postage, $6.95; and printing, $13.10.

1. Prepare the journal entry to record the establishment of the fund.

2. Prepare a summary of the petty cash payments similar to Exhibit 8.2 and then record the reimbursement on May 31.

3. Explain when the Petty Cash account would be credited in a journal entry.

QS 8-5 Petty cash LO⁴

WilsonArt set up a petty cash fund of $200 on March 1, 2014. On March 17, the petty cash box contained $19 and the following receipts: $75 for printing, $48 for taxi fare, and $55 for delivery expense. Record the reimbursement of the fund on March 17.

QS 8-6 Petty cash LO⁴

Canmore Consulting established a $100 petty cash fund on September 1, 2014. On September 23, the petty cash box contained $7 and receipts for the following expenses: $32 for entertainment expense (lunch with a client), $45 for computer repair, and $18 for delivery expense. Record the reimbursement of the fund on September 23.

QS 8-7 Credit card transactions LO⁵

Journalize the following transactions (assume a perpetual inventory system):

February 1	Recorded $75,000 of sales (cost $62,000) to customers using MasterCard. MasterCard charges the retailer 2.5% for credit card transactions.
February 10	Sold merchandise to customers who paid $28,000 in cash (cost $23,000).

QS 8-8 Debit card transactions LO⁵

Journalize the following transactions (assume a perpetual inventory system):

Oct.	1	Recorded sales of $14,000 (cost $8,000) to customers using debit cards. Assume the bank charges 0.25% for all debit card transactions.
	7	Sold merchandise to customers who paid $3,500 in cash (cost $2,800).

QS 8-9 Bank reconciliation LO⁶

1. Identify whether each of the following items affects the bank or book side of the reconciliation and indicate if the amount represents an addition or a subtraction:

   a. Deposits in transit.   e. Outstanding cheques.

   b. Interest on average monthly balance.   f. Debit memos.

   c. Credit memos.   g. NSF cheques.

   d. Bank service charges.

2. Which of the previous items require a journal entry?

QS 8-10 Bank reconciliation LO⁶

Bolton Company's October 31, 2014, bank statement showed a cash balance of $15,400, while the company's General Ledger Cash account for the same date showed a balance of $13,150. A bank deposit of October 31 for $1,200 does not appear on the bank statement. Cheques #150 for $980 and #169 for $2,515, both written in October, had not cleared the bank during October. Bank service charges for the month were $45. Prepare a bank reconciliation at October 31, 2014, and prepare the necessary entries.

*QS 8-11 Acid-test ratio LO⁷

Your company has a policy of granting credit only to customers whose acid-test ratio is greater than or equal to 1. Based on this policy, determine if the following companies would be granted credit (round to two decimal places). Why or why not?

	Company A	Company B
Cash	$1,200	$1,200
Accounts receivable	2,700	2,700
Inventory	5,000	5,000
Prepaid expenses	600	600
Accounts payable	3,100	4,750
Other current liabilities	250	950

An asterisk (*) identifies assignment material based on Appendix 8A.

Exercise 8-1 Analyzing internal control LO¹

Lombard Company is a young business that has grown rapidly. The company's bookkeeper, who was hired two years ago, left town suddenly after the company's manager discovered that a great deal of money had disappeared over the past 18 months. An audit disclosed that the bookkeeper had written and signed several cheques made payable to the bookkeeper's brother and then recorded the cheques as salaries expense. The brother, who cashed the cheques but had never worked for the company, left town with the bookkeeper. As a result, the company incurred an uninsured loss of $84,000.

Evaluate Lombard Company's internal control system and indicate which principles of internal control appear to have been ignored in this situation.

Exercise 8-2 Internal control objectives LO¹

As a member of the city's internal audit team, you have been instructed to observe the procedures regarding the collection of coins from the municipally owned parking meters. You accompany the civic employee on the collection route. The employee uses a key to open the locked coin compartment of the meter and empties its contents into a canvas bag that closes with a drawstring. When the bag is full, the employee closes it, and places it in the vehicle, which is parked along the route. At the end of the day, the civic employee delivers the bags to two individuals in a municipal office who are jointly responsible for counting the contents. Write a brief report regarding your observations and any concerns that you might have.

Exercise 8-3 Recommending internal control procedures LO¹

What internal control procedures would you recommend in each of the following situations?

a. A concession company has one employee who sells T-shirts and sunglasses at the beach. Each day, the employee is given enough shirts and sunglasses to last through the day and enough cash to make change. The money is kept in a box at the stand.

b. An antique store has one employee who is given cash and sent to garage sales each weekend. The employee pays cash for merchandise to be resold at the antique store.

Exercise 8-4 Internal control over cash receipts LO³

Some of Fannin Co.'s cash receipts from customers are sent to the company in the mail. Fannin's bookkeeper opens the letters and deposits the cash received each day. What internal control problem do you see in this arrangement? What changes would you recommend?

Exercise 8-5 Petty cash fund LO⁴

Cameron Co. established a $150 petty cash fund on January 1, 2014. One week later, on January 8, the fund contained $29.25 in cash and receipts for these expenditures: postage, $42.00; transportation-in, $27.00; store supplies, $32.75; and a withdrawal of $19.00 by Jim Cameron, the owner. Cameron uses the perpetual method to account for merchandise inventory.

a. Prepare the journal entry to establish the fund on January 1.

b. Prepare a summary of the petty cash payments similar to Exhibit 8.2 and record the entry to reimburse the fund on January 8.

Analysis Component: If the January 8 entry to reimburse the fund were not recorded and financial statements were prepared for the month of January, would net income be over- or understated?

Exercise 8-6 Petty cash fund LO⁴

Willard Company established a $400 petty cash fund on September 9, 2014. On September 30, the fund had $159.40 in cash along with receipts for these expenditures: transportation-in, $32.45; office supplies, $113.55; and repairs expense, $87.60. Willard uses the perpetual method to account for merchandise inventory. The petty cashier could not account for the $7.00 shortage in the fund.

a. Prepare the September 9 entry to establish the fund.

b. Prepare a summary of the petty cash payments similar to Exhibit 8.2 and record the entry on September 30 to reimburse the fund and reduce it to $250.

Analysis Component: You are the senior marketing manager and are reviewing the unadjusted account balances for your division. You notice the $7.00 cash shortage recorded on September 30 regarding petty cash. The current petty cash custodian has been in place for three months. What should be done, if anything? Explain.

Exercise 8-7 Petty cash fund LO⁴

Conway Designs established a $200 petty cash fund on October 1, 2014. Prepare the entry to replenish the fund at the end of each of the following months of activity:

a. The petty cash box contained $23 on October 31 along with receipts for $100 for cleaning, $26 for postage, and $45 for delivery expense.

b. On November 30, the petty cash box contained only two receipts, for a $78 computer repair and a $95 entertainment expense. The petty cash custodian counted cash remaining of $32.

c. The petty cash box contained $18 on December 31 plus receipts for $49 for gas expense, $92 for office supplies, and $41 for entertainment expense. In addition to replenishing the fund, it was increased by $50.

Exercise 8-8 Credit card and debit card transactions LO⁵

Journalize the following transactions for Stillwater Spa Consultants:

Oct.	1	Sold services for $160,000 to customers using debit cards. Assume the bank charges 0.5% for all debit card transactions.
	7	Sold services to customers for $19,000 cash.
	8	Recorded Visa credit card sales totalling $92,000. Visa applies fees of 2%.
	10	Sold $68,000 of services to Edson Community Health Clinic, terms 2/15, n/30.
	25	Collected the amount owing regarding the October 10 sale.

Exercise 8-9 Credit card and debit card transactions LO⁵

On January 15, Tundra Co. sold merchandise to customers for cash of $42,000 (cost $28,500). Merchandise costing $10,500 was sold to customers for $15,800 on January 17; terms 2/10, n/30. Sales totalling $296,000 (cost $198,000) were recorded on January 20 to customers using MasterCard, a credit card that charges a 2% fee. On January 25, sales of $72,000 (cost $48,200) were made to debit card customers. The bank charges Tundra a flat fee of 0.5% on all debit card transactions.

Required Prepare journal entries for each of the transactions described (assume a perpetual inventory system).

Analysis Component: Identify the advantages and disadvantages of each type of sale: cash sale, credit sale, credit card sale, or debit card sale. Explain why Tundra would likely accept all these types of sales.

Exercise 8-10 Preparation of bank reconciliation LO[6]

The bank reconciliation prepared by Winfield Construction on June 30, 2014, appeared as follows:

Winfield Construction
Bank Reconciliation
June 30, 2014

Bank statement balance	$9,200	Book balance	$9,770
Add:			
Deposit of June 30 in transit	1,350		
	$10,550		
Deduct:			
Outstanding cheque #14............................	780		
Adjusted bank balance	$ 9,770	Adjusted book balance..	$9,770

The Cash account in the General Ledger appeared as follows on July 31:

Cash					Acct. No. 101
Date	Explanation	PR	Debit	Credit	Balance
2014					
June 30	Balance				9,770
July 31		CR3	5,040		14,810
31		CD6		3,142	11,668

A list of deposits made and cheques written during July, taken from the Cash Receipts Journal and Cash Disbursements Journal, is shown below:

Deposits Made			Cheques Written	
July 8.......................................	$1,280	No. 52.......................................	$1,796
11	1,675	53.......................................	964
24.......................................	1,445	54.......................................	382
31	640		
Total July Cash Receipts..............	$5,040	Total July Cash Disbursements.....	$3,142

The following bank statement is available for July:

Bank Statement

To: Winfield Construction

July 31, 2014
Bank of Montreal

Cheques/Charges			Deposits/Credits		Balance
					9,200
NSF	07/02	465	07/02	1,350	10,085
#52	07/08	1,796	07/08	1,280	9,569
#96	07/11	420	07/11	1,675	10,824
			07/24	1,445	12,269
#54	07/31	382	07/31		11,887

NSF = Not Sufficient Funds	SC = Service Charge	PMT = Principal Payment	INT = Interest

In reviewing cheques returned by the bank, the bookkeeper noted that cheque #96 written by Winburn Construction in the amount of $420 was charged against Winfield's account in error by the bank. The NSF cheque was regarding a customer account, Jim Anderson.

Required

1. Prepare a bank reconciliation at July 31.
2. Prepare the necessary journal entries to bring the General Ledger Cash account into agreement with the adjusted balance on the bank reconciliation.

Analysis Component: If the journal entries in Part 2 were not recorded, what financial statement elements (net income, assets, liabilities, and equity) would be over- or understated?

Exercise 8-11 Bank reconciliation LO[6]

Kesler Co. deposits all receipts intact on the day received and makes all payments by cheque. On July 31, 2014, after all posting was completed, its Cash account showed an $11,042 debit balance. However, Kesler's July 31 bank statement showed only $9,860 on deposit in the bank on that day along with the following information.

a. Outstanding cheques, $2,695.

b. Included with the July cancelled cheques returned by the bank was a $42 debit memorandum for bank services.

c. Cheque #919, returned with the cancelled cheques, was correctly drawn for $892 in payment of the utility bill and was paid by the bank on July 15. However, it had been recorded with a debit to Utilities Expense and a credit to Cash as though it were for $982.

d. The July 31 cash receipts, $3,925, were placed in the bank's night depository after banking hours on that date and were unrecorded by the bank at the time the July bank statement was prepared.

Required

a. Prepare a bank reconciliation for Kesler Co. at July 31.

b. Give the journal entries that Kesler Co. should make as a result of having prepared the bank reconciliation in part (a).

Analysis Component: Identify whether net income, assets, liabilities, and equity would be over- or understated if the journal entires in part (b) were not recorded.

Exercise 8-12 Bank reconciling items and required entries LO[6]

Set up a table with the following headings for a bank reconciliation as of September 30:

Bank Balance		Book Balance			Not Shown on the Reconciliation
Add	Deduct	Add	Deduct	Must Adjust	

For each item that follows, place an X in the appropriate columns to indicate whether the item should be added to or deducted from the book or bank balance, or whether it should not appear on the reconciliation. If the book balance is to be adjusted, place a Dr. or Cr. in the Must Adjust column to indicate whether the Cash balance should be debited or credited.

1. Interest earned on the account.

2. Deposit made on September 30 after the bank was closed.

3. Cheques outstanding on August 31 that cleared the bank in September.

4. NSF cheque from customer returned on September 15 but not recorded by the company.

5. Cheques written and mailed to payees on September 30.

6. Deposit made on September 5 that was processed on September 8.

7. Bank service charge.

8. Cheques written and mailed to payees on October 5.

9. Cheques written by another depositor but charged against the company's account.

10. Principal and interest on a note receivable collected by the bank but not recorded by the company.

11. Special charge for collection of note in Item 10 on company's behalf.

12. Cheque written against the account and cleared by the bank; not recorded by the bookkeeper.

*Exercise 8-13 Acid-test ratio LO[7]

Calculate the acid-test ratio in each of the following cases:

	Case X	Case Y	Case Z
Cash	$ 800	$ 910	$1,100
Short-term investments..	-0-	-0-	500
Receivables	-0-	990	800
Inventory	2,000	1,000	4,000
Prepaid expenses	1,200	600	900
Total current assets	$4,000	$3,500	$7,300
Current liabilities..	$2,200	$1,100	$3,650

Required Which case is in the best position to meet short-term obligations most easily? Explain your choice. *Round calculations to two decimal places.*

PROBLEMS

Problem 8-1A Principles of internal control LO[1]

For the following five scenarios, identify the principle of internal control that is violated. Next, make a recommendation as to what the business should do to ensure adherence to principles of internal control.

1. At Stratford Iron Company, Jill and Joan alternate lunch hours. Normally Jill is the petty cash custodian, but if someone needs petty cash when Jill is at lunch, Joan fills in as custodian.

2. Nadine McDonald does all the posting of patient charges and payments at the Northampton Medical Clinic. Every night, Nadine backs up the computerized accounting system to a tape and stores the tape in a locked file at her desk.

3. Jack Mawben prides himself on hiring quality workers who require little supervision. As office manager, Jack gives his employees full discretion over their tasks and has seen no reason to perform independent reviews of their work for years.

4. Bill Clark's manager has told him to "reduce overhead" no matter what! Bill decides to raise the deductible on the plant's property insurance from $5,000 to $10,000. This cuts the property insurance premium in half. In a related move, he decides that bonding of the plant's employees is really a waste of money since the company has not experienced any losses due to employee theft. Bill saves the entire amount of the bonding insurance premium by dropping the bonding insurance.

5. Catherine Young records all incoming customer cash receipts for her employer and also posts the customer payments to their accounts.

Problem 8-2A Establishing, reimbursing, and increasing the petty cash fund LO[4]

Milton Consulting completed the following petty cash transactions during February 2014:

Feb. 2 Prepared a $400 cheque, cashed it, and gave the proceeds and the petty cash box to Nick Reed, the petty cashier.
5 Purchased paper for the copier, $22.45.
9 Paid $36.80 COD charges on merchandise purchased for resale. *Assume Milton Consulting uses the perpetual method to account for merchandise inventory.*
12 Paid $15.65 postage to express mail a contract to a client.
14 Reimbursed Kim Marn, the manager of the business, $135.00 for business auto expenses.
20 Purchased stationery, $58.70.
23 Paid a courier $32.45 to deliver merchandise sold to a customer.
25 Paid $37.80 COD charges on merchandise purchased for resale.
28 Paid $50.00 for stamps.
28 Reed sorted the petty cash receipts by accounts affected and exchanged them for a cheque to reimburse the fund for expenditures. However, there was only $8.15 in cash in the fund. In addition, the size of the petty cash fund was increased to $500.

Required

1. Prepare a journal entry to record establishing the petty cash fund.

2. Prepare a summary of petty cash payments, similar to Exhibit 8.2, that has these categories: delivery expense, auto expense, postage expense, merchandise inventory, and office supplies. Sort the payments into the appropriate categories and total the expenditures in each category.

3. Prepare the journal entry to record the reimbursement and the increase of the fund.

Analysis Component: One of your responsibilities as an employee with Milton Consulting is to handle the petty cash fund. You are concerned about the auto expense claims made regularly by Kim Marn, the manager who hired you: Kim tells you how much the expenditures were and you give her the cash out of petty cash. Kim has never given you receipts to substantiate her claims. The owner of the business is visiting and asks you how things are going. What should you do, if anything? Explain.

Problem 8-3A Petty cash fund reimbursement and analysis of errors LO[4]

Capital Irrigation has only a General Journal in its accounting system and uses it to record all transactions. However, the company recently set up a petty cash fund to facilitate payments of small items. The following petty cash transactions were noted by the petty cashier as occurring during April 2014:

Apr. 1 Received a company cheque for $300 to establish the petty cash fund.
15 Received a company cheque to replenish the fund for the following expenditures made since April 1 and to increase the fund to $400.
a. Paid $82 for janitorial service.
b. Purchased office supplies for $78.15.
c. Purchased postage stamps for $25.00.
d. Paid $92.50 to *The County Crier* for an advertisement in the newspaper.
e. Discovered that $24.35 remained in the petty cash box.
30 The petty cashier noted that $244.95 remained in the fund and decided that the April 15 increase in the fund was too large. Therefore, a company cheque was issued to replenish the fund for the following expenditures made since April 15 and to reduce the fund to $350.
f. Purchased office supplies for $94.65.
g. Reimbursed office manager for business auto, $45.60.
h. Paid $14.80 courier charges to deliver merchandise to a customer.

Required Prepare journal entries to record the establishment of the fund on April 1 and its replenishments on April 15 and April 30.

Analysis Component: Explain how the company's financial statements would be affected if the petty cash fund were not replenished and no entry were made on April 30. (*Hint: The amount of office supplies that appears on a balance sheet is determined by a physical count of the supplies on hand.*)

CHECK FIGURE:
Adjusted book
balance = $2,401.54

Problem 8-4A Preparation of bank reconciliation and recording adjustments LO[6]

The bank reconciliation prepared by Gatz Company on May 31, 2014, appeared as follows:

Gatz Company Bank Reconciliation May 31, 2014				
Bank statement balance		$ 9,564.35	Book balance	$20,056.03
Add:			Deduct:	
Deposit of April 30 in transit		982.17	NSF cheque plus service	
		$10,546.52	charge $11,900.50	
Deduct:			Bank service charge 65.00	11,965.50
Outstanding cheques:			Adjusted book balance...................	$ 8,090.53
#876...	$ 655.99			
#882:..	1,800.00	2,455.99		
Adjusted bank balance		$ 8,090.53		

The Cash account in the General Ledger appeared as follows on June 30 (Gatz uses only a General Journal to record transactions):

Cash					Acct. No. 101
Date	Explanation	PR	Debit	Credit	Balance
2014					
May 31	Balance				8,090.53
June 1	Cheque #883	GJ16		1,865.30	6,225.23
1	Cheque #884	GJ16		112.70	6,112.53
3	Cheque #885	GJ16		650.84	5,461.69
4	Cheque #886	GJ16		2,018.45	3,443.24
9	Deposit	GJ16	4,285.26		7,728.50
12	Cheque #887	GJ16		425.15	7,303.35
12	Cheque #888	GJ16		3,040.60	4,262.75
12	Cheque #889	GJ16		974.12	3,288.63
18	Deposit	GJ16	3,515.60		6,804.23
20	Cheque #890	GJ16		2,640.00	4,164.23
21	Cheque #891	GJ16		1,406.24	2,757.99
24	Cheque #892	GJ16		2,590.81	167.18
26	Cheque #893	GJ16		75.99	91.19
29	Deposit	GJ16	1,845.35		1,936.54

The following bank statement is available for June:

Bank Statement					
To: Gatz Company				June 30, 2014 Bank of Montreal	
Cheques/Charges			Deposits/Credits		Balance
			05/31		9,564.35
#884	06/01	112.70	06/01	982.17	10,433.82
#883	06/04	1,865.30			8,568.52
#876	06/09	655.99	06/09	4,285.26	12,197.79
#889	06/12	974.12			11,223.67
#882	06/14	1,800.00			9,423.67
#887	06/18	245.15	06/18	3,515.60	12,694.12
#885	06/20	650.84			12,043.28
#891	06/21	1,046.24			10,997.04
#886	06/29	2,018.45			8,978.59
SC	06/30	75.00	06/30		8,903.59
NSF = Not Sufficient Funds		SC = Service Charge	PMT = Principal Payment		INT = Interest

Required

a. Prepare a bank reconciliation at June 30, 2014. Assume that any errors made were by the bookkeeper (cheque #887 was for office supplies; cheque #891 was for utilities expense).
b. Prepare the necessary entries resulting from the bank reconciliation.

Analysis Component: You have been employed with Gatz Company since June 1, 2014, and part of your job is writing and recording cheques as well as preparing the bank reconciliation. To your surprise, the person you replaced brought in the June bank statement as it had been mailed to her home. While preparing the June bank reconciliation, you notice that cheque #882 for $1,800 cleared the bank in June but is not among the cancelled cheques. What should you do? Explain.

Problem 8-5A Preparation of bank reconciliation and recording adjustments LO[6]

The bank reconciliation prepared by Gemma Tours on March 31, 2014, appeared as follows:

Gemma Tours Bank Reconciliation March 31, 2014					
Bank statement balance		$14,800	Book balance		$32,710
Add:					
Deposit of March 31 in transit		21,050			
		$35,850			
Deduct:					
Outstanding cheques:					
#79	$1,250				
#84:	1,890	3,140			
Adjusted bank balance		$32,710	Adjusted book balance..		$32,710

The Cash account in the General Ledger appeared as follows on April 30:

Cash					Acct. No. 101
Date	Explanation	PR	Debit	Credit	Balance
2014					
March 31	Balance				32,710.00
April 30		CR11	34,049.00		66,759.00
30		CD14		43,643.00	23,116.00

A list of deposits made and cheques written during April, taken from the Cash Receipts Journal and Cash Disbursements Journal, is shown below:

Deposits Made			Cheques Written		
April 7.......................................	$14,200		No. 91.....................................	$ 1,200	
13.......................................	850		92.....................................	5,230	
18.......................................	13,600		93.....................................	2,590	
23.......................................	945		94.....................................	3,452	
27.......................................	1,890		95.....................................	2,900	
30.......................................	2,564		96.....................................	1,811	
Total April Cash Receipts...........	$34,049		97.....................................	8,470	
			98.....................................	2,900	
			99.....................................	8,590	
			100.....................................	6,500	
			Total April Cash Disbursements..	$43,643	

The following bank statement is available for April:

Bank Statement					
To: Gemma Tours				April 30, 2014 Bank of Montreal	
Cheques/Charges			Deposits/Credits		Balance
					14,800
#93	04/02	2,509	04/03	21,050	33,341
#92	04/07	5,230	04/07	14,200	42,311
#84	04/13	1,890	04/13	850	41,271
NSF	04/18	6,540	04/18	13,600	48,331
#95	04/23	2,900	04/23	945	46,376
#99	04/27	8,590	04/27	1,890	39,676
#96	04/30	1,811	04/30	2,564	40,429
#97	04/30	8,470	04/30	46	32,005
#94	04/30	3,452			28,553
PMT	04/30	9,420			19,133
INT	04/30	35			19,098
SC	04/30	55			19,043
NSF = Not Sufficient Funds		SC = Service Charge	PMT = Principal Payment		INT = Interest

In reviewing cheques returned by the bank, the bookkeeper discovered that cheque #93, for delivery expense, was recorded in the Cash Disbursements Journal incorrectly as $2,590. The NSF cheque was that of customer Laura Clark, deposited in April.

Required

a. Prepare a bank reconciliation at April 30.

b. Prepare the necessary journal entries to bring the General Ledger Cash account into agreement with the adjusted balance on the bank reconciliation.

CHECK FIGURE:
1. Adjusted book
balance = $32,439

Problem 8-6A Preparation of bank reconciliation and recording adjustments LO[6]

The following information was available to reconcile Montrose Company's book balance of Cash with its bank statement balance as of October 31, 2014:

a. After all posting was completed on October 31, the company's Cash account had a $13,254 debit balance, but its bank statement showed a $29,436 balance.

b. Cheques #296 for $1,340 and #307 for $12,809 were outstanding on the September 30 bank reconciliation. Cheque #307 was returned with the October cancelled cheques, but cheque #296 was not. It was also found that cheque #315 for $897 and cheque #321 for $2,010, both written in October, were not among the cancelled cheques returned with the statement.

c. In comparing the cancelled cheques returned by the bank with the entries in the accounting records, it was found that cheque #320 for the October rent was correctly written for $3,070 but was erroneously entered in the accounting records as $3,700.

d. A credit memorandum enclosed with the bank statement indicated that the bank had collected a $22,000 non-interest–bearing note for Montrose, deducted a $120 collection fee, and credited the remainder to the account. This transaction was not recorded by Montrose before receiving the statement.

e. A debit memorandum for $3,250 listed a $3,200 NSF cheque plus a $50 NSF charge. The cheque had been received from a customer, Jefferson Tyler. Montrose had not recorded this bounced cheque before receiving the statement.

f. Also enclosed with the statement was a $75 debit memorandum for bank services. It had not been recorded because no previous notification had been received.

g. The October 31 cash receipts, $7,250, were placed in the bank's night depository after banking hours on that date and this amount did not appear on the bank statement.

Required

1. Prepare a bank reconciliation for the company as of October 31, 2014.

2. Prepare the General Journal entries necessary to bring the company's book balance of Cash into agreement with the reconciled balance.

Analysis Component: Assume that an October 31, 2014, bank reconciliation for the company has already been prepared and some of the items were treated incorrectly in preparing the reconciliation. For each of the following errors, explain the effect of the error on: (1) the final balance that was calculated by adjusting the bank statement balance, and (2) the final balance that was calculated by adjusting the Cash account balance.

a. The company's Cash account balance of $13,254 was listed on the reconciliation as $12,354.

b. The bank's collection of a $22,000 note less the $120 collection fee was added to the bank statement balance.

CHECK FIGURE:
1. Adjusted book
balance, $4,871.89

Problem 8-7A Preparation of bank reconciliation and recording adjustments LO[6]

Pelzer Company reconciled its bank and book statement balances of Cash on August 31 and showed two cheques outstanding at that time, #5888 for $6,220.00 and #5893 for $1,485.65. The following information was available for the September 30, 2014, reconciliation:

From the September 30, 2014, bank statement

BALANCE OF PREVIOUS STATEMENT ON AUG. 31/14	10,674.50
6 DEPOSITS AND OTHER CREDITS TOTALLING................	22,417.05
9 CHEQUES AND OTHER DEBITS TOTALLING	26,296.05
CURRENT BALANCE AS OF SEPT. 30/14............................	6,795.50

Chequing Account Transactions

Date	Amount	Transaction Description	Date	Amount	Transaction Description
Sept. 05	5,643.20	+Deposit	Sept. 25	4,230.60	+Deposit
12	2,561.45	+Deposit	30	45.00	+Interest
17	1,176.50	−NSF cheque	30	3,500.00	+Credit memo
21	6,436.80	+Deposit			

Date	Cheque No.	Amount	Date	Cheque No.	Amount
Sept. 03	5904	9,340.55	Sept. 22	5888	6,220.00
07	5901	1,450.00	24	5909	2,140.40
08	5905	338.25	28	5907	3324.60
10	5903	1320.15	29	5902	985.60

From Pelzer Company's accounting records:

Cash   Acct. No. 101

Date	Explanation	PR	Debit	Credit	Balance
2014					
Aug. 31	Balance				2,968.85
Sept. 30		CR12	20,005.75		22,974.60
30		CD23		15,071.21	7,903.39

Deposits Made	
Sept. 5...............................	$ 5,643.20
12...............................	2,561.45
21...............................	6,436.80
25...............................	4,230.60
30...............................	1,133.70
Total Sept. Cash Receipts	$20,005.75

Cheques Written	
No. 5901	$ 1,450.00
5902	985.60
5903	1,320.15
5904	3,940.55
5905	338.25
5906	715.26
5907	3,324.60
5908	856.40
5909	2,140.40
Total Sept. Cash Disbursements	$15,071.21

Cheque #5904 was correctly written for $9,340.55 to pay for computer equipment; however, the book-keeper misread the amount and entered it in the accounting records with a debit to Computer Equipment and a credit to Cash as though it were for $3,940.55.

The NSF cheque was originally received from a customer, Lisa Willis, in payment of her account. Its return was not recorded when the bank first notified the company. The credit memorandum resulted from the collection of a $3,550 note for Pelzer Company by the bank. The bank had deducted a $50 collection fee. The collection has not been recorded.

Required

1. Prepare a September 30 bank reconciliation for the company.
2. Prepare the General Journal entries needed to adjust the book balance of cash to the reconciled balance.

Analysis Component: The preceding bank statement discloses three places where the cancelled cheques returned with the bank statement are not numbered sequentially. In other words, some of the prenumbered cheques in the sequence are missing. Several possible situations would explain why the cancelled cheques returned with a bank statement might not be numbered sequentially. Describe three possible explanations.

CHECK FIGURE:
a. Adjusted book
balance = $100,488

Problem 8-8A Preparation of a bank reconciliation and recording adjustments LO6

Stewart Recording Studio, owned by Ron Stewart, showed the following bank reconciliation at March 31:

Stewart Recording Studio Bank Reconciliation March 31, 2014					
Bank statement balance		$22,100	Book balance		$30,945
Add:					
Deposit of March 31 in transit		10,000			
		$32,100			
Deduct:					
Outstanding cheques:					
#14	$840				
#22	315	1,155			
Adjusted bank balance		$30,945	Adjusted book balance...		$30,945

Cash					Acct. No. 101
Date	Explanation	PR	Debit	Credit	Balance
2014					
Mar. 31	Balance				30,945
Apr. 30		CR17	71,440		102,385
30		CD13		91,172	11,213

A list of deposits made and cheques written during April, taken from the Cash Receipts Journal and Cash Disbursements Journal, is shown below:

Deposits Made			Cheques Written		
April 7..	$ 690		No. 23.....................................	$ 5,200	
13..	4,600		24.....................................	3,150	
18..	5,900		25.....................................	940	
23..	13,900		26.....................................	310	
27..	1,750		27.....................................	4,230	
30..	44,600		28.....................................	4,900	
Total April Cash Receipts............	$71,440		29.....................................	19,630	
			30.....................................	41,000	
			31.....................................	412	
			32.....................................	11,400	
			Total April Cash Disbursements ..	$91,172	

The following bank statement is available for April:

Bank Statement					
To: Stewart Recording Studio				April 30, 2014 Bank of Canada	
Cheques/Charges			**Deposits/Credits**		**Balance**
					22,100
#31	04/03	412	04/03	10,000	31,688
#28	04/07	9,400	04/07	690	22,978
#26	04/13	310	04/13	4,600	27,268
NSF	04/18	14,200	04/18	5,900	18,968
#24	04/23	3,150	04/23	13,900	29,718
#23	04/27	5,200	04/27	1,750	26,268
#29	04/30	19,630	04/30	120,000	126,638
PMT	04/30	15,900			110,738
INT	04/30	450			110,288
SC	04/30	175			**110,113**
NSF = Not Sufficient Funds		SC = Service Charge	PMT = Payment of Principal on the Loan		INT = Interest on Bank Loan

In reviewing cheques returned by the bank, the bookkeeper discovered that cheque #28, for delivery expense, was recorded in the Cash Disbursements Journal correctly as $4,900. The NSF cheque for $14,200 was that of customer Oprah Winney, deposited in March.

On the bank statement, the payment for $15,900 is regarding a note payable. There is also a deposit of $120,000 dated April 30. It is an investment made by the owner into the business (the bank transferred the funds electronically from the owner's personal account to his business account, which is why it was not recorded in the Cash Receipts Journal).

Required

a.   Prepare a bank reconciliation for Stewart Recording Studio at April 30.

b.   Prepare the necessary journal entries to bring the General Ledger Cash account into agreement with the adjusted balance on the bank reconciliation.

CHECK FIGURE:
a. Adjusted book balance = $82,994.99

Problem 8-9A Preparation of a bank reconciliation and recording adjustments LO[6]

Presented below is information related to Simalan Dive Company. The balance according to the books at October 31, 2014, was $99,657.29; cash receipts recorded during November were $64,805.69; and cash disbursements recorded for November were $76,850.30. The balance according to the bank statement on November 30, 2014, was $82,370.68.

The following cheques were outstanding at November 30:

Cheque	Amount
#920	947.29
#991	2,843.50
#1030	1,971.34
#1064	824.66

Included with the November bank statement and not recorded by the company were a bank debit memo for $32.26 covering bank charges for the month, a debit memo for $5,200.75 for a customer's cheque (Marnie Wiesen) returned and marked NSF, and a credit memo for $615.32 representing interest collected by the bank for Simalan Dive Company. Cash on hand at November 30, which has been recorded and is awaiting deposit, amounted to $7,211.10.

Required

a.   Prepare a bank reconciliation at November 30, 2014.

b.   Prepare any journal entries required to adjust the Cash account at November 30.

Problem 8-10A Preparation of a bank reconciliation and recording adjustments LO[6]

The following is information for Dundee Realty:

a. Balance per the bank statement dated October 31, 2014, is $26,830.

b. Balance of the Cash account on the company books as of October 31, 2014, is $5,575.

c. $14,680 of customer deposits were outstanding as of September 30; this amount had been deposited to Dundee's account in October.

d. Cheques written in October that had not cleared the bank as of October 31 were:

#8700, $985

#8709, $12,600

#8801, $620

#8815, $145.

e. The bank charged Dundee's account for a $2,350 cheque of the E-Zone Networks; the cheque was found among the cancelled cheques returned with the bank statement.

f. Bank service charges for October amount to $65.

g. A customer's cheque (Teresa Krant) for $7,050 had been deposited in the bank correctly but was recorded in the accounting records as $7,500.

h. Among the cancelled cheques is one for $260 given in payment of an account payable to Decker Company; the bookkeeper had recorded the cheque incorrectly at $620 in the company records.

i. The bank had collected a $22,000 note plus interest of $880. A fee of $50 was charged for this service.

j. A bank deposit of October 31 for $13,420 does not appear on the bank statement.

Required

1. Prepare a bank reconciliation statement as of October 31, 2014.

2. Prepare the necessary entries to make the Cash account agree with the bank reconciliation adjusted Cash balance as of October 31.

Analysis Component: Identify the effects on the income statement and balance sheet if the entries in Part 2 were not recorded.

ALTERNATE PROBLEMS

Problem 8-1B Principles of internal control LO[1]

For the following five scenarios, identify the principle of internal control that is violated. Next, recommend what the business should do to ensure adherence to principles of internal control.

1. Tamerick Company is a fairly small organization but has segregated the duties of cash receipts and cash disbursements. However, the employee responsible for cash disbursements also reconciles the bank account monthly.

2. Stan Spencer is the most computer literate employee in his company. His boss has recently asked him to put password protection on all the office computers. Stan's main job at the company is to process payroll. Stan has put a password in place that now only allows his boss access to the file where pay rates are changed and personnel are added or deleted from the company payroll.

3. Starlight Theatre has a computerized order-taking system for its tickets. The system is active all week and backed up every Friday night.

4. Trek There Company has two employees handling acquisitions of inventory. One employee places purchase orders and pays vendors. The second employee receives the merchandise.

5. The owner of Holiday Helper uses a cheque protector to perforate cheques, making it difficult for anyone to alter the amount of the cheque. The cheque protector sits on the owner's desk in an office that houses company cheques and is often unlocked.

Problem 8-2B Establishing, reimbursing, and increasing the petty cash fund LO⁴

Stihl Repairs completed the following petty cash transactions during July 2014:

July	5	Prepared a $500 cheque, cashed it, and turned the proceeds and the petty cash box over to Bob Stuart, the petty cashier.
	6	Paid $108.00 COD charges on merchandise purchased for resale. *Stihl Repairs uses the perpetual inventory method to account for merchandise inventory.*
	11	Paid $23.75 delivery charges on merchandise sold to a customer.
	12	Purchased file folders, $8.50.
	14	Reimbursed Collin Dodge, the manager of the business, $8.26 for office supplies purchased.
	18	Purchased paper for printer, $12.15.
	27	Paid $21.60 COD charges on merchandise purchased for resale.
	28	Purchased stamps, $23.00
	30	Reimbursed Collin Dodge $64.80 for business car expenses.
	31	Bob Stuart sorted the petty cash receipts by accounts affected and exchanged them for a cheque to reimburse the fund for expenditures. However, there was $233.94 in cash in the fund. In addition, the size of the petty cash fund was decreased to $300.

Required

1. Prepare a General Journal entry to record establishing the petty cash fund.

2. Prepare a summary of petty cash payments similar to Exhibit 8.2 that has these categories: delivery expense, auto expense, postage expense, merchandise inventory, and office supplies.

3. Prepare the General Journal entry to record the reimbursement and the increase of the fund.

Analysis Component: You supervise Bob Stuart, the petty cashier, and while reviewing the accounts you notice that the Cash Over/Short Expense account has a balance for the seven months ended July 31, 2014, of $300. Given the size of the petty cash account, does this balance appear to be unusual? Explain and identify any concerns that you might have.

Problem 8-3B Petty cash fund; reimbursement and analysis of errors LO⁴

The accounting system used by Dartmouth Sales and Service requires that all entries be journalized in a General Journal. To facilitate payments for small items, Dartmouth established a petty cash fund. The following transactions involving the petty cash fund occurred during February 2014.

Feb.	3	A company cheque for $200 was prepared and made payable to the petty cashier to establish the petty cash fund.
	14	A company cheque was prepared to replenish the fund for the following expenditures made since February 3 and to increase the fund to $250.
		a. Purchased office supplies, $65.82.
		b. Paid $75.00 COD charges on merchandise purchased for resale. Dartmouth uses the perpetual method to account for merchandise inventory.
		c. Paid $36.40 to Data Services for minor repairs to a computer.
		d. Paid $15.23 for postage expenses.
		e. Discovered that only $5.55 remained in the petty cash box.
	28	The petty cashier noted that $39.30 remained in the fund, and decided that the February 14 increase in the fund was not large enough. A company cheque was prepared to replenish the fund for the following expenditures made since February 14, and to increase it to $300.
		f. Paid $45 to *The Smart Saver* for an advertisement in a monthly newsletter.
		g. Paid $96.35 for office supplies.
		h. Paid $69.35 to Best Movers for delivery of merchandise to a customer.

Required Prepare General Journal entries to record the establishment of the fund on February 3 and its replenishment on February 14 and February 28.

Analysis Component: Explain how the company's financial statements would be affected if the petty cash fund is not replenished and no entry is made on February 28. (*Hint: The amount of Office Supplies that appears on a balance sheet is determined by a physical count of the supplies on hand.*)

Problem 8-4B Preparing a bank reconciliation and recording adjustments LO[6]

Mae Telford, the controller of the Baylor Company, provided the following information:

Baylor Company
Bank Reconciliation
October 31, 2014

Bank statement balance		$19,687.60	Book balance		$45,548.66
Add:					
Deposit of Oct. 31 in transit..........		4,280.45			
		$23,968.05			
Deduct:			Deduct:		
Outstanding cheques:			NSF cheque plus		
#537	$ 725,00		service charge	$25,140.95	
#542	2,965.34	3,690.34	Bank service charges......................	130.00	25,270.95
Adjusted bank balance		$20,277.71	Adjusted book balance......................		$20,277.71

The Cash account in the General Ledger appeared as follows on November 30 (Baylor Company uses only a General Journal to record transactions):

Cash					Acct. No. 101
Date	Explanation	PR	Debit	Credit	Balance
2014					
Oct. 31	Balance				20,277.71
Nov. 1	Cheque #543	GJ5		6,505.12	13,772.59
1	Cheque #544	GJ5		854.71	12,917.88
1	Cheque #545	GJ5		1,156.94	11,760.94
1	Cheque #546	GJ5		2,564.24	9,196.70
1	Cheque #547	GJ5		1,345.68	7,851.02
1	Cheque #548	GJ6		56.45	7,794.57
1	Cheque #549	GJ6		564.23	7,230.34
9	Deposit	GJ6	1,548.97		8,779.31
9	Cheque #550	GJ6		3,457.15	5,322.16
9	Cheque #551	GJ6		985.64	4,336.52
18	Deposit	GJ6	5,649.85		9,986.37
20	Cheque #552	GJ6		5,556.71	4,429.66
27	Cheque #553	GJ6		964.25	3,465.41
29	Deposit	GJ6	1,250.65		4,716.06

The following bank statement is available for November 2014:

Bank Statement					
To: Baylor Company				**November 30, 2014** **Bank of Canada**	
Cheques/Charges			**Deposits/Credits**		**Balance**
			10/31		19,687.60
#549	11/01	564.23	11/01	4,280.45	23,403.82
#543	11/02	6,505.12			16,898.70
#537	11/07	725.00			16,173.70
#551	11/09	985.64	11/09	1,584.97	16,773.03
#542	11/12	2,965.34			13,807.69
#544	11/14	854.71			12,952.98
#547	11/18	3,145.68	11/18	5,649.85	15,457.15
#545	11/20	1,156.94			14,300.21
#546	11/29	2,564.24			11,735.97
SC	11/30	115.00	11/30		11,620.97
NSF = Not Sufficient Funds		SC = Service Charge	PMT = Principal Payment		INT = Interest

Required

a. Prepare a bank reconciliation for Baylor Company for the month of November 2014. Assume that any errors made were by the bookkeeper (cheque #547 was for advertising expense; the deposit of November 9 was regarding a credit customer, Val Pacino).

b. Prepare the necessary entries resulting from the bank reconciliation.

Analysis Component: You have been employed with Baylor Company since November 1, 2014, and part of your job is writing and recording cheques as well as preparing the bank reconciliation. In reviewing the cheques returned by the bank, you notice that the payee on cheque #543 is the employee you recently replaced. You investigate further and find that the journal entry recording cheque #543 debited Office Supplies Expense. What should you do? Explain.

CHECK FIGURE:
a. Adjusted book
balance = $13,929

Problem 8-5B Preparing a bank reconciliation and recording adjustments LO⁶

The bank reconciliation prepared by Village-on-the-Lake Condos on May 31, 2014, is shown below:

Village-on-the-Lake Condos Bank Reconciliation May 31, 2014					
Bank statement balance		$ 2,060	Book balance		$3,910
Add:					
Deposit of May 31 in transit		12,500			
		$14,560			
Deduct:					
Outstanding cheques:					
#103	$6,520				
#120	4,130	10,650			
Adjusted bank balance		$ 3,910	Adjusted book balance		$3,910

The Cash account in the General Ledger appeared as follows on June 30:

Cash					Acct. No. 101
Date	Explanation	PR	Debit	Credit	Balance
2014					
May 31	Balance				3,910
June 30		CR21	38,680		42,590
30		CD16		31,861	10,729

A list of deposits made and cheques written during June, taken from the Cash Receipts Journal and Cash Disbursements Journal, is shown below:

Deposits Made			Cheques Written	
June 5	$ 590		No. 127	$ 2,100
10	1,120		128	450
15	5,690		129	680
20	4,510		130	9,750
27	7,830		131	196
30	12,600		132	6,420
30	6,340		133	4,550
Total June Cash Receipts	$38,680		134	6,780
			135	820
			136	115
			Total June Cash Disbursements ..	$31,861

The following bank statement is available:

Bank Statement					
To: Village-on-the-Lake Condos				**June 30, 2014**	
				Bank of Nova Scotia	
Cheques/Charges			**Deposits/Credits**		**Balance**
					2,060
#133	06/02	4,550	06/02	12,500	10,010
#136	06/05	115	06/05	590	10,485
#129	06/10	680	06/10	1,120	10,925
#130	06/15	9,750	06/15	5,690	6,865
#103	06/20	6,520	06/20	4,510	4,855
#134	06/27	6,780	06/27	7,830	5,905
#128	06/30	450	06/30	16,200	21,655
SC	06/30	400			**21,255**
NSF = Not Sufficient Funds		SC = Service Charge	PMT = Principal Payment		INT = Interest

In reviewing deposits recorded by the bank, the bookkeeper discovered that the deposit from customer Darla Smith dated June 30, recorded in the Cash Receipts Journal incorrectly as $12,600, was recorded by the bank correctly as $16,200.

Required

a. Prepare a bank reconciliation at June 30.

b. Prepare the necessary journal entries to bring the General Ledger Cash account into agreement with the adjusted balance on the bank reconciliation.

CHECK FIGURE:
1. Adjusted book balance = $20,374

Problem 8-6B Preparing a bank reconciliation and recording adjustments LO[6]

The following information was available to reconcile Frogbox Moving's book Cash balance with its bank statement balance as of December 31, 2014:

a. The December 31 Cash balance according to the accounting records was $12,644, and the bank statement balance for that date was $13,650.

b. Cheque #3115 for $1,213 and cheque #3201 for $694, both written and entered in the accounting records in December, were not among the cancelled cheques returned. Two cheques, #3207 for $3,260 and #3221 for $984, were outstanding on November 30 when the bank and book statement balances were last reconciled. Cheque #3207 was returned with the December cancelled cheques, but cheque #3221 was not.

c. When the December cheques were compared with entries in the accounting records, it was found that cheque #3199 had been correctly written for $3,910 to pay for office supplies, but was errone-ously entered in the accounting records as though it were written for $9,310.

d. Two debit memoranda were included with the returned cheques and were unrecorded at the time of the reconciliation. One of the debit memoranda was for $1,620 and dealt with an NSF cheque for $1,570 that had been received from a customer, Tork Industries, in payment of its account. It also assessed a $50 fee for processing. The second debit memorandum covered cheque printing and was for $35. These transactions had not been recorded by Frogbox before receiving the statement.

e. A credit memorandum indicated that the bank had collected a $4,000 note receivable for the com-pany, deducted a $15 collection fee, and credited the balance to the company's account. This trans-action was not recorded by Frogbox before receiving the statement.

f. The December 31 cash receipts, $9,615, had been placed in the bank's night depository after bank-ing hours on that date and did not appear on the bank statement.

Required

1. Prepare a bank reconciliation for the company as of December 31.

2. Prepare the General Journal entries necessary to bring the company's book balance of Cash into conformity with the reconciled balance.

Analysis Component: Explain the nature of the messages conveyed by a bank to one of its depositors when the bank sends a debit memo and a credit memo to the depositor.

CHECK FIGURE:
1. Adjusted book
balance = $35,201.35

Problem 8-7B Preparing a bank reconciliation and recording adjustments LO[6]

Yardworx reconciled its book balance of Cash with its bank statement balance on April 30 and showed two cheques outstanding at that time, #1771 for $15,463.10 and #1780 for $955.65. The following information is available for the May 31, 2014, reconciliation:

From the May 31, 2014, bank statement:

BALANCE OF PREVIOUS STATEMENT ON APR. 30/14	$ 61,045.95
5 DEPOSITS AND OTHER CREDITS TOTALLING	26,088.10
9 CHEQUES AND OTHER DEBITS TOTALLING	57,005.40
CURRENT BALANCE AS OF THIS STATEMENT	30,128.65

Chequing Account Transactions

Date	Amount	Transaction Description	Date	Amount	Transaction Description
May 04	14,662.30	+Deposit	May 25	5,200.00	+Credit memo
14	849.25	+Deposit	26	4,210.10	+Deposit
18	15,600.40	−NSF cheque	31	135.00	−Service charge
22	1,166.45	+Deposit			

Date	Cheque No.	Amount	Date	Cheque No.	Amount
May 01	1784	7,600.00	May 26	1785	620.15
02	1783	1,465.80	28	1771	15,463.10
15	1787	2,334.75	29	1788	985.65
16	1782	12,800.55			

From Yardworx's accounting records:

Cash　　　　　Acct. No. 101

Date	Explanation	PR	Debit	Credit	Balance
2014					
Apr. 30	Balance				44,627.20
May 31		CR7	29,289.05		73,916.25
31		CD8		28,089.50	45,826.75

Deposits Made

May 4	$14,662.30
14	849.25
22	1,166.45
26	4,210.10
31	8,400.95
Total May Cash Receipts	$29,289.05

Cheques Written

No. 1782	$ 12,800.55
1783	1,465.80
1784	7,600.00
1785	620.15
1786	974.35
1787	2,334.75
1788	895.65
1789	1,398.25
Total May Cash Disbursements	$ 28,089.50

Cheque #1788 was correctly written for $985.65 to pay for May utilities; however, the bookkeeper misread the amount and entered it in the accounting records with a debit to Utilities Expense and a credit to Cash as though it were for $895.65. The bank paid and deducted the correct amount.

The NSF cheque was originally received from a customer, Gertie Mayer, in payment of her account. Its return was unrecorded. The credit memorandum resulted from a $5,300 note that the bank had collected for the company. The bank had deducted a $100 collection fee and deposited the remainder in the company's account. The collection has not been recorded.

Required

1. Prepare a bank reconciliation for Yardworx.
2. Prepare the General Journal entries needed to adjust the book balance of Cash to the reconciled balance.

Analysis Component: The preceding bank statement discloses two places where the cancelled cheques returned with the bank statement are not numbered sequentially. In other words, some of the prenumbered cheques in the sequence are missing. Several possible situations would explain why the cancelled cheques returned with a bank statement might not be numbered sequentially. Describe three possible reasons why this might occur.

Problem 8-8B Preparing a bank reconciliation and recording adjustments LO[6]

Lyryx Co. reconciled its bank statement balances of Cash on October 31 and showed two cheques outstanding at that time, #1388 for $14,650 and #1393 for $9,800. The following information was available for the November 30, 2014, reconciliation:

From the November 30 bank statement:

BALANCE OF PREVIOUS STATEMENT ON OCT. 31/14	106,980
5 DEPOSITS AND OTHER CREDITS TOTALLING	63,568
9 CHEQUES AND OTHER DEBITS TOTALLING	123,873
CURRENT BALANCE AS OF NOVEMBER 30/14	46,675

Chequing Account Transactions

Date	Amount	Transaction Description	Date	Amount	Transaction Description
Nov. 05	21,640	+Deposit	Nov. 25	29,008	+Deposit
12	956	+Deposit	30	250	+Interest
17	1,810	−NSF cheque	30	10,550	+Credit memorandum
21	1,164	+Deposit			

Date	Cheque No.	Amount	Date	Cheque No.	Amount
Nov. 03	1402	9,325	Nov. 17	1409	12,125
04	1403	11,500	20	1405	14,850
08	1388	14,650	27	1407	38,412
12	1401	18,600	29	1404	2,601

From Lyryx Co.'s accounting records:

Cash					Acct. No. 101
Date	Explanation	PR	Debit	Credit	Balance
2014 Oct. 31	Balance				82,530
Nov. 30		CR12	86,145		168,675
30		CD23		149,733	18,942

Deposits Made	
Nov. 5..............................	$21,640
12..............................	956
21..............................	1,164
25..............................	29,008
30..............................	33,377
Total November Cash Receipts	$86,145

Cheques Written	
No.1401	$ 18,600
1402..............................	9,325
1403..............................	11,500
1404..............................	6,201
1405..............................	14,850
1406..............................	12,980
1407..............................	38,412
1408..............................	25,740
1409..............................	12,125
Total November Cash Disbursements	$149,733

Cheque #1404 was correctly written for $2,601 to pay for computer equipment: however, the book-keeper misread the amount and entered it in the accounting records with a debit to Computer Equipment and a credit to Cash as though it were for $6,201.

The NSF cheque was originally received from a customer, Jerry Skyles, in payment of his account. Its return was not recorded when the bank first notified the company. The credit memorandum resulted from the collection of a $10,700 note for Lyryx by the bank. The bank had deducted a $150 collection fee. The collection has not been recorded.

Required

1. Prepare a November 30 bank reconciliation for the company.
2. Prepare the General Journal entries needed to adjust the book balance of Cash to the reconciled balance.

CHECK FIGURE:
1. Adjusted book balance = $24,370

Problem 8-9B Preparing a bank reconciliation and recording adjustments LO⁶

The following information was available to reconcile Shanghai Company's book balance of Cash with its bank statement balance as of February 28, 2014.

a. The bank statement at February 28 indicated a balance of $23,620. The General Ledger account for Cash showed a balance at February 28 of $9,400.

b. Of the cheques issued in February, the following were still outstanding:

Cheque	Amount
#202	$ 960
#205	1,075
#213	610
#240	840

c. Two cheques, #136 for $1,036 and #200 for $2,600, were outstanding on Jan. 31 when the bank and book balances were last reconciled. Cheque #136 was returned with the February cancelled cheques but cheque #200 was not.

d. Included with the February bank statement was an NSF cheque for $6,250 that had been received from a customer, Mrs. Loni Fung, in payment of her account.

e. Cheque #219 was correctly written for $1,910 in payment for office supplies but was erroneously entered as $9,110 in the Cash Payments Journal.

f. A debit memorandum for $35 was enclosed with the bank statement. This charge was for printing the chequebook for Shanghai Company.

g. Included with the bank statement was a $120 credit memorandum for interest earned on the bank account in February.

h. The February 28 cash receipts amounting to $6,835 had been placed in the bank's night depository after banking hours on that date and did not appear among the deposits on the February bank statement.

i. Included with the bank statement was a credit memorandum, which indicated that the bank had collected a $14,000 note receivable for the company, deducted a $65 collection fee, and credited the balance to the company's account.

Required

1. Prepare a bank reconciliation for the Shanghai Company as of February 28, 2014.
2. Prepare the entries needed to adjust the book balance of Cash to the reconciled balance.

Problem 8-10B Preparing a bank reconciliation and recording adjustments LO[6]

The following is information for the Timbits Cafe:

a. Balance per the bank statement dated December 31, 2014, is $50,860.

b. Balance of Cash account on the company books as of December 31, 2014, is $57,285.

c. A cheque from customer Della Armstrong for $7,860 that had been deposited in the bank was erroneously recorded by the bookkeeper as $8,760.

d. A cheque made out by Neon Company for $10,140 deposited on December 21 is returned by the bank marked NSF; no entry has been made on the company records to reflect the returned cheque.

e. Among the cancelled cheques is one for $692 given in payment of an account payable to CT Financial; the bookkeeper had incorrectly recorded the cheque at $962 in the company records.

f. Bank service charges for December amount to $35.

g. The bank erroneously charged the Timbits Cafe account for a $5,000 cheque of HRD Company; the cheque was found among the cancelled cheques returned with the bank statement.

h. The bank had collected a $14,000 note plus accrued interest amounting to $150; $14,150 was credited to the Timbits Cafe's account; a collection fee of $50 was debited to the Timbits Cafe's account.

i. The bank deposit of December 31 for $6,860 does not appear on the bank statement.

j. Outstanding cheques as of December 31: #197, $920; #199, $1,220.

Required

1. Prepare a bank reconciliation as of December 31, 2014.

2. Prepare the necessary entries to make the Cash account agree with the bank reconciliation adjusted Cash balance as of December 31.

Analysis Component: Identify the effects on the income statement and balance sheet if the adjustments in Part 2 were not recorded.

ANALYTICAL AND REVIEW PROBLEMS

A & R Problem 8-1

You are a college student and have just been hired to work part-time in the accounting department of Candy's Cleaning Services. The person you are replacing had difficulty preparing the bank reconciliation for April 30, which is shown below.

Candy's Cleaning Services Bank Reconciliation April 30, 2014						
Bank balance..		$33,452	Book balance			$28,934
			Add:			
Deduct:...			Interest......................................	$47		
NSF, customer Bonne	$ 412		Error Chq #93	99		146
						$29,080
Outstanding cheques:			Deduct:			
#879	2,600		Service Charge			40
#100	1,400	4,412	Adjusted book balance.....................			$29,040
Adjusted bank balance		$29,040				

In comparing the bank reconciliation to the Cash account in the General Ledger, you notice a problem. You investigate further and come up with some additional information as follows:

a. The Cash account in the General Ledger showed the following:

Cash					Acct. No. 101
Date	Explanation	PR	Debit	Credit	Balance
2014					
March 31	Balance				28,934
April 30		CR16	56,000		84,934
30		CD21		63,883	21,051

b. The error in cheque #93, for Utilities Expense, resulted from the bank incorrectly debiting our account for $99; the correct amount entered in the accounting records is $199.

c. The bank statement showed interest expense of $47; there was no other interest.

d. The bank debited our account for cheque #879 written by Candy's Hair Salon.

e. Cheque #86 for $14,000 listed as outstanding on last month's bank reconciliation was not returned with the April 30 bank statement.

Required

1. Prepare a corrected bank reconciliation for April 30, 2014.

2. Record the journal entries resulting from the corrected bank reconciliation.

CHECK FIGURE:
1. Adjusted book balance = $10,014

A & R Problem 8-2

Your assistant prepared the following bank reconciliation statement. It appears that the statement is unacceptable and the task of preparing a proper reconciliation falls upon you.

Brandon Company Bank Reconciliation May 31, 2014		
Balance per books May 31		$ 9,500
Add:		
Note collected	$1,000	
Interest on note	60	
Deposit in transit	2,455	3,515
		$13,015
Deduct:		
Bank charges	$ 10	
NSF cheque, Rhonda Teal	500	
Outstanding cheques	1,800	
Error in cheque #78 issued for $762 and recorded in the books as $726 (Accounts Payable–Delta Co.)	36	2,346
Indicated bank balance		$10,669
Balance per bank statement		9,359
Discrepancy		$ 1,310

Required

1. Prepare a proper bank reconciliation showing the true Cash balance.

2. Prepare the necessary journal entries.

A & R Problem 8-3

Wanda White acquired a sports equipment distribution business with a staff of six salespeople and two clerks. Because of the trust that Wanda had in her employees—after all, they were all her friends and just like members of the family—she believed that an honour system in regard to the operation of the petty cash fund was adequate. Consequently, Wanda placed $300 in a coffee jar, which, for convenience, was kept in a cupboard in the common room. All employees had access to the petty cash fund and withdrew amounts as required. No vouchers were required for withdrawals. As required, additional funds were placed in the coffee jar and the amount of the replenishment was charged to "miscellaneous selling expense."

Required

1. From the internal control point of view, discuss the weaknesses of the petty cash fund operation and suggest steps necessary for improvement.

2. Does the petty cash fund operation as described above violate any of the generally accepted accounting principles? If yes, which, and how are the principles violated?

ETHICS CHALLENGE

EC 8-1

Marge Page, Dot Night, and Colleen Walker work for a dentist, Dr. Linda Thomen, who is in a private practice. Dr. Thomen is fairly knowledgeable about sound office management practices and has segregated the cash receipt duties as follows. Marge opens the mail and prepares a triplicate list of money received. She sends one copy of the list to Dot, the cashier, who deposits the receipts daily in the bank. Colleen, the recordkeeper, also receives a copy of the list and posts payments to patients' accounts. About once a month the office clerks decide to have an expensive lunch compliments of Dr. Thomen. Dot endorses a patient's cheque in Dr. Thomen's name and cashes it at the bank. Marge destroys the remittance advice accompanying the cheque. Colleen posts the payment to the customer's account as a miscellaneous credit. The clerks justify their actions given their relatively low pay and knowing that Dr. Thomen will likely never miss the payment.

Required

1. Who would be the best person in Dr. Thomen's office to reconcile the bank statement?

2. Would a bank reconciliation detect the office fraud scheme?

3. What are some ways of uncovering this type of scheme?

4. Suggest additional internal controls that Dr. Thomen might want to implement.

FOCUS ON FINANCIAL STATEMENTS

FFS 8-1

CHECK FIGURES:
Current assets =
$68,190, Total assets
= $112,540

Ellis Worton, the owner of Worton Consulting, showed the following unadjusted account balances at December 31, 2014, the business's year-end (accounts have been listed in alphabetical order):

Account	Account Balance*
Accounts payable	$ 31,500
Accounts receivable	46,250
Accumulated depreciation, store fixtures	61,000
Cash	19,340
Cost of goods sold	469,000
Delivery expense	11,330
Ellis Worton, capital	89,560
Ellis Worton, withdrawals	69,000
Interest expense	2,240
Notes payable (principal of $20,000 to be paid in 2015)	56,000
Petty cash	350
Prepaid rent	16,200
Rent expense	11,250
Salaries expense	213,000
Salaries payable	17,750
Sales	721,400
Sales returns and allowances	6,000
Store fixtures	113,250

*Assume normal account balances.

Other information:

1. There were two reconciling items on the bank reconciliation: an outstanding cheque in the amount of $620 and an NSF cheque for $2,835.

2. A review of the Prepaid Rent account showed that the unexpired portion was $2,250.

3. Annual depreciation on the store fixtures is $7,900.

Required

Prepare the December 31, 2014, classified balance sheet.

Analysis Component:

a. Calculate Worton Consulting's current ratio and acid-test ratio at December 31, 2014. Compare and comment. Round calculations to two decimal places.

b. Recalculate the current ratio and acid-test ratio assuming the current portion of the note payable was reported as part of the long-term liabilities. Compare your results to part (a) and comment. Round calculations to two decimal places.

FFS 8-2   Refer to **WestJet's** December 31, 2011, balance sheet in Appendix II at the end of the textbook.

Required

Answer the following questions.

1. WestJet shows *cash and cash equivalents* on its December 31, 2011, balance sheet. Explain the meaning of *cash and cash equivalents*.

2. How much *cash and cash equivalents* did WestJet have on December 31, 2011?

3. By how much did WestJet's cash and cash equivalents increase or decrease from December 31, 2010, to December 31, 2011?

Analysis Component: Is it possible for there to be excessive *cash and cash equivalents*? Explain.

CRITICAL THINKING MINI CASE

You are the newly elected vice-president of campus life for the business students' association at your institution. The first big event of the year is a party that has three live bands playing from 5:00 p.m. to midnight; tickets are $20 (cash only). A number of people are helping you sell tickets during the two weeks prior to the event. At the end of each day, you collect the cash from each seller and reconcile it against the tickets sold (the tickets are sequentially numbered). You place your records and the cash in a locked filing cabinet in your office, which is always locked. In less than two weeks, all of the tickets are sold. After collecting the cash from the ticket sellers on the day of the sellout, you're feeling terrific about the success of the sales campaign you organized for the event and go to your office, unlock the door, and immediately notice that the filing cabinet has been tampered with . . . all of the money is gone . . . over $35,000!!

Required Using the elements of critical thinking described on the inside front cover, comment.

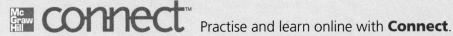

Practise and learn online with **Connect**.

Receivables

LEARNING OBJECTIVES

LO¹ Describe accounts receivable and how they occur and are recorded.

LO² Apply the allowance method to account for uncollectible accounts receivable.

LO³ Estimate uncollectible accounts receivable using approaches based on sales and accounts receivable.

LO⁴ Describe and record a short-term note receivable and calculate its maturity date and interest.

*Appendix 9A

LO⁵ Explain how receivables can be converted to cash before maturity.

*Appendix 9B

LO⁶ Calculate accounts receivable turnover and days' sales uncollected to analyze liquidity.

TWO COMPANIES, DIFFERENT RECEIVABLES EXPERIENCES

Sun-Rype Products Ltd., with its head office in Kelowna, British Columbia, is a manufacturer and marketer of juice-based beverages and fruit snacks. It reported net sales of $147,529,000 for the year ended December 31, 2011. Accounts receivable at December 31, 2011, totalled $13,672,000; no uncollectible accounts were noted, implying that this figure must be immaterial.

With its head office in Toronto, the **Canadian Imperial Bank of Commerce (CIBC)** is one of Canada's largest banks. Its primary source of revenue is from interest, and during the year ended October 31, 2011, the bank reported $10,099,000,000 of interest earned. The CIBC's October 31, 2011, balance sheet shows credit card receivables of $10,408,000,000 along with estimated uncollectible accounts of $411,000,000—yes, almost half a billion dollars!

Both companies have receivables, yet Sun-Rype and CIBC have different experiences in terms of uncollectible accounts. Why? Because of what each company is selling and to whom. The credit managers for both organizations require a solid understanding of collection risk in their specific industry; they must develop policies and procedures to maximize the effective and efficient collection of receivables while minimizing bad debts, which, in the banking industry, can have a huge total dollar value.

 CRITICAL THINKING CHALLENGE How are Sun-Rype's customers different from CIBC's? Why would CIBC experience a higher rate of uncollectible accounts than Sun-Rype does?

CHAPTER PREVIEW

This chapter focuses on accounts receivable and short-term notes receivable. We describe each of these assets, their use in practice, and how they are accounted for and reported in financial statements. This knowledge helps us use accounting information to make better decisions, and can also help in predicting bad debts.

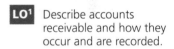

Student Success *Cycle*

Read the material
Do the exercises
Check your answers
Apply your critical thinking skills

ACCOUNTS RECEIVABLE

A *receivable* refers to an amount due from another party. The two most common receivables are accounts receivable and notes receivable. Other receivables include interest receivable, rent receivable, tax refund receivable, and amounts due from other parties such as officers and employees.

Accounts receivable are amounts due from customers for credit sales. They are also referred to as **trade receivables** because they result from customers with whom we *trade*. This section begins by describing how accounts receivable arise and their various sources. These sources include sales when customers use the seller's credit cards, and when a company gives credit directly to customers. When a company extends credit directly to customers, it must (1) maintain a separate account receivable for each customer and (2) account for bad debts from credit sales.

Recognizing Accounts Receivable

Accounts receivable arise from credit sales to customers. The amount of credit sales over cash sales has increased in recent years, reflecting several factors including an efficient banking system and a sound economy. Exhibit 9.1 shows the dollar amounts of accounts receivable and their percent of total assets for five companies.

LO¹ Describe accounts receivable and how they occur and are recorded.

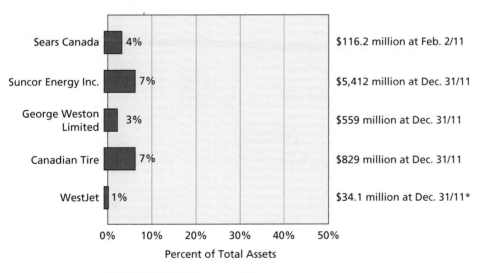

Company	Percent of Total Assets	Amount
Sears Canada	4%	$116.2 million at Feb. 2/11
Suncor Energy Inc.	7%	$5,412 million at Dec. 31/11
George Weston Limited	3%	$559 million at Dec. 31/11
Canadian Tire	7%	$829 million at Dec. 31/11
WestJet	1%	$34.1 million at Dec. 31/11*

*NOTE: This is 0.98% (less than 1%).

EXHIBIT 9.1

Accounts Receivable for Selected Companies

Sales on Credit

To review how accounts receivable from credit sales are recognized, we will record two transactions in the accounting records for TechCom, a small electronics wholesaler. TechCom's *Accounts Receivable controlling account* in the General Ledger and *Accounts Receivable Subledger* prior to recording these transactions are illustrated in Exhibit 9.2.

EXHIBIT 9.2

Accounts Receivable Controlling Account and the Accounts Receivable Subledger

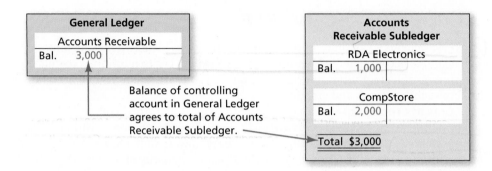

The first transaction to be recorded on July 15 is a credit sale of $950 to CompStore (cost of sales to TechCom is $630 assuming a perpetual inventory system). The second is a collection of $720 from RDA Electronics from prior credit sales. Both transactions are reflected in Exhibit 9.3. Note that these transactions would typically be recorded in the appropriate Sales and Cash Receipts Journals. We use the General Journal format here for simplicity.

EXHIBIT 9.3

Accounts Receivable Transactions

July	15	Accounts Receivable—CompStore..................	950	
		Sales		950
		To record credit sales.		
	15	Cost of Goods Sold	630	
		Merchandise Inventory		630
		To record cost of sales.		
	15	Cash	720	
		Accounts Receivable—RDA Electronics...		720
		To record collection of credit sales.		

Exhibit 9.4 shows the Accounts Receivable controlling account and the Accounts Receivable Subledger after posting these two transactions.

EXHIBIT 9.4

Accounts Receivable Controlling Account and the Accounts Receivable Subledger

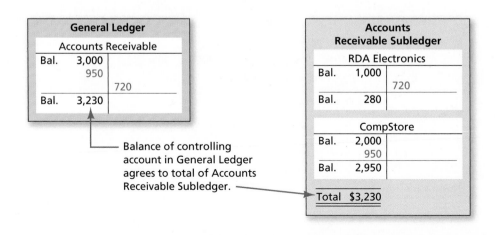

Like many companies, TechCom grants credit directly to qualified customers. Many large retailers such as **Canadian Tire** maintain their own credit card. This allows them to grant credit to approved customers and to earn interest on any balance not paid within a specified period of time, as well as to avoid the fee charged by credit card companies. The entries in this case are the same as those above except for the possibility of added interest revenue. If a customer owes interest on the bill, then we debit Accounts Receivable and credit Interest Revenue for this amount.

DECISION INSIGHT

Credit management involves establishing policies and procedures around approving credit customers, resolving invoice issues, collecting receivables, and controlling cash flow. The Credit Institute of Canada was created on June 11, 1928, by Parliament for the purpose of developing credit management expertise in Canada. Its mission is to provide credit management resources, education, and certification to its members and it offers the CCP (Certified Credit Professional) program which leads to the professional designation FCI (Fellow Credit Institute).

SOURCE: www.creditedu.org

CHECKPOINT

1. Where on the balance sheet are accounts receivable reported?

Do Quick Study question: QS 9-1

Valuing Accounts Receivable

When a company grants credit to its customers, there are usually a few customers who do not pay what they promised. The accounts of these customers are **uncollectible accounts**, commonly called **bad debts**. The total amount of uncollectible accounts is an expense of selling on credit. Why do companies sell on credit if it is likely some accounts will prove uncollectible? Companies believe granting credit will increase revenues and profits to offset bad debts. They are willing to incur bad debt losses if the net effect is to increase sales and profits.

Two methods are used by companies to account for uncollectible accounts: (1) allowance method, and (2) direct write-off method. Exhibit 9.5 summarizes these methods.

EXHIBIT 9.5

Methods for Writing Off Bad Debts

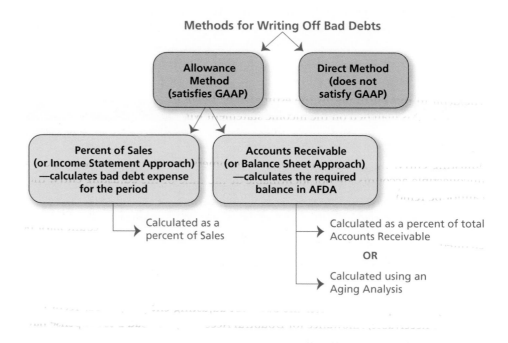

Methods for Writing Off Bad Debts

Allowance Method (satisfies GAAP)

Direct Method (does not satisfy GAAP)

Percent of Sales (or Income Statement Approach) —calculates bad debt expense for the period

Accounts Receivable (or Balance Sheet Approach) —calculates the required balance in AFDA

Calculated as a percent of Sales

Calculated as a percent of total Accounts Receivable

OR

Calculated using an Aging Analysis

Allowance Method

 LO² Apply the allowance method to account for uncollectible accounts receivable.

The matching principle requires that expenses be reported in the same accounting period as the sales they helped produce. This means that if extending credit to customers helped produce sales, any bad debt expense linked to those sales should be matched and reported in the same period as the sales. The **allowance method of accounting for bad debts** satisfies the matching principle by matching the expected loss from uncollectible accounts receivable against the sales they helped produce in that period. How? Since the seller is unable to identify in advance which of the credit sales will become uncollectible, an estimate based on past experience and the experience of similar companies must be used. This means that at the end of each period, the total bad debts expected to result from that period's sales are estimated. An allowance is then recorded for this expected loss. As well as matching, the allowance method satisfies the requirement of the prudence principle. To avoid overstatement, the allowance reduces accounts receivable on the balance sheet to an amount that is expected to be collected. Overstating assets could cause users of the information to make inappropriate business decisions.

Recording Estimated Bad Debt Expense

The allowance method estimates bad debt expense at the end of each accounting period and records it with an adjusting entry. TechCom, for instance, had credit sales of approximately $300,000 during its first year of operations. At the end of the first year, $20,000 of credit sales remained uncollected. Based on the experience of similar businesses, TechCom estimated bad debt expense to be $1,500. This estimated expense is recorded with the following adjusting entry at the end of the accounting period:

Dec. 31	Bad Debt Expense...	1,500	
	Allowance for Doubtful Accounts..........		1,500
	To record estimated bad debts.		

The debit in this entry means the estimated bad debt expense of $1,500 from selling on credit is matched on the income statement with the $300,000 sales it helped produce. The credit in this entry is to a contra asset called **Allowance for Doubtful Accounts**. A contra account is used because at the time of the adjusting entry, we do not know which customers will not pay. Because specific uncollectible accounts are not identifiable at the time of the adjusting entry, they cannot be removed from the Accounts Receivable Subledger. Because the customer accounts are left in the subledger, the controlling account for Accounts Receivable cannot be reduced. Instead, the Allowance for Doubtful Accounts account *must* be credited.

Bad Debts and Related Accounts in Financial Statements

Recall that TechCom has $20,000 of outstanding accounts receivable at the end of its first year of operations. After the bad debt adjusting entry is posted, TechCom's Accounts Receivable, Allowance for Doubtful Accounts, and Bad Debt Expense have balances as shown in Exhibit 9.6.

EXHIBIT 9.6

General Ledger Balances After Bad Debts Adjustment

Accounts Receivable and *Allowance for Doubtful Accounts* are BOTH balance sheet accounts shown under current assets.

Accounts Receivable		
Dec. 31	20,000	

Allowance for Doubtful Accounts		
	1,500	Dec. 31

Bad Debt Expense is an income statement account and is normally listed as a selling expense.

Bad Debt Expense		
Dec. 31	1,500	

Although $20,000 is legally owed to TechCom by its credit customers, $18,500 (= $20,000 − $1,500) is the **realizable value**, or the estimated amount to be realized in cash collections from customers.

On the balance sheet, the Allowance for Doubtful Accounts is subtracted from Accounts Receivable to show the realizable value. This information is often reported as shown in Exhibit 9.7.

Current assets:		
Accounts receivable...	$20,000	
Less: Allowance for doubtful accounts	1,500	18,500

EXHIBIT 9.7

Balance Sheet Presentation of Allowance for Doubtful Accounts

Often the contra account to Accounts Receivable is not reported separately. This alternative presentation is shown in Exhibit 9.8.

EXHIBIT 9.8

Alternative Presentation of
Allowance for Doubtful Accounts

Current assets:
    Accounts receivable (net of $1,500 estimated uncollectible accounts).................. $18,500

Writing Off a Bad Debt

When specific accounts receivable are identified as uncollectible, they must be removed from accounts receivable. This is done by writing them off against the Allowance for Doubtful Accounts. For instance, after spending a year trying to collect from Jack Kent, TechCom finally decides that his $520 account is uncollectible and makes the following entry to write it off:

Jan.	23	Allowance for Doubtful Accounts...................	520	
		Accounts Receivable—Jack Kent............		520
		To write off an uncollectible account.		

After this entry is posted, the General Ledger accounts appear as shown in Exhibit 9.9.

EXHIBIT 9.9

General Ledger Balances After
Posting Write-Off

Accounts Receivable			
Dec. 31	20,000		
		520	Jan. 23
Balance	19,480		

Allowance for Doubtful Accounts			
		1,500	Dec. 31
Jan. 23	520		
		980	Balance

Note that the expense account is not debited, because bad debt expense is previously estimated and recorded with an adjusting entry at the end of the period in which the sale occurred. While the write-off removes the amount of the account receivable from the ledgers, it does not affect the estimated realizable value of TechCom's net accounts receivable as shown in Exhibit 9.10.

EXHIBIT 9.10

Realizable Value Before and
After Write-Off

	Before Write-Off (Dec. 31)	After Write-Off (Jan. 23)
Accounts receivable	$20,000	$19,480
Less: Allowance for doubtful accounts......................	1,500	980
Estimated realizable accounts receivable...................	$18,500	$18,500

Neither total assets nor net income is affected by the write-off of a specific account. But both total assets and net income are affected by recognizing the year's bad debt expense in the adjusting entry.

Recovery of a Bad Debt

When a customer fails to pay and the account is written off, his or her credit standing is jeopardized. The customer sometimes chooses to pay all or part of the amount owed after the account is written off as uncollectible. This payment helps restore credit standing. When a recovery of a bad debt occurs, it is recorded in the customer's subsidiary account where this information is retained for use in future credit evaluation.

If on March 11 Jack Kent pays in full his account that TechCom previously wrote off, the entries to record this bad debt recovery are:

Mar.	11	Accounts Receivable—Jack Kent	520	
		Allowance for Doubtful Accounts		520
		To reinstate the account of Jack Kent previously written off.		
	11	Cash	520	
		Accounts Receivable—Jack Kent		520
		In full payment of account.		

Jack Kent paid the entire amount previously written off, but in some cases a customer may pay only a portion of the amount owed. A question then arises of whether the entire balance of the account is returned to accounts receivable or just the amount paid. The answer is a matter of judgement. If we believe this customer will later pay in full, the entire amount owed is returned to accounts receivable. But only the amount paid is returned if we expect no further collection.

To summarize, the transactions discussed in this chapter[1] that cause changes in Accounts Receivable and Allowance for Doubtful Accounts are illustrated using T-accounts in Exhibit 9.11.

Accounts Receivable		Allowance for Doubtful Accounts	
(a) Sales on credit	(b) Collections received from credit customers		
	(c) Write-off of accounts receivable identified as uncollectible	(c) Write-off of accounts receivable identified as uncollectible	
(d) Recovery (reinstatement of accounts previously written off)	(e) Recovery (collection of reinstated accounts)		(d) Recovery (reinstatement of accounts previously written off)
			(f) Adjusting entry to estimate uncollectible accounts

EXHIBIT 9.11

Summary of Accounts Receivable and Allowance for Doubtful Accounts Transactions

---

1   Remember that Sales Returns and Allowances also cause Accounts Receivable to decrease.

CHECKPOINT

2. Why does the matching principle require that bad debt expenses be estimated?
3. What term describes the balance sheet valuation of accounts receivable less the allowance for doubtful accounts?
4. Why is estimated bad debt expense credited to a contra account rather than to the Accounts Receivable controlling account?
5. Record entries for the following transactions:

January 10, 2014   The $300 account of customer Cool Jam is determined to be uncollectible.

April 12, 2014   Cool Jam pays in full its account that was deemed uncollectible on January 10, 2014.

Do Quick Study questions: QS 9-2, QS 9-3

Estimating Bad Debt Expense

LO³ Estimate uncollectible accounts receivable using approaches based on sales and accounts receivable.

There are two general approaches for estimating bad debt expense. These were introduced briefly in Exhibit 9.5.

Percent of Sales Approach

The **percent of sales approach** (or **income statement approach**) uses income statement relations to estimate bad debts. It is based on the idea that a percentage of a company's credit sales for the period are uncollectible.[2] To demonstrate, assume MusicLand has credit sales of $400,000 in 2014. Based on experience, MusicLand estimates 0.6% of credit sales to be uncollectible. Using this prediction, MusicLand expects $2,400 of bad debt expense from 2014's sales ($400,000 × 0.006 = $2,400). The adjusting entry to record this estimated expense is:

Dec.	31	Bad Debt Expense	2,400	
		Allowance for Doubtful Accounts		2,400
		To record estimated bad debts.		

For demonstration purposes, assume that the Allowance for Doubtful Accounts (AFDA) had an unadjusted credit balance of $200 on December 31. Bad Debt Expense and Allowance for Doubtful Accounts would appear as in Exhibit 9.12 *after* the December 31 adjustment.

EXHIBIT 9.12

Accounts Receivable and Allowance for Doubtful Accounts Balances After the December 31 Adjustment

Bad Debt Expense			**Allowance for Doubtful Accounts**		
				200	Unadjusted Balance Dec. 31
Dec. 31 Adjustment	2,400			2,400	Dec. 31 Adjustment
Adjusted Balance Dec. 31	2,400			2,600	Adjusted Balance Dec. 31

---

2 Note that the focus is on credit sales. Cash sales do not produce bad debts, and they are generally not used in this estimation. But if cash sales are relatively small compared to credit sales, there is no major impact of including them.

Note that the unadjusted balance of AFDA could be a zero balance, a credit balance, or a debit balance depending on the circumstances. If MusicLand were in its first period of operations, the AFDA would have a zero beginning balance. In the next accounting periods, if write-offs are *greater* than what had been estimated, a *debit* unadjusted balance will result. If *fewer* write-offs occur than what was estimated, as in Exhibit 9.12, a *credit* unadjusted balance will result. If the estimate for bad debts is too high or too low, the percentage used to estimate bad debts can be adjusted in future periods.

Accounts Receivable Approach

The **accounts receivable approach**, also known as the **balance sheet approach**, uses balance sheet relations (Accounts Receivable and the Allowance for Doubtful Accounts) to estimate bad debts. It is based on the idea that some portion of the end-of-period accounts receivable balance is not collectible. The objective for the bad debt adjusting entry is to make the Allowance for Doubtful Accounts balance equal to the portion of outstanding accounts receivable estimated to be uncollectible. To obtain this required balance for the Allowance for Doubtful Accounts account, we compare its balance before the adjustment with the required balance. The difference between the two is debited to Bad Debt Expense and credited to Allowance for Doubtful Accounts. Estimating this required balance for the allowance account is done in one of two ways:

1. By using a simple percent estimate of uncollectibles from the total outstanding accounts receivable, or
2. By aging accounts receivable.

1. *Percent of Accounts Receivable*

Estimating the required balance in the Allowance for Doubtful Accounts by calculating the **percent of accounts receivable** assumes that a percent of a company's outstanding receivables is uncollectible. This estimated percent is based on past experience and the experience of similar companies, and is also affected by recent economic conditions and difficulties faced by customers. The total dollar amount of all outstanding receivables is multiplied by an estimated percent to get the estimated dollar amount of uncollectible accounts. This is the amount to be reported in the balance sheet as the balance for Allowance for Doubtful Accounts. To accomplish this, we prepare the adjusting entry in the amount necessary to give us the required balance in Allowance for Doubtful Accounts.

Assume RGO, an office furniture supplier, has $50,000 of outstanding accounts receivable on December 31. Past experience suggests that 5% of outstanding receivables are uncollectible.

Therefore, we want the Allowance for Doubtful Accounts to show a $2,500 credit balance (5% of $50,000). Assume that the unadjusted balance in the Allowance for Doubtful Accounts at December 31 is currently a $500 credit.

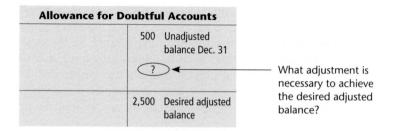

Allowance for Doubtful Accounts

	500 Unadjusted balance Dec. 31
	⟨ ? ⟩
	2,500 Desired adjusted balance

What adjustment is necessary to achieve the desired adjusted balance?

The adjusting entry to give the required $2,500 balance is:

Dec.	31	Bad Debt Expense..	2,000	
		Allowance for Doubtful Accounts..........		2,000
		To record estimated bad debts.		

After this entry is posted, the allowance has a $2,500 credit balance as shown in Exhibit 9.13.

EXHIBIT 9.13

Allowance for Doubtful Accounts After Bad Debt Adjusting Entry

Allowance for Doubtful Accounts

	500 Unadjusted balance Dec. 31
	2,000 From Dec. 31 adjusting entry
	2,500 Adjusted balance Dec. 31

Accounts receivable would then be reported as follows on RGO's balance sheet:

Current assets:		
Accounts receivable	$50,000	
Less: Allowance for doubtful accounts	2,500	$47,500
or		
Current assets:		
Accounts receivable (net of $2,500 estimated uncollectible accounts)....		$47,500

2. *Aging of Accounts Receivable*

Normally, the older the account receivable the more likely that it will become uncollectible. An **aging of accounts receivable**, or **aging analysis**, estimates uncollectible accounts by grouping accounts receivable according to how much time has passed since they were created. Groupings depend on the judgement of management but are often based on 30-day periods. Estimated rates of uncollectibility are applied to each class and totalled to get the required balance of the Allowance for Doubtful Accounts. This calculation is illustrated in Exhibit 9.14 for DeCor, an interior design company whose total outstanding accounts receivable at December 31 were $49,900.

EXHIBIT 9.14

Aging of Accounts Receivable

DeCor Schedule of Accounts Receivable by Age December 31, 2014						
Customer's Name	Total	Not Yet Due	1 to 30 Days Past Due	31 to 60 Days Past Due	61 to 90 Days Past Due	Over 90 Days Past Due
Charles Abbot	$ 450	$ 450				
Frank Allen	710			$ 710		
George Arden	500	300	$ 200			
Paul Baum	740				$ 100	$ 640
ZZ Services	1,000	810	190			
Totals	$49,900	$37,000	$6,500	$3,500	$1,900	$1,000
Percent Uncollectible		× 2%	× 5%	× 10%	× 25%	× 40%
Estimated Uncollectible Accounts	$ 2,290	$ 740	$ 325	$ 350	$ 475	$ 400

Notice the percent of uncollectibility increases with the age of the accounts to reflect the increasing risk of noncollection.

The total in the first column tells us the adjusted balance in DeCor's Allowance for Doubtful Accounts should be $2,290 (= $740 + $325 + $350 + $475 + $400). Because DeCor's allowance account as shown below has an unadjusted *debit balance* of $200, the required adjustment to the Allowance for Doubtful Accounts needs to be calculated as follows:

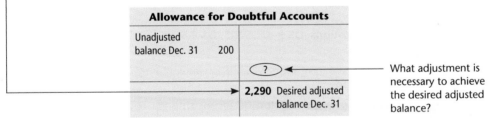

Allowance for Doubtful Accounts	
Unadjusted balance Dec. 31 200	
	?
	2,290 Desired adjusted balance Dec. 31

What adjustment is necessary to achieve the desired adjusted balance?

DeCor records the following adjusting entry:

Dec. 31	Bad Debt Expense	2,490	
	Allowance for Doubtful Accounts		2,490
	To record estimated bad debts;		
	$2,290 + $200 = $2,490.		

On the balance sheet, DeCor's accounts receivable would be reported as follows:

Current assets:
  Accounts receivable $49,900
  Less: Allowance for doubtful accounts 2,290 $47,610

or

Current assets:
  Accounts receivable (net of $2,290 estimated uncollectible accounts) $47,610

Exhibit 9.15 summarizes the principles guiding the estimation approaches and their focus of analysis.

EXHIBIT 9.15

Approaches to Estimate Bad Debts

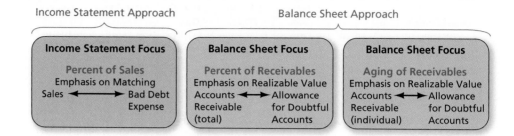

Using an aging of receivables is the most reliable of the three calculations because it is based on a more detailed examination of specific accounts. In many cases, the aging analysis is supplemented with information about specific customers, allowing management to decide whether those accounts should be classified as uncollectible. This information is often supplied by the sales and credit department managers.

CHECKPOINT

6. SnoBoard Company's end-of-period Dec. 31, 2014, balance in the Allowance for Doubtful Accounts is a credit of $440. It estimates from an aging of accounts receivable that $6,142 is uncollectible. Prepare SnoBoard's year-end adjusting entry for bad debts.

Do Quick Study questions: QS 9-4, QS 9-5, QS 9-6, QS 9-7

Direct Write-Off Method

An alternative to the allowance method of accounting for bad debts is the *direct write-off method*. The **direct write-off method** records the loss from an uncollectible account receivable at the time it is determined to be uncollectible. No attempt is made to estimate uncollectible accounts or bad debt expense. For example, if Tech-Com determines on January 23 that it cannot collect $520 owed by an individual named Jack Kent, this loss is recognized using the direct write-off method in the following entry:

Jan.	23	Bad Debt Expense...	520	
		Accounts Receivable—Jack Kent............		520
		To write off uncollectible accounts under the direct write-off method.		

The allowance method satisfies the requirement for faithful representation and matching; the direct write-off method does not.

1. An aspect of faithful representation demands that caution be exercised to prevent the overstatement of assets and net income. Overstated assets and/or net income could result in bad lending or investing decisions. The allowance method, in recognizing that less than 100% of the accounts receivable will be collected (Accounts Receivable less Allowance for Doubtful Accounts), reduces the risk of overstating receivables. Under the direct write-off method, Accounts Receivable are reported on the balance sheet at 100%, which is more than what will typically be collected.

2. Matching requires that expenses be reported in the period in which the revenue was recorded. Often, an uncollectible account receivable is not discovered until the next accounting period. The allowance method attempts to match the expense of uncollectible accounts to the period in which the revenue was recorded by recording an estimate at the end of the period. The direct write-off method does *not* achieve matching since the expense is recorded when an account is identified as uncollectible, which is normally *not* in the period in which the revenue was recorded.

Although the direct write-off method is not in accordance with faithful representation and matching, *a business may choose to use it* instead of the allowance method. This would occur when uncollectible accounts are not material. The materiality principle states that an amount can be ignored if its effect on the financial statements is unimportant to users. The materiality principle permits the matching principle to be ignored when bad debt expenses are very small in relation to a company's other financial statement items. So the direct write-off method would be used when bad debt expense is unimportant for decisions made by users of the company's financial statements.

CHECKPOINT

7. The direct write-off method is recorded by debiting Bad Debt Expense and crediting the Allowance for Doubtful Accounts.
   a. True
   b. False

Do Quick Study question: QS 9-8

DECISION MAKER   Answer—End of chapter

Labour Union Chief

You are representing your employee union in contract negotiations with management. One week prior to contract discussions, management released financial statements showing zero growth in earnings. This is far below the 10% growth predicted earlier. In your review of the financial statements, you find the company increased its "allowance for uncollectible accounts" from 1.5% to 4.5% of accounts receivable. Apart from this change, earnings would show a 9% growth. Does this information affect your negotiations?

MID-CHAPTER DEMONSTRATION PROBLEM

Delcor Industries, a distributor of electrical supplies, had outstanding accounts receivable on December 31, 2014, of $450,000 aged as follows:

Delcor Industries Schedule of Accounts Receivable by Age December 31, 2014						
Customer's Name	Total	Not Yet Due	1 to 30 Days Past Due	31 to 60 Days Past Due	61 to 90 Days Past Due	Over 90 Days Past Due
Alton Group.............	$ 90,000		$ 90,000			
Filby's Electrical Service	48,000			$22,000	$26,000	
GDP Servicing..........	162,000	$120,000	42,000			
Parker's Electrical......	80,000	80,000				
Trenton Construction .	15,000					$15,000
Xeon Developments .	55,000	30,000	25,000			
Totals	$450,000	$230,000	$157,000	$22,000	$26,000	$15,000
Percent uncollectible		× 1%	× 4%	× 8%	× 25%	× 60%
Estimated uncollectible accounts						

During the year 2014, the company had sales of $3,720,000, of which $38,000 were cash sales. The Allowance for Doubtful Accounts had an unadjusted debit balance on December 31, 2014, of $3,050.

Required

Prepare the adjusting entry to estimate uncollectible accounts on December 31, 2014, under each of the following independent assumptions, and show the resulting balance sheet presentation for accounts receivable:

a.   Bad debts are estimated to be 0.6% of credit sales.

b.   Bad debts are estimated to be 4% of outstanding accounts receivable.

c.   Bad debts are based on an aging analysis (part of the required information is provided in the schedule above).

Analysis Component:

d.   If Delcor did not record the adjusting entry to estimate uncollectible accounts receivable, what effect would this have on current assets, equity, and net income?

e.   Assume Delcor's competitors report uncollectible accounts receivable of 1% of outstanding receivables. How does Delcor's experience compare?

SOLUTION

a.   0.6% × ($3,720,000 − $38,000 = $3,682,000 credit sales) = $22,092

	2014			
Dec.	31	Bad Debt Expense...	22,092	
		Allowance for Doubtful Accounts..........		22,092
		To record estimated bad debts.		

Current assets:
Accounts receivable.. $450,000
Less: Allowance for doubtful accounts 19,042* $430,958

or

Current assets:
Accounts receivable (net of $19,042* estimated uncollectible accounts).... $430,958

*$22,092 credit adjustment − $3,050 debit balance = $19,042.

b. The required balance in the Allowance for Doubtful Accounts is $18,000
    (= 4% × $450,000)

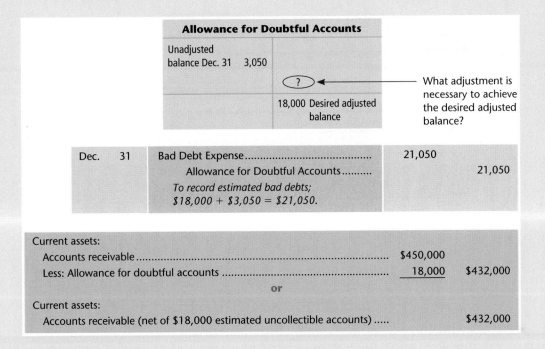

Allowance for Doubtful Accounts

Unadjusted balance Dec. 31	3,050	
		?
		18,000 Desired adjusted balance

What adjustment is necessary to achieve the desired adjusted balance?

Dec.	31	Bad Debt Expense...	21,050	
		Allowance for Doubtful Accounts..........		21,050
		To record estimated bad debts; $18,000 + $3,050 = $21,050.		

Current assets:
Accounts receivable.. $450,000
Less: Allowance for doubtful accounts 18,000 $432,000

or

Current assets:
Accounts receivable (net of $18,000 estimated uncollectible accounts) $432,000

c. First, calculate total estimated uncollectible accounts by completing the bottom
    of the aging schedule as follows:

Totals	$450,000	$230,000	$157,000	$22,000	$26,000	$15,000
Percent uncollectible		× 1%	× 4%	× 8%	× 25%	× 60%
Estimated uncollectible accounts	$ 25,840	$ 2,300	$ 6,280	$ 1,760	$ 6,500	$ 9,000

Allowance for Doubtful Accounts

Unadjusted balance Dec. 31	3,050	
		?
		25,840 Desired adjusted balance Dec. 31

What adjustment is necessary to achieve the desired adjusted balance?

Second, determine what adjustment is necessary to achieve the desired balance of $25,840 in the Allowance for Doubtful Accounts as follows:

Dec.	31	Bad Debt Expense..	28,890	
		Allowance for Doubtful Accounts..........		28,890
		To record estimated bad debts;		
		$25,840 + $3,050.		

Current assets:		
Accounts receivable..	$450,000	
Less: Allowance for doubtful accounts	25,840	$424,160

or

Current assets:	
Accounts receivable (net of $25,840 estimated uncollectible accounts)	$424,160

Analysis Component:

d.   If Delcor did not record the adjusting entry to estimate uncollectible accounts receivable, current assets would be overstated, equity would be overstated, and net income would be overstated.

e.   Delcor's competitors are experiencing a lower rate of uncollectible accounts receivable which, on the surface, appears to be favourable. However, additional information is required. Perhaps Delcor has an aggressive credit policy, granting credit to a wider range of customers, which increases revenues but at the same time increases the risk of uncollectibility but overall increases net income. It may also be that Delcor's experience is the result of weak credit policies that grant credit to riskier customers (regarding collectibility).

SHORT-TERM NOTES RECEIVABLE

LO⁴ Describe and record a short-term note receivable and calculate its maturity date and interest.

A **promissory note**, as illustrated in Exhibit 9.16, is a written promise to pay a specified amount of money either on demand or at a definite future date. A **short-term note receivable** (or **note receivable**) is a promissory note that becomes due within the next 12 months or within the business's operating cycle if greater than 12 months.

EXHIBIT 9.16

Terminology Related to a Promissory Note

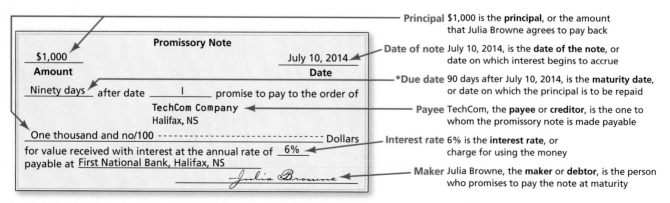

*   Note: The **due date** of a note is also referred to as the **maturity date**. The **period** of this note is 90 days, the time from the *date of the note* to its *maturity date* or *due date*.

Calculations for Notes

We need to know two calculations related to notes:

1. How to determine the maturity date, and
2. How to calculate interest.

Maturity Date

A note dated on July 10 with a specified maturity date of July 15 is a five-day note (calculated as July 15 − July 10 = 5 days). A 10-day note dated July 10 would have a maturity date of July 20 (calculated as July 10 + 10 days = July 20). The promissory note dated July 10 in Exhibit 9.16 is a 90-day note and the maturity date is calculated as shown in Exhibit 9.17.

Days in July	31
Minus date of note	10
Days remaining in July	21
Add days in August	31
Add days in September	30
Days to equal 90 days or **Maturity Date, October 8**	8
Period of the note in days	90

EXHIBIT 9.17
Maturity Date Calculation

The period of a note is sometimes expressed in months or years. When months are used, the note matures and is payable in the month of its maturity on the *same day of the month* as its original date. A three-month note dated July 10, for instance, is payable on October 10. The same analysis applies when years are used.

Interest Calculation

Interest is an annual rate unless otherwise stated. The formula for calculating interest is shown in Exhibit 9.18.

$$\text{Interest} = \begin{array}{c}\text{Principal}\\\text{of the}\\\text{note}\end{array} \times \begin{array}{c}\text{Annual}\\\text{interest}\\\text{rate}\end{array} \times \begin{array}{c}\text{Time}\\\text{expressed}\\\text{in years}\end{array} \quad \textbf{or} \quad i = Prt$$

EXHIBIT 9.18
Formula for Calculating Interest

Interest on a $1,000, 6%, six-month note is calculated as:

$$\$1,000 \times 6\% \times \frac{6}{12} = \$30$$

Using the promissory note in Exhibit 9.16 where the term of the note is in days, interest is calculated as follows:

$$\text{Interest} = \text{Principal} \times \text{Rate} \times \frac{\text{Exact days}}{365}$$

or

$$\$1,000 \times 6\% \times \frac{90}{365} = \$14.79$$

Unless otherwise instructed, you are to solve problems using the specific number of days and a 365-day year. Interest calculations should be rounded to the nearest whole cent.

Receipt of a Note

To illustrate recording the receipt of a note, we use the $1,000, 90-day, 6% promissory note in Exhibit 9.16. Assume that TechCom receives this note at the time of a product sale to Julia Browne (cost of sales $630). This transaction is recorded as (assuming a perpetual inventory system):

July	10	Notes Receivable...	1,000	
		Sales		1,000
		Sold merchandise in exchange for a 90-day, 6% note.		
	10	Cost of Goods Sold	630	
		Merchandise Inventory		630
		To record cost of sales.		

A note receivable can also arise when a company accepts a note from an overdue customer as a way of granting a time extension on a past-due account receivable. When this occurs, a company may collect part of the past-due balance in cash. This partial payment forces a concession from the customer, reduces the customer's debt (and the seller's risk), and produces a note for a smaller amount. TechCom, for instance, agreed to accept $1,000 in cash and a $3,000, 60-day, 6% note on December 16 from Jo Cook to settle her $4,000 past-due account. TechCom made the following entry to record receipt of this cash and note:

Dec.	16	Cash	1,000	
		Notes Receivable...	3,000	
		Accounts Receivable—Jo Cook		4,000
		Received cash and note in settlement of account.		

End-of-Period Interest Adjustment

When notes receivable are outstanding at the end of an accounting period, accrued interest is calculated and recorded. This recognizes both the interest revenue when it is earned and the added asset (interest receivable) owned by the note's holder. When TechCom's accounting period ends on December 31, $7.40 of interest accrues on the note dated December 16 ($3,000 \times 6\% \times 15/365$). The following adjusting entry records this revenue:

Dec.	31	Interest Receivable	7.40	
		Interest Revenue		7.40
		To record accrued interest.		

This adjusting entry means that interest revenue appears on the income statement of the period when it is earned. It also means that interest receivable appears on the balance sheet as a current asset.

Honouring a Note

When the note dated December 16 is paid on the maturity date of February 14, the maker of the note, Jo Cook, is **honouring** the note. TechCom's entry to record the cash receipt is:

Feb.	14	Cash	3,029.59	
		Interest Revenue		22.19
		Interest Receivable		7.40
		Notes Receivable.....................................		3,000.00
		Received payment of a note and its interest.		

Total interest earned on this note is $29.59 (= $3,000 \times 6\% \times 60/365$). On February 14, Interest Receivable is credited for $7.40 to record the collection of the interest accrued on December 31. The interest revenue in this period is $22.19 (= $29.59 total interest less $7.40 interest accrued on December 31) and reflects TechCom's revenue from holding the note from January 1 to February 14.

Dishonouring a Note

Sometimes the maker of a note does not pay the note at maturity; this is known as **dishonouring** the note. The act of dishonouring does not relieve the maker of the obligation to pay. The payee should use every legitimate means to collect. Assume Julia Browne did not pay the note dated July 10 when it matured on October 8. TechCom removes the amount of the note from the Notes Receivable account and charges it back to an account receivable from its maker as follows:

Oct.	8	Accounts Receivable—Julia Browne	1,014.79	
		Interest Revenue		14.79
		Notes Receivable.....................................		1,000.00
		To charge the account of Julia Browne for a dishonoured note including interest; $1,000 \times 6\% - 90/365$.		

Charging a dishonoured note back to the account of its maker serves two purposes. First, it removes the amount of the note from the Notes Receivable account, leaving in the account only notes that have not matured, and records the dishonoured note in the maker's account. Second, and most important, if the maker of the dishonoured note applies for credit in the future, his or her account will show all past dealings, including the dishonoured note. Restoring the account also reminds the company to continue collection efforts for both principal and interest. If the restored account receivable is later identified as being uncollectible, it is written off as follows:

Oct.	31	Allowance for Doubtful Accounts	1,014.79	
		Accounts Receivable—Julia Browne		1,014.79
		To write off an uncollectible account.		

 CHECKPOINT

8. Wiley purchases $7,000 of merchandise from Stamford Company on December 16, 2014. Stamford accepts Wiley's $7,000, 90-day, 12% note as payment. Stamford's annual accounting period ends on December 31 and it doesn't make reversing entries. Prepare entries for Stamford Company on December 16, 2014, and December 31, 2014.

9. Using the information in Checkpoint 8, prepare Stamford's March 16, 2015, entry if Wiley dishonours the note.

Do Quick Study questions: QS 9-9, QS 9-10, QS 9-11

CRITICAL THINKING CHALLENGE | Refer to the Critical Thinking Challenge questions at the beginning of the chapter. Compare your answers to those suggested on Connect.

IFRS AND ASPE—THE DIFFERENCES

Difference	International Financial Reporting Standards (IFRS)	Accounting Standards for Private Enterprises (ASPE)
There are no significant differences between IFRS and ASPE related to this chapter.		

SUMMARY

LO¹ Describe accounts receivable and how they occur and are recorded. Accounts receivable are amounts due from customers for credit sales. The subledger lists the amounts owed by individual customers. Credit sales arise from at least two sources: (1) sales on credit and (2) non-bank credit card sales. Sales on credit refers to a company granting credit directly to customers. Non-bank credit card sales involve use of a third party issuing a credit card.

LO² Apply the allowance method to account for uncollectible accounts receivable. Under the allowance method, bad debt expense is estimated at the end of the accounting period by debiting Bad Debt Expense and crediting the Allowance for Doubtful Accounts. When accounts are later identified as being uncollectible, they are written off by debiting the Allowance for Doubtful Accounts and crediting Accounts Receivable.

LO³ Estimate uncollectible accounts receivable using approaches based on sales and accounts receivable. Uncollectibles are estimated by focusing on either (a) the income statement relation between bad debt expense and credit sales or (b) the balance sheet relation between accounts receivable and the Allowance for Doubtful Accounts. The first approach emphasizes the matching principle for the income statement. The second approach can include either a simple percent relation with accounts receivable or the aging of accounts

receivable and emphasizes realizable value of accounts receivable for the balance sheet. Although not acceptable according to GAAP, the direct write-off method debits Bad Debt Expense and credits Accounts Receivable when accounts are determined to be uncollectible. It is used when the amount of bad debt expense is immaterial.

LO⁴ Describe and record a short-term note receivable and calculate its maturity date and interest. A short-term note receivable is a written promise to pay a specified amount of money either on demand or at a definite future date, normally within the next 12 months or the business's operating cycle if greater than one year. The maturity date of a note is the day the note (principal and interest) must be repaid. Interest rates are typically stated in annual terms. When a note's time to maturity is more or less than one year, the amount of interest on a note is calculated by expressing time as a fraction of one year and multiplying the note's principal by this fraction and the annual interest rate. It is recorded at its principal amount by debiting the Notes Receivable account and is credited to the asset or service provided in return for the note. Interest earned is recorded for the time period it is held in the accounting period reported on. When a note is honoured, the payee debits the money received and credits both Notes Receivable and Interest Revenue. Dishonoured notes are credited to Notes Receivable and Interest Revenue and debited to Accounts Receivable.

GUIDANCE ANSWER TO **DECISION MAKER**

Labour Union Chief

Yes, this information is likely to affect your negotiations. The obvious question is why the company increased the allowance to such a large extent. This major increase in allowance means a substantial increase in bad debt expense *and* a decrease in earnings. Also, this change coming immediately prior to labour contract discussions raises concerns since it

reduces the union's bargaining power for increased compensation. You want to ask management for supporting documentation justifying this increase. Also, you want data for two or three prior years, and similar data from competitors. These data should give you some sense of whether the change in the allowance for uncollectibles is justified or not.

1. Accounts receivable are typically due within the current accounting period so would be reported on the balance sheet as a current asset.

2. Bad debt expense must be estimated to match it with the sales that gave rise to the accounts receivable. This requires that companies estimate bad debts before they learn which accounts are uncollectible.

3. Realizable value.

4. The estimated amount of bad debt expense cannot be credited to the Accounts Receivable account because the specific customer accounts that will prove uncollectible cannot be identified and removed from the Accounts Receivable Subledger. If the controlling account were credited directly, its balance would not equal the sum of the subsidiary account balances.

5.

2014			
Jan. 10	Allowance for Doubtful Accounts......	300	
	Accounts Receivable—Cool Jam ...		300
	To record write-off of uncollectible account.		
Apr. 12	Accounts Receivable—Cool Jam........	300	
	Allowance for Doubtful Accounts ..		300
	To reinstate account previously written off.		
12	Cash...	300	
	Accounts Receivable—Cool Jam ...		300
	To record collection.		

6.

2014			
Dec. 31	Bad Debt Expense	5,702	
	Allowance for Doubtful Accounts ..		5,702
	To record estimated bad debts; $6,142 − $440.		

7. False. The direct write-off method is recorded by debiting Bad Debt Expense and crediting Accounts Receivable.

8.

2014			
Dec. 16	Notes Receivable	7,000.00	
	Sales...................................		7,000.00
	To record 90-day, 12% note.		
31	Interest Receivable.................	34.52	
	Interest Revenue...............		34.52
	To record accrued interest; $7,000 × 12% × 15/365.		

9.

2015			
Mar. 16	Accounts Receivable—Wiley ...	7,207.12	
	Interest Revenue................		172.60
	Interest Receivable.............		34.52
	Notes Receivable		7000.00
	To record dishonouring of a bad note; $7,000 × 12% × 90/365 = $207.12.		

DEMONSTRATION PROBLEM

Garden Company had a number of transactions involving receivables during the year 2014. Each of them follows.

Required

Prepare journal entries to record these independent transactions on the books of Garden Company. Garden Company's year-end is December 31.

a. On November 15, 2014, Garden Company agreed to accept $500 in cash and a $2,000, 90-day, 8% note from Argo Company to settle its $2,500 past-due account. Determine the maturity date and record the entry on November 15, on December 31, and on the date of maturity.

b. Garden Company held an $1,800, 6%, 45-day note of Altamira Industries. At maturity, December 15, Altamira dishonoured the note. Record the dishonouring of the Note Receivable.

c. Elko Purchasing Consultants estimates bad debts to be 3.5% of net credit sales. During 2014, total sales were $6,200,000, of which 35% were for cash. Sales returns and allowances for the year were $128,000, all related to credit sales. Accounts receivable in the amount of $130,000 were identified as uncollectible and written off during 2014. Calculate the adjusted balance in the allowance for doubtful accounts at December 31, 2014, assuming a credit balance on January 1, 2014, of $160,000.

Analysis Component:

In (b) the note receivable was dishonoured. How should this be classified on the balance sheet?

Planning the Solution

*   Examine each item to determine which accounts are affected and perform the required calculations.
*   Prepare required journal entries.
*   Prepare an answer to the analysis component.

SOLUTION

a.

Days in November	30
Minus date of note	15
Days remaining in November	15
Add days in December	31
	46
Add days in January	31
Days to equal 90 days or **Maturity date, February 13**	13
Period of the note in days	90

2014				
Nov. 15	Cash		500.00	
	Notes Receivable		2,000.00	
	Accounts Receivable—Argo Company			2,500.00
	Received cash and note in settlement of account.			
Dec. 31	Interest Receivable		20.16	
	Interest Revenue			20.16
	To record accrued interest;			
	$2,000 × 46/365 × 8% = $20.16.			
2015				
Feb. 13	Cash		2,039.45	
	Interest Receivable			20.16
	Interest Revenue			19.29
	Notes Receivable			2,000.00
	Collected note with interest;			
	$2,000 × 90/365 × 8% = $39.45.			

b.

	2014			
Dec.	15	Accounts Receivable—Altamira	1,813.32	
		Interest Revenue		13.32
		Note Receivable....................................		1,800.00
		To charge the account of Altamira for a dishonoured note including interest; $1,800 \times 6\% \times 45/365 = $13.32.		

c.

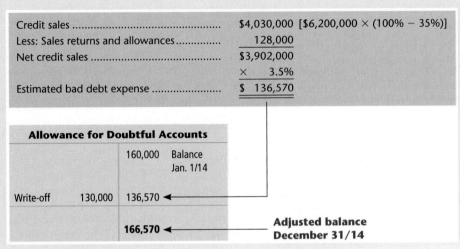

Credit sales	$4,030,000 [$6,200,000 × (100% − 35%)]
Less: Sales returns and allowances..............	128,000
Net credit sales	$3,902,000
	× 3.5%
Estimated bad debt expense	$ 136,570

Allowance for Doubtful Accounts

		160,000	Balance Jan. 1/14
Write-off	130,000	136,570 ◄	
		166,570 ◄	**Adjusted balance December 31/14**

Analysis Component:

The dishonoured note receivable in (b) is technically recorded as a current asset on December 15. However, given the high risk of uncollectibility of this receivable, the Allowance for Doubtful Accounts should be adjusted appropriately or the account should be written off or some other appropriate course of action should be taken to ensure that accounts receivable are not overstated at year-end because of this note.

APPENDIX 9A

Converting Receivables to Cash Before Maturity

LO⁵ Explain how receivables can be converted to cash before maturity.

Sometimes companies convert receivables to cash before they are due. Reasons for this include the need for cash or a desire not to be involved in collection activities. Converting receivables is usually done either (1) by selling them or (2) by using them as security for a loan. A recent survey showed that about 20% of large companies obtain cash from either the sale of receivables or the pledging of receivables as security. In some industries, such as textiles and furniture, this is common practice. Recently, this practice has spread to other industries, especially the apparel industry. Also, many small companies use sales of receivables as an immediate source of cash. This is especially the case for those selling to companies and government agencies that often delay payment.

Selling Accounts Receivable

A company can sell its accounts receivable to a finance company or bank. The buyer, called a **factor**, charges the seller a *factoring fee* and then collects the receivables as they come due. By incurring a factoring fee, the seller receives cash earlier and passes the risk of bad debts to the factor. The seller also avoids costs of billing and accounting for the receivables.

If TechCom, for instance, sells $20,000 of its accounts receivable on August 15 and is charged a 2% factoring fee, it records this sale as:

Aug.	15	Cash	19,600	
		Factoring Fee Expense.....................................	400	
		Accounts Receivable		20,000
		Sold accounts receivable for cash, less a 2% factoring fee.		

Pledging Accounts Receivable as Loan Security

A company can also raise cash by borrowing money and then *pledging* its accounts receivable as security for the loan. Pledging receivables does not transfer the risk of bad debts to the lender. The borrower retains ownership of the receivables. But if the borrower defaults on the loan, the lender has a right to be paid from cash receipts as the accounts receivable are collected. When TechCom borrowed $35,000 and pledged its receivables as security, it recorded this transaction as:

Aug.	20	Cash	35,000	
		Notes Payable		35,000
		Borrowed money with the note secured by pledging accounts receivable.		

Because pledged receivables are committed as security for a specific loan, the borrower's financial statements should disclose the pledging of accounts receivable. TechCom, for instance, includes the following note with its financial statements regarding its pledged receivables: "Accounts receivable in the amount of $40,000 are pledged as security for a $35,000 note payable to First National Bank."

Discounting Notes Receivable

Notes receivable can be converted to cash before they mature. Companies who may need cash sooner to meet their obligations can discount (or sell) notes receivable at a financial institution or bank. TechCom, for instance, discounted a $3,000, 90-day, 10% note receivable at First National Bank. TechCom held the note for 50 of the 90 days before discounting it. The bank applied a 12% rate in discounting the note. TechCom received proceeds of $3,033.55 from the bank calculated as:

Principal of Note	$3,000.00
+ Interest from Note ($3,000 × 10% × 90/365)	73.97
= Maturity Value	$3,073.97
− Bank Discount ($3,073.97 × 12% × 40/365)	40.42
= Proceeds...	$3,033.55

TechCom recorded the discounting of this note as:

Aug. 25	Cash	3,033.55	
	Interest Revenue		33.55
	Notes Receivable		3,000.00
	Discounted a note receivable.		

Computer programs are used in practice to calculate bank proceeds easily. Notes receivable are discounted without recourse or with recourse. When a note is discounted *without recourse*, the bank assumes the risk of a bad debt loss and the original payee does not have a *contingent liability*. A **contingent liability**[3] is a potential obligation dependent on an uncertain future event arising out of a past transaction. A note discounted without recourse is like an outright sale of an asset. If a note is discounted *with recourse* and the original maker of the note fails to pay the bank when it matures, the original payee of the note must pay for it. This means a company discounting a note with recourse has a contingent liability until the bank is paid. A company should disclose contingent liabilities in notes to its financial statements. TechCom included the following note: "The Company is contingently liable for a $3,000 note receivable discounted with recourse."

Full Disclosure

The disclosure of contingent liabilities in notes is consistent with the full disclosure principle. Contingent liabilities are discussed in more detail in Chapter 11.

CHECKPOINT

10. A company needs cash and has substantial accounts receivable. What alternatives are available for getting cash from its accounts receivable prior to receiving payments from credit customers?

Do Quick Study questions: *QS 9-12, *QS 9-13

---

3   IFRS 2012, IAS 37, para. 10.

APPENDIX 9B

Using the Information

ACCOUNTS RECEIVABLE TURNOVER AND DAYS' SALES UNCOLLECTED

LO⁶ Calculate accounts receivable turnover and days' sales uncollected to analyze liquidity.

For a company selling on credit, we want to assess both the *quality* and *liquidity* of its accounts receivable. Quality of receivables refers to the likelihood of collection without loss. Experience shows that the longer receivables are outstanding beyond their due date, the lower the likelihood of collection. Liquidity of receivables refers to the speed or efficiency of collection. Therefore, tools to help monitor receivables are critical to their timely collection.

Accounts Receivable Turnover

The **accounts receivable turnover** is a measure of both the quality and liquidity of accounts receivable. It indicates how often, on average, receivables are received and collected during the period. Accounts receivable turnover also helps us evaluate how well management is doing in granting credit to customers in a desire to increase sales revenues. A high turnover in comparison with competitors suggests that management should consider using more liberal credit terms to increase sales. A low turnover suggests management should consider more strict credit terms and more aggressive collection efforts to avoid having its resources tied up in accounts receivable.

The formula for this ratio is shown in Exhibit 9B.1.

EXHIBIT 9B.1

Accounts Receivable Turnover Formula

$$\text{Accounts receivable turnover} = \frac{\text{Net sales}}{\text{Average accounts receivable}}$$

Although the numerator of this ratio is more precise if credit sales are used, total net sales are usually used by external users because information about credit sales is typically not reported. The denominator includes accounts receivable and all short-term receivables (including notes receivable) from customers. Average accounts receivable is calculated by adding the balances at the beginning and end of the period and dividing the sum by 2. Some users prefer using gross accounts receivable, before subtracting the allowance for doubtful accounts, but many balance sheets report only the net amount of accounts receivable.

DECISION MAKER
Answer—End of appendix

Private Health Care Investor
You have invested in a private diagnostic imaging clinic so you and your fellow investors hire a health care analyst. The analyst highlights several points including the following: "Accounts receivable turnover is too low. Tighter credit policies are recommended along with discontinuing service to those most delayed payments."
How do you interpret these recommendations? What actions do you take?

Days' Sales Uncollected

We use the number of **days' sales uncollected** (also known as **days' sales in receivables**) to assess the liquidity of receivables by estimating how much time is likely to pass before we receive cash from credit sales equal to the *current amount* of accounts receivable.[4] The formula for this ratio is shown in Exhibit 9B.2.

$$\text{Days' sales uncollected} = \frac{\text{Accounts receivable}}{\text{Net sales}} \times 365$$

EXHIBIT 9B.2

Days' Sales Uncollected Formula

Days' sales uncollected is more meaningful if we know the company's credit terms. A rough guideline is that days' sales uncollected should not exceed one and one-third times the days in its: (1) credit period, if discounts are not offered; (2) discount period, if discounts are offered.

Analysis

To perform an analysis using the receivable ratios, we select data from the annual reports of two Canadian food manufacturers, **High Liner Foods Incorporated**, and **Maple Leaf Foods Inc.**, as shown in Exhibit 9B.3.

		($ thousands)	
		December 31, 2011	**January 1, 2011**
High Liner Foods Inc.	Accounts receivable	$ 84,920	$ 50,452
	Net sales	668,589	584,715
Maple Leaf Foods Inc.	Accounts receivable	133,504	108,739
	Net sales	4,893,624	4,968,119

EXHIBIT 9B.3

Comparison of Accounts Receivable Turnover and Days' Sales Uncollected for High Liner Foods Incorporated and Maple Leaf Foods Inc.

Results for December 31, 2011		
	Accounts Receivable Turnover	**Days' Sales Uncollected**
High Liner Foods Inc.	$\dfrac{\$668,589}{(\$84,920 + \$50,452)/2} = 9.88$ times	$\dfrac{\$84,920}{\$668,589} \times 365 = 46.36$ days
Maple Leaf Foods Inc.	$\dfrac{\$4,893,624}{(\$133,504 + \$108,739)/2} = 40.40$ times	$\dfrac{\$133,504}{\$4,893,624} \times 365 = 9.96$ days

Maple Leaf Foods' accounts receivable turnover of 40.40 times tells us that in 2011 it collected receivables more than four times as fast as High Liner Foods. The days' sales uncollected ratio indicates that High Liner Foods will take 46.36 days to collect the January 1, 2011, balance in accounts receivable as compared to Maple Leaf's 9.96 days to collect its receivables balance on December 31, 2011. Although both companies are in a similar industry, their credit management appears to be significantly different based on a review of the receivables ratios.

---

4   When days' sales uncollected is calculated using *average* accounts receivable, the result tells us how many days, *on average*, it takes to collect receivables. The formula in Exhibit 9B.2 tells us how many days it will take to collect the current receivables balance.

11. WebCor reported an accounts receivable turnover at March 31, 2014, of 11. The industry average is 10 for the same date. At March 31, 2013, WebCor reported an accounts receivable turnover of 13. Did WebCor improve regarding its collection of receivables?

Do Quick Study question: *QS 9-14

SUMMARY OF APPENDIX 9A AND APPENDIX 9B

LO⁵ Explain how receivables can be converted to cash before maturity. There are three usual means to convert receivables to cash before maturity. First, a company can sell accounts receivable to a factor, who charges a factoring fee. Second, a company can borrow money by signing a note payable that is secured by pledging the accounts receivable. Third, notes receivable can be discounted at a bank, with or without recourse. The full disclosure principle requires companies to disclose the amount of receivables pledged and the contingent liability for notes discounted with recourse.

LO⁶ Calculate accounts receivable turnover and days' sales uncollected to analyze liquidity. Accounts receivable turnover and days' sales uncollected are measures of both the quality and liquidity of accounts receivable. The accounts receivable turnover indicates how often, on average, receivables are received and collected during the period and is calculated as sales divided by average accounts receivable for the period. Days' sales uncollected is calculated as (Accounts receivable ÷ Net sales) × 365 and is used to estimate how much time is likely to pass before cash receipts from net sales are received equal to the average amount of accounts receivable. Both ratios are compared to those for other companies in the same industry, and with prior years' estimates.

GUIDANCE ANSWER TO DECISION MAKER

Private Health Care Investor
The recommendations are twofold. First, the analyst suggests more stringent screening of clients' credit standing. Second, the analyst suggests dropping clients who are most overdue in payments. You are likely bothered by both suggestions. They are probably financially wise recommendations but you are troubled by eliminating services to those less able to pay. One alternative is to follow a care program directed at clients less able to pay for services. This allows you to continue services to clients less able to pay and lets you discontinue services to clients able but unwilling to pay.

GUIDANCE ANSWERS TO CHECKPOINT

10. Alternatives are:
1. Selling their accounts receivable to a factor,
2. Pledging accounts receivable as loan security, and
3. Discounting notes receivable at a bank with or without recourse.

11. At March 31, 2014, WebCor collected its receivables faster than what was reported for the industry average. However, in comparison to its performance in the previous year, WebCor's efficiency in its collection of receivables decreased.

GLOSSARY

Accounts receivable Amounts due from customers for credit sales. Also referred to as *trade receivables*.

Accounts receivable approach A method of estimating bad debts using balance sheet relations. Also known as the *balance sheet approach*.

Accounts receivable turnover A measure of both the quality and liquidity of accounts receivable; it indicates how often, on average, receivables are received and collected during the period; calculated by dividing credit sales (or net sales) by the average accounts receivable balance.

Aging analysis See *aging of accounts receivable*.

Aging of accounts receivable A process of classifying accounts receivable in terms of how long they have been outstanding for the purpose of estimating the amount of uncollectible accounts.

Allowance for Doubtful Accounts A contra asset account with a balance equal to the estimated amount of accounts receivable that will be uncollectible; also called the *Allowance for Uncollectible Accounts*.

Allowance method of accounting for bad debts An accounting procedure that (1) estimates and reports bad debt expense from credit sales during the period of the sales, and (2) reports accounts receivable as the amount of cash proceeds that are expected from their collection (their estimated realizable value).

Bad debts The accounts of customers who do not pay what they have promised to pay; the amount is an expense of selling on credit; also called *uncollectible accounts*.

Balance sheet approach See *accounts receivable approach*.

Contingent liability A potential liability that depends on a future event arising out of a past transaction.

Creditor See *payee*.

Date of a note The date on which interest begins to accrue.

Days' sales uncollected A measure of the liquidity of receivables calculated by taking the balance of receivables and dividing by the credit (or net) sales over the year just completed, and then multiplying by 365 (the number of days in a year); also called *days' sales in receivables*.

Days' sales in receivables See *days' sales uncollected*.

Debtor See *maker of a note*.

Direct write-off method A method of accounting for bad debts that is not generally accepted that records the loss from an uncollectible account receivable at the time it is determined to be uncollectible; no attempt is made to estimate uncollectible accounts or bad debt expense.

Dishonouring a note receivable When a note's maker is unable or refuses to pay at maturity.

Due date of a note See *maturity date*.

Factor The buyer of accounts receivable.

Honouring a note receivable When the maker of the note pays the note in full at maturity.

Income statement approach See *percent of sales approach*.

Interest rate The charge for using (not paying) money until a later date.

Maker of a note One who signs a note and promises to pay it at maturity.

Maturity date of a note The date on which a note and any interest are due and payable.

Note receivable See *short-term note receivable*.

Payee of a note The one to whom a promissory note is made payable.

Percent of accounts receivable An approach to estimating bad debts that assumes a percent of outstanding receivables is uncollectible.

Percent of sales approach Uses income statement relations to estimate bad debts. Also known as the *income statement approach*.

Period of a note The time from the date of the note to its maturity date or due date.

Principal of a note The amount that the signer of a promissory note agrees to pay back when it matures, not including the interest.

Promissory note A written promise to pay a specified amount of money either on demand or at a definite future date.

Realizable value The expected proceeds from converting assets into cash.

Short-term note receivable A promissory note that becomes due within the next 12 months or within the business's operating cycle if greater than 12 months.

Trade receivables See *accounts receivable*.

Uncollectible accounts See *bad debts*.

 Visit **Connect** for additional study tools, practice quizzes, to search an interactive eBook, and much more.

CONCEPT REVIEW QUESTIONS

1. Explain why writing off a bad debt against the allowance account does not reduce the estimated realizable value of a company's accounts receivable.

2. Why does the Bad Debt Expense account usually not have the same adjusted balance as the Allowance for Doubtful Accounts?

3. Why does the direct write-off method of accounting for bad debts commonly fail to match revenues and expenses?

4. What is the essence of the accounting principle of materiality?

5. Why might a business prefer a note receivable to an account receivable?

6. Review the balance sheet for **Danier Leather** in Appendix II. Did accounts receivable increase or decrease from 2010 to 2011 and by how much? **DANIER**

*7. What does it mean to sell a receivable without recourse?

QUICK STUDY

QS 9-1 Entries for sale on credit and subsequent collection LO[1]

Journalize the following transactions for Kimmel Company (assume a perpetual inventory system):

a. On March 1, Kimmel Company sold $40,000 of merchandise costing $32,000 on credit terms of n/30 to JP Holdings.

b. On March 27, JP Holdings paid its account in full.

QS 9-2 Bad debts, write-off, recovery LO[2]

Record the following selected transactions for Allistar Company during its first two months of operations:

Mar.	4	Performed services for various customers on account; $165,000.
	15	Collected $80,000 from credit customers.
	20	Determined that Tom Williams, a credit customer, would not be paying his $5,000 account; wrote it off.
	25	Tom Williams came into an inheritance and paid Allistar the amount written off on March 20.
Apr.	2	Performed services for various customers on account; $280,000.
	9	Collected $110,000 from credit customers.
	30	Allistar estimated bad debt expense to be $8,000.

QS 9-3 Balance sheet presentation LO[2]

From the following alphabetized list of adjusted account balances, prepare the current asset section of Biatech's December 31, 2014, balance sheet.

Account	Debit	Credit
Accounts receivable	29,000	
Allowance for doubtful accounts		1,300
Bad debt expense	800	
Cash	10,000	
Machinery	52,000	
Office supplies	400	
Prepaid insurance	950	

An asterisk (*) identifies assignment material based on Appendix 9A or Appendix 9B.

QS 9-4 Adjusting entry to estimate bad debts—percent of sales LO²,³

Lexton Company uses the allowance method to account for uncollectible accounts receivable. At year-end, October 31, it was estimated that 0.6% of net credit sales were uncollectible based on past experience. Net sales were $690,000, of which 2/3 were on credit. Record the entry at year-end to estimate uncollectible receivables.

QS 9-5 Adjusting entry to estimate bad debts—percent of receivables LO²,³

Foster Company uses the allowance method to account for uncollectible accounts receivable. At year-end, December 31, the unadjusted balance in the Allowance for Doubtful Accounts was $450 credit. Based on past experience, it was estimated that 2.5% of the Accounts Receivable balance of $640,000 was uncollectible. Record the adjusting entry to estimate bad debts at December 31.

QS 9-6 Accounts receivable allowance method of accounting for bad debts LO²,³

Duncan Company's year-end trial balance shows accounts receivable of $89,000, allowance for doubtful accounts of $500 (credit), and net credit sales of $270,000. Uncollectibles are estimated to be 1.5% of outstanding accounts receivable.

a. Prepare the December 31 year-end adjustment.

b. What amount would have been used in the year-end adjustment had the allowance account had a year-end debit balance of $200?

c. Assume the same facts, except that Duncan estimates uncollectibles as 1% of net credit sales. What amount would be used in the adjustment?

QS 9-7 Aging analysis LO²,³

Delcom had total accounts receivable on December 31, 2014, of $160,000 aged as follows:

December 31, 2014 Accounts Receivable	Age of Accounts Receivable	Expected Percentage Uncollectible
$110,000	Not due (under 45 days)	2%
40,000	1 to 30 days past due	5%
10,000	Over 30 days past due	40%

Prepare the December 31, 2014, adjusting entry to estimate uncollectible accounts receivable assuming an unadjusted credit balance in Allowance for Doubtful Accounts of $800.

QS 9-8 Direct write-off method LO³

Winston Abbott operates Abbott Small Engine Repair on his cattle farm, greatly supplementing his farm income. Most of his customers pay cash, so he uses the direct write-off method to account for uncollectible accounts receivable. On March 28, 2014, he determined that the $1,100 account for Jim Patterson is uncollectible. Record the write-off.

QS 9-9 Notes receivable LO⁴

On August 2, 2014, SLM Company received a $5,500, 90-day, 5% note from customer Will Carr as payment on his account. Determine the maturity date and prepare the August 2 and maturity date entries, assuming the note is honoured by Carr.

QS 9-10 Notes receivable LO⁴

Seaver Company's December 31 year-end trial balance shows an $8,000 balance in Notes Receivable. This balance is from one note dated December 1, with a term of 45 days and 4.5% interest. Determine the maturity date and prepare the December 31 and maturity date entries, assuming the note is honoured.

QS 9-11 Dishonouring of a note receivable LO⁴

Ajax Company had a $17,000, 7%, 30-day note of Beatrice Inc. At maturity, April 4, Beatrice dishonoured the note. Record the entry on April 4.

*QS 9-12 **Sale of accounts receivable** LO[5]

On June 4, Maltex sold $108,000 of its accounts receivable to a collection agency, which charges a 2.5% factoring fee. Record the entry on June 4.

*QS 9-13 **Discounting a note receivable** LO[5]

Tallcrest discounted a $50,000, 45-day, 5% note receivable on August 10 at the local bank, which applies an 8% discount rate. Tallcrest had held the note for 25 days before discounting it. Record the entry on August 10.

*QS 9-14 **Accounts receivable turnover and days' sales uncollected** LO[6]

Mega Company and Holton Company are similar firms that operate within the same industry. The following information is available:

	Industry Average	Mega Company			Holton Company		
		2014	2013	2012	2014	2013	2012
Accounts receivable turnover	12	14.9	12.2	11.5	10.6	13.1	13.5
Days' sales uncollected	30	24.5	29.9	31.7	34.4	27.9	27.1

a. Which company has the *more favourable* accounts receivable turnover in 2014?

b. Which company has the *greater* number of days in uncollected accounts in 2014? Is this generally favourable or unfavourable?

c. Which company is showing an *unfavourable* trend in terms of managing accounts receivable?

EXERCISES

Exercise 9-1 **Subledger accounts** LO[1]

Wallace Contracting recorded the following transactions during November 2014:

Nov.	3	Accounts Receivable—ABC Shop....................	8,500	
		Sales*...		8,500
	8	Accounts Receivable—Colt Enterprises	2,600	
		Sales*...		2,600
	11	Accounts Receivable—Red McKenzie	1,560	
		Sales*...		1,560
	19	Sales Returns and Allowances*	214	
		Accounts Receivable—Red McKenzie		214
	28	Accounts Receivable—ABCShop....................	4,980	
		Sales*...		4,980

*Cost of goods sold (or COGS) has been ignored for the purpose of maintaining focus on accounts receivable.

Required

1. Open a General Ledger having T-accounts for Accounts Receivable, Sales, and Sales Returns and Allowances. Also, open an Accounts Receivable Subledger having a T-account for each customer. Post the preceding entries to the General Ledger accounts and the customer accounts.

2. List the balances of the accounts in the subledger, total the balances, and compare the total with the balance of the Accounts Receivable controlling account.

An asterisk (*) identifies assignment material based on Appendix 9A or Appendix 9B.

Exercise 9-2 Write-off and subsequent partial recovery LO²

Foster Company uses the allowance method to account for uncollectibles. On October 31, it wrote off a $1,200 account of a customer, Gwen Rowe. On December 9, it received an $800 payment from Rowe.

a. Make the appropriate entry or entries for October 31.

b. Make the appropriate entry or entries for December 9.

Exercise 9-3 Allowance for doubtful accounts LO²,³

At the end of its annual accounting period, Midi Company estimated its bad debts as 0.75% of its $1,750,000 of credit sales made during the year. On December 31, Midi made an addition to its Allowance for Doubtful Accounts equal to that amount. On the following February 1, management decided that the $2,600 account of Catherine Hicks was uncollectible and wrote it off as a bad debt. Four months later, on June 5, Hicks unexpectedly paid the amount previously written off. Give the journal entries required to record these transactions.

CHECK FIGURE:
b. Bad Debt Expense
= $7,515

Exercise 9-4 Bad debt expense LO²,³

At the end of each year, Deutch Supply Co. uses the simplified balance sheet approach (i.e., percent of accounts receivable) to estimate bad debts. On December 31, 2014, it has outstanding accounts receivable of $159,000 and estimates that 3.5% will be uncollectible.

Required

a. Give the entry to record bad debt expense for 2014 under the assumption that the Allowance for Doubtful Accounts has a $1,950 credit balance before the adjustment.

b. Give the entry under the assumption that the Allowance for Doubtful Accounts has a $1,950 debit balance before the adjustment.

Exercise 9-5 Analyzing receivables and allowance for doubtful accounts LO¹,²,³

Accounts Receivable				Allowance for Doubtful Accounts		
Dec. 31/13					2,900	Dec. 31/13
Balance	78,000					Balance
	420,000	448,000			210	
		3,250		3,250	2,600	
	210	210				
Dec. 31/14					2,460	Dec. 31/14
Balance	46,750					Balance

Required Analyzing the information presented in the T-accounts above, identify the dollar value related to each of the following:

a. Credit sales during the period.

b. Collection of credit sales made during the period.

c. Write-off of an uncollectible account.

d. Recovery of the account previously written off.

e. The adjusting entry to estimate bad debts.

Exercise 9-6 Balance sheet presentation LO[2,4]

From the following alphabetized list of adjusted account balances, prepare the current asset section of LisTel's March 31, 2014, balance sheet.

Account	Balance*
Accounts receivable	$110,000
Accumulated depreciation, building	29,000
Allowance for doubtful accounts	2,350
Bad debt expense	2,100
Building	375,000
Cash	19,000
Merchandise inventory	82,000
Notes receivable, due May 1, 2016	61,000
Notes receivable, due Nov. 30, 2014	14,300
Supplies	5,260

*Assume all balances are normal.

CHECK FIGURE:
d. Accounts receivable
(net) = $232,700

Exercise 9-7 Estimating bad debt expense—percent of sales LO[3]

Selected unadjusted account balances at December 31, 2014, are shown below for Demron Servicing.

Account	Debit	Credit
Accounts receivable	$70,000	
Allowance for doubtful accounts		$ 1,100
Sales (all on credit)		480,000
Sales discounts	8,000	

Required

a. Demron estimates that 1.5% of net credit sales will prove to be uncollectible. Prepare the adjusting entry required on December 31, 2014, to estimate uncollectible receivables.

b. During 2015, credit sales were $620,000 (cost of sales $406,500); sales discounts of $12,000 were taken when accounts receivable of $440,000 were collected; and accounts written off during the year totalled $10,000. Prepare the entries for these transactions.

c. Record the adjusting entry required on December 31, 2015, to estimate uncollectible receivables assuming it is based on 1.5% of net credit sales.

d. Show how accounts receivable would appear on the December 31, 2015, balance sheet.

Analysis Component: Comment on the advantages and disadvantages of using the income statement approach for estimating uncollectibles.

CHECK FIGURE:
d. Accounts receivable
(net) = $235,200

Exercise 9-8 Estimating bad debt expense—percent of receivables LO[3]

Refer to the information in Exercise 9-7.

Required

a. Assume that Demron estimates uncollectible accounts as 2% of receivables. Prepare the adjusting entry required on December 31, 2014, to estimate uncollectible receivables.

b. During 2015, credit sales were $620,000 (cost of sales $406,500); sales discounts taken were $12,000; accounts receivable collected were $440,000; and accounts written off during the year totalled $10,000. Prepare the entries to record these transactions.

c. Record the adjusting entry required on December 31, 2015, to estimate uncollectible receivables assuming it is based on 2% of receivables.

d. Show how accounts receivable would appear on the December 31, 2015, balance sheet.

Analysis Component: Comment on the advantages and disadvantages of using the balance sheet approach for estimating uncollectibles.

Exercise 9-9 Aging analysis LO³

Winfrey Designs had an unadjusted credit balance in its Allowance for Doubtful Accounts at December 31, 2014, of $1,800.

Required

a. Prepare the adjusting entry assuming that Winfrey estimates uncollectible accounts based on an aging analysis as follows:

December 31, 2014 Accounts Receivable	Age of Accounts Receivable	Expected Percentage Uncollectible
$120,000	Not due (under 30 days)	0.75%
35,000	1 to 30 days past due	4%
8,000	31 to 60 days past due	10%
2,000	Over 60 days past due	60%

b. During 2015, credit sales were $1,200,000; sales discounts taken were $22,000; accounts receivable collected were $995,000; and accounts written off during the year totalled $24,000. Prepare the adjusting entry required on December 31, 2015, to estimate uncollectible receivables assuming it is based on the following aging analysis.

December 31, 2015 Accounts Receivable	Age of Accounts Receivable	Expected Percentage Uncollectible
$240,000	Not due (under 30 days)	0.75%
75,000	1 to 30 days past due	4%
20,000	31 to 60 days past due	10%
11,000	Over 60 days past due	60%

c. Show how accounts receivable would appear on the December 31, 2015, balance sheet.

Analysis Component: Comment on the advantages and disadvantages of using an aging analysis for estimating uncollectible accounts.

Exercise 9-10 Direct write-off method LO³

Delores Cooper operates Cooper Garden Designs. Most of her customers pay cash so she uses the direct write-off method to account for uncollectible accounts receivable. On May 3, 2014, she determined that the $2,600 account for Wilma Benz was uncollectible. During 2014, she had total credit sales of $265,000. The December 31, 2014, balance in accounts receivable was $42,000.

Required Record the May 3 write-off using the direct write-off method.

Analysis Component: Delores wants to compare the effect of using the allowance method versus the direct write-off method for recording uncollectible accounts. If uncollectible accounts were estimated at (a) 2% of credit sales or (b) 4% of outstanding accounts receivable, prepare a comparison of the effects on net income of using the allowance methods versus the direct write-off method.

Exercise 9-11 Dishonouring a note LO⁴

Prepare journal entries to record these transactions:

Mar.	21	Accepted a $6,200, six-month, 4% note dated today from Bradley Brooks in granting a time extension on his past-due account.
Sept.	21	Brooks dishonoured his note when presented for payment.
Dec.	31	After exhausting all legal means of collection, wrote off Brooks's account against the Allowance for Doubtful Accounts.

Exercise 9-12 Honouring a note LO⁴

Prepare journal entries to record these transactions (round the answer to two decimal places):

Oct.	31	Accepted a $15,000, six-month, 4.5% note dated today from Leann Grimes in granting a time extension on her past-due account.
Dec.	31	Adjusted the books for the interest due on the Grimes note.
Apr.	30	Grimes honoured her note when presented for payment.

CHECK FIGURE:
May 31, 2015: Interest
Revenue = $78.90

Exercise 9-13 Accounting for notes receivable transactions LO⁴

Following are transactions of The Barnett Company (round the answer to two decimal places):

2014

Dec.	16	Accepted a $22,000, 60-day, 5% note dated this day in granting Carmel Karuthers a time extension on her past-due account.
	31	Made an adjusting entry to record the accrued interest on the Karuthers note.
	31	Closed the Interest Revenue account.

2015

Feb.	14	Received Karuthers' payment for the principal and interest on the note dated December 16.
Mar.	2	Accepted an $8,000, 4%, 90-day note dated this day in granting a time extension on the past-due account of ATW Company.
	17	Accepted a $3,200, 30-day, 4.5% note dated this day in granting Leroy Johnson a time extension on his past-due account.
May	31	Received ATW's payment for the principal and interest on the note dated March 2.

Required Prepare journal entries to record The Barnett Company's transactions.

*Exercise 9-14 Selling and pledging accounts receivable LO⁵

On July 31, Konrad International had $125,900 of accounts receivable. Prepare journal entries to record the following August transactions. Also, prepare any footnotes to the August 31 financial statements that should be reported as a result of these transactions.

2014

Aug.	2	Sold merchandise to customers on credit, $6,295. Cost of sales was $3,150.
	7	Sold $18,770 of accounts receivable to Fidelity Bank. Fidelity charges a 1.5% fee.
	15	Received payments from customers, $3,436.
	25	Borrowed $10,000 from Fidelity Bank, pledging $14,000 of accounts receivable as security for the loan.

CHECK FIGURE:
Feb. 19: Interest
Revenue = $487.58

*Exercise 9-15 Discounting notes receivable LO⁵

Prepare journal entries to record the following transactions by Ericton Industries:

2014

| Jan. | 20 | Accepted a $170,000, 90-day, 9% note dated this day in granting a time extension on the past due account of Steve Soetart. |
| Feb. | 19 | Discounted the Steve Soetart note at the bank at 11.5%. |

An asterisk (*) identifies assignment material based on Appendix 9A or Appendix 9B.

*Exercise 9-16 Accounts receivable turnover and days' sales uncollected LO6

The following information was taken from the December 31, 2014, annual report of WestCon Developments.

	($ millions)			Industry Average
	2014	2013		
Net sales	$7,280	$5,410	Accounts receivable turnover	16.2
Accounts receivable	598	486	Days' sales uncollected	21.0

Required

1. Calculate accounts receivable turnover and days' sales uncollected for the year 2014.*

2. Compare your calculations in (1) to the industry average and comment on WestCon's relative performance as F (Favourable) or U (Unfavourable).*

*Round the answer to two decimal places.

PROBLEMS

CHECK FIGURES:
1b. Bad Debt Expense
= $138,000
2. Accounts receivable
(net) = $1,962,000

Problem 9-1A Estimating bad debt expense LO2,3

On December 31, 2014, Corotel Company's year-end, the unadjusted trial balance included the following items:

Account	Debit	Credit
Accounts receivable	$2,100,000	
Allowance for doubtful accounts	33,000	
Sales ($2,850,000 cash sales)...		$11,400,000

Required

1. Prepare the adjusting entry needed in Corotel's books to recognize bad debts under each of the following independent assumptions:

   a. Bad debts are estimated to be 2% of credit sales.

   b. An analysis suggests that 5% of outstanding accounts receivable on December 31, 2014, will become uncollectible.

2. Show how Accounts Receivable and the Allowance for Doubtful Accounts would appear on the December 31, 2014, balance sheet given the facts in requirement 1(a).

3. Show how Accounts Receivable and the Allowance for Doubtful Accounts would appear on the December 31, 2014, balance sheet given the facts in requirement 1(b).

Analysis Component: If bad debts are not adjusted for at the end of the accounting period, identify which GAAP are violated and why.

An asterisk (*) identifies assignment material based on Appendix 9A or Appendix 9B.

Problem 9-2A Aging accounts receivable LO^{2,3}

On December 31, 2014, Toro Company's Allowance for Doubtful Accounts had an unadjusted credit balance of $31,000. The accountant for Toro has prepared a schedule of the December 31, 2014, accounts receivable by age and, on the basis of past experience, has estimated the percentage of the receivables in each age category that will become uncollectible. This information is summarized as follows:

December 31, 2014 Accounts Receivable	Age of Accounts Receivable	Expected Percentage Uncollectible
$1,500,000	Not due (under 30 days)	1.25%
708,000	1 to 30 days past due	2.00
152,000	31 to 60 days past due	6.50
98,000	61 to 90 days past due	32.75
24,000	Over 90 days past due	68.00

Required

1. Calculate the amount that should appear in the December 31, 2014, balance sheet as the allowance for doubtful accounts.

2. Prepare the journal entry to record bad debt expense for 2014.

Analysis Component: On June 30, 2015, Toro Company concluded that a customer's $7,500 receivable (created in 2014) was uncollectible and that the account should be written off. What effect will this action have on Toro's 2015 net income? Explain your answer.

Problem 9-3A Accounts receivable transactions and bad debt adjustments LO^{1,2,3}

BeleVu Supplies showed the following selected adjusted balances at its December 31, 2013, year-end:

Accounts Receivable		Allowance for Doubtful Accounts	
Dec. 31/13			16,400 Dec. 31/13
Balance 490,000			Balance

During the year 2014, the following selected transactions occurred:

a. Sales totalled $2,800,000, of which 25% were cash sales (cost of sales $1,804,000).

b. Sales returns were $108,000, half regarding credit sales. The returned merchandise was scrapped.

c. An account for $24,000 was recovered.

d. Several accounts were written off; $26,000.

e. Collections from credit customers totalled $1,790,000 (excluding the recovery in (c) above).

Part A

Required

1. Journalize transactions (a) through (e). You may find it useful to post your entries to T-accounts for Accounts Receivable and Allowance for Doubtful Accounts.

Part B

Required

2. Prepare the December 31, 2014, adjusting entry to estimate bad debts assuming that uncollectible accounts are estimated to be 1% of net credit sales.

3. Show how accounts receivable will appear on the December 31, 2014, balance sheet.

4. What will bad debt expense be on the income statement for the year ended December 31, 2014?

Part C (independent of Part B)

Required

5. Prepare the December 31, 2014, adjusting entry to estimate bad debts assuming that uncollectible accounts are estimated to be 3% of outstanding receivables.

6. Show how accounts receivable will appear on the December 31, 2014, balance sheet.

7. What will bad debt expense be on the income statement for the year ended December 31, 2014?

Problem 9-4A Recording accounts receivable transactions and bad debt adjustments LO[1,2,3]

Peru Industries began operations on January 1, 2014. During the next two years, the company completed a number of transactions involving credit sales, accounts receivable collections, and bad debts (assume a perpetual inventory system). These transactions are summarized as follows:

2014

a. Sold merchandise on credit for $2,250,000, terms n/30 (COGS = $1,240,000).

b. Wrote off uncollectible accounts receivable in the amount of $34,000.

c. Received cash of $1,330,000 in payment of outstanding accounts receivable.

d. In adjusting the accounts on December 31, concluded that 1.5% of the outstanding accounts receivable would become uncollectible.

2015

e. Sold merchandise on credit for $2,940,000, terms n/30 (COGS = $1,592,000).

f. Wrote off uncollectible accounts receivable in the amount of $53,000.

g. Received cash of $2,210,000 in payment of outstanding accounts receivable.

h. In adjusting the accounts on December 31, concluded that 1.5% of the outstanding accounts receivable would become uncollectible.

Required Prepare journal entries to record Peru's 2014 and 2015 summarized transactions and the adjusting entries to record bad debt expense at the end of each year.

Problem 9-5A Uncollectible accounts LO[2,3]

Aaron Servicing showed the following partial unadjusted results at October 31, 2014, its year-end:

Account	Debit	Credit
Sales		$1,650,000
Accounts receivable	$148,000	
Allowance for doubtful accounts	3,200	

Part 1

Required

a. Assuming Aaron estimates bad debts to be 1.5% of sales, prepare the adjusting entry at October 31, 2014.

b. Show how accounts receivable would be shown on the October 31, 2014, balance sheet using your calculations in (a).

Part 2

Required

c. Instead of (a), assume that Aaron estimates bad debts to be 5% of outstanding accounts receivable. Prepare the adjusting entry at October 31, 2014.

d. Show how accounts receivable would be shown on the October 31, 2014, balance sheet using your calculations in (c).

Problem 9-6A Bad debt expense LO³

The following is information taken from the June 30, 2014, balance sheet of Tippleton Company:

Accounts receivable	$320,000	
Less: Allowance for doubtful accounts...	14,000	$306,000

Part 1

During July, Tippleton Company recorded total sales of $850,000, all on credit. There were $30,000 of sales returns and allowances. Collections during July were $920,000. Total receivables identified as being uncollectible and written off during July were $15,000. Tippleton estimates bad debts as 1% of net credit sales.

Required Prepare the adjusting entry to record estimated bad debts for July.

Part 2

During August, total sales of $845,000 were recorded, all on credit. Sales returns and allowances totalled $14,000. Collections during the month were $710,000, which included the recovery of $1,950 from a customer account written off in a previous month. No accounts were written off during August. Tippleton Company changed its method of estimating bad debts to the balance sheet approach because the new accountant said it more accurately reflected uncollectible accounts. The resulting aging analysis determined total estimated uncollectible accounts at August 31 to be $14,250.

Required Prepare the August 31 adjusting entry to record estimated bad debts for August.

Problem 9-7A Estimating bad debts LO³

The following information is available regarding the outstanding accounts receivable of Mufu Contracting at September 30, 2014:

Month of Credit Sale*					
Customer	**May**	**June**	**July**	**Aug.**	**Sept.**
B. Axley	$32,000	$ -0-	$ -0-	$ -0-	$ -0-
T. Holton	-0-	-0-	68,000	33,000	15,000
W. Nix	-0-	21,000	-0-	9,000	11,000
C. Percy	-0-	-0-	5,000	-0-	14,000
K. Willis	-0-	-0-	-0-	-0-	82,000

*All services are performed on terms of n/30. Assume all sales occurred on the last day of the month.

Mufu estimates bad debts using the following rates:

Not yet due	1 to 29 days past due	30 to 59 days past due	60 to 89 days past due	90 to 119 days past due	Over 119 days past due
0.5%	1%	4%	10%	20%	50%

Required

a. Complete a Schedule of Accounts Receivable by Age at September 30, 2014 (similar to Exhibit 9.14).

b. The Allowance for Doubtful Accounts showed an unadjusted balance on September 30, 2014, of $1,600. Record the adjusting entry at September 30, 2014, to estimate uncollectible accounts.

Problem 9-8A Uncollectible accounts LO³

At year-end, December 31, 2014, Corolla Sales showed unadjusted balances of: $394,000 in Accounts Receivable; $13,800 debit in Allowance for Doubtful Accounts; and $1,940,000 in Sales. Uncollectible accounts are estimated to be 2.5% of sales.

Unadjusted balances at December 31, 2015, were: Accounts Receivable, $514,000; Allowance for Doubtful Accounts, $1,000 credit; and Sales, $3,280,000. Corolla Sales changed the method of estimating uncollectible accounts to 4% of outstanding accounts receivable.

At December 31, 2016, the General Ledger showed unadjusted balances of: $460,000 in Accounts Receivable; $700 debit in Allowance for Doubtful Accounts; and $3,400,000 in Sales. Corolla prepared an aging analysis on December 31, 2016, that estimated total uncollectible accounts to be $26,500.

Required Prepare the 2014, 2015, and 2016 year-end adjusting entries to estimate uncollectible accounts.

Analysis Component: On December 31, 2014, the unadjusted balance in Allowance for Doubtful Accounts was a debit of $13,800. What is the normal balance for the Allowance for Doubtful Accounts account? What would cause Allowance for Doubtful Accounts to have an unadjusted debit balance?

Problem 9-9A Notes receivable LO⁴

Vauxall Holdings showed the following information regarding its notes receivable:

Note	Date of Note	Principal	Interest Rate	Term	Maturity Date	Days of Accrued Interest at Dec. 31, 2014	Accrued Interest at Dec. 31, 2014*
1	Nov. 1/13	$240,000	4.0%	180 days			
2	Jan. 5/14	100,000	5.0%	90 days			
3	Nov. 20/14	90,000	4.5%	45 days			
4	Dec. 10/14	120,000	5.5%	30 days			

*Round calculations to the nearest whole cent.

Required For each note:

a. Determine the maturity date.

b. Calculate the *days* of accrued interest, if any, at December 31, 2014 (Vauxall Holdings' year-end).

c. Calculate the *amount* of accrued interest, if any, at December 31, 2014.

For Note 3:

d. Prepare the entry to record the accrued interest at December 31, 2014.

e. Prepare the entry to record the collection on the maturity date. Assume that both interest and principal are collected at maturity.

Problem 9-10A Accrued interest calculation and dishonouring note receivable LO⁴

Following are transactions of The Purple Onion Company (round calculations to the nearest whole cent):

2013

Dec. 16 Accepted a $20,000, 60-day, 5.5% note dated this day in granting Hal Krueger a time extension on his past-due account.

31 Made an adjusting entry to record the accrued interest on the Krueger note.

31 Closed the Interest Revenue account.

2014

Feb. 14 Received Krueger's payment for the principal and interest on the note dated December 16.

Mar. 2 Accepted a $15,000, 3.75%, 90-day note dated this day in granting a time extension on the past-due account of ARC Company.

17 Accepted a $6,500, 30-day, 4% note dated this day in granting Penny Bobek a time extension on her past-due account.

Apr. 16 Bobek dishonoured her note when presented for payment.

Required

a. Prepare journal entries to record The Purple Onion's transactions.

b. Determine the maturity date of the note dated March 2. Prepare the entry on the maturity date, assuming ARC Company honours the note.

Problem 9-11A Short-term notes receivable LO⁴

Seerden Servicing monitors its accounts receivable carefully. A review determined that a customer, John Daley, was unable to pay his $130,000 past-due account. Seerden accepted a 90-day promissory note dated April 15, 2014, bearing interest of 5% in exchange for Daley's account. Another customer, ABC Drilling, signed a 4.75%, six-month note dated May 1 in place of its $50,000 past-due accounts receivable. On May 31, Seerden's year-end, accrued interest was recorded on the notes receivable. John Daley honoured his note on the maturity date. ABC Drilling dishonoured its note on the maturity date. On November 15, Seerden Servicing wrote off ABC Drilling's account as it was determined to be uncollectible.

Required Prepare Seerden Servicing's entries for each of the following dates (round calculations to the nearest whole cent):

a. April 15, 2014

b. May 1, 2014

c. May 31, 2014

d. Maturity date of John Daley's note

e. Maturity date of ABC Drilling's note

f. November 15, 2014

Analysis Component: Assuming a $4,000 debit balance in the Allowance for Doubtful Accounts on November 14, 2014, calculate the balance after posting the entry in (f) above. Comment on the adequacy of the Allowance for Doubtful Accounts.

*Problem 9-12A Discounting notes receivable LO⁵

Required Prepare entries to record the following transactions of Wipe-Out Company:

Mar.	2	Accepted a $10,240, 5%, 90-day note dated this day in granting a time extension on the past-due account of JNC Company.
Apr.	21	Discounted, with recourse, the JNC Company note at BancFirst at a cost of $50.
June	2	Received notice from BancFirst that JNC Company defaulted on the note due May 31. Paid the bank the principal plus interest due on the note. *(Hint: Create an account receivable for the maturity value of the note.)*
July	16	Received payment from JNC Company for the maturity value of its dishonoured note plus interest for 45 days beyond maturity at 5%.
Sept.	3	Accepted a $4,160, 60-day, 5% note dated this day in granting Cecile Duval a time extension on her past-due account.
	18	Discounted, without recourse, the Duval note at BancFirst at a cost of $25.

Analysis Component: What reporting is necessary when a business discounts notes receivable with recourse and these notes have not reached maturity by the end of the fiscal period? Explain the reason for this requirement and what accounting principle is being satisfied.

*Problem 9-13A Discounting notes receivable LO⁵

Required Prepare General Journal entries to record the following transactions of Leduc Company:

2014

Dec. 11 Accepted a $15,000, 6%, 60-day note dated this day in granting Fred Calhoun a time extension on his past-due account.

31 Made an adjusting entry to record the accrued interest on the Fred Calhoun note.

31 Closed the Interest Revenue account.

2015

Jan. 10 Discounted the Fred Calhoun note at the bank at 7%.

Feb. 10 The Fred Calhoun note was dishonoured. Paid the bank the maturity value of the note plus a $30 fee.

Mar. 5 Accepted a $4,500, 5.5%, 60-day note dated this day in granting a time extension on the past-due account of Donna Reed.

29 Discounted the Donna Reed note at the bank at 7.5%.

May 7 The Donna Reed note had been received by the bank and paid by Donna Reed.

June 9 Accepted a $6,750, 60-day, 5% note dated this day in granting a time extension on the past-due account of Jack Miller.

Aug. 8 Received payment of the maturity value of the Jack Miller note.

11 Accepted an $8,000, 60-day, 5% note dated this day in granting Roger Addison a time extension on his past-due account.

31 Discounted the Roger Addison note at the bank at 6.5%.

Oct. 12 The Roger Addison note was dishonoured. Paid the bank the maturity value of the note plus a $30 fee.

Nov. 19 Received payment from Roger Addison of the maturity value of his dishonoured note, the fee, and interest on both for 40 days beyond maturity at 5%.

Dec. 23 Wrote off the Fred Calhoun account against Allowance for Doubtful Accounts.

ALTERNATE PROBLEMS

Problem 9-1B Estimating bad debt expense LO²,³

On December 31, 2014, Stilton Service Company's year-end, the unadjusted trial balance included the following items:

Account	Debit	Credit
Accounts receivable	$239,000	
Allowance for doubtful accounts		$ 3,100
Sales ($470,000 cash sales)		1,128,000

Required

1. Prepare the adjusting entry on the books of Stilton Service Company to estimate bad debts under each of the following independent assumptions:

   a. Bad debts are estimated to be 3% of credit sales.

   b. An analysis suggests that 6% of outstanding accounts receivable on December 31, 2014, will become uncollectible.

2. Show how Accounts Receivable and the Allowance for Doubtful Accounts would appear on the December 31, 2014, balance sheet given the facts in requirement 1(a).

3. Show how Accounts Receivable and the Allowance for Doubtful Accounts would appear on the December 31, 2014, balance sheet given the facts in requirement 1(b).

Analysis Component: Would you recommend to Stilton that it use the income statement or the balance sheet approach to estimate uncollectible accounts receivable? Explain why, identifying advantages and disadvantages for each approach.

An asterisk (*) identifies assignment material based on Appendix 9A or Appendix 9B.

Problem 9-2B Aging accounts receivable LO[2,3]

On December 31, 2014, RCA Company's Allowance for Doubtful Accounts had an unadjusted debit balance of $7,800. The accountant for RCA has prepared a schedule of the December 31, 2014, accounts receivable by age and, on the basis of past experience, has estimated the percentage of the receivables in each age category that will become uncollectible. This information is summarized as follows:

December 31, 2014 Accounts Receivable	Age of Accounts Receivable	Expected Percentage Uncollectible
$620,000	Not due (under 30 days)	1.75%
355,600	1 to 30 days past due	2.5
91,000	31 to 60 days past due	8.5
11,500	61 to 90 days past due	35
7,600	Over 90 days past due	60

Required

1. Calculate the amount that should appear in the December 31, 2014, balance sheet as the Allowance for Doubtful Accounts.

2. Prepare the journal entry to record bad debt expense for 2014.

Analysis Component: On July 31, 2015, RCA concluded that a customer's $4,200 receivable (created in 2014) was uncollectible and that the account should be written off. What effect will this action have on RCA's 2015 net income? Explain your answer.

Problem 9-3B Accounts receivable transactions and bad debt adjustments LO[1,2,3]

Wondra Supplies showed the following selected adjusted balances at its December 31, 2013, year-end:

Accounts Receivable		Allowance for Doubtful Accounts	
Dec. 31/13			12,300 Dec. 31/13
Balance 490,000			Balance

During the year 2014, the following selected transactions occurred:

a. Sales totalled $1,800,000, of which 85% were credit sales (cost of sales $987,000).

b. Sales returns were $31,000, all regarding credit sales. The returned merchandise was scrapped.

c. An account for $29,000 was recovered.

d. Several accounts were written off, including one very large account; the total was $65,500.

e. Collected accounts receivable of $1,630,000 (excluding the recovery in (c) above). Sales discounts of $22,000 were taken.

Part A
Required

1. Journalize transactions (a) through (e). You may find it useful to post your entries to T-accounts for Accounts Receivable and Allowance for Doubtful Accounts.

Part B
Required

2. Prepare the December 31, 2014, adjusting entry to estimate bad debts, assuming uncollectible accounts are estimated to be 8% of net credit sales.

3. Show how accounts receivable will appear on the December 31, 2014, balance sheet.

4. What will bad debt expense be on the income statement for the year ended December 31, 2014?

Part C (independent of Part B)
Required

5. Prepare the December 31, 2014, adjusting entry to estimate bad debts, assuming uncollectible accounts are estimated to be 4% of outstanding receivables.

6. Show how accounts receivable will appear on the December 31, 2014, balance sheet.

7. What will bad debt expense be on the income statement for the year ended December 31, 2014?

Problem 9-4B Recording accounts receivable transactions and bad debt adjustments LO[1,2,3]

Selzer Products Co. began operations on January 1, 2014, and completed a number of transactions during 2014 and 2015 that involved credit sales, accounts receivable collections, and bad debts. Assume a perpetual inventory system. These transactions are summarized as follows:

2014

a. Sold merchandise on credit for $1,640,000, terms n/30 (COGS = $1,070,000).

b. Received cash of $1,175,000 in payment of outstanding accounts receivable.

c. Wrote off uncollectible accounts receivable in the amount of $7,500.

d. In adjusting the accounts on December 31, concluded that 1% of the outstanding accounts receivable would become uncollectible.

2015

e. Sold merchandise on credit for $1,876,000, terms n/30 (COGS = $1,224,000).

f. Received cash of $1,444,000 in payment of outstanding accounts receivable.

g. Wrote off uncollectible accounts receivable in the amount of $8,600.

h. In adjusting the accounts on December 31, concluded that 1% of the outstanding accounts receivable would become uncollectible.

Required Prepare General Journal entries to record the 2014 and 2015 summarized transactions of Selzer Products Co., and the adjusting entries to record bad debt expense at the end of each year.

Problem 9-5B Uncollectible accounts LO[2,3]

Littlerock Surveying showed the following partial unadjusted results at May 31, 2014, its month-end:

Account	Debit	Credit
Sales		$860,000
Accounts receivable	$132,000	
Allowance for doubtful accounts		1,800

Part 1

Required

a. Assuming Littlerock estimates bad debts to be 2.5% of sales, prepare the adjusting entry at May 31, 2014.

b. Show how accounts receivable would be shown on the May 31, 2014, balance sheet using your calculations in (a).

Part 2

Required

c. Instead of (a) above, prepare the adjusting entry at May 31, 2014, assuming that Littlerock estimates bad debts to be based on the following aging analysis.

May 31, 2014 Accounts Receivable	Age of Accounts Receivable	Expected Percentage Uncollectible
$98,000	Not due (under 30 days)	1%
27,000	1 to 30 days past due	4%
7,000	Over 60 days past due	50%

d. Show how accounts receivable would be shown on the May 31, 2014, balance sheet using your calculations in (c).

Problem 9-6B Bad debt expense LO³

The following is information regarding adjusted account balances for Leonardo Painters at September 30, 2014:

Accounts Receivable		Allowance for Doubtful Accounts	
235,000			13,700

Part 1

During October, Leonardo Painters recorded $1,746,000 in total revenues, all on credit. Collections during October were $1,532,000. Included in the $1,532,000 collections was the recovery of $6,100 from a customer account written off in September. Total receivables identified as being uncollectible and written off during October were $14,700. Leonardo Painters estimates bad debts to be 0.5% of net credit revenues.

Required Prepare the adjusting entry to record estimated bad debts for October.

Part 2

During November, revenues totalled $1,680,000, all on credit. Collections during the month were $1,890,000. An account for $5,400 was identified as being uncollectible and written off on November 28. It was recommended to Leonardo Painters that the method of estimating bad debts be changed to the balance sheet approach. As a result, it was estimated that 5% of the November 30 accounts receivable balance was uncollectible.

Required Prepare the adjusting entry to record estimated bad debts for November.

Problem 9-7B Estimating bad debts LO³

The following information is available regarding the accounts receivable of ClubLink Holdings at August 31, 2014:

	Month of Credit Sale*				
Customer	April	May	June	July	Aug.
A. Leslie	$ -0-	$ 24,000	$ -0-	$ 58,000	$32,000
T. Meston	52,000	-0-	-0-	-0-	-0-
P. Obrian	-0-	-0-	-0-	104,000	42,000
L. Timms	-0-	126,000	52,000	-0-	28,000
W. Victor	-0-	-0-	166,000	122,000	64,000

*All services are performed on terms of n/60. Assume all sales occurred on the last day of the month.

ClubLink estimates uncollectibility of accounts receivable using the following rates:

Not yet due	1 to 29 days past due	30 to 59 days past due	60 to 89 days past due	90 to 119 days past due	Over 119 days past due
1.5%	2%	5%	20%	35%	50%

Required

a. Complete a Schedule of Accounts Receivable by Age at August 31, 2014, similar to Exhibit 9.14.

b. The Allowance for Doubtful Accounts showed an unadjusted balance on August 31, 2014, of $9,600 (debit). Record the adjusting journal entry at August 31, 2014, to estimate uncollectible accounts.

Problem 9-8B Uncollectible accounts LO³

At year-end, March 31, 2014, Waterton Contractors showed unadjusted balances of: $243,000 in Accounts Receivable; $1,100 debit in Allowance for Doubtful Accounts; and $4,640,000 in Sales. Uncollectible accounts are estimated to be 0.4% of sales.

Unadjusted balances at March 31, 2015, were: Accounts Receivable, $298,000; Allowance for Doubtful Accounts, $900 debit; and Sales, $3,971,000. Waterton changed the method of estimating uncollectible accounts to 5.5% of outstanding accounts receivable.

At March 31, 2016, the General Ledger showed unadjusted balances of: $253,000 in Accounts Receivable; $4,600 credit in Allowance for Doubtful Accounts; and $3,750,000 in Sales. Waterton prepared an aging analysis on March 31, 2016, that estimated total uncollectible accounts to be $12,900.

Required Prepare the 2014, 2015, and 2016 year-end adjusting entries to estimate uncollectible accounts.

Analysis Component: List the adjusted balances in Allowance for Doubtful Accounts for each of March 31, 2014, 2015, and 2016. Beside each, show the respective Accounts Receivable and Sales balances. Comment on the change in Allowance for Doubtful Accounts and Accounts Receivable relative to the change in Sales.

Problem 9-9B Notes receivable LO⁴

Shostak showed the following details regarding its notes receivable:

Note	Date of Note	Principal	Interest Rate	Term	Maturity Date	Days of Accrued Interest at Dec. 31, 2014	Accrued Interest at Dec. 31, 2014
1	Sept. 20/13	$490,000	3.0%	120 days			
2	June 01/14	240,000	3.5%	45 days			
3	Nov. 23/14	164,000	4.5%	90 days			
4	Dec. 18/14	120,000	4.0%	30 days			

*Round calculations to the nearest whole cent.

Required

For each note:

a. Determine the maturity date.

b. Calculate the *days* of accrued interest, if any, at December 31, 2014, Shostak's year-end.

c. Calculate the *amount* of accrued interest, if any, at December 31, 2014.

For Note 4:

d. Prepare the entry to record the accrued interest at December 31, 2014.

e. Prepare the entry to record the collection on the maturity date. Assume that interest and principal are collected at maturity.

Problem 9-10B Accrued interest calculation and dishonouring note receivable LO[4]

Following are transactions of Rural Company (round calculations to the nearest whole cent):

2014

Nov. 16   Accepted a $74,000, 90-day, 4% note dated this day in granting Bess Parker a time extension on her past-due account.

Dec. 31   Made an adjusting entry to record the accrued interest on the Parker note.

31   Closed the Interest Revenue account.

2015

Feb. 14   Received Parker's payment for the principal and interest on the note dated November 16.

28   Accepted a $36,000, 5.5%, 30-day note dated this day in granting a time extension on the past-due account of The Simms Co.

Mar. 1   Accepted a $62,000, 60-day, 4.75% note dated this day in granting Bedford Holmes a time extension on his past-due account.

30   The Simms Co. dishonoured its note when presented for payment.

Required

a. Prepare journal entries to record Rural's transactions.

b. Determine the maturity date of the note dated March 1. Prepare the entry at maturity assuming Bedford Holmes honours the note.

Problem 9-11B Short-term notes receivable LO[4]

Asiatic Electroplating analyzes its accounts receivable weekly. On November 17, 2014, Asiatic accepted a 5.5%, 90-day, $90,000 note receivable from RoadWorks in exchange for its past-due account. On December 1, Ellen Huskey's $36,000 overdue account was converted to a four-month, 5.5% note receivable. On January 31, 2015, Asiatic's year-end, accrued interest was recorded on the notes. RoadWorks honoured its note on the maturity date but Ellen Huskey's note was dishonoured. Huskey's account was determined to be uncollectible and written off on July 15, 2015.

Required Prepare Asiatic Electroplating's entries for each of the following dates:

a. November 17, 2014

b. December 1, 2014

c. January 31, 2015

d. Maturity date of RoadWorks' note

e. Maturity date of Huskey's note

f. July 15, 2015

Analysis Component: Assuming a $50,000 credit balance in the Allowance for Doubtful Accounts on July 14, 2015, calculate the balance after posting the entry in (f) above. Assuming no additional write-offs were made prior to year-end, comment on the adequacy of the Allowance for Doubtful Accounts.

*Problem 9-12B Discounting notes receivable LO[5]

Required Prepare entries to record the following transactions of Ibscon Company:

Mar. 1   Accepted a $50,000, 60-day, 4.5% note dated this day in granting Bolton Company a time extension on its past-due account.

23   Discounted, without recourse, the Bolton note at Security Bank at a cost of $100.

June 21   Accepted a $22,000, 90-day, 5% note dated this day in granting Vince Soto a time extension on his past-due account.

July 5   Discounted, with recourse, the Soto note at Security Bank at a cost of $475.

Sept. 25   Received notice from Security Bank that the Soto note had been paid.

Analysis Component: What reporting is necessary when a business discounts notes receivable with recourse and these notes have not reached maturity by the end of the fiscal period? Explain the reason for this requirement and what accounting principle is being satisfied.

An asterisk (*) identifies assignment material based on Appendix 9A or Appendix 9B.

*Problem 9-13B Discounting notes receivable LO[5]

Required Prepare General Journal entries to record the following transactions of Billington Company.

	2014	
Jan	10	Accepted a $3,000, 60-day, 6% note dated this day in granting a time extension on the past-due account of David Huerta.
Mar.	14	David Huerta dishonoured his note when presented for payment.
	19	Accepted a $2,100, 90-day, 5% note dated this day in granting a time extension on the past-due account of Rose Jones.
	28	Discounted the Rose Jones note at the bank at 8%.
Jun.	20	Received word from the bank that the Rose Jones note had been paid.
	27	Accepted $700 in cash and a $1,300, 60-day, 6% note dated this day in granting a time extension on the past-due account of Jake Thomas.
July	24	Discounted the Jake Thomas note at the bank at 7%.
Aug.	29	The Jake Thomas note was dishonoured. Paid the bank the maturity of the note plus a $10 fee.
Sept.	4	Accepted a $1,500, 60-day, 5.5% note dated this day in granting a time extension on the past-due account of Ginnie Bauer.
Oct.	13	Discounted the Ginnie Bauer note at the bank at 7%.
Nov.	6	The Ginnie Bauer note was dishonoured. Paid the bank the maturity value of the note plus a $10 fee.
Dec.	6	Received payment from Ginnie Bauer of the maturity value of her dishonoured note, the fee, and interest at 5.5% on both for 30 days beyond maturity.
	28	Decided the accounts of David Huerta and Jake Thomas were uncollectible and wrote them off against Allowance for Doubtful Accounts.

ANALYTICAL AND REVIEW PROBLEMS

A & R Problem 9-1

Reproduced below from Farthington Supply's accounting records is the Accounts Receivable Subledger along with selected General Ledger accounts.

General Ledger

Accounts Receivable				Allowance for Doubtful Accounts			
Dec. 31/13 Balance	158,500					200	Dec. 31/13 Balance
		7,000	Jan. 4/14				
Credit sales in 2014	????	????	Collections in 2014	July 15/14	14,000		
		14,000	July 15/14			????	Dec. 31/14
Dec. 31/14 Balance	????					????	Dec. 31/14 Balance

Accounts Receivable Subledger

JenStar Company				Indigo Developments			
Dec. 31/13 Balance	48,000			Dec. 31/13 Balance	-0-		
		48,000	Jan. 20/14	Mar. 1/14	17,000	17,000	Mar. 20/14
Nov. 15/14	????			Nov. 28/14	39,000		
				Dec. 2/14	4,000		
Dec. 31/14 Balance	104,000			Dec. 31/14 Balance	43,000		

Lomas Industries				PDQ Servicing			
Dec. 31/13 Balance	????			Dec. 31/13 Balance	14,000		
		7,000	Jan. 4/14				
		????	Jan. 7/14				
Apr. 21/14	52,000	52,000	May 5/14			14,000	July 15/14
Dec. 7/14	21,000						
Dec. 31/14 Balance	21,000			Dec. 31/14 Balance	-0-		

During the year 2014, there were no recoveries of accounts previously written off. Only one account, that of PDQ Servicing, was identified as being uncollectible on July 15, 2014. On January 4, 2014, Farthington issued a $7,000 credit memo to Lomas Industries regarding damaged goods returned.

Required Analyzing the accounts, determine the following amounts:

a. The December 31, 2013, balance in Lomas Industries' account.

b. The January 7, 2014, collection from Lomas Industries.

c. The December 31, 2014, balance in the Accounts Receivable controlling account.

d. The November 15, 2014, transaction in JenStar Company's account.

e. Collections during 2014.

f. Credit sales during 2014.

g. Adjusting entry on December 31, 2014, to estimate uncollectible accounts based on a rate of 2.5% of outstanding receivables.

h. The December 31, 2014, balance in the Allowance for Doubtful Accounts.

i. Show how accounts receivable should appear on the balance sheet on December 31, 2014.

Analysis Component: Why does Farthington maintain an Accounts Receivable Subledger? What other subledgers might the company be using and why?

A & R Problem 9-2

Sullivan Equipment Sales showed the following.

	2014	
Jan.	15	Sold $25,000 of merchandise for $29,000 to JanCo; terms 3/5, n/15.
	16	Wrote off Fedun's account in the amount of $15,000.
	20	Collected the amount owing from the January 15 sale.
Mar.	1	Accepted a $12,000, 60-day, 7% note dated this day in granting Parker Holdings a time extension on its past-due account.
Apr.	15	Sold merchandise costing $62,000 for $71,000 to customers who used their Visa credit cards. Visa charges a 1% fee and deposits the cash electronically into the retailer's account immediately at the time of sale.
	?	Parker Holdings honoured the note dated March 1.
Nov.	1	Accepted a $24,000, three-month, 6% note dated this day in granting Grant Company a time extension on its past-due account.
Dec.	31	Sullivan's year-end. Interest was accrued on outstanding notes receivable.
	31	Bad debts are based on an aging analysis that estimated $9,700 of accounts receivable are uncollectible. Allowance for Doubtful Accounts showed an unadjusted credit balance of $1,600 on this date.
	2015	
	?	Grant Company dishonoured its note dated November 1, 2014.
Mar.	5	Recovered $1,500 from Derek Holston that was previously written off.
	14	Wrote off the Grant Company account.

Required

a. Determine the maturity dates of the March 1 and November 1 notes.

b. Prepare entries as appropriate for each date.

Analysis Component: Sullivan's receivable turnovers at December 31, 2014 and 2015, were 7 and 7.5, respectively. Explain what this ratio measures and whether the change in the ratio for Sullivan was favourable or unfavourable.

ETHICS CHALLENGE

EC 9-1

Randy Meyer is the chief executive officer of a medium-sized company in Regina, Saskatchewan. Several years ago, Randy persuaded the board of directors of his company to base a percent of his compensation on the net income the company earns each year. Each December, Randy estimates year-end financial figures in anticipation of the bonus he will receive. If the bonus is not as high as he would like, he offers several accounting recommendations to his controller for year-end adjustments. One of his favourite recommendations is for the controller to reduce the estimate of doubtful accounts. Randy has used this technique with success for several years.

1. What effect does lowering the estimate for doubtful accounts have on the income statement and balance sheet of Randy's company?

2. Do you think Randy's recommendations to adjust the allowance for doubtful accounts is within his right as CEO or do you think this action is an ethics violation? Justify your response.

3. What type of internal control might be useful for this company in overseeing the CEO's recommendations for accounting changes?

FOCUS ON FINANCIAL STATEMENTS

FFS 9-1

Clara Dover, the owner of Dover Plumbing Sales and Service, showed the following adjusted account balances for the year ended March 31, 2014 (listed alphabetically):

Account	Account Balance*
Accounts payable	$ 6,900
Accounts receivable	28,000
Accumulated depreciation, tools	11,000
Accumulated depreciation, truck	14,000
Allowance for doubtful accounts	1,800
Bad debt expense	5,600
Cash	16,000
Cash over/short expense	20**
Clara Dover, capital	248,770
Clara Dover, withdrawals	72,000
Cost of goods sold	103,000
Depreciation expense, tools	2,000
Depreciation expense, truck	5,000
Insurance expense	7,100
Interest expense	250
Merchandise inventory	9,000
Notes payable, due August 31, 2017	17,000
Notes payable, due February 1, 2015	6,000
Notes receivable, due December 1, 2016	14,000
Petty cash	400
Plumbing fees earned	121,000
Prepaid insurance	3,800
Prepaid rent	6,500
Rent expense	23,000
Salaries expense	118,000
Salaries payable	3,200
Sales	124,000
Tools	82,000
Truck	67,000
Unearned plumbing fees	9,000

*Assume all account balances are normal unless otherwise stated.
**Debit balance.

Required Prepare a classified balance sheet based on the information provided.

Analysis Component: Dover Plumbing had total *Plumbing fees earned* for the year ended March 31, 2013, of $86,000 and net accounts receivable at March 31, 2013, of $21,200. Calculate and compare days' sales uncollected for March 31, 2013, and March 31, 2014. Round calculations to two decimal places.

FFS 9-2

Refer to **Danier Leather**'s balance sheet and income statement in Appendix II at the end of the textbook.

DANIER

Required Answer the following questions.

1. The balance sheet shows accounts receivable of $385,000 at June 25, 2011, and $543,000 at June 26, 2010. What type of asset is accounts receivable? Explain how accounts receivable arise.

2. Refer to the income statement. Does the change in receivables appear to correspond to the change in total sales? Explain your answer.

CRITICAL THINKING MINI CASE

You are the finance officer at a bank where the owner of Delta Designs is applying for a $600,000 loan. In reviewing the account information for the year ended June 30, 2014, you are concerned by the following selected adjusted account information:

Account	Debit	Credit
Accounts receivable[1]	$472,000	
Allowance for doubtful accounts		$ 7,080
Sales[2]		3,980,000

[1] 85% of this balance represents receivables that are not yet due. Delta Designs offers credit terms of 2/10, n/30.

[2] All sales are on credit and sales occur evenly throughout the year.

Required Using the elements of critical thinking described on the inside front cover, respond.

Payroll Liabilities

GUILTY

Edmundston—The Canada Revenue Agency (CRA) announced that a dentist was fined $3,000 in Edmundston provincial court after pleading guilty to three charges of failing to remit over $8,000 in monies deducted and withheld from wages and salaries paid to employees.

Montreal—A director on the board of two companies was fined $541,870 and sentenced to a 12-month prison term following a CRA investigation that showed payroll deductions from the salaries of employees were not remitted to the Receiver General for Canada.

In each of the above cases, unpaid deductions had to be paid in addition to the fines. Failure to do so would result in imprisonment. The CRA takes non-payment of source deductions very seriously, as the amounts deducted from employees are deemed to be held in trust until remitted to CRA on their behalf. Canadians have to be confident that the tax system is fair, and know that CRA will prosecute those individuals who cheat.

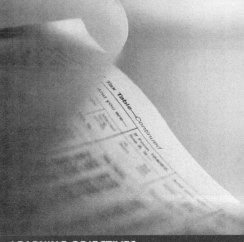

LEARNING OBJECTIVES

LO1 Identify the taxes and other items frequently withheld from employees' wages.

LO2 Make the calculations necessary to prepare a payroll register and prepare the entries to record and pay payroll liabilities.

LO3 Calculate the payroll costs levied on employers and prepare the entries to record the accrual and payment of these amounts.

LO4 Calculate and record employee fringe benefit costs.

CRITICAL THINKING CHALLENGE If payroll liabilities are not recorded, what is the effect on the financial statements?

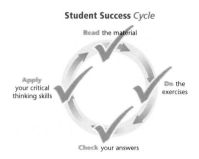

Student Success *Cycle*

Read the material

Apply your critical thinking skills

Do the exercises

Check your answers

APPENDIX PREVIEW

Wages or salaries generally amount to one of the largest expenses incurred by a business. Accounting for employees' wages and salaries is one task that is shared by almost all business entities.

Payroll accounting:

- Records cash payments to employees.
- Provides valuable information regarding labour costs.
- Accounts for amounts withheld from employees' pay.
- Accounts for employee (fringe) benefits and payroll costs paid by the employer.
- Provides the means to comply with governmental regulations on employee compensation.

As you study this appendix, you will learn the general processes that all businesses follow to account for these items.

ITEMS WITHHELD FROM EMPLOYEES' WAGES

 LO¹ Identify the taxes and other items frequently withheld from employees' wages.

An understanding of payroll accounting and the design and use of payroll records requires some knowledge of the laws and programs that affect payrolls. Many of these require **payroll deductions**, amounts withheld from the wages of employees, and are discussed in the first portion of this appendix.

DECISION INSIGHT

The Canadian Payroll Association (CPA) represents more than 10,000 members of the professional payroll community in Canada, the United States, and abroad. With over 18 million Canadian employees paid through CPA member companies, its mission is to provide payroll leadership through advocacy and education. The two qualifications granted through the country's only nationally recognized Payroll Management Certificate Program are Payroll Compliance Practitioner (PCP) and Certified Payroll Manager (CPM).

CPA ACP 25 1978-2003

SOURCE: www.payroll.ca.

Withholding Employees' Income Tax

Employers are required to calculate, collect, and remit to the Receiver General for Canada the income taxes of their employees. Historically, when the first federal income tax law became effective in 1917, it applied to only a few individuals having high earnings. It was not until the Second World War that income taxes were levied on almost all wage earners. At that time, Parliament recognized that many individual wage earners could not be expected to save the money needed to pay their income taxes once each year, so Parliament began a system of pay-as-you-go withholding of taxes at their source each payday. This pay-as-you-go withholding of employee income taxes requires an employer to act as a tax collecting agent of the federal government. Failure to cooperate results in severe consequences.

The amount of income taxes to be withheld from an employee's wages is determined by his or her wages and the amount of **personal tax credits**. Based on rates in effect January 1, 2012, each individual is entitled, in 2012, to some or all of the following annual amounts that are subject to tax credits (as applicable):

1. Basic Personal Amount................. $10,822
2. Married or Equivalent................... 10,822
   (with maximum earnings stipulated)

The total of each taxpayer's personal tax credits is deducted from income to determine the level of income tax deductions from the individual's gross pay. For example, based on rates effective January 1, 2012, a Saskatchewan resident with a gross weekly salary of $400 and personal tax credits of $10,822 (2012 net claim code 1 on the *TD1* form) would have $31.84 of total income taxes withheld. Another individual with the same gross salary but with personal tax credits of $17,027 (claim code 5) would have $10.96 withheld.

Employers withhold income tax owed by each employee every payday based on an employee's completed Personal Tax Credits Return, Form **TD1**. There are federal and provincial/territorial TD1 forms. The taxpayer must file revised TD1 forms each time the exemptions change during a year. The federal TD1 form is shown in Extend Your Knowledge A-1 online.

In determining the amounts of income taxes to be withheld from the wages of employees, employers use payroll deductions tables provided by the Canada Revenue Agency (CRA). The to-be-withheld amounts include both federal and provincial income taxes except for the province of Quebec, which levies and collects its own income tax and its own pension plan contributions. Provincial income tax rates vary from province to province. Therefore, for consistency, all examples and problems making use of tax tables in this appendix will be based on Saskatchewan's tables. Calculation of deductions is simplified for computer users if they access the "Payroll Deductions Online Calculator" (PDOC) at https://apps.cra-arc.gc.ca/ebci/rhpd/start Language.do?lang=English. Employers are required to remit the withheld taxes to the Receiver General for Canada each month.

EYK
A-1

Canada (or Quebec) Pension Plan (CPP or QPP)

Every working person between the ages of 18 and 70 with few exceptions must make contributions in required amounts to the **Canada Pension Plan** (CPP) or Quebec Pension Plan (QPP).

Effective December 9, 2011, contributions are based on earnings as follows:

Canada Pension Plan Contributions		
Effective Dec. 9, 2011	**Employee Contributions**	**Employer Contributions**
Rate	4.95%*	4.95%*
Maximum	$2,306.70	$2,306.70

*4.95% of earnings greater than $3,500 and less than $50,100.

Employers are responsible for making the proper deductions from their employees' earnings. They remit these deductions each month, together with their own contributions, to the Receiver General for Canada.

Self-employed individuals pay the combined rate for employees and employers, or 9.9% on annual earnings between $3,500 and the exempt ceiling of $50,100.

Employment Insurance (EI)

To assist the unemployed, the federal government began an employee/employer-financed unemployment insurance plan. Under the revised 1996 *Employment Insurance Act*, compulsory **Employment Insurance** (EI) coverage was extended to all Canadian workers who are not self-employed. Over 13 million employees, including teachers, hospital workers, and top-level executives, are covered by the insurance plan.

The Employment Insurance fund from which benefits are paid is jointly financed by employees and their employers. At January 1, 2012, employers are required to deduct from their employees' wages 1.83% of insured earnings, to add a contribution of 1.4 times the amount deducted from employees' wages, and to remit both amounts to the Receiver General for Canada. The system is summarized as follows:

Employment Insurance Contributions		
Effective Jan. 1, 2012	**Employee Contributions**	**Employer Contributions**
Rate	1.83%	1.4 times employee rate
Maximum	$839.97	$1,175.96
Note: maximum insurable earnings for 2012 are $45,900.		

Insured earnings, in most instances, refer to gross earnings. An employee may receive taxable benefits or allowances that would be included in gross earnings but would not be considered insurable earnings. However, in this text, gross earnings will be insurable earnings.

The *Employment Insurance Act* also requires that an employer complete a "record of employment" because of termination of employment, illness, injury, or pregnancy and keep a record for each employee that shows among other things wages subject to employment insurance and taxes withheld.

Use of Withholding Tables

Employers may use **wage bracket withholding tables** in determining Canada Pension Plan and Employment Insurance to be withheld from employees' gross earnings. These tables are available from CRA.

Alternatively, determining the amount of withholdings from an employee's gross wages is quite easy when the Payroll Deductions Online Calculator is used. Extend Your Knowledge A-2 online shows the screens used to determine withholding amounts using the Payroll Deductions Online Calculator.

EYK
A-2

The T-4 Form

Employers are required to report wages and deductions both to each employee and to the local office of CRA. On or before the last day of February, the employer must give each employee a T-4 statement that tells the employee:

- Total wages for the preceding year.
- Taxable benefits received from the employer.
- Income taxes withheld.
- Deductions for registered pension plan.
- Canada Pension Plan contributions.
- Employment Insurance deductions.

On or before the last day of February the employer must forward to the district taxation office copies of the employee's T-4 statements plus a T-4 that summarizes the information contained on the employee's T-4 statements. The T-4 form is shown in Exhibit A.1.

EXHIBIT A.1

2012 T-4 Form

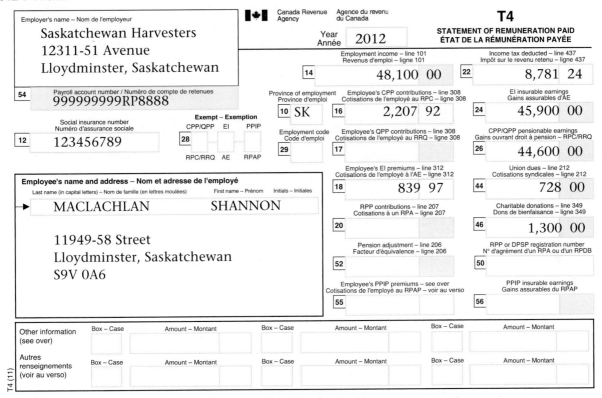

Reproduced with permission of the Minister of Public Works and Government Services Canada, 2012.

Wages, Hours, and Union Contracts

All provinces have laws establishing maximum hours of work and minimum pay rates. And, while the details vary with each province, generally employers are required to pay an employee for hours worked in excess of 40 in any one week at the employee's regular pay rate plus an overtime premium of at least one-half of his or her regular rate. In addition, employers commonly operate under contracts with their employees' union that provide even better terms.

In addition to specifying working hours and wage rates, union contracts often provide that the employer shall deduct dues from the wages of each employee and remit the amounts deducted to the union.

Other Payroll Deductions

Employees may individually authorize additional deductions such as:

1. Deductions to accumulate funds for the purchase of Canada Savings Bonds.
2. Deductions to pay health, accident, hospital, or life insurance premiums.
3. Deductions to repay loans from the employer or the employees' credit union.
4. Deductions to pay for merchandise purchased from the company.
5. Deductions for donations to charitable organizations such as the United Way.

CHECKPOINT

1. What is the purpose of the federal Employment Insurance scheme?
2. When must T-4 statements be given to employees?
3. What are other typical nonmandatory payroll deductions?

Do Quick Study question: QS A-1

THE PAYROLL REGISTER

 LO² Make the calculations necessary to prepare a payroll register and prepare the entries to record and pay payroll liabilities.

Each pay period the total hours worked are summarized in a payroll register, an example of which is shown in Exhibit A.2. The illustrated register is for a weekly pay period and shows the payroll data for each employee on a separate line.

In Exhibit A.2, the columns under the heading Daily Time show the hours worked each day by each employee. The total of each employee's hours is entered in the column headed Total Hours. If hours include overtime hours, these are entered in the column headed O.T. Hours.

The Regular Pay Rate column shows the hourly pay rate of each employee. Total hours worked multiplied by the regular pay rate equals regular pay. Overtime hours multiplied by the overtime premium rate (50% in this case) equals overtime premium pay (O.T. Premium Pay column). And regular pay plus overtime premium pay is the **employee's gross pay**.

The amounts withheld from each employee's gross pay are recorded in the Deductions columns of the payroll register. For example, you determine the income tax deductions by matching the gross pay of each employee to the tax deduction tables and then enter the results in the tax deduction column. Income tax deductions are based on the gross pay less the amounts deducted for EI and CPP (or QPP). The tax tables allow for these adjustments and separate books are available for each province. Exhibit A.2 assumes that income tax deductions are based on the tables provided in Exhibit A.3 assuming the employees are resident in Saskatchewan.

For example, you can use the tables in Exhibit A.3 to determine the appropriate CPP, EI, and income tax deductions for John Auer's $400 pay. In the CPP table, under the *Pay* column, find $400. The CPP deduction according to the table is $16.47 for the pay range $399.93–$400.12. Using the EI table, go to the *Insurable Earnings* column and find $400. The table shows that the EI deduction for the range $399.73–$400.27 is $7.32. Finally, using each of the federal and provincial tax deductions tables, go to the Pay column and find $400. Now follow the numbers across to the claim code 1 column (assume a claim code of 1 unless otherwise specified). The tables show a total income tax to be deducted of $32.00[1] (federal tax of $22.20 + provincial tax of $9.80). You can use the tables to determine the CPP, EI, and income tax deductions for the remaining employees.

---

1   The Payroll Deductions Online Calculator produces marginally more accurate results since the table values are based on ranges vs. specific dollar amounts.

EXHIBIT A.2

Payroll Register

													Earnings				
													Payroll Week Ended				
Employees	Clock Card No.	Daily Time							Total Hours	O.T. Hours	Reg. Pay Rate	Regular Pay	O.T. Premium Pay	Gross Pay		
		M	T	W	T	F	S	S								
Auer, John	118	8	8	8	8	8			40		10.00	400.00		400.00	1
Cheung, Joen	109	0	8	8	8	8	8		40		12.00	480.00		480.00	2
Daljit, Moe	121	8	8	8	8	8	8	4	52	12	15.00	780.00	90.00	870.00	3
Lee, Shannon	104	8	8		8	8	8	4	44	4	14.00	616.00	28.00	644.00	4
Prasad, Sunil	108		8	8	8	8	4	8	44	4	15.00	660.00	30.00	690.00	5
Rupert, Allan	105	8	8	8	8	8			40		12.00	480.00		480.00	6
Totals												3,416.00	148.00	3,564.00	

Register March 9, 2012

	Gross Pay	Deductions					Payment		Distribution	
		EI Premium	Income Taxes	Hospital Insurance	CPP	Total Deductions	Net Pay	Cheque Number	Sales Salaries	Office Salaries
1	400.00	7.32	32.00	18.00	16.47	73.79	326.21	754	400.00	
2	480.00	8.78	51.30	18.00	20.43	98.51	381.49	755	480.00	
3	870.00	15.92	150.45	24.00	39.73	230.10	639.90	756		870.00
4	644.00	11.79	91.50	18.00	28.55	149.84	494.16	757		644.00
5	690.00	12.63	102.00	24.00	30.82	169.45	520.55	758	690.00	
6	480.00	8.78	51.30	18.00	20.43	98.51	381.49	759	480.00	
	3,564.00	65.22	478.55	120.00	156.43	820.20	2,743.80		2,050.00	1,514.00

EXHIBIT A.3

Excerpts From CPP, EI, and Income Tax Tables Effective January 1, 2012.

Canada Pension Plan Contributions
Weekly (52 pay periods a year)

Cotisations au Régime de pensions du Canada
Hebdomadaire (52 périodes de paie par année)

Pay Rémunération		CPP RPC	Pay Rémunération		CPP RPC	Pay Rémunération		CPP RPC	Pay Rémunération		CPP RPC
From - De	To - À		From - De	To - À		From - De	To - À		From - De	To - À	
399.93 -	400.12	16.47	643.57 -	643.76	28.53	867.20 -	867.40	39.60	903.57 -	903.76	41.40
400.13 -	400.33	16.48	643.77 -	643.96	28.54	867.41 -	867.60	39.61	903.77 -	903.96	41.41
400.34 -	400.53	16.49	643.97 -	644.16	28.55	867.61 -	867.80	39.62	903.97 -	904.16	41.42
400.54 -	400.73	16.50	644.17 -	644.37	28.56	867.81 -	868.00	39.63	904.17 -	904.37	41.43
400.74 -	400.93	16.51	644.38 -	644.57	28.57	868.01 -	868.20	39.64	904.38 -	904.57	41.44
400.94 -	401.13	16.52	644.58 -	644.77	28.58	868.21 -	868.41	39.65	904.58 -	904.77	41.45
401.14 -	401.34	16.53	644.78 -	644.97	28.59	868.42 -	868.61	39.66	904.78 -	904.97	41.46
401.35 -	401.54	16.54	644.98 -	645.17	28.60	868.62 -	868.81	39.67	904.98 -	905.17	41.47
401.55 -	401.74	16.55	645.18 -	645.38	28.61	868.82 -	869.01	39.68	905.18 -	905.38	41.48
479.93 -	480.12	20.43	689.02 -	689.21	30.78	869.02 -	869.21	39.69	934.48 -	934.67	42.93
480.13 -	480.33	20.44	689.22 -	689.42	30.79	869.22 -	869.42	39.70	934.68 -	934.87	42.94
480.34 -	480.53	20.45	689.43 -	689.62	30.80	869.43 -	869.62	39.71	934.88 -	935.07	42.95
480.54 -	480.73	20.46	689.63 -	689.82	30.81	869.63 -	869.82	39.72	935.08 -	935.27	42.96
480.74 -	480.93	20.47	689.83 -	690.02	30.82	869.83 -	870.02	39.73	935.28 -	935.48	42.97
480.94 -	481.13	20.48	690.03 -	690.22	30.83	870.03 -	870.22	39.74	935.49 -	935.68	42.98
481.14 -	481.34	20.49	690.23 -	690.43	30.84	870.23 -	870.43	39.75	935.69 -	935.88	42.99
481.35 -	481.54	20.50	690.44 -	690.63	30.85	870.44 -	870.63	39.76	935.89 -	936.08	43.00
481.55 -	481.74	20.51	690.64 -	690.83	30.86	870.64 -	870.83	39.77	936.09 -	936.28	43.01

Employee's maximum CPP contribution for the year 2012 is $2,306.70

La cotisation maximale de l'employé au RPC pour l'année 2012 est de 2 306,70 $

Employment Insurance Premiums

Cotisations à l'assurance-emploi

Insurable Earnings Rémunération assurable		EI premium Cotisation d'AE	Insurable Earnings Rémunération assurable		EI premium Cotisation d'AE	Insurable Earnings Rémunération assurable		EI premium Cotisation d'AE	Insurable Earnings Rémunération assurable		EI premium Cotisation d'AE
From - De	To - À		From - De	To - À		From - De	To - À		From - De	To - À	
398.64 -	399.18	7.30	639.62 -	640.16	11.71	683.88 -	684.42	12.52	865.85 -	866.39	15.85
399.19 -	399.72	7.31	640.17 -	640.71	11.72	684.43 -	684.97	12.53	866.40 -	866.93	15.86
399.73 -	400.27	7.32	640.72 -	641.25	11.73	684.98 -	685.51	12.54	866.94 -	867.48	15.87
400.28 -	400.81	7.33	641.26 -	641.80	11.74	685.52 -	686.06	12.55	867.49 -	868.03	15.88
400.82 -	401.36	7.34	641.81 -	642.34	11.75	686.07 -	686.61	12.56	868.04 -	868.57	15.89
401.37 -	401.91	7.35	642.35 -	642.89	11.76	686.62 -	687.15	12.57	868.58 -	869.12	15.90
401.92 -	402.45	7.36	642.90 -	643.44	11.77	687.16 -	687.70	12.58	869.13 -	869.67	15.91
402.46 -	403.00	7.37	643.45 -	643.98	11.78	687.71 -	688.25	12.59	869.68 -	870.21	15.92
403.01 -	403.55	7.38	643.99 -	644.53	11.79	688.26 -	688.79	12.60	870.22 -	870.76	15.93
477.33 -	477.86	8.74	644.54 -	645.08	11.80	688.80 -	689.34	12.61	870.77 -	871.31	15.94
477.87 -	478.41	8.75	645.09 -	645.62	11.81	689.35 -	689.89	12.62	871.32 -	871.85	15.95
478.42 -	478.96	8.76	645.63 -	646.17	11.82	689.90 -	690.43	12.63	871.86 -	872.40	15.96
478.97 -	479.50	8.77	646.18 -	646.72	11.83	690.44 -	690.98	12.64	872.41 -	872.95	15.97
479.51 -	480.05	8.78	646.73 -	647.26	11.84	690.99 -	691.53	12.65	872.96 -	873.49	15.98
480.06 -	480.60	8.79	647.27 -	647.81	11.85	691.54 -	692.07	12.66	873.50 -	874.04	15.99
480.61 -	481.14	8.80	647.82 -	648.36	11.86	692.08 -	692.62	12.67	874.05 -	874.59	16.00
481.15 -	481.69	8.81	648.37 -	648.90	11.87	692.63 -	693.16	12.68	874.60 -	875.13	16.01
481.70 -	482.24	8.82	648.91 -	649.45	11.88	693.17 -	693.71	12.69	875.14 -	875.68	16.02

Yearly maximum insurable earnings are $45,900
Yearly maximum employee premiums are $839.97
The premium rate for 2012 is 1.83%

Le maximum annuel de la rémunération assurable est de 45 900 $
La cotisation maximale annuelle de l'employé est de 839,97 $
Le taux de cotisation pour 2012 est de 1,83 %

EXHIBIT A.3

Excerpts From CPP, EI, and Income Tax Tables Effective January 1, 2012. (continued)

Federal tax deductions
Effective January 1, 2012
Weekly (52 pay periods a year)
Also look up the tax deductions in the provincial table

Retenues d'impôt fédéral
En vigueur le 1er janvier 2012
Hebdomadaire (52 périodes de paie par année)
Cherchez aussi les retenues d'impôt dans la table provinciale

Pay / Rémunération		Federal claim codes/Codes de demande fédéraux										
		0	1	2	3	4	5	6	7	8	9	10
From De	Less than Moins de	Deduct from each pay / Retenez sur chaque paie										
391 -	395	52.30	21.10	18.10	12.15	6.15	.20					
395 -	399	52.85	21.65	18.65	12.70	6.70	.75					
399 -	403	53.40	22.20	19.20	13.25	7.30	1.30					
403 -	407	53.95	22.75	19.75	13.80	7.85	1.90					
407 -	411	54.55	23.30	20.35	14.35	8.40	2.45					
471 -	475	63.50	32.25	29.30	23.30	17.35	11.40	5.40				
475 -	479	64.05	32.80	29.85	23.85	17.90	11.95	6.00				
479 -	483	64.60	33.40	30.40	24.45	18.45	12.50	6.55	.55			
483 -	487	65.15	33.95	30.95	25.00	19.05	13.05	7.10	1.15			
487 -	491	65.70	34.50	31.50	25.55	19.60	13.60	7.65	1.70			
611 -	619	83.35	52.10	49.15	43.15	37.20	31.25	25.30	19.30	13.35	7.40	1.40
619 -	627	84.45	53.25	50.25	44.30	38.30	32.35	26.40	20.45	14.45	8.50	2.55
627 -	635	85.55	54.35	51.35	45.40	39.45	33.50	27.50	21.55	15.60	9.60	3.65
635 -	643	86.70	55.50	52.50	46.55	40.55	34.60	28.65	22.65	16.70	10.75	4.75
643 -	651	87.80	56.60	53.60	47.65	41.70	35.70	29.75	23.80	17.80	11.85	5.90
651 -	659	88.95	57.70	54.75	48.75	42.80	36.85	30.85	24.90	18.95	12.95	7.00
659 -	667	90.05	58.85	55.85	49.90	43.90	37.95	32.00	26.00	20.05	14.10	8.15
667 -	675	91.15	59.95	56.95	51.00	45.05	39.05	33.10	27.15	21.15	15.20	9.25
675 -	683	92.30	61.05	58.10	52.10	46.15	40.20	34.20	28.25	22.30	16.35	10.35
683 -	691	93.40	62.20	59.20	53.25	47.25	41.30	35.35	29.40	23.40	17.45	11.50
851 -	859	119.25	88.05	85.05	79.10	73.15	67.15	61.20	55.25	49.25	43.30	37.35
859 -	867	120.95	89.75	86.75	80.80	74.80	68.85	62.90	56.90	50.95	45.00	39.00
867 -	875	122.60	91.40	88.40	82.45	76.50	70.55	64.55	58.60	52.65	46.65	40.70
875 -	883	124.30	93.10	90.10	84.15	78.15	72.20	66.25	60.25	54.30	48.35	42.40
883 -	891	126.00	94.75	91.80	85.85	79.85	73.90	67.95	61.95	56.00	50.05	44.05

*You normally use claim code "0" only for non-resident employees. However, if you have non-resident employees who earn less than the minimum amount shown in the "Pay" column, you may not be able to use these tables. Instead, refer to the "Step-by-step calculation of tax deductions" in Section "A" of this publication.

Saskatchewan provincial tax deductions
Effective January 1, 2012
Weekly (52 pay periods a year)
Also look up the tax deductions in the federal table

Retenues d'impôt provincial de la Saskatchewan
En vigueur le 1er janvier 2012
Hebdomadaire (52 périodes de paie par année)
Cherchez aussi les retenues d'impôt dans la table fédérale

Pay / Rémunération		Provincial claim codes/Codes de demande provinciaux										
		0	1	2	3	4	5	6	7	8	9	10
From De	Less than Moins de	Deduct from each pay / Retenez sur chaque paie										
393 -	395	40.75	9.15	7.15	3.05							
395 -	397	40.95	9.35	7.35	3.25							
397 -	399	41.20	9.55	7.55	3.45							
399 -	401	41.40	9.80	7.75	3.65							
401 -	403	41.60	10.00	7.95	3.90							
473 -	477	49.05	17.45	15.45	11.35	7.30	3.25					
477 -	481	49.50	17.90	15.85	11.75	7.70	3.65					
481 -	485	49.90	18.30	16.25	12.20	8.10	4.05					
485 -	489	50.30	18.70	16.65	12.60	8.55	4.45	.40				
489 -	493	50.70	19.10	17.05	13.00	8.95	4.85	.80				
633 -	641	65.70	34.10	32.05	28.00	23.90	19.85	15.75	11.70	7.65	3.55	
641 -	649	66.50	34.90	32.85	28.80	24.75	20.65	16.60	12.50	8.45	4.40	.30
649 -	657	67.35	35.70	33.70	29.60	25.55	21.50	17.40	13.35	9.30	5.20	1.15
657 -	665	68.15	36.55	34.50	30.45	26.35	22.30	18.25	14.15	10.10	6.05	1.95
665 -	673	68.95	37.35	35.35	31.25	27.20	23.10	19.05	15.00	10.90	6.85	2.80
673 -	681	69.80	38.20	36.15	32.10	28.00	23.95	19.85	15.80	11.75	7.65	3.60
681 -	689	70.60	39.00	36.95	32.90	28.85	24.75	20.70	16.65	12.55	8.50	4.40
689 -	697	71.45	39.80	37.80	33.70	29.65	25.60	21.50	17.45	13.40	9.30	5.25
697 -	705	72.25	40.65	38.60	34.55	30.45	26.40	22.35	18.25	14.20	10.15	6.05
705 -	713	73.05	41.45	39.45	35.35	31.30	27.20	23.15	19.10	15.00	10.95	6.90
833 -	841	86.75	55.15	53.10	49.05	45.00	40.90	36.85	32.80	28.70	24.65	20.60
841 -	849	87.75	56.15	54.10	50.05	45.95	41.90	37.85	33.75	29.70	25.60	21.55
849 -	857	88.70	57.10	55.10	51.00	46.95	42.90	38.80	34.75	30.65	26.60	22.55
857 -	865	89.70	58.10	56.05	52.00	47.90	43.85	39.80	35.70	31.65	27.60	23.50
865 -	873	90.70	59.05	57.05	52.95	48.90	44.85	40.75	36.70	32.65	28.55	24.50

The column headed Hospital Insurance in Exhibit A.2 shows the amounts withheld to pay for hospital insurance for the employees and their families. The total withheld from all employees is a current liability of the employer until paid to the insurance company. Likewise, the total withheld for employees' union dues is a current liability until paid to the union.

Additional columns may be added to the payroll register for any other deductions that occur sufficiently often to warrant special columns. For example, a company that regularly deducts amounts from its employees' pay for Canada Savings Bonds may add a special column for this deduction.

An employee's gross pay less total deductions is the **employee's net pay** and is entered in the Net Pay column. The total of this column is the amount the employees are to be paid. The numbers of the cheques used to pay the employees are entered in the column headed Cheque Number.

The Distribution columns are used to classify the various salaries in terms of different kinds of expense. Here you enter each employee's gross salary in the proper column according to the type of work performed. The column totals then indicate the amounts to be debited to the salary expense accounts.

Recording the Payroll

The entry to record the payroll shown in Exhibit A.2 is:

March 10	Sales Salaries Expense	2,050.00	
	Office Salaries Expense....................................	1,514.00	
	EI Payable		65.22
	Employees' Income Taxes Payable.........		478.55
	Employees' Hospital Insurance Payable .		120.00
	CPP Payable...		156.43
	Salaries Payable......................................		2,743.80
	To record the March 10 payroll.		

The debits of the entry were taken from the payroll register's distribution column totals. They charge the employees' gross earnings to the proper salary expense accounts. The credits to EI Payable, Employees' Income Taxes Payable, Employees' Hospital Insurance Payable, and CPP Payable record these amounts as current liabilities. The credit to Salaries Payable (also called Payroll Payable, Wages Payable, or Accrued Salaries Payable, etc.) records as a liability the net amount to be paid to the employees.

CHECKPOINT

4. What constitutes the employee's gross pay?
5. What is the employee's net pay?

Do Quick Study questions: QS A-2, QS A-3, QS A-4, QS A-5, QS A-6

Paying the Employees

Almost every business pays its employees by cheque or through electronic funds transfer (EFT). Employers give each employee an earnings statement each payday showing the hours worked, gross pay, deductions, and net pay, as shown in Exhibit A.4.

EXHIBIT A.4

A Payroll Cheque

Employee	Total Hours	O.T. Hours	Reg. Pay Rate	Regular Pay	O.T. Prem. Pay	Gross Pay	EI Premium	Income Taxes	CP Plan	Hosp. Ins.	Total Deductions	Net Pay
John Auer	40		10.00	400.00		400.00	7.32	32.00	16.47	18.00	73.79	326.21

STATEMENT OF EARNINGS AND DEDUCTIONS FOR EMPLOYEE'S RECORDS—DETACH BEFORE CASHING CHEQUE

GRASSLAND INDUSTRIES
Loon Lake, Saskatchewan

No. 1517

PAY TO THE
ORDER OF ___ John Auer _____ Date _March 6, 2012_ $ ___326.21___

___Three hundred twenty-six dollars and twenty-one cents_ – – – – – – – – –

Lloydminster Credit Union
Lloydminster, Saskatchewan

GRASSLAND INDUSTRIES

Jane R. Morris

Employee's Individual Earnings Record

An **employee's individual earnings record**, as shown in Exhibit A.5, provides for each employee, in one record, a full year's summary of the employee's working time, gross earnings, deductions, and net pay. In addition, it accumulates information that:

> **1.** Serves as a basis for the employer's payroll tax returns.
> **2.** Indicates when an employee's earnings have reached the maximum amounts for CPP and EI deductions.
> **3.** Supplies data for the T4 slip, which must be given to the employee at the end of the year.

The payroll information on an employee's individual earnings record is posted from the payroll register. Note the last column of the record. It shows an employee's earnings to date and is used to determine when the earnings reach maximum amounts and are no longer subject to the various deductions such as CPP and EI.

EXHIBIT A.5

Employee's 2012 Individual Earnings Record

Employee's Name __John Auer__   SIN No. __123-456-789__   Employee No. __114__

Home
Address __Box 68, Loon Lake__   Notify in Case
of Emergency __Margaret Auer__   Phone
No. __964-9834__

Employed __May 15, 1999__   Date of
Termination _____   Reason _____

Date of
Birth __June 6, 1972__   Date
Becomes 65 __June 6, 2037__   Male (X)
Female ( )   Married ( )
Single (X)   Number of
Exemptions __0__   Pay
Rate __$10.00__

Occupation __Clerk__   Place __Warehouse__

Date			Time Lost	Time Worked												
Per. Ends	Paid	Hrs.	Rea-son	Total	O.T. Hours	Reg. Pay	O.T. Pay	Gross Pay	EI Prem	Income Taxes	Hosp. Ins.	CPP	Total Deduc-tions	Net Pay	Cheque No.	Cumu-lative Earnings
6-Jan	6-Jan			40		400.00		400.00	7.32	32.00	18.00	16.47	73.79	326.21		400.00
13-Jan	13-Jan			40		400.00		400.00	7.32	32.00	18.00	16.47	73.79	326.21		800.00
20-Jan	20-Jan			40		400.00		400.00	7.32	32.00	18.00	16.47	73.79	326.21		1,200.00
27-Jan	27-Jan	4	Sick	36		360.00		360.00	6.59	22.25	18.00	14.49	61.33	298.67		1,560.00
3-Feb	3-Feb			40		400.00		400.00	7.32	32.00	18.00	16.47	73.79	326.21		1,960.00
10-Feb	10-Feb			40		400.00		400.00	7.32	32.00	18.00	16.47	73.79	326.21		2,360.00
25-May	25-May			40		400.00		400.00	7.32	32.00	18.00	16.47	73.79	326.21		8,400.00

DECISION MAKER   Answer—End of chapter

Lawn Worker
You take a summer job working for a family friend who runs a small lawn mow-ing service. When the time arrives for your first paycheque, the owner slaps you on the back, gives you full payment in cash, winks, and adds: "No need to pay those high taxes, eh?" What are your responsibilities in this case? Do you take any action?

CHECKPOINT

6. What is the purpose of the employee's individual earnings record?

Do Quick Study questions: QS A-7, QS A-8

MID-APPENDIX DEMONSTRATION PROBLEM

On January 27, the end of its fourth weekly pay period in 2012, Saskat Company's payroll record showed that its one office employee and two sales employees had earned $481 (claim code 2), $645 (claim code 3), and $868 (claim code 4), respectively. Each employee has $40 of hospital insurance premiums withheld plus $15 of union dues.

Required

a. Prepare a schedule similar to the register in Exhibit A.2 to summarize deductions by employee and in total. Use the tables in Exhibit A.3 to determine the appropriate CPP, EI, and income tax to be withheld.

b. Give the journal entry to record the payroll on January 27.

Analysis Component:
What effect does the entry in part (b) have on the balance sheet?

SOLUTION

a.

	Gross Pay	EI Premium	Income Taxes	Hospital Insurance	CPP	Union Dues	Total Deductions	Net Pay	Cheque Number	Sales Salaries	Office Salaries
	Deductions							**Payment**		**Distribution**	
2	481.00	8.80	46.25	40.00	20.48	15.00	130.53	350.47	754	481.00	
4	645.00	11.80	76.45	40.00	28.60	15.00	171.85	473.15	758		645.00
4	868.00	15.88	125.40	40.00	39.63	15.00	235.91	632.09	759		868.00
	1,994.00	36.48	248.10	120.00	88.71	45.00	538.29	1,455.71		481.00	1,513.00

b.

January 27	Office Salaries Expense...................................	481.00	
	Sales Salaries Expense	1,513.00	
	EI Payable..		36.48
	Employees' Income Taxes Payable.........		248.10
	Employees' Hospital Insurance Payable ..		120.00
	CPP Payable...		88.71
	Employees' Union Dues Payable............		45.00
	Salaries Payable.....................................		1,455.71
	To record payroll deductions for pay period ending January 27.		

Analysis Component:
The entry in part (b) will cause liabilities, specifically current liabilities, to increase and equity to decrease.

PAYROLL DEDUCTIONS REQUIRED OF THE EMPLOYER

Under the previous discussion of the Canada (or Quebec) Pension Plan (CPP or QPP), it was pointed out that pension deductions are required in like amounts on both employed workers and their employers. A covered employer is required by law to deduct from the employees' pay the amounts of their CPP (or QPP), but in addition, the employer must pay an amount equal to the sum of the employees' CPP (or QPP). Commonly, the amount deducted by the employer is recorded at the same time as the payroll to which it relates is recorded. Also, since both the employees' and employer's shares are reported on the same form and are paid in one amount, the liability for both is normally recorded in the same liability account, the CPP (or QPP) Payable account.

An employer is also required to pay Employment Insurance (EI) that is 1.4 times the sum of the employees' EI deductions. Most employers record both of these payroll deductions with a journal entry that is made at the time of recording the payroll to which they relate. For example, the entry to record the employer's amounts on the payroll in Exhibit A.2 is:

LO³ Calculate the payroll costs levied on employers and prepare the entries to record the accrual and payment of these amounts.

March 10	EI Expense (1.4 × $65.22)	91.31	
	CPP (or QPP) Expense	156.43	
	EI Payable		91.31
	CPP (or QPP) Payable		156.43
	To record the employer's payroll taxes.		

The debit in the entry records as an expense the payroll taxes levied on the employer, and the credits record the liabilities for the taxes.

Paying the Payroll Deductions

Income tax, EI, and CPP (or QPP) amounts withheld each payday from the employees' pay plus the employer's portion of EI and CPP (or QPP) are current liabilities until paid to the Receiver General for Canada. The normal method of payment is to pay the amounts due at any chartered bank or remit them directly to the Receiver General for Canada. Payment of these amounts is usually required to be made before the 15th of the month following the month that deductions were made from the earnings of the employees. Large employers are required to remit on the 10th and 25th of each month.

For simplicity, we assume the payment of the March 10 amounts recorded above is made the following day. Recall, however, that the employer must remit the amounts withheld from the employee as determined in Exhibit A.2 *plus* the employer's portion recorded above. The following T-accounts summarize all of these amounts:

EI Payable	
	65.22*
	91.31**
	156.53

Employees' Income Taxes Payable	
	478.55*

Hospital Insurance Payable	
	120.00*

CPP (or QPP) Payable	
	156.43*
	156.43**
	312.86

*Employees' portion per Exhibit A.2   ** Employer's portion

A-14   APPENDIX I Payroll Liabilities

The entry to record remittance to the Receiver General for Canada is then:

March 11	EI Payable	156.53	
	Employees' Income Taxes Payable..................	478.55	
	CPP (or QPP) Payable.....................................	312.86	
	Cash		947.94
	To record the remittance of payroll liabilities to the Receiver General for Canada.		

The entry to record remittance to the hospital insurance plan authority is then:

March 11	Employment Hospital Insurance Payable	120.00	
	Cash		120.00
	To record the remittance of employees' hospital insurance premiums.		

Notice that the payment of payroll liabilities is recorded in the same manner as payment of any other liabilities.

Accruing Payroll Deductions on Wages

Mandatory payroll deductions are levied *only on wages actually paid.* Accrued wages are not subject to payroll deductions until they are paid. However, to satisfy the matching principle, both accrued wages and the related accrued deductions should be recorded at the end of an accounting period. In reality, because the amounts of such deductions vary little from one accounting period to the next and often are small in amount, many employers apply the materiality principle and do not accrue payroll deductions.

CHECKPOINT

7. When are the payments for employee deductions due to the Receiver General for Canada?

Do Quick Study questions: QS A-9, QS A-10

EMPLOYEE (FRINGE) BENEFIT COSTS

LO⁴ Calculate and record employee fringe benefit costs.

Many companies pay for a variety of benefits called **employee fringe benefits** in addition to the wages earned by employees and the related amounts paid by the employer. For example, an employer may pay for part (or all) of the employees' medical insurance, life insurance, and disability insurance. Another typical employee benefit involves employer contributions to a retirement income plan. Workers' compensation and vacation pay are required to be paid by employers according to the legislation in each province.

Workers' Compensation

Legislation is in effect in all provinces for payments to employees for an injury or disability arising out of or in the course of their employment. Under the provincial workers' compensation acts, employers are required to insure their employees against injury or disability that may arise as a result of employment. Premiums are normally based on (1) accident experience of the industrial classification to which each business is assigned and (2) the total payroll.

Procedures for payment are as follows:

---

1. At the beginning of each year, every covered employer is required to submit to the Workers' Compensation Board[2] an estimate of the expected payroll for the coming year.

2. Provisional premiums are then established by the board relating estimated requirements for disability payments to estimated payroll. Provisional premium notices are then sent to all employers.

3. Provisional premiums are normally payable in three to six installments during the year.

4. At the end of each year, actual payrolls are submitted to the board, and final assessments are made based on actual payrolls and actual payments. Premiums are normally between 1% and 3% of gross payroll and are borne by the employer.

Employer Contributions to Employee Insurance and Retirement Plans

The entries to record employee benefits costs depend on the nature of the benefit. Some employee retirement plans are quite complicated and involve accounting procedures that are too complex for discussion in this introductory course. In other cases, however, the employer simply makes periodic cash contributions to a retirement fund for each employee and records the amounts contributed as expense. Other employee benefits that require periodic cash payments by the employer include employer payments of insurance premiums for employees.

In the case of employee benefits that simply require the employer to make periodic cash payments, the entries to record the employer's obligations are similar to those used for payroll deductions.[3] For example, assume that an employer with five employees has agreed to pay medical insurance premiums of $40 per month for each employee. The employer will also contribute 10% of each employee's salary to a retirement program. If each employee earns $2,500 per month, the entry to record these employee benefits for the month of March is:

March 31	Benefits Expense	1,450	
	Employees' Medical Insurance Payable		200
	Employees' Retirement Program Payable		1,250
	To record employee benefits; *($2,500 × 5) × 10% = $1,250.*		

---

2 In Ontario, the Workers' Compensation Board is called the Workplace Safety and Insurance Board (WSIB). In BC, it is called WorkSafeBC.

3 Some payments of employee benefits must be added to the gross salary of the employee for the purpose of calculating income tax, CPP, and EI payroll deductions. However, in this chapter and in the problems at the end of the chapter, the possible effect of employee benefit costs on payroll taxes is ignored to avoid undue complexity in the introductory course.

Vacation Pay

Employers are required to allow their employees paid vacation time (at a minimum rate of 4% of gross earnings) as a benefit of employment. For example, many employees receive two weeks' vacation in return for working 50 weeks each year. The effect of a two-week vacation is to increase the employer's payroll expenses by 4% (2/50 = 0.04). After five years of service, most employees are entitled to a three-week vacation (i.e., 3/49 = 6.12%). However, new employees often do not begin to accrue vacation time until after they have worked for a period of time, perhaps as much as a year. The employment contract may say that no vacation is granted until the employee works one year, but if the first year is completed, the employee receives the full two weeks. Contracts between the employer and employee may allow for vacation pay in excess of the 4% minimum.

To account for vacation pay, an employer should estimate and record the additional expense during the weeks the employees are working and earning the vacation time. For example, assume that a company with a weekly payroll of $20,000 grants two weeks' vacation after one year's employment. The entry to record the estimated vacation pay is:

Date			
	Benefits Expense	800	
	Estimated Vacation Pay Liability.................		800
	To record estimated vacation pay;		
	$20,000 × 0.04 = $800.		

As employees take their vacations and receive their vacation pay, the entries to record the vacation payroll take the following general form:

Date			
	Estimated Vacation Pay Liability......................	xxx	
	EI and CPP (or QPP) Payable		xxx
	Employees' Income Taxes Payable.............		xxx
	Other Withholding Liability Accounts		
	Such as Employees' Hospital		
	Insurance Payable......................................		xxx
	Salaries Payable...		xxx
	To record payroll.		

Mandatory payroll deductions and employee benefits costs are often a major category of expense incurred by a company. They may amount to well over 25% of the salaries earned by employees.

CHECKPOINT

8. How is the cost of Workers' Compensation determined?

Do Quick Study question: QS A-11

CRITICAL THINKING CHALLENGE | Refer to the Critical Thinking Challenge questions at the beginning of the appendix. Compare your answers to those suggested on Connect.

SUMMARY

LO¹ Identify the taxes and other items frequently withheld from employees' wages. Amounts withheld from employees' wages include federal income taxes, Canada (or Quebec) Pension Plan (CPP or QPP), and Employment Insurance (EI). Payroll costs levied on employers include EI and CPP (or QPP).

An employee's gross pay may be the employee's specified wage rate multiplied by the total hours worked plus an overtime premium rate multiplied by the number of overtime hours worked. Alternatively, it may be the given periodic salary of the employee. Taxes withheld and other deductions for items such as union dues, insurance premiums, and charitable contributions are subtracted from gross pay to determine the net pay.

LO² Make the calculations necessary to prepare a payroll register and prepare the entries to record and pay payroll liabilities. A payroll register is used to summarize all employees' hours worked, regular and overtime pay, payroll deductions, net pay, and distribution of gross pay to expense accounts during each pay period. It provides the necessary information for journal entries to record the accrued payroll and to pay the employees.

LO³ Calculate the payroll costs levied on employers and prepare the entries to record the accrual and payment of these amounts. When a payroll is accrued at the end of each pay period, payroll deductions and levies should also be accrued with debits and credits to the appropriate expense and liability accounts.

LO⁴ Calculate and record employee fringe benefit costs. Fringe benefit costs that involve simple cash payments by the employer should be accrued with an entry similar to the one used to accrue payroll levies. Legislated employee benefits related to Workers' Compensation and vacation pay are paid for by the employer.

GUIDANCE ANSWER TO **DECISION MAKER**

Lawn Worker

You need to be concerned about being an accomplice to unlawful payroll activities. Not paying federal and provincial taxes on wages earned is unlawful and unethical. Such payments won't provide CPP and EI contributions. The best course of action is to request payment by cheque. If this fails to change the owner's payment practices, you must consider quitting this job.

GUIDANCE ANSWERS TO **CHECKPOINT**

1. Employment Insurance is designed to alleviate hardships caused by interruptions in earnings through unemployment.
2. On or before the last day in February.
3. Deductions for Canada Savings Bonds, health or life insurance premiums, loan repayments, and donations to charitable organizations.
4. Regular pay plus overtime pay.
5. Gross pay less all the deductions.
6. An employee's individual earnings record serves as a basis for the employer's tax returns, indicates when the maximum CPP (or QPP) and EI deductions have been reached, and supplies the data for the employees' T-4 slips.
7. Normally by the 15th of the following month; large employers must remit on the 10th and 25th of each month.
8. Premiums are based on the accident experience in the specific industry and on the size of the employer's payroll.

DEMONSTRATION PROBLEM

Presented below are various items of information about three part-time employees of the Saskatchewan Consulting Company for the week ending March 30, 2012.

	Billings	Dephir	Singe
Wage rate (per hour)...................................	$ 75.00	$ 60.00	$ 18.00
Overtime premium (when >40 hours).........	50%	50%	50%
Annual vacation	2.5 weeks	2.5 weeks	2.5 weeks
Cumulative wages as of March 30, 2012:....................................	$28,500.00	$52,600.00	$10,800.00
For the week (pay period) ended March 30, 2012:			
Hours worked......................................	8	22	48
Medical insurance:			
Employer's contribution....................	$ 25.00	$ 25.00	$ 25.00
Withheld from employee	18.00	18.00	18.00
Union dues withheld	50.00	70.00	50.00
Income tax withheld	86.40	321.05	185.60
Employment Insurance withheld	10.98	—	17.18
Canada Pension withheld....................	26.37	—	43.00
Payroll deduction rates:			
Employment Insurance	1.83% to an annual maximum of $839.97		
Canada Pension Plan	4.95% less annual exemption of $3,500; maximum per year is $2,306.70		

Required

In solving the following requirements, round all amounts to the nearest whole penny. Prepare schedules that determine, for each employee and for all employees combined, the following information:

1. Wages earned for the week, total overtime pay (if any), and gross wages.
2. Vacation pay accrued for the week.
3. Costs imposed on the employer.
4. Employees' net pay for the week.
5. Employer's total payroll-related cost (wages, mandatory deductions, and fringe benefits).

Present journal entries to record the following:

6. Payroll expense.
7. Payroll deductions and employees' benefits expense.
8. Remittance to the Receiver General for Canada on April 15.

Analysis Component:

What percentage of the total payroll-related cost to the employer represents deductions and fringe benefits versus gross pay? Round your answers to two decimal places.

Planning the Solution

- Calculate the gross pay for each employee.
- Calculate the amounts deducted for all employees and their net pay.
- Calculate the employer's share of payroll deductions.
- Prepare the necessary journal entries.
- Address the analysis component.

SOLUTION

1. The gross wages (including overtime) for the week:

	Billings	Dephir	Singe	Total
Regular wage rate	$ 75.00	$ 60.00	$ 18.00	
Regular hours...	× 8	× 22	× 48	
Regular pay...	$600.00	$1,320.00	$864.00	$2,784.00
Overtime premium..................................	$ 37.50	$ 30.00	$ 9.00	
Overtime hours..	-0-	× -0-	× 8	
Total overtime pay	$ -0-	$ -0-	$ 72.00	$ 72.00
Gross wages..	$600.00	$1,320.00	$936.00	$2,856.00

2. The vacation pay accrued for the week:

	Billings	Dephir	Singe	Total
Annual vacation	2.5 weeks	2.5 weeks	2.5 weeks	
Weeks worked in year........................	49.5 weeks	49.5 weeks	49.5 weeks	
Vacation pay as a percentage of regular pay	5.05%	5.05%	5.05%	
Regular pay this week........................	× $600.00	× $1,320.00	× $936.00	
Vacation pay this week	$ 30.30	$ 66.66	$ 47.27	$144.23

The information in the following table is needed for part 3:

			Earnings Subject to	
Employees	Earnings Through March 30	Earnings This Week	CPP	Employment Insurance
Billings	$28,500.00	$ 600.00	$ 532.69[3]	$ 600.00
Dephir[1]	52,600.00	1,320.00	—	—
Singe[2]	10,800.00	936.00	868.69[3]	936.00
Totals		$2,856.00	$1,402.00	$1,536.00

[1]Dephir's earnings have exceeded the CPP maximum of $50,100 and EI maximum of $45,900 and the maximum deductions of $2,306.70 (CPP) and $839.97 (EI). Therefore, neither CPP nor EI is deducted.
[2]Deductions would cease when the yearly maximum deduction of $839.97 was reached.
[3]Recall that the first $3,500 of income is exempt from CPP. This represents $67.31/week (= $3,500/52 weeks).

3. The costs imposed on the employer.

	Billings	Dephir	Singe	Total
CPP (1.0)	$26.37	—	$43.00	$ 69.37
Employment Insurance (1.4)	15.37	—	24.05	39.42
Totals	$41.74	—	$67.05	$108.79

4. The net amount paid to the employees:

	Billings	Dephir	Singe	Total
Regular pay	$600.00	$1,320.00	$864.00	$2,784.00
Overtime pay	-0-	-0-	72.00	72.00
Gross pay	$600.00	$1,320.00	$936.00	$2,856.00
Withholdings:				
Income tax withholding	$ 86.40	$ 321.05	$185.60	$ 593.05
CPP withholding	26.37	—	43.00	69.37
EI withholding	10.98	—	17.18	28.16
Medical insurance	18.00	18.00	18.00	54.00
Union dues	50.00	70.00	50.00	170.00
Total withholdings	$191.75	$ 409.05	$313.78	$ 914.58
Net pay to employees	$408.25	$ 910.95	$622.22	$1,941.42

5. The total payroll-related cost to the employer.

	Billings	Dephir	Singe	Total
Regular pay	$600.00	$1,320.00	$ 864.00	$2,784.00
Overtime pay	-0-	-0-	72.00	72.00
Gross pay	$600.00	$1,320.00	$ 936.00	$2,856.00
Deductions and fringe benefits:				
CPP	$ 26.37	$ —	$ 43.00	$ 69.37
EI	15.37	—	24.05	39.42
Vacation	30.30	66.66	47.27	144.23
Medical insurance	25.00	25.00	25.00	75.00
Total deductions and fringe benefits	$ 97.04	$ 91.66	$ 139.32	$ 328.02
Total payroll-related cost	$697.04	$1,411.66	$1,075.32	$3,184.02

6. Journal entry for payroll expense:

2012			
March 27	Salary Expense	2,856.00	
	Employees' Income Taxes Payable		593.05
	CPP Payable		69.37
	EI Payable		28.16
	Employees' Medical Insurance Payable		54.00
	Employees' Union Dues Payable		170.00
	Salaries Payable		1,941.42
	To record payroll expense.		

7. Journal entry for payroll deductions and employees' benefit expense:

2012			
March 27	CPP Expense	69.37	
	EI Expense	39.42	
	Benefits Expense	219.23	
	CPP Payable		69.37
	EI Payable		39.42
	Accrued Vacation Pay Payable		144.23
	Employees' Medical Insurance Payable		75.00
	To record employer's share of payroll deductions and benefits expense.		

8. Journal entry to record the remittance to the Receiver General for Canada:

	2012			
Apr.	15	EI Payable[1]	67.58	
		CPP Payable[2]	138.74	
		Employees' Income Taxes Payable...................	593.05	
		Cash		799.37
		Calculations:		
		1. $28.16 (Employees' Portion) + $39.42		
		(Employer's Portion) = $67.58		
		2. $69.37 (Employees' Portion) + $69.37		
		(Employer's Portion) = $138.74		

Analysis Component:

Deductions and fringe benefits represent 10.30% (= $328.02/$3,184.02) of total payroll-related costs, and gross pay is 89.70% (= $2,856.00/$3,184.02).

GLOSSARY

Canada Pension Plan A national contributory retirement pension scheme.

Employee fringe benefits Payments by an employer, in addition to wages and salaries, that are made to acquire employee benefits such as insurance coverage and retirement income.

Employee's gross pay The amount an employee earns before any deductions for taxes or other items such as union dues or insurance premiums.

Employee's individual earnings record A record of an employee's hours worked, gross pay, deductions, net pay, and certain personal information about the employee.

Employee's net pay The amount an employee is paid, determined by subtracting from gross pay all deductions for taxes and other items that are withheld from the employee's earnings.

Employment Insurance An employee/employer–financed unemployment insurance plan.

Payroll deductions Amounts deducted from an employee's pay, usually based on the amount of an employee's gross pay.

Personal tax credits Amounts that may be deducted from an individual's income taxes and that determine the amount of income taxes to be withheld.

TD1 A form, known as the Personal Tax Credit Return, that determines how much income tax is to be withheld by the employer based on the employee's exemptions.

Wage bracket withholding table A table showing the amounts to be withheld from employees' wages at various levels of earnings.

 Visit **Connect** for additional study tools, practice quizzes, to search an interactive eBook, and much more.

CONCEPT REVIEW QUESTIONS

1. Who pays the contributions to the Canada Pension Plan?

2. Who pays premiums under the Workers' Compensation laws?

3. Who pays federal Employment Insurance? What is the rate?

4. What are the objectives of Employment Insurance laws?

5. To whom and when are payroll deductions remitted?

6. What determines the amount that must be deducted from an employee's wages for income taxes?

7. What is a tax withholding table?

8. What is the Canada Pension Plan deduction rate for self-employed individuals?

9. What information is accumulated on an employee's individual earnings record? Why must this information be accumulated? For what purposes is the information used?

10. What payroll charges are levied on the employer? What amounts are deducted from the wages of an employee?

11. What are employee fringe benefits? Name some examples.

QUICK STUDY

QS A-1 Payroll expenses LO¹

A company deducts $260 in Employment Insurance and $205 in Canada Pension from the weekly payroll of its employees. How much is the company's expense for these items for the week?

QS A-2 Preparing payroll journal entries LO²

Tracon Co. has six employees, each of whom earns $3,000 per month. Income taxes are 20% of gross pay and the company deducts EI and CPP. Prepare the March 31 journal entry to record payroll for the month.

QS A-3 Paying employees LO²

Use the information in QS A-2 to record the payment of the wages to the employees for March.

QS A-4 Completing a payroll register LO²

	Deductions					Pay	Distribution	
Employee	Gross Pay	EI Premium	Income Taxes	CPP	Total Deductions	Net Pay	Office Salaries	Sales Salaries
Johnson, S.	1,200.00	21.96	266.95	56.07				
Waverley, N.	530.00	9.70	63.30	22.90				
Zender, B.	675.00	12.35	98.15	30.08				
Totals	2,405.00	44.01	428.40	109.05				

Required Prairie Rigging's three employees are paid weekly. Waverley works in the office and Johnson and Zender are sales representatives. Complete the payroll register above for the week ended March 9, 2012.

QS A-5 Completing a payroll register using tables LO²

	Deductions					Pay	
Employee	Gross Pay	EI Premium	Income Taxes	CPP	Total Deductions	Net Pay	Salaries Expense
Bentley, A.	2,010.00						
Craig, T.	2,115.00						
Totals	4,125.00						

Required Meadow Lake Groceries has two employees who are paid monthly. Using the tables at the end of the appendix, complete the payroll register above for the month ended March 31, 2012, assuming both employees' TD1 claim code is 1.

QS A-6 Completing a payroll register by calculating deductions LO²

	Deductions					Pay	Distribution	
Employee	Gross Pay	EI Premium	Income Taxes	CPP	Total Deductions	Net Pay	Office Salaries	Sales Salaries
Withers, S.	2,500.00						2,500.00	
Volt, C.	1,800.00							1,800.00
Totals								

Required Maidstone Plumbing Services' two employees are paid biweekly. Assuming a tax rate of 30%, complete the payroll register above for the two-week period ended February 24, 2012.

QS A-7 Payroll journal entry LO²

Racon Co. has eight employees, each of whom earns $3,500 per month. Income taxes are 20% of gross pay and the company deducts EI and CPP. Prepare the March 31, 2012, journal entry to record Racon's salaries expenses for the month.

QS A-8 Payroll journal entry LO²

Chandler Tailors pays its three part-time employees monthly. The following information is available for the February 2012 payroll:

| Employee | Deductions | | | | | Pay | Distribution | |
	Gross Pay	EI Premium	Income Taxes	CPP	Total Deductions	Net Pay	Office Salaries	Sales Salaries
Berkley, M.	575.00	10.52	0.00	14.03	24.55	550.45	575.00	
Cander, O.	840.00	15.37	0.00	27.14	42.51	797.49		840.00
Meister, P.	1,020.00	18.67	0.00	36.05	54.72	965.28		1,020.00
Totals	2,435.00	44.56	0.00	77.22	121.78	2,313.22	575.00	1,860.00

Required Prepare the journal entry to record payroll expenses for the month.

QS A-9 Recording employer's payroll deductions LO³

Refer to the information in QS A-8. Prepare a journal entry to record Chandler Tailors' share of payroll deductions.

QS A-10 Payment of payroll deductions LO³

Refer to the information in QS A-8 and QS A-9. Prepare a journal entry to record payment by Chandler Tailors to the Receiver General for Canada on March 15.

QS A-11 Recording fringe benefit costs LO⁴

Racon Co. (see QS A-7) contributes 8% of an employee's salary to a retirement program, pays medical insurance premiums of $60 per employee, and pays vacation allowance equivalent to 5% of the employee's salary. Prepare a journal entry to record the fringe benefit costs for March.

EXERCISES

CHECK FIGURE:
Net pay = $1,830.28

Exercise A-1 Calculating gross and net pay LO²

Julie Leung, an employee of the Import Company, worked 172 hours during the month of January 2012. Her pay rate is $12.50 per hour, and her wages are subject to no deductions other than income taxes, EI, and CPP. The overtime premium is 50% and is applicable to any time greater than 160 hours per month. Calculate her regular pay, overtime premium pay, gross pay, total deductions, and net pay. Use the tables at the end of the appendix to determine the EI, CPP, and income tax deductions (assume claim code 1).

CHECK FIGURE:
Total EI withholding = $70.64

Exercise A-2 Calculating payroll deductions and recording the payroll LO²

The following information as to earnings and deductions for the weekly pay period ended March 9 was taken from a company's payroll records:

Employees' Names	Weekly Gross Pay	Earnings to End of Previous Week	Income Taxes	Health Insurance Deductions
Hellena Chea.........	$ 720	$12,510	$115.50	$ 24.00
Joseph Lim	610	10,320	88.30	24.00
Dino Patelli	830	15,500	148.95	36.00
Sharl Qulnata........	1,700	29,500	460.70	24.00
	$3,860		$813.45	$108.00

Required Calculate the employees' EI and CPP withholdings, the amounts paid to each employee, and prepare a General Journal entry to record the payroll. Assume all employees work in the office.

Exercise A-3 Completing a payroll register LO²

Lendrum Servicing's four employees are paid every two weeks. Akerley runs the office and the remaining employees are sales representatives.

Employee	Gross Pay	EI Premium	Income Taxes	United Way	CPP	Total Deductions	Net Pay	Admin. Salaries	Sales Salaries
				Deductions			**Pay**	**Distribution**	
Akerley, D.	1,900.00	34.77	381.95	80.00	87.39				
Nesbitt, M.	1,260.00	23.06	187.95	50.00	55.71				
Trent, F.	1,680.00	30.74	304.85	40.00	76.50				
Vacon, M.	3,000.00	54.90	768.50	300.00	141.84				
Totals	7,840.00	143.47	1,643.25	470.00	361.44				

Required Complete the payroll register above for the biweekly period ended March 16, 2012.

Exercise A-4 Completing a payroll register using tables LO²

D&D Stockyards' four employees are paid monthly. Each employee donates 5% of gross pay to the United Way through payroll deductions. Crimson and Peterson purchase Canada Savings Bonds through monthly payroll deductions of $150 and $200 respectively.

Employee	Gross Pay	EI Premium	Income Taxes	Canada Savings Bonds	CPP	United Way	Total Deductions	Net Pay	Office Salaries	Sales Salaries
				Deductions				**Pay**	**Distribution**	
Crimson, L.	1,995.00								1,995.00	
Long, M.	2,040.00									2,040.00
Morris, P.	2,000.00									2,000.00
Peterson, B.	2,280.00									2,280.00
Totals										

Required Using the tables at the end of the appendix, complete the payroll register above for the monthly pay period ended February 29, 2012, assuming the following TD1 claim codes for each employee: Crimson (2), Long (1), Morris (1), and Peterson (3).

Exercise A-5 Completing a payroll register by calculating deductions LO²

Employee	Gross Pay	EI Premium	Income Taxes	Medical Ins.	CPP	United Way	Total Deductions	Net Pay	Office Salaries	Guide Salaries
				Deductions				**Pay**	**Distribution**	
Wynne, L.	1,200.00			65.00		40.00				1,200.00
Short, M.	950.00			65.00		100.00			950.00	
Pearl, P.	1,150.00			65.00		-0-				1,150.00
Quince, B.	875.00			65.00		50.00				875.00
Totals										

Required Piperel Lake Resort's four employees are paid weekly. Assume an income tax rate of 20%. Complete the payroll register above for the month ended January 31, 2012.

Exercise A-6 Other payroll deductions LO²

Sharon Von Hatton is the only employee of a self-employed businessperson. She earned a monthly salary of $2,050 in February 2012, her first month of employment. In response to a citywide effort to obtain charitable contributions to the local United Way programs, Von Hatton has requested that her employer withhold 2% of her salary (after CPP, EI, and income taxes have been deducted).

Required Prepare the journal entry to record payroll expenses for the month of February 2012. Use the tables at the end of the appendix to determine CPP, EI, and income tax deductions (assume claim code 1).

Exercise A-7 Payroll journal entry LO²

Paradise Hills Berry Farm has 25 employees who are paid biweekly. The payroll register showed the following payroll deductions for the pay period ending March 23, 2012.

Gross Pay	EI Premium	Income Taxes	CPP	Medical Ins.	United Way
65,950.00	1,207.00	9,095.00	3,097.93	1,150.00	1,319.00

Required Using the information provided, prepare the journal entry to record the payroll expenses.

Exercise A-8 Recording employer's payroll deductions LO³

Refer to the information in Exercise A-7. Prepare a journal entry to record the employer's share of payroll deductions.

Exercise A-9 Payment of payroll deductions LO³

Refer to the information in Exercise A-7 and Exercise A-8. Prepare a journal entry to record payment by the employer to the Receiver General for Canada on April 15.

Exercise A-10 Calculating and recording payroll deductions LO³,⁴

Use the information provided in Exercise A-2 to complete the following requirements:

1. Prepare a General Journal entry to record the employer's payroll costs resulting from the payroll.

2. Prepare a General Journal entry to record the following employee benefits incurred by the company: (a) health insurance costs equal to the amounts contributed by each employee and (b) contributions equal to 10% of gross pay for each employee's retirement income program.

CHECK FIGURE:
Total CPP
contributions
= $11,479.05

Exercise A-11 Analyzing total labour costs LO²,³,⁴

O'Riley Company's payroll costs and fringe benefit expenses include the normal CPP and EI contributions, retirement fund contributions of 10% of total earnings, and health insurance premiums of $120 per employee per month. Given the following list of employees' projected 2012 annual salaries, payroll costs and fringe benefits are what percentage of salaries?

Doherty	$ 52,000
Fane	61,000
Kahan	59,000
Martin...........................	49,000
Poon	76,000
Total	$297,000

Exercise A-12 Calculating and recording payroll costs (using tables) LO²,³,⁴

Milly's Drive-In's 12 employees earn a gross pay of $2,050 each per month. Milly's Drive-In contributes 8% of gross pay to a retirement program for employees and pays a medical insurance premium of $50 per month per employee.

Required Prepare the entries to record the employer's payroll costs for the month of March 2012. Use the tables at the end of the appendix to determine CPP, EI, and income tax deductions (assume claim code 1).

Exercise A-13 Calculating fringe benefits costs LO⁴

Bellward Company grants vacation time of two weeks to those employees who have worked for the company one complete year. After 10 years of service, employees receive four weeks of vacation. The monthly payroll for January totals $320,000, of which 70% is payable to employees with 10 or more years of service. On January 31, record the January expense arising from the vacation policy of the company. Round calculations to the nearest whole dollar.

PROBLEMS

CHECK FIGURE:
Total deductions
= $2,268.27

Problem A-1A Payroll register and payroll deductions LO^{2,3}

The payroll records of Brownlee Company provided the following information for the weekly pay period ended March 23, 2012:

												Payroll		
												Week Ended March 23, 2012		
Employees	**Employee No.**	**Daily Time**							**Pay Rate**	**Hospital Insurance**	**Union Dues**	**Earnings to End of Previous Week**		
		M	T	W	T	F	S	S						
Ray Loran	11	8	8	8	8	8	4	0	40.00	40.00	16.00	43,000		
Kathy Sousa	12	7	8	6	7	8	4	0	36.00	40.00	15.00	46,000		
Gary Smith	13	8	8	0	8	8	4	4	32.00	40.00	14.00	21,000		
Nicola Parton	14	8	8	8	8	8	0	0	40.00	40.00	16.00	32,000		
Diana Wood	15	0	6	6	6	6	8	8	36.00	40.00	15.00	36,000		
Totals										200.00	76.00			

Required

1. Enter the relevant information in the proper columns of a payroll register and complete the register; calculate CPP and EI deductions. Charge the wages of Kathy Sousa to Office Wages Expense and the wages of the remaining employees to Service Wages Expense. Calculate income tax deductions at 20% of gross pay. Employees are paid an overtime premium of 50% for all hours in excess of 40 per week.

2. Prepare General Journal entries to record the payroll register information, including the employer's expenses.

Problem A-2A Payroll register and journal entries LO^{2,3}

On January 13, at the end of the second weekly pay period of the year, a company's payroll register showed that its 30 employees had earned $19,570 of sales salaries and $6,230 of office salaries. Assume withholdings from the employees' salaries were to include $446.34 of EI, $1,177.14 of CPP, $5,310 of income taxes, $930 of hospital insurance, and $420 of union dues.

Required

1. Prepare the General Journal entry to record the January 13 payroll.

2. Prepare a General Journal entry to record the employer's payroll expenses resulting from the January 13 payroll.

Problem A-3A Journal entries—payroll taxes, and employee fringe benefits LO^{2,3,4}

A company showed the following information in its payroll register for the week ended March 16, 2012:

	Deductions					Payment		Distribution		
EI Premium	**Income Taxes**	**Medical Insurance**	**CPP**	**Union Dues**	**Total Deductions**	**Net Pay**	**Sales Salaries Expense**	**Office Salaries Expense**	**Shop Salaries Expense**	
21.96	265.40	47.50	44.96	90.00	469.82	730.18	1,200.00			
25.62	335.25	52.50	54.87	105.00	573.24	826.76			1,400.00	
31.11	441.00	25.00	69.71	127.50	694.32	1,005.68			1,700.00	
19.22	257.75	35.00	37.54	78.75	428.26	621.74		1,050.00		
97.91	**1,299.40**	**160.00**	**207.08**	**401.25**	**2,165.64**	**3,184.36**	**1,200.00**	**1,050.00**	**3,100.00**	

1. Prepare a General Journal entry to record the payroll register information.

2. Prepare a General Journal entry to record the employer's payroll expenses resulting from the payroll.

3. Prepare General Journal entries to accrue employee fringe benefit costs for the week. Assume that the company matches the employees' payments for medical insurance and contributes an amount equal to 8% of each employee's gross pay to a retirement program. Also, each employee accrues vacation pay at the rate of 6% of the wages and salaries earned. The company estimates that all employees eventually will be paid their vacation pay.

Problem A-4A Journal entries for payroll transactions LO^{2,3,4}

A company has three employees, each of whom has been employed since January 1, earns $2,600 per month, and is paid on the last day of each month. On March 1, the following accounts and balances appeared in its ledger.

a. Employees' Income Taxes Payable, $1,442.40 (liability for February).

b. EI Payable, $323.86 (liability for February).

c. CPP Payable, $685.58 (liability for February).

d. Employees' Medical Insurance Payable, $1,560.00 (liability for January and February).

During March and April, the company completed the following related to payroll.

| Mar. | 17 | Issued cheque #320 payable to the Receiver General for Canada. The cheque was in payment of the February employee income taxes, EI, and CPP amounts due. |
| | 31 | Prepared a General Journal entry to record the March payroll register, which had the following column totals: |

EI	Income Taxes	CPP	Medical Insurance	Total Deductions	Net Pay	Office Salaries	Shop Salaries
$142.74	$1,442.40	$357.23	$390.00	$2,332.37	$5,467.63	$2,600	$5,200

	31	Recorded the employer's $390.00 liability for its 50% contribution to the medical insurance plan of employees and 6% vacation pay accrued to the employees.
	31	Prepared a General Journal entry to record the employer's costs resulting from the March payroll.
Apr.	17	Issued cheque #375 payable to the Receiver General for Canada in payment of the March mandatory deductions.
	17	Issued cheque #376 payable to All Canadian Insurance Company in payment of the employee medical insurance premiums for the first quarter.

Required Prepare the entries to record the transactions.

ALTERNATE PROBLEMS

Problem A-1B Payroll register and payroll deductions LO[2,3]

The payroll records of Wailee Company provided the following information for the weekly pay period ended March 23, 2012:

												Payroll
												Week Ended March 23, 2012
Employees	**Employee No.**	**Daily Time**							**Pay Rate**	**Hospital Insurance**	**Union Dues**	**Earnings to End of Previous Week**
		M	T	W	T	F	S	S				
Ben Amoko	31	8	8	8	8	8	0	0	34.00	30.00	12.00	43,000
Auleen Carson	32	7	8	8	7	8	4	0	36.00	30.00	12.00	42,100
Mitali De	33	8	8	0	8	8	4	4	36.00	30.00	12.00	28,000
Gene Deszca	34	8	8	8	8	8	0	0	30.00	30.00	12.00	32,000
Ysong Tan	35	0	6	6	6	6	8	8	30.00	30.00	12.00	36,000
Totals										150.00	60.00	

Required

1. Enter the relevant information in the proper columns of a payroll register and complete the register; calculate CPP and EI deductions. Charge the wages of Auleen Carson to Office Wages Expense and the wages of the remaining employees to Service Wages Expense. Calculate income tax deductions at 20% of gross pay. Employees are paid an overtime premium of 50% for all hours in excess of 40 per week.

2. Prepare General Journal entries to record the payroll register information, including the employer's expenses.

Problem A-2B Payroll register and journal entries LO[2,3]

On January 13, at the end of the second weekly pay period of the year, a company's payroll register showed that its 45 employees had earned $23,400 of sales salaries and $5,820 of office salaries. Assume withholdings from the employees' salaries were to include $505.51 of EI, $1,296.46 of CPP, $6,180 of income taxes, $920 of hospital insurance, and $490 of union dues.

Required

1. Prepare the General Journal entry to record the January 13 payroll.

2. Prepare a General Journal entry to record the employer's payroll expenses resulting from the January 13 payroll.

Problem A-3B Journal entries—payroll taxes, and employee fringe benefits LO^{2,3,4}

A company showed the following information in its payroll register for the week ended March 16, 2012:

		Deductions				Payment		Distribution	
EI Premium	Income Taxes	Medical Insurance	CPP	Union Dues	Total Deductions	Net Pay	Sales Salaries Expense	Office Salaries Expense	Shop Salaries Expense
26.54	352.05	47.50	68.37	90.00	584.46	865.54	1,450.00		
36.23	552.05	52.50	94.61	105.00	840.39	1,139.61			1,980.00
32.21	464.65	25.00	83.72	127.50	733.08	1,026.92			1,760.00
31.48	450.85	35.00	81.74	78.75	677.82	1,042.18		1,720.00	
126.46	**1,819.60**	**160.00**	**328.44**	**401.25**	**2,835.75**	**4,074.25**	**1,450.00**	**1,720.00**	**3,740.00**

1. Prepare a General Journal entry to record the payroll register information.
2. Prepare a General Journal entry to record the employer's payroll expenses resulting from the payroll.
3. Prepare General Journal entries to accrue employee fringe benefit costs for the week. Assume that the company matches the employees' payments for medical insurance and contributes an amount equal to 8% of each employee's gross pay to a retirement program. Also, each employee accrues vacation pay at the rate of 6% of the wages and salaries earned. The company estimates that all employees eventually will be paid their vacation pay.

Problem A-4B Journal entries for payroll transactions LO^{2,3,4}

A company has three employees, each of whom has been employed since January 1, earns $2,600 per month, and is paid on the last day of each month. On March 1, the following accounts and balances appeared in its ledger.

a. Employees' Income Taxes Payable, $1,212.00 (liability for February).
b. EI Payable, $286.49 (liability for February).
c. CPP Payable, $595.58 (liability for February).
d. Employees' Medical Insurance Payable, $1,380.00 (liability for January and February).

During March and April, the company completed the following related to payroll:

Mar.   17   Issued cheque #635 payable to the Receiver General for Canada. The cheque was in payment of the February employee income taxes, EI, and CPP amounts due.

    31   Prepared a General Journal entry to record the March payroll register, which had the following column totals:

EI	Income Taxes	CPP	Medical Insurance	Total Deductions	Net Pay	Office Salaries	Shop Salaries
$126.27	$1,212.00	$341.55	$345.00	$2,024.82	$4,875.18	$2,300.00	$4,600.00

    31   Recorded the employer's $345.00 liability for its 50% contribution to the medical insurance plan of employees and 6% vacation pay accrued to the employees.

    31   Prepared a General Journal entry to record the employer's payroll costs resulting from the March payroll.

Apr.   14   Issued cheque #764 payable to the Receiver General for Canada in payment of the March mandatory deductions.

    14   Issued cheque #765 payable to National Insurance Company in payment of the employee medical insurance premiums for the first quarter.

Required Prepare the entries to record the transactions.

ANALYTICAL AND REVIEW PROBLEMS

A & R Problem A-1

Using the current year's withholding tables for Canada Pension Plan, Employment Insurance, and income tax, update the payroll register of Exhibit A.2. In calculating income tax withholdings, state your assumption as to each employee's personal deductions. Assume that hospital insurance deductions continue at the same amounts as in Exhibit A.2.

A & R Problem A-2

The following data were taken from the payroll register of Eastcoastal Company:

Gross Salary	xxx
Employees' Income Tax Deductions	xxx
EI Deductions	xxx
CPP Deductions	xxx
Hospital Insurance Deductions	xxx
Union Dues Deductions	xxx

Eastcoastal contributes an equal amount to the hospital insurance plan, in addition to the statutory payroll taxes, and 6% of the gross salaries to a pension retirement program.

Required Record in General Journal form the payroll, payment of the employees, and remittance to the appropriate persons amounts owing in connection with the payroll. (Note: All amounts are to be indicated as xxx.)

ETHICS CHALLENGE

EC A-1

Moe Daljit is the accountant for Valley Sales Company, which is currently experiencing a cash shortage because its Pacific Rim customers have not been paying their accounts on a timely basis. The owner has been unable to arrange adequate bank financing to cover the cash shortage and has suggested that Moe delay sending the amounts withheld from employees to the Receiver General for Canada for a few months, "until things clear up." Then he adds, "After all, we will be sending the money to the Receiver General eventually."

Required

1. What are the company's responsibilities with respect to amounts withheld from employees' wages and salaries?
2. What are the ethical factors in this situation?
3. Would you recommend that Moe follow the owner's "suggestion"?
4. What alternatives might be available to the owner if Moe does not delay sending the amounts to the Receiver General for Canada?

CRITICAL THINKING MINI CASE

Delta Yard Maintenance offers a variety of services to its customers, including lawn and garden care, tree pruning, exterior painting, fence building/installation, eavestrough cleaning, snow removal, and other miscellaneous tasks. Delta employs five full-time salaried individuals and 15 to 20 part-time wage employees. During the year just ended, $194,392 was paid in cash to the part-time employees "under the table," meaning that cash was paid to the employees and no payroll deductions were withheld. The part-time wage employees would not have paid income tax on the cash received because Delta would not have issued T4 slips. To cover up these payments, Delta claimed $194,392 in various other expenses that were not supported by documentation. You have just been hired by Delta as one of the five full-time individuals—the office manager. One of your many duties will be to keep the accounting records, including payroll.

Required Using the elements of critical thinking described on the inside front cover, comment.

Employment Insurance Premiums   ## Cotisations à l'assurance-emploi

Insurable Earnings Rémunération assurable From - De	To - À	EI premium Cotisation d'AE	Insurable Earnings Rémunération assurable From - De	To - À	EI premium Cotisation d'AE	Insurable Earnings Rémunération assurable From - De	To - À	EI premium Cotisation d'AE	Insurable Earnings Rémunération assurable From - De	To - À	EI premium Cotisation d'AE
1992.08	1992.62	36.46	2006.84	2007.37	36.73	2046.18	2046.72	37.45	2223.23	2223.77	40.69
1992.63	1993.16	36.47	2007.38	2007.92	36.74	2046.73	2047.26	37.46	2223.78	2224.31	40.70
1993.17	1993.71	36.48	2007.93	2008.46	36.75	2047.27	2047.81	37.47	2224.32	2224.86	40.71
1993.72	1994.26	36.49	2008.47	2009.01	36.76	2047.82	2048.36	37.48	2224.87	2225.40	40.72
1994.27	1994.80	36.50	2009.02	2009.56	36.77	2048.37	2048.90	37.49	2225.41	2225.95	40.73
1994.81	1995.35	36.51	2009.57	2010.10	36.78	2048.91	2049.45	37.50	2225.96	2226.50	40.74
1995.36	1995.90	36.52	2010.11	2010.65	36.79	2049.46	2049.99	37.51	2226.51	2227.04	40.75
1995.91	1996.44	36.53	2010.66	2011.20	36.80	2050.00	2050.54	37.52	2227.05	2227.59	40.76
1996.45	1996.99	36.54	2011.21	2011.74	36.81	2050.55	2051.09	37.53	2227.60	2228.14	40.77
1997.00	1997.54	36.55	2036.34	2036.88	37.27	2110.11	2110.65	38.62	2277.33	2277.86	41.68
1997.55	1998.08	36.56	2036.89	2037.43	37.28	2110.66	2111.20	38.63	2277.87	2278.41	41.69
1998.09	1998.63	36.57	2037.44	2037.97	37.29	2111.21	2111.74	38.64	2278.42	2278.96	41.70
1998.64	1999.18	36.58	2037.98	2038.52	37.30	2111.75	2112.29	38.65	2278.97	2279.50	41.71
1999.19	1999.72	36.59	2038.53	2039.07	37.31	2112.30	2112.84	38.66	2279.51	2280.05	41.72
1999.73	2000.27	36.60	2039.08	2039.61	37.32	2112.85	2113.38	38.67	2280.06	2280.60	41.73
2000.28	2000.81	36.61	2039.62	2040.16	37.33	2113.39	2113.93	38.68	2280.61	2281.14	41.74
2000.82	2001.36	36.62	2040.17	2040.71	37.34	2113.94	2114.48	38.69	2281.15	2281.69	41.75
2001.37	2001.91	36.63	2040.72	2041.25	37.35	2114.49	2115.02	38.70	2281.70	2282.24	41.76

Yearly maximum insurable earnings are $45,900
Yearly maximum employee premiums are $839.97
The premium rate for 2012 is 1.83%

Le maximum annuel de la rémunération assurable est de 45 900 $
La cotisation maximale annuelle de l'employé est de 839,97 $
Le taux de cotisation pour 2012 est de 1,83 %

Canada Pension Plan Contributions
Monthly (12 pay periods a year)

Cotisations au Régime de pensions du Canada
Mensuel (12 périodes de paie par année)

Pay Rémunération From - De	To - À	CPP RPC	Pay Rémunération From - De	To - À	CPP RPC	Pay Rémunération From - De	To - À	CPP RPC	Pay Rémunération From - De	To - À	CPP RPC
1993.38	1993.57	84.24	2009.75	2009.94	85.05	2049.75	2049.94	87.03	2224.29	2224.48	95.67
1993.58	1993.78	84.25	2009.95	2010.14	85.06	2049.95	2050.14	87.04	2224.49	2224.69	95.68
1993.79	1993.98	84.26	2010.15	2010.34	85.07	2050.15	2050.34	87.05	2224.70	2224.89	95.69
1993.99	1994.18	84.27	2010.35	2010.54	85.08	2050.35	2050.54	87.06	2224.90	2225.09	95.70
1994.19	1994.38	84.28	2010.55	2010.75	85.09	2050.55	2050.75	87.07	2225.10	2225.29	95.71
1994.39	1994.58	84.29	2010.76	2010.95	85.10	2050.76	2050.95	87.08	2225.30	2225.49	95.72
1994.59	1994.79	84.30	2010.96	2011.15	85.11	2050.96	2051.15	87.09	2225.50	2225.70	95.73
1994.80	1994.99	84.31	2011.16	2011.35	85.12	2051.16	2051.35	87.10	2225.71	2225.90	95.74
1995.00	1995.19	84.32	2011.36	2011.55	85.13	2051.36	2051.55	87.11	2225.91	2226.10	95.75
1998.84	1999.03	84.51	2038.84	2039.03	86.49	2113.38	2113.57	90.18	2278.84	2279.03	98.37
1999.04	1999.23	84.52	2039.04	2039.23	86.50	2113.58	2113.78	90.19	2279.04	2279.23	98.38
1999.24	1999.43	84.53	2039.24	2039.43	86.51	2113.79	2113.98	90.20	2279.24	2279.43	98.39
1999.44	1999.63	84.54	2039.44	2039.63	86.52	2113.99	2114.18	90.21	2279.44	2279.63	98.40
1999.64	1999.84	84.55	2039.64	2039.84	86.53	2114.19	2114.38	90.22	2279.64	2279.84	98.41
1999.85	2000.04	84.56	2039.85	2040.04	86.54	2114.39	2114.58	90.23	2279.85	2280.04	98.42
2000.05	2000.24	84.57	2040.05	2040.24	86.55	2114.59	2114.79	90.24	2280.05	2280.24	98.43
2000.25	2000.44	84.58	2040.25	2040.44	86.56	2114.80	2114.99	90.25	2280.25	2280.44	98.44
2000.45	2000.64	84.59	2040.45	2040.64	86.57	2115.00	2115.19	90.26	2280.45	2280.64	98.45

Employee's maximum CPP contribution for the year 2012 is $2,306.70

La cotisation maximale de l'employé au RPC pour l'année 2012 est de 2 306,70 $

Federal tax deductions
Effective January 1, 2012
Monthly (12 pay periods a year)
**Also look up the tax deductions
in the provincial table**

Retenues d'impôt fédéral
En vigueur le 1er janvier 2012
Mensuel (12 périodes de paie par année)
**Cherchez aussi les retenues d'impôt
dans la table provinciale**

Pay Rémunération		Federal claim codes/Codes de demande fédéraux										
From–Less than De–Moins de		0	1	2	3	4	5	6	7	8	9	10
		Deduct from each pay / Retenez sur chaque paie										
1933 - 1951		260.05	124.75	111.85	86.00	60.15	34.30	8.45				
1951 - 1969		262.55	127.25	114.35	88.50	62.65	36.80	10.95				
1969 - 1987		265.05	129.80	116.85	91.00	65.15	39.30	13.45				
1987 - 2005		267.60	132.30	119.40	93.55	67.70	41.85	16.00				
2005 - 2023		270.10	134.80	121.90	96.05	70.20	44.35	18.50				
2023 - 2041		272.60	137.35	124.40	98.55	72.70	46.85	21.00				
2041 - 2059		275.15	139.85	126.95	101.10	75.25	49.40	23.55				
2059 - 2077		277.65	142.35	129.45	103.60	77.75	51.90	26.05	.20			
2077 - 2095		280.15	144.90	131.95	106.10	80.25	54.40	28.55	2.70			
2095 - 2113		282.70	147.40	134.50	108.65	82.80	56.95	31.10	5.25			
2113 - 2131		285.20	149.90	137.00	111.15	85.30	59.45	33.60	7.75			
2131 - 2149		287.70	152.45	139.50	113.65	87.80	61.95	36.10	10.25			
2149 - 2167		290.25	154.95	142.05	116.20	90.35	64.50	38.65	12.80			
2167 - 2185		292.75	157.45	144.55	118.70	92.85	67.00	41.15	15.30			
2185 - 2203		295.25	160.00	147.05	121.20	95.35	69.50	43.65	17.80			
2203 - 2221		297.80	162.50	149.60	123.75	97.90	72.05	46.20	20.35			
2221 - 2239		300.30	165.00	152.10	126.25	100.40	74.55	48.70	22.85			
2239 - 2257		302.80	167.55	154.60	128.75	102.90	77.05	51.20	25.35			
2257 - 2275		305.35	170.05	157.15	131.30	105.45	79.60	53.75	27.90	2.05		
2275 - 2293		307.85	172.55	159.65	133.80	107.95	82.10	56.25	30.40	4.55		

Saskatchewan provincial tax deductions
Effective January 1, 2012
Monthly (12 pay periods a year)
**Also look up the tax deductions
in the federal table**

Retenues d'impôt provincial de la Saskatchewan
En vigueur le 1er janvier 2012
Mensuel (12 périodes de paie par année)
**Cherchez aussi les retenues d'impôt
dans la table fédérale**

Pay Rémunération		Provincial claim codes/Codes de demande provinciaux										
From–Less than De–Moins de		0	1	2	3	4	5	6	7	8	9	10
		Deduct from each pay / Retenez sur chaque paie										
1933 - 1951		200.75	63.75	54.95	37.30	19.70	2.05					
1951 - 1969		202.55	65.60	56.80	39.15	21.55	3.90					
1969 - 1987		204.40	67.45	58.65	41.00	23.40	5.75					
1987 - 2005		206.25	69.30	60.50	42.85	25.20	7.60					
2005 - 2023		208.10	71.15	62.35	44.70	27.05	9.45					
2023 - 2041		209.95	73.00	64.15	46.55	28.90	11.30					
2041 - 2059		211.80	74.85	66.00	48.40	30.75	13.15					
2059 - 2077		213.65	76.70	67.85	50.25	32.60	15.00					
2077 - 2095		215.50	78.50	69.70	52.10	34.45	16.85					
2095 - 2113		217.35	80.35	71.55	53.95	36.30	18.65	1.05				
2113 - 2131		219.20	82.20	73.40	55.75	38.15	20.50	2.90				
2131 - 2149		221.05	84.05	75.25	57.60	40.00	22.35	4.75				
2149 - 2167		222.85	85.90	77.10	59.45	41.85	24.20	6.60				
2167 - 2185		224.70	87.75	78.95	61.30	43.70	26.05	8.45				
2185 - 2203		226.55	89.60	80.80	63.15	45.55	27.90	10.25				
2203 - 2221		228.40	91.45	82.65	65.00	47.35	29.75	12.10				
2221 - 2239		230.25	93.30	84.45	66.85	49.20	31.60	13.95				
2239 - 2257		232.10	95.15	86.30	68.70	51.05	33.45	15.80				
2257 - 2275		233.95	97.00	88.15	70.55	52.90	35.30	17.65	.05			
2275 - 2293		235.80	98.85	90.00	72.40	54.75	37.15	19.50	1.85			

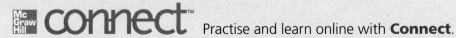

Practise and learn online with **Connect**.

II

Financial Statement Information

This appendix includes financial statement information from (a) Danier Leather Inc. and (b) WestJet Airlines Ltd. All of this information is taken from their annual reports. An **annual report** is a summary of the financial results of a company's operations for the year and its future plans. It is directed at external users of financial information, but also affects actions of internal users.

An annual report is also used by a company to showcase itself and its products. Many include attractive pictures, diagrams, and illustrations related to the company. But the *financial section* is its primary objective. This section communicates much information about a company, with most data drawn from the accounting information system.

The layout of each annual report's financial section that is included in this appendix is:

- Management's Report
- Auditor's Report
- Financial Statements
- Notes to Financial Statements

This appendix is organized as follows:

- Danier
- WestJet

There are questions at the end of each chapter that refer to information in this appendix. We encourage readers to spend extra time with these questions as they are especially useful in reinforcing and showing the relevance and diversity of financial reporting.

More current financial information about these and other Canadian corporations can be found online at: www.sedar.com.

ANNUAL REPORT 2011

DANIER

MANAGEMENT'S RESPONSIBILITY FOR FINANCIAL STATEMENTS

The accompanying financial statements and other financial information contained in this Annual Report are the responsibility of management. The financial statements have been prepared in conformity with Canadian generally accepted accounting principles using management's best estimates and judgments based on currently available information, where appropriate. The financial information contained elsewhere in this Annual Report has been reviewed to ensure consistency with that in the financial statements.

Management is also responsible for a system of internal controls which is designed to provide reasonable assurance that assets are safeguarded, liabilities are recognized and that financial records are properly maintained to provide timely and accurate financial reports.

The Board of Directors is responsible for ensuring that management fulfills its responsibility in respect of financial reporting and internal control. The Audit Committee of the Board, which is comprised solely of unrelated and outside directors, meets regularly to review significant accounting and auditing matters with management and the independent auditors and to review the interim and annual financial statements.

The financial statements have been audited by PricewaterhouseCoopers LLP, the independent auditors, in accordance with Canadian generally accepted auditing standards on behalf of the shareholders. The Auditors' Report outlines the nature of their examination and their opinion on the financial statements. PricewaterhouseCoopers LLP have full and unrestricted access to the Audit Committee to discuss their audit and related findings as to the integrity of the financial reporting.

Jeffrey Wortsman
President and CEO

Bryan Tatoff, C.A.
Senior Vice-President, CFO and Secretary

INDEPENDENT AUDITOR'S REPORT TO SHAREHOLDERS

To the Shareholders of Danier Leather Inc.

We have audited the accompanying consolidated financial statements of Danier Leather Inc. and its subsidiaries, which comprise the consolidated balance sheets as at June 25, 2011 and June 26, 2010 and the consolidated statements of net earnings and comprehensive earnings, cash flow, and changes in shareholders' equity for the 52-week periods then ended, and the related notes, which comprise a summary of significant accounting policies and other explanatory information.

Management's responsibility for the consolidated financial statements
Management is responsible for the preparation and fair presentation of these consolidated financial statements in accordance with Canadian generally accepted accounting principles, and for such internal control as management determines is necessary to enable the preparation of consolidated financial statements that are free from material misstatement, whether due to fraud or error.

Auditor's responsibility
Our responsibility is to express an opinion on these consolidated financial statements based on our audits. We conducted our audits in accordance with Canadian generally accepted auditing standards. Those standards require that we comply with ethical requirements and plan and perform the audit to obtain reasonable assurance about whether the consolidated financial statements are free from material misstatement.

An audit involves performing procedures to obtain audit evidence about the amounts and disclosures in the consolidated financial statements. The procedures selected depend on the auditor's judgment, including the assessment of the risks of material misstatement of the consolidated financial statements, whether due to fraud or error. In making those risk assessments, the auditor considers internal control relevant to the entity's preparation and fair presentation of the consolidated financial statements in order to design audit procedures that are appropriate in the circumstances, but not for the purpose of expressing an opinion on the effectiveness of the entity's internal control. An audit also includes evaluating the appropriateness of accounting policies used and the reasonableness of accounting estimates made by management, as well as evaluating the overall presentation of the consolidated financial statements.

We believe that the audit evidence we have obtained in our audits is sufficient and appropriate to provide a basis for our audit opinion.

Opinion
In our opinion, the consolidated financial statements present fairly, in all material respects, the financial position of Danier Leather Inc. and its subsidiaries as of June 25, 2011 and June 26, 2010 and the results of their operations and their cash flows for the years then ended in accordance with Canadian generally accepted accounting principles.

PricewaterhouseCoopers LLP
Chartered Accountants, Licensed Public Accountants
Toronto, Ontario August 10, 2011

CONSOLIDATED FINANCIAL STATEMENTS

For The Years Ended June 25, 2011 And June 26, 2010

CONSOLIDATED STATEMENTS OF NET EARNINGS AND COMPREHENSIVE EARNINGS (thousands of dollars, except per share amounts)

	Years Ended	
	June 25, 2011	June 26, 2010
Revenue	$ 157,621	$ 164,217
Cost of sales (Note 7)	71,333	77,438
Gross profit	86,288	86,779
Selling, general and administrative expenses (Note 7)	75,500	75,867
Interest (income) expense - net	(57)	116
Restructuring costs (Note 8)	-	(153)
Earnings before income taxes	10,845	10,949
Provision for income taxes (Note 9)		
Current	3,101	3,714
Future	106	16
	3,207	3,730
Net earnings and comprehensive earnings	**$7,638**	**$7,219**
Net earnings per share:		
Basic	$1.63	$1.30
Diluted	$1.57	$1.28
Weighted average number of shares outstanding:		
Basic	4,673,944	5,545,918
Diluted	4,880,010	5,638,389
Number of shares outstanding at period end	4,678,135	4,568,169

See accompanying notes to the consolidated financial statements.

CONSOLIDATED BALANCE SHEETS (thousands of dollars)

	June 25, 2011	June 26, 2010
ASSETS		
Current Assets		
Cash	$ 28,698	$ 26,563
Accounts receivable	385	543
Inventories (Note 2)	28,964	26,539
Prepaid expenses	901	1,140
Future income tax asset (Note 9)	422	456
	59,370	55,241
Other Assets		
Property and equipment (Note 3)	15,061	16,349
Intangible assets (Note 4)	1,054	1,417
Future income tax asset (Note 9)	992	1,064
	$ 76,477	$ 74,071
LIABILITIES		
Current Liabilities		
Accounts payable and accrued liabilities	$ 12,217	$ 14,005
Income taxes payable	278	3,900
	12,495	17,905
Deferred lease inducements and rent liability	1,318	1,345
	13,813	19,250
SHAREHOLDERS' EQUITY		
Share capital (Note 6)	15,160	14,176
Contributed surplus	898	1,106
Retained earnings	46,606	39,539
	62,664	54,821
	$ 76,477	$ 74,071

CONTINGENCIES & GUARANTEES (Note 11)

See accompanying notes to the consolidated financial statements.

Approved by the Board

Edwin F. Hawken, Director

Jeffrey Wortsman, Director

CONSOLIDATED STATEMENTS OF CASH FLOW (thousands of dollars)

	Years Ended	
	June 25, 2011	June 26, 2010
OPERATING ACTIVITIES		
Net earnings	$7,638	$7,219
Items not affecting cash:		
Amortization of property and equipment	3,518	3,677
Amortization of intangible assets	523	568
Amortization of deferred lease inducements	(213)	(234)
Straight line rent expense	31	89
Stock-based compensation	203	302
Future income taxes	106	16
Net change in non-cash working capital items (Note 10)	(7,438)	2,265
Proceeds from deferred lease inducements	155	101
Cash flows from operating activities	**4,523**	**14,003**
FINANCING ACTIVITIES		
Subordinate voting shares issued (Note 6)	902	37
Subordinate voting shares repurchased (Note 6)	(900)	(9,433)
Cash flows from (used in) financing activities	**2**	**(9,396)**
INVESTING ACTIVITIES		
Acquisition of property and equipment	(2,230)	(2,415)
Acquisition of intangible assets	(160)	(257)
Cash flows used in investing activities	**(2,390)**	**(2,672)**
Increase in cash	2,135	1,935
Cash, beginning of period	26,563	24,628
Cash, end of period	**$28,698**	**$26,563**
Supplementary cash flow information:		
Interest paid	218	13
Income taxes paid	6,961	67

See accompanying notes to the consolidated financial statements.

CONSOLIDATED STATEMENTS OF CHANGES IN SHARESHOLDERS' EQUITY
(thousands of dollars)

	Years Ended	
	June 25, 2011	June 26, 2010
SHARE CAPITAL		
Balance, beginning of period	$14,176	$19,853
Shares repurchased	(329)	(5,733)
Shares issued on exercise of stock options	1,313	56
Balance, end of period	**$15,160**	**$14,176**
CONTRIBUTED SURPLUS		
Balance, beginning of period	$1,106	$823
Stock-based compensation related to stock options	203	302
Exercise of stock options	(411)	(19)
Balance, end of period	**$898**	**$1,106**
RETAINED EARNINGS		
Balance, beginning of period	$39,539	$36,020
Net earnings	7,638	7,219
Share repurchases	(571)	(3,700)
Balance, end of period	**$46,606**	**$39,539**
ACCUMULATED OTHER COMPREHENSIVE INCOME		
Balance, beginning of period	$-	$-
Balance, end of period	**$-**	**$-**
TOTAL SHAREHOLDERS' EQUITY	**$62,664**	**$54,821**

See accompanying notes to the consolidated financial statements.

NOTES TO CONSOLIDATED FINANCIAL STATEMENTS

For the Years Ended June 25, 2011 and June 26, 2010

(dollar amounts in thousands except per share amounts and where otherwise indicated)

Danier Leather Inc. ("Danier" or the "Company") is a corporation existing under the *Business Corporations Act (Ontario)* and is a vertically integrated designer, manufacturer, distributor and retailer of leather apparel and accessories.

NOTE 1: SUMMARY OF SIGNIFICANT ACCOUNTING POLICIES

The consolidated financial statements have been prepared in accordance with Canadian generally accepted accounting principles ("GAAP").

(a) Basis of consolidation:

The consolidated financial statements include the accounts of the Company and its wholly-owned subsidiary companies. On consolidation, all intercompany transactions and balances have been eliminated.

(b) Year-end:

The fiscal year end of the Company consists of a 52 or 53 week period ending on the last Saturday in June each year. The fiscal year for the consolidated financial statements presented is the 52-week period ended June 25, 2011, and comparably, the 52-week period ended June 26, 2010.

(c) Revenue recognition:

Revenue includes sales of merchandise, alteration services and gift cards to customers through stores operated by the Company and sales of incentive and promotional product merchandise to a third party distributor. Revenue is measured at the fair value of consideration received, net of estimated returns and discounts. The Company bases its estimates on historical results and the type of transaction.

Sales of merchandise to customers through stores operated by the Company is recorded net of returns and discounts and is recognized when the significant risks and rewards of ownership have been transferred to the buyer, which is the time the transaction is entered into the point-of-sale register.

Alteration revenue is recorded based on the percentage of completion method. Due to alteration revenue representing less than one percent of merchandise revenue, the short time required to complete an alteration and the fact that at any point in time there is an immaterial amount of partially processed alterations, alteration revenue is recorded at the same time the sale of merchandise transaction is entered into the point-of-sale register.

Sales to a third party distributor are recorded when the significant risks and rewards of ownership have been transferred to the buyer which is at the time of shipment.

Revenue from gift cards is recognized at the time of redemption. When a customer purchases a gift card, a liability is recorded based on the dollar value of the gift card purchased. Unredeemed balances on gift cards that are more than three years old from the date of issuance (or "breakage") are recorded in the consolidated statement of earnings. Historically, breakage has not been material.

(d) Cash:

Cash consists of cash on hand, bank balances and money market investments with maturities of three months or less.

(e) Inventories:

Merchandise inventories are valued at the lower of cost, using the weighted average cost method, and net realizable value. For inventories manufactured by the Company, cost includes direct labour, raw materials, manufacturing and distribution centre costs related to inventories and transportation costs that are directly incurred to bring inventories to their present location and condition. For inventories purchased from third party vendors, cost includes the cost of purchase, duty and brokerage, quality assurance costs, distribution centre costs related to inventories and transportation costs that are directly incurred to bring inventories to their present location and condition. The Company estimates the net realizable value as the amount at which inventories are expected to be sold, taking into account fluctuations in retail prices due to seasonality, less estimated costs necessary to make the sale. Inventories are written down to net realizable value when the cost of inventories is not estimated to be recoverable due to obsolescence, damage or declining selling prices. When circumstances that previously caused inventories to be written down below cost no longer exist, the amount of the write-down previously recorded is reversed. Storage costs, administrative overheads and selling costs related to the inventories are expensed in the period the costs are incurred.

f) Property and equipment:

Property and equipment are recorded at cost and annual amortization is provided at the following rates:

Building...4% declining balance
Furniture and equipment.....................................20% declining balance
Computer hardware ....30% declining balance

Leasehold improvements are amortized on a straight line basis over the term of the lease, unless the Company has decided to terminate the lease, at which time the unamortized balance is written off.

Property and equipment are reviewed for recoverability whenever events indicate an impairment may exist. An impairment loss is measured as the amount by which the carrying value of an asset or a group of assets exceeds its fair value. If such assets or group of assets are considered impaired, an impairment loss is recognized and the carrying value of the asset is adjusted.

g) Intangible assets:

Intangible assets consist of computer software and annual amortization is provided at a rate of 30% declining balance.

h) Deferred lease inducements and rent liability:

Deferred lease inducements represent cash benefits received from landlords pursuant to store lease agreements. These lease inducements are amortized against rent expense over the term of the lease, not exceeding 10.5 years.

Rent liability represents the difference between minimum rent as specified in the lease and rent calculated on a straight line basis.

i) Income taxes:

Income taxes are determined using the asset and liability method of accounting. This method recognizes future tax assets and liabilities that arise from differences between the accounting basis of the Company's assets and liabilities and their corresponding tax basis. Future taxes are measured at the balance sheet date using the enacted or substantially enacted income tax rates and laws that are expected to apply when the asset is realized or the liability settled. The Company provides a valuation allowance for future tax assets when it is more likely than not that some or all of the future tax assets will not be realized.

j) Earnings per share:

Basic earnings per share is calculated by dividing the net earnings available to shareholders by the weighted average number of shares outstanding during the year (see Note 6). Diluted earnings per share is calculated using the treasury stock method, which assumes that all outstanding stock options with an exercise price below the average monthly market price of the Subordinate Voting Shares on the Toronto Stock Exchange (the "TSX") are exercised and the assumed proceeds are used to purchase the Company's Subordinate Voting Shares at the average monthly market price on the TSX during the fiscal year.

k) Translation of foreign currencies:

Accounts in foreign currencies are translated into Canadian dollars. Monetary balance sheet items are translated at the rates of exchange in effect at year-end and non-monetary items are translated at historical exchange rates. Revenues and expenses are translated at the rates in effect on the transaction dates or at the average rates of exchange for the reporting period. The resulting net gain or loss is included in the consolidated statement of earnings (loss).

l) Financial instruments:

Financial instruments are recognized depending on their classification with changes in subsequent measurements being recognized in net earnings or other comprehensive income. The Company's financial assets and liabilities are classified as follows:

Cash is classified as "held-for-trading" and is measured at fair value. This financial asset is marked-to-market through net earnings and recorded as interest income at each period end.

Accounts receivable are classified as "loans and receivables" and are recorded at cost, which at initial measurement corresponds to fair value. After their initial fair value measurement, they are measured at amortized cost using the effective interest method.

Accounts payable and accrued liabilities and bank indebtedness are classified as "other liabilities". They are initially measured at fair value and subsequent revaluations are recorded at amortized cost using the effective interest method.

Transaction costs other than those related to financial instruments classified as held-for-trading, which are expensed as incurred, are amortized using the effective interest method.

Foreign currency option contracts, which are included in either accounts receivable or accounts payable and accrued liabilities, have been classified as held-for-trading and are measured at fair value. Fair value estimates are made at a specific point in time, using published price quotations or other available information where published price quotations are not available. These estimates are subjective in nature and involve uncertainties and the exercise of significant judgment.

Embedded derivatives (elements of contracts whose cash flows move independently from the host contract) are required to be separated and measured at fair values if certain criteria are met.

m) Stock option plan:

The Company has a Stock Option Plan which is described in Note 6 where options to purchase Subordinate Voting Shares are issued to directors, officers, employees and service providers. Effective with the commencement of its 2004 fiscal year, the Company accounts for stock-based compensation using the fair-value method. The fair value of options granted are estimated at the date of grant using the Black-Scholes Option Pricing Model and is recognized as an expense over the vesting period of the stock option with an offsetting credit to contributed surplus. When stock options are subsequently exercised, share capital is increased by the sum of the consideration paid together with the related portion previously added to contributed surplus when compensation costs were charged against income. The Company continues to use settlement accounting to account for stock options granted prior to June 29, 2003.

n) Restricted Share Units and Deferred Share Units:

The Company has Restricted Share Unit ("RSU") and Deferred Share Unit ("DSU") Plans, which are described in Note 6. RSUs and DSUs are settled in cash and are recorded as liabilities. The measurement of the compensation expense and corresponding liability for these awards is based on the fair value of the award, and is recorded as a charge to selling, general and administrative ("SG&A") expenses over the vesting period of the award. At the end of each financial period, changes in the Company's payment obligation due to changes in the market value of the Subordinate Voting Shares on the TSX are recorded as a charge to SG&A expenses. Dividend equivalent grants, if any, are recorded as a charge to SG&A expenses in the period the dividend is paid.

o) Use of estimates:

The preparation of financial statements in conformity with Canadian GAAP requires management to make estimates and assumptions that affect the reported amounts of assets and liabilities and disclosure of contingent assets and liabilities in the consolidated financial statements and the reported amounts of revenues and expenses during the reporting period. Estimates and assumptions are based on management's historical experience, best knowledge of current events and actions that the Company may undertake in the future. Illiquid credit markets, volatile equity and foreign currency markets and declines in consumer spending have combined to increase the uncertainty inherent in such estimates and assumptions. Significant areas requiring the use of management estimates relate to the determination of inventory valuation, realizable value of property and equipment and intangible assets, stock based compensation, future tax assets, harmonized sales tax, goods and services tax, provincial sales tax, gift card breakage and income tax provisions. By their nature, these estimates are subject to measurement uncertainty and the impact on the consolidated financial statements of future periods could differ materially from those estimated.

p) Comparative figures:

Certain amounts included in the June 26, 2010 comparative figures were reclassified to conform with the current year's financial statement presentation. Reclassification of these amounts had no effect on previously reported shareholders' equity or net earnings.

NOTE 2: INVENTORIES

	June 25, 2011	June 26, 2010
Raw materials	$ 2,655	$ 1,451
Work-in-process	265	105
Finished goods	26,044	24,983
	$ 28,964	$ 26,539

	June 25, 2011	June 26, 2010
Cost of inventory recognized as an expense	$70,420	$76,473
Write-downs of inventory due to net realizable value being lower than cost	$1,549	$2,267
Write-downs recognized in previous periods that were reversed	$45	$25

NOTE 3: PROPERTY AND EQUIPMENT

	June 25, 2011			June 26, 2010		
	Cost	Accumulated Amortization	Net Book Value	Cost	Accumulated Amortization	Net Book Value
Land	$ 1,000	$ -	$ 1,000	$ 1,000	$ -	$ 1,000
Building	7,124	2,571	4,553	7,064	2,380	4,684
Leasehold improvements	23,453	17,681	5,772	23,574	16,700	6,874
Furniture and equipment	8,984	6,203	2,781	8,504	5,671	2,833
Computer hardware	3,180	2,225	955	3,110	2,152	958
	$ 43,741	$ 28,680	$ 15,061	$ 43,252	$ 26,903	$ 16,349

NOTE 4: INTANGIBLE ASSETS

Intangible assets consist of computer software.

	June 25, 2011	June 26, 2010
Cost	$ 4,041	$ 4,169
Accumulated amortization	2,987	2,752
Net book value	$ 1,054	$ 1,417

NOTE 5: BANK FACILITIES

The Company has an operating credit facility for working capital and for general corporate purposes to a maximum amount of $25 million that is committed until June 27, 2014 and bears interest at prime plus 0.75%. Standby fees of 0.50% are paid on a quarterly basis for any unused portion of the operating credit facility. The operating credit facility is subject to certain covenants and other limitations that, if breached, could cause a default and may result in a requirement for immediate repayment of amounts outstanding. Security provided includes a security interest over all personal property of the Company's business and a mortgage over the land and building comprising the Company's head office/distribution facility.

The Company also has an uncommitted letter of credit facility (the "LC Facility") to a maximum amount of $10 million ($14 million between September 1, 2011 and December 15, 2011) and an uncommitted demand overdraft facility in the amount of $0.5 million to be used exclusively for issuance of letters of credit for the purchase of inventory. Any amounts outstanding under the overdraft facility will bear interest at the bank's prime rate. The LC Facility is secured by the Company's personal property from time to time financed with the proceeds drawn thereunder.

NOTE 6: SHARE CAPITAL

(a) Authorized

1,224,329 Multiple Voting Shares
Unlimited Subordinate Voting Shares
Unlimited Class A and B Preference Shares

(b) Issued

Multiple Voting Shares

	Number	Consideration
Balance June 27, 2009	1,224,329	Nominal
Balance June 26, 2010	1,224,329	Nominal
Balance June 25, 2011	1,224,329	Nominal

Subordinate Voting Shares

	Number	Consideration
Balance June 27, 2009	4,684,940	$ 19,853
Shares repurchased	(1,352,700)	(5,733)
Shares issued upon exercising of stock options	11,600	56
Balance June 26, 2010	3,343,840	$ 14,176
Shares repurchased	(75,000)	(329)
Shares issued upon exercising of stock options	184,966	1,313
Balance June 25, 2011	3,453,806	$ 15,160

The Multiple Voting Shares and Subordinate Voting Shares have identical attributes except that the Multiple Voting Shares entitle the holder to ten votes per share and the Subordinate Voting Shares entitle the holder to one vote per share. Each Multiple Voting Share is convertible at any time, at the holder's option, into one fully paid and non-assessable Subordinate Voting Share. The Multiple Voting Shares are subject to provisions whereby, if a triggering event occurs, then each Multiple Voting Share is converted into one fully paid and non-assessable Subordinate Voting Share. A triggering event may occur if, among other things, Mr. Jeffrey Wortsman, President and Chief Executive Officer: (i) dies; (ii) ceases to be a Senior Officer of the Company; (iii) ceases to own 5% or more of the aggregate number of Multiple Voting Shares and Subordinate Voting Shares outstanding; or (iv) owns less than 918,247 Multiple Voting Shares and Subordinate Voting Shares combined.

(c) Earnings per share

Basic and diluted per share amounts are based on the following weighted average number of shares outstanding:

	June 25, 2011	June 26, 2010
Weighted average number of shares for basic earnings per share calculations	4,673,944	5,545,918
Effect of dilutive options outstanding	206,066	92,471
Weighted average number of shares for diluted earnings per share calculations	4,880,010	5,638,389

The computation of dilutive options outstanding only includes those options having exercise prices below the average market price of Subordinate Voting Shares on the TSX during the period. The number of options excluded was 58,000 as at June 25, 2011 and 115,000 as at June 26, 2010.

(d) Substantial Issuer Bid and Normal Course Issuer Bids

During the past several years, the Company has received approval from the TSX to commence various normal course issuer bids ("NCIBs"). On May 5, 2011, the Company received approval from the TSX to commence its fifth normal course issuer bid (the "2011 NCIB"). The Company's previous normal course issuer bid expired on May 6, 2011 (the "2010 NCIB"). The 2011 NCIB permits the Company to acquire up to 176,440 Subordinate Voting Shares, representing approximately 5% of the Company's issued and outstanding Subordinate Voting Shares at the date of acceptance of the notice of intention in respect of the 2011 NCIB filed with the TSX, during the period from May 9, 2011 to May 8, 2012, or such earlier date as the Company may complete its purchases under the 2011 NCIB. During the fourth quarter of fiscal 2011, the Company repurchased 75,000 Subordinate Voting Shares for cancellation at a weighted average price of $12.00 per share under the 2011 NCIB. During the fourth quarter of fiscal 2010, the Company repurchased 232,700 Subordinate Voting Shares for cancellation at a weighted average price of $8.49 per share under the 2010 NCIB.

On January 29, 2010, the Company commenced a substantial issuer bid ("SIB" or the "Offer") by filing and mailing a formal offer to purchase and accompanying circular dated January 26, 2010, pursuant to which the Company offered to purchase for cancellation up to $7 million in value of its Subordinate Voting Shares from shareholders by way of a modified "Dutch Auction" at a range of Offer prices between $6.10 and $6.45 per share. The minimum and maximum Offer prices corresponded with the fair market range of values per Subordinate Voting Share determined, as of January 20, 2010, by Deloitte and Touche LLP, the independent valuator engaged by the Special Committee of independent directors of the Board of Directors to prepare a formal valuation of the Subordinate Voting Shares. The Offer expired on March 8, 2010 and a total of 1,845,592 Subordinate Voting Shares were validly deposited and not withdrawn under the Offer. As the aggregate value of Subordinate Voting Shares deposited under the Offer exceeded the $7 million maximum value of consideration payable by the Company pursuant to the Offer, a pro-ration factor of 0.6088 was applied to deposited Subordinate Voting Shares (except for odd lot deposits, which were not subject to pro-ration), and the Company purchased for cancellation 1,120,000 Subordinate Voting Shares at a price of $6.25 per share.

The following Subordinate Voting Shares were repurchased for cancellation under the SIB and NCIBs then in effect during the years ended June 25, 2011 and June 26, 2010, respectively:

	June 25, 2011	June 26, 2010
Number of shares repurchased under SIB	-	1,120,000
Number of shares repurchased under NCIBs	75,000	232,700
Amount charged to share capital	$329	$5,733
Amount charged to retained earnings representing the excess over the average paid-in value	$571	$3,700
Total cash consideration	$900	$9,433

(e) Stock option plan

The Company maintains a Stock Option Plan, as amended, for the benefit of directors, officers, employees and service providers, pursuant to which granted options are exercisable for Subordinate Voting Shares. As at June 25, 2011, the Company has reserved 638,934 Subordinate Voting Shares for issuance under its Stock Option Plan. The granting of options and the related vesting periods are at the discretion of the Board of Directors, on the advice of the Governance, Compensation, Human Resources and Nominating Committee of the Board (the "Committee"), at exercise prices determined as the weighted average of the trading prices of the Company's Subordinate Voting Shares on the TSX for the five trading days preceding the effective date of the grant. In general, options granted under the Stock Option Plan vest over a period of one year from the grant date for options issued to directors and between two years and four years from the grant date for options issued to officers, employees and service providers, and expire no later than the tenth anniversary of the date of grant (subject to extension in accordance with the Stock Option Plan if the options would otherwise expire during a blackout period).

A summary of the status of the Company's Stock Option Plan as of June 25, 2011 and June 26, 2010 and changes during the fiscal years ended on those dates is presented below:

	June 25, 2011		June 26, 2010	
Stock Options	Shares	Weighted Average Exercise Price	Shares	Weighted Average Exercise Price
Outstanding at beginning of year	553,400	$6.19	577,000	$6.13
Granted	-	-	-	-
Exercised	(184,966)	$4.87	(11,600)	$3.15
Forfeited	(20,000)	$10.40	(12,000)	$6.02
Outstanding at end of year	348,434	$6.65	553,400	$6.19
Options exercisable at end of year	238,429	$8.25	324,641	$8.18

The following table summarizes the distribution of these options and the remaining contractual life as at June 25, 2011:

	Options Outstanding			Options Exercisable	
Exercise Prices	Outstanding #	Weighted Average Remaining Contractual Life	Weighted Average Exercise Price	# of Shares Exercisable	Weighted Average Exercise Price
$3.15	169,767	7.4 years	$3.15	66,429	$3.15
$3.97	6,667	7.9 years	$3.97	-	$3.97
$6.25	50,000	7.0 years	$6.25	50,000	$6.25
$7.80	45,000	5.6 years	$7.80	45,000	$7.80
$8.68	15,000	5.9 years	$8.68	15,000	$8.68
$10.96	4,000	2.1 years	$10.96	4,000	$10.96
$15.85	58,000	1.1 years	$15.85	58,000	$15.85
	348,434	6.0 years	$6.65	238,429	$8.25

During the years ended June 25, 2011 and June 26, 2010, there were no stock options granted.

The compensation expense recorded for the year ended June 25, 2011 in respect of stock options was $203 (June 26, 2010 - $302). The counterpart is recorded as contributed surplus. Any consideration paid by optionees upon the exercise of stock options is credited to share capital.

(f) Deferred Share Unit Plan

The DSU Plan, as amended, was established by the Company for non-management directors. Under this Plan, non-management directors of the Company may receive an annual grant of DSUs and can also elect to receive their annual retainers and meeting fees in DSUs. A DSU is a notional unit equivalent in value to one Subordinate Voting Share of the Company based on the five-day average trading price of the Company's Subordinate Voting Shares on the TSX immediately prior to the date on which the value of the DSU is determined.

After retirement from the Board of Directors, a participant in the DSU Plan receives a cash payment equal to the market value of the accumulated DSUs in their account. The value of the DSU liability is adjusted to reflect changes in the market value of the Company's Subordinate Voting Shares on the TSX.

The following transactions occurred with respect to the DSU Plan during years ended June 25, 2011 and June 26, 2010, respectively:

	June 25, 2011	June 26, 2010
Outstanding at beginning of period	103,920	78,920
Granted	-	25,000
Redeemed	-	-
Outstanding at end of period	103,920	103,920
Danier stock price at end of period	$11.00	$8.86
Liability at end of period	$1,143	$921
Compensation expense recorded in SG&A	$222	$546

(g) Restricted Share Unit Plan

The Company established a RSU Plan, as amended, as part of its overall compensation plan. The RSU Plan is administered by the Board of Directors, with the advice of the Committee. Under this plan, certain eligible participating employees and directors of the Company are eligible to receive a grant of RSUs that vest over periods not exceeding three years as determined by the Committee. An RSU is a notional unit equivalent in value to one Subordinate Voting Share of the Company based on the average of the daily closing price of the Subordinate Voting Shares on the TSX for the last five consecutive trading days immediately preceding the payment date. Upon the exercise of the vested RSUs, a cash payment equal to the market value of the exercised vested RSUs will be paid to the participant. The value of the vested RSU liability is adjusted to reflect changes in the market value of the Company's Subordinate Voting Shares on the TSX.

The following transactions occurred with respect to the RSU Plan during the years ended June 25, 2011 and June 26, 2010, respectively:

	June 25, 2011	June 26, 2010
Outstanding at beginning of period	105,479	133,300
Granted	122,300	
Redeemed	(104,479)	(27,821)
Forfeited	(1,000)	-
Outstanding at end of period	122,300	105,479
RSU vested at end of period	-	93,355
Liability at end of period	$411	$836
Compensation expense recorded in SG&A	$973	$597

NOTE 7: AMORTIZATION

Amortization included in cost of sales and SG&A is summarized as follows:

	June 25, 2011	June 26, 2010
Cost of sales	$226	$183
SG&A	3,815	4,062
	$4,041	$4,245

NOTE 8: RESTRUCTURING COSTS

Restructuring costs of approximately $1,466 were originally recorded during fiscal 2009 and represented severance costs in connection with the Toronto manufacturing facility workforce reduction of approximately 56 employees and head office staff reduction of more than 20 employees. Approximately $1,313 of the restructuring costs were paid during fiscal 2009 and $153 of restructuring costs were reversed during fiscal 2010 as these costs are not expected to be incurred as all severances have been paid.

NOTE 9: INCOME TAXES

Future income tax asset is summarized as follows:

	June 25, 2011	June 26, 2010
Amortization	$ 655	$ 710
Deferred lease inducements and rent liability	337	354
Stock based compensation	422	456
	$ 1,414	$ 1,520

The Company's effective income tax rate consists of the following:

	June 25, 2011	June 26, 2010
Combined basic federal and provincial average statutory rate	29.1%	31.5%
Non-deductible expenses	0.9%	1.3%
Future federal and provincial rate changes	0.2%	1.1%
Other	(0.6%)	0.2%
	29.6%	34.1%

NOTE 10: CHANGES IN NON-CASH OPERATING WORKING CAPITAL ITEMS

	June 25, 2011	June 26, 2010
Decrease (increase) in:		
Accounts receivable	$158	($192)
Income taxes recoverable	-	631
Inventories	(2,425)	(5,494)
Prepaid expenses	239	16
Increase (decrease) in:		
Accounts payable and accrued liabilities	(1,788)	3,404
Income taxes payable	(3,622)	3,900
	($7,438)	$2,265

NOTE 11: CONTINGENCIES & GUARANTEES

(a) Legal proceedings

In the course of its business, the Company from time to time becomes involved in various claims and legal proceedings. In the opinion of management, all such claims and suits are adequately covered by insurance, or if not so covered, the results are not expected to materially affect the Company's financial position.

(b) Guarantees

The Company has provided the following guarantees to third parties and no amounts have been accrued in the consolidated financial statements for these guarantees:

(i) In the ordinary course of business, the Company has agreed to indemnify its lenders under its credit facilities against certain costs or losses resulting from changes in laws and regulations or from a default in repaying a borrowing. These indemnifications extend for the term of the credit facilities and do not provide any limit on the maximum potential liability. Historically, the Company has not made any indemnification payments under such agreements.

(ii) In the ordinary course of business, the Company has provided indemnification commitments to certain counterparties in matters such as real estate leasing transactions, director and officer indemnification agreements and certain purchases of non-inventory assets and services. These indemnification agreements generally require the Company to compensate the counterparties for costs or losses resulting from legal action brought against the counterparties related to the actions of the Company. The terms of these indemnification agreements will vary based on the contract and generally do not provide any limit on the maximum potential liability.

(iii) The Company sublet one location during the first quarter of fiscal 2011 and provided the landlord with a guarantee in the event the sub-tenant defaults on its obligations under the lease. The guarantee terminates at the time of lease expiry, which is March 31, 2013, and the Company's maximum exposure is approximately $246.

NOTE 12: COMMITMENTS

(a) Operating leases:

Minimum rentals for the next five fiscal years and thereafter, excluding rentals based upon revenue are as follows:

2012	$9,879
2013	$7,889
2014	$6,460
2015	$4,568
2016	$3,325
Thereafter	$8,595

(b) Letters of credit:

The Company had outstanding letters of credit in the amount of $11,827 (June 26, 2010 - $11,118) for the importation of finished goods inventories to be received.

NOTE 13: FINANCIAL INSTRUMENTS

(a) Fair value disclosure

The following table presents the carrying amount and the fair value of the Company's financial instruments.

| | Maturity | June 25, 2011 | | June 26, 2010 | |
		Carrying value	Fair value	Carrying value	Fair value
Cash	Short-term	$28,698	$28,698	$26,563	$26,563
Accounts receivable	Short-term	$385	$385	$435	$435
Accounts payable and accrued liabilities	Short-term	$12,077	$12,077	$14,005	$14,005
Derivative financial instruments(1)	Short-term	($140)	($140)	$108	$108

(1) Included in accounts payable and accrued liabilities for the fiscal year ended June 25, 2011 and included in accounts receivable for the fiscal year ended June 26, 2010.

The fair value of a financial instrument is the estimated amount that the Company would receive or pay to settle the financial assets and financial liabilities as at the reporting date. These estimates are subjective in nature, often involve uncertainties and the exercise of significant judgment and are made at a specific point in time, using available information about the financial instrument and may not reflect fair value in the future. The estimated fair value amounts can be materially affected by the use of different assumptions or methodologies.

The methods and assumption used in estimating the fair value of the Company's financial instruments are as follows:

- The derivative financial instruments, which consist of foreign exchange collar contracts, have been marked-to-market and are categorized as Level 2 in the fair value hierarchy. Factors included in the determination of fair value include the spot rate, forward rates, estimates of volatility, present value factor, strike prices, credit risk of the Company and credit risk of counterparties. As at June 25, 2011, a $140 loss (June 26, 2010 - $108 gain) was recorded in SG&A for the contracts outstanding at year-end.

- The fair value of cash is determined using Level 2 inputs in the fair value hierarchy which include interest rates for similar instruments which are obtained from independent publications and market exchanges.

- Given their short-term maturity, the fair value of cash, accounts receivable and accounts payable and accrued liabilities approximates their carrying values.

(b) Financial instrument risk management

Exposure to foreign currency risk, interest rate risk, equity price risk, liquidity risk and credit risk arise in the normal course of the Company's business and are discussed further below:

Foreign Currency Risk

Foreign currency risk is the risk that the fair value or future cash flows of a financial instrument will fluctuate because of changes in foreign currency exchange rates. The Company purchases a significant portion of its leather and finished goods inventory from foreign vendors with payment terms in U.S. dollars. The Company uses a combination of foreign exchange option contracts and spot purchases to manage its foreign exchange exposure on cash flows related to these purchases. A foreign exchange option contract represents an option with a counterparty to buy or sell a foreign currency to meet its obligations. Credit risk exists in the event of failure by a counterparty to fulfill its obligations. The Company reduces this risk by dealing only with highly-rated counterparties such as major Canadian financial institutions.

Outstanding foreign exchange option contracts as at June 25, 2011 included contracts with notional amounts of US$18,500 expiring between July 15, 2011 and December 16, 2011. As at June 26, 2010, there were outstanding foreign exchange option contracts with notional amounts of US$15,000 that expired between July 2, 2010 and December 6, 2010.

As at June 25, 2011, a sensitivity analysis was performed on the Company's U.S. dollar denominated financial instruments which principally consist of US$0.5 million of cash to determine how a change in the U.S. dollar exchange rate would impact net earnings. A 500 basis point rise or fall in the Canadian dollar against the U.S. dollar, assuming that all other variables, in particular interest rates, remained the same, would have resulted in a $19 decrease or increase, respectively, in the Company's net earnings for the year ended June 25, 2011.

Interest Rate Risk

Interest rate risk is the risk that the fair value or future cash flows of a financial instrument will fluctuate because of changes in market interest rates. The Company's exposure to interest rate fluctuations is primarily related to cash borrowings under its existing credit facility which bears interest at floating rates and interest earned on its cash balances. The Company has performed a sensitivity analysis on interest rate risk as at June 25, 2011, to determine how a change in interest rates would have impacted net earnings. As at June 25, 2011, the Company's cash balance available for investment was approximately $28.7 million and an increase or decrease of 100 basis points in interest rates would have increased or decreased net earnings by approximately $0.2 million. This analysis assumes that all other variables, in particular foreign currency rates, remain constant.

Equity Price Risk

Equity price risk is the risk that the fair value or future cash flows of a financial instrument will fluctuate because of changes in market equity prices. The Company's exposure to equity price fluctuations is primarily related to the RSU and DSU liability included in accounts payable and accrued liabilities. The value of the vested DSU and RSU liability is adjusted to reflect changes in the market value of the Company's Subordinate Voting Shares on the TSX. The Company has performed a sensitivity analysis on equity price risk as at June 25, 2011 to determine how a change in the price of the Company's Subordinate Voting Shares would have impacted net earnings. As at June 25, 2011, a total of 122,300 RSUs and 103,920 DSUs have been granted and are outstanding. An increase or decrease of $1.00 in the market price of the Company's Subordinate Voting Shares would have increased or decreased net earnings by approximately $0.2 million. This analysis assumes that all RSUs and DSUs were fully vested and other variables remain constant.

Liquidity Risk

Liquidity risk is the risk that the Company will not be able to meet its financial obligations as they become due. The Company's approach to managing liquidity risk is to ensure, to the extent possible, that it will have sufficient liquidity to meet its liabilities when due. As at June 25, 2011, the Company had $28.7 million of cash; an operating credit facility of $25 million that is committed until June 27, 2014; and a $10 million ($14 million between September 1, 2011 and December 15, 2011) uncommitted letter of credit facility which includes an uncommitted demand overdraft facility in the amount of $0.5 million related thereto. The credit facilities are used to finance seasonal working capital requirements for merchandise purchases and other corporate purposes. The Company expects that the majority of its accounts payable and accrued liabilities will be discharged within 90 days.

Credit Risk

Credit risk is the risk that a customer or counterparty to a financial instrument will cause a financial loss to the Company by failing to meet its obligations. The Company's financial instruments that are exposed to concentrations of credit risk are primarily cash (which includes cash and money market investments with maturities of three months or less), accounts receivable and foreign exchange option contracts. The Company limits its exposure to credit risk with respect to cash and money market investments by investing in short-term deposits and bankers' acceptances with major Canadian financial institutions and Government of Canada treasury bills. The Company's accounts receivable consist primarily of credit card receivables from the last few days of the fiscal period end, which are settled within the first few days of the new fiscal period. Accounts receivable also consist of accounts receivable from distributors and corporate customers. Accounts receivable are net of applicable allowance for doubtful accounts, which is established based on the specific credit risks associated with the distributor, each corporate customer and other relevant information. The allowance for doubtful accounts is assessed on a quarterly basis. Concentration of credit risk with respect to accounts receivable from distributors and corporate customers is limited due to the relatively insignificant balances outstanding.

As at June 25, 2011, the Company's exposure to credit risk for these financial instruments was cash of $28.7 million and accounts receivable of $0.4 million. Cash included $24.1 million of short-term deposits.

NOTE 14: CAPITAL DISCLOSURE

The Company defines its capital as shareholders' equity. The Company's objectives in managing capital are to:

- Ensure sufficient liquidity to support its current operations and execute its business plans;
- Enable the internal financing of capital projects; and
- Maintain a strong capital base so as to maintain investor, creditor and market confidence.

The Company's primary uses of capital are to finance non-cash working capital along with capital expenditures for new store additions, existing store renovation or relocation projects, information technology software and hardware purchases and production machinery and equipment purchases. The Company maintains a $25 million operating credit facility and a $10 million ($14 million between September 1, 2011 and December 15, 2011) uncommitted letter of credit facility that it uses to finance seasonal working capital requirements for merchandise purchases and other corporate purposes. The Company does not have any long-term debt and therefore net earnings generated from operations are available for reinvestment in the Company. The Board of Directors does not establish quantitative return on capital criteria for management, but rather promotes year-over-year sustainable profitable growth. On a quarterly basis, the Board of Directors monitors share repurchase program activities. Decisions on whether to repurchase shares are made on a specific transaction basis and depend on the Company's cash position, estimates of future cash requirements, market prices and regulatory restrictions. The Company does not currently pay dividends.

Externally imposed capital requirements include a debt-to-equity ratio covenant as part of the operating credit facility. The Company was in compliance with this covenant as at June 25, 2011 and June 26, 2010. There has been no change with respect to the overall capital risk management strategy during the year ended June 25, 2011.

NOTE 15: SEGMENTED INFORMATION

Management has determined that the Company operates in one dominant industry which involves the design, manufacture, distribution and retail of fashion leather clothing and accessories.

Expanding Our Reach

WestJet Annual Report 2011

WESTJET

MANAGEMENT'S REPORT TO THE SHAREHOLDERS

The consolidated financial statements have been prepared by management in accordance with International Financial Reporting Standards. When a choice between accounting methods exists, management has chosen those they deem conservative and appropriate in the circumstances. Financial statements will, by necessity, include certain amounts based on estimates and judgments. Management has determined such amounts on a reasonable basis so that the consolidated financial statements are presented fairly in all material respects. All information in this report is the responsibility of management.

Management has established systems of internal control, including disclosure controls and procedures and internal controls over financial reporting, which are designed and operated to provide reasonable assurance that financial and non-financial information that is disclosed is timely, complete, relevant and accurate. These systems of internal control also serve to safeguard the Corporation's assets. The systems of internal control are monitored by management, and further supported by an internal audit department whose functions include reviewing internal controls and their applications.

The Board of Directors is responsible for the overall stewardship and governance of the Corporation, including ensuring management fulfills its responsibility for financial reporting and internal control, and reviewing and approving the consolidated financial statements. The Board carries out this responsibility principally through its Audit Committee.

The Audit Committee of the Board of Directors, composed of independent Directors, meets regularly with management, the internal auditors and the external auditors to satisfy itself that each is properly discharging its responsibilities, and to review the consolidated financial statements and management's discussion and analysis. The Audit Committee reports its findings to the Board of Directors prior to the approval of such statements for issuance to the shareholders. The Audit Committee also recommends, for review by the Board of Directors and approval of shareholders, the reappointment of the external auditors. The internal and external auditors have full and free access to the Audit Committee.

The consolidated financial statements have been audited by KPMG LLP, the independent external auditors, in accordance with Canadian generally accepted auditing standards on behalf of the shareholders. The auditors' report outlines the scope of their examination and sets forth their opinion.

Gregg Saretsky

President and
Chief Executive Officer

Vito Culmone

Executive Vice-President, Finance and
Chief Financial Officer

Calgary, Canada
February 7, 2012

INDEPENDENT AUDITORS' REPORT

To the Shareholders of WestJet Airlines Ltd.

We have audited the accompanying consolidated financial statements of WestJet Airlines Ltd., which comprise the consolidated statements of financial position as at December 31, 2011, December 31, 2010 and January 1, 2010, the consolidated statement of earnings, other comprehensive income, changes in equity and cash flows for the years ended December 31, 2011 and December 31, 2010, and notes, comprising a summary of significant accounting policies and other explanatory information.

Management's Responsibility for the Consolidated Financial Statements

Management is responsible for the preparation and fair presentation of these consolidated financial statements in accordance with International Financial Reporting Standards, and for such internal control as management determines is necessary to enable the preparation of consolidated financial statements that are free from material misstatement, whether due to fraud or error.

Auditors' Responsibility

Our responsibility is to express an opinion on these consolidated financial statements based on our audits. We conducted our audits in accordance with Canadian generally accepted auditing standards. Those standards require that we comply with ethical requirements and plan and perform the audit to obtain reasonable assurance about whether the consolidated financial statements are free from material misstatement.

An audit involves performing procedures to obtain audit evidence about the amounts and disclosures in the consolidated financial statements. The procedures selected depend on our judgment, including the assessment of the risks of material misstatement of the consolidated financial statements, whether due to fraud or error. In making those risk assessments, we consider internal controls relevant to the entity's preparation and fair presentation of the consolidated financial statements in order to design audit procedures that are appropriate in the circumstances, but not for the purpose of expressing an opinion on the effectiveness of the entity's internal controls. An audit also includes evaluating the appropriateness of accounting policies used and the reasonableness of accounting estimates made by management, as well as evaluating the overall presentation of the consolidated financial statements.

We believe that the audit evidence we have obtained in our audits is sufficient and appropriate to provide a basis for our audit opinion.

Opinion

In our opinion, the consolidated financial statements present fairly, in all material respects, the consolidated financial position of WestJet Airlines Ltd. as at December 31, 2011, December 31, 2010 and January 1, 2010, and its consolidated financial performance and its consolidated cash flows for the years then ended in accordance with International Financial Reporting Standards.

KPMG LLP

Chartered Accountants

Calgary, Canada

February 7, 2012

Consolidated Statement of Earnings
For the years ended December 31
(Stated in thousands of Canadian dollars, except per share amounts)

	Note	2011	2010
Revenues:			
Guest		2,790,299	2,390,887
Other		281,241	216,407
		3,071,540	2,607,294
Expenses:			
Aircraft fuel		915,878	674,608
Airport operations		421,561	388,112
Flight operations and navigational charges		344,442	325,582
Sales and distribution		273,364	255,732
Marketing, general and administration		209,880	194,481
Depreciation and amortization		174,751	170,462
Aircraft leasing		165,571	143,381
Maintenance		146,260	117,057
Inflight		139,478	124,303
Employee profit share		23,804	22,222
		2,814,989	2,415,940
Earnings from operations		256,551	191,354
Non-operating income (expense):			
Finance income	16	15,987	9,910
Finance costs	16	(60,911)	(70,914)
Gain on foreign exchange		2,485	2,579
(Loss) gain on disposal of property and equipment		(54)	570
Loss on derivatives		(6,052)	(34)
		(48,545)	(57,889)
Earnings before income tax		208,006	133,465
Income tax expense:	12		
Current		1,236	1,573
Deferred		58,068	41,695
		59,304	43,268
Net earnings		148,702	90,197
Earnings per share:	15		
Basic		1.06	0.62
Diluted		1.06	0.62

The accompanying notes are an integral part of the consolidated financial statements.

Consolidated Statement of Financial Position
(Stated in thousands of Canadian dollars)

	Note	December 31 2011	December 31 2010	January 1 2010
Assets				
Current assets:				
Cash and cash equivalents	5	1,243,605	1,159,316	994,989
Restricted cash	6	48,341	28,583	10,192
Accounts receivable	20	34,122	17,518	27,654
Prepaid expenses, deposits and other	20	66,936	53,761	64,868
Inventory	20	31,695	26,095	31,505
		1,424,699	1,285,273	1,129,208
Non-current assets:				
Property and equipment	7	1,911,227	1,989,522	2,108,351
Intangible assets	8	33,793	13,018	14,087
Other assets	20	103,959	96,167	98,451
Total assets		3,473,678	3,383,980	3,350,097
Liabilities and shareholders' equity				
Current liabilities:				
Accounts payable and accrued liabilities	20	307,279	287,710	228,911
Advance ticket sales	20	432,186	336,926	297,720
Non-refundable guest credits	20	43,485	36,381	63,164
Current portion of long-term debt	10	158,832	178,337	165,111
Current portion of obligations under finance leases	11	75	108	744
		941,857	839,462	755,650
Non-current liabilities:				
Maintenance provisions	9	151,645	113,206	97,722
Long-term debt	10	669,880	848,465	1,028,165
Obligations under finance leases	11	3,174	3,249	3,358
Other liabilities	20	10,449	8,958	9,517
Deferred income tax	12	326,456	266,407	223,509
Total liabilities		2,103,461	2,079,747	2,117,921
Shareholders' equity:				
Share capital	13	630,408	647,637	633,075
Equity reserves		74,184	66,726	75,866
Hedge reserves		(3,353)	(10,470)	(14,852)
Retained earnings		668,978	600,340	538,087
Total shareholders' equity		1,370,217	1,304,233	1,232,176
Commitments	18			
Total liabilities and shareholders' equity		3,473,678	3,383,980	3,350,097

The accompanying notes are an integral part of the consolidated financial statements.

On behalf of the Board:

Gregg Saretsky, Director

Hugh Bolton, Director

Consolidated Statement of Cash Flows
For the years ended December 31
(Stated in thousands of Canadian dollars)

	Note	2011	2010
Operating activities:			
Net earnings		148,702	90,197
Items not involving cash:			
Depreciation and amortization		174,751	170,462
Change in long-term maintenance provisions		38,522	27,927
Change in other liabilities		(313)	(685)
Amortization of hedge settlements		1,400	1,400
Loss on derivative instruments		6,052	34
Loss (gain) on disposal of property and equipment	13	54	(763)
Share-based payment expense		12,553	15,497
Income tax credit		—	(1,667)
Deferred income tax expense		58,068	41,695
Unrealized foreign exchange loss		1,453	337
Change in non-cash working capital		88,410	98,382
Change in restricted cash		(19,758)	(18,391)
Change in other assets		(3,510)	(5,659)
		506,384	418,766
Investing activities:			
Aircraft additions		(61,265)	(29,884)
Other property and equipment and intangible additions		(57,108)	(18,675)
		(118,373)	(48,559)
Financing activities:			
Repayment of long-term debt	13	(199,225)	(164,989)
Decrease in obligations under finance leases	14	(108)	(744)
Shares repurchased	13	(74,570)	(31,391)
Dividends paid		(35,000)	—
Issuance of common shares		34	520
Change in other assets		(836)	(2,947)
Change in non-cash working capital		7,106	(4,526)
		(302,599)	(204,077)
Cash flow from operating, investing and financing activities		85,412	166,130
Effect of foreign exchange on cash and cash equivalents		(1,123)	(1,803)
Net change in cash and cash equivalents		84,289	164,327
Cash and cash equivalents, beginning of year		1,159,316	994,989
Cash and cash equivalents, end of year	5	1,243,605	1,159,316
Cash taxes (paid) received		26	(2,958)
Cash interest received		14,631	8,343
Cash interest paid		(51,722)	(61,280)

The accompanying notes are an integral part of the consolidated financial statements.

Consolidated Statement of Changes in Equity
For the years ended December 31
(Stated in thousands of Canadian dollars)

	Note	2011	2010
Share capital:	13		
Balance, beginning of year		647,637	633,075
Issuance of shares pursuant to stock option plan		34	520
Transfer of share-based payment expense		5,095	24,637
Shares repurchased		(22,358)	(10,595)
		630,408	647,637
Equity reserves:	13		
Balance, beginning of year		66,726	75,866
Share-based payment expense		12,553	15,497
Transfer of share-based payment expense		(5,095)	(24,637)
		74,184	66,726
Hedge reserves:			
Balance, beginning of year		(10,470)	(14,852)
Other comprehensive income		7,117	4,382
		(3,353)	(10,470)
Retained earnings:			
Balance, beginning of year		600,340	538,087
Dividends declared	14	(27,852)	(7,148)
Shares repurchased	13	(52,212)	(20,796)
Net earnings		148,702	90,197
		668,978	600,340
Total shareholders' equity		1,370,217	1,304,233

The accompanying notes are an integral part of the consolidated financial statements.

Consolidated Statement of Comprehensive Income
For the years ended December 31
(Stated in thousands of Canadian dollars)

	2011	2010
Net earnings	148,702	90,197
Items to be reclassified to net earnings:		
Other comprehensive income, net of tax:		
Amortization of hedge settlements to aircraft leasing	1,400	1,400
Net unrealized gain (loss) on foreign exchange derivatives under cash flow hedge accounting [i]	2,532	(3,460)
Reclassification of net realized loss on foreign exchange derivatives to net earnings [ii]	3,590	1,557
Net unrealized loss on interest rate derivatives under cash flow hedge accounting [iii]	(397)	—
Net unrealized gain (loss) on fuel derivatives under cash flow hedge accounting [iv]	1,966	(1,778)
Reclassification of net realized (gain) loss on fuel derivatives to net earnings [v]	(1,974)	6,663
	7,117	4,382
Total comprehensive income	155,819	94,579

(i)   Net of income taxes of $(870) (2010 – $1,224).
(ii)   Net of income taxes of $1,250 (2010 – $(586)).
(iii)   Net of income taxes of $135 (2010 – $nil).
(iv)   Net of income taxes of $(679) (2010 – $670).
(v)   Net of income taxes of $682 (2010 – $(2,509)).

The accompanying notes are an integral part of the consolidated financial statements.

Notes to Consolidated Financial Statements
For the years ended December 31, 2011 and 2010
(Stated in thousands of Canadian dollars, except share and per share amounts)

1. Statement of significant accounting policies

The consolidated annual financial statements of WestJet Airlines Ltd. (the Corporation) for the years ended December 31, 2011 and 2010, were authorized for issue by the Board of Directors on February 7, 2012. The Corporation is a public company incorporated and domiciled in Canada. The Corporation provides airline service and travel packages. The Corporation's shares are publicly traded on the Toronto Stock Exchange. The principal business address is 22 Aerial Place N.E., Calgary, Alberta, T2E 3J1 and the registered office is Suite 1400, 350 - 7 Avenue SW, Calgary, Alberta, T2P 3N9.

(a) Basis of presentation

These consolidated annual financial statements and the notes thereto have been prepared in accordance with IAS 1 – Presentation of financial statements under International Financial Reporting Standards (IFRS) as issued by the International Accounting Standards Board (IASB).

These are the Corporation's first consolidated annual financial statements prepared in accordance with IFRS. For all periods up to and including December 31, 2010, the Corporation prepared its consolidated financial statements in accordance with Canadian Generally Accepted Accounting Principles (GAAP). In accordance with IFRS 1 – First-time adoption of IFRS, the Corporation has restated all required prior period financial information to be in accordance with IFRS.

For a description of the accounting policy and financial statement presentation transitional adjustments together with the reconciliation of financial statement balances from Canadian GAAP to IFRS refer to note 22.

These consolidated annual financial statements have been prepared on a historical cost basis except for certain financial assets and liabilities, including derivative financial instruments that are measured at fair value. Where applicable, these differences have been described in the notes hereto.

Amounts presented in these consolidated annual financial statements and the notes hereto are in Canadian dollars, the Corporation's reporting currency, unless otherwise stated. The Corporation's functional currency is the Canadian dollar.

(b) Principles of consolidation

The accompanying consolidated financial statements include the accounts of the Corporation and its wholly owned subsidiaries, as well as the accounts of five special-purpose entities (SPEs), which are utilized to facilitate the financing of aircraft. The Corporation has no equity ownership in the SPEs; however, the substance of the relationship between the Corporation and the SPEs indicates that they are controlled by the Corporation. Accordingly, the accounts of the SPEs have been consolidated in the Corporation's financial statements and all intercompany balances and transactions have been eliminated.

(c) Seasonality

The airline industry is sensitive to general economic conditions and the seasonal nature of air travel. The Corporation experiences increased domestic travel in the summer months and more demand for transborder and international travel over the winter months, thus reducing the effects of seasonality on net earnings.

(d) Revenue recognition

(i) Guest

Guest revenues, including the air component of vacation packages, are recognized when air transportation is provided. Tickets sold but not yet used are reported in the consolidated statement of financial position as advance ticket sales.

(ii) Other

Other revenues include charter revenue, cargo revenue, net revenues from the sale of the land component of vacation packages, ancillary revenues and other.

Charter and cargo revenue is recognized when air transportation is provided.

Revenue for the land component of vacation packages is generated from providing agency services equal to the amount paid by the guest for products and services, less payment to the travel supplier, and is reported at the net amount received. Revenue from the land component is deferred as advance ticket sales and recognized in earnings on completion of the vacation.

Ancillary revenues are recognized when the services and products are provided to the guests. Included in ancillary revenues are fees associated with guest itinerary changes or cancellations, second checked baggage fees, excess baggage fees, buy-on-board sales, pre-reserved seating fees, and ancillary revenue from the Frequent Guest Program (FGP).

Notes to Consolidated Financial Statements
For the years ended December 31, 2011 and 2010
(Stated in thousands of Canadian dollars, except share and per share amounts)

1. Statement of significant accounting policies (continued)

(d) Revenue recognition (continued)

(iii) Frequent Guest Program

The Corporation has a frequent guest program that allows guests to accumulate credits that entitle them to a choice of various rewards, primarily discounted travel. Revenue received in relation to credits issued is deferred as a liability at fair value until a reward is ultimately utilized at which time it is recognized in guest revenue. Revenue associated with credits expected to expire (breakage) is recognized in other revenue at the time the revenue is received.

The Corporation also has a co-branded MasterCard with the Royal Bank of Canada (RBC). RBC issues FGP credits to cardholders as a percentage of their total retail spend. The fair value of these credits is deferred and recognized on redemption as described above. Ancillary revenue from the issuance of FGP credits on the credit card is measured as the difference between the cash received and the fair value of the credit issued and is recognized in other revenue at the time a credit is issued. Revenue related to new cards issued is recognized in other revenue immediately upon activation.

(iv) Non-refundable guest credits

The Corporation issues future travel credits to guests for flight changes and cancellations as well as for gift certificates. Where appropriate, future travel credits are also issued for flight delays, missing baggage and other inconveniences. All credits are non-refundable and have expiry dates dependent upon the nature of the credit, except for gift certificates which do not contain an expiry date. The Corporation records a liability at the face value for credits issued for flight changes, cancellations and gift certificates. No liability is recorded at issuance for travel credits related to flight delays, missing baggage or other inconveniences as these credits are issued as goodwill gestures by the Corporation and do not represent a performance obligation. Revenue related to flight changes, cancellations and gift certificates is recorded in other revenue when the credit is utilized or upon expiry. Credits issued as a sign of goodwill are recorded as a reduction to guest revenue when the credit is utilized.

(e) Financial instruments

A financial instrument is any contract that gives rise to a financial asset of one entity and a financial liability to another entity or equity instrument of another entity. Financial assets and liabilities, including derivatives, are recognized in the consolidated statement of financial position at the time the Corporation becomes a party to the contractual provisions. Upon initial recognition, financial instruments are measured at fair value. Subsequent measurement is based on designation in one of the following five categories: at fair value through profit or loss, held-to-maturity, loans and receivables, available-for-sale or other financial liabilities.

The following table lists the Corporation's financial instruments and the method of measurement subsequent to initial recognition:

Financial instrument	Category	Measurement method
Cash and cash equivalents	At fair value through profit or loss	Fair value
Restricted cash	At fair value through profit or loss	Fair value
Deposits	At fair value through profit or loss	Fair value
Accounts receivable	Loans and receivables	Amortized cost
Accounts payable and accrued liabilities	Other financial liabilities	Amortized cost
Long-term debt	Other financial liabilities	Amortized cost
Finance lease obligations	Other financial liabilities	Amortized cost
Derivative instruments	At fair value through profit or loss	Fair value

Financial assets and liabilities at fair value through profit or loss include financial assets and liabilities held-for-trading and financial assets and liabilities designated upon initial recognition at fair value through profit or loss. Financial assets and liabilities are classified as held-for-trading if they are acquired for the purpose of selling or repurchasing in the near term. This category includes derivative financial instruments entered into by the Corporation that are not designated as effective hedging instruments. As at December 31, 2011, 2010, and January 1, 2010, the Corporation did not hold any financial instruments classified as held-for-trading. Financial assets and liabilities designated upon initial recognition at fair value through profit or loss are initially measured at fair value with subsequent changes in fair value recorded in net earnings. The Corporation uses trade-date accounting for initial recognition of financial instruments in this category.

Financial assets classified as loans and receivables are measured at amortized cost using the effective interest method. Impairment, if any, is recorded in net earnings.

Notes to Consolidated Financial Statements
For the years ended December 31, 2011 and 2010
(Stated in thousands of Canadian dollars, except share and per share amounts)

1. Statement of significant accounting policies (continued)

(e) Financial instruments (continued)

Other financial liabilities are measured at amortized cost using the effective interest method and include all liabilities other than derivatives, which are designated as cash flow hedges.

The Corporation will, from time to time, use various financial derivatives to reduce market risk exposure from changes in foreign exchange rates, interest rates and jet fuel prices. Derivatives are recorded at fair value on the consolidated statement of financial position with changes in fair value recorded in net earnings unless designated as effective hedging instruments. Similarly, embedded derivatives are recorded at fair value on the consolidated statement of financial position with the changes in fair value recorded in net earnings unless exempted from derivative treatment as a normal purchase and sale or the host contract and derivative are deemed to be clearly and closely related. When financial assets and liabilities are designated as part of a hedging relationship and qualify for hedge accounting, they are subject to measurement and classification requirements as cash flow hedges. The Corporation's policy is not to utilize derivative financial instruments for trading or speculative purposes.

At each reporting period, the Corporation will assess whether there is any objective evidence that a financial asset, other than those classified as at fair value through profit or loss, is impaired.

The Corporation offsets qualifying transaction costs incurred in relation to the acquisition of financial assets and liabilities not measured at fair value through profit or loss against those same financial assets and liabilities.

(f) Cash flow hedges

The Corporation uses various financial derivative instruments such as forwards, swaps, collars and call options to manage fluctuations in foreign exchange rates, interest rates and jet fuel prices.

The Corporation's derivatives that have been designated and qualify for hedge accounting are classified as cash flow hedges. The Corporation formally documents all relationships between hedging instruments and hedged items, as well as the risk-management objective and strategy for undertaking the hedge transaction. This process includes linking all derivatives that are designated in a cash flow hedging relationship to a specific firm commitment or forecasted transaction. The Corporation also formally assesses, both at inception and at each reporting date, whether derivatives used in hedging transactions have been highly effective in offsetting changes in cash flows of hedged items and whether those derivatives may be expected to remain highly effective in future periods.

Under cash flow hedge accounting, the effective portion of the change in the fair value of the hedging instrument is recognized in other comprehensive income (OCI) and presented within shareholders' equity in hedge reserves. The ineffective portion of the change in fair value is recognized in non-operating income (expense). Upon maturity of the financial derivative instrument, the effective gains and losses previously accumulated in hedge reserves within shareholders' equity are recorded in net earnings under the same caption as the hedged item.

The Corporation excludes time value from the measurement of effectiveness; accordingly, changes in time value are recognized in non-operating income (expense) during the period the change occurs.

If the hedging relationship ceases to qualify for cash flow hedge accounting, any change in fair value of the instrument from the point it ceases to qualify is recognized in non-operating income (expense). Amounts previously accumulated in hedge reserves within shareholders' equity will remain in shareholders' equity until the anticipated transaction occurs, at which time, the amount is recorded in net earnings under the same caption as the hedged item. If the transaction is no longer expected to occur, amounts previously accumulated in hedge reserves within shareholders' equity will be reclassified to non-operating income (expense).

(g) Foreign currency

Monetary assets and liabilities, denominated in foreign currencies, are translated into Canadian dollars at the rate of exchange in effect at the consolidated statement of financial position date, with any resulting gain or loss recognized in net earnings. Non-monetary assets, non-monetary liabilities, revenues and expenses arising from transactions denominated in foreign currencies are translated into Canadian dollars at the rates prevailing at the time of the transaction.

(h) Cash and cash equivalents

Cash and cash equivalents consist of cash and short-term investments that are highly liquid in nature and have maturity dates of up to 97 days.

Notes to Consolidated Financial Statements
For the years ended December 31, 2011 and 2010
(Stated in thousands of Canadian dollars, except share and per share amounts)

1. Statement of significant accounting policies (continued)

(i) Inventory

Inventories are valued at the lower of cost and net realizable value, with cost being determined on a first-in, first-out basis and a specific item basis depending on the nature of the inventory. The Corporation's inventory balance consists of aircraft fuel, de-icing fluid, retail merchandise and aircraft expendables.

(j) Property and equipment

Property and equipment is stated at cost and depreciated to its estimated residual value. Assets under finance leases are initially recorded at the present value of minimum lease payments at the inception of the lease. Expected useful lives and depreciation methods are reviewed annually.

Asset class	Basis	Rate
Aircraft, net of estimated residual value	Straight-line	20 years
Engine, airframe and landing gear overhaul	Straight-line	8 to 15 years
Live satellite television equipment	Straight-line	10 years/Term of lease
Ground property and equipment	Straight-line	5 to 25 years
Spare engines and rotables, net of estimated residual value	Straight-line	20 years
Buildings	Straight-line	40 years
Leasehold improvements	Straight-line	Term of lease
Assets under finance leases	Straight-line	Term of lease

Estimated residual values of the Corporation's aircraft range between $4,000 and $6,000 per aircraft. Spare engines have a residual value equal to 10% of the original purchase price. Residual values, where applicable, are reviewed annually against prevailing market rates at the consolidated statement of financial position date.

Major overhaul expenditures are capitalized and depreciated over the expected life between overhauls. All other costs relating to the maintenance of fleet assets are charged to the consolidated statement of earnings on consumption or as incurred.

Rotable assets are purchased, depreciated and disposed of on a pooled basis. When parts are purchased, the cost is added to the pool and depreciated over its useful life of 20 years. The cost to repair rotable parts is recognized in maintenance expense as incurred.

(k) Intangible assets

Included in intangible assets are costs related to software and landing rights. Software and landing rights are carried at cost less accumulated amortization and are amortized on a straight-line basis over their respective useful lives of five and 20 years. Expected useful lives and amortization methods are reviewed annually.

(l) Impairment

Property and equipment and intangible assets are grouped into cash generating units (CGUs) and reviewed annually for impairment when events or changes in circumstances indicate that the carrying value of the CGU may not be recoverable. When events or circumstances indicate that the carrying amount of the CGU may not be recoverable, the long-lived assets are tested for recoverability by comparing the recoverable amounts, defined as the greater of the CGU's fair value less cost to sell or value-in-use, with the carrying amount of the CGU. Fair value is defined as the amount for which an asset could be exchanged, or a liability settled, between knowledgeable willing parties, in an arm's length transaction. Value-in-use is defined as the present value of the cash flows expected from the future use or eventual sale of the asset at the end of its useful life. If the carrying value of the CGU exceeds the greater of the fair value less cost to sell and value-in-use, an impairment loss is recognized in net earnings for the difference. Impairment losses may subsequently be reversed and recognized in earnings due to changes in events and circumstances, but only to the extent of the original carrying amount of the asset, net of depreciation or amortization, had the original impairment not been recognized.

Notes to Consolidated Financial Statements
For the years ended December 31, 2011 and 2010
(Stated in thousands of Canadian dollars, except share and per share amounts)

1.   Significant accounting policies (continued)

(m) Maintenance provisions and reserves

Provisions are made when it is probable that an outflow of economic benefits will be required to settle a present legal or constructive obligation in respect of a past event and where the amount of the obligation can be reliably estimated.

The Corporation's aircraft operating lease agreements require leased aircraft to be returned to the lessor in a specified operating condition. This obligation requires the Corporation to record a maintenance provision liability for certain return conditions specified in the operating lease agreements. Certain obligations are based on aircraft usage and the passage of time, while others are fixed amounts regardless of aircraft usage or passage of time. Expected future costs are estimated based on contractual commitments and company specific history. Each period, the Corporation recognizes additional maintenance expense based on increased aircraft usage, the passage of time and any changes to judgments or estimates, including discount rates and expected timing of maintenance activities. The unwinding of the discounted present value is recorded as a finance cost on the consolidated statement of earnings. The discount rate used by the Corporation is the current pre-tax risk-free rate approximated by the corresponding term of a Government of Canada Bond to the remaining term until cash flow. Any difference between the provision recorded and the actual amount incurred at the time the maintenance activity is performed is recorded to maintenance expense.

A certain number of aircraft leases also require the Corporation to pay a maintenance reserve to the lessor. Payments are based on aircraft usage. The purpose of these deposits is to provide the lessor with collateral should an aircraft be returned in an operating condition that does not meet the requirements stipulated in the lease agreement. Maintenance reserves are refunded to the Corporation when qualifying maintenance is performed, or if not refunded, act to reduce the end of lease obligation payments arising from the requirement to return leased aircraft in a specific operating condition. Where the amount of maintenance reserves paid exceeds the estimated amount recoverable from the lessor, the non-recoverable amount is recorded as maintenance expense in the period it is incurred.

(n) Leases

The determination of whether an arrangement is, or contains, a lease is made at the inception of the arrangement based on the substance of the arrangement and whether (i) fulfillment of the arrangement is dependent on the use of a specific asset and (ii) whether the arrangement conveys a right to use the asset.

Finance leases transfer substantially all the risks and rewards incidental to ownership. Finance leases are recognized as assets and liabilities on the consolidated statement of financial position at the fair value of the leased property or, if lower, the present value of the minimum lease payments, each determined at the inception of the lease. Any costs directly attributable to the finance lease are added to the cost of the leased asset. Minimum lease payments are apportioned between a finance charge, which produces a constant rate of interest on the outstanding liability, and a principal reduction of the lease liability. Depreciation of finance lease assets follows the same methods used for other similar owned assets over the term of the lease.

Operating leases do not result in the transfer of substantially all risks and rewards incidental to ownership. Non-contingent lease payments are recognized as an expense in the consolidated statement of earnings on a straight-line basis over the term of the lease.

(o) Borrowing costs

Interest and other borrowing costs are capitalized to a qualifying asset provided they are directly attributable to the acquisition, construction or production of the qualifying asset. For specific borrowings, any investment income on the temporary investment of borrowed funds is offset against the capitalized borrowing costs.

To the extent the Corporation borrows funds generally for the purpose of obtaining a qualifying asset, a capitalization rate is determined and added to the cost of the qualifying asset.

Interest and other borrowing costs are capitalized beginning when the Corporation incurs expenditures for the qualifying asset, and undertakes activities necessary to prepare the asset for its intended use. Capitalization ceases during any extended periods of suspension of development or when substantially all activities necessary to prepare the qualifying asset for its intended use are complete.

Notes to Consolidated Financial Statements
For the years ended December 31, 2011 and 2010
(Stated in thousands of Canadian dollars, except share and per share amounts)

1.   Significant accounting policies (continued)

(p) Income taxes

Current tax assets and liabilities are recognized based on amounts receivable from or payable to a tax authority within the next 12 months. A current tax asset is recognized for a benefit relating to an unused tax loss or unused tax credit that can be carried back to recover current tax of a previous period.

Deferred tax assets and liabilities are recognized for temporary differences between the tax and accounting bases of assets and liabilities on the consolidated statement of financial position using the tax rates that are expected to apply in the period in which the deferred tax asset or liability is expected to settle. The tax rates that are expected to be applied in future periods are based on the enacted or substantively enacted rates known at the end of the reporting period. Deferred tax assets are only recognized to the extent that it is probable that a taxable profit will be available when the deductible temporary differences can be utilized. A deferred tax asset is also recognized for any unused tax losses and unused tax credits to the extent that it is probable that future taxable profit will be available for use against the unused tax losses and unused tax credits. Deferred tax assets and liabilities are not discounted.

Current and deferred tax benefit or expense is recognized in the same period as the related transaction or event is recognized in net earnings. Current and deferred tax benefit or expense related to transactions or events in other comprehensive income or equity are recognized directly in those accounts.

Current tax assets and liabilities are offset on the consolidated statement of financial position to the extent the Corporation has a legally enforceable right to offset and the amounts are levied by the same taxation authority or when the Corporation has the right to offset and intends to settle on a net basis or realize the asset and settle the liability simultaneously. Deferred tax assets and liabilities are classified as long-term.

(q) Share-based payment plans

Equity-settled share-based payments to employees are measured at the fair value of the equity instrument granted. An option valuation model is used to fair value stock options issued to employees on the date of grant. The market value of the Corporation's voting shares on the date of the grant is used to determine the fair value of the equity-based share units issued to employees on the date of grant.

The cost of the equity-settled share-based payments is recognized as compensation expense with a corresponding increase in equity reserves over the related service period provided to the Corporation. The service period may commence prior to the grant date with compensation expense recognition being subject to specific vesting conditions and the best estimate of equity instruments expected to vest. Estimates related to vesting conditions are reviewed regularly with any adjustments recorded to compensation expense. On the vesting date, the Corporation revises, if necessary, the estimate to equal the number of equity instruments ultimately vested and adjusts the corresponding compensation expense and equity reserves accordingly.

Market conditions attached to certain equity-settled share-based payments are taken into account when estimating the fair value of the equity instruments granted.

Upon exercise or settlement of equity-settled instruments, consideration received, if any, together with amounts previously recorded in the equity reserves, are recorded as an increase in share capital.

Cash-settled share-based payments are measured based on the fair value of the cash liability. The amount determined is recorded as compensation expense and recognized over the service period. The liability is remeasured each period with a corresponding adjustment to the related compensation expense until the date of settlement.

(r) Earnings per share

Basic earnings per share is calculated by dividing net earnings attributable to equity holders by the weighted average number of voting shares outstanding during the period.

Diluted earnings per share is calculated by dividing net earnings attributable to equity holders by the weighted average number of voting shares outstanding adjusted for the effects of all potential dilutive voting shares. Potential dilutive voting shares are only those shares that would result in a decrease to earnings per share or increase to loss per share. The calculation of potential dilutive voting shares assumes the exercise of all dilutive instruments at the average market price during the period with the proceeds received from exercise assumed to reduce the number of dilutive voting shares otherwise issued.

Notes to Consolidated Financial Statements
For the years ended December 31, 2011 and 2010
(Stated in thousands of Canadian dollars, except share and per share amounts)

1. Statement of significant accounting policies (continued)

(s) Critical accounting judgments and estimates (continued)

Judgments

(i) Componentization

The componentization of the Corporation's assets, namely aircraft, are based on management's judgment of what components constitute a significant cost in relation to the total cost of an asset and whether these components have similar or dissimilar patterns of consumption and useful lives for purposes of calculating depreciation and amortization.

(ii) Depreciation and amortization

Depreciation and amortization methods for aircraft and related components as well as other property, plant and equipment and intangible assets are based on management's judgment of the most appropriate method to reflect the pattern of an asset's future economic benefit expected to be consumed by the Corporation. Among other factors, these judgments are based on industry standards, manufacturers' guidelines and company specific history and experience.

(iii) Impairment

Assessment of impairment is based on management's judgment of whether there are sufficient internal and external factors that would indicate that an asset or CGU is impaired. The determination of CGUs is also based on management's judgment and is an assessment of the smallest group of assets that generate cash inflows independently of other assets. Factors considered include whether an active market exists for the output produced by the asset or group of assets as well as how management monitors and makes decisions about the Corporation's operations.

(iv) Lease classification

Assessing whether a lease is a finance lease or an operating lease is based on management's judgment of the criteria applied in IAS 17 – Leases. The most prevalent leases of the Corporation are those for aircraft. Management has determined that all of the Corporation's leased aircraft are operating leases.

Estimates

(v) Depreciation and amortization

Depreciation and amortization are calculated to write off the cost, less estimated residual value, of assets on a systematic and rational basis over their expected useful lives. Estimates of residual value and useful lives are based on data and information from various sources including vendors, industry practice, and company-specific history. Expected useful lives and residual values are reviewed annually for any change to estimates and assumptions.

(vi) Maintenance provisions

The Corporation has a legal obligation to adhere to certain maintenance conditions set out in its aircraft operating lease agreements relating to the condition of the aircraft when it is returned to the lessor. To fulfill these obligations, a provision is made during the lease term. Estimates related to the maintenance provision include the likely utilization of the aircraft, the expected future cost of the maintenance, the point in time at which maintenance is expected to occur, the discount rate used to present value the future cash flows and the lifespan of life-limited parts. These estimates are based on data and information obtained from various sources including the lessor, current maintenance schedules and fleet plans, contracted costs with maintenance service providers, other vendors and company-specific history.

(vii) Fair value of awards and breakage associated with the Frequent Guest Program

Estimates are required in determining the amount of revenue to be recognized or deferred from revenue received in relation to credits awarded under the FGP. These estimates are based on the amount of FGP credits expected to expire (breakage). Management bases its estimates on company specific redemption history, industry results and future forecasts of expected redemption.

Notes to Consolidated Financial Statements
For the years ended December 31, 2011 and 2010
(Stated in thousands of Canadian dollars, except share and per share amounts)

1. Statement of significant accounting policies (continued)

(s) Critical accounting judgments and estimates (continued)

(viii) Income taxes

Deferred tax assets and liabilities contain estimates about the nature and timing of future permanent and temporary differences as well as the future tax rates that will apply to those differences. Changes in tax laws and rates as well as changes to the expected timing of reversals may have a significant impact on the amounts recorded for deferred tax assets and liabilities. Management closely monitors current and potential changes to tax law and bases its estimates on the best available information at each reporting date.

(ix) Impairment of assets

Impairment assessments may require the Corporation to determine the recoverable amount of a CGU, defined as the smallest identifiable group of assets that generates cash inflows independent of other assets. This determination requires significant estimates in a variety of areas including: the determination of fair value, selling costs, timing and size of cash flows, and discount and interest rates. The Corporation documents and supports all assumptions made in the determination of a recoverable amount and updates these assumptions to reflect the best information available to the Corporation if and when an impairment assessment requires the recoverable amount of a CGU to be determined.

(x) Fair value of share-based payments

The Corporation uses an option pricing model to determine the fair value of certain share-based payments. Inputs to the model are subject to various estimates about volatility, interest rates, dividend yields and expected life of the units issued. Fair value inputs are subject to market factors as well as internal estimates. The Corporation considers historic trends together with any new information to determine the best estimate of fair value at the date of grant.

Separate from the fair value calculation, the Corporation is required to estimate the expected forfeiture rate of equity-settled share-based payments. The Corporation has assessed forfeitures to be insignificant based on the underlying terms of its payment plans.

(xi) Fair value of derivative instruments

The fair value of derivative instruments is estimated using inputs, including forward prices, foreign exchange rates, interest rates and historical volatilities. These inputs are subject to change on a regular basis based on the interplay of various market forces. Consequently, the fair value of the Corporation's derivative instruments are subject to regular changes in fair value each reporting period.

Notes to Consolidated Financial Statements
For the years ended December 31, 2011 and 2010
(Stated in thousands of Canadian dollars, except share and per share amounts)

2. New accounting standards and interpretations

The IASB and International Financial Reporting Interpretations Committee (IFRIC) have issued the following standards that have not been applied in preparing these consolidated financial statements as their effective dates fall within annual periods beginning subsequent to the current reporting period.

Proposed standards	Description	Previous standard	Effective date (i)
IFRS 10 – Consolidated Financial Statements	Builds on the existing principles of control and elaborates on the definition of control when determining whether an entity should be consolidated or not.	SIC-12 – Consolidation – Special Purpose Entities; IAS 27 – Consolidated and Separate Financial Statements	January 1, 2013
IFRS 11 – Joint Arrangements	Focuses on the rights and obligations of an arrangement rather than its legal form and requires a single method to account for interests in jointly controlled entities.	IAS 31 – Interests in Joint Ventures; SIC 13 – Jointly Controlled Entities – Non-Monetary Contributions by Venturers	January 1, 2013
IFRS 12 – Disclosure of Interests in Other Entities	A new standard detailing disclosure requirements for all forms of interests in other entities, including joint arrangements, associates, special purpose entities and other off-statement of financial position vehicles.	Various – no direct replacement	January 1, 2013
IFRS 13 – Fair Value Measurement	Sets out a single framework for measuring fair value and disclosure requirements surrounding the inputs and assumptions used in determining fair value.	Various – no direct replacement	January 1, 2013
IFRS 9 – Financial Instruments	Initially issued in November 2009 to address the classification and measurement of financial assets. Additional guidance issued in October 2010 on the classification and measurement of financial liabilities.	IAS 39 – Financial Instruments: Recognition and Measurement	January 1, 2015

(i) Effective for annual periods beginning on or after the stated date.

Management continues to evaluate the potential qualitative and quantitative impact of these new standards on the Corporation's financial statement measurements and disclosures. The Corporation does not anticipate early adopting these standards at this time.

Notes to Consolidated Financial Statements
For the years ended December 31, 2011 and 2010
(Stated in thousands of Canadian dollars, except share and per share amounts)

3. Capital management

The Corporation's policy is to maintain a strong capital base in order to maintain investor, creditor and market confidence and to sustain the future development of the airline. The Corporation manages its capital structure and makes adjustments in light of changes in economic conditions and the risk characteristics of the underlying assets.

In order to maintain the capital structure, the Corporation may, from time to time, purchase shares for cancellation pursuant to normal course issuer bids, issue new shares, pay dividends and adjust current and projected debt levels.

In the management of capital, the Corporation includes shareholders' equity (excluding hedge reserves), long-term debt, finance leases, cash and cash equivalents and the Corporation's off-balance-sheet obligations related to its aircraft operating leases, all of which are presented in detail below.

The Corporation monitors its capital structure on a number of bases, including adjusted debt-to-equity and adjusted net debt to earnings before net finance costs, taxes, depreciation and amortization and aircraft leasing (EBITDAR). EBITDAR is a non-IFRS financial measure commonly used in the airline industry to evaluate results by excluding differences in the method an airline finances its aircraft. In addition, the Corporation will adjust EBITDAR for one-time special items, for non-operating gains and losses on derivatives and for gains and losses on foreign exchange. The calculation of EBITDAR is a measure that does not have a standardized meaning prescribed under IFRS and therefore may not be comparable to similar measures presented by other issuers. The Corporation adjusts debt to include its off-balance-sheet aircraft operating leases. Common industry practice is to multiply the trailing 12 months of aircraft leasing expense by 7.5 to derive a present-value debt equivalent. The Corporation defines adjusted net debt as adjusted debt less cash and cash equivalents. The Corporation defines equity as total shareholders' equity, excluding hedge reserves.

	2011	2010	Change
Adjusted debt-to-equity			
Long-term debt (i)	828,712	1,026,802	(198,090)
Obligations under finance leases (ii)	3,249	3,357	(108)
Off-balance-sheet aircraft leases (iii)	1,241,783	1,075,358	166,425
Adjusted debt	2,073,744	2,105,517	(31,773)
Total shareholders' equity	1,370,217	1,304,233	65,984
Add: Hedge reserves	3,353	10,470	(7,117)
Adjusted equity	1,373,570	1,314,703	58,867
Adjusted debt-to-equity	1.51	1.60	(5.6%)
Adjusted net debt to EBITDAR (iv)			
Net earnings	148,702	90,197	58,505
Add:			
Net finance costs (v)	44,924	61,004	(16,080)
Taxes	59,304	43,268	16,036
Depreciation and amortization	174,751	170,462	4,289
Aircraft leasing	165,571	143,381	22,190
Other (vi)	3,567	(2,545)	6,112
EBITDAR	596,819	505,767	91,052
Adjusted debt (as above)	2,073,744	2,105,517	(31,773)
Less: Cash and cash equivalents	(1,243,605)	(1,159,316)	(84,289)
Adjusted net debt	830,139	946,201	(116,062)
Adjusted net debt to EBITDAR	1.39	1.87	(25.7%)

(i) As at December 31, 2011, long-term debt includes the current portion of long-term debt of $158,832 (2010 – $178,337) and long-term debt of $669,880 (2010 – $848,465).

(ii) As at December 31, 2011, obligations under finance leases includes the current portion of obligations under finance leases of $75 (2010 – $108) and obligations under finance leases of $3,174 (2010 – $3,249).

(iii) Off-balance-sheet aircraft leases is calculated by multiplying the trailing 12 months of aircraft leasing expense by 7.5. As at December 31, 2011, the trailing 12 months of aircraft leasing costs totaled $165,571 (2010 – $143,381).

(iv) The trailing 12 months are used in the calculation of EBITDAR.

(v) As at December 31, 2011, net finance costs includes the trailing 12 months of finance income of $15,987 (2010 – $9,910) and the trailing 12 months of finance costs of $60,911 (2010 – $70,914).

(vi) As at December 31, 2011, other includes the trailing 12 months foreign exchange gain of $2,485 (2010 – gain of $2,579) and the trailing 12 months non-operating loss on derivatives of $6,052 (2010 – loss of $34).

Notes to Consolidated Financial Statements
For the years ended December 31, 2011 and 2010
(Stated in thousands of Canadian dollars, except share and per share amounts)

3. Capital management (continued)

As at December 31, 2011 and 2010, the Corporation exceeded its internal targets of an adjusted debt-to-equity measure of no more than 3.00 and an adjusted net debt to EBITDAR measure of no more than 3.00.

There are no financial covenant compliance requirements for the facilities guaranteed by the Export-Import Bank of the United States (Ex-Im Bank) related to aircraft purchases.

4. Employee counts and compensation

The Corporation employed 7,141 full-time equivalent employees as at December 31, 2011 (2010 – 6,877). The following table reconciles the Corporation's compensation expense items to where the amounts are presented on the consolidated statement of earnings:

	Note	2011	2010
Salaries and benefits (i)		481,211	439,617
Employee share purchase plan	13	58,682	52,643
Employee profit share (ii)		23,804	22,222
Share-based payment expense	13	12,553	15,497
		576,250	529,979

Presented on the consolidated statement of earnings as follows:

	2011	2010
Airport operations	83,067	78,679
Flight operations and navigational charges	184,143	171,403
Sales and distribution	46,915	46,349
Marketing, general and administration	86,066	76,353
Maintenance	43,772	38,919
Inflight	108,483	96,054
Employee profit share	23,804	22,222
	576,250	529,979

(i) Salaries and benefits expense is classified in the consolidated statement of earnings based on the related nature of the service performed.
(ii) Employee profit share expense is a variable payment based on a percentage of pre-tax earnings available to all employees.

5. Cash and cash equivalents

	December 31 2011	December 31 2010	January 1 2010
Cash and cash equivalents (i):			
Bank balances	337,289	201,234	181,774
Short-term investments	906,316	958,082	813,215
	1,243,605	1,159,316	994,989

(i) Included in these balances, as at December 31, 2011, the Corporation has US-dollar cash and cash equivalents totaling US $55,357 (December 31 2010 – US $111,351; January 1 2010 – US $32,858).

6. Restricted cash

	December 31 2011	December 31 2010	January 1 2010
Restricted cash:			
Cash held in trust for WestJet Vacations Inc.	41,438	21,578	4,564
Security on facilities for letters of guarantee	6,610	6,691	4,491
Passenger facility charges	293	314	1,137
	48,341	28,583	10,192

Notes to Consolidated Financial Statements
For the years ended December 31, 2011 and 2010
(Stated in thousands of Canadian dollars, except share and per share amounts)

7. Property and equipment

	January 1 2011	Net additions	Depreciation (i)	Transfers	December 31 2011
Aircraft (ii)	1,616,263	32,164	(149,021)	15,227	1,514,633
Ground property and equipment	60,298	9,669	(10,843)	539	59,663
Spare engines and rotables	72,952	18,904	(6,305)	4,865	90,416
Deposits on aircraft	98,344	23,880	–	(11,979)	110,245
Buildings	122,662	6	(3,432)	–	119,236
Leasehold improvements	6,617	2,648	(761)	2,851	11,355
Assets under finance leases	3,243	–	(138)	–	3,105
Assets under development	9,143	4,934	–	(11,503)	2,574
	1,989,522	92,205	(170,500)	–	1,911,227

	January 1 2010	Net additions	Depreciation (i)	Transfers	December 31 2010
Aircraft (ii)	1,748,250	10,483	(145,635)	3,165	1,616,263
Ground property and equipment	67,591	3,429	(10,741)	19	60,298
Spare engines and rotables	71,846	6,334	(5,228)	–	72,952
Deposits on aircraft	81,001	17,343	–	–	98,344
Buildings	126,385	324	(3,312)	(735)	122,662
Leasehold improvements	7,009	115	(507)	–	6,617
Assets under finance leases	3,672	–	(429)	–	3,243
Assets under development	2,597	9,772	–	(3,226)	9,143
	2,108,351	47,800	(165,852)	(777)	1,989,522

(i) For the year ended December 31, 2011, total aircraft depreciation expense was $61,659 (2010 - $60,739) for overhaul components and $87,362 (2010 - $94,896) for aircraft, including live satellite television equipment.
(ii) Aircraft includes (a) aircraft (b) engine, airframe and landing gear overhauls, and (c) live satellite television equipment.

December 31, 2011	Cost	Accumulated depreciation	Net book value
Aircraft	2,510,811	(996,178)	1,514,633
Ground property and equipment	130,543	(70,880)	59,663
Spare engines and rotables	130,675	(40,259)	90,416
Deposits on aircraft	110,245	–	110,245
Buildings	135,822	(16,586)	119,236
Leasehold improvements	15,462	(4,107)	11,355
Assets under finance leases	4,221	(1,116)	3,105
Assets under development	2,574	–	2,574
	3,040,353	(1,129,126)	1,911,227

December 31, 2010	Cost	Accumulated depreciation	Net book value
Aircraft	2,463,536	(847,273)	1,616,263
Ground property and equipment	124,674	(64,376)	60,298
Spare engines and rotables	106,903	(33,951)	72,952
Deposits on aircraft	98,344	–	98,344
Buildings	135,817	(13,155)	122,662
Leasehold improvements	9,965	(3,348)	6,617
Assets under finance leases	4,413	(1,170)	3,243
Assets under development	9,143	–	9,143
	2,952,795	(963,273)	1,989,522

Notes to Consolidated Financial Statements
For the years ended December 31, 2011 and 2010
(Stated in thousands of Canadian dollars, except share and per share amounts)

7. Property and equipment (continued)

January 1, 2010	Cost	Accumulated depreciation	Net book value
Aircraft	2,449,634	(701,384)	1,748,250
Ground property and equipment	122,675	(55,084)	67,591
Spare engines and rotables	100,567	(28,721)	71,846
Deposits on aircraft	81,001	—	81,001
Buildings	136,228	(9,843)	126,385
Leasehold improvements	9,886	(2,877)	7,009
Assets under finance leases	5,882	(2,210)	3,672
Assets under development	2,597	—	2,597
	2,908,470	(800,119)	2,108,351

The net book value of the property and equipment pledged as collateral for the Corporation's long-term debt was $1,403,422 as at December 31, 2011 (December 31, 2010 – $1,592,871; January 1, 2010 – $1,731,123).

8. Intangible assets

Cost	Software	Landing rights	Assets under development	Total
Balance at January 1, 2010	36,307	—	4,085	40,392
Additions	2,230	—	1,393	3,623
Disposals	(435)	—	(31)	(466)
Transfers	3,296	—	(3,296)	—
Balance at December 31, 2010	41,398	—	2,151	43,549
Additions	2,788	17,782	4,465	25,035
Disposals	(4,782)	—	—	(4,782)
Transfers	5,741	—	(5,741)	—
Balance at December 31, 2011	45,145	17,782	875	63,802
Accumulated amortization				
Balance at January 1, 2010	(26,305)			(26,305)
Amortization	(4,610)			(4,610)
Disposals	384			384
Balance at December 31, 2010	(30,531)			(30,531)
Amortization	(4,251)			(4,251)
Disposals	4,773			4,773
Balance at December 31, 2011	(30,009)			(30,009)
Net book value				
At January 1, 2010	10,002		4,085	14,087
At December 31, 2010	10,867		2,151	13,018
At December 31, 2011	15,136	17,782	875	33,793

Notes to Consolidated Financial Statements
For the years ended December 31, 2011 and 2010
(Stated in thousands of Canadian dollars, except share and per share amounts)

9. Maintenance provisions and reserves

The Corporation's operating aircraft lease agreements require leased aircraft to be returned to the lessor in a specified operating condition. The maintenance provision liability represents the present value of the expected future cost. A maintenance expense is recognized over the term of the provision based on aircraft usage and the passage of time, while the unwinding of the present value discount is recognized as a finance cost.

	2011	2010
Opening balance (i)	125,578	105,753
Additions	27,758	24,275
Change in estimate (ii)	8,675	—
Foreign exchange	2,775	(6,372)
Accretion (iii)	5,078	4,725
Settled	(17,974)	(2,803)
Ending balance	151,890	125,578
Current portion (iv)	(245)	(12,372)
Long-term portion	151,645	113,206

(i) At January 1, 2010, includes current portion of $8,031 and long-term portion of $97,722.

(ii) Reflects changes to the timing and scope of maintenance activities and the discount rate used to present value the liability.

(iii) At December 31, 2011, all of the Corporation's aircraft lease maintenance provisions are discounted using a weighted average risk-free rate of approximately 1.20% to reflect the weighted average remaining term of approximately 43 months until cash outflow.

(iv) The current portion of maintenance provisions is included in accounts payable and accrued liabilities.

A certain number of operating aircraft leases also require the Corporation to pay a maintenance reserve to the lessor. Maintenance reserves are either refunded when qualifying maintenance is performed or offset against end of lease obligations for returning leased aircraft in a specified operating condition. Where the amount of maintenance reserves paid exceeds the estimated amount recoverable from the lessor, the non-recoverable amount is recorded as maintenance expense in the period it is incurred.

As at December 31, 2011, the current portion of maintenance reserves included in prepaid expenses, deposits and other is $nil (December 31, 2010 – $12,045; January 1, 2010 – $8,629) and the long-term portion of maintenance reserves included in other assets is $49,655 (December 31, 2010 – $41,736; January 1, 2010 – $44,084).

10. Long-term debt

	December 31 2011	December 31 2010	January 1 2010
Term loans – purchased aircraft (i)	828,104	985,571	1,142,304
Term loan – purchased aircraft (ii)	—	25,729	33,207
Term loan – flight simulator (iii)	—	5,575	6,392
Term loan – live satellite television equipment (iv)	—	41	493
Term loan – Calgary hangar facility (v)	—	8,707	9,202
Term loan – Calgary hangar facility (vi)	608	1,179	1,678
	828,712	1,026,802	1,193,276
Current portion	158,832	178,337	165,111
	669,880	848,465	1,028,165

(i) 52 individual term loans, amortized over a 12-year term, repayable in quarterly principal instalments totaling $40,676, at an effective weighted average fixed rate of 5.96%, maturing between 2014 and 2020. These facilities are guaranteed by Ex-Im Bank and secured by one 800-series aircraft, 38 700-series aircraft and 13 600-series aircraft.

(ii) US dollar denominated term loan paid in full in November 2011. Total amount settled was US $21,804 which consisted of US $21,571 in aggregate outstanding principal of the loan and US $233 in transaction costs on the loan accrued to the scheduled payoff date. This facility was secured by one 800 series aircraft.

(iii) Five-year term loan matured in September 2011 with a final payment of $5,123. This facility was secured by one flight simulator.

(iv) Five-year term loan matured in January 2011 with a final payment of $41. This facility was for the purchase of live satellite television equipment, was guaranteed by the Ex-Im Bank and was secured by certain 700-series and 600-series aircraft.

(v) Ten-year term loan matured in April 2011 with a final payment of $8,575. This facility was secured by the Calgary hangar.

(vi) Term loan repayable in monthly instalments of $50, including floating interest at the bank's prime rate plus 0.50%, with an effective interest rate of 3.50% as at December 31, 2011, maturing April 2013, secured by the Calgary hangar facility.

Notes to Consolidated Financial Statements
For the years ended December 31, 2011 and 2010
(Stated in thousands of Canadian dollars, except share and per share amounts)

10. Long-term debt (continued)

Future scheduled repayments of long-term debt as at December 31, 2011 are as follows:

Within 1 year	158,832
1 – 3 years	319,100
3 – 5 years	222,194
Over 5 years	128,586
	828,712

Held within the special-purpose entities, as identified in note 1, Summary of significant accounting policies, are liabilities of $842,976 (December 31, 2010 – $1,005,719; January 1, 2010 – $1,168,907) related to the acquisition of the 52 purchased aircraft and live satellite television equipment, which are included above in the long-term debt balances.

11. Obligations under finance leases

The Corporation has entered into finance leases relating to a fuel storage facility and ground handling equipment. Future scheduled repayments of obligations under finance leases as at December 31, 2011 are as follows:

Within 1 year	245
1 – 3 years	490
3 – 5 years	490
Over 5 years	4,371
Total minimum lease payments	5,596
Less: Weighted average imputed interest at 5.28%	(2,347)
Net minimum lease payments	3,249
Less: Current portion of obligations under finance leases	(75)
Long term obligations under finance leases	3,174

12. Income taxes

(a) Reconciliation of total tax expense

The effective rate on the Corporation's earnings before income tax differs from the expected amount that would arise using the combined Canadian federal and provincial statutory income tax rates. A reconciliation of the difference is as follows:

	2011	2010
Earnings before income tax	208,006	133,465
Combined Canadian federal and provincial income tax rate	27.26%	29.46%
Expected income tax provision	56,702	39,319
Add (deduct):		
Non-deductible expenses	3,344	2,380
Non-deductible share-based payment expense	3,430	4,534
Effect of tax rate changes	(4,539)	(3,726)
Other	367	761
Actual income tax provision	59,304	43,268
Effective tax rate	28.51%	32.42%

The decrease in the effective tax rate for year ended December 31, 2011 was primarily due to higher comparative earnings. As earnings increase, the impact of relatively fixed permanent differences on the overall effective tax rate is less pronounced, resulting in a corresponding decrease in the effective tax rate.

The Corporation has included in its reconciliation a deduction of $4,539 for the year ended December 31, 2011 (2010 – $3,726) for the effect of tax rate changes. This amount primarily reflects the impact of changes to the timing of when the Corporation expects certain temporary differences to reverse and differences between current statutory rates used in the reconciliation and future rates at which the deferred income tax liability is recorded.

Notes to Consolidated Financial Statements
For the years ended December 31, 2011 and 2010
(Stated in thousands of Canadian dollars, except share and per share amounts)

12. Income taxes (continued)

(b) Tax on earnings from continuing operations

	2011	2010
Current tax:		
Current tax	1,443	1,573
Adjustments of current tax of a prior year	(207)	–
	1,236	1,573
Deferred tax:		
Origination and reversal of temporary differences	57,991	41,695
Change in tax rate[i]	89	–
Adjustment for prior year	(12)	–
	58,068	41,695
	59,304	43,268

(i) Effect of substantively enacted corporate income tax rate changes

(c) Deferred tax

Components of the net deferred tax liability are as follows:

	December 31 2011	December 31 2010	January 1 2010
Deferred tax liability:			
Property and equipment	(278,003)	(280,899)	(274,853)
Deferred partnership income	(67,473)	(43,437)	(11,913)
Net unrealized gain on derivatives designated in a hedging relationship	(1,062)	–	–
Deferred tax asset:			
Share issue costs	747	1,143	1,561
Net unrealized loss on effective portion of derivatives designated in a hedging relationship	–	919	2,120
Non-capital losses[i]	7,348	45,010	50,200
Credit carry forwards[ii]	11,987	10,857	9,376
	(326,456)	(266,407)	(223,509)

(i) Non-capital losses will begin to expire in 2014.
(ii) Credit carry forwards recognized for unused corporate minimum tax credits will begin to expire in 2013.

Notes to Consolidated Financial Statements
For the years ended December 31, 2011 and 2010
(Stated in thousands of Canadian dollars, except share and per share amounts)

13. Share capital

(a) Authorized

Unlimited number of common voting shares

The common voting shares may be owned and controlled only by Canadians and shall confer the right to one vote per common voting share at all meetings of shareholders of the Corporation.

If a common voting share becomes beneficially owned or controlled by a person who is not a Canadian, such common voting share shall be converted into one variable voting share automatically and without any further act of the Corporation or the holder.

Unlimited number of variable voting shares

The variable voting shares may be beneficially owned and controlled only by a person who is not Canadian and are entitled to one vote per variable voting share unless (i) the number of issued and outstanding variable voting shares exceed 25% of the total number of all issued and outstanding variable voting shares and common voting shares collectively, including securities currently convertible into such a share and currently exercisable options and rights to acquire such shares (or any higher percentage the Governor in Council may specify pursuant to the *Canada Transportation Act*) or (ii) the total number of votes cast by or on behalf of the holders of variable voting shares at any meeting exceeds 25% (or any higher percentage the Governor in Council may specify pursuant to the *Canada Transportation Act*) of the total number of votes cast that may be cast at such meeting.

If either of the thresholds described in the paragraph above is surpassed at any time, the vote attached to each variable voting share will decrease automatically and without further act or formality to equal the maximum permitted vote per variable voting share. In the circumstance described in (i) in the paragraph above, the variable voting shares as a class cannot carry more than 25% (or any higher percentage the Governor in Council may specify pursuant to the *Canada Transportation Act*) of the aggregate votes attached to all variable voting shares and common voting shares collectively, including securities currently convertible into such a share and currently exercisable options and rights to acquire such shares. In the circumstance described in (ii) in the paragraph above, the variable voting shares as a class cannot, for a given shareholders' meeting, carry more than 25% (or any higher percentage the Governor in Council may specify pursuant to the *Canada Transportation Act*) of the total number of votes that can be exercised at the meeting.

Each issued and outstanding variable voting share shall be automatically converted into one common voting share without any further intervention on the part of the Corporation or of the holder if (i) the variable voting share is or becomes owned and controlled by a Canadian or if (ii) the provisions contained in the *Canada Transportation Act* relating to foreign ownership restrictions are repealed and not replaced with other similar provisions in applicable legislation.

Unlimited number of non-voting shares and unlimited number of non-voting first, second and third preferred shares

The non-voting shares and non-voting preferred shares may be issued, from time to time in one or more series, each series consisting of such number of non-voting shares and non-voting preferred shares as determined by the Corporation's Board of Directors who may also fix the designations, rights, privileges, restrictions and conditions attached to the shares of each series of non-voting shares and non-voting preferred shares. There are no non-voting shares or non-voting preferred shares issued and outstanding.

(b) Issued and outstanding

	2011 Number	2011 Amount	2010 Number	2010 Amount
Common and variable voting shares:				
Balance, beginning of year	142,958,414	647,637	144,359,383	633,075
Issuance of shares pursuant to stock option plan	173,584	34	741,014	520
Share-based payment expense on stock options exercised	–	4,011	–	21,860
Issuance of shares pursuant to key employee and pilot plan	18,681	–	2,298	–
Share-based payment expense on settled key employee and pilot units	–	252	–	29
Issuance of shares pursuant to executive share unit plan	55,967	–	194,449	–
Share-based payment expense on executive share units exercised	–	832	–	2,748
Shares repurchased	(4,926,090)	(22,358)	(2,338,730)	(10,595)
Balance, end of year	138,280,556	630,408	142,958,414	647,637

As at December 31, 2011, the number of common voting shares outstanding was 130,827,446 (2010 – 137,489,456) and the number of variable voting shares was 7,453,110 (2010 – 5,468,958).

On November 2, 2010, the Corporation filed a notice with the Toronto Stock Exchange (TSX) to make a normal course issuer bid to purchase outstanding shares on the open market. As approved by the TSX, the Corporation was authorized to purchase up to 7,264,820 shares (representing 5% of its issued and outstanding shares at the time of the bid) during the period of November 5, 2010, to November 4, 2011, or until such earlier time as the bid was completed or terminated at the option of the Corporation. Shares purchased under the bid were purchased on the open market through the facilities of the TSX at the prevailing market price at the time of the transaction. Shares acquired under the bid were cancelled. As of August 9, 2011, the Corporation successfully completed the 2010 bid.

During the year ended December 31, 2011, the Corporation purchased and subsequently cancelled 4,926,090 shares under its normal course issuer bid for total consideration of $74,570. The average book value of the shares repurchased of $4.54 per share was charged to share capital with the $52,212 excess of the market price over the average book value, including transaction costs, charged to retained earnings.

(c) Stock option plan

The Corporation has a stock option plan, whereby at December 31, 2011, 11,520,284 (2010 – 11,693,868) voting shares were reserved for issuance to officers and employees of the Corporation, subject to the following limitations:

(i) the number of common voting shares reserved for issuance to any one optionee will not exceed 5% of the issued and outstanding voting shares at any time;

(ii) the number of common voting shares reserved for issuance to insiders shall not exceed 10% of the issued and outstanding voting shares; and

(iii) the number of common voting shares issuable under the stock option plans, which may be issued within a one-year period, shall not exceed 10% of the issued and outstanding voting shares at any time.

In May 2011, the Board approved amendments to the stock option plan to extend the maximum permitted expiry date from five years to seven years for all new options granted. Stock options are granted at a price equal to the five day weighted average market value of the Corporation's voting shares preceding the date of grant and vest completely or on a graded basis on the first, second and third anniversary from the date of grant.

Notes to Consolidated Financial Statements
For the years ended December 31, 2011 and 2010
(Stated in thousands of Canadian dollars, except share and per share amounts)

13. Share capital (continued)

(c) Stock option plan (continued)

Changes in the number of options, with their weighted average exercise prices, are summarized below:

	2011		2010	
	Number of options	Weighted average exercise price	Number of options	Weighted average exercise price
Stock options outstanding, beginning of year	8,083,431	14.21	11,521,844	13.42
Granted	1,856,471	14.85	2,024,143	12.78
Exercised	(1,033,254)	12.56	(5,100,279)	11.83
Forfeited	(21,564)	13.36	(32,607)	12.58
Expired	(1,534,328)	16.32	(329,670)	14.77
Stock options outstanding, end of year	7,350,756	14.17	8,083,431	14.21
Exercisable, end of year	5,044,598	14.03	3,348,164	16.49

Under the terms of the Corporation's stock option plan, with the approval of the Corporation, option holders can either (i) elect to receive shares by delivering cash to the Corporation in the amount of the exercise price of the options, or (ii) choose a cashless settlement alternative, whereby they can elect to receive a number of shares equivalent to the market value of the options over the exercise price. For the year ended December 31, 2011, option holders exercised 1,030,565 options (2010 – 5,056,288 options) on a cashless settlement basis and received 170,895 shares (2010 – 697,023 shares). For the year ended December 31, 2011, 2,689 options were exercised on a cash basis and received 2,689 shares (2010 – 43,991 options and 43,991 shares, respectively).

The following table summarizes the options outstanding and exercisable as at December 31, 2011:

	Outstanding options			Exercisable options	
Range of exercise prices	Number outstanding	Weighted average remaining life (years)	Weighted average exercise price	Number exercisable	Weighted average exercise price
$11.00–$12.50	2,017,450	1.58	12.48	1,992,745	12.48
$12.51–$15.50	3,572,614	4.46	13.88	1,291,161	12.79
$15.51–$19.99	1,760,692	0.35	16.69	1,760,692	16.69
	7,350,756	2.69	14.17	5,044,598	14.03

The fair value of the options is expensed over the service period, with an offsetting entry to equity reserves. The fair value of each option grant is estimated on the date of grant using the Black-Scholes option pricing model. Upon the exercise of stock options, consideration received, together with amounts previously recorded in equity reserves, is recorded as an increase to share capital.

The fair value of options granted during the years ended December 31, 2011 and 2010, and the assumptions used in their determination are as follows:

	2011	2010
Weighted average fair value per option	4.30	4.02
Weighted average risk-free interest rate	2.3%	2.5%
Weighted average expected volatility	38%	38%
Expected life of options (years)	4.0	3.6
Weighted average dividend yield	1.4%	0.02%

Notes to Consolidated Financial Statements
For the years ended December 31, 2011 and 2010
(Stated in thousands of Canadian dollars, except share and per share amounts)

13. Share capital (continued)

(d) Key employee and pilot plan

The Corporation has a key employee and pilot (KEP) plan, whereby restricted share units (RSUs) are issued to key employees and pilots of the Corporation. The fair market value of the RSUs at the time of grant is equal to the weighted average trading price of the Corporation's voting shares for the five trading days immediately preceding the grant date. Each RSU entitles the employee to receive payment upon vesting in the form of voting shares of the Corporation. The Corporation intends to settle all RSUs with shares either through the purchase of voting shares on the open market or the issuance of new shares from treasury; however, wholly at its own discretion, the Corporation may settle the units in cash. The RSU's time vest at the end of a two or three-year period, with compensation expense being recognized in net earnings over the service period. As at December 31, 2011, 979,021 (2010 – 997,702) voting shares of the Corporation were reserved for issuance under the KEP plan. For the year ended December 31, 2011, the Corporation settled all RSUs with shares issued from treasury.

	2011		2010	
	Number of units	Weighted fair value	Number of units	Weighted fair value
Units outstanding, beginning of year	171,129	12.77	–	–
Granted	201,391	14.77	177,440	12.77
Units, in lieu of dividends	5,308	13.31	–	–
Settled	(18,677)	13.62	(2,298)	12.77
Forfeited	(5,803)	13.48	(4,013)	12.77
Units outstanding, end of year	353,348	13.86	171,129	12.77
Vested, end of year	–		–	

(e) Executive share unit plan

The Corporation has an equity-based executive share unit (ESU) plan, whereby RSUs and performance share units (PSU) may be issued to senior executive officers. As at December 31, 2011, 959,425 (2010 – 805,551) voting shares of the Corporation were reserved for issuance under the ESU plan.

The fair market value of the RSUs and PSUs at the time of grant is equal to the weighted average trading price of the Corporation's voting shares for the five trading days immediately preceding the grant date.

Each RSU entitles the senior executive officers to receive payment upon exercise in the form of voting shares of the Corporation. RSUs time vest at the end of a three-year term, with compensation expense being recognized in net earnings over the service period.

Each PSU entitles the senior executive officers to receive payment upon exercise in the form of voting shares of the Corporation. PSU's time vest at the end of a three-year term and incorporate performance criteria established at the time of grant. Compensation expense is recognized in net earnings over the service period based on the number of units expected to vest.

	2011				2010			
	RSUs		PSUs		RSUs		PSUs	
	Number of units	Weighted fair value	Number of units	Weighted fair value	Number of units	Weighted fair value	Number of units	Weighted fair value
Units outstanding, beginning of year	187,875	13.73	199,486	13.73	143,461	14.10	191,276	14.10
Granted	75,213	15.39	91,450	15.44	127,750	13.57	119,323	13.79
Exercised	(55,321)	15.04	–	–	(83,336)	14.13	(111,113)	14.13
Forfeited	(6,051)	15.44	(39,995)	18.49	–	–	–	–
Units outstanding, end of year	201,716	13.94	250,941	13.94	187,875	13.73	199,486	13.90
Vested, end of year	46,902	14.20	50,087	13.28	17,211	14.16	22,948	14.16

Notes to Consolidated Financial Statements
For the years ended December 31, 2011 and 2010
(Stated in thousands of Canadian dollars, except share and per share amounts)

13. Share capital (continued)

(f) Share-based payment expense

The following table summarizes share-based payment expense for the Corporation's equity-based plans:

	2011	2010
Stock option plan	8,506	10,756
Key employee and pilot plan	2,378	1,153
Executive share unit plan	1,669	3,588
Total share-based payment expense	12,553	15,497
Presented on the consolidated statement of earnings as follows:		
Flight operations and navigational charges	5,042	8,785
Marketing, general and administration	7,511	6,712
Total share-based payment expense	12,553	15,497

(g) Deferred share units

The Corporation has a cash-settled deferred share unit (DSU) plan as an alternative form of compensation for independent members of the Corporation's Board of Directors. Each DSU entitles a participant to receive cash equal to the market value of the equivalent number of shares of the Corporation. The number of DSUs granted is determined based on the closing price of the Corporation's common shares on the trading day immediately prior to the date of grant. Total compensation expense is recognized at the time of grant. Fluctuations in the market value are recognized in the period in which the fluctuations occur. For the year ended December 31, 2011, 21,146 (2010 – 20,565) DSUs were granted, with $108 (2010 – $344) of expense included in marketing, general and administration expense. During the years ended December 31, 2011 and 2010, the Corporation did not settle any DSUs. The carrying amount of the liability, included in trade and other payables, relating to the cash-settled DSUs as at December 31, 2011 is $966 (2010 - $858). As at December 31, 2011, 82,134 (2010 – 60,988) DSUs are vested and outstanding. DSUs are redeemable upon the Director's retirement from the Board.

(h) Employee share purchase plan

The Corporation has an employee share purchase plan (ESPP), whereby the Corporation matches every dollar contributed by each employee. Under the terms of the ESPP, employees may contribute up to a maximum of 20% of their gross pay and acquire voting shares of the Corporation at the current fair market value of such shares. Shares acquired for the ESPP are restricted for one year. Employees may offer to sell shares, which have not been held for at least one year to the Corporation, four times per year. The purchase price of the voting shares shall be equal to 50% of the weighted average trading price of the Corporation's voting shares for the five trading days immediately preceding the employee's notice to the Corporation.

The Corporation has the option to acquire voting shares on behalf of employees through open market purchases or to issue new shares from treasury at the current market price, which is determined based on the volume weighted average trading price of the Corporation's voting shares for the five trading days preceding the issuance.

For the years ended December 31, 2011 and 2010, all shares were acquired through open market purchases.

The Corporation's share of the contributions in 2011 amounted to $58,682 (2010 – $52,643) and is recorded as compensation expense within the related business unit.

14. Dividends

During the year ended December 31, 2011 the Corporation declared quarterly cash dividends of $0.05 per share to its shareholders of common and variable voting shares. For the year ended December 31, 2011, the Corporation paid dividends totaling $35,000 (2010 - $nil). In aggregate, dividends of $27,852 (2010 - $7,148) were declared for the year ended December 31, 2011.

Subsequent to year end, on February 7, 2012, the Corporation's Board of Directors declared the 2012 first quarter dividend of $0.06 per common voting share and variable voting share, representing an increase of 20% from the Corporation's previous quarterly amount of $0.05 per share. The dividend is payable on March 30, 2012 to shareholders of record on March 14, 2012.

Notes to Consolidated Financial Statements
For the years ended December 31, 2011 and 2010
(Stated in thousands of Canadian dollars, except share and per share amounts)

15. Earnings per share

The following reflects the share data used in the computation of basic and diluted earnings per share:

	2011	2010
Weighted average number of shares outstanding – basic	139,902,637	144,852,548
Effect of dilution		
Employee stock options	332,489	26,077
Key employee and pilot - Restricted share units	226,704	73,433
Executive - Restricted share units	126,742	105,099
Executive - Performance share units	50,087	22,948
Weighted average number of shares outstanding – diluted	140,638,659	145,080,105

For the year ended December 31, 2011, 3,646,624 employee stock options (2010 – 7,105,619 employee stock options) were not included in the calculation of dilutive potential shares as the result would be anti-dilutive.

There have been no other transactions involving shares between the reporting date and the date of completion of these statements.

16. Finance income and cost

	Note	2011	2010
Finance income:			
Interest on cash and cash equivalents		15,987	9,910
Finance cost:			
Interest on term loans and finance leases		55,833	66,189
Accretion on aircraft lease return obligations	9	5,078	4,725
		60,911	70,914

Notes to Consolidated Financial Statements
For the years ended December 31, 2011 and 2010
(Stated in thousands of Canadian dollars, except share and per share amounts)

17. Financial instruments and risk management

(a) Fair value of financial assets and financial liabilities

The Corporation's financial assets and liabilities consist primarily of cash and cash equivalents, accounts receivable, derivatives both designated and not designated in an effective hedging relationship, deposits, accounts payable and accrued liabilities, long-term debt and obligations under finance leases. The following tables set out the Corporation's classification and carrying amount, together with the fair value, for each type of financial asset and financial liability as at December 31, 2011 and 2010, and January 1, 2010:

	Fair value		Amortized cost		Totals	
December 31, 2011	Through profit or loss	Derivatives	Loans and receivables	Other financial liabilities	Carrying amount	Fair value
Asset (liability):						
Cash and cash equivalents (i)	1,291,946	–	–	–	1,291,946	1,291,946
Accounts receivable	–	–	34,122	–	34,122	34,122
Foreign exchange derivatives (ii)	–	4,662	–	–	4,662	4,662
Fuel derivatives (iii)	–	7,611	–	–	7,611	7,611
Interest rate derivatives (iv)	–	(532)	–	–	(532)	(532)
Deposits (v)	28,386	–	–	–	28,386	28,386
Accounts payable and accrued liabilities (vi)	–	–	–	(284,902)	(284,902)	(284,902)
Long-term debt (vii)	–	–	–	(828,712)	(828,712)	(937,336)
Obligations under finance leases (viii)	–	–	–	(3,249)	(3,249)	(3,249)
	1,320,332	11,741	34,122	(1,116,863)	249,332	140,708

	Fair value		Amortized cost		Totals	
December 31, 2010	Through profit or loss	Derivatives	Loans and receivables	Other financial liabilities	Carrying amount	Fair value
Asset (liability):						
Cash and cash equivalents (i)	1,187,899	–	–	–	1,187,899	1,187,899
Accounts receivable	–	–	17,518	–	17,518	17,518
Foreign exchange derivatives (ii)	–	(3,579)	–	–	(3,579)	(3,579)
Fuel derivatives (iii)	–	4,889	–	–	4,889	4,889
Deposits (v)	28,258	–	–	–	28,258	28,258
Accounts payable and accrued liabilities (vi)	–	–	–	(264,136)	(264,136)	(264,136)
Long-term debt (vii)	–	–	–	(1,026,802)	(1,026,802)	(1,141,961)
Obligations under finance leases (viii)	–	–	–	(3,357)	(3,357)	(3,357)
	1,216,157	1,310	17,518	(1,294,295)	(59,310)	(174,469)

Notes to Consolidated Financial Statements
For the years ended December 31, 2011 and 2010
(Stated in thousands of Canadian dollars, except share and per share amounts)

17. Financial instruments and risk management (continued)

(a) Fair value of financial assets and financial liabilities (continued)

	Fair value		Amortized cost		Totals	
January 1, 2010	Through profit or loss	Derivatives	Loans and receivables	Other financial liabilities	Carrying amount	Fair value
Asset (liability):						
Cash and cash equivalents (i)	1,005,181	–	–	–	1,005,181	1,005,181
Accounts receivable	–	–	27,654	–	27,654	27,654
Foreign exchange derivatives (ii)	–	(1,249)	–	–	(1,249)	(1,249)
Fuel derivatives (iii)	–	(8,667)	–	–	(8,667)	(8,667)
Deposits (v)	27,264	–	–	–	27,264	27,264
Accounts payable and accrued liabilities (vi)	–	–	–	(210,687)	(210,687)	(210,687)
Long-term debt (vii)	–	–	–	(1,193,276)	(1,193,276)	(1,319,990)
Obligations under finance leases (viii)	–	–	–	(4,102)	(4,102)	(4,102)
	1,032,445	(9,916)	27,654	(1,408,065)	(357,882)	(484,596)

(i) Includes restricted cash of $48,341 (December 31, 2010 – $28,583; January 1, 2010 – $10,192)

(ii) Includes $4,662 (December 31, 2010 – $nil; January 1, 2010 – $181) classified in prepaid expenses, deposits and other, and $nil (December 2010 – $3,579; January 2010 – $1,430) classified in accounts payable and accrued liabilities.

(iii) Includes $7,611 (December 31, 2010 – $5,689; January 1, 2010 – $96) classified in prepaid expenses, deposits and other, and $nil (December 2010 – $800; January 2010 – $8,763) classified in accounts payable and accrued liabilities.

(iv) Includes current portion of interest rate derivatives of $112 included in accounts payable and accrued liabilities and long-term portion of interest rate derivatives of $420 included in other long-term liabilities.

(v) Includes $16,278 (December 31, 2010 – $14,752; January 1, 2010 – $11,249) classified in prepaid expenses, deposits and other, and $12,108 (December 31, 2010 – $13,506; January 1, 2010 – $16,015) classified in other assets.

(vi) Excludes current portion of maintenance provisions of $245 (December 31, 2010 – $12,372; January 1, 2010 – $8,031), deferred FGP revenue of $22,020 (December 31, 2010 – $6,823; January 1, 2010 – $nil), foreign exchange derivative liabilities of $nil (December 31, 2010 – $3,579; January 1, 2010 – $1,430), fuel derivative liabilities of $nil (December 31, 2010 – $800; January 1, 2010 – $8,763) and interest rate derivative liabilities of $112 (December 31, 2010 – $nil; January 1, 2010 – $nil).

(vii) Includes current portion of long-term debt of $158,832 (December 31, 2010 – $178,337; January 1, 2010 – $165,111) and long-term debt of $669,880 (December 31, 2010 – $848,465; January 1, 2010 – $1,028,165).

(viii) Includes current portion of obligations under finance leases of $75 (December 31, 2010 – $108; January 1, 2010 – $744) and obligations under finance leases of $3,174 (December 31, 2010 – $3,249; January 1, 2010 – $3,358).

The following items shown in the consolidated statement of financial position as at December 31, 2011 and 2010, and January 1, 2010, are measured at fair value on a recurring basis using level 1 or level 2 inputs. The fair value of the financial assets and liabilities at December 31, 2011, using level 3 inputs, was $nil (December 31, 2010 – $nil; January 1, 2010 – $nil).

December 31, 2011	Level 1	Level 2	Total
Asset (liability):			
Cash and cash equivalents	1,291,946	–	1,291,946
Foreign exchange derivatives	–	4,662	4,662
Fuel derivatives	–	7,611	7,611
Interest rate derivatives	–	(532)	(532)
Deposits	28,386	–	28,386
	1,320,332	11,741	1,332,073

Notes to Consolidated Financial Statements
For the years ended December 31, 2011 and 2010
(Stated in thousands of Canadian dollars, except share and per share amounts)

17. Financial instruments and risk management (continued)

(a) Fair value of financial assets and financial liabilities (continued)

Deposits: Relate to purchased aircraft and airport operations and are based on a floating market rate of interest. Classified in level 1 as the measurement inputs are unadjusted, observable inputs in an active market.

Long-term debt: The fair value of the Corporation's fixed-rate long-term debt is determined by discounting the future contractual cash flows under the current financing arrangements at discount rates presently available to the Corporation for loans with similar terms and remaining maturities. At December 31, 2011, the rates used in determining the fair value ranged from 1.28% to 1.61% (December 31, 2010 – 2.00% to 2.74%; January 1, 2010 – 2.28% to 3.27%).

(b) Risk management related to financial instruments

The Corporation is exposed to market, credit and liquidity risks associated with its financial assets and liabilities. From time to time, the Corporation will use various financial derivatives to reduce exposures from changes in foreign exchange rates, interest rates and jet fuel prices. The Corporation does not hold or use any derivative instruments for trading or speculative purposes.

The Corporation's Board of Directors has responsibility for the establishment and approval of the Corporation's overall risk management policies, including those related to financial instruments. Management performs continuous assessments so that all significant risks related to financial instruments are reviewed and addressed in light of changes to market conditions and the Corporation's operating activities.

Market Risk

Market risk is the risk that the fair value or future cash flows of a financial instrument will fluctuate due to changes in market prices. The Corporation's significant market risks relate to fuel price risk, foreign exchange risk and interest rate risk.

(i) Fuel price risk

The airline industry is inherently dependent upon jet fuel to operate and, therefore, the Corporation is exposed to the risk of volatile fuel prices. Fuel prices are impacted by a host of factors outside the Corporation's control, such as significant weather events, geopolitical tensions, refinery capacity, and global demand and supply. For the year ended December 31, 2011, aircraft fuel expense represented approximately 33% (2010 – 28%) of the Corporation's total operating expenses.

Under the Corporation's fuel price risk management policy, the Corporation is permitted to hedge a portion of its future anticipated jet fuel purchases for up to 36 months, as approved by the Board of Directors. The hedging program is designed to mitigate the risk of sudden and substantial movements in fuel prices causing volatility in earnings and cash flows. Management continuously reviews its hedging positions based on market conditions and competitors' positions. Financial derivatives in crude-oil-based commodities (including a variety of crude oil, heating oil and jet fuel benchmarks) that are traded directly on organized exchanges or are available over the counter are used by the Corporation to mitigate the risk of volatile fuel prices.

As at December 31, 2011, the Corporation had Canadian-dollar West Texas Intermediate (WTI) call options to hedge approximately 23% of its anticipated jet fuel requirements for the next 12 months. The following table outlines, per year, as at December 31, 2011, the notional volumes per barrel (bbl.) along with the weighted average contract prices:

Type	Period	Instrument	Notional volumes (bbl.)	WTI average strike price ($ CAD/bbl.)
WTI	Q1 2012	Call options	420,000	117
WTI	Q2 2012	Call options	430,000	112
WTI	Q3 2012	Call options	520,000	109
WTI	Q4 2012	Call options	240,000	115

Upon proper qualification, the Corporation accounts for its fuel derivatives as cash flow hedges.

Notes to Consolidated Financial Statements
For the years ended December 31, 2011 and 2010
(Stated in thousands of Canadian dollars, except share and per share amounts)

17. Financial instruments and risk management (continued)

(a) Fair value of financial assets and financial liabilities (continued)

December 31, 2010	Level 1	Level 2	Total
Asset (liability):			
Cash and cash equivalents	1,187,899	–	1,187,899
Foreign exchange derivatives	–	(3,579)	(3,579)
Fuel derivatives	–	4,889	4,889
Deposits	28,258	–	28,258
	1,216,157	1,310	1,217,467

January 1, 2010	Level 1	Level 2	Total
Asset (liability):			
Cash and cash equivalents	1,005,181	–	1,005,181
Foreign exchange derivatives	–	(1,249)	(1,249)
Fuel derivatives	–	(8,667)	(8,667)
Deposits	27,264	–	27,264
	1,032,445	(9,916)	1,022,529

During the years ended December 31, 2011 and 2010, there were no transfers between level 1, level 2 and level 3 classified assets and liabilities.

Cash and cash equivalents: Consist of bank balances and short-term investments, primarily highly liquid debt instruments, with terms up to 97 days. Classified in level 1, as measurement inputs are derived from observable, unadjusted quoted prices in active markets. Interest income is recorded in the consolidated statement of earnings as finance income. Due to their short-term nature, the carrying value of cash and cash equivalents approximates their fair value.

Foreign exchange derivatives: Foreign exchange derivatives consist of forward and option contracts. The fair value of the foreign exchange forward contracts is measured based on the difference between the contracted rate and the current forward price obtained from the counterparty. Classified in level 2, as the significant measurement inputs used in the valuation models are observable in active markets. At December 31, 2011, the average contracted rate on the forward contracts was 0.9914 (December 31, 2010 – 1.0264; January 1, 2010 – 1.0671) Canadian dollars to US dollars, and the average forward rate used in determining the fair value was 1.0201 (December 31, 2010 – 0.9995; January 1, 2010 – 1.0512) Canadian dollars to one US dollar.

The fair value of the foreign exchange option contracts is determined through a standard option valuation technique used by the counterparty based on market inputs, including foreign exchange rates, interest rates and volatilities. Classified in level 2, as the significant measurement inputs are observable in active markets. There are no foreign exchange option contracts outstanding at December 31, 2011 (December 31, 2010 – $nil; January 1, 2010 – $(211)).

Fuel derivatives: Fuel derivatives consist of swaps, collars and call option contracts. The fair value of the fuel derivatives is determined using inputs, including quoted forward prices for commodities, quoted volatility curves, foreign exchange rates and interest rates, which can be observed in the marketplace. The fair value of the swap contracts is estimated by discounting the difference between the contractual strike price and the current forward price. These instruments are classified in level 2, as the inputs noted above. These instruments are classified in level 2, as the significant measurement inputs are observable in an active market. As at December 31, 2011, for the period that the Corporation is hedged, the closing forward curve for crude oil averaged approximately US $99 per barrel (December 31, 2010 – US $94; January 1, 2010 – US $82), with the average forward foreign exchange rate used in determining the fair value being 1.0251 (December 31, 2010 – 1.0032; January 1, 2010 – 1.0536) Canadian dollars to one US dollar.

The fair value of the collar and call option derivatives are estimated by the use of a standard option valuation technique using the inputs noted above. These instruments are classified in level 2, as the significant measurement inputs are observable in an active market.

Interest rate derivatives: Interest rate derivatives consist of swap contracts that exchange a floating rate of interest with a fixed rate of interest. The fair value of the interest rate swaps is determined by measuring the difference between the fixed contracted rate and the forward curve for the applicable floating interest rates obtained from the counterparty. Classified in level 2, as the significant measurement inputs used in the valuation models, such as forward interest rate curves, are observable in active markets. At December 31, 2011, the weighted average fixed interest rate on the Corporation's contractual nominal notional debt is 2.19% and the closing average forward interest rate for the three month CDOR for the term of the debt is 2.60%.

Notes to Consolidated Financial Statements
For the years ended December 31, 2011 and 2010
(Stated in thousands of Canadian dollars, except share and per share amounts)

17. Financial instruments and risk management (continued)

(b) Risk management related to financial instruments (continued)

Market Risk (continued)

(i) Fuel price risk (continued)

The following table presents the financial impact and statement presentation of the Corporation's fuel derivatives on the consolidated statement of financial position:

	Statement presentation	December 31 2011	December 31 2010	January 1 2010
Receivable from counterparties for fuel derivatives	Accounts receivable/Prepaid expenses, deposits and other	27	445	96
Fair value of fuel derivatives	Prepaid expenses, deposits and other	7,611	5,244	–
Fair value of fuel derivatives	Accounts payable and accrued liabilities	–	–	(7,521)
Payable to counterparties for fuel derivatives	Accounts payable and accrued liabilities	–	(800)	(1,242)
Unrealized (gain)/loss from fuel derivatives (i)	Hedge reserves – before tax impact	–	(11)	6,713

(i) The estimated amount reported in hedge reserves that is expected to be reclassified to net earnings as a component of aircraft fuel expense, when the underlying jet fuel is consumed during the next 12 months, is $nil (December 31, 2010 – gain before tax of $11; January 1, 2010 – loss before tax of $6,713).

The following table presents the financial impact and statement presentation of the Corporation's fuel derivatives on the consolidated statement of earnings for the 12 months ended December 31, 2011 and 2010:

	Statement presentation	2011	2010
Realized gain (loss) on designated fuel derivatives	Aircraft fuel	2,656	(9,172)
Gain (loss) on designated fuel derivatives	Loss on derivatives	(6,052)	44

During the year ended December 31, 2011, the Corporation cash settled fuel derivatives in its favour of $2,732 (2010 – $8,980 in favour of the counterparties). The Corporation paid cash premiums for option contracts of $8,506 for the year ended December 31, 2011 (2010 – $6,189).

The following table presents the financial impact and statement presentation of the Corporation's fuel derivatives on the forward curve for WTI, the underlying commodity of the Corporation's fuel derivatives:

Year	Instrument	December 31 Fair Value	10% Increase in WTI Gain (Loss) Income	OCI	10% Decrease in WTI Gain (Loss) Income	OCI
2011	Fuel derivatives	7,611	–	4,974	–	(2,986)
2010	Fuel derivatives	5,244	–	4,896	–	(2,455)

This sensitivity analysis assumes that 100% of the change in price is considered effective under cash flow hedge accounting. Should some or all of the change in price be considered ineffective under hedge accounting, the ineffective portion would be recorded in non-operating income (expense). It also assumes that all other variables remain constant, particularly foreign exchange and interest rates. These assumptions may not be representative of actual movements.

Notes to Consolidated Financial Statements
For the years ended December 31, 2011 and 2010
(Stated in thousands of Canadian dollars, except share and per share amounts)

17. Financial instruments and risk management (continued)

(b) Risk management related to financial instruments (continued)

Market Risk (continued)

(ii) Foreign exchange risk

The Corporation is exposed to foreign exchange risks arising from fluctuations in exchange rates on its US-dollar-denominated monetary assets and liabilities and its US dollar operating expenditures, mainly aircraft fuel, aircraft leasing expense, and certain maintenance and airport operations costs.

US dollar monetary assets and liabilities

The gain on foreign exchange included in the Corporation's consolidated statement of earnings is mainly attributable to the effect of the changes in the value of the Corporation's US-dollar-denominated monetary assets and liabilities. As at December 31, 2011, US-dollar-denominated net monetary liabilities totaled approximately US $21,528 (December 31, 2010 – US $18,798; January 1, 2010 – US $32,867).

The Corporation estimates that a one-cent change in the value of the US dollar versus the Canadian dollar as at December 31, 2011, would have increased or decreased net earnings, net of tax, for the year ended December 31, 2011, by $154 (2010 – $127), as a result of the Corporation's US-dollar-denominated net monetary liability balance.

US dollar aircraft leasing costs

As at December 31, 2011 the Corporation has entered into foreign exchange forward contracts for an average of US $13,367 (2010 – US $11,535) per month for the period of January to December 2012 for a total of US $160,400 (2010 – US $138,420) at a weighted average contract price of 0.9914 Canadian dollars to US dollars to offset a portion of its US-dollar-denominated aircraft lease payments. As at December 31, 2011, no portion of the forward contracts was considered ineffective.

Upon proper qualification, the Corporation accounts for its foreign exchange derivatives as cash flow hedges.

The following table presents the financial impact and statement presentation of the Corporation's foreign exchange derivatives on the consolidated statement of financial position:

	Statement presentation	December 31 2011	December 31 2010	January 1 2010
Fair value of foreign exchange derivatives	Prepaid expenses, deposits and other	4,662	–	181
Fair value of foreign exchange derivatives	Accounts payable and accrued liabilities	–	(3,579)	(1,219)
Unrealized gain (loss) from foreign exchange derivatives	Hedge reserves – before tax impact	4,662	(3,579)	(1,038)

The following table presents the financial impact and statement presentation of the Corporation's foreign exchange derivatives on the consolidated statement of earnings for the 12 months ended December 31, 2011 and 2010:

	Statement presentation	2011	2010
Realized loss on designated foreign exchange derivatives	Aircraft leasing	(4,840)	(2,143)
Loss on undesignated foreign exchange derivatives	Loss on derivatives	–	(78)

A one-cent change in the US-dollar exchange rate for the year ended December 31, 2011, would impact OCI, net of taxes, by $1,192 (2010 – $1,028) as a result of the Corporation's foreign exchange derivatives.

(iii) Interest rate risk

Interest rate risk is the risk that the value or future cash flows of a financial instrument will fluctuate as a result of changes in market interest rates.

Cash and cash equivalents

The Corporation is exposed to interest rate fluctuations on its short-term investments, included in cash and cash equivalents. A change of 50 basis points in the market interest rate would have had an approximate impact on net earnings of $4,375 (December 31, 2010 – $3,762; January 1, 2010 – $2,555) as a result of the Corporation's short-term investment activities.

Notes to Consolidated Financial Statements
For the years ended December 31, 2011 and 2010
(Stated in thousands of Canadian dollars, except share and per share amounts)

17. Financial instruments and risk management (continued)

(b) Risk management related to financial instruments (continued)

Market Risk (continued)

(iii) Interest rate risk (continued)

Deposits

The Corporation is exposed to interest rate fluctuations on its deposits that relate to purchased aircraft and airport operations, which, as at December 31, 2011, totaled $28,386 (December 31, 2010 – $28,258; January 1, 2010 – $27,264). A reasonable change in market interest rates as at December 31, 2011, would not have significantly impacted the Corporation's net earnings due to the small size of these deposits.

Long-term debt

The fixed-rate nature of the majority of the Corporation's long-term debt mitigates the impact of interest rate fluctuations over the term of the outstanding debt. The Corporation accounts for its long-term fixed-rate debt at amortized cost, and, therefore, a change in interest rates as at December 31, 2011, would not impact net earnings.

At December 31, 2011, the Corporation had two interest rate swap contracts outstanding with a 12 year term beginning in February 2012 and June 2012, respectively, to fix the interest rate on future variable interest rate debt at 2.89% and 2.99% respectively, inclusive of a 75 basis point spread. The variable interest rate debt in question relates to the purchase of two future aircraft in 2012 and has yet to be drawn and is therefore not recorded in the Corporation's accounts at December 31, 2011. However, for purposes of valuing the interest rate derivatives at December 31, 2011, an average contractual nominal notional amount of $35,000 per swap contract was used.

Upon delivery of the two aircraft in 2012, the Corporation will draw on the available loan amounts. Once drawn, the contractual nominal notional amount becomes equal to the amount drawn on the loan.

Upon proper qualification, the Corporation accounts for its interest rate swap derivatives as cash flow hedges.

At December 31, 2011 the unrealized loss on interest rate derivatives recorded in accumulated other comprehensive income, before tax, was $532 (December 31, 2010 – $nil; January 1, 2010 – $nil) with $112 (December 31, 2010 – $336,926; January 1, 2010 – $297,720). Typically, the Corporation has cash and cash equivalents on hand to have sufficient liquidity to meet its liabilities, when due, – $nil) classified in accounts payable and accrued liabilities and $420 (December 31, 2010 – $nil; January 1, 2010 – $nil) classified in other long-term liabilities.

A reasonable change in market interest rates at December 31, 2011 would not significantly impact the earnings or equity of the Corporation due to the insignificant fair value balance of the interest rate derivative.

Notes to Consolidated Financial Statements
For the years ended December 31, 2011 and 2010
(Stated in thousands of Canadian dollars, except share and per share amounts)

17. Financial instruments and risk management (continued)

(b) Risk management related to financial instruments (continued)

Credit Risk

Credit risk is the risk that one party to a financial instrument will cause a financial loss for the other party by failing to discharge an obligation. As at December 31, 2011, the Corporation's credit exposure consists primarily of the carrying amounts of cash and cash equivalents, accounts receivable, deposits and the fair value of derivative financial assets.

The Corporation's maximum exposure to credit risk is represented by the balances in the aforementioned accounts:

	December 31 2011	December 31 2010	January 1 2010
Cash and cash equivalents [(i)]	1,243,605	1,159,316	994,989
Restricted cash[(i)]	48,341	28,583	10,192
Accounts receivable [(ii)]	34,122	17,518	27,654
Deposits [(iii)]	28,386	28,258	27,264
Derivative financial assets [(iv)]	12,273	5,689	277

(i) Consist of bank balances and short-term investments with terms of up to 97 days. Credit risk associated with cash and cash equivalents is minimized substantially by ensuring that these financial assets are invested primarily in debt instruments with highly rated financial institutions, some with provincial-government-backed guarantees. The Corporation manages its exposure by assessing the financial strength of its counterparties and by limiting the total exposure to any one individual counterparty.

(ii) All significant counterparties, both current and new, are reviewed and approved for credit on a regular basis under the Corporation's credit management policies. The Corporation does not hold any collateral as security, however, in some cases the Corporation requires guaranteed letters of credit with certain of its counterparties. Trade receivables are generally settled in less than 30 days. Industry receivables are generally settled within 30 to 60 days.

(iii) The Corporation is not exposed to counterparty credit risk on its deposits that relate to purchased aircraft, as the funds are held in a security trust separate from the assets of the financial institution. While the Corporation is exposed to counterparty credit risk on its deposit relating to airport operations, it considers this risk to be remote because of the nature and size of the counterparty.

(iv) Derivative financial assets consist of fuel derivative contracts and foreign exchange forward contracts. The Corporation reviews the size and credit rating of both current and any new counterparties in addition to limiting the total exposure to any one counterparty.

The Corporation's allowance for doubtful accounts provision relates to a disputed balance with a cargo operation counterparty that has yet to be settled. The provision was recorded in a prior year as a bad debt. There were no new bad debts recorded for the year ended December 31, 2011 and 2010.

Liquidity risk

Liquidity risk is the risk that the Corporation will encounter difficulty in meeting obligations associated with financial liabilities. The Corporation maintains a strong liquidity position and sufficient financial resources to meet its obligations as they fall due.

The table below presents a maturity analysis of the Corporation's undiscounted contractual cash flows for its non-derivative and derivative financial liabilities as at December 31, 2011. The analysis is based on foreign exchange and interest rates in effect at the consolidated statement of financial position date, and includes both principal and interest cash flows for long-term debt and obligations under finance leases.

	Total	Within 1 year	1–3 years	3–5 years	Over 5 years
Accounts payable and accrued liabilities [(i)]	284,902	284,902	–	–	–
Long-term debt	975,770	204,770	382,271	250,723	138,006
Obligations under finance leases	5,596	245	490	490	4,371
	1,266,268	489,917	382,761	251,213	142,377

(i) Excludes current portion of maintenance provisions of $245, deferred FGP revenue of $22,020 and interest rate derivative liabilities of $112.

A portion of the Corporation's cash and cash equivalents balance relates to cash collected with respect to advance ticket sales, for which the balance at December 31, 2011 was $432,186 (December 31, 2010 – $336,926; January 1, 2010 – $297,720). Typically, the Corporation has cash and cash equivalents on hand to have sufficient liquidity to meet its liabilities, when due, under both normal and stressed conditions. As at December 31, 2011 the Corporation had cash and cash equivalents on hand of 2.88 times (December 31, 2010 – 3.44; January 1, 2010 – 3.34) the advance ticket sales balance.

The Corporation aims to maintain a current ratio, defined as current assets over current liabilities, of at least 1.00. As at December 31, 2011, the Corporation's current ratio was 1.51 (December 31, 2010 – 1.53; January 1, 2010 – 1.49). As at December 31, 2011, the Corporation has not been required to post collateral with respect to any of its outstanding derivative contracts.

Notes to Consolidated Financial Statements
For the years ended December 31, 2011 and 2010
(Stated in thousands of Canadian dollars, except share and per share amounts)

18. Commitments

(a) Purchased aircraft

As at December 31, 2011, the Corporation is committed to purchase 35 737-700 and two 737-800 aircraft for delivery between 2012 and 2018. The remaining estimated amounts to be paid in deposits and purchase prices for the 37 aircraft in US dollars and Canadian dollar equivalents are as follows:

	USD	CAD
Within 1 year	99,550	101,240
1 – 3 years	421,238	428,392
3 – 5 years	703,952	715,907
Over 5 years	386,466	393,030
	1,611,206	1,638,569

(b) Operating leases and commitments

The Corporation has entered into operating leases and commitments for aircraft, land, buildings, equipment, computer hardware, software licenses and satellite programming. As at December 31, 2011 the future payments in US dollars, where applicable, and Canadian dollar equivalents under operating leases and commitments are as follows:

	USD	CAD
Within 1 year	191,462	219,271
1 – 3 years	371,634	400,588
3 – 5 years	262,846	279,747
Over 5 years	215,642	261,441
	1,041,584	1,161,047

As at December 31, 2011, the Corporation is committed to lease one additional 737-800 aircraft for a term of eight years in US dollars. This aircraft has been included in the above totals.

(c) Letters of guarantee

As at December 31, 2011, the Corporation has available two revolving letter of credit facilities with a Canadian charter bank totaling $38,000 (December 31, 2010 – $38,000; January 1, 2010 – $38,000). One facility is unsecured for $8,000 and the other is a facility for $30,000 that requires funds to be assigned and held in cash security for the full value of letters of guarantee issued by the Corporation. As at December 31, 2011 $6,610 (December 31, 2010 – $6,691; January 1, 2010 – $12,491) of letters of guarantee were issued under these facilities with restricted cash of $6,610 (December 31, 2010 – $6,691; January 1, 2010 – $4,491).

(d) Operating line of credit

The Corporation has available a three-year revolving operating line of credit with a syndicate of three Canadian banks. The line of credit is available for up to a maximum of $76,500 (December 31, 2010 – $80,750; January 1, 2010 – $85,000) and is secured by the Corporation's campus facility. The line of credit bears interest at prime plus 0.50% per annum, or a banker's acceptance rate at 2.0% annual stamping fee or equivalent, and is available for general corporate expenditures and working capital purposes. The Corporation is required to pay a standby fee of 15 basis points, based on the average unused portion of the line of credit for the previous quarter, payable quarterly. As at December 31, 2011, no amounts were drawn (December 31, 2010 – $nil; January 1, 2010 – $nil).

Notes to Consolidated Financial Statements
For the years ended December 31, 2011 and 2010
(Stated in thousands of Canadian dollars, except share and per share amounts)

19. Related parties

(a) Subsidiaries and partnership

The consolidated financial statements of WestJet Airlines Ltd., the parent company, include the accounts of the Corporation and its following three directly wholly-owned subsidiaries incorporated in Canada, as well as an indirectly wholly-owned Alberta partnership:

WestJet Investment Corp.
WestJet Operations Corp.
WestJet Vacations Inc.
WestJet Partnership

WestJet Partnership is the primary operating entity of the Corporation.

The Corporation utilizes five special purpose entities (SPEs) to facilitate the financing of aircraft. The Corporation has no equity ownership in the SPEs, however, the substance of the relationship between the Corporation and the SPEs indicates that they are controlled by the Corporation. Accordingly, the accounts of the SPEs have been consolidated in the Corporation's financial statements and all intercompany balances and transactions have been eliminated.

(b) Key management personnel

The Corporation has defined key management personnel as senior executive officers, as well as the Board of Directors, as they have the collective authority and responsibility for planning, directing and controlling the activities of the Corporation. The following table outlines the total compensation expense for key management personnel for the years ended December 31, 2011 and 2010.

	2011	2010
Short-term fees and other short-term benefits	4,401	3,546
Termination and post-employment benefits	1,116	1,618
Share-based payment expense [i]	3,293	5,354
	8,810	10,518

[i] Includes amounts expensed pursuant to the stock option plan, executive share unit plan, deferred share unit plan and employee share purchase plan.

(c) Transactions with other related parties

During 2010, the Corporation engaged a relocation firm to purchase a single family residence from the President and Chief Executive Officer (CEO) for a guaranteed price of US $1,525 in accordance with the Corporation's relocation policy, and in addition, granted RSUs pursuant to the Corporation's ESU plan in connection with the relocation. On September 30, 2011, the residence was sold for US $1,050 to a third party. The Corporation recognized an expense of US $475 plus closing charges of US $100 on the transaction, this difference was made payable to the relocation firm and recognized in 2011 under marketing, general and administrative expense.

Notes to Consolidated Financial Statements
For the years ended December 31, 2011 and 2010
(Stated in thousands of Canadian dollars, except share and per share amounts)

20. Additional financial information (continued)

(a) Assets

	Note	December 31 2011	December 31 2010	January 1 2010
Accounts receivable (i):				
Trade		19,193	12,620	15,940
Industry		15,665	5,242	11,384
Other		1,632	2,024	2,698
Allowance (ii)		(2,368)	(2,368)	(2,368)
		34,122	17,518	27,654
Prepaid expenses, deposits and other:				
Prepaid expenses		27,288	9,082	29,797
Short-term deposits (iii)		27,322	26,892	26,113
Maintenance reserves – current portion		–	12,045	8,629
Derivatives	17	12,273	5,689	276
Other		53	53	53
		66,936	53,761	64,868
Inventory:				
Fuel		21,479	17,967	24,777
Aircraft expendables		7,525	5,914	5,457
De-icing fluid		240	537	533
Other		2,451	1,677	738
		31,695	26,095	31,505
Other Assets:				
Aircraft deposits (iv)		45,515	45,268	50,975
Maintenance reserves – long term		49,655	41,736	44,084
Other		8,789	9,163	3,392
		103,959	96,167	98,451

(i) Trade receivables relate to day-to-day operations. Industry receivables include receivables relating to travel agents, interline agreements with other airlines and partnerships. All significant services and counterparties are reviewed and approved for credit on a regular basis. Trade receivables are generally settled in less than 30 days. Industry receivables are generally settled within 30 to 60 days.

(ii) The Corporation recorded a bad debt provision in 2009 in relation to its cargo operations. There were no new provisions recorded in 2011 or 2010.

(iii) Short-term deposits include deposits relating to aircraft fuel, airport operations and other operating costs.

(iv) Aircraft-related deposits include long-term deposits with lessors for the lease of aircraft and long-term US-dollar deposits, which relate to purchased aircraft.

Notes to Consolidated Financial Statements
For the years ended December 31, 2011 and 2010
(Stated in thousands of Canadian dollars, except share and per share amounts)

20. Additional financial information (continued)

(b) Liabilities

	Note	December 31 2011	December 31 2010	January 1 2010
Accounts payable and accrued liabilities:				
Trade and industry		268,624	237,668	198,828
Frequent guest program		22,020	6,823	–
Maintenance provision - current	9	245	12,372	8,031
Derivatives	17	112	4,379	10,193
Dividend payable		–	7,148	–
Other		16,278	19,320	11,859
		307,279	287,710	228,911
Other current liabilities:				
Advanced ticket sales		432,186	336,926	297,720
Non-refundable guest credits		43,485	36,381	63,164
		475,671	373,307	360,884
Other liabilities:				
Deferred contract incentives (i)		9,299	8,794	9,421
Derivatives	17	420	–	–
Other		730	164	96
		10,449	8,958	9,517

(i) Deferred contract incentives relate to discounts received on aircraft related items as well as land leases. Incentives are amortized over the terms of the related contracts.

21. Subsequent events

(a) Aircraft financing

On February 2, 2012, the Ex-Im Bank authorized a final commitment of $77,559 to support the financing of the two 737-800 aircraft to be delivered in February and June of 2012. The final commitment is drawn down at the time the Corporation takes delivery of the aircraft. Upon delivery of the second aircraft, any unused portion of the final commitment will be cancelled. In conjunction with the final commitment, the Corporation secured two new term credit facilities with a Canadian chartered bank. The facilities will be financed in Canadian dollars and amortized over a 12-year term, each repayable in fixed principal instalments plus a floating rate of interest equal to the three month Canadian dealer offer rate plus 75 basis points. As disclosed in note 17, the Corporation has entered into swap contracts to fix the interest rate over the 12 year term of the loans at a rate of 2.89% and 2.99%, respectively, inclusive of the 75 basis points.

(b) Normal course issuer bid

On February 7, 2012, the Corporation filed a notice with the TSX to make a normal course issuer bid to purchase outstanding shares on the open market. As approved by the TSX, the Corporation is authorized to purchase up to 6,914,330 common voting shares and variable voting shares (representing approximately 5 per cent of the Corporation's issued and outstanding shares at the time of the bid) during the period February 10, 2012 to February 9, 2013, or until such time as the bid is completed or terminated at the Corporation's option. Any shares purchased under this bid will be purchased on the open market through the facilities of the TSX at the prevailing market price at the time of the transaction. Common voting shares and variable voting shares acquired under this bid will be cancelled.

Notes to Consolidated Financial Statements
For the years ended December 31, 2011 and 2010
(Stated in thousands of Canadian dollars, except share and per share amounts)

22. Transition to IFRS

The following discussion describes the principal adjustments made by the Corporation in restating its Canadian GAAP consolidated financial statements to IFRS for the year ended December 31, 2010 as well as the opening statement of financial position as at January 1, 2010. Tables reconciling the balances from Canadian GAAP to IFRS are also provided following the narrative discussion below.

Exemptions applied

IFRS 1 contains mandatory and optional exemptions required by publicly accountable enterprises adopting IFRS for the first time. The Corporation has assessed each of the mandatory and optional exemptions in detail and concluded there was no impact to the recognition, measurement, presentation or disclosure of past transactions related to these exemptions.

The Corporation has applied the optional transitional exemption under IFRS 1 – First-time Adoption of International Financial Reporting Standards in the preparation of these consolidated financial statements. IFRS 1 provides the option to apply IFRIC 4, Determining Whether an Arrangement Contains a Lease, to arrangements existing at the transition date on the basis of facts and circumstances at that date. The result of this election is to allow the Corporation to determine whether an arrangement contains a lease at the date of transition based on the facts and circumstances existing at that date instead of making this determination at the original inception of the arrangement. Based on the analysis performed, there are no effects to the accounts of the Corporation from the adoption of IFRIC 4.

Transition impacts

IFRS employs a conceptual framework that is similar to Canadian GAAP; however, significant differences exist in certain matters of recognition, measurement and disclosure. While adoption of IFRS has not changed the Corporation's actual cash flows, it has resulted in changes to the Corporation's reported financial position and results of operations. In order to allow the users of the financial statements to better understand these changes, the Corporation's Canadian GAAP consolidated statement of financial position as at January 1, 2010 and December 31, 2010, and the Corporation's consolidated statement of earnings, consolidated statement of cash flows and consolidated statement of comprehensive income for the 12 months ended December 31, 2010, have been reconciled to IFRS with the resulting differences explained.

Recast information

Since the first IFRS interim condensed consolidated financial statements were reported by the Corporation as at and for the periods ending March 31, 2011 and 2010, the Corporation has amended its opening statement of financial position balance for maintenance provisions to reflect a correction to the pre-tax, risk-free discount rate as at January 1, 2010. This adjustment reflects a discount rate equal to the remaining term until cash flow instead of the full term of the aircraft lease. The resulting effect is an adjustment to the opening statement of financial position balances for long-term maintenance provisions of $6,495, $1,662 to deferred income tax and $4,833 to retained earnings from those amounts reported at March 31, 2011. The tables in this note reflect the amended opening statement of financial position.

Significant IFRS accounting policy differences

IAS 16 – Property, Plant and Equipment

(i) Componentization

Aircraft are required to have periodic maintenance performed at predetermined time intervals to maintain the integrity and efficiency of the aircraft and its major components, including the airframe, landing gear, and engines.

Canadian GAAP: Maintenance and repair costs for owned aircraft and aircraft under operating leases, including major overhauls, were charged to expense at the time maintenance was performed.

IFRS: For owned aircraft, each item of property and equipment with a significant cost in relation to the total cost and/or a different useful life is required to be depreciated separately. The costs of activities that restore the service potential of airframes, engines and landing gear are considered components of the aircraft and are separately capitalized and amortized over the period until the next overhaul.

For aircraft under operating leases, where the Corporation is required to return the aircraft to the lessor in a specified condition, a provision is recorded. See discussion under section IAS 37 – Provisions, contingent liabilities and contingent assets for more information.

Impact: More aircraft components with different useful lives were recognized under IFRS. This resulted in increased depreciation expense, as certain components have a shorter useful life than under Canadian GAAP. However, this increase is offset by a decrease in maintenance expense, as the costs to perform major maintenance are now capitalized whereas they were previously expensed. There is no change to the cost of maintenance activities and no overall impact on earnings over the life of the aircraft, only a timing difference in expense recognition.

Notes to Consolidated Financial Statements
For the years ended December 31, 2011 and 2010
(Stated in thousands of Canadian dollars, except share and per share amounts)

22. Transition to IFRS (continued)

Significant IFRS accounting policy differences (continued)

(ii) Depreciation

Canadian GAAP: Depreciation of owned aircraft was based on aircraft cycles. Aircraft were amortized over a range of 30,000 to 50,000 cycles with one cycle being defined as the aircraft leaving the ground and landing.

IFRS: As a result of componentization described above, the Corporation was required to assess the useful lives and depreciation methods of each newly identified aircraft component. The result was a change to the depreciation method for aircraft components to the straight-line method. The Corporation determined that the expected useful life of the aircraft under IFRS is 20 years based on the expected pattern of consumption of future economic benefits embodied in the aircraft components. The useful life of an overall component ranges depending upon the time intervals required between planned major maintenance events.

Impact: Total depreciation over the life of the aircraft is unchanged under IFRS. There is only a timing difference in expense recognition.

(iii) Asset retirement obligations (ARO)

Canadian GAAP: For aircraft under operating leases, amounts relating to future lease return obligations including the painting of the tail and the removal of the in-flight entertainment and passenger briefing system were initially measured at fair value and recorded as a liability with a corresponding increase to the carrying value of the related asset (aircraft), which was amortized on a straight line basis over the term of the lease.

IFRS: Future lease return obligations are assessed as a provision under IAS 37. There is no property and equipment asset recognized related to future lease return obligations for the Corporation's aircraft under operating lease.

Impact: On transition, the ARO asset and liability previously recorded under Canadian GAAP were written off to retained earnings. The amortization expense and accretion expense recognized on the ARO asset and liability under Canadian GAAP in 2010 was reversed under IFRS. The obligation to return aircraft under operating lease in a specified condition previously recorded as a liability under Canadian GAAP was reclassified as a provision under IAS 37.

IAS 37 – Provisions, Contingent Liabilities and Contingent Assets

(i) Maintenance provisions for aircraft under operating lease

Aircraft leasing agreements require the Corporation to return aircraft to the lessor in a specified condition. This requires the Corporation to incur maintenance costs related to the aircraft's engines, landing gear and airframe as well as the painting of the tail and the removal of the in-flight entertainment and passenger briefing systems.

Canadian GAAP: Maintenance costs on leased aircraft were expensed as incurred as the definition of a liability was not met under Canadian GAAP until the time the maintenance activity was performed.

IFRS: The definition of a provision under IFRS has a broader scope as compared to Canadian GAAP. As such, a maintenance provision is recognized for leased aircraft. Current and long-term provisions are recognized based on the expected timing of maintenance costs to be incurred. Accretion expense is recognized each period on the maintenance provisions for the unwinding of the present value discount. Provision amounts denominated in US dollars are revalued to Canadian dollars at each reporting period until settlement.

Impact: The adoption of this standard created a maintenance provision on the consolidated statement of financial position. There is no overall increase to maintenance expense over the term of the lease, only a timing difference in expense recognition. Finance costs are also increased due to the recording of accretion expense for the unwinding of the discount on the maintenance provision liabilities. A foreign exchange gain or loss is recognized on the revaluation of the US-dollar denominated maintenance liabilities at each reporting period.

(ii) Maintenance reserves

Certain aircraft lease agreements require the Corporation to pay maintenance deposits to the lessor based on predefined cycle and flight hour formulas. These payments are intended to provide the lessor with collateral should an aircraft not be returned to the condition specified in the lease agreement. When qualifying maintenance is performed, the Corporation is entitled to be reimbursed by the lessor up to a maximum of the amounts previously deposited with the lessor.

Canadian GAAP: Payments made to the lessor were expensed (maintenance expense) as incurred and reimbursements were recognized as receivables (and a related reduction to maintenance expense) when qualifying maintenance was performed.

Notes to Consolidated Financial Statements
For the years ended December 31, 2011 and 2010
(Stated in thousands of Canadian dollars, except share and per share amounts)

22. Transition to IFRS (continued)

Significant IFRS accounting policy differences (continued)

(ii) Maintenance reserves (continued)

IFRS: To the extent maintenance deposits paid to the lessor are expected to be recoverable through qualifying maintenance activities, a maintenance reserve asset is recorded. As qualifying maintenance is performed and reimbursed, the maintenance reserve is drawn down. Any amounts deposited that are not expected to be recoverable through future qualifying maintenance activities are expensed as incurred. The Corporation recognizes both a current and long-term maintenance reserve based on the expected timing of reimbursements. Maintenance deposits denominated in US dollars are revalued to Canadian dollars at each reporting period until settlement.

Impact: Creation of a maintenance reserve asset on the consolidated statement of financial position and a one-time reduction in maintenance expense recognized on transition. A foreign exchange gain or loss is recognized at each reporting period for the revaluation of the US-dollar denominated maintenance reserve asset.

(iii) Soft dollar credit files

Credit files are presented on the consolidated statement of financial position as non-refundable guest credits. These credits are made up of both soft dollar and hard dollar credit files. Soft dollar credit files are provided to guests for inconveniences such as flight and baggage delays as a sign of goodwill to be used towards future travel. Hard dollar credit files are provided to guests for flight changes and cancellations, as well as for the purchase of gift certificates.

Canadian GAAP: Soft dollar credit files issued were recorded as an expense and related liability upon issuance at the incremental cost of flying an additional guest.

IFRS: Soft dollar credit files do not require a performance obligation to be fulfilled by the Corporation nor are they issued as part of a sales transaction. As a result, no obligation or liability is recognized under IFRS at the time when a soft dollar credit file is issued. When soft dollar credit files are redeemed by the guest they are recognized as a reduction to guest revenue for the full amount of the credit.

Impact: Elimination of the soft dollar credit file liability on transition with a related increase to retained earnings. There was no effect on hard dollar credit files due to the adoption of IFRS.

IAS 39 – Financial Instruments: Recognition and Measurement

WestJet has incurred various transaction costs, including agency, advisory and legal fees, related to its aircraft debt financing.

Canadian GAAP: As permitted under Canadian GAAP, these transaction costs were expensed as incurred.

IFRS: Requires costs that are incremental and directly attributable to the acquisition of a financial liability to be included in the initial measurement of the financial liability. These costs are recorded against the liability and amortized using the effective interest rate method over the term of the debt. The expense is recorded as a finance cost in the consolidated statement of earnings.

Impact: On transition, current and long-term debt was reduced with a related increase to retained earnings. Finance costs are increased for the amortization of the transaction costs.

Notes to Consolidated Financial Statements
For the years ended December 31, 2011 and 2010
(Stated in thousands of Canadian dollars, except share and per share amounts)

22. Transition to IFRS (continued)

Significant IFRS accounting policy differences (continued)

Other IFRS Adjustments

Other IFRS transitional adjustments relate to changes in the measurement of share-based payment expense and leases, specifically sale and leaseback transactions, among others.

Share-based payment expense for the Corporation's stock options is now recognized over a longer service period for certain employees, and incorporates an estimated forfeiture rate on the number of instruments expected to vest at the date of grant. There is no change to total expense from these IFRS changes, only a difference in the period of expense allocation.

IFRS requires the gain from the sale and leaseback of aircraft to be recognized immediately. The Corporation previously deferred and amortized this gain over the term of the lease. There was no change to the total gain, only a timing difference in its recognition.

The share-based payment expense, lease and other changes under IFRS are not material individually or in aggregate to the consolidated financial statements.

Changes to deferred income tax assets and liabilities and the related deferred tax expense or benefit are the direct result of changes to the accounting values from Canadian GAAP to IFRS. There is no recognition and measurement difference between Canadian GAAP and IFRS related to the Corporation's deferred tax accounts. There are some presentation and disclosure differences under IFRS including the derecognition of any current deferred income tax assets or liabilities in favour of disclosing only a long-term deferred income tax asset or liability.

Notes to Consolidated Financial Statements

For the years ended December 31, 2011 and 2010
(Stated in thousands of Canadian dollars, except share and per share amounts)

22. Transition to IFRS (continued)

Reconciliation of Consolidated Statement of Financial Position as at January 1, 2010

	Canadian GAAP balance	IAS 16	IAS 37	IAS 39	Other	IFRS balance
Assets						
Current assets:						
Cash and cash equivalents	994,989	–	–	–	–	994,989
Restricted cash	10,192	–	–	–	–	10,192
Accounts receivable	27,654	–	–	–	–	27,654
Prepaid expenses, deposits and other	56,239	–	8,629	–	–	64,868
Inventory	26,048	–	–	–	5,457	31,505
Deferred income tax	2,560	–	–	–	(2,560)	–
	1,117,682	–	8,629	–	2,897	1,129,208
Non-current assets:						
Property and equipment	2,307,566	(199,215)	–	–	–	2,108,351
Intangible assets	14,087	–	–	–	–	14,087
Other assets	54,367	–	44,084	–	–	98,451
Total assets	3,493,702	(199,215)	52,713	–	2,897	3,350,097
Liabilities and shareholders' equity						
Current liabilities:						
Accounts payable and accrued liabilities	220,042	–	8,031	838	–	228,911
Advance ticket sales	297,720	–	–	–	–	297,720
Non-refundable guest credits	64,506	–	(1,342)	–	–	63,164
Current portion of long-term debt	171,223	–	–	(6,112)	–	165,111
Current portion of obligations under finance leases	744	–	–	–	–	744
	754,235	–	6,689	(5,274)	–	755,650
Non-current liabilities:						
Maintenance provisions	–	–	97,722	–	–	97,722
Long-term debt	1,048,554	–	–	(20,389)	–	1,028,165
Obligations under finance leases	3,358	–	–	–	–	3,358
Other liabilities	19,628	(4,926)	–	–	(5,185)	9,517
Deferred income tax	278,999	(49,318)	(13,093)	6,644	277	223,509
Total liabilities	2,104,774	(54,244)	91,318	(19,019)	(4,908)	2,117,921
Shareholders' equity:						
Share capital	633,075	–	–	–	–	633,075
Equity reserves	71,503	–	–	–	4,363	75,866
Hedge reserves	(14,852)	–	–	–	–	(14,852)
Retained earnings	699,202	(144,971)	(38,605)	19,019	3,442	538,087
Total shareholders' equity	1,388,928	(144,971)	(38,605)	19,019	7,805	1,232,176
Total liabilities and shareholders' equity	3,493,702	(199,215)	52,713	–	2,897	3,350,097

Notes to Consolidated Financial Statements
For the years ended December 31, 2011 and 2010
(Stated in thousands of Canadian dollars, except share and per share amounts)

22. Transition to IFRS (continued)

Reconciliation of Consolidated Statement of Financial Position as at December 31, 2010

	Canadian GAAP balance	IAS 16	IAS 37	IAS 39	Other	IFRS balance
Assets						
Current assets:						
Cash and cash equivalents	1,159,316	–	–	–	–	1,159,316
Restricted cash	28,583	–	–	–	–	28,583
Accounts receivable	17,518	–	–	–	–	17,518
Prepaid expenses, deposits and other	41,716	–	12,045	–	–	53,761
Inventory	20,181	–	–	–	5,914	26,095
Deferred income tax	1,396	–	–	–	(1,396)	–
	1,268,710	–	12,045	–	4,518	1,285,273
Non-current assets:						
Property and equipment	2,226,685	(237,163)	–	–	–	1,989,522
Intangible assets	13,018	–	–	–	–	13,018
Other assets	54,431	–	41,736	–	–	96,167
Total assets	3,562,844	(237,163)	53,781	–	4,518	3,383,980
Liabilities and shareholders' equity						
Current liabilities:						
Accounts payable and accrued liabilities	274,603	–	12,372	735	–	287,710
Advance ticket sales	337,002	–	(76)	–	–	336,926
Non-refundable guest credits	36,778	–	(397)	–	–	36,381
Current portion of long-term debt	183,681	–	–	(5,344)	–	178,337
Current portion of obligations under finance leases	108	–	–	–	–	108
	832,172	–	11,899	(4,609)	–	839,462
Non-current liabilities:						
Maintenance provisions	–	–	113,206	–	–	113,206
Long-term debt	863,496	–	–	(15,031)	–	848,465
Obligations under finance leases	3,249	–	–	–	–	3,249
Other liabilities	18,838	(5,903)	–	–	(3,977)	8,958
Deferred income tax	337,410	(58,667)	(18,082)	5,084	662	266,407
Total liabilities	2,055,165	(64,570)	107,023	(14,556)	(3,315)	2,079,747
Shareholders' equity:						
Share capital	647,637	–	–	–	–	647,637
Equity reserves	62,534	–	–	–	4,192	66,726
Hedge reserves	(10,470)	–	–	–	–	(10,470)
Retained earnings	807,978	(172,593)	(53,242)	14,556	3,641	600,340
Total shareholders' equity	1,507,679	(172,593)	(53,242)	14,556	7,833	1,304,233
Total liabilities and shareholders' equity	3,562,844	(237,163)	53,781	–	4,518	3,383,980

Notes to Consolidated Financial Statements
For the years ended December 31, 2011 and 2010
(Stated in thousands of Canadian dollars, except share and per share amounts)

22. Transition to IFRS (continued)

Reconciliation of Consolidated Statement of Earnings for the year ended December 31, 2010

	Canadian GAAP balance	IAS 16	IAS 37	IAS 39	Other	IFRS balance
Revenues:						
Guest	2,405,281	–	(14,394)	–	–	2,390,887
Other	203,980	–	12,427	–	–	216,407
	2,609,261	–	(1,967)	–	–	2,607,294
Expenses:						
Aircraft fuel	674,608	–	–	–	–	674,608
Airport operations	388,392	–	(280)	–	–	388,112
Flight operations and navigational charges	325,754	–	–	–	(172)	325,582
Sales and distribution	255,777	–	(45)	–	–	255,732
Marketing, general and administration	195,185	–	(773)	–	69	194,481
Depreciation and amortization	132,894	37,568	–	–	–	170,462
Aircraft leasing	142,242	–	–	–	1,139	143,381
Maintenance	100,339	(216)	17,391	–	(457)	117,057
Inflight	124,303	–	–	–	–	124,303
Employee profit share	22,222	–	–	–	–	22,222
	2,361,716	37,352	16,293	–	579	2,415,940
Earnings from operations	247,545	(37,352)	(18,260)	–	(579)	191,354
Non-operating income (expense):						
Finance income	9,910	–	–	–	–	9,910
Finance costs	(60,164)	–	(4,725)	(6,025)	–	(70,914)
Gain (loss) on foreign exchange	(780)	–	3,359	–	–	2,579
Gain on disposal of property and equipment	190	380	–	–	–	570
Loss on derivatives	(34)	–	–	–	–	(34)
	(50,878)	380	(1,366)	(6,025)	–	(57,889)
Earnings before income taxes	196,667	(36,972)	(19,626)	(6,025)	(579)	133,465
Income tax expense:						
Current	1,573	–	–	–	–	1,573
Deferred	58,374	(9,350)	(4,988)	(1,562)	(779)	41,695
	59,947	(9,350)	(4,988)	(1,562)	(779)	43,268
Net earnings	136,720	(27,622)	(14,638)	(4,463)	200	90,197
Earnings per share:						
Basic	0.94					0.62
Diluted	0.94					0.62

Notes to Consolidated Financial Statements
For the years ended December 31, 2011 and 2010
(Stated in thousands of Canadian dollars, except share and per share amounts)

22. Transition to IFRS (continued)

Reconciliation of Consolidated Statement of Cash Flows for the year ended December 31, 2010

	Canadian GAAP balance	IAS 16	IAS 37	IAS 39	Other	IFRS balance
Operating activities:						
Net earnings	136,720	(27,622)	(14,638)	(4,463)	200	90,197
Items not involving cash:						
Depreciation and amortization	132,894	37,568	–	–	–	170,462
Change in long-term maintenance provisions	–	–	27,927	–	–	27,927
Change in other liabilities	(1,891)	–	–	–	1,206	(685)
Amortization of hedge settlements	1,400	–	–	–	–	1,400
Loss on derivative instruments	34	–	–	–	–	34
Gain on disposal of property and equipment	(167)	(596)	–	–	–	(763)
Share-based payment expense	15,668	–	–	–	(171)	15,497
Income tax credit	(1,667)	–	–	–	–	(1,667)
Deferred income tax expense	58,374	(9,350)	(4,988)	(1,562)	(779)	41,695
Unrealized foreign exchange loss	3,696	–	(3,359)	–	–	337
Change in non-cash working capital	98,222	–	716	(101)	(455)	98,382
Change in restricted cash	(18,391)	–	–	–	–	(18,391)
Change in other assets	–	–	(5,658)	–	–	(5,658)
	424,892	–	–	(6,126)	–	418,766
Investing activities:						
Aircraft additions	(29,884)	–	–	–	–	(29,884)
Other property and equipment and intangible additions	(18,675)	–	–	–	–	(18,675)
	(48,559)	–	–	–	–	(48,559)
Financing activities:						
Repayment of long-term debt	(171,115)	–	–	6,126	–	(164,989)
Decrease in obligations under finance leases	(744)	–	–	–	–	(744)
Shares repurchased	(31,391)	–	–	–	–	(31,391)
Issuance of common shares	520	–	–	–	–	520
Change in other assets	(2,947)	–	–	–	–	(2,947)
Change in non-cash working capital	(4,526)	–	–	–	–	(4,526)
	(210,203)	–	–	6,126	–	(204,077)
Cash flow from operating, financing and investing activities	166,130	–	–	–	–	166,130
Effect of foreign exchange on cash and cash equivalents	(1,803)	–	–	–	–	(1,803)
Net change in cash and cash equivalents	164,327	–	–	–	–	164,327
Cash and cash equivalents, beginning of year	994,989	–	–	–	–	994,989
Cash and cash equivalents, end of year	1,159,316	–	–	–	–	1,159,316

Notes to Consolidated Financial Statements
For the years ended December 31, 2011 and 2010
(Stated in thousands of Canadian dollars, except share and per share amounts)

22. Transition to IFRS (continued)

Reconciliation of Consolidated Statement of Comprehensive Income for the year ended December 31, 2010

	Canadian GAAP balance	Adjustments	IFRS balance
Net earnings	136,720	(46,523)	90,197
Other comprehensive income, net of tax:			
Amortization of hedge settlements to aircraft leasing	1,400	–	1,400
Net unrealized loss on foreign exchange derivatives	(3,460)	–	(3,460)
Reclassification of net realized loss on foreign	1,557	–	1,557
Net unrealized loss on fuel derivatives under cash	(1,778)	–	(1,778)
Reclassification of net realized loss on fuel derivatives	6,663	–	6,663
	4,382	–	4,382
Total comprehensive income	141,102	(46,523)	94,579

(i)   Net of income taxes of $1,224.
(ii)   Net of income taxes of $(586).
(iii) Net of income taxes of $670.
(iv)   Net of income taxes of $(2,509).

Chart of Accounts

Assets

Current Assets

101 Cash
102 Petty cash
103 Short-term investments
104 _____ investments
106 Accounts receivable
107 Allowance for doubtful accounts
108 GST receivable
109 Interest receivable
110 Rent receivable
111 Notes receivable
119 Merchandise inventory
120 _____ inventory
124 Office supplies
125 Store supplies
126 _____ supplies
128 Prepaid insurance
129 Prepaid _____
131 Prepaid rent

Long-Term Investments

141 Investment in ____ shares
142 Investment in ____ bonds
144 Investment in _____

Property, Plant, and Equipment (PPE)

151 Automobiles
152 Accumulated depreciation, automobiles
153 Trucks
154 Accumulated depreciation, trucks
159 Library
160 Accumulated depreciation, library

161 Furniture
162 Accumulated depreciation, furniture
163 Office equipment
164 Accumulated depreciation, office equipment
165 Store equipment
166 Accumulated depreciation, store equipment
167 _____ equipment
168 Accumulated depreciation, _____ equipment
169 Machinery
170 Accumulated depreciation, machinery
173 Building _____
174 Accumulated depreciation, building _____
175 Land
176 Leasehold improvements
179 Land improvements, _____
180 Accumulated depreciation, land improvements _____

Intangible Assets

191 Patents
192 Accumulated amortization, patents
193 Leasehold
194 Accumulated amortization, leasehold
195 Franchise
196 Accumulated amortization, franchise
197 Copyright
198 Accumulated amortization, copyright

Goodwill

199 Goodwill

Liabilities

Current Liabilities

201 Accounts payable
202 Insurance payable
203 Interest payable
204 Legal fees payable
205 Short-term notes payable
206 Rent payable
207 Salaries payable
208 Wages payable
209 Estimated warranty liability
210 Income taxes payable
211 Common dividends payable
212 Preferred dividends payable
213 EI payable
214 CPP payable
215 Employees' medical insurance payable
216 PST payable
217 GST payable
218 _____ payable

Unearned Revenues

230 Unearned consulting fees
231 Unearned legal fees
232 Unearned _____

Long-Term Liabilities

250 Long-term notes payable
251 Long-term lease liability
252 Bonds payable
253 Discount on bonds payable
254 Premium on bonds payable

Equity

301 _____ , capital
302 _____ , withdrawals

Corporate Contributed Capital

307 Common shares
310 Common share dividends distributable
313 Contributed capital from the retirement of common shares
315 Preferred shares

Retained Earnings

318 Retained earnings
319 Cash dividends
320 Share dividends

Revenues

401 _____ fees earned
403 _____ services revenue
405 Commission earned
406 Rent earned
407 Dividends earned
408 Earnings from investment in _____
409 Interest earned
413 Sales
414 Sales returns and allowances
415 Sales discounts

Expenses

Cost of Sales

500 Cost of goods sold
501 Purchases
502 Purchases returns and allowances
503 Purchases discounts
504 Transportation-in

Depreciation/Amortization

600 Depreciation expense, automobiles
602 Depreciation expense, _____
603 Amortization expense, copyrights
604 Amortization expense, _____

Employee Related Expense

620 Office salaries expense
621 Sales salaries expense
622 Salaries expense
623 _____ wages expense
624 Employees' benefits expense

Financial Expenses

630 Brokerage fee expense
631 Cash over and short
633 Interest expense

Insurance Expenses

636 Insurance expense, building
637 Insurance expense, _____

Rental Expenses

640 Rent expense
641 Rent expense, office space
642 Rent expense, _____

Supplies Expense

650 Office supplies expense
651 _____ supplies expense

Other Expenses

655 Advertising expense
656 Bad debts expense
659 Collection expense
662 Credit card expense
663 Delivery expense
667 Equipment expense
668 Food and drinks expense
671 Gas and oil expense
673 Janitorial expense
674 Legal fees expense
676 Mileage expense
682 Postage expense
683 Property taxes expense
684 Repairs expense, _____
688 Telephone expense
689 Travel and entertaining expense
690 Utilities expense
691 Warranty expense
695 Income taxes expense
696 _____ expense

Gains and Losses

701 Gain on retirement of bonds
702 Gain on sale of machinery
703 Gain on sale of investments
705 Gain on _____
805 Loss on retirement of bonds
806 Loss on sale of investments
807 Loss on sale of machinery
809 Loss on _____
810 Unrealized holding gain
811 Unrealized holding loss

Clearing Accounts

901 Income summary

Credits

Chapter 1

Page 1: Courtesy of Vertically Inclined; page 10 logo: http://www.rbc.com

Chapter 2

Page 63: Used with permission from Black Feather; page 63 logo: Used with permission from Black Feather

Chapter 3

Page 121: Used with permission from Frogbox

Chapter 4

Page 187: © Tracy Leonard

Chapter 5

Page 255: NielsVK/Alamy/GetStock.com

Chapter 6

Page 331: Toronto Star/GetStock.com

Chapter 7

Page 385: Used with permission from Moxie Trades

Chapter 8

Page 432: Devonyu/Dreamstime.com/GetStock.com

Chapter 9

Page 490: Creatas/PunchStock

Appendix I

Page A-1: Duncan Smith/Getty Images

Index

SUMMARY OF FOCUS ON FINANCIAL STATEMENT ONLINE COMPANIES—VOLUME 1

EXTEND YOUR KNOWLEDGE (EYK) INDEX—VOLUME 1